Reclaiming Clio

Reclaiming Clio

Making American Women's History, 1900–2000

JENNIFER BANNING TOMÁS

The University of North Carolina Press
Chapel Hill

Manufactured in the United States of America
Set in Minion Pro by Jamie McKee, MacKey Composition

Cover art: Carlo Franzonis, *Car of History*, 1810. Courtesy
Craig Jack Photographic / Alamy Stock Photo.

Library of Congress Cataloging-in-Publication Data
Names: Tomás, Jennifer Banning, author
Title: Reclaiming Clio : making American women's history,
    1900–2000 / Jennifer Banning Tomás.
Description: Chapel Hill : The University of North Carolina Press,
    [2025] | Includes bibliographical references and index.
Identifiers LCCN 2025015431 | ISBN 9781469686004 (cloth) | ISBN 9781469686011
    (paperback) | ISBN 9781469686028 (epub) | ISBN 9781469686035 (pdf)
Subjects: LCSH: Women—United States—Historiography. | Women's studies—
    United States—History—20th century. | Historiography—United States—
    History—20th century. | BISAC: SOCIAL SCIENCE / Women's Studies |
    HISTORY / Women
Classification: LCC HQ1181.U5 T66 2025 | DDC 305.40973—dc23/eng/20250512
LC record available at https://lccn.loc.gov/2025015431

For product safety concerns under the European Union's General Product
Safety Regulation (EU GPSR), please contact gpsr@mare-nostrum.co.uk or
write to the University of North Carolina Press and Mare Nostrum Group
B.V., Mauritskade 21D, 1091 GC Amsterdam, The Netherlands.

For the pioneers, the founders, the institution builders, the allies, and all those who continue to labor in the vineyards of American women's history so that the majority is not lost to historical view

Contents

A section of illustrations begins on page 169

Tables

Acknowledgments

This book has been a long time coming. When I completed the history PhD program at Binghamton University (SUNY) and the first draft of the manuscript over a decade ago, the history job market was not good. The specter of unemployment or permanent adjunct status loomed large. However, the wide net I cast during an unrelenting two-year job search paid off: I accepted a full-time faculty position at a community college in Charlottesville, Virginia. Since then, I've had the privilege of working and teaching in the field for which I trained. The teaching was all-consuming at first. I often felt a strange combination of satisfaction and despair. The satisfaction was rooted in the teaching—as was the despair, as teaching a 5/5 course load left little time for research or writing, and I had a dissertation to turn into a book. Seven years passed by. The book remained but an aspiration. The blue-bound dissertation sat forlornly on the bookshelf above my desk.

My move south entailed some initial culture shock. My college sits at the bottom of the "little mountain" that is home to Thomas Jefferson's historic plantation. It felt strange teaching in the shadow of Jefferson's Monticello, encountering larger-than-life Confederate monuments in the town square, and being addressed as "Ma'am" by strangers and students alike. Hailing from Rochester, New York, I had been raised with different cultural and historical landmarks, including Frederick Douglass and Susan B. Anthony. Still, I quickly came to love this small city I had been lucky to land in. It was in many ways an idyllic college town, surrounded by natural beauty and blessed with a rich cultural life.

Things started getting weird around 2016. They became downright dystopian by summer 2017. In July 2017 the KKK came to town to protest the proposed removal of Confederate monuments from two town squares in the city. They were heckled and chased out by counterprotesters, among whom I was counted. In August, hundreds of white nationalists descended on the city and University of Virginia campus. They marched with tiki torches, angrily shouting anti-Semitic chants. They clashed with counterprotesters and assaulted locals. One young man plowed his muscle car into social justice activists demonstrating peacefully in the streets, killing a young woman and seriously injuring others. This escalating violence too was a reaction to community efforts to get Confederate monuments removed from the public square. History was at the white-hot center of the culture wars in this local historical moment. It received national attention. The shocking result of the 2016 presidential election, my own participation in the 2017 Women's March on Washington, the COVID-19 pandemic, the contentious 2020 presidential election, and the January 6 attack on the US Capitol were all profoundly affecting events, to put it mildly. The year I was hired at Piedmont Virginia Community College, the Voting Rights Act of 1965 had been rendered ineffective by the US Supreme Court. More recently, *Roe v. Wade* was overturned. Election denialism has endangered faith in our democratic institutions. The threat of political violence hangs in the air, buoyed by anger generated by disinformation, distortion, and outright lies. I've had outspoken white supremacists and misogynists in my courses state their opinion that women should not have the right to vote and parrot Nazi racial theories. I cannot be alone among American history educators in this regard. Even as this manuscript is being sent to production, the assaults keep coming, as exemplified by the recently proposed SAVE Act, yet another attempt to role back the gains made by women's rights and voting rights activists over the last century. All this recent historical change has required some rewriting of lectures and a reexamination of assumptions about what it means to be an American in the twenty-first century. It has given the teaching of American history added relevance and urgency. One silver lining has been that enrollment in my Women in American History survey class has become steady as young people, women and men, seek deeper understanding of how we've come to this point in our nation's history.

Despite all the weirdness and national trauma, I have been blessed to work in a wonderfully supportive community of colleagues who have since become friends. During the COVID-19 pandemic, I applied for a half-year sabbatical so I could finally make headway toward turning my dissertation into a book. The college awarded me this sabbatical leave for the spring of 2021. I gave up summer teaching to make time for writing. I thank my colleagues and the leadership at PVCC for their positivity, friendship, and moral and financial support as I've labored on this project and waxed on about how it's been shaping up over the last few years. I also thank my students who've expressed their enthusiasm for my course in American women's history and a genuine interest in reading the book when it is finally out. Here it is!

While historical research and writing can be a largely solitary activity, no historical monograph finds its way into print without benefiting from the insights of peers, reviewers, mentors, and editors. This book certainly did. I owe my biggest debt of gratitude to the historian who turned me on to this topic and introduced me, a first-generation college student, to what were once completely alien worlds to me—the ivory tower and the historical profession. Kathryn Kish Sklar, "Kitty," has been a role model, a mentor, an inspiration, a needle reminding me that my work told an important story. I had no idea what she was getting me into all those years ago in graduate school. But I'm glad she did. Kitty connects me, and many others, to the scholarly and feminist pioneers, founders, and institution builders featured in this book, going all the way back to the 1920s when Arthur Schlesinger Sr. threw his support to the study of women in American history. Schlesinger was the graduate advisor of Merle Curti, who was the graduate advisor of John Higham, who was the graduate advisor of Kitty Sklar, who became my dissertation advisor. In the final few years of her teaching career, she agreed to take on "one more" student if I agreed to work on the topic that has now become *Reclaiming Clio*. She was a conscientious and constructive dissertation advisor who helped me conceptualize the project, organize the chapters, and improve as a writer. She encouraged me to go to history conferences, thereby introducing me to the professional culture of historians. Kitty belongs to a remarkable generation of feminist historians who became superb models of professionalism in their dedication to the historian's craft. They forged paths and created spaces within the discipline's core institutions for the women coming after them and for women's history. Her partner, historian Tom Dublin, was part of this generation. Tom, too, served as an important mentor to me at Binghamton University. He kept me employed as a graduate assistant for several years, thereby making sure I could afford to complete graduate school. He served as an integral member of my dissertation committee who always offered incisive editorial feedback. Without these two powerhouse mentors, this book could not have come to fruition. I never would have had the courage, confidence, or endurance to bring it to light. Others at Binghamton University were supportive, including Leigh Ann Wheeler, who joined my dissertation committee in its final year of production. The late sociologist Benita Roth buoyed my confidence in the project with constructive feedback and hyperbolic praise in the wake of my dissertation defense. In retrospect, I think this pushed me into thinking I might be onto something that could be of interest to a broader audience.

The research for this book was largely funded by a series of travel grants. Binghamton University awarded me three separate grants: the Joan S. Dubofsky Research Travel Grant, the Kramer Research Travel Award, and the Rosa Collechio Travel Award. The Southern Historical Collection at the University of North Carolina at Chapel Hill awarded me the J. Carlyle Sitterson Visiting Scholar Grant. The Radcliffe Institute for Advanced Study at Harvard University awarded me a Schlesinger Library Dissertation Research Grant. The librarians and archivists at these and other university special collections at Indiana University–Purdue University, Winthrop University, Duke University, and Texas Woman's University rendered invaluable assistance in person and from afar. Research and oral histories I gathered for the *Journal of Women's History* twenty-fifth anniversary enhanced my treatment of the *JWH* as an example of how historians of women created their own institutions.

I was fortunate to be connected to a first-rate copy editor who has much improved the prose. I thank Michael Strange for her incisive editorial work on the manuscript as the project reached its penultimate phase of completion. She helped rein in tedious, long-winded prose and eliminate redundancies. Thanks go to the University of North Carolina Press and Andrew Winters for seeing value in the project, introducing me to the world of academic publishing, and bringing it to print. I'm appreciative of the peer reviewers who encouraged me to expand key areas of the text and improve the structure and organization of the manuscript in places. Thanks also go to those who provided me with the photographic treasures included on the pages within. I hope these snapshots convey both the solitary satisfaction and collective joy that doing women's history can bring.

My two children grew up and into young adulthood alongside this dissertation-turned-book. If I accomplish nothing else in this life, I've left three legacies behind, whether I ever write another book. Gratitude and love go to Francisco, who has watched me labor over the project like an on-again, off-again obsessive-compulsive for years. I'm so incredibly grateful to my aunties and ancestors. Each has had my back in their own special way. They have supported me in good times and bad and taught me so much about the power of sisterly support and models of maternal love. I hope this book makes them proud.

No book can be all things to all people. The questions and sources I have centered have pushed some individuals and elements of the story to the fore while undoubtedly obscuring others. The conceptual choices and any errors made are my own. I trust others will come along to flesh out elements of the story that have been referenced but leave some readers wanting more. I've tried to provide readers with the broad contours and content of a single academic field's development in one country, across generations, and inclusive of the major areas of historical work that professional historians do: research, writing, teaching, and institution building; professional service in academic societies; and dissemination of knowledge via public history. American women's history, as an academic field, has moved from the intellectual margins in the eyes of professional historians to the very center of historical discourse in the United States. With every new generation, it takes on new dimensions. We must do a better job of sharing the field's insights with the American public and conveying its significance in the broader culture. As the history of the majority, women's history must continue to serve contemporary women as they face the challenge of maintaining the human rights for which women before us fought long and hard.

Finally, I thank the pioneers, founders, and fellow laborers in the vineyards of women's history—both those I've been able to weave into this narrative and those who formed part of the much broader tapestry that made up the twentieth-century movement for women's history in the United States and around the world. They have collectively done a powerful thing in helping the majority find its past. What a priceless gift.

Author's Note

Both the cover and the title of this book invoke Clio, the mythical Greek muse of history. A statue of Clio in a winged chariot overlooks the great men honored in Statuary Hall in the US Capitol building. No doubt her presence is meant as an acknowledgment of the role that written history plays in shaping our national identity and our nation's legal and cultural institutions. How ironic that a female figure should be placed in such an elevated position in the halls of the US Congress, a governing body overwhelmingly made up of male legislators since the nation's founding and a body from which women were categorically excluded until 1917. How ironic too that she should serve as the symbolic inspiration for an academic discipline long dominated by men writing about the history of men. By reclaiming Clio and a place among the history professors for themselves, twentieth-century historians of American women claimed a place for women in the narratives of American history. In doing so, they staked a claim to women's place in the body politic as the coauthors of American civilization. Now more than ever we need Clio to inspire us to shed light on our collective past so that we don't squander away the hard-won progress achieved by dint of 190 years of sustained effort to advance human and civil rights.

Reclaiming Clio

Forward out of error
Leave behind the night
Forward through the darkness
Forward into light!

—motto of the National Woman's Party, between 1911 and 1920

PART I

Frameworks

Introduction

Looking Back at the Making of US Women's History from 2025

The role of women in American history has long been ignored.

—Gerda Lerner, 1971

The history of the Afro-American woman and her role in the making of America has been neglected by historians, just as the history of women in the United States has been neglected.

—Sharon Harley and Rosalyn Terborg-Penn, 1978

Just fifteen years ago, the field of women's history did not exist.

—Mary Beth Norton, 1986

In December 1971, Duke University history professor Anne Firor Scott wrote to Harvard dean and historian Barbara Miller Solomon,

> The whole business of women's history is in such a state of change and excitement that I hardly know where to begin among the things I would like to talk over with you. . . . The question keeps coming up: Why haven't we been training graduate students all these years so that there would be dozens of young women ready now to take jobs with a specialty in the field! . . . The question would have been pooh-poohed . . . not long ago. . . . Many department chairmen seem to have undergone a change comparable to Paul on the road to Damascus.[1]

Scott and Solomon would go on to have that long conversation in the years to come as they both worked to mentor younger historians and foster the development of a rapidly burgeoning field. Both women had earned their doctorates in American history in the 1950s at Radcliffe College, studying with Harvard's Oscar Handlin. Scott's note suggested that women's history was undergoing a profound transformation in 1971, rather than experiencing its moment of creation. This stands in stark contrast to the common wisdom about when the academic field of American women's history began. When and how did women become a recognized part of the narratives of American history, and who were the first professional historians in the United States to work toward that goal? *Reclaiming Clio* offers a new interpretation of the field's origins story.

The book revises the timeline of the field's emergence to consider the professional and scholarly contributions made by multiple generations of historians and archivists over the full course of the twentieth century.[2]

The field's deepest academic roots can be found in work begun by scholars and archivists who operated within the boundaries of the historical and archival disciplines much earlier than is commonly understood. In pioneering the field, they created a stable foundation for what later became a thriving academic enterprise. Then, during the last three decades of the twentieth century, women's history exploded and became well-integrated into the canons of American history. In large part, this was because historians of women embraced the historical profession's craft traditions, because they were incredibly productive, and because they had the benefit of the foundations laid earlier.

But women's history was also inspired by the zeitgeist of each era in which it was produced. The professional activism and scholarly foci of late twentieth-century historians of women were particularly animated by the social justice movements of the time. Participation in the Black civil rights movement, movements for economic justice and peace, and the modern women's movement led historians of American women to develop an "intersectional feminist" approach to their work well before that term was coined by legal scholar Kimberlé Crenshaw in 1989 as shorthand for analyzing the complex ways that race, class, gender, and other markers of difference have operated in societies past and present.[3] In seeking to incorporate women fully into the narratives of American history, many feminist historians of this era broke down the barriers created by androcentric, elitist, and racist practices and perspectives in the ivory tower. Historians of women in America today are thus the inheritors of a rich tradition of engagement with, and struggle against, androcentrism, racism, elitism, heteronormativity, and sexism in the discipline of history.

During much of the twentieth century, the American ivory tower and the historical profession were predominantly male, white, and marked by pervasive androcentrism. For example, when Marc Bloch wrote his influential tract *The Historian's Craft* in the 1940s, he specifically framed the craft as a masculine pursuit, titling his opening essay "History, Men, and Time."[4] Here he shared a conversation he had with his son, who inquired, "Daddy, what is the use of history?" The subtitle of the book was "Reflections on the Nature and Uses of History and the Techniques and Methods of the Men Who Write It."[5] The editor of the volume opened his introduction with two words: "Western man." Title, subtitle, father-son exchange, and editor's note all signaled that male historians understood history writing to be a masculine pursuit of knowledge about men in the Western world. Similarly, Jack H. Hexter, in reviewing Mary Beard's *Woman as Force in History* for the *New York Times Book Review* in 1946, stated that it was not the fault of male historians that history had primarily been "stag affairs."[6] Instead, he argued, men predominated in the written remains of history that scholars had to work with. He repeated this sentiment with somewhat different implications in 1979, in *On Historians*, which he dedicated to his Yale University "colleagues, living and dead, gentlemen, and scholars."[7] Feminist scholars who later made observations about how androcentric the formal history profession was had plenty of evidence to support this contention and confirm their impressions. In short, historians' scholarly focus had been the political, military, intellectual, and economic activities of men.

Women entering the historical profession during the first half of the twentieth century were a distinct minority with limited influence over the focus of historical study. The first American woman history PhD was Kate Everest Levi, who earned her degree at the University of Wisconsin in 1893 when she submitted her dissertation on German immigrants in Wisconsin.[8] Between 1893 and 1935, white women earned 16 percent of the 2,055 history PhDs awarded in the United States. Only 4 of these pioneering 334 women, Elisabeth Anthony Dexter, Virginia Gearhart, Helen Marshall, and Mary Sumner Benson, are known to have written dissertations pointedly focused on women in America. Of these four, only Marshall and Benson found permanent places in the historical profession as full professors, Marshall at Illinois State Normal University and Benson at Mt. Holyoke College for women. There was only one African American woman history PhD in the United States in 1935: Anna Julia Cooper, a graduate of Oberlin College, earned a PhD in history in France at the Sorbonne in 1925 at the age of sixty-seven. Had she gone knocking, her age, race, and gender undoubtedly would have conspired to keep the doors of American history departments closed to her. Despite her remarkable achievement, her dissertation on French ideas about slavery could not win her a place among the ranks of American history professors. Black women historians would remain marginal as they entered the profession thereafter in very small numbers, beginning with Marion Thompson Wright. In 1940, she was the first Black woman awarded a history PhD by an American university—Teachers College, Columbia University. She went on to teach at Howard University. Neither Cooper nor Wright had made women the focus of her scholarship. The male mainstream of the profession demonstrated little interest in the history of women in these same years, and the female minority in the profession mostly followed suit. All that changed during the second half of the twentieth century due to the innovation, persistence, hard work, scholarly productivity, professional activism, and struggle of feminist historians.[9]

The struggle for women's history was waged both within the broader historical profession and among historians of women with distinct, always evolving visions for the future of the field. The work was exciting and rewarding, challenging and difficult, often affirming, at times painful.[10] Ultimately, it gave women in the United States and around the world an enduring place in written human history, a canon that now forms part of humanity's collective cultural legacy. Along the way, feminist historians have collaborated and clashed with one another over the content of their field, understanding that, as Lisa Tetrault and others have suggested, the stakes of women's history are very high.[11] The histories we choose to make visible through our work have great cultural power and resonance. This book tells the story of the field's remarkable trajectory during the twentieth century, detailing the contributions of several generations of feminist historians as they searched for usable pasts and scholarly legitimacy and worked to expand and diversify the scope of their field. They did the heavy lifting of building American women's history into a robust field and making it the relatively diverse and inclusive enterprise that it is today. Feminist historians ultimately shifted the gendered paradigms of the American historical profession. The story ahead considers feminist historians' impact on academic culture and the content of American history. It is a story long overdue and clearly much needed as the modern field of women's and gender history is the product of at least three full generations of feminist scholars who ought to be understood in historical relation to one another. Their accomplishments were considerable.

Indeed, women's history experienced particularly remarkable growth in the final third of the century. From 1969 to 2005, the number of women's and gender historians in American history departments rose from less than 1 percent of historians to nearly 9 percent of all specialists listed in the *American Historical Association Directory of History Departments, Historical Organizations, and Historians in the United States and Canada*—making them the single largest group of specialists in the country in 2005.[12] From 1975 to 2005, the number of history departments in the United States and Canada with one or more specialists in women's and gender history rose from 18 percent to 80 percent. The scholarly output of these historians was prolific. Working both within the academy and outside it, feminist historians made space for their field within the discipline, within academia, and in society more broadly. While there were male allies on the scene, feminist historians often pursued their work in the face of indifference, skepticism, and ridicule from their male peers. Yet, they were energized and supported by the modern women's movement as students, scholars, and professors.

Taking a longer perspective, the field's development over the course of the century paralleled the ebb and flow of the feminist movement and reflected the various strains of feminism that developed from 1920 forward. Historians of women and feminists alike saw the work of constructing a usable past as essential to women's pursuit of equality. Their epistemological project first recognized women as worthy of scholarly attention by virtue of their active influence on human history and then worked to re-center dominant historical narratives, presenting a fuller, more accurate vision of the past by incorporating the female half of humanity.[13]

Debates over the content of American history have been central to America's national identity and have figured prominently in our culture wars since the early twentieth century. Joan Marie Johnson and Christine Erickson have shown that women—Black and white, conservative and progressive—have long seen the content of the American history curriculum as an important front in the culture wars.[14] Public discourse has been particularly contentious since the 1960s as marginalized Americans sought to claim their rightful places in history as the makers of our society.[15] Most recently this has been reflected in heated, even violent controversies surrounding the removal of Confederate monuments, in conservative anger against initiatives like the 1619 Project, in fears regarding the teaching of "critical race theory" in public schools, and in scholarly scorn for the Trump administration's reactionary and ahistorical 1776 Commission. Even presidents of prestigious historical societies have gotten caught up in these controversies.[16]

The furor over what elements of American history should be at the center of our collective history, and anxiety surrounding who has been doing history right or wrong, suggest that no matter where one is on the political spectrum, or whether one is a trained professional, most people understand that the history we write, acknowledge, and honor reflects and defines our cultural values and shapes our national and individual identities. This, of course, includes the histories of men, women, sex, gender, and gender inequality alongside *and intersecting with* the histories of race, racism, and white supremacy; the place of immigrants and LGBTQ Americans in American life; and the history of the working classes. To see women's history in all its rich and intersectional diversity is to value women and envision them as active participants in all areas of American life. Yet, a world without women's history was a reality not so long ago. Women's role in history was not valued, and women were largely absent from scholarly history books and the K–16 school curriculum. As one participant in the women's history movement framed it in 1974, students of history had been sold a "male fantasy" and might legitimately demand their money back. The majority found its past in the second half of the twentieth century when feminist historians excavating in the archives individually, collectively, and systematically brought the facts to light, interpreting them for the history-reading public.[17]

Reclaiming Clio considers the development of women's history in the United States during three overlapping chronological periods marked by individual, institutional, and collective strategies of knowledge production. It argues that the field's development was not the work of a single generation of late twentieth-century scholars. Instead, the book offers a generationally, regionally, and racially inclusive interpretation of women's history in the United States. First, it examines how individual historians of women contributed to knowledge production from 1900 to 1968, when the field's legitimacy and even existence was not recognized by most historians; the term "women's history" didn't exist for most of this period. It then examines 1943–68 as a critical field-building period within discrete educational institutions where major women's archives were established, providing the first building blocks and foundation for the emerging field. Finally, it charts the collective work of historians in the women's history movement from 1969 to 2000 by examining how scholarship, institution building, teaching, and other forms of history production served to re-envision women's place in American history.

While *Reclaiming Clio* primarily situates the work of feminist historians within the context of the professional culture of historians working in the ivory tower, it also considers this work in the gendered context of American political culture. It examines the political underpinnings of women's history as an endeavor ongoing before, during, and after the crest of late twentieth-century feminism. From 1900 to 1968, the history of women often informed feminist activism and vice versa, even though academic historians were at pains to keep their politics out of their scholarship in their search for legitimacy within academia. The field's meteoric rise to prominence after 1969 is to be attributed to the energy of participants in the "women's history movement" who drew inspiration from the modern women's movement in their bid to open the historical profession to women and women's history. In doing so, they did not lose sight of their responsibilities to uphold scholarly standards and craft traditions. Yet, their feminist adaptations to the professional practice of history had enormous implications for how we see women and the past—not least of which was to assert the historical and cultural value of women in all their diversity. The women's history movement was an intellectual and professional movement within the historical profession in which feminist scholars organized collectively to expand, legitimize, and diversify the history of women through scholarly production, professional service, teaching, and institution building. This book undertakes to explain how historians of women gained a place for their field within a professional culture dominated by men who had hitherto produced histories mostly about men. It suggests why that process of legitimization mattered to feminist historians and women in general.

A major thread woven into this narrative considers the impact of systemic racism and gender discrimination on the historical profession. It explores how and when historians of American women addressed these inequities. If, during most of the century, the historical profession was overwhelmingly male, it was also overwhelmingly white in terms of practitioners and subject matter. This left people of color, and especially women of color, marginalized or excluded for the most part, with some significant exceptions. Historians only began to work to remedy this situation toward the end of the century. Feminist historians, particularly women of color, were active on this front.

The intellectual, professional, and political roots of the field are deeper than usually acknowledged and spread across several fields of activity. In 1922, progressive historian Arthur Schlesinger Sr. urged historians to attend more closely to "the roles and contributions of women in American society."[18] Few professionally credentialed historians—meaning holders of PhDs in history—responded to his call until 1970. Yet, those who did respond laid down an important foundation, which included writing women into cultural, political, and social histories, establishing manuscript collections and archives about women, and publishing a small body of monographic work on the history of American women between the 1920s and 1960.[19] In the 1960s scholars wrote a little more, and in the 1970s feminist historians unleashed a flood of new and innovative work on women, transforming American history as we knew it.

Historiography

Most historical studies that examine women and other marginalized groups in academia emphasize how a given group's exclusion from or incursion into an academic discipline impacts the production of knowledge about that group. Following in that model, this volume focuses on women within the American historical profession. Despite the marginalizing effects of sex discrimination, these women found ways to create historical knowledge about women. They developed professional strategies that advanced and deepened that knowledge between 1900 and 2000. From 1969 forward, historians of women came to understand that to change the content of history more comprehensively, they would have to change the professional culture of historians—an insight that earlier generations had not acted upon.

Historians have paid considerable attention to the way that the professionalization of history and other academic disciplines in the United States and western Europe from the 1880s to the 1940s marginalized women in those disciplines. For example, Margaret Rossiter and Julie Des Jardins have written compelling accounts of the gendered nature of medical and scientific fields and reported on women's experiences and strategies for working in an increasingly masculinized environment.[20] Their analyses of the sciences extend up to 1970 to show that processes of masculinization and female exclusion were pervasive. Rosalind Rosenberg has written two major accounts about women social scientists' impact on their disciplines. In *Beyond Separate Spheres*, she focused on how they contributed to the understanding of sex differentiation.

In *Changing the Subject*, she described the educational and professional experiences and scholarly insights developed by women of Columbia University in the disciplines of psychology, anthropology, sociology, the law, and history in the early to middle twentieth century.[21] Rosenberg's studies suggested that when women asked the questions, framed the studies, and posited answers, the results were attuned to the impact of sex and gender on society and politics. Penina Migdal Glazer and Miriam Slater examined the uneven playing field that women found in a variety of professions requiring advanced degrees like history, science, and medicine from 1890 to 1940.[22]

Similarly, accounts of women in the historical profession look at women's professional status and discuss how women historians have shaped, or failed to shape, historical discourse by including scholarship about women and gender. These studies have focused on either the period up to 1945 or the period after 1969. This more than twenty-year lacuna in the field's historiography and the study of women in the historical profession is odd since it was between 1943 and 1969 that about two dozen credentialed scholars turned their gaze to women. During these same years, two preeminent women's history archives were established: the Radcliffe Women's Archives, now called the Arthur and Elizabeth Schlesinger Library on the History of Women in America, and the Sophia Smith Collection of Women's History at Smith College.

Bonnie Smith and Julie Des Jardins have offered major statements on women as both professional and popular historians and on the historical study of women in the period before 1945. In *The Gender of History*, Smith compellingly argues that as the practice of writing history professionalized in the late nineteenth century, it became an exclusive, university-based masculine pursuit. Male historians in universities in the United States and Europe developed standards for writing scientific, allegedly objective history based on official state archival research and dispassionate analysis of historical documents. This development recast history written in a popular literary style by those without university training, particularly women "scribblers," as amateur. Exacerbating this masculinizing process, men of status generally controlled access to higher education and the seminar-style training required to earn credentials, essentially excluding most women (and most racial and ethnic minorities in the American context) from professional historical practice.[23] Historians in the United States based their history programs and early craft traditions on the German model developed by Leopold von Ranke. This model departed from older literary traditions of historical writing. It made history into a "scientific" discipline; history was to be written "as it was," based on official sources, and without value judgments, biases, or a personally informed perspective.[24]

The centrality of the Rankean model of history to scholarly discourse in the United States was featured in Peter Novick's influential work *That Noble Dream:*

The "Objectivity Question" and the American Historical Profession. In striving to achieve the proper level of objectivity, the historian had to be dispassionate, which precluded the historian being inspired by "presentist," politically motivated, personal concerns. Rankean objectivists cautioned that scholars should take special care when writing about their own particular social group lest they produce biased, unreliable history. As an example, Novick observed that Black historians who studied Black history during the first half of the twentieth century were automatically suspected of bias.[25] This extended to women who chose to write about women in history. To be a woman studying the history of women could delegitimize a publication and jeopardize a career. In this process, native-born white men of the middle and upper classes—the majority of faculty in history departments—were universalized as the norm: the only group capable of writing about themselves objectively and with the proper level of detachment.[26]

Further considering the pre-1945 period that Smith and Des Jardins evaluated, Robert Townsend contends in *History's Babel* that the professionalization of the historical enterprise in America was in fact fractured and contested. Between 1910 and 1940, what had once been an intellectual community open to archivists, precollegiate educators, and local and state historical societies became increasingly esoteric and specialized in terms of research and scholarly standards.[27] It wouldn't be until after 1940 that the historical profession began to open to significant numbers of people of the working class, immigrants and their children, people of color, and women. William Palmer suggests that this shift turned the historical profession from a "gentleman's club" into a more inclusive, representative professional body between 1940 and 1980. This shift also increased scholarly interest in the histories of these same groups of Americans.[28]

Julie Des Jardins's *Women and the Historical Enterprise in America* focuses on women writers of history and other historical workers in the United States from 1880 to 1945. Her major focus, though, is on marginalized professional and amateur historians writing popular, local, regional, institutional, race, and movement histories. Some of these writers produced histories on African Americans, women, Native Americans, and other marginalized groups. Others, such as those working with the Daughters of the American Revolution or the United Daughters of the Confederacy, wrote in a more filiopietistic, conservative vein. They worked at or beyond the fringes of the historical discipline, in archives and historical societies, on public school curriculum projects, and in historical preservation. Des Jardins argues that they made important contributions to historical knowledge as shapers of popular memory. Moreover, she suggests that these "amateurs," as they were considered by professional scholars, may have had a larger impact than academic historians, since they influenced curriculum development and textbook selection in schools throughout the country, wrote bestsellers, and participated in historic preservation projects more readily accessible to the public than the scholarly tomes of academic history.[29] Women's history was produced by suffragists, feminists, and African American, white, and other women active in affiliative, reform, and civic associations. Many simply hoped to leave to posterity histories undistorted by outsiders or detractors of their movements. Others were particularly invested in developing origins stories of the women's movement that centered their own involvement. Lisa Tetrault's work, for example, considers how Elizabeth Cady Stanton and Susan B. Anthony constructed the first history of the American woman suffrage movement.[30] They centered their own contributions and actions, thereby rendering less visible, or invisible, the work of rival activists and most women of color. These women and their peers understood the cultural power that inhered in the construction of national historical narratives. They hoped to incorporate women into them intentionally and with positive effects. African American women, for instance, developed a positive Black history K–12 curriculum as part of their broader work of racial uplift and their desire to counter white supremacist history narratives. Important as these types of history writing are as objects of historical study, though, this book is about the scholarly history of women that was produced by those working in universities and colleges during the twentieth century and how and why they produced it.

For thirty years, Judith Zinsser's 1993 *History and Feminism: A Glass Half Full* has served as the one historical monograph explaining the field's emergence and development. She argued that this was due to the combination of the "new" social history of the 1960s and the impact of second-wave feminism on the historical discipline. Explaining that new social historians of the 1960s paid little attention to the subject of women and were often hostile to it, Zinsser's work has two foci—the status of women in the historical profession and the development of women's and gender history since 1970. Drawing on a more limited fount of archival sources than is now available, she provided a helpful first draft of feminist historians' efforts to build and legitimize the field while pursuing greater access to professional institutions. When she wrote, the movement was still in full swing, just beginning to take stock of its enormous advances, and reaping the rewards of two decades of intense work.[31]

Zinsser's opening pages rather sweepingly claimed that "in discovering and writing women's history, feminist scholars challenged every aspect of the historian's craft."[32] We will see that women's and gender historians integrated rapidly into the discipline between 1970 and 2000 precisely because they embraced historians' craft traditions and professional culture, albeit modified through the application of feminist principles and collective action on behalf of the field. Professional academic cultures shape intellectual cultures and therefore knowledge.[33] History, as an academic discipline, has its own craft traditions and professional culture. Most historians are socialized into this professional culture through gradual acculturation—by living up to standards of professional behavior and conduct modeled by peers and mentors. The *craft traditions* of historians are a basic set of practices that have evolved since the 1880s, when historians in Europe and the Western world first tried to regularize or "discipline" their work through the development of research and writing standards, methodologies, and stylistic conventions. Yet, as Marc Bloch argued in *The Historian's Craft*, the "science" of history, concerned with the relationship between historical phenomena and their connection to the present, has remained as much art as "science."[34] Nevertheless, historians hold to a standard that demands research in original archival sources, critical analysis and interpretation of the evidence, careful documentation, and the written and oral presentation of scholarship for peer review. Essential is the willingness to change an interpretation when new or reexamined evidence contradicts or significantly complicates a prior thesis. The overall goal of historians is to explain change and stasis over time and how events, periods, and trends relate to one another. Many would argue that historians must also explain the contradictions inherent in the historical record and the relevance of key events, people, periods, and historical trends to the present.[35]

In addition to adhering to these craft traditions, historians have their own professional culture.[36] Common work experiences, patterns, and beliefs within the historical profession have guided historians' behavior and attitudes as they have gone about their work since the 1880s.[37] The professional culture of American historians is transmitted in graduate schools, history departments, formal and informal scholarly networks, academic journals, and professional societies, such as the American Historical Association (AHA, founded in 1884), the Organization of American Historians (OAH, founded in 1907 as the Mississippi Valley Historical Association), and the Southern Historical Association (SHA, founded in 1935).[38] Smaller or more specialized associations have also proliferated since the early twentieth century, such as the Association for the Study of Negro Life and History, founded in 1915. It was renamed the Association for the Study of Afro-American Life and History in the 1970s before taking its current name, the Association for the Study of African American Life and History. Transmission of the profession's cultural values and expectations was accomplished through these institutions' executive boards and councils, via their committees, and in the pages of their journals and newsletters. While recognition primarily rests upon the quality of historians' scholarly work, professional service in the associational life of the discipline has also been a path to recognition. University history departments and presses uphold the standards generated by these structures that support the production of historical knowledge.

The story ahead is by and large a story about historians of women who acculturated successfully to their chosen profession—a profession long dominated by middle-class and elite white men operating within a framework colloquially referred to as an "old boy network." These women were few in number before 1970 because most would-be historians of women had limited access to mentors willing to guide them and the larger professional culture was not interested in the questions they were asking. After 1970, feminist historians of the era were dedicated scholars with a shared mission, certainly. But they did not "discover" and write "women's history" for the first time any more than Columbus "discovered" the "New World." They had a small body of foundational work in archives and scholarship to build on as they reimagined and redirected the field. They needed to find and interpret the archival materials necessary to further develop the field, define its topical and theoretical parameters, and insist on women's rightful place within the narratives of American history.

Existing scholarship on the historical profession in the United States does little to help us understand the place of women in American historiography in the twentieth century. A few examples will suffice. Peter Novick's important study *That Noble Dream* includes only a very brief section on the emergence of women's history as a "subfield" in the 1970s.[39] He frames the field in reference to the impact contemporary politics had on a variety of "revisionist" histories. He pays negligible attention to women or the study of women in the profession before the 1970s. And the very absurdity of Novick referring to the history of half of humanity as a "subfield" must be called out. John Higham's classic 1965 study, *History: The Development of Historical Studies in the United States*, ignored women historians and the history of women completely.[40] This is especially ironic since Higham had studied under Merle Curti, who in turn studied under Arthur Schlesinger Sr., both of whom had been early prominent, vocal, and active supporters of developing women's history. Moreover, Higham was the graduate advisor of Kathryn Kish Sklar, who is widely regarded as a founder of the "new women's history" of the late 1960s and early 1970s.[41] This may suggest that while he was certainly aware of this emerging field of inquiry, and at least tolerant of his advisees' interest in the history of women, he didn't deem the subject worthy of inclusion in his general work on historical studies in the United States. A more current example of how women and gender are treated is found in a commonly assigned 1997 text. George Iggers's otherwise crisp and comprehensive *Historiography in the Twentieth Century: From Scientific Objectivity to the Postmodern Challenge* pays scant attention to women and gender.[42] In this otherwise wide-ranging overview of the topic, he gives only passing acknowledgment to women historians and gender history. Women's history registers as a faint blip. As a measure, out of roughly 376 index entries, only 12 (3 percent) refer to significant women historians, women's history, feminism, or gender history. Both traditional historiographies and feminist historiographies thus leave us relatively uninformed as to the state of the field and its practitioners prior to 1969 or after.

The first part of this book recovers the work of these historians and archivists. Where possible, it links them to the subsequent generation of scholar activists. Later chapters examine the exciting story of the women's history movement launched at the annual meeting of the American Historical Association in December 1969. Chapter 1 of *Reclaiming Clio* considers how participants in the women's history movement have understood, explained, and problematized the rise of their specialization to the heights of legitimacy and recognition within the American historical profession since the 1970s. It suggests that a closer examination of the record is in order, an examination that can offer the field's students and practitioners a cohesive narrative spanning the twentieth century and demonstrating how the work of each generation of scholars built on the shoulders of the previous generation. In essence, the chapter interrogates the "origins story" of the academic field of American women's history in much the same spirit as Lisa Tetrault does that of the women's movement in *The Myth of Seneca Falls*. This is not to discredit or refute the collective memory of participants in the women's history movement but rather to give their movement and generational perspectives the serious scholarly attention they deserve and place them in longer historical context. Chapters 2 and 3 address the field's early development through the lens of historians of women writing regional, cultural, progressive, and social history, some of whom worked within the historical discipline's central institutions and whose work was welcomed by its arbiters of legitimacy. They did so in an era when women were a marginalized minority within the historical profession.

In chapters 4 and 5, I show how the establishment of women's archives at Radcliffe College/Harvard and at Smith College in 1943 allowed "women's history" to gain ground at the center of American academic life. I explore this in the broader context of efforts to collect and preserve archival records on women: Black women archivists' and librarians' work to create the Bethune Museum Archives, for example; efforts at the Huntington Library in California; and work at other collecting institutions. For too long the historiography has remained stuck at the beginning of the story with Mary Beard's seminal efforts to foster women's archives in the 1930s and 1940s. Here, we examine how others ultimately brought her vision to fruition. Chapter 5 moves the story forward to document the construction of an ambitious encyclopedia project in the history of American women, *Notable American Women, 1607–1950: A Biographical Dictionary*.[43] This massive project, sponsored by Radcliffe College and the Belknap Press of Harvard University Press from 1955 to 1971, drew on the support of hundreds of established professional historians who lent their legitimacy to the emerging field, paving the way for its increasing recognition within the historical discipline.

Chapter 6 considers the political activism and affiliations of the historians of women featured in chapters 2–5 and establishes the connection between the content of their historical work and their engagement in politics. There were feminists of every stripe working in the field at midcentury. The record demonstrates that though muted in their academic historical writing, these historians' political commitments resonated in their scholarship in the best tradition of progressive and social history. What's more, they incorporated their historical perspectives on women into the literature they wrote for the civic, volunteer, and governmental institutions with which they worked. These scholars and activists developed a distinct sensibility that women's progress depended on understanding women's past and appreciating their evolving place in the world. I am labeling this sensibility *feminist historicism*. In this they worked in the tradition of previous, nonacademic history writers. But as credentialed academics they did not yet bridge the feminist and professional streams of their work. That bridge would not be built until the women's history movement coalesced.

Chapters 7 through 11 construct a narrative of the women's history movement—its goals, its struggles, and its successes between 1969 and 2000. Each chapter identifies major participants and initiatives, organizational strategies, and distinct arenas of activity. Chapter 7 reconstructs the history of the seminal meeting of feminist historians at the December 1969 American Historical Association annual conference. Here the opening salvos of the movement were launched, and the groups formed in response immediately started to attract a multigenerational following of historians committed to developing and promoting women's history. Chapter 8 delves deeper into the history of the movement by examining the emergence of a women's history professional subculture within the historical profession comprised of regional history organizations and informal networks. It also offers a history of the early Berkshire Conference on the History of Women. It considers the topical areas of investigation that were featured in the work of participants and the demographic composition of those active in organizing the conference over the years. Still predominantly white, feminist historians in the movement by the mid- to late 1970s were often keenly focused on race, ethnicity, and class in their work and eager to diversify their ranks. Women of color scholars took pains to remind them to include their work as part of the emerging canon and participated actively in these conferences and the broader life of the profession. In light of the controversy that erupted over a panelist making racially offensive remarks at the 2023 Big Berkshire Conference, it is my hope that this chapter can offer some fuller and deeper context about the history of the conference that can help contemporary historians gain historical perspective on its place in the broader nexus of feminist historians' organizational activity over the last ninety years.[44]

Chapter 9 considers the ways in which women's historians worked to incorporate their scholarly insights into collegiate and graduate teaching, textbooks, and curricula in the 1970s and 1980s. By 1989, leading lights could proclaim that "Women's History had finally been recognized as legitimate"; it had "arrived," and what was left to consider were the new directions the field should take.[45] By this time too, more women of color had become vital participants in the movement. Chapters 10 and 11 detail some of these new directions, including a discussion of efforts to more fully and critically explore the differences among American women through the lenses of race, class, sexual orientation, and ideological proclivities. Furthermore, in the 1980s and 1990s, feminist historians more fully recognized the need to extend the reach of women's history into the realm of public history and public discourse. In doing so they hoped to enrich and illuminate women's profile in history and society as part of their broader political and cultural project. Feminist historians redoubled their efforts to incorporate women in museum collections and in national park representations. They also raised their voices as public intellectuals. But this raised profile did not come without risks. Women's history was increasingly caught up in the culture wars over the content of history education in the United States in much the same way that Black history has been. Detractors of both fields have resented that traditional white and male-centered history must now share the historical stage with other categories of Americans, whose stories complicate and enrich simplistic patriotic narratives of American exceptionalism.

Sources and Analytic Frameworks

This study relies upon previously untapped archival sources, oral histories, and the published record of the field to understand the trajectory of women's history within the American historical profession over a 100-year period. The institutional records of the major historical associations were an essential part of the research plan and included the records of the Organization of American Historians, the Southern Historical Association, the American Historical Association, the Berkshire Conference of Women Historians, the Berkshire Conference on the History of Women, the Coordinating Committee on Women in the Historical Profession–Conference Group on Women's History, the Southern Association for Women Historians, and the Association of Black Women Historians; the records of the Sophia Smith Collection and the Schlesinger Library on the History of Women in America were also heavily used. Newspapers, magazines, organizational newsletters, and academic publications were consulted. The papers of individual historians of women active both before the emergence of the women's history movement in 1969 and after were an important component of the research plan. Both professional correspondence and the front matter of publications, especially the acknowledgments and prefaces of books, offered clues and endearing insights into the texture of historians' mutually supportive relationships with one another.

Oral histories, historiographic essays, and personal memoirs of women's historians provided another major line of research.[46] Key among these is the oral history collection housed at the Sophia Smith Collection at Smith College, the Living US Women's History Oral History Project.[47] This collection contains fifty-one oral history interviews on videotapes, audiotapes, and in transcription with many of the field's founders and most powerful voices. They are an important collective statement of the remembered experiences of several generations of scholars in the field. The oral histories formed my original conception of the history contained herein—a history characterized partly by struggle and conflict with a resistant masculine professional culture and a history closely linked to the fortunes of the late twentieth-century women's movement in the United States. However, my research in the archives revealed a more complex set of gendered professional and intellectual dynamics at play from 1943 to the 1980s than the oral histories and reflective publications suggested to me *at first*. Instead of resulting from one particularly productive generation of feminist scholars, women's history developed from a long series of dialogues, collaborations, debates, and conflicts over the place of women in American history from 1920 forward. These exchanges occurred between men and women in the discipline, between different generations of "women's historians," and between those holding distinct historical and political philosophies. In each generation, though, historians of women sought to create scholarship that was both *responsible*, according to the craft traditions of the discipline, and *useful* to American women as their participation in public life and society transformed and expanded over the course of the century. For academic women's historians, doing scholarship that was recognized by their professional peers as legitimate was the cornerstone to achieving these dual goals. And so, learning to navigate the professional culture and master the craft traditions of historians was critical to their success.

The analytic framework for this study rests on three interrelated factors: a basic understanding of historians' professional culture and how individuals navigated it; an understanding of what makes a social and intellectual movement; and an awareness of historical shifts in the definition of feminism and its varieties. Historians of women developed their field within the discipline of history, at its margins, or outside it, in relation to these three factors in the United States. For much of the twentieth century, the professional culture was marked by the relative marginalization of women—and for that matter, the exclusion of people of color from the profession and from participation in its organizational life.[48] While many women historians recognized this problem, none organized against it until 1969. Even the women of the small Northeastern Berkshire Conference of Women Historians, established between 1928 and 1930, did little to challenge their professional marginalization during the organization's first four decades in existence.[49] Most women scholars at midcentury practiced an equal rights approach to gaining recognition; that is, they asked to be judged and rewarded on their individual merits with no special consideration of the woman scholar as a class of worker confronting significant structural barriers to advancement. This stance made it difficult to push for an end to discriminatory patterns or for the study of their marginalized group. This approach persisted despite considerable evidence that pointed to its ineffectiveness right up until December 1969.[50]

In combining their commitments to their craft and to improving women's place in history, participants in the late twentieth century's *women's history movement* recognized these problems as endemic and moved decisively to offer solutions. They formed separate professional associations like the Coordinating Committee on Women in the Historical Profession or the Southern Association for Women Historians. These new women's institutions worked to meet the needs of women in the profession by providing networks, newsletters, recognition of women's scholarship, and scholarly conferences to showcase and vet new work. At the same time, historians of women sought to make history's overall professional culture less hierarchical, more inclusive, more transparent, and more participatory.[51] In this they echoed the women's liberation movement with its consciousness-raising, emphasis on democratic process, and anti-hierarchical traditions.[52] Since mainstream institutions were the ones they were trying to change, they also worked within them, demanding the establishment of status of women committees and more representation of their work in history journals and on conference programs. The creation of these committees in the historical profession's chief institutions from 1970 forward was undoubtedly inspired by the status of women commissions created by the Kennedy administration and the fifty states during the 1960s.

The women's history movement was an intellectual and professional movement for women's history within the historical profession.[53] While it was linked to the broader twentieth-century social movements for women's rights and women's equality, it cannot be properly defined as a social movement. Confined as it was to the historical profession and academic institutions, it did not have a mass base. Nevertheless, since the 1970s, participants in the women's history movement have reached beyond the ivory tower to raise Americans' historical consciousness about women—seeing their work as inspired by, even part of, the modern feminist movement.

In 1961, the women's movement was revitalized when progressive feminists active in the Democratic Party convinced John F. Kennedy to establish the President's Commission on the Status of Women. This commission was, in fact, the brainchild of midcentury feminists, some of whom had been professional historians. The revived women's movement after 1961 prompted recognition of and assault on the structural inequalities that women academics had hitherto confronted as lone scholars. By 1968, the coming of age of the baby boomers and the emergence of the women's liberation movement led to rising female enrollment in higher education and entry of increasing numbers of young radical feminists into graduate history programs. As these new historians navigated the historical profession, their politics influenced the strategies they developed to challenge structural inequalities within the profession. Their politics also inspired their interest in the history of women. The emphasis on "personal politics" and "sexual politics" in women's liberation and a commitment to civil rights and antiwar activism likewise influenced the direction of women's history scholarship after 1969. Thus, the picture emerges of several generations of feminist historians uncovering the history of women in their own ways. Historians of women from each of these generations, credentialed and otherwise, recognized the value of "women's history" and were determined to write and disseminate it.

Chapter 1

Rethinking the Midcentury Doldrums Narrative of American Women's History

> Those of us who began teaching US women's history in the early 1970s can well remember our efforts to invent the wheel.
>
> —Ann Boylan, 1992

> The contributors to this volume grew up into a world in which history was rigidly limited. It paid limited attention to social relationships, to issues of race, to the concerns of the poor, and virtually none to women.
>
> —Linda Kerber, Alice Kessler-Harris, and Kathryn Kish Sklar, 1995

> When I entered the profession in the late 1960s, there was no such field as "women's history" and only a few enterprising souls were willing to explore the arena.
>
> —Alice Kessler-Harris, 2007

It is often taken as a truism among historians of women in America that the academic field of women's history only came into being in the United States during the 1970s.[1] Yet, what appears to be a clear generational consensus about the newness of the field in the 1970s is not so clear upon closer examination. A perfect example comes from historian Carol Lasser. In 1987 Lasser analyzed the impact of Eleanor Flexner's prescient 1959 publication, *Century of Struggle: The Woman's Rights Movement in the United States*, on the emergence of the women's history field. Calling the years between 1940 and 1969 "pre-history" in the field of American women's history, she rhetorically set this period apart from the boom in women's history that came after. Despite Lasser's recognition of a handful of professional academic historians working on the subject in the "pre-women's history" period, she suggested that the field of women's history did not begin during these years.[2] Many other late twentieth-century historians of women searching for the field's founders and origins looked to Flexner and to Mary Beard, a well-known author and early advocate for women's history in the archives field. Neither woman held a PhD nor pretensions to becoming a history professor. Beard and Flexner operated at the margins of the historical profession. On the other hand, when late twentieth-century feminist historians encountered the work of professional historians of American women from the earlier era, they tended to dismiss their work as "compensatory" and lacking in analytical rigor. In denying that the field existed between 1900 and 1968, feminist historians of the 1970s and 1980s dismissed an entire generation of scholars, marking out their work as of little importance in the field's development. Yet, it was during these years that a host of women's history archives were founded in the United States. The work of nearly two dozen historians of American women with a PhD made it into print from 1920 to 1968. What began in the early 1970s as the effort of a new generation of feminist historians to distinguish themselves intellectually from an earlier generation had, by the late 1980s, become an oversimplified historiography in which a few pioneers and marginal noncredentialed historians merely prefigured what was to come. This simplified narrative claimed there was no field before the second wave of the feminist movement generated support for its development.[3]

In the 1970s, historians of women constructed their intellectual identities as women's historians in dialogue with each other and with their male counterparts in their respective fields. Their identity was also formed by setting themselves apart from an earlier generation of specialists in the field. In the 1990s, as women's history became a permanent and legitimate part of history departments in the United States, analyses of the field's development focused on the period between 1969 and 1989, showing how historians of women coped with issues of careerism and professional status, as well as how they gradually incorporated class, race, ethnicity, sexual orientation, and other differences among women into their scholarship. Nevertheless, as these analyses assumed that the field began after 1969, they missed important aspects of the field's earlier development.

Lise Vogel's 1991 essay "Telling Tales: Historians of Our Own Lives" offered an early critique of this historiographic interpretation. Vogel challenged the view that mainstream American women's history had evolved seamlessly from a model focused primarily on the experiences of white middle-class Northeastern women whose lives were shaped by the ideology of separate spheres in the 1970s to a model that increasingly incorporated people of color, race, class, gender, and sexuality in the 1980s.[4] Instead, Vogel suggested that these factors had been part of the scholarship since the field's emergence around 1969. She argued that this somewhat teleological history of a progressively more sophisticated and inclusive women's history was "sanitized" and "self-congratulatory." But more importantly, she said that this tale of progress failed to recognize the interventions that 1970s scholarship had made in the history of race, class, and gender. Yet, at the same time, Vogel did not acknowledge scholarship produced before the 1970s, some of which did in fact also attend to matters of race, class, and regional differences among American women. Each new cohort of women's historians, including those entering the profession in the 1970s, the 1980s, and the 1990s, seems either to have been unaware of earlier work in the field, to have dismissed predecessors' scholarship as inadequate, or to have ignored it, failing altogether to recognize that same scholarship as a foundation and springboard for newer work.

A kind of generational myopia led new historians of women in the 1970s—and again, those in the 1980s and 1990s—to overlook their field's deeper roots. Their discursive process of creating, challenging, reformulating, re-theorizing, and "reinventing" has served to fertilize and propel the field of women's history to prominence. Nevertheless, historians of women should not let the process of clearing historiographic space for new approaches, arguments, and subjects result in inaccurate assertions that no one was studying women's history before the late 1960s or that the field of women's history in the 1970s essentially ignored race, class, sexuality, and other differences among women. By interrogating the first of these two rhetorical fictions, this chapter seeks to clear up some common misconceptions and thereby make some historiographic space for earlier generations of scholars in the field. They deserve to be recognized for their early, critical interventions in the history of American women.

Two of the most prominent leaders of the women's history movement that developed in the 1970s, Gerda Lerner and Anne Firor Scott, helped construct this narrative by telling and retelling their own stories in their advocacy of their field's development.[5] Lerner once quipped that in 1963 the number of professional historians interested in women's history when she tried to offer her first women's history course as a graduate student "could have fit into a telephone booth."[6] Yet, Lerner and Scott also offered evidence indicating there had been a quiet ferment in the field. Situated at generational crossroads between the old and the new women's history, these two leading historians figure prominently in the story of the field's origins. Their multiple retellings of the field's emergence modify and complicate the 1970s generational perspective that holds that the field emerged only after 1969. The 1970s perspective, rooted in the rhetorical imagery of "inventing wheels," "no women's history before the second wave," and "discovery" emerging from the women's movement, did not recognize the work of an entire generation of scholars and archivists who established a firm foundation for the field between 1943 and 1968. Some likely were simply unfamiliar with the earlier generations' work, while others saw it as precursory work, too epistemologically disjointed, limited, and random to constitute the beginnings of an emerging academic field. In the rush to claim historiographic ground in the 1970s, the earlier work was perhaps unconsciously and unintentionally buried in the footnotes or left sitting on the dusty shelves of libraries unnoticed. Whatever the reason, the work of the older generations was soon drowned out by a tidal wave of new scholarship.

———————

Women who earned doctorates in the field of American history between 1958 and 1976 were, for the most part, a generation of scholars who were profoundly affected by the social movements and politics of their time. Their personal involvement in civil rights, antiwar activism, liberal feminism, women's liberation, and other movements of the Left and New Left was deeply entwined with their identities as scholars and drove them to the topics they studied. Entering academia in these years, either as graduate students or as early career academics, they were acutely aware of the discrimination women faced as students and professionals. Many were also aware of racial discrimination in academia but probably had little direct exposure to it as aspiring academics, unless they themselves were not white. When the federal government conducted studies under the President's Commission on the Status of Women from 1961 to 1963, revealing deep inequalities confronted by American women in law, education, and the economy, legislators followed with a series of mandates under Title VII of the Civil Rights Act of 1964 banning sex discrimination in employment. Women in multiple academic disciplines took notice and action. Certainly, they understood that the Civil Rights Act of 1964 was first and foremost intended to address racial discrimination, but the prohibition of both racial and sexual discrimination in the law was meant to provide remedies for people of color, women, and those who fell into both categories. Female academics throughout higher education started demanding an end to discriminatory practices in admissions, hiring, and promotions. By 1968 their actions took the form of organizing caucuses and committees on the status of women in academia. All of these caucuses addressed the issue of sex discrimination in academic women's employment. Some also addressed the need to refocus scholarship on women, sex, and gender in their respective fields.[7] History was one discipline in which activist women placed roughly equal emphasis on each of these goals.[8]

Many women entering the field of American history in these years had limited or no knowledge of prior scholarship on women. The body of scholarship remained small, and as it was not widely recognized by male historians, it was not offered as part of most graduate or undergraduate courses and programs across the nation. Before the internet and the digitization of publishing and archives, access to sources and perspectives not available in one's own institution proved difficult. Additionally, because sources on women often did not fit into traditional library categorization schemes, the access problem was magnified. Aspiring scholars entering graduate school in the 1960s were not likely to be pointed to older work, archives, or topics dealing with women. Only a few had a male advisor interested in social, economic, or cultural history and curious about women's part in that history. Most female graduate students in history in the 1960s who would by the 1970s turn their scholarly gaze to women did so cautiously because they accepted what Carroll Smith-Rosenberg called in 1975 "traditional hierarchies of historical significance."[9] By this, Smith-Rosenberg meant a male-centered political history of public events. In turn, this meant that many women graduate students remained unaware of the work on women being done since the 1940s by a small number of dedicated scholars and archivists at Radcliffe and Smith Colleges and scattered across the nation's colleges and universities.

When they embarked on the mission to recover the history of women in the late 1960s, most of these emerging historians understood the field to be new and essentially needing to be built from the ground up. As they proceeded, however, they discovered the extant archival sources and scholarship of earlier generations, even as the politics of the modern women's movement shaped their understanding of that scholarship as the product of a more conservative, even anti-feminist midcentury academic and intellectual culture and therefore suspect or uninteresting. One trio of young feminist historians—Mari Jo Buhle, Ann Gordon, and Nancy Schrom—explained in 1971, for example, that "the rise and fall of concern for women's history has followed the intensity of organized women's movements. Not since 1920, when the suffrage movement ended, has there been the interest evident today."[10]

Furthermore, the need to clear historiographic space for their new interests and the pressure on them to create convincing justifications for their focus on women as subjects led them to dismiss earlier work as inadequate, merely compensatory history. Thus, the new feminist historians often disregarded the more established historians of women, only later to recognize the importance of the contributions they had made in an era before the 1960s resurgence of the women's movement generated support for the field.[11] A closer look at how two late twentieth-century leaders in the field, Gerda Lerner and Anne Firor Scott, remembered the expansion of women's history is illuminating, both because of their professional prominence as feminist historians and because their work bridged several generations of scholars.

In Gerda (Kronstein) Lerner's multiple descriptions of her mission to recover women's history between 1963 and 2009, the details of her personal narrative remain consistent. Lerner, born into an upper-middle-class Jewish family in Vienna in 1920, fled her country in 1939 during the Nazi occupation. In the United States, after marrying and divorcing her first husband, she married writer and film editor Carl Lerner. She worked at a series of jobs that included housekeeper, secretary, and X-ray technician. She was briefly a member of the popular front, left-wing group the Congress of American Women in the late

1940s and maintained her association with fellow members, including Eleanor Flexner and Eve Miriam, after the group disbanded in 1950.[12] The Congress of American Women was the American branch of the Women's International Democratic Federation, a pro-communist, anti-fascist organization.[13] Lerner remembered joining these groups because of their commitment to racial, economic, and social justice. Before becoming a historian, Lerner was a peace activist and involved in interracial neighborhood politics in New York City, had two children, and dabbled in writing.[14] While working on a piece of historical fiction about the abolitionist, feminist Grimké sisters of South Carolina, she determined that she didn't know enough about the period and signed up for history courses at the New School for Social Research.[15] In her 2002 autobiography, *Fireweed*, Lerner revealed the extent to which her political activism on the left during the 1950s inspired her interest in the history of women.[16]

Lerner enrolled full time at the New School and conceived of her first course in the history of American women in 1962, while still an undergraduate. The course ran for the first time at the New School in 1963, the year she earned her BA.[17] In 1963, she decided to continue her education in the history program at Columbia University and in her application to the program informed the department of her intent to focus on women's history. She planned to write a dissertation on the Grimké sisters. When asked by the historians considering her admission why she wanted to study history, she remembered replying that she wanted to continue the work of Mary Beard and develop and legitimize women's history. Perplexed, the Columbia historians reportedly asked, "What was women's history?" but accepted her into the program.[18] Though she presents this accomplishment as unusual, there were other women at Columbia in this decade doing dissertations related to the history of women. Aileen Kraditor published her 1962 Columbia dissertation as *The Ideas of the Woman Suffrage Movement, 1890–1920* in 1965.[19] Between 1966 and 1968 Carroll Smith-Rosenberg was working on her dissertation, dealing largely with women moral reformers in New York City. At Columbia's women's coordinate, Barnard College, between 1965 and 1967, Annette Baxter and Barbara Cross proposed and offered early courses in "The History of American Women."[20]

Lerner has suggested that in the twenty years prior to her entry into the profession, only a handful of historians, including the noncredentialed scholars Mary Beard and Eleanor Flexner, had attended to the history of women. Underscoring the power of finding role models in the history books, Lerner identified Beard as her primary historical role model, even though Beard had died in 1958 and the two historians never met. Lerner knew Flexner personally. There were in fact several working professional historians of women rising to prominence within the field during the 1950s and1960s (Anne Firor Scott, Mary Elizabeth Massey, and A. Elizabeth Taylor, for example). If she was aware of them, they did not enter into the narrative of her own professional trajectory as a feminist historian. Through feminist Miriam Holden's goodwill, Lerner had access to what she called the best private collection of sources on women's history in the country, an obvious boon since many archives did not yet collect or effectively catalog material on women.[21] Lerner also carried out research on the history of American women at the Schlesinger Library at Harvard's Radcliffe College and at the Boston Public Library.

Lerner remembered herself as an embattled outsider. Nevertheless, she entered the historical profession in 1966, against the odds, given the ground that women had been losing in terms of their proportional representation among the American history professoriate since 1920. They had gone from making up 16 percent of history faculty in 1920 to only 9 percent in 1969. To be sure, this was a period fraught with professional obstacles and inequities for women, not least of which was male historians' apparent lack of interest in the subject of women.[22] Despite these obstacles, though, Lerner made her way into college-level teaching relatively quickly. She taught part-time at the New School for Social Research while still a Columbia graduate student (1963–65). She then acquired a full-time position at Long Island University in Brooklyn in 1966—the same year she earned her PhD. In 1968 she moved to Sarah Lawrence College, where she later founded the first MA program in women's history with Europeanist Joan Kelly. In 1981 she moved to a major research institution, the University of Wisconsin–Madison.[23] By 1969, Gerda Lerner launched a lifelong project of forceful advocacy for the "new women's history," after which she was recognized as a leader of feminist historians. Those in the mainstream of the profession recognized her significance when they elected her to be president of the Organization of American Historians for 1981–82. She was only the second woman in the organization's history to attain that post, a full fifty-one years after the first woman, Louise Kellogg.[24]

Lerner's representations of the early days of the field are dominated by themes of professional struggle and feminist politics, and with good reason. One anecdote shows Lerner at a professional conference in 1968 suggesting to a certain publisher's representatives that a textbook on the history of women needed to be written. The story concludes with her being heartily ridiculed by those representatives, who laughed and asked, "Is there enough to fill a book?"[25] She didn't let such petty humiliations deter her, although it's easy to imagine that women with less forceful personalities and determination were discouraged and dissuaded from becoming historians in the face of similar denigration. And though she perceived herself to be in a struggle against the historical profession's dominant androcentric paradigm, she was also deeply committed to its craft traditions and was quick to admonish younger historians when she thought their conduct might jeopardize the field's future. For example, she once worried privately that younger women leaders working in the Organization of American Historians and the American Historical Association might fail in their obligations to be unimpeachable models of scholarly professionalism and to do nothing to threaten the newly won place of women within the profession.[26]

Lerner's first essays on the state of the field, published between 1969 and 1979, unevenly acknowledged the work of earlier scholars. She recognized a few historians who, she said, wrote "compensatory" or "contribution" history in the mid- to late 1960s. In her classic anthology of essays, *The Majority Finds Its Past*, she names Mary Beard's and Elisabeth Dexter's work and then moves to the mid-1960s contributions of Keith Melder, Aileen Kraditor, and William O'Neill, asserting this was the only work done on women in American history.[27] Her essays emphasize the dearth of scholarship and chart a direction for the field. Though she conducted research in the archives of the Schlesinger Library, the Sophia Smith Collection, and other archives throughout the nation, these sites of "women's history" activism do not figure prominently in her first "tellings" of the early days of the field. To a certain degree, she corrected this representation in 1981, when she produced an American Historical Association pamphlet detailing a historiography of the field, *Teaching Women's History*. In it, Lerner included ample footnotes from dozens of scholars working in the field over the course of the twentieth century.[28] Though the notes did not include all scholars publishing in the field, they were much more extensive than in her earlier works. Because of her position as a leader and guiding voice for the women's history movement in the early 1970s, Lerner's early formulations of the field's history resonated through the 1970s and beyond. The same can be said of one of her contemporaries, Anne Firor Scott.

Scott, a Georgian who had finished her undergraduate studies during World War II and worked as a congressional intern and then as a writer for the League of Women Voters, entered the historical profession in 1958, having written a dissertation at Radcliffe (Harvard) under Oscar Handlin. Her focus was on Southern progressives, many of whom were women, though she paid scant attention to them in the dissertation itself.[29] As a married woman academic, with an academic husband and a young family in the 1950s, she moved to follow her husband's career. After holding temporary teaching posts at Haverford College and the University of North Carolina at Chapel Hill, she took a full-time teaching position at Duke University in 1961. Between 1961 and 1970, she rose to a position of leadership within the emerging field of American women's history on the strength of her scholarship and professional activism. While she herself worked in an intellectual community in North Carolina that had a history of supporting scholarship on women, if not professional women scholars, she would later refer to Southern women's historians in the first half of the twentieth century as the "unheard voices" that had gotten lost.[30]

Scott once suggested in an interview that the only two women's historians she knew of in the 1960s went totally unrecognized and that, by 1971, "there were no books [about women in history]" that she could assign in her classes.[31] Which two historians she meant is not made clear. But she could not have been referring to Mary Massey or A. Elizabeth Taylor, two prominent historians of women in the South, because both were widely published and each held prominent positions in the Southern Historical Association in the 1950s and 1960s.[32] Both had been recognized by leading Southern historians and were gainfully employed as full professors in women's colleges. Indeed, Massey's election to the vice presidency of the SHA in 1971 showed she was "recognized" by the Southern wing of the infamous "old boy network." What the Scott interview did acknowledge was Taylor's "indispensable but ever so boring" work. In another interview—in an act as much dismissal as recognition—Scott included Taylor in a list of five historians of women working in the field before there was much of a field in the late 1960s. Scott concluded the interview by conceding, "I didn't have sense enough to realize that I should think only about the strong point, which was her excellent research, and I should forget the fact that, by my lights, she didn't interpret her material. Then, I'm afraid there were a couple of panels on which I was really hard on her, which I now regret. I was young and full of beans, and she was older and deserved more respect. She was the only person doing Southern women's history at that point."[33]

Scott's memories of the early days of the field offer a cautionary tale about accepting the common wisdom or the memory of any one person. Scott's version of the story is powerful but personal and therefore limited by whom she knew, who formed her professional circles, and what she remembered as significant. These told and retold memories raise many compelling questions, both general and specific. When *did* the field emerge? Why does Scott remember one early historian of Southern women but fail to acknowledge Mary Elizabeth Massey—arguably the most prominent historian of Southern women in the 1960s? How can we account for the fluctuating number of women in Scott's remembrances of the "pre-history" of the field? Her numbers ranged from one to several to five or six. Such inconsistencies can be attributed to the vagaries of memory, and historians should be grateful for Scott's willingness to share hers. But above all, these intriguing inconsistencies invite historians to check them against the historical record.

Though some leading women's historians acknowledged the presence of a few specialists in the history of women before 1969, the consensus seemed to be that these scholars were so professionally and intellectually marginal and so unwilling to challenge traditional male "hierarchies of historical significance" that their early work did not represent the beginnings of a new field of historical inquiry but merely an unsatisfactory precursor. The narrative of "no field of women's history before the second wave" was quickly established after 1979 and went largely unchallenged thereafter. Second-wave feminism, as the phase of the modern women's movement that emerged from 1961 to 1979 is sometimes called, and its influence on an incredibly productive cohort of scholars emerged as the major causal factor explaining the rise of women's history, and few would have said there was a field before there was a movement to support it. Academic historians coming out of this movement gained prominence in the telling of the history of the field. Because the 1970s generation became the women's history "establishment" by the late 1980s, contesting its self-constructed history became a challenging prospect.[34]

The narrative of the marginal nature of the field's midcentury scholars has been repeated since 1970, though the details sometimes change, and few can resist sprinkling their narrative with women historians not working in the history of women. Depending on which historian is relating the early historiography, Mary Beard and Eleanor Flexner are most often named, followed by Julia Cherry Spruill, Caroline Ware, and Elisabeth Anthony Dexter. Then, there is generally a leap to the pioneering efforts of Gerda Lerner and Anne Firor Scott, though the publications of Aileen Kraditor (1965) and Barbara Welter (1966) are sometimes noted in passing. The narratives are unified in emphasizing the impact of modern social movements on academic historians' decisions to recover the history of women. They all stress—through implication, omission, or direct argument—that until the late 1960s, there was no field of women's history. Male historians who published in the field in the 1960s are typically overlooked or relegated to footnotes. Carl Degler, William O'Neill, Keith Melder, and Page Smith are all examples of male historians who had written dissertations or published books on women's history by 1970.

In the usual narrative, the work done between 1920 and 1969 becomes unimportant for the study of "women's history," with the only exception being Eleanor Flexner's *Century of Struggle* in 1959. Yet, it was during these years that the two great archives on the history of women in America were founded and built. Moreover, during these years several historians of women reached professional prominence in the South. Nationally, nearly two dozen scholars wrote women's history. In Washington, DC, the Archives Committee of the National Council of Negro Women began an archival initiative on sources in Black women's history during these postwar years that would result in the founding of the National Archives for Black Women's History.[35] In the Northeast, some made use of the recently founded Women's Archives at Radcliffe to conduct the Radcliffe Seminars on Women in the 1950s, while others completed PhD dissertations on the history of American women. From 1955 to 1971, the landmark biographical dictionary *Notable American Women* was conceived by Arthur Schlesinger Sr. and produced by Edward James, Janet James, and Paul

Boyer with the contributions of over 600 scholars and the institutional support of Radcliffe College. A few male historians produced some early scholarship in the field during these years and encouraged their graduate students to do the same. Clearly, the history of American women as a field of academic study was evolving well before the late 1960s, even if it was in a formative stage and lacked a satisfactory label.

A small but significant number of scholars in the history of women was active between 1920 and 1969. These historians led professional lives, though gendered hierarchies throughout academia limited their professional opportunities and determined the way they categorized their work on women. Racial exclusion within the academy, of course, kept women of color out of the ranks of the historical profession for the most part, and those who found professional footholds within historically Black colleges or universities or specialized libraries rarely focused on women in their work. Yet, the work of these historians ultimately created a foundation upon which the formal field of women's history could be built. They gave the 1970s generation of historians a body of work against which to juxtapose and launch more sophisticated interpretations. Many of these older scholars were still on the professional scene in the 1970s and were willing to support emerging women's history scholars. The work of the earlier historians and archivists remains a stage in the field's development that demands further study. This book is, in part, a departure in that direction.

Another part of the predominant narrative suggests that the field emerged in struggle with the male mainstream of the historical profession. Even when recognizing the existence of sympathetic men, such as Carl Degler, Arthur Schlesinger Sr., or David Potter, this narrative creates an image of the historical profession as hostile not only to women as professionals but also to women's history as a worthy subject.[36] Anecdotal examples of this narrative of struggle came from Gerda Lerner, Louise Tilly, and Alice Kessler-Harris. Recall Lerner's 1968 suggestion that a publisher sponsor a survey textbook on women's history, only to be met with derisive laughter from Houghton Mifflin representatives.[37] In a later example from 1989, Louise Tilly listened as Joan Scott was challenged at a conference panel to explain to a "crusty old historian of the French revolution . . . what difference it made" to history to prove that women had existed.[38] And in 1974, prominent labor historian Melvyn Dubofsky reacted negatively to Kessler-Harris's paper on women in labor unions at a labor history conference, questioning the relevance of her study and taking issue with its distorting effect on the field.[39]

This anecdotal evidence of widespread skepticism toward the field and its new practitioners certainly indicates the historical profession was by default an unwelcoming place for feminist historians trying to make professional and scholarly inroads. Yet, we can also acknowledge that it wasn't monolithically so by the late 1960s. There were small numbers of men willing to accept women into the profession and to support the development of the women's history field. For example, in 1961, Dubofsky both consulted on and contributed a biographical sketch to the historical encyclopedia *Notable American Women.*[40] Houghton Mifflin's representatives were not interested in Lerner's 1968 textbook proposal but by 1970 had published Anne Firor Scott's *Women in American Life: Selected Readings.*[41] By 1971, Addison-Wesley had taken up Lerner's textbook idea, publishing a survey titled *The Woman in American History.*[42] Moreover, Lerner's pathbreaking documentary history, *Black Women in White America*, was brought out by Pantheon Books shortly after, in 1972.[43] And in 1970, the executive boards of both the American Historical Association and the Organization of American Historians, *when pressed*, voted in support of demands for action on behalf of women historians and women' history. Thus, the historical profession was not monolithic in its hostility to women historians, nor to the idea of supporting the development of women's history—despite clear patterns of sex discrimination and the mainstream's lack of interest in women's history. To be sure, the men had to be pressed and historians of women had to earn their place in the profession. And earn their place they did. But key features of the profession and key male individuals aided the emergence of the field, especially after 1943. Then, during the 1970s, as a critical mass of women's historians became active in the profession, some male scholars helped legitimize women's history by throwing their support behind the new field. But the major protagonists of this story are feminist historians—mostly women.

It is also true that the heightened political climate of the 1960s and 1970s caused potential allies of women's history to react defensively to its newest generation of practitioners, recoiling from what they saw as the politicization of the discipline. Thus, Bennett Wall, longtime secretary-treasurer of the SHA, rankled at a 1972 letter from New York feminist historian Sandi Cooper. She demanded the SHA recognize the Coordinating Committee on Women in the Historical Profession. In response he accused her of "hounding" the SHA men and complained about Cooper's abrasiveness.[44] Eleven years later he bristled at June Burton, member of the SHA Committee on the Status of Women, after she criticized him. He defended his forty-year administration, track record with women in the organization, and ability to keep records in a point-by-point refutation of Burton's critique. He closed with the taunt, "Incidentally, that is the third time your hang-up has shown."[45] He privately described Anne Firor Scott as "nuts" to a close female colleague of his who had identified Scott as "highly competent" but a member of the "women's lib faction."[46] These derogatory and defensive reactions to scholars whom Wall perceived as radical, "abrasive, nutty feminists with personal hang-ups" came in spite of his long and cordial professional relationship with Southern historians A. Elizabeth Taylor and Mary

Elizabeth Massey.[47] In 1972, John Hope Franklin, the first African American president of the SHA, shot a barb at the young feminist historians when he introduced incoming SHA president Mary Massey by explaining that "she did not need to become a part of the feminist revolt in order to understand and appreciate women's role in history."[48] It would seem, then, that while some men were opposed or indifferent to the field, others were open to American women's history but disagreed with the strategies and ideologies of the younger and more radical generation joining the profession. Still others seemed to have their own hang-ups, discomfited by the feminism of the "new women's historians" and the challenge to long-established academic traditions they represented. To be sure, women's history of the 1970s presented a profound epistemological challenge to the androcentric discipline of history in its rejection of traditional hierarchies of historical significance. The new women's history was not satisfied with simply adding women into historical scholarship while leaving the framework and outline of traditional history intact. Feminist historians suggested, rather, that until women's experiences and perspectives were fully incorporated into historical narratives, there could be no accurate, truthful accounting of the past. What had been seen as "history" to that point—these feminist historians argued—had been a distortion, a "male fantasy."[49]

The flurry of historical scholarship about women that began in the late 1960s often defined a rhetorical division between the "new women's history" and the "old celebratory," "contribution," or "compensatory" model of women's history.[50] This division itself, however, suggests that the field had emerged quite a bit earlier, while questions remained about its centrality to American historiography, its legitimacy, and its status as a distinct field. If the new women's historians did not always recognize the work of earlier credentialed scholars, between 1969 and 1989 they did emphasize the foundational influence of the noncredentialed historians Mary Beard and Eleanor Flexner. Between 1969 and 1989 they also acknowledged that most women's history produced during the 1960s was part of a transitional stage of women's history that was necessary but inadequate.[51] By the 1980s and as late as 2007, historians of women discussing the origins of the field increasingly omitted reference to most of the work done in the 1960s and appeared oblivious to work done during the 1950s. They accepted the narrative of a field begun in the late 1960s or even the 1970s and made the case that the pre-1970 pioneers in the history of women were intellectual anomalies whose work had never gained enough traction to be of significance.[52]

Numerous historians have written on the work of Mary Beard and Eleanor Flexner, effectively heralding them as the "founding mothers" of the field.[53] While their work was influential, overemphasizing their work and highlighting their lack of professional success does not explain the field's path to legitimacy. Flexner and Beard weren't full-fledged members of the historical profession.

They lacked doctoral degrees and wrote for a public audience rather than for an academic one. The saga of the field of women's history ought to be narrated in equal measure by pointing to the work of credentialed historians as well as to that of archivists and others writing from 1943 to 1970. These years were an important foundational period for the field. Archives were built. Monographs were published. Both male and female scholars turned their attention to the historical experiences of women, which they considered legitimate and fully part of American historical discourse. The study of women steadily gained adherents up through the time when scholars in the 1970s were able to establish "women's history" on firmer and more analytically complex ground. As many as two dozen largely unheralded pioneers in the history of American women were professionally active and even successful between 1943 and 1969. In many cases, they were linked to those who became recognized leaders of the women's history movement from 1969 forward.

The midcentury generation of historians of women and those who came into the profession after 1969 did not always appreciate or acknowledge one another. With a few important exceptions, generational differences were difficult to bridge. As a result, midcentury historians of women have not been fully represented in historiographic accounts of the field.[54] An examination of this foundational period offers a window into the tensions that existed between professionalism, feminism, and scholarship, as well as between generations of historians. It brings to light the work lives, professional strategies, and experiences of midcentury scholars of women in history and features the success of major women's archives projects during these years.

As midcentury historians and archivists matured and a new generation of scholars entered the discipline in the late 1960s, generational divisions emerged that would shape the field in the highly prolific decades that followed. One midcentury woman historian perceived the younger scholars in 1971 as part of "an amazing number of instant specialists in all the 'in' fields" who seemed to be eclipsing the "real scholars" in the field of women's history.[55] Meanwhile, a member of the younger generation expressed her initial opinion of those women she saw working in the Schlesinger Library at Radcliffe in the late 1960s as nonserious, dismissing them as amateurs. She admitted that she and her contemporaries were somewhat arrogant toward them.[56] Some of the midcentury historians got recognized by the new generation, while others disappeared from accounts of the field's founding. Why?

Those entering the field of women's history from 1969 forward found an area of study that had been pioneered by a dozen or more scholars and archivists before there was a mass movement to support the field. The field had not been abandoned after Mary Beard failed in her efforts to establish a World Center for Women's Archives in 1940 as one historian has suggested.[57] The period 1943 to 1968 was one of attrition for women historians in the United States, but it was nevertheless a critical building period for the study of women in history.[58] The 1970s generation of scholars did not invent the study of women in history after a long period of silence and neglect. Rather, they undertook a dramatic transformation and expansion of the field within an academic setting. And they gave the field an independent identity when they advocated for a new label for the field—"women's history."

From 1970 to 2000, an intellectually powerful and productive generation of women's historians wrote their field's historiography. As part of the normal practice of clearing historiographic space for new work, they tended to downplay the work of older historians of women. Others simply appeared unaware of the older work—work that in fact provided a stable foundation for the growing field. In the first two decades of the twenty-first century, feminist historians have produced reflective accounts in scholarly journals and edited anthologies and oral history initiatives documenting their own individual and collective accounts of the women's history movement.[59] This body of evidence must be understood within its longer historical context and read against the traditional archival record.

Finally, the new feminist historians of the 1970s were right when they recognized that scholarship on women (or other groups) was never divorced from the gendered politics of any given era but was, instead, fundamentally influenced by the broader culture and society in which it was produced. This calls our attention again to the influential 1971 essay in *Radical America* by Mari Jo Buhle, Ann Gordon, and Nancy Schrom. They linked interest in women's history to the ebb and flow of feminist movements in America. Feminist historians of the 1970s were likely predisposed to thinking women's history would not have been produced during the midcentury "doldrums" of the American feminist movement.[60] Histories revealing the widespread civic, organizational, and even feminist activism of midcentury American women was still two decades in the future.[61] Influenced and propelled by the ideas and energy of the women's liberation movement, the new generation did not at first appreciate the logic behind midcentury women's professional strategies or the muted feminist perspectives offered in their writings; they could not decipher the bonds of the midcentury professional culture, which precluded activism. We turn our attention now to this earlier generation of historians of women who did much to lay the groundwork for the scholarly field of American women's history.

PART II

Pioneers

Chapter 2

Pioneer Scholars, Masculine Paradigms, Northern Contexts, 1900–1960s

Between 1900 and 1960, some of the earliest specialists in the history of American women became professional historians. Their work built a modest foundation for the field in the decades before women's history was widely recognized as forming a distinct area of historical study. Some of these historians of women were relatively successful as academics, graduating from prestigious history departments like those at the University of North Carolina at Chapel Hill, Columbia University, and Harvard's female coordinate, Radcliffe College. Some found full-time work in lower-ranking colleges and universities, and often in women's colleges. Others were underemployed at best. All struggled to navigate the gendered hierarchies of the profession. Whatever their individual circumstances, all were deeply affected and influenced by the male-dominated professional, cultural, and political milieus in which they worked. They developed professional survival strategies that enabled them to carve out a place for themselves in academia, when so many others could not. Not least of their strategies was their tendency to classify their scholarship on women within non-gender-specific topical categories to gain acceptance as scholars. As midcentury historian A. Elizabeth Taylor once explained, she never considered herself a "true disciple of women's history" but rather a specialist in American political history who gave proper attention to women.[1] Everything Taylor had ever published had been on the woman suffrage movement in the South. This strategy of identifying one's work with established subfields, rather than emphasizing its focus on women, enabled them to connect as professionals to the male-dominated mainstream, even as they built a modest foundation for the history of women. The inroads they made for women and the field may seem small in retrospect, but they were hard-won in a time when the historical profession and ivory tower were exceedingly unwelcoming to women and their history.

Women's status in American higher education from 1900 to 1960 fluctuated. Women were a distinct but growing minority as students in undergraduate and graduate schools across the land. In 1900, women earned 19 percent of bachelor's degrees, 6 percent of master's degrees, and 6 percent of doctoral degrees. In the 1920s and '30s, women broke into the double digits, earning as many as 15 percent of doctoral degrees each year. By 1940 they were earning 40 percent of bachelor's and master's degrees but only 10 percent of PhDs. By 1950, the numbers went into decline, with women earning nearly 24 percent of bachelor's degrees and 9.6 percent of doctoral degrees in the United States that year. Those numbers ticked upward again between 1960 and 1970 for women earning BAs and MAs but barely budged in the PhD category.[2] This was undoubtedly the result of several factors. First, the influence of exclusionary admissions policies and a highly androcentric academic culture played a role. Anne Firor Scott, who broke into the profession in the late 1950s, surmised that the men who could accept women as undergraduate students could not generally accept them as peers and colleagues. As evidence she noted the disparaging tone of a 1943 report on women history doctorates. In the report, two male historians explained that the accomplishments of women history PhDs in America were "not impressive" and "not productive" and that women held "poorer positions," had higher unemployment rates, and didn't contribute significantly to the life of the profession.[3] They offered no structural explanation for this state of affairs.

During much of the twentieth century, the historical profession could fairly have been described as a "gentleman's club."[4] While its exclusion of people of color was far more pronounced than its exclusion of white women, gender discrimination was by most accounts pervasive. Access was guarded by gatekeepers who envisioned the work of the historian as the work of gentleman scholars.[5] The profession was shaped by highly gendered cultural expectations. During the early to middle twentieth century, when a working woman history PhD married, she would generally be expected to withdraw from professional life, though she might find work in academe on a part-time, contingent basis, especially if she were a faculty wife.[6] This was a reality that discouraged most women from seeking advanced degrees by forcing them to make difficult choices and weigh the relative payoff of an advanced degree; they could have a professional and intellectual life as a working scholar or have a family. They could only rarely do both. This was a choice that no man was forced to make. Other discriminatory practices were baked into the system. Many prestigious history departments, like that of the University of North Carolina at Chapel Hill, made it a policy to not hire women as faculty as late as the 1960s.[7] Microaggressions against women seeking to join the ranks of the history professoriate were commonplace, as when a female UNC Chapel Hill history graduate student in the 1930s overheard a history faculty member say women were categorically unqualified to teach history at the college level; or when a female graduate student at Columbia in the 1960s was told by a potential dissertation advisor that he didn't want to waste his time advising someone who would just get married, have babies, and leave the profession; or when a graduate student at an HBCU was told by a male professor that her research interest in Black woman suffragists was "Mickey Mouse" in the mid-1970s; or when, in the spring of 1964, a married

Rutgers history graduate student who had carefully planned the birth of her child to fall in June, learned that her fellowship for the coming academic year had been pulled. When she went to ask the graduate director why, he pointed to her pregnant belly and reportedly said, "We don't need any other reason why." Gerda Lerner, a leading figure in the late twentieth-century movement for women's history, reflected on her early experience in the profession and said that it was hard to convey to younger historians the extent to which women of her era were subjected to denigration and dismissal when trying to break into the profession in the 1960s and 1970s. These anecdotes are but representative of broader patterns that pushed all but the most tenacious female academics to the professional margins or off the academic path.[8]

To be sure, after 1940, exclusion from the profession for women, whether of color or white, was never absolute. Both the Mississippi Valley Historical Association (renamed the Organization of American Historians in 1965) and the American Historical Association had many women members who were social studies teachers, librarians, archivists, public historians, or faculty at women's and state colleges or at HBCUs. Yet the leadership of the organizations and the contents of the *American Historical Review* and other mainline history journals were unmistakably white, masculine, and androcentric prior to 1970. It's hardly surprising when considering the demographics of the historical profession at the time. According to official studies conducted by the AHA in 1970, 1980, and 1995, the ranks of the full-time female history professoriate in America shrank dramatically in proportional terms between 1920 and 1970, from a high of 16 percent to less than 1 percent in coeducational colleges and universities and to 9 percent in all colleges and universities. During this same time span, history graduate programs had been awarding between 11 percent and 15 percent of their doctoral degrees to women in each decade.[9] And as Deborah Gray White and others have shown, as difficult as it was for white women to break in and remain in the historical profession, Black women only started entering in small numbers in the 1940s and 1950s. In *Telling Histories*, White identifies only eight professionally trained Black women historians with a PhD in the country by the 1950s, as compared with the several hundred white women historians working in the lower ranks of the American history professoriate. As late as 1991, while white women made up 34 percent of new history PhDs each year and 18.7 percent of all academically employed historians, minority women represented merely 3.1 percent of all history PhDs. In 1995, the AHA Committee on Women Historians saw the problem as acute enough to make it a priority to encourage graduate history programs to recruit minority graduate students, especially women, into their programs.[10]

The gains that women made in academia between 1900 and 1945 were partly reversed during the postwar era when the broader culture shifted in ways that discouraged women from combining professional aspirations with family formation. A postwar new "cult of domesticity" gripped the nation and scolded women into narrowing their aspirations to marriage and family. If they didn't, the experts warned, catastrophic social forces threatened to destroy American families and civilization. Educated professional women pushed back by either trying to combine work and family anyway or remaining unmarried, but the messaging had its effect. The issue was debated by social scientists like Marynia Farnham, coauthor of the infamous tract *Modern Woman: The Lost Sex*, and journalist Betty Friedan in *The Feminine Mystique* for over two decades.[11] These prevailing cultural attitudes and prescriptions combined with policies and practices in higher education institutions to create added barriers to women.

While many colleges and universities accepted women into their programs, many others excluded them as a matter of official policy. This included nearly all the Ivy League schools with prestigious history departments such as Yale, Harvard, Dartmouth, and Princeton, which were determined, as Nancy Weiss Malkiel has shown, to "keep the damned women out" well into the 1960s.[12] But it wasn't just the Ivy League. When, for example, a young Georgian named Eleanor Boatright was searching for a college to attend in 1914, she couldn't apply to the University of Georgia, as it didn't yet accept women students. Instead, the history major went off to attend the University of Tennessee, transferred to Columbia Teachers College, graduated with a BA in 1918, and took up a high school history teaching career in South Carolina. Sixteen years later, in 1934, she pursued an MA in history at Duke University, completing in 1941 a thesis on women in Georgia from 1783 to 1860. She continued to teach high school history but longed to be "a real historian," to be accepted as a member of the Georgia Historical Society, and to find a publisher for her 300-page MA thesis. After almost a decade of trying to achieve these goals but being rebuffed and ignored, she committed suicide in 1950.[13] This harrowing example is extreme perhaps, but it conveys the frustrating and depressing barriers this generation of potential historians of women were confronted with and the toll it might take on them. It makes all the more remarkable the tales of survival and success featured in the pages ahead.

The changing intellectual and political milieus in which historians of women worked during the first half of the twentieth century influenced their professional strategies and intellectual perspectives no less than this environment influenced their male peers. As they entered the American historical profession in small but increasing numbers over these decades, they imbibed and ascribed to various schools of historical thinking. Early in the century, the Rankean "objectivists" who had formalized the American historical profession in the late Gilded Age and Progressive Era dominated the discipline of history. They believed they could interpret official records and facts without bias. Soon, this perspective on history was challenged by progressive historians of the 1910s and beyond who engaged in economic and class analyses and were more forthright about the political implications of their interpretations. Some went so far as to see history as a tool for progress. Adding to these competing interpretive approaches were social and cultural historians of the 1930s and 1940s who sought to broaden the topical scope of history to include ordinary folk and new types of source material. Then in the 1950s, consensus school historians of the World War II and Cold War eras worked to recenter national narratives on politics. While social historians of the 1930s forward sought to understand the American experience by expanding knowledge about ordinary people and culture, midcentury conservative consensus historians reasserted the primacy of traditional unified national narratives over histories focused on difference and conflict.[14] Later, new social historians of the 1960s continued in their predecessors' paths but added to the historian's toolbox innovative quantitative methodologies, consideration of new types of evidence such as oral history, and new frameworks of analysis that by the 1960s included race and by the 1970s included gender.

Where did the history of American women fit within this broad historiographic sweep of competing interpretative schools? Certainly not with the more traditional "objectivists" and later "consensus" historians who contended that historians should assiduously avoid topics in which they might be too personally invested, lest they produce histories with "biased" perspectives.[15] This proscription discouraged scholars from marginalized groups from focusing on the history of their own group, an obstacle that especially restricted women historians, historians of color, and historians from the working class. Studying one's own group could delegitimize the work, exposing one to charges of bias—unless of course one was a white man studying the history of powerful white men.[16] Within this framework the historical actions, experiences, and perspectives of elite white men were held up as relevant and as the norm. Everyone else was anomalous and irrelevant. This created something of a bind for historians of women and minority groups seeking entry and acceptance within the discipline. Yet, as we shall see, the historians of American women featured here did find a home among progressive and social historians.

Professional women historians were also influenced by the state of women's politics and feminism during these years. Even as the nation weathered two world wars and a severe economic depression bookended by decades of prosperity, American women made slow but steady gains in higher education and labor force participation. As they did so, they struggled to balance work and family and debated the best ways to go about this. Women academics were part of this debate. For much of the twentieth century, regardless of their personal political beliefs, professional women historians were guided by an ethos of equal rights feminism in education and the labor force. This ethos recognized structural barriers to women's participation in education and the history labor market but often left it up to professional women to overcome these barriers on their own.[17] In *The Grounding of Modern Feminism*, Nancy Cott suggests that after women earned the vote in 1920, they entered the professions assuming that formal barriers to their participation in politics had been eliminated and they would be able to gain equal access and status by proving they were competent, professional, rational, scientific, and worthy. Accordingly, at midcentury, male and female scholars both frowned on women academics taking a feminist stance in which they "developed grievances and constantly aired them."[18] Women academics believed women would achieve recognition and equality by "developing a more professional attitude" and "by displaying professional competence and tenacity of the highest order and . . . refusing to accept either privilege or disabilities on the grounds of sex."[19] These attitudes were not favorable to collective professional action by women scholars for women scholars. Nor did they encourage women historians to claim they were specialists in the history of women, even when it was their research specialty. While a scholar of the stature of Carl Becker might assert in 1931 that it was unavoidable that "everyman" would, should, or could be "his own historian," most women and African Americans in the discipline faced the pressure of other historians to eschew their own histories, lest their work be deemed irrelevant, biased, and therefore illegitimate.[20] In response, African American scholars built their own professional institutions and body of historical scholarship in the New Negro History movement of the early twentieth century, supported by the existence of HBCUs and the founding of the Association for the Study of Negro Life and History. White women historians sought entry into the mainstream of the profession, while Black women history workers worked in segregated libraries and K–12 schools, in Black archives, and occasionally as professors in HBCUs after 1940.[21] White or Black, most women historians didn't focus on the history of women primarily.

As a result of all these factors, between 1920 and 1960 most women scholars with an interest in the history of American women relied on individual professional strategies for survival and success. They fit their work into the accepted epistemological parameters of the historical profession so they would be considered legitimate scholars. They were at pains to situate their work within the mainstream of social, progressive, and political history to overcome total intellectual marginalization in an androcentric discipline. Their struggles were emblematic, too, of the post-suffrage period during which professional women worked to find ways to balance family and career and achieve legitimate status in their disciplines, whether they were feminists or not.[22] Usually this meant crafting professional/intellectual identities based on the male models available to them and minimizing the appearance of differences based on sex. Nevertheless, the subjects they chose to study often mirrored their social location and political interests. Their subjects and perspectives reflected the wide range of social, economic, civic, political, and feminist activities American women engaged in between 1920 and 1960, and they allowed their politics to permeate their scholarship and their professional lives to varying degrees. Who were these scholars, and how did they carve out academic lives for themselves as historians of women in times not terribly friendly to their work?

Historians of women with advanced degrees in history and aspirations to a traditional career in academia were not the only writers focusing on women of the past in the early to mid-twentieth century. Black and white women writers of popular histories like Ishbel Ross, Sadie Daniel St. Clair, Alma Lutz, Hallie Quinn Brown, Mary Beard, and Eleanor Flexner all published popular books about women in history, as had women writing institutional histories of the major women's clubs and organizations of the early twentieth century.[23] Their topics ranged from the history of Black women in women's clubs and communities, to suffrage and labor activists, to women in various trades and professions.[24]

But popular history writing for non-scholarly audiences is not where the early roots of the field found purchase in academia. Instead, it was with those committed to the tenets of the historical profession. The academics were at once bound by the craft traditions of the profession and limited by its customary patterns of class, racial, and gender exclusion in ways that popular history writers were not. Their audiences were the scholarly history communities to which they belonged and from which they sought favorable peer review, legitimization, and acceptance. They relied on individual professional strategies to work and lead scholarly lives, often working in relative intellectual isolation from other women as they carved out niches for themselves in academia. As professional historians with PhDs, some were marginally employed, but a fair number held academic tenure in colleges or universities—most frequently at women's colleges—and many belonged to a variety of professional associations. As late as the 1960s they were all, as far as I've been able to ascertain, white. Not only were Black women history PhDs few and far between during these decades, but they had no access to the employment opportunities white women had in women's colleges or as lower-ranking and contingent faculty in predominantly white colleges and universities. They even found posts in HBCUs elusive at best. Marion Thompson Wright, who specialized in the history of education, became the first academically employed Black woman history PhD in the United States in 1940. She was followed by diplomatic historian Merze Tate in 1943.[25] As Pero Dagbovie has suggested, given their extreme marginalization within academia, it's not surprising they didn't flock to a field that was yet to be recognized.[26]

Others have shown that the gendered nature of the historical discipline of the early twentieth century relegated most women, even when fully credentialed, to the margins of the profession.[27] They have observed that these women were employed predominantly in women's colleges and had heavy teaching loads, lower pay and status than equally qualified men, limited access to research opportunities, and no incentive to work in the not-yet-legitimate area of the history of women, since they were attempting to fit into masculine professional and intellectual paradigms.[28]

However, a dozen female historians of women, active between 1920 and 1968, managed to carve out academic and intellectual lives for themselves, ultimately building a small foundation for the field of American women's history. These women came out of three elite institutional hubs that allowed for their interests to develop. In the North, the history departments at Harvard University and Columbia University served as two nodes in a network of progressive and social historians open to allowing graduate students to study women. In the South, the University of North Carolina at Chapel Hill—at the time a racially segregated institution—created space for historical research on women, Black Americans, and economically marginalized groups. In the 1920s, both Columbia and Chapel Hill had established innovative social science research centers that supported examination of social, economic, and cultural problems, inclusive of those affecting women, in various social science disciplines. These regional nodes of scholarship were then further amplified through national networks of historians, extending to history departments in the Midwest and West, including, for instance, the University of Wisconsin–Madison. Male and female scholars who wrote about women in history, but for whom the subject was not the center of their scholarly pursuits, contributed to the field's early development but didn't stake their entire academic careers on this unusual focus.[29]

Columbia University and Radcliffe College at Harvard were early sites of activity for emerging Northern historians of women between 1900 and 1960. Starting with Lucy Maynard Salmon's early twentieth-century shift into social history and Elisabeth Anthony Dexter's work on colonial working women, the history of American women began to gain toeholds in academia. It was given a high-profile boost with progressive historian Arthur Schlesinger Sr.'s 1922 direct call for more attention to the history of women in his *New Viewpoints in American History*. This early period of development for the field culminated with the launch of Radcliffe graduate Anne Firor Scott's career in 1958. After studying with Harvard University's Oscar Handlin, Scott turned her attention in the early 1960s to the history of American women and became an effective advocate for the field's development thereafter. These two institutions, along with other Northern colleges, graduated a cluster of pioneering historians of women in the intervening decades. Many of these historians of women had traditional history careers. Some worked at the professional margins, sporadically, or in quiet obscurity within mainline institutions. Typical of the fate of the rare, relatively fortunate woman historian of the era was Mary Sumner Benson. Benson wrote a single scholarly monograph on women in colonial America.[30] She was a member of the Berkshire Conference of Women Historians and the major history associations in the United States. She had a long teaching career at Mt. Holyoke College for women in the 1950s and 1960s, but she left an extremely limited record of her activities there, preventing even a partial reconstruction of her part in this history.[31]

Elisabeth Anthony Dexter left us with more records and falls in the category of women scholars who worked on the profession's margins but maintained an active scholarly agenda throughout her adult life. Dexter was born in 1887 in Maine and was a distant relative of suffragist Susan B. Anthony, her grandfather's cousin. She earned a BA from Bates College and a master's degree from Columbia University in 1911. After marrying, she and her husband earned doctorates in 1923 from Clark University, Elisabeth's in history.[32] In 1925, she published *Colonial Women of Affairs*, which ran into a second edition in 1931. In 1950 she published *Career Women of America, 1776–1840*.[33] Dexter taught history only briefly, heading the history department at Skidmore College from 1923 to 1927, where her husband also taught. But her husband's career choices, and probably the social expectations of the day, caused her to resign from the Skidmore faculty and start a family. She pursued her scholarly interests on a sporadic basis after she became involved in internationally focused civic organizations as a corollary to her husband's overseas career from 1940 to 1948. She worked for the Unitarian Universalist Service Committee rescuing Holocaust refugees. She also did intelligence work for the Office of Strategic Services in Portugal during World War II—historian, wife, humanitarian, mother, spy rolled into one person.[34]

Correspondence between Dexter and Smith College librarian Margaret Grierson in the 1940s reveals that Dexter maintained her scholarly interest in the history of American women and was hoping to complete the sequel to her first book, even while abroad. Between 1945 and 1960, Grierson, who was busy building a women's history archive at Smith, repeatedly invited Dexter to the college to give talks on her work, share lunch, and chat about women in history. Dexter developed closer connections to the new Radcliffe Women's Archives in Cambridge in these same years. Radcliffe presented the opportunity for scholarly exchange in a pioneering series of seminars on women in American history, which met weekly from 1951 to 1959.[35] Dexter served on Radcliffe's Advisory Board of the Women's Archives periodically from the 1950s until her death in 1972.[36] The work being done at Smith and Radcliffe will feature in coming chapters. Here the work of individual scholars is the focus.

Dexter's concern with her own scholarly legitimacy and that of her specialization was evident. In the preface to the 1972 edition of *Career Women of America*, she shared the hope that she had achieved an acceptable standard of objectivity: "I have tried to give an objective presentation of the facts as I found them, with a minimum of explanation and generalization; but opinions, clearly labeled I trust, have now and then broken through. That these opinions are always justified would be too much to hope."[37] As a scholar trained in scientific history, when progressive historians had begun their intellectual ascent and social history was still on the horizon, she would naturally be concerned with these issues. Her disclaimer shows how even a marginal figure in the historical profession situated herself within the mainline intellectual discourse of the era, even as the gendered cultural milieu of midcentury America militated against her having a traditional career in academia while she established and raised a family. Then in the 1940s she took part in the sweeping events that overtook the world.

Perhaps the earliest, most direct call to attend to women's history in a sustained manner from within the discipline came in 1922 from Arthur Meier Schlesinger Sr. While on the faculty of Iowa State University, before his move to Harvard in 1924, Schlesinger had published an essay on American women in his widely read *New Viewpoints in American History*. The essay, "The Role of Women in American History," was one of twelve chapters identifying and summarizing for the nonspecialist new areas of research in American history. Included in the book were essays on immigration, geography as it impacted historical development, economic influences in history, radicalism, and conservatism, among others. In his essay on women, Schlesinger outlined their participation in wars, westward expansion, reform, and the women's rights movement; their rising educational attainment; and their workforce participation in the industrial age. In his bibliographical notes, Schlesinger pointed out that "historians have generally ignored woman as a positive influence in American history and have usually omitted even any mention of her struggle for sex equality. This task has fallen to other hands."[38] Those other hands, he suggested, had for the most part been amateur scholars and suffragists. Yet his 1922 call for more scholarly attention to the history of American women marks the launch of the first phase in legitimizing the field. He went on to mentor a number of pioneering historians of women, and his efforts and those of others culminated in the creation of the women's history archive at Harvard University's female coordinate college, Radcliffe. Schlesinger's 1922 claim that the field had not been cultivated by professional historians was mostly accurate.

But at least one professional woman scholar had been writing women into her studies prior to Schlesinger's clarion call. Lucy Maynard Salmon, though not a self-declared specialist in the history of women, was known to incorporate everyday history, what she referred to as "history in a backyard," into her writing and teaching at Vassar College.[39] Her use of primary sources and material culture introduced women's daily activities into historical study. Once she was well-established in her Vassar professorship and recognized as an expert in constitutional history, she turned away from studying American political history and published two books, *Domestic Service* in 1897 and *Progress in the Household* in 1906, both decidedly female subjects.[40] Her final 1929 publication, *Why Is History Rewritten?*, explained why historians need to revisit past interpretations and consider overlooked sources and groups to arrive at ever more complete and accurate explanations of the past. These works earned mixed reviews, and professional historians gave her little acclaim for breaking new ground. But her work was prescient. She was also the first woman to serve on the executive board of the American Historical Association, and her innovative approach to teaching social history with a documents-based approach inspired her students and colleagues. Historian Louise Fargo Brown, a founding member of the Berkshire Conference of Women Historians, published a biography of Salmon in 1943, *Apostle of Democracy: The Life of Lucy Maynard Salmon*.[41] In it she explained the significance of Salmon's scholarship and her influence as a professor during her four decades at Vassar (1887–1927).

Caroline Farrar Ware was one of Salmon's students. She also published scholarship that, while not identified as "women's history," focused substantively on women's experiences. After earning her BA at Vassar in 1920, Ware spent two years teaching at the Baldwin School for girls in Bryn Mawr, Pennsylvania. During these years, Bryn Mawr College instituted a "Summer School for Women Workers in Industry." Ware joined the school's staff in 1922 in a move that foreshadowed her lifelong interest in labor reform, education, and women's rights. The following year she attended Oxford on a Vassar fellowship to get an MA She returned home before finishing due to her mother's poor health. Ware, a Bostonian whose family had connections to the Harvard community, determined to enroll at its women's coordinate, Radcliffe College, in the fall of 1923. This was just one year before Arthur Schlesinger Sr. arrived at Harvard. She hoped to study under historian Frederick Jackson Turner, but he retired that year. Instead, she worked under the guidance of Frederick Merk, another historian of westward expansion. Merk would later marry Radcliffe graduate student Lois Bannister, who returned to Radcliffe to earn a PhD in the 1950s, writing a dissertation on the Massachusetts woman suffrage movement.[42] Ware was influenced first by Salmon and then by Turner's work and by economic historian Edwin Gay. She does not appear to have worked with Arthur Schlesinger, though surely she was aware of his essays in *New Viewpoints in American History*.[43]

Ware published her 1925 dissertation as *The Early New England Cotton Manufacture* in 1931.[44] This study in American women's labor history is an important early landmark in the field. The last 100 pages detail the labor force in New England's textile mills, a largely female labor force in the 1830s and 1840s. Ware described how the industry challenged family work practices, altered American work culture, and distressed gender roles. She detailed the eventual competition for jobs between native-born women and Irish immigrant laborers. The epistemological framework did not yet exist for her to identify herself as a "women's historian." Instead, she paid attention to women's lives as part of economic, social, and cultural history. In this way she was able to establish a strong reputation as a scholar.

While working to turn her dissertation into a book, Ware took a faculty position at Vassar College, and she married economist Gardiner Means in 1927. When Means entered the graduate program in economics at Columbia University, Ware took a leave from Vassar to direct a study at the new Columbia Council for Research in the Social Sciences in 1931. The study examined demographic changes in New York's Greenwich Village. Primarily a study of urban change and ethnic communities, Ware again gave attention to gender issues, analyzing the changing culture of Italian immigrants in New York and describing the impact of acculturation on Italian women as daughters, wives, and workers.[45] The Council for Research in the Social Sciences also sponsored a small number of women scholars and works focusing on women, gender, and sexuality in a variety of disciplines, including anthropology, sociology, history, economics, languages, and psychology.[46] Studies on women and gender conducted at the council between 1925 and 1955 included studies about fertility, the psychological impact of hormone treatments on women, family life in particular societal groups, and marital ideals in the lower-middle class; a historical study of Harriet Martineau by Robert K. Webb; and Mirra Komarovsky's study of voluntary associations.[47]

From 1935 to 1940 Ware taught part-time at Sarah Lawrence College and American University. She also worked full-time as a consumer advocate in the Democratic administration's New Deal programs.[48] In 1942, Ware accepted an academic post at Howard University in Washington, DC, a historically Black college. Here, she met a student named Pauli Murray who was already a civil rights activist and who would go on to become a pioneering feminist lawyer and legal theorist, coining the term "Jane Crow" in an analogy between sexism and the systemic racism of "Jim Crow."[49] The two developed a lifelong friendship, with the older woman bringing the younger Murray onto the staff of the President's Commission on the Status of Women in 1961. Ware was widely respected, married, and steadily employed in both government and academia—a rare combination for a midcentury woman scholar.

Ware's success was evidenced by the recognition accorded her by the nation's premier history organization, the American Historical Association. The AHA selected Ware to organize and edit a set of papers presented in sessions at the 1939 AHA convention. The volume was published in 1940 as *The Cultural Approach to History* and has since become a classic in cultural history, cementing Ware's scholarly reputation.[50] Yet, as Thomas Dublin put it, "The field of history could not contain her energies."[51] Ware moved into a life of political activism, though she did not abandon academia completely.[52] As we will see, Ware's background in history informed her work as a feminist activist from the 1920s to the 1960s. She was not unique in this regard.

Ware's choice to redirect the bulk of her energies toward civic and political activism after World War II was not based on the professional barriers she encountered as a woman. As Ware had given attention to women in history and framed her work as belonging to recognized subfields, her peers did not question her scholarly legitimacy, proving it was possible to incorporate women into academic histories and remain legitimate as a scholar. Even so, her work, and that of other scholars treading quietly in the recovery of women's past, did not launch a robust new field between 1920 and 1968, when the gendered hierarchies of the historical profession were not favorable to the emergence of women's history as a distinct domain. For that to occur, more women needed to enter the profession and work collectively toward that goal.

Caroline Ware's academic and intellectual roots at Vassar, Harvard, and Columbia point to connections between her work and that of progressive historians, like Charles and Mary Beard, Arthur M. Schlesinger, Frederick Jackson Turner, and Frederick Merk. Charles and Mary Beard had been at Columbia University until 1917, when Charles resigned his faculty position in protest of violations of academic freedom during the First World War. Even before that, Mary had dropped out of the graduate history program at Columbia due partly to the department's unwelcoming attitude toward women, her own family responsibilities, and possibly her political preoccupation with the progressive and woman suffrage movements.[53] Arthur Schlesinger's wife, Elizabeth, also a progressive, suffragist, and feminist, was also deeply interested in the history of women. She published many history articles. Married to intellectually and politically active women, two of these four historians, Charles Beard and Arthur Schlesinger, lent their names or energies to the development of the history of American women. Arthur Schlesinger and Mary Beard became particularly important advocates for the field after 1922. Thus, these Northern-based historians of women had intellectual roots sunk firmly in the progressive, economic, and cultural schools of American history. The history of women as a field emerged in protean form from these broad intellectual streams. In both Northern and, as we will see in the next chapter, Southern intellectual communities, the fledgling field had strong ties to scholars in the professional and intellectual mainstream of the discipline.

Perhaps the most significant historian of women to emerge from the Northern midcentury context was Anne Firor Scott. Scott became a nationally recognized historian of Southern women in the mid-1960s, after earning a PhD in history from Radcliffe. She was well-connected to Southern, Northern, and national networks of prominent historians; proved adept at bridging generational differences through mentorship and role modeling; and was skilled at the kind of professional politicking needed to succeed in academia. Scott would become a key mediator between established male members of the historical profession and the younger generation of feminist historians. Scott was also a self-identified feminist who embraced the modern women's movement in the post–World War II era when this was not exactly in vogue. Here, though, we will focus on her early career path, since her role in midcentury women's politics and the later women's history movement will feature later.

Anne Byrd Firor was born April 24, 1921, in Georgia. Her father, John William Firor, was a professor of agricultural economy at the state university, and her parents encouraged her to get an education. Her mother, Mary Valentine Moss, had graduated from Simmons College, and her aunt Judith had graduated from Boston University, majoring in history and then marrying a history professor who later took an appointment at Syracuse University.[54] Anne Firor lived for a year with her aunt and historian uncle in Syracuse at the age of twelve. She later attended the University of Georgia in the late 1930s, originally intending to become a journalist. At her father's suggestion she took courses in liberal arts and graduated with a history degree in 1940.

After college she worked as a secretary for IBM for a year. She applied for and received a fellowship to take her MA in personnel administration at Northwestern, but the program did not ignite her intellectually. She became enthusiastic upon learning about an internship at the National Institute of Public Affairs in Washington, DC. She applied and was accepted as an intern for 1943, working for Democratic California congressman Jerry Voorhis.[55] These internships opened for women during World War II because so many men were serving in the military. She found herself working in DC alongside many other women. Under pressure from her father to finish her MA, she returned the next year to Northwestern as a political science major. At Northwestern she met and talked frequently with political scientist Mary Earhart Dillon, who had just published a history of Frances Willard, the dynamic leader of the temperance movement. Scott finished her master's degree in the spring of 1944, writing a thesis on international organizations, which she later described as "unremarkable."[56]

She then returned to Washington, where a friend helped her find work with the League of Women Voters. Until 1946, she worked on the league's staff writing on international affairs for its newsletter, *Trends*, and traveling around the eastern half of the country as a national representative at branch meetings.[57] Scott credited her years with the league with teaching her how to lead discussions and giving her an appreciation of the importance of women's voluntary organizations in American society and politics.[58] These experiences developed her administrative capacities, her feminist sensibilities, and her historical consciousness of women's part in political history. She later recalled that the younger generation of historians in the 1970s had thought of league women as "fuddy-duddies in tennis shoes" but that her experience working with them in the 1940s and then again in 1953 had taught her that they were to be taken seriously as political activists.[59] Her league years also accustomed *her* to being taken seriously, having been included in luncheons with men and women on Capitol Hill. Thus, when she reentered academia as a graduate student and then history professor in the late 1950s, the gender discrimination she encountered in some of these academic communities surprised her.[60]

In 1946, Anne Firor met and became engaged to Andrew Scott, a political scientist who had decided on a career in academia. She had intended to take a fellowship to study political science at the University of Chicago, but when Andrew Scott determined to take a PhD in government at Harvard, Anne Firor decided to marry and go with him. She entered the PhD program in American civilization at Radcliffe College, the university's female coordinate. This is how Anne Firor Scott found her way into American history, ending up with Oscar Handlin as her dissertation advisor.[61] Scott's relationship with Handlin would prove a critical turning point for her professionally, as Handlin treated her as he would any other talented graduate student by advocating for her as her mentor and advisor in her early career.

While at Radcliffe, Anne Scott also became aware of the newly established Radcliffe Women's Archives through her contact with Handlin and through university publicity. Thus, she became acquainted with the library's great efforts to build the preeminent manuscript archive on women in American history in the country. Here she became acquainted with the role of Arthur Schlesinger Sr. in promoting the history of American women and coincided with two other women graduate students in the program, Barbara Miller Solomon and Janet Wilson James, who will occupy our attention later.[62] Scott's research on Southern progressives was going well when Andrew Scott finished his PhD and took work in Washington, DC. The Scotts then moved to Dartmouth College in New Hampshire in 1954 and then to Haverford College in Philadelphia in 1956. Anne Scott followed her husband's career. They started a family. Beginning to worry about finishing her dissertation, she fortuitously came upon an advertisement for an American Association of University Women dissertation fellowship in 1955. She applied for, received, and used the fellowship to pay for childcare so that she could finish her degree.[63]

With her degree finally in hand in 1958, she managed to obtain a one-year appointment teaching American history survey courses when a Haverford College history professor went on leave. In the summer of 1959, with a year of teaching behind her, Scott decided to pick up on research she had wanted to pursue on Jane Addams. When she was working on her Southern progressives dissertation, her friend Louise Young, a League of Women Voters activist and English professor at American University from 1953 to 1971, had called Addams "America's greatest woman."[64] The next year Andrew Scott was hired by the political science department at UNC Chapel Hill. The Scotts made a permanent move to Chapel Hill, leaving Anne Scott once again in professional limbo and taking her away from the Jane Addams papers at Swarthmore College in Pennsylvania.

This limbo would be short-lived. Scott had heard rumors that "the history department at the University of North Carolina has never had a woman, and never will." When the chair of the department, Fletcher Green, traveled to the annual American Historical Association meeting in December 1958 and met with Oscar Handlin to inquire whether Handlin could send any recent Harvard PhDs to come teach the survey at Chapel Hill, Handlin might have dropped the name of some promising young man. Instead, Handlin replied that he already had sent a qualified candidate to North Carolina and gave Green Anne Scott's name. Anne Scott was offered a non-tenure-track appointment, which she held from the spring of 1959 through the spring of 1960. When Andrew Scott received a Fulbright Scholarship, Scott resigned her position to accompany him to Italy in the summer of 1960. Upon her return the next year, a new department chair had "reverted to the old standard which was no women in this department." Thinking she was about to be unemployed again, she was instead contacted by Duke University with an offer that she come on as a temporary replacement for a historian who had accepted a job offer elsewhere just before the start of the term. Offered the position of "instructor," Scott was able to parlay her experience at Haverford and UNC Chapel Hill into an assistant professor position. She thus became a Duke faculty member in the fall of 1961. By the spring of 1963, the department offered her a tenured position, which she accepted "with delight." Anne Scott took up her teaching duties with energy, incorporating women into her course content in the early 1960s. One undergraduate from Scott's early teaching days, Sara Evans, recalled that Scott had "always incorporated women into her courses." Scott also began giving papers and turning out articles on women in Southern history.[65]

In her last semester at Chapel Hill in the spring of 1960, a colleague had asked her to present a paper at the department seminar. She agreed and presented a paper on Jane Addams, which she prepared from her research at Swarthmore and at the Southern Historical Collection. Whether it was his knowledge of this paper or something else that cued him to Scott's interest in the history of women, George Tindall then contacted Scott before her family returned from Italy with the request that she give a paper on Southern women at the fall meeting of the Southern Historical Association in 1961. Scott agreed and began work on the essay that became "The 'New Woman' in the New South."[66] Meeting with Oscar Handlin for a long lunch during the SHA meeting that November, Scott remembered that by the end of the lunch she had committed herself to writing a monograph on Southern white women. She would spend the next nine years working on the book *The Southern Lady: From Pedestal to Politics, 1830–1930.*[67] It became a classic that shaped the field of American women's history.

Why George Tindall and Oscar Handlin would suddenly solicit work about women in history is not certain. But surely the archive-building activities at Radcliffe had an impact on Handlin's consciousness of the subject. Handlin participated in the launching of a massive reference work project—*Notable American Women*—from 1957 forward, and he had favorably evaluated Eleanor Flexner's manuscript about the first phase of the American women's movement, *Century of Struggle*, in 1959.[68] Tindall was also friend and peer to Mary Elizabeth Massey, who specialized in the history of Southern women during the Civil War. What is certain is that Anne Scott was encouraged to pursue the subject of women by her male mentors and colleagues and that this encouragement came well before the modern women's movement took the historical profession by storm in the 1970s. Scott found some powerful allies in her corner.[69] She maintained a long collegial correspondence from her graduate school years at Harvard with history heavyweights Handlin and Bernard Bailyn and from 1963 with Carl Degler and Dick Lowitt, indicating in these early career years for Scott collegial relationships with these male scholars.[70] Scott had an assertive professional style and when called for would directly and systematically challenge the "old boy network," the gender hierarchies that served as barriers to women historians, and the inadequate treatment of women in the field of US history.

By 1966, Anne Firor Scott had made a steady journey from the margins to the center of the American historical profession. In a twist of professional irony that illustrates this powerfully, a letter arrived on her desk in January 1966 from President Alan Simpson of Vassar College (not coincidentally, where her friend Carl Degler taught). The letter was an offer of employment for Mr. and Mrs. Scott. Anne Scott was offered the position of dean of faculty and tenured professor of history with an annual salary of $20,000 and the perk of an "attractive rent-free residence for the dean and family." Andrew was offered a $17,000 salary and a nine-month tenured faculty position. The Scotts declined, preferring to remain in the South.[71] Over the next twenty years other institutions would try unsuccessfully to recruit her away from Duke. By 1966, she had grown from being a marginalized scholar wife, tagging along after her husband's career, into an academic with the reputation to command substantial employment offers and appointments in professional associations.

Anne Scott's Harvard connections and early entry as a historian of women into the Southern wing of the historical profession was fortunate for a small host of budding young feminist historians about to burst onto the professional scene. She would prove a powerful advocate, mediator, and leader for their movement for women's history. Yet, Anne Scott's early career reveals her as a historian entering the profession at a transitional time both for women and the field. Historians of women who were able to establish themselves professionally before 1969 were critical participants in the field's rise to legitimacy in the following decades.

The first small Northern cohort of professionally trained historians of women featured here represent of range of experiences both typical and atypical of women academics of the early to middle twentieth century. They ranged in terms of marital status. Some remained single. Others struggled to combine family with higher education careers and developed individual solutions for doing so. Professionally successful historians of women worked often from the haven of women's colleges, or in the case of Ware, an HBCU. They offered little challenge to the predominant masculine professional paradigms during the first six decades of the twentieth century. They strove to be consummate history professionals, in tune with the intellectual currents of their time, and entirely committed to the craft's traditions and standards of legitimacy. They tended not to claim feminism as their creed openly in professional settings. Nor did they narrowly define their scholarly specialization in gendered terms.

Even those women who famously formed the Berkshire Conference of Women Historians between 1928 and 1930 did not express any interest in developing historical studies about women, preferring instead to focus on research in traditional fields, teaching, and their collective sense of professional isolation.[72] From 1928 through the 1950s, the Berkshire Conference of Women Historians was a relatively informal Northeast association of professionally marginalized women historians with a tiny membership from New England and New York. They didn't open their membership to women outside of the Northeast until the late 1940s because they didn't want to be obligated to travel that far should new members push to hold meetings outside the region. When the group opened its membership to women around the nation in the late 1940s and finally got around to writing a formal constitution, membership was open to any woman historian who wanted to join and pay the annual dues of one dollar per year. By 1955, membership had grown to 102 women history professors, a large number of whom worked in Northeastern women's colleges.[73]

Up through the 1960s, the membership appears to have been all-white. This fact was noted by Deborah Gray White in *Telling Histories* to demonstrate Black women's exclusion from the historical profession and its organizations during the long Jim Crow era.[74] Did active racism on the part of the Berkshire Conference of Women Historians play a role in shaping its membership? No direct evidence exists that would allow us to evaluate the racial attitudes of the women in that group. No reference to race can be found in their institutional records. They were overall a circumspect group when it came to expressing opinions and personal views. It seems more likely that seeking out African American women historians simply didn't occur to them. Call it a blind spot or a product of systemic racism—both de facto and de jure—and its pervasive influence on American cultural institutions. Had the Berkshire Conference of Women Historians sought out Black members in its first thirty years, it would have found fewer than ten Black women historians with the PhD in the entire country prior to 1960. They were scattered across the nation, mostly in the mid-Atlantic states and the South, clustered within historically Black colleges and libraries, and often intensely focused on their work in Black education and within the Black history movement, though this was not always the case, as the work of diplomatic historian Merze Tate demonstrates.[75] Black women historians had other proverbial fish to fry during the long Jim Crow era.[76] It's also quite possible that Black women historians were not interested in joining white women historians in the Berkshire Conference for their own reasons, like the hundreds of other women history PhDs and professors who didn't join the group during its first three decades.

While the Berkshire Conference of Women Historians was the only women's organization of its kind in the historical profession up through 1968, it must be acknowledged that the group didn't initially have broad national appeal because of its own limited scope. It had only a very modest professional agenda on behalf of women historians before the 1960s, which included trying to get at least one woman on the nominating and program committees of the AHA each year. Members essentially gathered for one weekend every year in the mountains of eastern New York and New England to hike, socialize, drink, informally discuss history and professional matters, and soothe their shared feelings of alienation from the male-dominated profession. They also met informally for a breakfast at the annual meeting of the AHA each year. The fact that the early records of the Berkshire Conference of Women Historians are very limited has left women historians with little evidence to help them piece together the organization's early history or the attitudes of its members—but it does not appear to have actively organized to demand the historical profession redress grievances regarding women's professional status; did not develop even a list of grievances; and did not, until the 1970s, sponsor the field of women's history.[77] Professionally marginal as these women historians were, they were limited by the racially segregated, sometimes sex-segregated, and androcentric academic systems within which they had secured isolated toeholds for themselves. They hadn't constructed these systems, but they were playing by the rules the gentleman scholars of the era had put in place. It is perhaps ironic that Berkshire Conference members were not, as a group, active in the earliest efforts to develop the history of American women into a recognized research field. But it was, after all, an organization of women historians, not an organization of historians of women.

———————

Early work on women in American history represents a noteworthy stage in the development of women's history. These scholars pioneered the field. They secured toeholds and constructed footbridges to the mainstream of the discipline. By the end of the period under consideration here, the women scholars' willingness to perform professional service and their skill at making enduring connections with prominent male historians was a double-edged sword. It enabled a few historians of women to establish careers. It also fostered unwillingness to pose a direct challenge to sex-based inequities within the discipline of history. Finally, many of their male allies, mentors, and colleagues agreed that their focus on women was valid—when properly framed. The debate over whether there should be something called "women's history" did not ensue in this early period, and the distinct field did not emerge.

Chapter 3

Pioneer Scholars, Masculine Paradigm, Southern Contexts, 1920s–1960s

> Now that you have your [history] Ph.D., go home and learn
> how to bake a chocolate cake.
>
> —R. D. W. Connor to Guion Griffis Johnson, 1927

While individual historians trained at Radcliffe and Columbia ventured tenta- tively into the study of American women during the first half of the twentieth century, others were doing the same in the South. We've seen that it was pos- sible—if difficult—for women who studied women to make a place for them- selves in the historical profession in the United States between 1900 and the 1960s but that women were generally a marginalized minority in the historical profession throughout these decades. This pattern held true in the South, even though the Southern Historical Association had already elected two women presidents in its roughly thirty-year history by 1969—a track record twice as good as that of the American Historical Association and the Organization of American Historians. These were Ella Lonn of Goucher College and Kathryn Abbey Hannah of Florida State Women's College. Lonn had specialized in US immigration history, while Hannah had specialized in the history of Florida and Spanish America. As Carol Bleser suggested in 1981, they were elected president not because they were women, nor despite it, but because they had paid their dues through professional service and scholarship.[1] Yet, as Ella Lonn's 1924 study of academic women's status shows, these successful women knew of the tough and discriminatory patterns of employment faced by women in academia.[2] This makes it all the more surprising that the South produced sev- eral well-regarded historians of American women during the middle decades of the twentieth century. The most notable were A. Elizabeth Tayor and Mary Elizabeth Massey.

In the South, those historians of women who did become established early were native Southerners, productive historians of Southern women, committed to professional service, and not afraid to speak up to their male colleagues. When considered in national scope, both the SHA and the MVHA/OAH were predominantly associations of Americanists, a factor significant in the devel- opment of American women's history, given the perceptible undercurrent of support for a potentially fruitful new field of inquiry within these societies of Americanists and regionalists. This was an undercurrent that was largely absent from the AHA. Historians active with the SHA and the MVHA/OAH did not build a distinct cohesive field around women in history in these years, but they did allow space for the production of a body of foundational work on American women from 1922 to 1965 rooted in regional, cultural, social, and progressive history.[3]

Work completed by graduates of the history department and the Institute for Research in Social Science (IRSS) at the University of North Carolina at Chapel Hill is illustrative of how established progressive and social historians in the South fostered the work of emerging historians of women between 1924 and 1960. Since the discipline of history was still overwhelmingly masculine, historians of women had little choice but to embrace that profession on its own terms; some were relatively successful, while others were less so. The more successful women were connected to both regional and national networks of prominent historians and built traditional academic careers as single women. Since family concerns could limit the choices open to married women PhDs in these decades, those who married were forced to carve out intellectual niches for themselves at the margins of academia.[4]

The histories of Julia Cherry Spruill, Marjorie Mendenhall Applewhite, Virginia Gearhart Gray, Guion Griffis Johnson, A. Elizabeth Taylor, and Mary Elizabeth Massey highlight the way that both traditional hierarchies of historical significance and traditional gender and family roles limited the potential of women historians.[5] While their scholarship on women was sometimes recognized, they were not generally rewarded with faculty appointments unless they could overcome or sidestep those gendered barriers.

Arguably, of those whose talents went unrewarded, Julia Cherry Spruill was the most recognized for her work. Her example is illustrative. In 1922, Julia Cherry of Rocky Mount, North Carolina, and a recent graduate of North Carolina College for Women (now UNC Greensboro), married her college beau, Corydon Spruill. The couple set up house in Chapel Hill, where Corydon had a position as an economics professor and later as dean of the College of Arts and Sciences. Mrs. Spruill was active in campus life for many years as a faculty wife and, according to Anne Firor Scott, defined herself primarily as "the wife of Corydon Spruill who dabbled in history."[6] She was a gifted researcher and writer. Spruill conducted research for her 1938 book, *Women's Life and Work in the Southern Colonies*, as a graduate student and paid research assistant for the IRSS at UNC Chapel Hill from 1925 to 1927, during which time she worked to earn her MA in history.[7] At the time, she worked under the guidance of sociologist Howard Odum and historians R. D. W. Connor and W. W. Pierson. Spruill's work was also encouraged by progressive historians Mary Beard and Arthur M. Schlesinger Sr., both of whom she met while her husband studied at Harvard from 1929 to 1930.[8] She thus connected with Schlesinger and Beard before they began the efforts that resulted in the establishment of both the Radcliffe Women's Archives and the Sophia Smith Collection in 1943.[9] She kept a foot in historical work, teaching high school history and government in Chapel Hill and sometimes social science courses at the university on a part-time, contingent basis. She was well-regarded enough by North Carolina historians that in 1948 she was elected to the elite Historical Society of North Carolina on the basis of her pathbreaking publication. She remained a member until her death in 1986. The exclusive society included only the most prominent historians, such as Fletcher Green, James Patton, and Bell Wiley.[10] Spruill maintained a lively interest in history throughout her life. But she never pursued the PhD nor a career in history, likely because she perceived the barriers presented by her status as a married woman and a faculty wife.

Another marginal scholar, Virginia Gearhart Gray, completed her PhD dissertation, "The Southern Woman, 1840–1860," in 1927 under Carl Russell Fish at the University of Wisconsin. She married a zoologist that same year and went with him to Tulane University. Despite having a degree from a well-regarded graduate school and excellent references, she did not find work. Conforming to the cultural expectations of the era, she took many years off to raise her children. The family moved to Durham, North Carolina, in 1930 when her husband, Irving Gray, was hired by Duke University. Duke later hired her to teach part-time in the nursing school and in the English department. In 1955, she began work in the manuscript department of the Duke University Libraries.[11] Gearhart Gray and Cherry Spruill were limited in their career options by their decision to marry and have families. Though they never eschewed scholarly life completely, the profession did not offer them the sort of opportunities their married male peers could expect.

Marjorie Mendenhall Applewhite earned a 1926 MA in history from Radcliffe, where she studied under Arthur Schlesinger Sr. She taught at a variety of colleges, including Winthrop University in South Carolina and Vassar College, before completing her PhD at UNC Chapel Hill in 1939. Her dissertation was not on women's history, though she later wrote a biography of Varina Davis and reviewed works in women's history. Over the years, Arthur Schlesinger Sr., Ulrich B. Phillips, and Hugh T. Lefler recommended her to publishers who needed essays and reviews on the history of women. Yet she was unable to land a faculty appointment in history, despite her academic pedigree and her efforts to do so. Anne Firor Scott suggested that Mendenhall Applewhite had a personality that would not allow her to dissemble and flatter male colleagues. Scott's assertion that she had "determined [that] the men who ran the university were unwilling to hire women" is probably fair. Nevertheless, Mendenhall Applewhite was able to make a belated career move when she was hired by the University of Maryland in 1960. Her death in 1961 ended her career.[12] The thwarted career aspirations of the fully credentialed Marjorie Mendenhall Applewhite and Virginia Gearhart Gray show how hiring practices and social conventions could prevent a woman's career from launching; Julia Cherry Spruill shows us that gendered cultural conventions discouraged women's educational and career aspirations. Yet, a few Southern historians of women fared better. They belonged to important networks of historians, were well-published and well-respected, and participated actively in the associational life of historians. They even had careers as professional historians. In the South, this network's center was at UNC Chapel Hill.

Guion Griffis Johnson is a good example of how talented, credentialed women academics at midcentury tried to balance their intellectual and professional lives with their family lives and political commitments. Guion Griffis was born in 1900 in Wolfe City, Texas.[13] She attended Baylor College for Women and earned her AB in journalism in 1921. From 1921 until 1924, she taught at Baylor, built the journalism department as its chair, and completed her MA during summers at the University of Missouri. In 1923 she married Guy Benton Johnson, then a PhD candidate in sociology at the University of Chicago.[14] In 1923, Guy Johnson was offered a position at Baylor College and he took it, sharing his wife's office space during their tenure there. In 1924 Guy Johnson was recruited to work as a research assistant in Howard Odum's Institute for Research in Social Science, an innovative new interdisciplinary program at UNC that focused on researching North Carolina's social and economic problems. The Johnsons negotiated a research assistantship for Guion as well. The couple moved to Chapel Hill that year, intent upon completing their doctorates and intending to return to their positions at Baylor.

At Chapel Hill, Guy Johnson conducted a sociological study of African American culture. Guion Griffis Johnson made a decisive switch from journalism to history, after she found a dissertation topic that absorbed her more than North Carolina newspapers—the topic that Odum had initially assigned her. Her dissertation, "Social Conditions in North Carolina, 1800–1860," was completed in history.[15] Odum was initially reluctant to allow the change to a different discipline and a new advisor, R. D. W. Connor. Nevertheless, he supported her decision after he got Connor to agree that Johnson not be distracted from the ongoing work she was doing for Odum by Connor's own research projects. As a graduate student Johnson reported overhearing a professor say, "No woman is competent to teach a class in history. No matter how qualified, no woman is competent to teach courses except on the public-school level—elementary or high school, but in the university, no." Nevertheless, twenty years later she explained that she persisted in history despite such negative attitudes toward women because she was "naïve and deeply committed to scholarship."[16]

Between 1924 and 1927 she completed coursework for her PhD, conducted her research, and wrote her dissertation. The dissertation won the university-wide Smith Research Award in 1927, beating out Fletcher Green's dissertation on state constitutions, among others. Green would soon rise to professional prominence in American history, join the faculty at UNC Chapel Hill, and later become its chair. During his tenure at Chapel Hill, he mentored two pioneer historians of women, A. Elizabeth Taylor and Mary Elizabeth Massey.

After Johnson earned her doctorate, the IRSS promoted her to the position of research associate, an appointment equivalent in rank and pay to that of associate professor but without teaching responsibilities. Johnson proceeded to publish several articles, and her first book, *A History of the South Carolina Sea Islands*, appeared in 1930.[17] The research and writing of these works, her primary job responsibility, was funded by the IRSS. Nevertheless, the university did not appoint her to a teaching position, as they had some male research associates. Johnson took this as the discrimination that it was, since she aspired to become a history professor. Frustrated for years by this inequity, according to a 1974 interview, Johnson nevertheless continued her association with the IRSS and the Chapel Hill history department until 1943.[18]

In 1937 Johnson published her second book, *Ante-Bellum North Carolina: A Social History*. This book, whose research and writing had been funded by the IRSS, was an elaboration of her dissertation. In this book and her work on the Sea Islands, she gave considerable attention to women's lives, even if the personal pronoun "he" is used as a substitute for "the average North Carolinian" in her opening pages. "He" had seen a long list of developments between 1800 and 1860, according to Johnson's two-and-a-half-page summary of the history she was about to describe in 813 detailed pages. But this gendering of "the average North Carolinian" as primarily male was deceptive, for Johnson thoroughly integrated the lives of North Carolinian women into her narrative. As her "average North Carolinian" observed in passing, "On the small farms he still saw women laboring by day and by night, both in the house and in the field, to aid their husbands in feeding and clothing the family. Despite divorce suits and the agitation for larger property rights of the married woman, the wife's personality was still legally merged in that of the husband."[19]

Johnson offered a chapter titled "Courtship and Marriage" that explored social customs, extramarital relations, divorce, and alimony. Another titled "Family Life" discussed women's legal status, wage earning, housewifery, and children. Within the other twenty-four chapters women appear frequently as members of elite and laboring social classes, in Black and white families, and as active participants in education, churches, reform movements, the economy, and other areas of North Carolina life.[20] Johnson did not identify herself as a "women's historian," as this classification did not yet exist. But she featured women as full participants in society. Johnson's attention to race and economic conditions was also notable, reflecting her own research interests and those of the IRSS more generally. Her *History of the South Carolina Sea Islands* was a study of the Gullah people and gave equal attention to men, women, and children.[21] Both of Guion Griffis Johnson's major books were reviewed favorably in history journals in the 1930s.[22]

During her most productive years as a scholar, the Johnsons raised two children, born in 1928 and 1933.[23] They hired full-time household help to care for the children so that Guion could continue with her work. She recalled that when their older child began throwing temper tantrums as she left for work, she and Guy disagreed over whether the arrangement was satisfactory. Guy suggested she should stay home with the boy, but Guion remained firm and found a care provider more attuned to the needs of their son, and the issue faded.[24]

Having by 1939 established their reputations as scholars and Southern liberals, first Guy and then Guion Griffis Johnson were recruited in 1939 to work on Gunnar Myrdal's renowned study on American race relations, *An American Dilemma*. The book, which would become a classic and eventually help overturn the segregationist doctrine of "separate but equal" established by the 1896 Supreme Court ruling *Plessy v. Ferguson*, drew on the research of thirty or more social scientists.[25] Myrdal asked Guion to join the project at the suggestion of Guy, who had already accepted a full-time staff position. Myrdal wrote to her hoping that she could prepare research and a report on some area of interest to her and trusted she would be able to devote enough time to it, given her parenting responsibilities. It seems, however, that before he asked her to work with the project, he had already listed her in a memorandum to the Carnegie Corporation as one of six scholars he had engaged as an "outside expert . . . [who] will be asked to make major contributions in cooperation with the staff and under my direction."[26] Guion agreed to the assignment and in 1940 was paid $2,000 for her research and analysis on racial ideologies. In 2023 dollars that would be equivalent to $43,000, suggesting that she indeed made a substantial research contribution.[27]

Guion Johnson produced a 300-page manuscript on the development of Southern white racial ideologies. Myrdal asked her permission to publish her research as one of his chapters but wanted another staff member to cut its length and be listed as lead author. Johnson refused to release her rights to the material. She was incensed that Myrdal would give another author credit for the work she had done. She later regretted her refusal, as Myrdal listed her in the preface to *An American Dilemma* as merely "one of those who had also helped."[28] In 1974 she recalled, "I was so angry with Gunnar Myrdal that I actually have not read the manuscript through. I've used the index and the table of contents to find the parts that I'm interested in, to trace my materials through."[29] Guion Johnson here demonstrated that she was willing to advocate for her intellectual property rights. Being relegated to a footnote in her own work conflicted with her sense of her own worth.

Johnson published some of her research on racial ideologies in 1949 as a chapter in an edited volume and as an article in the *Journal of Southern History* in 1957.[30] Both the chapter and the article contain well-crafted analyses of white racial ideologies. They recognize the inherent racism in even the more benevolent forms of white paternalism toward Southern Blacks. Johnson stood up against the very concept of race, drawing on the work of anthropologists Franz Boas and Melville Herskovitz, who asserted that there was no such thing as a pure race.[31] She also drew on the work of psychologists Otto Klineberg, Abram Kardiner, and Lionel Ovesey, who challenged earlier claims that racial traits were biological and genetic. Instead, they argued that the cultural and social characteristics of American "negroes" that earlier race theorists had posited were biological traits were instead the product of their adaptations to difficult social conditions. Johnson embraced their idea that race was socially constructed rather than biologically determined. Her writing on these themes in the most prominent Southern history journal during an increasingly active period in the civil rights movement marks her as politically progressive and assertive—a stance she may have felt freer to take in 1957 because she was no longer employed as an academic historian and thus had little reason to fear professional reprisals.

Johnson finally got an opportunity to teach her own history courses at Chapel Hill during World War II. In 1943 she was asked to teach a semester of American History and Naval Strategy in the history department. After nineteen years at Chapel Hill, she finally negotiated a regular appointment as associate professor. The next year, however, Guy Johnson accepted appointment as director of the Southern Regional Conference, a group committed to interracial cooperation in solving the South's race problems. This new job meant the Johnsons would have to move to Atlanta. Guion reluctantly resigned her faculty position, and from 1944 to 1947 she worked as executive secretary for the Georgia Conference on Social Welfare, traveling frequently to New York for her work. As Johnson's tenure with this organization drew to a close, in 1947 Guion was offered the chair of the history department at Agnes Scott College. She felt the offered salary, $125 per month, was woefully insufficient. Weighing the low salary at Agnes Scott College with the prospect of an arduous commute if she were to live in North Carolina where Guy was to resume his teaching post, she rejected the college's offer of employment, to the dismay of the college president.[32] Guion Griffis Johnson was still hoping to re-establish herself as a history professor at Chapel Hill.

During the Johnsons' absence from Chapel Hill from 1944 to 1947, the political climate had changed at the university. The onset of the Cold War adversely affected Guion's plans.[33] In Chapel Hill, Guy Johnson was increasingly under attack from local conservatives for his liberal racial and economic ideas. Several college trustees seemed determined to oust him from his professorship, alleging he supported communism and racial integration. It was in this context that Guion attempted to negotiate being rehired by the history department. The department's answer was conveyed by R. D. W. Connor, who told her that the department was divided by bitterness and strife and there was no position to be had. When she appealed to the chancellor, Bob House, he suggested that she focus on getting in good with the wives of college administrators and trustees who might convince their husbands to allow Guy to keep his job.[34] She then joined a plethora of women's volunteer groups. Johnson was no stranger to volunteer work but had focused on research, writing, and parenting for most of her adult life. She took the chancellor's advice, however, abandoning her pursuit of a professorship at Chapel Hill in 1947. She moved to take up a life of civic activism.

Guion Griffis Johnson had been a marginally employed historian from 1924 to 1943. Her early work on women, race, and social history, though reviewed positively, had not landed her a long-term professorship in a university. The situation was a result of her husband's career, their mutual commitment to progressive politics, the Cold War political climate of the late 1940s, her own high standard for employment, and pervasive cultural prescriptions requiring married women to subordinate their ambitions to the needs of their families. Johnson was marginally employed, to be sure. By some measures, though, she was right in the center. Her scholarship was recognized as a major contribution to Southern history. Her election to the Historical Society of North Carolina in 1948 placed her at the center of North Carolina's history community with the likes of R. D. W. Connor, Fletcher Green, James Patton, and other esteemed historians. The Historical Society of North Carolina was an elite society of scholars that some joked was "harder to get into . . . than it is into heaven"; until the 1960s it had only fifty members who held life tenure.[35] As a member of this historical society from 1948 to 1989, Johnson maintained contact with her former Chapel Hill colleagues even as she shifted her attention to work in myriad civic organizations.[36]

Johnson's curtailed history career has been interpreted rightly by historians as a product of how gender discrimination professionally marginalized women. Yet, she had creatively managed to carve out a niche for herself at the center of North Carolina academic life over the course of twenty years. She worked for the Institute for Research in Social Science, first as research assistant and then as associate from 1924 to 1934. She left paid employment there, but not her office or her work, only when the Depression caused the program to cut back its staff, married women first. When the war created demand for an American history professor, she was invited to teach American History and Naval Strategy in the V-12 military program for the Chapel Hill history department in 1943 and offered a permanent position.[37] Johnson's research work and her prominent presence in this intellectual community suggest that she was in some ways quite central to contemporary historical practice in North Carolina. She found satisfying remunerative alternatives to a career as a history professor, though occasionally she dabbled in teaching when the opportunity presented itself. Her ability to maintain membership in this community, even while unable to attain employment she found suitable as a teaching professor, demonstrates she was able to adapt to the intellectual culture at Chapel Hill while juggling family and civic commitments. Moreover, she was able to publish her books through the university press and published widely in peer-reviewed scholarly journals of the South, including the *Journal of Southern History*.[38]

While Johnson did receive offers of professorships from Duke University, the University of North Carolina at Chapel Hill, and Agnes Scott College in Georgia during the 1940s, she rejected the Duke and Agnes Scott offers because they paid poorly. After she had taught successfully for a year at Chapel Hill during the war, the history department chair, Dr. A. R. Newsome, finally offered her an associate professorship in 1944, which she accepted. Yet, she was compelled to resign this position, settling for a position as the executive secretary of the Georgia Conference for Social Welfare. She took this job to join her husband in Georgia, sacrificing her hard-won opportunity at Chapel Hill. When her duties in this position were completed in 1947, Johnson interviewed for a position in sociology at Duke at the suggestion of a colleague. During the interview she and the chair determined she was overqualified for the position, and he suggested she apply instead for a job as dean of women. During the interview with Dean Alice Baldwin, Baldwin was apparently scandalized by the fact that the skirt Johnson wore rose above her knee when she sat down. Johnson believed this disqualified her in Baldwin's eyes. This anecdote suggests that female academics were as capable of imposing gendered and generational professional expectations for demeanor and self-presentation on women colleagues as male colleagues might have been. Baldwin, nevertheless, called on Johnson's expertise in the following decade, working with her in the state branch of the American Association of University Women and frequently meeting for lunch.[39]

Johnson was keenly aware of the gendered hierarchies she confronted. Being just as qualified as male colleagues (if not more) was not enough to get more than a foot in the door of the Chapel Hill history department. Johnson even had her title downgraded from associate professor to lecturer by Fletcher Green, chair of the UNC history department, in the annual department bulletin that reported on former faculty members' activities.[40] Recall that Green and Johnson earned PhDs in the same year and that his dissertation had lost to Johnson's in the 1927 Smith Research Award competition at UNC. Johnson believed this nominal demotion in departmental literature may have been indicative of lingering competitive feelings on the part of Green, in combination with the "rigid attitudes" toward women that prevailed within the department through the 1960s.[41] Still, Green edited the volume in which Johnson published her essay on white racial ideologies in 1949.[42] Paradoxically, then, Johnson was both an intellectual threat to her male colleagues, a respected scholar who could be called on when her research and teaching services fit the bill, and somewhat disposable as a faculty member. Small wonder that Johnson made her move into public service and volunteering a permanent one. In this line of work, there was no question that she was a respected expert and, as we will see, an organizational powerhouse.

A few points of comparison between Johnson and her contemporary, Caroline Ware, may be helpful. These scholars earned their PhDs within two years of one another. Ware, like Johnson, was a married woman academic in a period when this was unusual. Ware, unlike Johnson, however, found her jobs at Vassar and later Howard acceptable professional options. She also remained childless. Like Johnson, Ware forged a connection to a major coeducational institution through her work in an innovative social science research institute. Indeed, the Columbia Council for Research in the Social Sciences was modeled on Howard Odum's Institute for Research in Social Science at Chapel Hill, and the two institutes shared a source of funding in the Rockefeller Foundation.[43] Like the IRSS, the Columbia council also sponsored a small number of women scholars and works focusing on women, gender, and sexuality in a variety of disciplines, including anthropology, sociology, history, economics, languages, and psychology.[44] Other projects focused on matters of class and race. But the Columbia council took a much more global approach than the IRSS, which was focused primarily on the state of North Carolina and, later, on the Southern United States.[45]

Despite Ware's success, marital status was clearly a key factor in determining a woman's career trajectory in history and other academic disciplines during these years.[46] Married women historians—Cherry Spruill, Gearhart Gray, Mendenhall Applewhite, and Johnson—were professionally stymied; many if not most employed professional women historians remained single.[47] This was no doubt a conscious choice, a sacrifice they made knowing the obstacles placed in the path of married professional women. It wasn't until civil rights legislation of the 1960s included women that the occupational landscape for women professionals would begin to shift, which makes the few survival and success stories ahead all the more remarkable.[48]

Though women's opportunities were truncated by considerations of marital status, UNC Chapel Hill produced at least five scholars specializing in the history of Southern women by midcentury. What was it about the intellectual culture of this institution between 1927 and 1947 that made this possible? Foremost was Chapel Hill's renown, a liberal institution in a conservative region of the country. Guy Johnson's struggles during the McCarthy era revealed that even within the Chapel Hill community, divisions between liberals and conservatives could be bitter, but the university, as a public institution, was still a major point of access for white women who wanted to take up advanced study in the South. This fact alone may have rankled social conservatives, but work done at institutes like the IRSS remained a lightning rod for social and political controversy in the local community, the state, and the South.[49] The IRSS was designed as an interdisciplinary institute that would sponsor and publish research on social, economic, and political problems in the state of North Carolina. It was, however, most closely associated with sociology, the field of its founder, Howard Odum. Conservatives in the South often conflated sociology with socialism when they attacked the IRSS to try to discredit it. Researchers at the IRSS set out to investigate race, poverty, and the social, economic, and political development of the state. Because the institute's mandate was to conduct research that could then be used to develop solutions to those problems, its work threatened conservatives who sought to maintain racial segregation, the economic status quo, and social and religious conservatism. Guy and Guion Johnson's professional lives were thus deeply affected by the racial, Cold War, and gender politics of the era.

Studies at the IRSS during its first fifty years supported a few women scholars and a select number of investigations into women's status and history.[50] Historians made up a small share of the institute's staff, but it is worth noting that both Johnson and Julia Cherry Spruill produced some of the most pathbreaking social history of the region while on staff. Both women placed a major focus on women in their research, and their work remains foundational to the field of Southern women's history. It came out of a socially progressive institution of higher learning, dominated by male liberals, funded by the Laura Spellman Rockefeller Foundation, and dedicated to making scholarship, historical or otherwise, a vehicle for Southern progress.[51] These factors, then, help explain what made Chapel Hill a place where scholars might focus on women. But Southern liberals were not alone in allowing space for the study of women in history, as we will see.

Academic women who studied women were also able to find some success within the prescribed boundaries of the history discipline at midcentury, as the lives of A. Elizabeth Taylor and Mary Elizabeth Massey make clear. Taylor and Massey entered the discipline just as Johnson was making her shift into a life of civic activism in the mid-1940s. Unlike Johnson, they do not appear to have been politically active. Rather, they participated in historical associations, served their home institutions, and focused tightly on scholarship and teaching. Like Johnson, both had done graduate work at the University of North Carolina. Their formative professional experiences were rooted at UNC, where Fletcher Green served as advisor to both.[52] Neither historian married, leaving them free of family responsibilities and career-track pitfalls that marriage created for the midcentury career woman.

A. Elizabeth Taylor embarked on a path to preeminence as an expert on woman suffrage in the American South. Born in 1917 in Columbus, Georgia, to a middle-class family, Taylor was expected to attend college. A graduate of the University of Georgia in 1938, she studied under Fletcher Green at Chapel Hill for her MA before going into the PhD program in history at Vanderbilt University, where there was a strong contingent of social historians. At Vanderbilt she studied under William B. Hesseltine, Frank Owsley, and Daniel Robison.[53] The political milieu Taylor encountered at Vanderbilt was more conservative than that of UNC Chapel Hill, where the IRSS had great influence.

The historians at Vanderbilt took an intellectual stand opposed to the IRSS view of Southern regionalism, which focused on the South's distinct racial makeup, the cultural contributions of Black Americans, and the lag in economic development due to the region's agrarianism. A group of Vanderbilt scholars known as the Agrarians had published *I'll Take My Stand* in 1930, a polemical response to Howard Odum and the IRSS opposing the more liberal social, economic, and political agenda of the institute.[54] *I'll Take My Stand* lauded the South's distinct white, yeoman, and fundamentalist identity and defended racial segregation. Frank Owsley's essay in this book and in later publications revealed that he had backward views on race. Taylor, his student, does not seem to have taken any open stand on matters of race. In her many essays on woman suffrage, she invariably described typical Southern suffragist arguments, most of which echoed those of national suffrage organizations. But in the South, white women suffragists had to contend with questions related to how woman suffrage might upset the racial status quo of segregation. Anti-suffrage forces warned that African American women voters would vote in high numbers and could topple white (male) supremacy in the region. White suffragists in the South perforce and often by inclination operated within a racially exclusionary and segregated framework in the Jim Crow South.[55] Taylor was circumspect in her treatment of these arguments and in the way she presented other details of the movement, preferring to chronicle and describe, not to analyze or assess. It is thus difficult to ascertain her personal views on race inequality in America.

Taylor's interest in the woman suffrage movement was sparked when she made an important intellectual discovery while completing her doctorate and teaching at Judson College, a Baptist women's college: She discovered the multivolume *History of Woman Suffrage*, compiled by former suffragists, in the

Judson College library.[56] Taylor felt chagrined that she had not known of this source. Once found, she determined to make the study of woman suffrage in the South the topic of her dissertation. Because of the relative difficulty of traveling to archives and the limited duplication technologies available in the 1940s, she limited her dissertation to the suffrage movement in Tennessee. She described her advisors as not particularly interested in her subject matter but sympathetic. In retrospect, she was clear that she had not defined her field as "women's history," saying that no such field existed. Rather, she considered her specializations to be US history, Southern history, and political history.[57] She recalled that her advisors thought of her work as a peripheral study in American political history. She completed the PhD in 1943 and took a one-year appointment at Texas State College for Women, which was renamed Texas Woman's University in 1957. This job would turn into a permanent position the next year and be her academic home for the rest of her career.[58]

While at Texas State College for Women, Taylor continued her study of woman suffrage in the South, writing a pathbreaking article on the movement in Texas. She gained access to the papers of Jane Y. McCallum and Minnie Fisher Cunningham, two leaders of the movements in that state. McCallum allowed Taylor to borrow her private collection of material to complete her research.[59] Eventually Taylor wrote and published essays on the suffrage movement in most of the Southern states. She made a conscious decision to focus on women and was not derailed by her women colleagues' concern that her specialization put her at a professional disadvantage.[60] She reported that she had no idea whether focusing on a more traditional topic might have helped her professionally. But her unique field of specialization ensured her a place in the literature, and her professional activism accorded her some recognition within the Southern Historical Association.

Taylor was a career-long member of the SHA, the MVHA/OAH, the AHA, and other regional professional associations.[61] She developed connections to networks of historians and was a close friend of Southern historian of women Mary Elizabeth Massey. The commonalities they shared in having been graduate students of Fletcher Green, women scholars, Southerners, and specialists in the history of Southern women drew them together. They addressed each other as "Mary Lib" and "Lib."[62] Retrospectively, Taylor acknowledged she was in contact with other women historians but did not think of them as her network, nor did she consider that she had a "network," a term that would come into usage by women historians in the 1970s.[63] What did constitute Taylor's network was made up primarily of other women historians, like Massey and Doris King, who taught history at North Carolina State University. In 1963 she reported to her friend Mary Massey, "I enjoyed [the MVHA] convention and saw lots of our friends. It was a little lonely with neither you nor Doris King to pal around with. . . . Oh, well, I guess someone has to hold down the home front."[64] Taylor's career-long involvement in the SHA suggests that it was her primary professional affiliation. Throughout the 1950s and 1960s she served the SHA on several committees, including its executive council from 1963 to 1964. Here she worked with secretary-treasurer Bennett Wall, who essentially ran the organization for four decades.[65] At Texas Woman's University, Taylor, known as a wonderful though exacting teacher, was actively involved in the life of the college, becoming a leader in the regional branch of the American Association of University Professors and other regional professional associations.[66] In 1976 a younger generation of Southern women scholars founded the Southern Association for Women Historians and elected Taylor as vice president.

Taylor was aware of the pitfalls that a heavy teaching load and active professional service represented to the scholar. In 1963 she advised Mary Massey of Winthrop University to be cautious in agreeing to large classes: "I was interested in the fact that your large section had grown. I think that a big section like that would beat me down. I feel the weight of numbers in lectures as well as grading, etc. Don't tell your dean that you can lecture to 500 as easily as 100. He'll have you doing it. I plan to keep griping whenever my freshman sections get over 50. Our administration will pile as much on you as they think you will take."[67] Taylor was happy at Texas Woman's University but by 1963 was also somewhat stuck there, as moving to another school, like Converse College, which briefly courted her, wasn't economically viable.[68]

Taylor published numerous articles and gave papers at the annual conventions of the SHA and MVHA/OAH.[69] In 1972 she reported that the AHA frustrated her because even though she had been a member for thirty years, she had "never gotten anywhere with them."[70] Nevertheless, she rendered professional service to these organizations, and as a published, recognized scholar, she was well-placed to promote women's history and its younger practitioners when they arrived on the scene. Between 1969 and 1974, she lent her name and presented her work to early women's history panels. Still, until the end of her life, she insisted, "As for women's history, I guess I've never been a true disciple of women's history: just focus on US history with proper attention given to women and their role."[71] The irony is that everything she published was about woman suffrage in the South. This statement represents her rejection of the terms the younger generation of scholars was using, not a rejection of the value of women's history. She simply had come of age in an era when accepting women's history as epistemologically distinct was not a part of the discipline's intellectual paradigm.

Taylor's essays offer detailed chronologies of the movement in each state she examined. There is ample evidence of meticulous research, but she did not extend her interpretation of materials very far, preferring to let the facts speak for themselves. Yet, it is painfully clear that some effort to extend her analysis or incorporate the historical contexts in which her subjects operated would have greatly enriched her work. For example, essays written in the racially charged era of the 1950s and 1960s would have benefited if she had not simply listed the racial arguments of both suffragists and anti-suffragists but had also elaborated on the early Jim Crow era context of the arguments. We would like to hear her explanation of why the arguments made sense to Southerners, or why Northerners tolerated them or might not have set forth the same racial arguments.[72] In her essay on the woman suffrage movement in Texas, for example, she let stand the following sentence, making no attempt to contextualize or explain it: "Other leaflets stated that woman suffrage and socialism went 'hand in hand,' that women already had adequate legal rights, and that woman suffrage would result in negro rule in those sections of the South where colored women outnumbered white women."[73] What accounts for this interpretive weakness? Taylor seems simply to have omitted her own explanation of the motivations, ideas, and backgrounds of the suffragists and anti-suffragists, even though she could describe their movement in detail. A survey of Taylor's reviews of other people's work reveals a similar cut-and-dried style. She summarizes but does not critically assess the material under review.[74] This scholarly detachment may have been preferred by the history discipline, or Taylor may simply have wished to avoid revealing her views during the conservative era in which she launched her career. We will never know whether she was racially progressive, a feminist, or simply a white Southerner bound by a segregationist culture.

Taylor did not link her intellectual interest in politically active women to contemporary politics. In fact, she was wary of the women's liberation movement and the damage she perceived it might inflict on the reputations of women scholars, especially those specializing in the subject of women. Taylor's generation of women academics, having fought to achieve career footholds, were aware of the need to keep up appearances in a male-dominated professional culture. For women scholars, this could entail walking a fine line between feminine manners and dress and professional self-presentation in a masculine environment. In remembering her good friend Mary Massey in 1992, Taylor recalled that Massey had been adept at professional politicking:

> She dressed beautifully, had a wonderful sense of humor, was an interesting person, a hard worker, and highly intelligent. She could get along with men in a way that I've never noticed another woman brought up in the South could. . . . She knew what was going on, and would tell them, and do it in a way that they would take it or just laugh it off. She was strong for women, too, but she didn't believe in favoring women just

because they're women. I don't believe in that either, but I certainly want them to have a fair deal.[75]

Indeed, Massey had written Bennett Wall regarding organizational appointments she had in mind for vice president of the SHA in 1971: "I suppose there should be a woman on it [the nominating committee], but I'm opposed to appointing one just because she is a woman."[76] The reference to not favoring women just because of their sex is important here, perhaps indicative of an equal rights bent in Massey's thinking; to succeed, women had to be acceptable in standards of conduct, achievement, dress, and manners while not losing their femininity. Thus, Taylor's reference to Massey as beautifully dressed, humorous, interesting, intelligent, and able to "tell men off" in an acceptable way isn't just superfluous chatter. Rather, it illustrates how difficult it was for women academics to navigate gendered behavioral expectations.

Another example of this gendered perspective comes from historian Betty Fladeland of Southern Illinois University. In a 1983 letter to leaders in the Southern Association for Women Historians, she stated, "In all the years that I have been working for women's equal rights, I have advocated integration rather than segregation and therefore have preferred to work through the general committee structures of the historical organizations to which I belong. Please do not interpret this as being critical of your group, as I am not trying to convert anyone else to my point of view. All of us must take the approach we think best to reach our common goal."[77]

While Fladeland rejected "segregationist" tactics, by 1983 she and Taylor had come to recognize the benefit of separate women's groups in the profession. Taylor had come to that conclusion earlier. In 1976, when she was elected to the vice presidency of the Southern Association for Women Historians, she observed, "As a general rule, men tend to band together, excluding women. Women now have a means of supporting each other. . . . The organization also provides some socialization among women historians. . . . The new feminist movement has allowed the acceptability of the promotion of women by women. . . . Women used to be caught between accusals of either promoting other women only because they are women or trying to surround herself by men in a man's world."[78] Yet during her thirty-year career, Taylor had accepted the gendered hierarchies of the historical profession. She coped with the realities of a gendered job market by spending her entire career at a women's college.

Women historians most frequently found employment in women's colleges along with a good number of male historians. Though some of these institutions might have seemed marginal relative to the top schools in the country, they provided an important institutional base from which women and men could conduct professional lives. Unlike Johnson, political and civic activism was not a part of Taylor's life. She was active in the Union of University Professors and was a member of the American Association of University Women, but beyond that, she left little evidence to indicate an interest in matters beyond the internal politics of her profession and her home institution of Texas Woman's University. Late in her career, she went on the record with her struggles to overcome gendered hierarchies.[79]

Mary Elizabeth Massey in contrast, left no evidence that she felt held back professionally.[80] Born in 1915 in Morrilton, Arkansas, Massey earned her BA from Hendrix College in 1937. She took her MA in 1940 and PhD in 1947, both from the University of North Carolina at Chapel Hill.[81] Taylor and Massey overlapped at Chapel Hill as graduate students between 1938 and 1940. Guion Griffis Johnson coincided briefly with both between 1938 and 1942, but it is unclear whether Johnson was acquainted with the two younger women. All three shared a connection to Fletcher Green; Johnson and Green earned their PhDs in the same year at UNC (1927), and Massey and Taylor overlapped as Green's students between 1938 and 1947.

The esteem in which Green was held by his former students was great, and Massey was no exception. They corresponded regularly and with obvious mutual respect and affection until her death in 1974. He continued to write recommendations for her as her career progressed, even after his health began to fail. When his former students set out to honor Green's mentorship, Massey, as the most successful of Green's female students, was asked to contribute to *Writing Southern History: Essays in Historiography in Honor of Fletcher M. Green.*[82] She was formally asked to write an essay for the volume in July 1961 by Arthur Link, though she had discussed it with Bennett Wall of the SHA earlier that year.[83] In January 1962, Rembert Patrick, another collaborator on the project, requested her participation in a letter laden with Southern cultural references to "turkey, hog jowl, black-eyed peas, fatback, grits, corn bread, and the debtor class," meant to inspire the authors to complete their essays. Patrick further urged, "You know that Fletcher has given freely of his time to graduate students. . . . Rather than writing texts, he has concentrated on helping his students while they were in graduate school and after they had entered the profession."[84] Most importantly, Massey's inclusion in this volume suggests that by 1961, she was a recognized figure among Southern historians.

Her work up to that time centered on the Confederate home front and Confederate refugees, focusing primarily on the experiences and activities of women. Her doctoral dissertation was written on the impact of wartime shortages on the Confederate home front. Published as *Ersatz in the Confederacy* in 1952, it was essentially about women's strategies for dealing with shortages of household commodities during the Civil War. The book is still in print. After 1947, Massey held several one-year appointments in Southern high schools and colleges before accepting an appointment in the history department of Winthrop University, the state women's college in Rock Hill, South Carolina, in 1950. She remained at Winthrop for the rest of her career. By 1962 she had been the department chair for several years and published several articles and a second book, *Refugee Life in the Confederacy*. In 1963 she received a Guggenheim grant to complete the research for her third book on the Civil War, focusing on women in both the North and the South.[85]

Allan Nevins recruited Massey to write the book for his Impact of the Civil War on Society series. In an initial letter to her, he pointed out, "It is a topic of the utmost importance, which has been rather shockingly neglected. . . . A wealth of unused material upon it can be reached without colossal effort."[86] Her colleague from the Southern Historical Association C. Vann Woodward also wrote in support of her involvement on the Nevins project, noting that her topic was particularly "great," asking her advice on literature on women during the Civil War and Reconstruction that he might assign to "a bright graduate student," and suggesting she pay attention to the impact of the war on Negro women.[87] Massey's work on this book established her reputation as a scholar on a national level and expanded her professional network well beyond the South. In researching the book, she established links to the archives on women in America at Smith College and Radcliffe, as well as to the prestigious Huntington Library in California. At the time she agreed to write the book she was busy as chair of the 1961 SHA program committee and was finishing her manuscript that would become *Refugee Life in the Confederacy*.[88] She was so busy in fact that she worried about taking on the new project. But her colleagues in the SHA, in particular Arthur Link, prevailed upon her, reminding her that she would soon need something to occupy her considerable energies.

The secrets to Massey's success are threefold. First, her graduate experience, choice of advisor, and willingness to actively participate in the scholarly network were key. Second, she did exceptional work and was able to effectively place it within traditional hierarchies of significance, namely Southern and Civil War history. Furthermore, she did not have the entanglement of marriage nor the family distractions that marriage entails.

Mary Elizabeth Massey was a cultural insider in the South. She had similar historical interests and values as her mentors and colleagues. She practiced the kind of cordial but assertive interaction that was expected of a professional historian, and she made her gender and status work for her. She was personally warm with peers and was both socially and professionally adept. She was also professionally tough, willing to confront men who would impede her work. In one instance when an archivist was not being helpful, she chastised him, beginning her sentence, "Now listen here buster."[89]

Massey benefited from the friendship and mentoring of her senior colleagues. Aside from Fletcher Green, most significant among these was Bell Wiley of Emory University. Wiley encouraged her interest in the history of women and was influential in recommending her as a contributor to the Impact of the Civil War on Society series and subsequently urging her to take on the project.[90] Wiley also advised her to apply for Guggenheim and Social Science Research Council grants to complete the Northern half of the research for the book, which became *Bonnet Brigades* in 1966. He wrote letters of support on her behalf for these grants and even secured an application deadline extension for her. When she was awarded the Guggenheim, Wiley wrote to her department chair suggesting she be given a research leave. It was the first time her university had agreed to a leave with pay in its history.[91] Wiley, who served as president of the Southern Historical Association in 1955, is a good example of an unsung male supporter of the study of women in history.

In 1959, in the lead-up to the Civil War Centennial celebrated nationally, Wiley made a strong appeal for the recognition of women's experiences and contributions to the war. In a speech delivered in Richmond on April 17, 1959, he pressed organizers of the centennial to "recognize women who played important roles in the war," noting some key women from Northern and Southern states but also "some of the less-known women [who] ought to be known." Citing some examples of the importance of the lesser-known women, he asserted, "The greatest heroism of the war was not that of the men who marched to battle. Rather it was the devotion and sacrifice of the women, North and South, who looked after large families, often plowing fields, cutting the wood, cooking the food, nursing the sick and burying the dead. These women were the stalwart characters of the period we seek to commemorate, and their magnificent work ought to be recognized."[92]

When Massey was invited in 1958 to join the Civil War Centennial Commission as a specialist on women in the Civil War, Wiley pointed her to the work done by Francis B. Simkins and James Patton, two prominent historians. He also referred her to a major reference work on American women then in progress at the Radcliffe Women's Archives, *Notable American Women*.[93] Thus, twelve years into her career, Massey knew a lot of people who encouraged her work on the history of women and who helped clear the path so she could do it. Her correspondence files show that her relationships with Wiley, Green, Nevins, and Wall were professional but often endearingly personal in nature. They were friends and colleagues, commiserating over difficulties and exhaustion while untiringly aiding each other in mutual intellectual and professional endeavors.

If Massey's intellectual secret to success was her ability to effectively work on women within the more recognized fields of Southern, Civil War, and social history, her first book, *Ersatz in the Confederacy*, is illustrative of how she did that. A study of the Confederate home front, Massey examined Southern women's strategies for overcoming the shortage of food and other goods as the war wore on. She emphasized the daily heroism and struggles of ordinary as well as upper-class women, placing her study firmly in the school of social history. While *Ersatz* was well within dominant intellectual streams, Massey was clear that women were her main interest. In 1955 she wrote to a correspondent, "I am very pleased to hear that you are interested in publishing a volume dealing with Confederate women. . . . Earlier in the century several things were done along the lines of sketches. . . . Some pertained to women's contributions in specific states, such as the one dealing with South Carolina women in the war, but most of these were emotional and biased. Then in the 1930s James Patton and Francis Simkins wrote 'Women of the Confederacy.' . . . I have been interested in this topic because I believe women had great influence in the Confederacy."[94] Here, Massey reveals her commitment to professionally written history over what she calls "biased" and "emotional" work. She then suggests that women's history was an area of scholarship that sparked her personal interest. Six years later, re-emphasizing her commitment to social history as part of her ongoing work on the Civil War Centennial Commission and using the term "plain folk" borrowed from the title of Frank Owsley's book on Southern white yeoman farmers, she urged Texas congressman Fred Schwengel,

> I sincerely hope that some way can be devised to bring into focus the little-known women. Many who represented the planter classes in the South are famous only because of their name, but if you analyze what they did to assist the Confederacy it was often little or nothing of note. They were the ones who tended to leave the records but their importance has been overemphasized. . . . One of the saddest things about the job of our committee is that so many deserving women will go unrecognized because their deeds were not publicized. I am very interested in the "plain folk" but because they are usually less articulate than others, they fail to get their place in history.[95]

Massey also suggested to the same congressman, "While meaning no disrespect, I do believe we should be very careful about accepting nominees from certain regional and state organizations which are rooted in prejudices and are inclined toward emotionalism and ancestor worship."[96] Here she was undoubtedly referring to the historical preservation work of patriotic groups like the United Daughters of the Confederacy and the Daughters of the American Revolution, neither of which lived up to Massey's standards of historical scholarship. The passing reference to their work being rooted in prejudices implies she rejected those prejudices.

Massey, too, revealed her fear that feminine subjects might not interest male scholars, acknowledging that a talk she was scheduled to give on home management in the Confederacy might not hold much appeal to men unless she shaped it properly. She reassured the organizer of the event, "I trust the gentlemen will not be completely disgusted and bored. I'll endeavor to add material that will be of interest."[97]

It appears that Massey's professional life contained all the elements one would expect of a successful historian. The primary indication that professional gender hierarchies affected her career is that she never moved to teach at a more prestigious university. She died at Winthrop in 1974 at the age of fifty-nine from heart disease and kidney failure.[98] It must be said, however, that in one of the profession's ultimate signs of recognition, she was elected to the presidency of the Southern Historical Association in 1972.

Massey's brief relationship with the "new women's historians" indicates a slight discomfort with what her friend Taylor called their "bra burning, marching" tactics.[99] Massey did not want to be embarrassed as president of the SHA and feared the new feminists in the profession might be viewed by her male colleagues as radical while she herself identified with the historical establishment. Her fear was well-grounded. In her correspondence with Bennett Wall in 1971 regarding committee appointments in the SHA, she attempted to appoint appropriate women, including those representing the "women's lib" group. Yet, she repeatedly stated that she was not a "women's libber." Letters between Massey, Taylor, and Doris King reveal a disconnect with the younger generation of women's scholars. To Grady McWhiney, chair of the program committee, Massey suggested Anne Firor Scott as a possible nominee, offering the caveat, "I'd like to get your reaction to having Anne Scott of Duke to serve. She has been very active in the association, has served on several committees, and she is absorbed in the women's 'lib' movement. Confidentially, she is of the more belligerent type, and we should give that group some representation even though I am not one of them. More important, I know she is both capable and efficient. Whether or not she will serve, I do not know. I'm not insisting . . . if there is another you would prefer."[100]

Bell Wiley had suggested Scott's name to Massey.[101] Bennett Wall, meanwhile, responded negatively when asked about Scott, stating that Scott had rejected two previous opportunities to serve on SHA committees and writing in the margins of Massey's letter "nuts!" and "out!" near sentences proposing Scott as a program committee member.[102] Wall then put forward the name of Mollie Davis, whom he thought was less radical. Davis, a member of the newly formed Coordinating Committee on Women in the Historical Profession, was working to establish the Caucus of Women in History of the SHA. Wall believed she would equally "appease" these overlapping groups.[103] Wall's use of the word "appease" in relation to the younger generation of women scholars in at least two letters suggests that he was looking to preempt any accusations that this "faction" might make of sex discrimination within the SHA. Despite Wall's preemptive strategy, Massey joined the Women's Caucus of the SHA in 1972, and at least one colleague believed she would have continued to support the work of this younger group of women.[104] The year after she was SHA president, her health declined precipitously. Having been warned by her doctors against overwork, she characteristically threw herself into the work of the SHA and no doubt harmed her chance of remaining well. She died in 1974, a day before her sixtieth birthday.[105]

Though Southern women historians were aware of Massey's success, she was not regularly recognized as a founding pioneer in women's history by the new generation during her lifetime. It would take years before she was credited as an important professional role model and scholar of women's history, and this was primarily among historians of Southern women.[106] She died at the very early stages of the women's history movement, but her scholarship on women was current, and she was the most prominent officer in the SHA in 1972. One would think her death would bring attention to her life and scholarship. Yet, there was much that separated her from the emerging women's history movement. Her Southernness, her generation's adaptational professional strategies, her lack of political activism, and her disavowal of the "women's libbers" all clashed with the radical strains of feminism ascendant in the late 1960s and early '70s. Furthermore, she was not marginal. "Rehabilitation" of marginalized yet pathbreaking historians like Flexner, Beard, or Cherry Spruill was what was on the historiographic agenda in women's history circles. Massey's brand of professionalism, which accepted the rules of the "old boy network," was not about to be embraced by the most vocal wing of the new generation of women's historians.

Perhaps Massey's focus on Confederate history also made her less attractive as an intellectual role model for the younger historians. As active supporters of Black civil rights, they may have felt an aversion to a historian whose avowed interests were Southern whites during the Confederacy. Yet, she was indeed a successful role model, specializing in the study of women. Moreover, she held at least moderate views on race, supporting Bennett Wall in his efforts to attract more African Americans into the Southern Historical Association. So, while her friend and colleague John Hope Franklin could speak of her importance in 1972 when he introduced her as the new president of the SHA, he also recognized that she "did not need to become a part of the feminist revolt in order to understand and appreciate women's role in history."[107] Though she is under-recognized in the main narrative of the field's history, her story complicates and illuminates the gendered intellectual and professional realities facing women historians prior to 1970.

The successes of these Southern historians of women hint at an important aspect of the nature of the historical discipline in America. The study of history was and is still highly compartmentalized by field of specialization, as well as by regional and institutional affiliations. Scholars are generally most closely linked and in dialogue with each other when they study in the same place and field. While this has become less pronounced since the 1970s and more so since the intense development of new communication technology in the 1990s, this may explain why some scholarly circles were less resistant to the study of women and the recognition of select women scholars than others. Furthermore, the way these scholars framed their work on women was in step with their contemporaries. At midcentury, there were strong trends in the study of both national and regional histories and an evolution in the dialogue between consensus and progressive historians, all of which led to more complex interpretations of national histories. The new interpretations considered culture, economics, and social history, what Frank Owsley of Vanderbilt dubbed in the Southern context the history of "plain folk."[108] The early credentialed historians of women were part of these intellectual streams; they were in dialogue with other scholars in the mainstream, and all were grappling with contemporary political, social, and racial contexts. And of course, in the South especially, the racial politics of the era made it impossible for Black women scholars to find entrée into these mainstream white academic communities. Instead, as Julie Des Jardins and Pero Dagbovie have shown, they engaged in parallel activities within the Black history movement. And as we will consider, they worked in historically Black colleges, universities, and archives—sometimes surfacing the history of Black women.

The early successful historians of women featured in chapters 2 and 3—Lucy Maynard Salmon, Mary Sumner Benson, Mary Elizabeth Massey, and A. Elizabeth Taylor—maintained strong regional identities, remained unmarried, and embraced the life of professional scholars with vigor, publishing, networking, and doing professional service from their strongholds at women's colleges. They worked effectively within the boundaries of the profession's gendered hierarchies. Guion Griffis Johnson, Elisabeth Anthony Dexter, and Julia Cherry Spruill were academics who juggled marriage and a scholarly life. The result was that they were professionally stymied but able to achieve some recognition for their work. Marjorie Mendenhall Applewhite and Virginia Gearhart Gray remained professionally and intellectually marginal as historians, according to Anne Firor Scott's findings, but eventually managed to find academic homes. Caroline Ware, a married but childless academic, carved out a unique professional and intellectual niche as a recognized scholar. Anne Firor Scott, a

Southern historian trained in the North, would return to the South and launch a highly successful career from 1958 forward. Each of these historians succeeded as historians of women to the extent that they were able to effectively embrace, emulate, and adapt to the masculine academic culture of history at midcentury while making compromises about marriage and family. Rare was the newly minted woman PhD, like Johnson or Ware, who could resist the not-so-subtle and pervasive cultural pressure to sublimate their professional ambitions and withdraw to family life and chocolate cake baking.[109]

Taylor and Massey received professional recognition. Their unique fields of specialization may have aided their professional progress. Yet, because they framed their work in Southern history as social history (in the case of Massey) and political history (in the case of Taylor), they did not openly challenge the androcentric paradigm. They placed their work in the center of historical discourse rather than at the margins. In so doing, they were primarily in dialogue with the men at that center and not with specialists in something called "women's history." Successful historians of women, whether in the North or the South, often belonged to prestigious networks of historians, operating effectively at the center of the historical profession. Yet they were unable to launch the field of American women's history, as they were a small minority without the collective clout, epistemological framework, or institutional backing to do so. To find the roots of a distinct field—American women's history—we have to look northward again, where the conceptualization of women's history as a distinct field was happening within the ivy-covered walls of Harvard University, Radcliffe College, and Smith College.

Chapter 4

Seeds Were Planted

Women in the Archives, 1935–1970

The first concrete steps taken toward developing the history of American women into a sustained formal area of scholarly inquiry emerged in the archives field. Women's organizations in the United States had been moving to preserve their own records and write their own histories since the late nineteenth century, including for example such groups as the National American Woman Suffrage Association, the Woman's Christian Temperance Union, and the National Association of Colored Women.[1] This work was begun at the same time that academic men were working to formalize the historical profession, though of course quite apart from it. It wouldn't be until the 1930s that anyone would try to bridge the two streams of historical knowledge production by proposing a specialized archive about women for use by academic researchers. In 1935, Mary Beard and a group of like-minded feminists, which included African American educator and activist Mary McLeod Bethune, attempted to launch a World Center for Women's Archives that ultimately collapsed in 1940. In the aftermath of this collapse, Bethune continued to push to establish an archive for Black women's history as leader of the National Council of Negro Women. An array of mainstream historians, librarians, and college administrators set about establishing permanent historical archives more broadly focused on women, including those of diverse backgrounds from the United States and around the world. Their collective efforts, supported by brick-and-mortar institutions that could sustain the initiative, helped create a distinct area of historical inquiry focused on women, well before the term "women's history" came into wide usage.

The two most significant initial collections were housed at elite women's colleges— Smith College in Northampton, Massachusetts, and Radcliffe College, Harvard University's women's coordinate in Cambridge, Massachusetts.[2] The institutional base and financial backing provided by these prestigious colleges created a firm foothold for the emerging field, provided the literal real estate upon which they were built, and made enduring sites of knowledge production. Since the ability of historians to systematically focus on any topic depends upon the identification, collection, storage, and accessibility of available evidence, these two archival centers were responsible for constructing an early framework for the new field. A host of smaller efforts across the United States amplified their endeavors.

Together, the women's collections at Smith and Radcliffe animated the heart of the emerging field. Both archives initially had the support and counsel of Mary Beard, but over time they went beyond bringing Beard's vision to fruition. They also reshaped, refined, and expanded it according to their own collecting frameworks. In their first two decades, the archives' directors built up their holdings, publicized their mission, and encouraged students and scholars to conduct research in their growing holdings. Overall, the collections can be credited with shifting the gendered paradigm in the archives field by proving the value of building archives focused exclusively on women and creating physical and intellectual space for individual and collaborative work in the history of women. Key early scholars in the history of American women whose stories do not typically form part of the historiographic origins story of American women's history were nurtured by the Harvard endeavor in the period from 1950 to 1965. As pioneering historians, some would act as intergenerational bridges whose initial efforts in the field would buttress and legitimize the work of a younger generation in the 1970s. Here, their stories are integrated into American women's historiography.[3]

The Enduring Influence of Mary Ritter Beard

Mary Ritter Beard's efforts to encourage the historical study of women and the creation of women's archives in the first half of the twentieth century are well-studied territory.[4] An undergraduate history major and 1897 graduate of DePauw University, Mary Ritter married her college beau, Charles Beard, in 1900. Charles spent two years in England studying at Oxford. There, the couple lived across the street from militant suffragists Emmeline and Christabel Pankhurst, with whom they associated. When they returned to the United States in 1902, both enrolled in the history graduate program at Columbia University. Mary withdrew soon after starting the program, partly to care for their one-year-old daughter and partly because the Columbia history department was unwelcoming to women.[5] From 1901 to 1917, Charles rose to prominence as a leading figure in the progressive school of history, publishing his controversial *Economic Interpretation of the Constitution* in 1913. Mary, meanwhile, raised their two young children and became increasingly involved in progressive reform via the Women's Trade Union League and the Equality League of Self-Supporting Women, a woman suffrage organization. She was also active in the major national woman suffrage organizations, belonging first to the National American Woman Suffrage Association and then to the National Woman's Party. Her progressive politics blended with her interest in history, as it also did for her husband.

Mary's earliest historical publication was her 1915 book, *Women's Work in Municipalities*.[6] She also regularly wrote for the various suffrage and progressive organizations with which she was affiliated. Together, the Beards wrote several influential and popular history textbooks between 1921 and 1939.[7] Charles Beard repeatedly insisted that Mary had made major contributions to these works, but reviewers and historiographers persisted in downplaying her role as coauthor.[8] In these textbooks, the Beards' progressive philosophy of history was on full display. History, they believed, must be of use to society and promote human progress. For Mary, that increasingly meant progress for women and history about women. In 1931 she published *On Understanding Women*; in 1933, *America through Women's Eyes*; and in 1946, *Woman as Force in History*. The few reviews that appeared were mixed, but they appeared in serious academic journals.[9] *Woman as Force in History* called for a rejection of what Mary Beard called the "feminist perspective" on history, that is, "assuming women's past oppression, rather than proving it."[10] She also asserted that women were coequal with men in influencing the course of history. Mary Beard was nothing if not prescient. Her claims about women shaping culture, society, and history as half the population, and alongside men, anticipated a later generation's restoration of women's past activities to their full and proper place in history. While Beard's publications were significant, her work in the archives field was perhaps even more so.

In 1935, when Hungarian feminist pacifist Rosika Schwimmer approached Beard about developing an archive of manuscript sources on women far from the war clouds threatening continental Europe, Beard agreed to take up the work. Schwimmer was concerned about rising fascist governments in Europe and the threat they posed to women's rights and status everywhere. Believing that the preservation of records documenting women's activities and progress could provide a bulwark against reaction and regression, Schwimmer offered her personal archive as the founding nucleus for a World Center for Women's Archives (WCWA) in the United States.[11] From 1935 to 1940, Beard, Schwimmer, and leaders of both the American Association of University Women and the International Federation of Business and Professional Women, among others, attempted to raise funds, designed publicity, and secured promises from prominent women to leave their papers to the WCWA.[12] Beard took on the bulk of this work, and the WCWA operated out of headquarters in New York City. Beard's vision for the WCWA was expansive and inclusive in that she sought records from around the world; from all major racial, ethnic, and cultural groups; and from women of all socioeconomic backgrounds. She actively solicited collaboration with prominent African American women, who responded positively.[13] But internal conflicts within the WCWA hindered the group's progress. By 1939, Beard grew frustrated and exhausted by the lack of interest shown by wealthy donors, by organizational and political conflicts within the WCWA board, and by having to work almost alone to secure archival materials.[14] In 1940, the WCWA disbanded due to lack of adequate funding and the outbreak of World War II. Beard did not give up her vision for a women's archive.[15] But this vision needed willing institutional partners to become reality.

Beard's group wasn't the only one about the business of trying to establish women's archives, and similar challenges plagued Black women's efforts to build Black women's archives. Acquiring historical records, financial resources, real estate, and the people to do the administrative and promotional work in a sustained manner was not so easy. African American women's sensibility about history's power to elevate and enfranchise marginalized peoples grew out of their own experiences as educators and community activists. They were further inspired by African American scholars' work to develop scholarly Black history and build archives, the most notable efforts being found in Carter G. Woodson's Association for the Study of Negro Life and History, formed in 1915, and the Schomburg Center for Research in Black Culture, a branch of the New York Public Library established in New York City in 1905. Black women's clubs and local librarians throughout the country preserved, collected, and taught their own history and participated in the broader Black history movement.[16] Indeed, historical consciousness often permeated their work as community and racial uplift activists.[17]

Mary McLeod Bethune, Dorothy Porter Wesley, and Sue Bailey Thurman were particularly keen to gather sources that would make writing the history of African American women possible. Their first efforts to that effect were made under the auspices of the National Council of Negro Women (NCNW). Bethune, Thurman, and Porter worked to create the Bethune Museum and the National Archives for Black Women's History from 1939 forward, though their efforts came to fruition only after forty years of effort in 1979.[18] Their early work was nudged forward by overtures from Mary Beard to bring them into the WCWA.

In 1938, Mary Beard reached out to Bethune, who as a prominent educator, president of the Association for the Study of Negro Life and History (1936–50), and head of the recently formed NCNW (1935) had long been interested in gathering and preserving the records of Black history. Beard hoped that Bethune would join the board of the WCWA, and in 1938 she sent a representative of the group, Marjorie White, to the NCNW's annual convention in Washington, DC, to speak with the council's leader. Bethune expressed support for the WCWA's work and responded by recommending Juanita Mitchell Jackson of Minnesota for the board position, undoubtedly because Bethune herself was already leading several major organizations. In the spring of 1939, Beard reported to WCWA board member Miriam Holden that 4 Black women, among 500 others, had attended a luncheon in DC at which luminaries such as Eleanor Roosevelt and Frances Perkins were also present. Beard remarked that their presence produced no "disruption." Clearly, she was worried that the realities of Jim Crow culture would create dissension among the white WCWA board members and trouble a group already dealing with ideological tensions between progressive, feminist, and conservative board members. She was right to be worried.[19]

Juanita Mitchell Jackson soon withdrew from WCWA work, unable to participate from so far away, and Bethune tapped Howard University librarian Dorothy Porter and Sue Bailey Thurman to take her place, alongside the more prominent Mary Church Terrell and Elizabeth Brooks Carter. As new WCWA members, these women were supposed to join their local WCWA unit in Washington, DC. But the DC branch was racially segregated, creating an immediate crisis. Beard's workaround was to ask the Black women to act independently of the Washington branch, as a "Negro Women's Committee" that would work directly with the national WCWA headquarters. While white New York feminist progressive Miriam Holden thought Beard needed to take a firmer, more principled stance on the race issue and stand up to the white DC branch, Beard decided to bypass it for fear the conflict that might ensue would toll the final bell for the WCWA. Beard enthusiastically proposed that the WCWA Negro Women's Committee be expanded to at least ten members dedicated to acquiring records from around the country. Dorothy Porter agreed to the arrangement, undoubtedly understanding all too well the binds of the Jim Crow era and the traditional rifts among white women regarding race. But by 1940 the WCWA was already collapsing. The African American women carried on independently. Indeed, according to Bettye Collier-Thomas, even before it was obvious that the WCWA was in its final death throes, Bethune encouraged Porter to identify herself principally as the chair of the NCNW's Negro Women's Committee on Archives.[20]

Dorothy Porter's hope of securing donations of materials for the WCWA and then for the NCNW Archives Committee did not materialize during her tenure between 1940 and 1942. Of the twenty-five women she contacted in 1940 with the dual request that they loan materials for a women's exhibit at the upcoming Chicago Negro Exposition and for deposit with the WCWA, none were willing to donate their materials to the WCWA. This was just as well, considering its imminent demise. But Porter was the supervisor of the Moorland Foundation, the progenitor of the Moorland-Spingarn Research Center at Howard University. In that role she was committed to collecting sources on African American history more broadly.[21]

In 1939, Sue Bailey Thurman, the spouse of a Howard University dean, joined the NCNW efforts to promote Black women's history and archives development, which she did first primarily as editor of the NCNW's organ, *Aframerican Woman's Journal*, and later as chair of the group's archives committee. A major focus of the journal was the historical contributions of African American women. Her efforts fell mostly in the realm of generating public interest in the subject matter and organizing public history events, such as a 1945 visual information series, "Negro Women in History." Thurman worked with Bethune to promote the cause of Black women's history. Her publicity-generating ideas included hosting local radio interviews and scripted history programs in Washington, DC; an essay contest in local schools on "Negro women in America"; and fundraising for the establishment of a museum and archives. A building was purchased in 1948 to serve as the national NCNW headquarters.[22]

In the 1950s, the NCNW was increasingly preoccupied with the growing mass civil rights movement. But Thurman continued to promote the archives cause. In 1952, she proposed that a small brick structure behind the NCNW national headquarters be dedicated to housing future archival holdings. The first items to be added to these holdings between 1955 and 1957 were a Harriet Tubman quilt and a collection of Black historical dolls. Thurman and the NCNW also published *Historical Cookbook of the American Negro* in 1958. It featured recipes and historical vignettes about significant African American women. After 1955 and the death of Bethune, the NCNW archives initiative narrowed its scope to the preservation of its own records and to publicizing its own activities. Conversely, the NCNW expanded their general "Heritage Education Program" in the 1960s with a broader focus on general Afro-American history. This latter work developed history kits that included curriculum guides, a bibliography, and pamphlets in consultation with professional historians but with no particular focus on women. It wouldn't be until 1979 that the Mary McLeod Bethune Memorial Museum and National Archives for Black Women's History would be formally established.[23] By then, women's archives established at Smith College, Radcliffe, and the Library of Congress were also busy adding Black women's manuscripts and oral history archives to their growing collections in the field.[24]

Mary Beard's vision for women's archives was ultimately accomplished by a cast of actors more willing to work within institutional limitations imposed by the colleges that came to house the earliest women's archives in the United States. These institutions and the women they recruited to do the work had the resources that had eluded the women working for the WCWA and the NCNW. Beard herself was skeptical of male-dominated institutions and did not trust them to be adequate guardians of women's archives. This skepticism was rooted in her negative experiences with male historians in a male-dominated profession. As a graduate history student at Columbia in 1904, she and other women encountered open hostility in a department run by John W. Burgess.

The disinterest with which the history of women was received by the male mainstream of history probably disinclined Beard to think that male-dominated institutions could provide a suitable home for women's archives.[25] Thus, it makes sense that Beard was willing to collaborate with administrators, historians, and librarians at women's colleges where women administrators and librarians might temper masculine influences.

After 1943, Mary Beard bequeathed her archives mission to Margaret Grierson, a newly appointed librarian at Smith College, and to Wilbur K. Jordan, Harvard historian and president of Radcliffe College.[26] Mary Beard's initial hopes were high for a women's archive at Radcliffe. This was due to the involvement of progressive historian Arthur M. Schlesinger Sr. and his wife, fellow former suffragist Elizabeth Bancroft Schlesinger, herself a widely published writer of histories focused on women.[27] But Beard's connection to Smith College grew stronger over time. She was a member of the Friends of the Smith College Library and believed that her global vision for a women's collection was more fully shared and faithfully executed by Grierson than by the Radcliffe team. These collections—dedicated exclusively to manuscripts of and about women—are widely recognized today as the United States' pioneering collections of historical records of women. Understanding the groundwork that these two great archives laid for the field of women's history is essential to understanding the field's historiography.

While the women's archives at Smith and Radcliffe were each formally founded in 1943, the spark for each was different, and each had a prehistory rooted in specific institutional contexts that dated back to the 1920s. Both archives were further inspired by the nationwide historical preservation movement that had emerged out of the New Deal's National Archives Act of 1934.[28] At Smith College, Margaret Storrs Grierson, with Mary Beard as her frequent consultant, was the main force behind the repository that came to be called the Sophia Smith Collection. She worked largely without the input of trained historians.[29] At Radcliffe, Arthur M. Schlesinger Sr., Ada Comstock, and Wilbur K. Jordan created the founding nucleus of their women's archive by acquiring the papers of Maud Wood Park, a prominent former suffragist and cofounder and leader of the League of Women Voters. They enjoyed a wide collaboration with feminists, historians, librarians, and women scholars thereafter.

The Sophia Smith Collection

At Smith College, the inspiration for an archive pertaining to women in history had several roots. The deepest reached back to the establishment of the Smith College Archives (SCA) in 1921.[30] The purpose of the SCA was to document the history of the college and preserve some record of alumnae achievements.[31]

This meant that most of the materials contained in the SCA referred to women, their education, and the college. The SCA was conceived of primarily as a repository for the institution, not as a women's collection, and so it contained records of male faculty, administrators, and benefactors. In 1941 the Friends of the Smith College Library Committee formed, Smith College president Herbert Davis proposed that the library develop a collection of writings by women authors, and Margaret Storrs Grierson was appointed director of the library.[32] The Friends Committee approved Davis's proposal. The stage was set for the women's collection.

Soon after, Mary Beard, who had joined the Friends of the Smith College Library, read and responded to Grierson's first annual report to the Friends of the Smith College Library for 1942–43. Grierson's report suggested a reconceptualization of the "Works of Women Writers" collection. While she intended this collection to become part of the broader Smith College Archives, the library would create, in addition to "Works of Women Writers," a special collection gathering manuscripts focused on women. Grierson explained to the Friends on March 1, 1943,

> With regard to the Collection of the Works of Women Writers, some
> restatement of aim is perhaps desirable. The project is only begun
> and offers opportunity for development particularly appropriate to a
> woman's college. The work of women, in the fields of literature and art,
> of government and social service, of science and the professions, are of
> especial interest to an institution founded to give women an education,
> and subsequent opportunities in life, equal to those afforded to their
> brothers. . . . It should be of interest to collect for our library the written
> records of the milestones and significant steps taken by women through
> the years.[33]

This passage heralds the founding of the special women's archives. Later library reports and publicity campaigns date the official start of the special women's collection at Smith to 1942. The record suggests, however, that it was conceived of as a women's archive per se in the spring of 1943. After 1943, Grierson was at pains to distinguish her efforts at Smith from the initiative established at Radcliffe College that same year.

In 1943, Grierson was still figuring out what sort of materials should be included and how to justify a gender-specific collecting framework. In her first report to the college she explained, "One alumna, in protest, writes, 'Aren't women people?' The purpose of the collection is certainly not to sharpen the distinction between the sexes . . . but further to diminish the distinction by gathering an imposing evidence of work of women comparable in every way to that of men. We do not want any book merely because it comes from the pen of a woman; we want books of permanent interest and significance and delight, by 'people,' whether male or female."[34] With the project just getting started, the fact that Grierson did not more specifically refer to books or manuscripts *about* women points to her early uncertainty about the focus of the collection. Until that fateful spring, the collection was of women's published writings housed alongside the archive dedicated to Smith College history, which included the papers of Smith alumnae. Grierson was herself grappling with the justification for establishing a separate women's collection.

The very notion of a separate women's archive did indeed need some justification even among those who were promoting equal opportunity with men at midcentury. The alumna objection that women were "people," just like men, reflected one mainstream version of equal rights feminism at midcentury in which the relative sameness of women and men bolstered women's claim to equal opportunity in education and work. For equal rights feminists, emphasizing women's difference from men was historically associated with their subordination. Other women activists saw gender differences as a basis for understanding women's distinct experiences in the world and valuing women's distinct contributions to society. Grierson perceived this alumna's objection as a call to justify creating a segregated archival repository for women. Might such a historical archive highlight women's difference from men in ways that could contribute to women's continued subordination? Or might it show—echoing Mary Beard's historical philosophy—that their work was comparable to that of men and equally historically significant? Grierson concluded that the women's collection would not segregate the new field of knowledge but rather illustrate women's force in history; it would diminish rather than sharpen the distinctions between men and women.

Grierson's 1943 report referred to a broad range of sources that she wanted to include in the new archive. Mary Beard found Grierson's defense of the concept of a women's collection encouraging. Letters between Beard and Grierson, beginning in April 1943, shed light on the emergence of the Sophia Smith Collection, named as such in 1946.[35] Beard encouraged the broad scope and integrative perspective that Grierson was developing for Smith's new collection. Beard wrote to Grierson first on April 11, 1943: "I have read very carefully and with great interest your report on the growing library collections and your appeal to the Friends of the Library. . . . That you have felt compelled to meet the protest of an alumna, relative to stress on women's archives and books, gives me the fellow-feeling which attends the effort to make women realize that to be 'people' they must be recognized as such and not lost to view."[36] In June, Beard followed up by soliciting a meeting: "I would enjoy discussing a model archive with you and steps toward the ideal—such steps as might be taken. . . . I shall be very happy to have you in my home if you would find a visit with me equally inciting to a review of the challenge and a way of meeting it."[37] Grierson agreed to the meeting.

In July 1943 she reported to former Smith College librarian Nina Browne the source of her newfound clarity about the shape of the new collection:

> I think you know that Mrs. Mary Beard has been a member of the Friends of the Library since its formation. She has written frequently . . . but finally decided that an oral conversation would be more profitable and asked me to visit her in New Milford. I am sure that you know of her project for a world center for Women's Archives which was given up. . . . I had read "On Understanding Women." I went to see her, a little dubious of some of her claims for her thesis, a little fearful of her designs on our library. I came back all enthusiasm![38]

Thus, by July 1943, after her meeting with Beard, Grierson was convinced that Smith "might well fall in with Mrs. Beard's proposal, and redefine the collection *to include works about, as well as by women* and at the same time have a basis for exclusion of much written by women."[39] The notion of a women's archive collection had matured for Grierson. The Smith collection would not merely amass material written by women; it would bring together materials that preserved evidence about women in the past.

In August 1943, still feeling uncertain about the Smith College library's acceptance of her new collecting focus, Grierson wrote again to Browne: "I feel . . . we must first get the new librarian's views on the subject of the collection, for its scope and position depends upon her cooperation. . . . I am hoping to have specific plans to put before the Trustees at their October [1943] meeting, and I hope that we may get underway."[40] In February 1944, the Council of the Friends of the Smith College Library Committee finally gave assurance of its support for Grierson's revised idea of a women's collection. In a follow-up letter to Browne, Grierson showed confidence that "interest was shown in the women's collection, and I think that plans can be better furthered out of committee now that I have the general approval of this meeting."[41] The Smith College Archives began in 1921, and President Herbert Davis's plan for a specialized collection of books and writings by women was underway by 1942. These initiatives provided rich soil for the cultivation of a special women's archival collection. The kernel for Smith's women's manuscripts collection, though, was planted in the spring of 1943. It germinated in 1944 with Mary Beard's facilitation of the donation of several manuscript collections.[42]

Beard also donated materials to the collection shaping up at Radcliffe, but Grierson was not particularly concerned with Radcliffe's activities at first. Grierson's first mention of Radcliffe's new Woman's Rights Collection came in a 1944 letter she wrote to Nina Browne: "You are wonderful to interest Mrs. [Maud

Wood] Park in our project. I am eager to talk to you about it. Yes, I know the Radcliffe collection and hope to see it. One of the members of our faculty helped initiate their scheme. I believe that it is on quite different lines from ours, but we should be of good assistance to one another."[43] This letter shows Grierson's unfamiliarity with the Radcliffe Woman's Rights Collection. At that point, Radcliffe's materials consisted mainly of the manuscripts donated in 1943 by Radcliffe alumna Maud Wood Park. Thanks to the efforts of college president Ada Comstock, Park gave her papers to Radcliffe in 1942. Her materials concerned Park's work in the women's movement, including her role in the suffrage movement and as first president of the League of Women Voters.[44] Grierson's reference to the Smith "faculty [who] helped initiate their scheme" was likely a reference to Merle Curti, who had been a student of Arthur Schlesinger Sr. at Harvard and then taught at Smith from 1927 to 1937 before taking a position at the University of Wisconsin–Madison.[45]

Grierson paid a visit to Radcliffe's Woman's Rights Collection on June 13 to meet Edna Stantial. During this period, Stantial, a feminist who would spend the next thirty years working to preserve records of the woman suffrage movement, was Maud Wood Park's representative at Radcliffe. She prepared the Park donation.[46] Grierson also met Radcliffe librarian Georgiana Hinckley. Stantial and Hinckley gave her a tour and explained that the collection was to be the "nucleus for a broader collection of women's material in the main library." Grierson assessed the work at Radcliffe: "I think that we are essentially in the same pursuit, but I don't find this discouraging to our enterprise. After all, the introduction into the educational program of women's colleges of neglected material on women's activities is something which might be generally adopted. I should say that a widespread movement would only stimulate activity on individual campuses. I understand that both Northwestern and California are busy building up such collections for immediate academic use."[47] Grierson suggested it was not problematic that Smith and Radcliffe were "both laboring in this vineyard, especially since about ten other libraries in the country are busy in the field" too.[48] She soon took a more negative view of the Radcliffe effort, however, affronted by what she saw as "Radcliffe's ignoring of our project and those elsewhere," which seemed to her "to smack of an arrogance that only Harvard could match."[49]

Grierson's concern over what the Radcliffe collection might mean for Smith soon intensified. She was at pains to distinguish Smith's women's collection from the Radcliffe Women's Archives. Grierson's main concern was to justify her own project's continuation. She also shared Mary Beard's disenchantment with Radcliffe's more narrow focus on American women and its early emphasis on women's rights. By November 1950, Grierson was bothered enough to draft a testy report on the Radcliffe Women's Archives for the Friends of the

Smith College Library Committee titled "The Present Situation at Radcliffe." This somewhat anxious four-page report is critical of the Radcliffe Women's Archives, which she pointed out was briefly named, "COW (Collection On Women)!"[50]

Citing Radcliffe's promotional literature about its archives, Grierson said the scope of Radcliffe's collection was in fact more broadly defined than previously understood. Rather than narrowly focusing on the women's rights movement, Radcliffe, as Grierson pointed out, would accumulate a "strong and well-equipped body of sources in this essential area of knowledge" for the purpose of scholarly research by independent scholars and graduate and undergraduate students at Harvard and Radcliffe. Of course, the archive would "enjoy the benefits of the great supporting collections in Harvard University." According to Grierson, Radcliffe was collecting both primary and secondary sources for the library and surmised that Radcliffe was "singularly fortunate" to be "building on the great American history collections at Harvard which include many thousands of printed volumes that would have to be acquired were it not for the organic relation existing between Radcliffe and Harvard." Grierson acknowledged the collection had very decent physical facilities, though she observed its materials were scattered on the fringes of the campus. For every advantage she identified, she expressed a criticism that allowed her to assert the superiority of the Sophia Smith Collection.[51]

For example, Grierson countered Radcliffe's claim of steady use of its archive by scholars and found it "questionable in the light of personal reports of local friends and of my conversation with the librarians last week."[52] For Grierson, the fact that the archive's newly appointed director, Mrs. Elizabeth Borden, had only just completed her BA at Radcliffe implied that she was not yet adequately prepared for the job.[53] Grierson followed with a sharp barb: "Naturally, she is as yet unfamiliar with the collection and field of the archives. ... I question that the word 'archives' aptly applies to such a collection as theirs." Indeed, Borden could devote only half her energies to the archives, as she was also director of the Radcliffe Seminars, a continuing education program. The Radcliffe Women's Archives may have been slowed in its earliest years by lack of a full-time director and its reliance on librarians with other work duties. It may also have been stunted by the control exercised by Maud Wood Park over possible additions to the Woman's Rights Collection. But Grierson's questioning of Radcliffe's right to call its repository an archive at all suggests that she was concerned about having to compete with Harvard. The potential that Harvard would share its wealth with the Radcliffe archive, the number of graduate students and distinguished historians on campus who could make use of its collections, and Harvard's overall status as one of the nation's premier educational institutions seems to have intimidated her. Nevertheless, Grierson persisted. By her retirement in 1965, the Sophia Smith Collection was firmly established as an important archival repository.

Grierson's 1950 report also illuminated the distinct frameworks of the two collections. As part of her assertion that Smith was "years ahead of" Radcliffe, she revealed the two archives' philosophical differences. "We are years ahead of them and advance here can justly be measured in time as well as in money. *Woman's history* is a generally unfamiliar *field* and a director must do a lot of reading even to get on the fruitful track. Even if Harvard professors and those distinguished American historians . . . give their assistance, someone must mold the fragments into some balanced unity, and no one is apparently on hand for this work who at present is competent for the job—It will take time for Mrs. Borden to learn her own materials."[54] Aspects of Smith's collecting mission certainly set it apart from Radcliffe's. The Sophia Smith Collection sought materials of international scope and of a much longer chronological sweep. Grierson believed this gave Smith's records a "sounder value from the setting in a wider field and from a more truly objective historical point of view." In Grierson's estimation,

> The Radcliffe enterprise is one where point of view, goals and methods of conventional scholarship are applied to a new field, and interesting and valuable as it is, it seems to me that they are missing a great opportunity. At a time when such lively popular as well as professional interest is directed to the problems of women, the[ir] proper nature, their higher education, their preparation for life "as women," such a collection should be used as [a] source of a theory of education. It is not the story of woman's victorious admission to professions and vocations of a "man's world" that will solve the problem but a review of women of all lands through the ages, with a truer understanding of the nature of their influences and activities, the quality of their peculiar gifts and contributions to society, or "civilization."[55]

Grierson's critique of Radcliffe's collecting in the "new field" was not limited to its reliance on conventional methods of scholarship.

Grierson agreed with Mary Beard when she took issue with the Radcliffe Women's Archives' "familiar point of view, miscalled 'feminist.'" She elaborated,

> The opening statement of the [Radcliffe] leaflet relating to the "historical role and contributions of women" again echoes ours, but thereafter it refers to the cultural revolution of the 19th and 20th centuries "as women won places in professions and spheres heretofore reserved principally to men," and to records of "women who by their persistence and ability opened important areas of activity to their sex." Although they are

developing their field beyond the Maud Wood Park nucleus, it sounds as though it were still directed to the theme of the late movement for woman's rights and looked upon 1848 as the year of creation. . . . Mary Beard exaggerates her thesis, but she has something in her insistence that what is needed is a fresh survey of women through "long history."[56]

First, while Grierson wrote that Radcliffe's promotional literature echoed Smith's framework, implying Smith was first in the business of establishing women's archives, it's clear that language about "the role and contributions of women" echoed Harvard historian Arthur M. Schlesinger's seminal 1922 essay in *New Viewpoints in American History*. Grierson thought that Radcliffe placed too many limits on its collecting mission. She called its central focus on the women's rights movement and on US history in the relatively recent past a narrow point of view, "miscalled 'feminist.'" Issues of perspective, objectivity, feminist definition, and whether to take a theoretical, temporal, or geographical approach are still hotly debated today.[57] And while it is common to say the field emerged only after 1969 when scholars intensified their attention to women's past, Radcliffe had already referred to women's history in a 1950 pamphlet as "this essential area of knowledge." In that same year, Grierson too identified the archive work at Smith and Radcliffe as a "new field," which she dubbed "woman's history."

Even earlier references to "women's history" as a field of study is found in the letters of Grierson, Beard, Wilbur K. Jordan, Nina Browne, and others in 1944 and 1945.[58] One 1945 letter from Grierson to Browne reads, "Have you heard of the Radcliffe announcement of [its] plan to develop the world's great research center in the *women's field*, with the help of Harvard? That caused a short flurry here, but we have decided to go straight ahead with our women's collection."[59] Another early use of the term "women's history" appears in a note from Beard to Jordan. The note refers to Beard's efforts to solicit the endowment of a research fellowship program at Radcliffe by the National Business and Professional Women's Clubs: "You are perfectly right in respect of freedom to select research scholars and their freedom to elect their research projects. Of course. I want to incite the B&PW to an interest in *women's history* as a possible education which may lead them to evaluate their own labors and careers. . . . I SHALL CONTINUE TO TRY TO PERSUADE THEM TO HELP FINANCE A WOMAN SCHOLAR as a *free scholar* at Radcliffe, on the ground that Radcliffe is sponsoring studies of women in American history."[60] That the study of women in American history was being conceived of as a developing field is bolstered in another of Beard's 1944 letters. She wrote to Grierson,

> As for the University of North Carolina, . . . [Mrs. Elizabeth Cotten] of the library there . . . has written me since she took up work at Chapel Hill of the women's materials that have come there and she says that among

the most interesting documents of the whole collection are numerous letters of Southern women. . . . I had persuaded Dr. Luther Evans, with the help of Mrs. Ellen Woodward who was then his superior officer in the Federal Works Project, to instruct the field workers in the Historical Records Survey to make a note of women's records when they found them. The note was to take the form of a WH in the margins of their reports (Woman's History). Some of this reporting went along all right but when it came with the WH, Mrs. Cotten, whose eyes were always open for it, found that some of her superiors were exceedingly cross and said it had no place in the reports.[61]

The use of the terms "woman's history," "women's history," and "field" in this circle of scholars and archivists and the passing reference to the "cross" reaction of one of Elizabeth Cotten's superiors are suggestive of a debate over the new field's existence, its legitimacy, and uncertainty about what to call it. Not surprisingly, Radcliffe and Smith were at the center of this debate.

In finishing up her "Present Situation at Radcliffe" report, Grierson acknowledged that "the value of Harvard's support is, of course, incomparable." Yet, she quickly followed that she was "skeptical" that Harvard would fulfill its promise of assistance. She quipped, "Seeing is believing and there is nothing yet to see. If Harvard changes its traditional point of view to this extent, quickly, it will be a miracle."[62] Her skepticism was justified since Harvard offered the Radcliffe archive no financial support. But it may also have reflected her own experience with Smith administrators and faculty. Though the Smith collection found some support, there was little interest in those early years from the college president or faculty to make the women's collection available to researchers and students. Nor was there any inclination to develop courses on the history of women.[63]

As early as 1943 Mary Beard suggested that Grierson push for a course at Smith on women in history. Nothing ever came of Beard's proposal, which she repeated annually up through 1956 when the two women stopped corresponding.[64] Indeed, Smith's faculty and administrators were against the idea of introducing women into the college curriculum at all. Beard was familiar with this attitude and told of a talk she gave to the Vassar faculty to promote women's history. She reported that they cried "as if with one voice, 'The time has come to forget women! We are becoming human beings now!'"[65] Grierson herself may have been unwilling to push for a course on women. As archive director from 1941 to 1965, she felt her role was one of "building up a fine collection of material in the field, certain that . . . it would become known and . . . widely used . . . and would forward a movement toward revision of the curriculum of women's colleges. . . . You will see that mine was a purely scholarly undertaking, or a preparing of the way for scholars, and not in any sense activist."[66]

The contradiction inherent in disclaiming personal activism while expressing certainty her work would "forward a movement" suggests an ambivalence about the relationship of professionalism and scholarship to activism.

Grierson's ambivalence was explicitly expressed in her reasons for refusing to be added to an early edition of *Who's Who of American Women* in 1959. She wrote the publisher,

> I am strongly opposed to the principle of publishing such biographical reference works, selected from artificially limited groups. I believe that race, religion and sex are characteristics which are irrelevant to a person's work, contribution to society, or personal distinction in any field. . . . I should hope that in succeeding editions of these [*Who's Who in America*] publications, increasing attention be given to the inclusion of individuals who are Jew, Negro, woman, etc. I am strongly opposed to separate biographical dictionaries for these groups not only because I believe the distinction irrelevant to your purposes, but because I believe that it harmfully implies the concept of segregation.[67]

This statement in the context of her roughly twenty years of work to build a collection limited by and segregated along lines of sex is remarkable. It is possible that she did not want to participate in the women's *Who's Who* because she knew of Radcliffe's active assistance to the publication between 1956 and 1959 and of Radcliffe's developing plans to produce just such a sex-segregated biographical dictionary. Regardless, Margaret Grierson proceeded steadily to build the women's archives at Smith as the repository's director, consciously tempering Mary Beard's more activist orientation and tailoring a project more palatable to the college administration.

The Sophia Smith Collection grew in stature during these years, becoming a significant factor in the emergence of the field of "woman's history." Interest in developing that field, however, remained relatively low at Smith through the 1950s despite the growing archive. Grierson never worked at publicizing the collection, and no courses, seminars, or research initiatives were launched at Smith in the archive's first two decades. As late as 1958, Grierson was faced with opposition from the college president, who didn't consider the undergraduate institution an appropriate site for a research library. Limited funding and lack of faculty interest in the developing field followed from the president's notion. Furthermore, with no graduate program at Smith, the archive's mission was constrained to collecting and maintaining its facility rather than developing programs to encourage its use.[68] Grierson was for some time at pains to distinguish the Sophia Smith Collection from the Radcliffe Women's Archives. And she was faced with justifying her collection given Harvard/Radcliffe's wider publicity efforts and the higher profile of the institution and historians backing the parallel endeavor. Nevertheless, developing an archive on the history of women through all of human history and across the globe was irrefutably a significant accomplishment for this one institution.

Women's Rights, Women's Archives, and the Schlesinger Library

In contrast to Smith College, interest at Harvard in developing the history of American women predated the Radcliffe women's collection founded in 1943. From 1924, when Arthur M. Schlesinger Sr. joined the Harvard history faculty, his powerful voice advocated for the study of women. His 1922 essay "The Role of Women in American History," in *New Viewpoints in American History*, was something of a clarion call for professional historians to research and write about women and to rescue the subject from writers of popular history.[69] Schlesinger outlined women's participation in wars, westward settlement, reform, and the women's rights movement; their rising educational attainment; and their workforce participation in the industrial age. He pointed out that historians had "ignored woman as a positive influence in American history," thus leaving the field to amateur writers and suffragists.[70] This assertion was mostly accurate, though as we have already seen, historian Lucy Maynard Salmon had incorporated women into her histories and teaching at Vassar in substantive ways.[71] Yet, it was the combined effort of Schlesinger, Mary Beard, and their disciples that ultimately made the academic field, "American women's history," possible. Their championing of women's archives and specialization in the field were seminal. Harvard's prestige and its central place in American higher education uniquely positioned the Radcliffe Women's Archives to become a launchpad for the field of American women's history.

The importance of Schlesinger to the development of the Radcliffe archive and of the early academic field cannot be overestimated. Janet Wilson James, one of his students in women's history in the 1940s, recalled, "Schlesinger's professional eminence and the weight of his personality allowed little doubt as to the wisdom of the undertaking."[72] Had Schlesinger had more than a few female graduate students over the course of his thirty years of teaching at Harvard and Radcliffe, the field may have developed at a quicker pace, even despite the fact that women scholars' professional lives were often hobbled by difficult choices regarding how to combine career, marriage, and family. Janet James, who began her dissertation focused on women in history in 1945, suggested that "probably nowhere but at Harvard would she have been steered into such a topic, and nowhere else would its viability as a springboard into the profession have been taken for granted."[73] This can largely be credited to Arthur Schlesinger's presence on the faculty. Yet, there were other Harvard faculty sympathetic to the development of the field and other male scholars, notably at the University of North Carolina at Chapel Hill, who supported their female students' interest in women in history and helped them launch careers.

If the Sophia Smith Collection had the more encompassing vision, Radcliffe had more historians (credentialed and non-credentialed) turning the raw data in its collection into historical knowledge. Moreover, Radcliffe's women's collection was more widely publicized. Grierson believed that the Smith collection was far ahead of Radcliffe's in 1950. Yet the resources housed at the Radcliffe Women's Archives grew explosively in the ensuing decades. In 2022, it held more than 3,200 manuscript collections in addition to 100,000 books, periodicals, photos, and audiovisual sources. The Sophia Smith Collection contained 814 manuscript collections in 2021.[74] Regardless of their respective sizes, both were heavily influenced by the feminist politics debated by educated women at midcentury. And there was a strong undercurrent of feminism motivating the women's archives movement of midcentury.

Everyone from administrators to scholars toiling to create women's archives at midcentury saw their work as a corollary to feminist politics in its many variants, a theme that will be explored in a separate chapter.[75] The historian and National Woman's Party activist Alma Lutz reported in 1954,

> Interest in the preservation of such records goes far beyond Smith and Radcliffe. There are more than fifty collections of material about women in this country, several of them in private hands. The Galatea Collection . . . [Boston Public Library] is one of the most notable. . . . California points with pride to the collection at the Henry E. Huntington Library, to the McPherson Collection of the Scripps College Library and the Susan B. Anthony Collection at the Los Angeles Public Library. The Library of Congress, the New York Public Library, and the Vassar College Library all have valuable collections of books and manuscripts on women's work and influence.[76]

Lutz went on to identify other collections. She touted the pioneering work of the Beards and Schlesingers and of women activists who had recorded and published their own work. Still other archival efforts initiated during this period included those at women's colleges, such as Texas Woman's University and the University of North Carolina at Greensboro.[77] She drew attention to early instruction on women in history in Arthur Schlesinger's survey courses at Harvard, mentioning also Goucher College's Latin Americanist Mary Wilhelmine Williams and Syracuse University dean M. Eunice Hilton.[78]

Lutz noted how the postwar generation of women scholars and archivists understood that they were making the historical study of women possible through their collecting efforts. "Until there is a wider knowledge and appreciation of women's heritage among both men and women, women will continue under a psychological handicap, lacking confidence, initiative, and self-respect, and men will distrust women's qualifications for leadership. Without this ground of self-confidence in citizenship, today's women cannot make their maximum contribution to society."[79] Lutz, like Mary Beard, linked understanding women's active role in history to the contemporary part they played as citizens in a democratic society.

Lutz became an active consultant to Radcliffe's archive in the late 1940s, maintaining a place on the library's advisory board for twenty years. As a member of the National Woman's Party, she subscribed to "equal rights feminism," setting her apart from progressive feminists like Beard. They all agreed, however, on the cultural and political value of recovering their own past: building archives to educate and inspire women to struggle for equality in American society. Lutz, a native of North Dakota, graduated from Vassar College in 1912, undoubtedly crossing paths with Lucy Maynard Salmon there. She then worked as a writer for the National Woman's Party from the 1920s to the 1940s and wrote popular books on women in American history. These books included biographies of Susan B. Anthony, Elizabeth Cady Stanton, and Emma Willard; an edited volume of letters of American women during World War II; and a study of women's participation in the antislavery movement.[80] Lutz also frequently contributed articles to newspapers and magazines with broad readership, like the *Christian Science Monitor*. Lutz never earned a PhD and therefore did not seek a place on the faculty of any history department. However, she was active, along with Mary Beard and Elizabeth Schlesinger, the two other non-credentialed historians who supported the development of archives focused on women. She did so through her publications and her place on the Advisory Board of the Women's Archives at Radcliffe and several of its major initiatives in the 1940s and 1960s.[81] Lutz's work in women's political organizations, her scholarly focus on past activist women, and her work establishing the women's archive at Radcliffe illustrate the connection between the emergence of American women's history as a field and women's wide-ranging political and civic engagement in the mid-twentieth century.

From 1943 to 1960, the key actors building the field through archive development at Radcliffe included Radcliffe president Ada Comstock, Harvard historian Arthur M. Schlesinger Sr., and Harvard historian and president of Radcliffe College Wilbur K. Jordan. Much of the work of building the archive, though, fell to women staff and directors. Librarians Georgiana Hinckley and Mary Howard worked on staff at the Radcliffe Women's Archives from the beginning. The archive's first director, Elizabeth Borden, was appointed in 1950. The archive's second and third directors were both trained historians. Barbara Miller Solomon (1960–64) and Janet Wilson James (1965–69) completed

Radcliffe PhDs under Oscar Handlin and Arthur Schlesinger Sr. in the 1950s.[82] Elizabeth Schlesinger, who held only a BA in history but was widely published in history periodicals, was active enough in the work of establishing the archive that the library was renamed for both her and her husband in 1965.

College president Ada Louise Comstock was instrumental in securing the initial manuscript donation for Radcliffe that heralded the founding of the archive.[83] In the year before the collection's inauguration she convinced suffragist and League of Women Voters founder Maud Wood Park to give her papers to Radcliffe. Park had also been approached in early 1942 by Professor Mary Earhart Dillon of Northwestern University, who wanted the Park papers for the planned suffrage collection there.[84] Dillon, a political scientist, had written a dissertation on temperance movement leader Frances Willard, later published in 1944. Park ultimately preferred to leave her papers with Radcliffe—her alma mater.[85] Comstock wooed Park by assuring her that her papers would have a permanent home and be publicized and that Radcliffe was clear about their historical and contemporary relevance to American women.[86] Comstock wrote potential sponsors in 1943, "We hope that the establishment of this collection will not only commemorate the long and successful struggle for woman suffrage, but will also serve as an incentive to women who will be called upon to carry increasing responsibilities in the post-war world."[87] Comstock, along with feminist Edna Stantial and others, viewed the Park collection as historically important and worthy of scholarly attention. The records were relevant as part of a usable past, and they could shape women's participation in contemporary American life and in the foreseeable future.

When Comstock retired from the presidency the same year the archive was founded, the support and leadership of Harvard history professor and incoming Radcliffe College president, Wilbur Kitchener Jordan, became vital. He lent his enthusiastic support, and between 1943 and 1960 the collection transformed from a small archive focused primarily on woman suffrage into the broader repository renamed in 1944 the Radcliffe Women's Archives. Jordan's support is one more example of how influential male scholars and college administrators at midcentury played a role in the early emergence of the field. He joins Fletcher Green, Bell Wiley, Oscar Handlin, and Arthur Schlesinger in the group of midcentury male allies to the field's creation. In major history departments during these decades, a few male historians encouraged female graduate students to study women.[88] Sometimes the influence was less direct. For example, one of Jordan's graduate students at Radcliffe, Natalie Zemon Davis, credited him with her shift from intellectual to social history. Davis had earned her BA at Smith College in 1949, just six years after the Sophia Smith Collection was launched.[89] She subsequently became a preeminent European women's and gender historian.[90]

In 1943 and 1944, Jordan, in consultation with Beard, Arthur Schlesinger, and feminists Edna Stantial and Miriam Holden, among others, made plans to house materials about women in American history and assemble the pre-eminent archive in the field at Radcliffe. And, whereas Beard earlier had a low opinion of professional historians and academics because of their inability to see women as the co-makers of history, by 1943, three years after the WCWA closed, she had come to appreciate the necessity of institutional backing. If her lifelong project of promoting a better understanding of women's historical importance were to take shape, the scaffolding could be erected only at a college or university and be buttressed by the legitimizing authority of scholars within the ivory tower. Beard lent her name, time, and influence to the work of the Radcliffe archive even while she was an advisor on the Smith project. She donated materials gathered earlier for the WCWA to each school. As Julie Des Jardins has revealed, Beard preferred the Sophia Smith Collection's broader approach, which included sources from around the world and which avoided giving pride of place to the "Seneca Falls, 1848" narrative of women's history.[91] Yet, she never completely gave up on Radcliffe or on Wilbur K. Jordan, even when she showed impatience with the speed of development of the collection or displayed her anxiety that Harvard's influence over Radcliffe might derail and "corrupt" the new archive.[92]

The Radcliffe archive grew rapidly from 1943 forward through continued acquisitions, publicity, and promoting use of its materials by scholars and students. For instance, Radcliffe encouraged scholars to use the archive by setting up a fund for fellowships. In the 1950s, the Radcliffe Seminars on Women were added to the work of the archive. Early in the decade, Beard and Grierson had conceived of a similar seminar project, referred to as the "The Woman's Institute," at the Sophia Smith Collection. The Beard/Grierson seminars would have challenged masculine forms of knowing, learning, and knowledge production, but the project ultimately came to naught.[93]

During the Radcliffe archive's first three decades, each of its directors encouraged and shaped the direction of the new field: American women's history. These directors' careers and relatively marginal position within the profession can be compared to those of their Southern counterparts.[94] Based on their writings, professional experiences, and activities, it is possible to show a direct connection between the midcentury movement for women's archives and the feminist-inspired women's history movement of the 1970s.

In its first years, the Radcliffe archive primarily consisted of Maud Wood Park's donation, which was named "The Woman's Rights Collection" and emphasized the work of the National American Woman Suffrage Association. College president Ada Louise Comstock saw the impending forty-fifth class reunion of Park ('98) as an opportunity to introduce the new collection to the

Radcliffe community and to "feature a step forward in the recognition of women as citizens" in light of what was "being said about the utilization of women in the war effort." Comstock hoped that the new collection would "lead to desirable developments for the college."[95] Park's representative, Edna Stantial, and librarian Georgiana Hinckley organized the collection, with Park holding considerable influence over the types of materials that could be added and the nature of any future publicity. Park was opposed to adding materials related to the National Woman's Party, the group headed by Alice Paul. Edna Stantial and other feminists, such as Carrie Chapman Catt, sought to preserve the records of the sharp disagreements between factions within the women's movement in the interest of a well-rounded representation of the full movement.[96]

The inauguration of the collection on August 26, 1943, at Radcliffe's Longfellow Hall was attended by about 100 people. It had been announced widely within the Radcliffe community and was touted the following day in the *Boston Herald*.[97] Letters of invitation to the grand opening were sent to those whose woman suffrage work was highlighted in the collection and especially to Radcliffe alumnae who might sponsor the collection through the donation of materials or money. Guests included "white haired ladies" from the suffrage movement, younger Radcliffe students, and alumnae.[98] Comstock's invitation emphasized the relevance of the collection regarding how it might inform and inspire women's contemporary responsibilities as citizens in the coming postwar world.[99] When the guests arrived at Longfellow Hall, a banner greeted them with Abigail Adams's now famous phrase, "Remember the ladies . . ." An exhibit contained images and memorabilia outlining the nineteenth-century struggle for women's rights, and a catalog was available that described the cultural, political, and scholarly purposes of the collection: "First to arouse greater appreciation and use of present opportunities for women by spreading knowledge of the efforts and sacrifices required to secure them; second to supply factual information on special subjects for students of history, government, education and economics."[100]

At a subsequent 1945 open house event for the exhibit, guests were overheard asking questions that librarian Georgiana Hinckley considered "thoughtful" and exclaiming positively, "Just think!" in reference to the Adams quote. They eagerly took in the visual exhibit and said things like, "1770 [*sic*]!" "Did she say that?"[101] The "hostesses" for this event were Edna Stantial, Elizabeth Bancroft Schlesinger, and future historian of women Lois Bannister Merk. By 1945, the fledgling archive had started to attract a core of scholars and archivists dedicated to ensuring its permanence and publicizing its relevance. Schlesinger and Merk would maintain strong ties to the archive, Schlesinger as a high-profile advocate along with her husband. They also regularly used the archive's collections. Georgiana Hinckley reported positively to Maud Park in 1946, "We have visitors and students very often inquiring about the collection and using it. So far, Mrs. Merk is the only steady user."[102] Merk earned her PhD in history at Radcliffe in 1961, completing a dissertation on the Massachusetts suffrage movement, a topic she worked on while a participant in the Radcliffe Seminars on the Role of Women in American History in the 1950s. Before that, she had taught at Wheaton College and Northeastern University after earning an MA in history in 1931. When she married prominent Harvard historian Frederick Merk, she combined teaching with raising two children. Merk also coauthored and edited her husband's work during these years. After earning her PhD, Lois became Frederick's official collaborator/coauthor, which enabled him to publish works long delayed by his active teaching career.[103] In the foreword to her dissertation, she acknowledged her husband and the Radcliffe Women's Archives staff. She reserved special acknowledgment for Arthur Schlesinger:

> The source of my interest in woman suffrage is to be found in
> Professor Arthur Meier Schlesinger's attention to reform movements,
> conveyed to me through his course in American Social History. To
> him I am also indebted for reading a portion of the first draft, and for
> his encouragement to go forward. To Professor Arthur Holcombe, a
> participant himself in the suffrage movement, and to President Wilbur K.
> Jordan, who has done so much to expand the Radcliffe Women's Archives,
> I am indebted for reading the manuscript as a 1956 Ph.D. dissertation. To
> each of them I am also grateful for constructive suggestions.[104]

She also expressed gratitude to archive director Elizabeth Borden for "opportunities offered by the Radcliffe Women's Workshop for exchange of ideas about women," an obvious reference to the Radcliffe Seminars on Women in American History.[105]

The first few years of the archive were imbued with its feminist creators' political and academic enthusiasm for the "Woman's Rights Collection." Theirs was an enthusiasm marked by a deep sense of historical consciousness and faith that the collection would inspire future generations to lead politically active lives. The collection owes its early existence to the persistence of these women and their fundraising efforts. The Harvard administration offered no financial backing, and Radcliffe provided only a limited budget. Radcliffe president Wilbur Jordan, however, gave strong support to the archive, and Radcliffe did provide physical space and the publicity that nurtured the fledgling repository.[106]

On May 1, 1946, the Radcliffe archive stopped accepting further additions to the Woman's Rights Collection. The mutual decision of President Jordan and Maud Wood Park was designed to avoid the "inevitable dilution of the collection and a distortion of the purposes [that Park] . . . held so clearly in mind." This move freed Jordan and the archive staff to accept new donations—in money or materials—destined for the general archive "relating to the historical and cultural contributions of American women." Park and Stantial had a narrower vision for the collection and had hitherto circumscribed what the archive could become.[107] Jordan's vision, though, was to establish a "national center for research in the historical role and cultural contributions of women in the United States . . . broadly defined . . . in close collaboration with the Harvard University Library."[108] This moment represented an important transition for the Radcliffe Women's Archives. In essence, it heralded a broader scope for the project and signaled Radcliffe's full commitment to its development.

Between 1943 and 1950 the archive was directed by Jordan, Hinckley, and Howard, who later became head archivist. In 1950, Jordan officially appointed the archive's first director, Mrs. Elizabeth Borden. Borden had been a nontraditional undergraduate at Radcliffe from 1948 to 1950. After attending Vassar College in 1930, she left her studies to marry and raise children. Her businessman husband was for a time a textile manufacturer, later turning to the production of documentary films. The family lived in Cambridge. As Elizabeth Borden's child-rearing duties lessened, she worked on hospital boards and committees but eventually felt compelled to complete her education. She enrolled at Radcliffe in 1948 and finished her AB in two years. Jordan, noting Borden's administrative experience, tagged her as the new director of the Women's Archives and the Radcliffe Seminars, an adult education program aimed at middle-class Boston and Cambridge women. It was under the auspices of this adult education program that the annual seminar "The Role of Women in American History" was conceived and became a graduate-level forum for original research and writing. Essentially an informal workshop that met at the library, Radcliffe never funded the enterprise. Participants were selected on an invitation-only basis.

Borden had majored in social relations as an undergraduate. As director, she felt inadequately prepared in history to effectively do her job and enrolled in the MA program in American history in 1953. She took a one-year leave of absence from her duties to complete her courses. In describing her duties as director, Borden told one news reporter that her job was primarily developing contacts with women's organizations and individuals in order to procure funding but more importantly manuscript collections, diaries, and papers. She reported that a steady number of researchers used the archives through the 1950s, including Radcliffe and Harvard undergraduate and graduate students and journalists, like Ishbel Ross, who wrote both *Ladies of the Press* and a biography of Elizabeth Blackwell. Scholar Louise Hall Tharp, biographer of the Ward family, and reform historian Arthur Mann also used the collection.[109]

Arguably the most important initiative Borden developed as director was the graduate-level seminar on women in American history. Designed to make use of the archive's holdings, the seminar was titled variously "Workshop on Women," "The Role of Women," or "The Role of Women in American History." Borden's original conception was a seminar that was part of the larger noncredit adult education program. The lack of a suitable instructor, however, meant that the seminar was offered only once to the general public in 1955. It was when Borden and a group of scholars convened the seminar independently of the college's adult education program that they were able to use the archives to conduct serious scholarship and discussion on the direction of the field. Most of the research and papers presented over the nine years of the seminar's life were never published. But some were, and many of the topics discussed became core topics for women's history scholars twenty years later.[110] These topics ranged from women in education, suffrage work, women workers, women in organized religion, institutional histories, study of household work, women pioneers in science and industry, frontier women, and examinations of individual women such as Susan B. Anthony or Fanny Fern. One participant wrote a biographical essay about early women historians in the United States.[111]

In the seminar's first year, 1951–52, ten women formed a core group that included six historians and archivists and four others. Borden and her colleagues struggled to create a framework for structured study, disagreeing over whether the seminar should take a contemporary, sociological approach or a historical one. The historically oriented members of the group were Elisabeth Anthony Dexter, Elizabeth Bancroft Schlesinger, Alma Lutz, Frieda Ullian, Lois Bannister Merk, and head archivist Mary Howard. The non-historians included Mary Volkmann, Mrs. John Fairbank, Mrs. Robert Treat, and Mrs. F. J. Ingelfinger. These four were more concerned with contemporary issues. They wanted the seminar to focus on the undergraduate curriculum to help prepare Radcliffe students for postgraduate life, especially how they would cope with family and career.[112] Drawing on her training in social relations, Borden tried to keep both groups happy. Linking the fields of sociology and psychology, she was initially torn between the two approaches, inclined toward the sociological faction but also wanting to encourage use of the archives for historical scholarship. As a result, the papers and discussions coming out of the first twelve-week seminar were not cohesive. Borden reported that the meetings were fraught. There was a serious lack of an experienced and informed seminar leader. There was a lack of common content background and of common interest in the topics, resulting in an unwillingness to do the background reading that would facilitate group discussion.

The historians in the group were not satisfied with the sociological approach and appear to have won out in determining the next year's program. Schlesinger,

Lutz, Merk, and Dexter strongly supported focusing on specific historical periods and doing original research. Schlesinger asked whether it would be possible to develop an undergraduate course in American women's history.[113] At the final meeting of the first year, participants discussed whether the focus should be chronologically narrow or thematic and broad. Lutz and Dexter suggested a balance between original research and summary of selected topics. Frieda Ullian concurred, expressing a concern that too broad a focus would dilute the seminar, noting, "After all, the 'history of women' covers the entire history of the world." Ullian joined the seminar early on; she held a PhD in economics, taught at Simmons College, and was active on Radcliffe boards and committees, as well as in women's civic and political organizations.[114] Members suggested possible topics—women and peace, women workers, women and education, women's organizations.[115] After the seminar's first year, the group decided to focus on the period 1860–1900 to inspire in-depth research,[116] and members drew up a reading list of over 130 books and other publications on history, economics, anthropology, and sociology.[117]

According to Borden's next annual report, the papers given were more novel and scholarly. Rather than summarizing their earlier work in the field, the participants produced original research. There was no tension in the group because the non-scholars had not returned. Borden was hopeful that the work done in the first two years could be published in a single volume.[118] This never materialized, but Radcliffe printed out selected essays and had them bound in two volumes. During this year Borden and the other participants drew up diagrams, outlines, and reading lists in their efforts to give shape to the seminar and to the vast new field opening before them.[119] They began to consider whether an undergraduate course on women's history could be developed and what materials it should include.

Records for the seminar years 1954–59 are scant. Only seventeen of the papers have survived. Participants and guest speakers for these years included Margaret Storrs Grierson, Cecilia Kenyon, Gladys Hosmer, Bess Bloodworth, Helen Maud Cam, Dorothy Thayer Green, and the original core members.[120] The papers range in topic: Jane Addams's work at Hull House, the Alcotts, industrial personnel work, women historians up to 1900, Dolley Madison, women teachers in Boston's public schools, a history of Radcliffe College, women in a variety of professions including teaching, pharmacy, botany, and agriculture.[121] Each year, Lois Merk, already in her fifties, presented research on her dissertation about the Massachusetts woman suffrage movement.[122]

Borden resigned her position as the archive's director in 1959 to accept a new position as a Radcliffe dean. Institutional financial support for the self-motivated and unfunded seminar never materialized. Unwilling to continue without this support, and with most of its strongest participants reaching advanced ages, the group that had dedicated itself to formal study of women's history for eight years decided to disband in 1959. But the seminars then began to reconvene on a monthly basis in 1961 independently of the Radcliffe archive. Elisabeth Dexter reported that Barbara Miller Solomon, the archive's new director, and archivist Mary Howard agreed to attend whenever possible.[123] Most of the seminar papers were never published, and discussions on the developing field were never aired publicly.[124]

In 1960, Solomon was appointed director of the archive. A Harvard PhD and published historian, she attended the ongoing seminars in the early 1960s. Her work promoting the archives won national recognition when she was invited to speak at a White House luncheon hosted by Lady Bird Johnson in 1964. Solomon was a native of Boston. She was married to a shoe manufacturer and, like her predecessor, had interrupted her education after receiving a Radcliffe AB in 1940 to raise her three children. Solomon returned to Radcliffe to earn her PhD in the history of American civilization in 1953, studying under Oscar Handlin and Arthur M. Schlesinger.[125] After earning her PhD, Solomon's scholarly interests and publications focused on immigrants, Jewish history, and women in higher education. She taught American history at Wheelock College from 1957 to 1959 and published two books, *Ancestors and Immigrants* and *Pioneers in Service*, a book about Jewish philanthropies in Boston.[126] She held memberships in a number of important professional associations, including the American Historical Association, the Mississippi Valley Historical Association, the American Association of University Women, the Committee on the History of Social Welfare, and the Berkshire Conference of Women Historians, suggesting she was an active participant in the life of the profession.[127] Lillian Handlin wrote about her upon her death,

> She represented the era before coeducational classes with Harvard, when parietal rules were strictly enforced. . . . She remembered Radcliffe President Ada Louise Comstock still greeting students with the admonition to wear hats and gloves when venturing out into the forbidden territory of Harvard Square. Proper appearance and manners would ease relations with Harvard neighbors, since the word "lady" was not yet a pejorative term. If in later years Barbara Solomon came to doubt the wisdom of these tactics, she retained her ladylike behavior for the rest of her life. . . . Barbara Solomon remained a firm believer in gentle persuasion, proper etiquette, and quiet persistence.[128]

Solomon represented an era for academic women in which they presented themselves as both feminine and scholarly professionals.[129] Most practiced feminism by deed, lifestyle, and advocacy for women's access to education and not by directly voicing grievances or legally challenging the professional gender status quo. This would be left to their second-wave successors. While appearing "genteel," Solomon and her generation broke down professional barriers. The generation of feminist scholars who came after challenged both the performance of femininity and the gendered hierarchy.

Solomon had seen progress in women's education during her lifetime. Ada Comstock waged a successful campaign to open Harvard classes to Radcliffe students in 1943. As a graduate student in the 1950s, Solomon herself attained educational and professional success. Unlike Mary Elizabeth Massey and A. Elizabeth Taylor, the two Southern historians of women with traditional history careers, she accomplished these feats while married and raising three young children.[130] Her youngest was only three years old when she completed her PhD in 1953; her oldest was eleven. When in 1965 Radcliffe offered her a deanship, she was also serving on the Massachusetts Commission on the Status of Women.[131] In 1970 Harvard made her the first female dean in its history, also appointing her a senior lecturer in American history and literature. At Harvard she introduced the first full-fledged women's history course in 1972.[132] In 1971 she served on a second State Commission on the Status of Women. Solomon was able to make her brand of feminine social and professional behavior work for her; she applied her women's history insights to her own feminist activism when she engaged in public discourse. Historian Susan Ware has suggested that Solomon "forged a professional style that was consciously feminist, but also effective within male-dominated institutions."[133]

Solomon was also an adept publicist for the archive. Her most high-profile act of publicity was a talk she gave at a White House luncheon hosted by Lady Bird Johnson in February 1964. The luncheon was part of a series of events for and about "Lady Doers" in the United States.[134] It was reported on nationally in numerous newspapers.[135] Coverage ranged in tone, some describing the luncheons as "the newest status symbol for career women" and others dedicating considerable space to details like dining room decor and the elegant menu.[136] Yet reporters also captured the significance of the work taking place at the Radcliffe Women's Archives. They identified the archive as "the outstanding collection in the United States centering on the development of the American woman from colonial times to the present."[137] Reporters recognized that Mrs. Johnson was acknowledging some of the "best" women in the country by inviting them to these luncheons. Moreover, Solomon's advice to women to "preserve those scribbles" was correctly understood by the reporters to be a shout-out to housewives, as well as to public figures and professionals, to keep the records of their lives.[138]

At the luncheon at which Solomon spoke, for example, the other guests included famed hat designer Sally Victor; a British historian visiting from London, Mrs. L. B. Wedgwood; Dr. Geraldine Woods, an African American scientist specializing in neuro-embryology; Dr. Leona Baumgartner, deputy director for the US Agency for International Development; Diana MacArthur of the Peace Corps; and the wives of some prominent politicians and officeholders in the Johnson administration. These politicians' wives included the wife of Secretary of Defense Robert McNamara; Mrs. Endicott Peabody, wife of the governor of Massachusetts; Mrs. Thomas Dodd, wife of the Connecticut senator; and a few others.[139] Solomon spoke about the Women's Archives. Leona Baumgartner described the archivists as "delightful naggers" because they had been pursuing her papers for some time.

When Solomon returned from her White House sojourn, she reported on the event to the Advisory Board of the Women's Archives and some seminar participants. This discussion was recorded. Just as the newspapers had, they discussed menu and decor. But the conversation quickly turned to the matter of whether the cause of the archive had been served.[140] Solomon expressed that she was sure Lady Bird Johnson had contacted her because of the network of activists in women's collecting. She acknowledged one of her colleagues:

> I'd like to say Betty, that I see this whole thing as a continuity really of something that you began in all your wonderful Washington trips. I think that what happened was that my archives report had gone out . . . and that it got into various hands of our friends in Washington and many of these friends were really due to you, there's no question of it, and so that really, this is in a real sense a fruition of that and somebody showed it to Mrs. Carpenter [Mrs. Johnson's secretary] and Mrs. Carpenter was interested, but more important showed it to Mrs. Johnson, and I think that from our total view the thing that's interesting is that Mrs. Johnson cared about this enough to have somebody to come and talk about the archives.[141]

"Betty" may refer to Elizabeth Borden, who still held a Radcliffe deanship in 1964, but it could have been Elizabeth Schlesinger or Elisabeth Anthony Dexter, who were both still quite involved with the archive and the seminar. "Betty" responded to the acknowledgment of her earlier efforts by elaborating, "Well, thank you. We planted seeds. You're planting some that will bear fruit ten years from now and seeds were planted before I came that took root later."[142]

Solomon continued her report by explaining that the substance of her talk had described the contents of the Women's Archives with emphasis placed on women in Texas and "Indian" women in a nod to the First Lady's Texas roots. She wrapped up her report by saying, "I just felt well, the seeds are planted, I mean a few more seeds are planted. We've since had a good deal of interesting correspondence as a result of this, . . . including National Archivist Alan Aldridge who thought the cause of all archives had been furthered."[143]

Solomon reported being invited to appear on the TV show *To Tell the Truth*. She declined, thinking it wasn't the right venue to publicize the archive, though one woman in the meeting questioned her decision, "because you never know who might pick up on it." From there the discussion turned to women's role in partisan politics. The names India Edwards, Eleanor Poland, and Katherine Elkis White came up as three women in party politics, as did Women's Bureau official Esther Peterson. Discussion returned to the archive. A comment was made on how wide the news coverage on the archive had been. One discussant asked who was currently working in the archive and what was being written. Seminar papers were being written by Frank Freidel's students; British scholar Anderson Clair was writing about Lydia Maria Child; a few graduate students were busy in the archive, including Helen Lefkowitz [Horowitz], who was working on her Wellesley honors thesis. Finally, what the discussants referred to as "the James Foundation over there," meaning the *Notable American Women* project, was recognized to be the collection's biggest user as its contributors were about at the midpoint in the production of the biographical encyclopedia. *Notable American Women* formed a nexus of links to the explosion that the field was about to experience. It would be hard to overestimate the importance of *Notable American Women* to the field's development and legitimization. At the Radcliffe Women's Archives, it was seen as a means by which to publicize and legitimize the archive. But, as we will see, *Notable American Women* was so much more. This hour-long discussion illustrates the deep roots growing from the Radcliffe Women's Archives. The roots were fertilized by scholarly interest and by political sensibilities and skills.

When Solomon took a teaching position at Harvard in 1970 and then introduced the first women's history course at Harvard in 1972, she was clearly at the pinnacle of her powers as a specialist in women's history. These midcentury historians of women felt both a connection to and a degree of difference from the generation coming up in the late 1960s. Anne Firor Scott wrote Solomon in 1971,

> The whole business of women's history is in such a state of change and excitement that I hardly know where to begin among the things I would like to talk over with you. . . . The question keeps coming up: Why haven't we been training graduate students all these years so that there would be dozens of young women ready now to take jobs with a specialty in the field! . . . The question would have been pooh poohed . . . not long ago. . . . Many department chairmen seem to have undergone a change comparable to Paul on the road to Damascus. . . . I've sent out three or four vitae I have of young women who can move around about ten times. . . . I hear that there were numbers of young scholars at the Schlesinger

Library, and at the L[ibrary] of C[ongress] this summer who were able to run an informal seminar because there were enough of them. (Shades of you & me sitting in your office in the old Women's Archives having *our seminar* . . .) I am sure you met the ones in Cambridge and have some idea what they are up to.[144]

Scott reminisced about the informal one-on-one meetings with Solomon during Solomon's tenure as director, and she marveled at the dramatic attitudinal changes male academics were undergoing. There was continuity between the two generations struggling for women's history. Scholars like Scott and Solomon were on hand to promote both the field and the young scholars coming up. This was critical in launching the next stage of the field's development.

The next director of the archive, Janet Wilson James, also became a key figure in women's history in the 1970s. By the time she entered the profession, more academic women were combining career and family without having to make the difficult compromises made by most women in prior decades. The 1960s saw the rise of several dual career academic historian couples, like Mary Maples Dunn and Richard Dunn, Anne Firor Scott and Andrew Scott, Carroll Smith-Rosenberg and Charles Rosenberg, Lois Banner and James Banner, and Jane De Hart Mathews and Donald Mathews. This reflected the upsurge in the number of women seeking advanced degrees and the dramatic expansion in hiring caused by increased college enrollment as the baby boomers came of age. This opened opportunities for women scholars married to academics— something that was curtailed in earlier decades. Janet James's story will be told more fully in the next chapter in the context of her editorship of a pathbreaking reference work in women's history.

———————

As pioneering efforts in the field, the Radcliffe Women's Archives and the Sophia Smith Collection were critical sites for cultivating the field of women in American history. They were first to get substantial institutional backing, and the prestige of the institutions bolstered the legitimacy of the endeavor. The archival collections enabled and promoted knowledge production in the field. Some of these historians and archivists were aware of the political implications inherent in collecting material, supporting research, and building institutions that would provide a foundation for the study of women in history. And all of this predated the activism of "second-wave" feminist historians who took the lead after 1969. While these later scholars broadened the conceptual frameworks of the field, advocated for professional gender equity, and expanded women's history scholarship, the field had been plowed and made ready for cultivation, and the first seeds planted at midcentury had sprouted.

Two significant areas of development predated the emergence of the women's history movement in 1969—the work of individual scholars focusing on women but functioning within traditional academic hierarchies between the 1920s and the 1950s, and the development of women's history archives beginning in the 1940s. By the early 1960s, a small body of scholarship on the history of American women existed. The most significant work done in the field had been by female scholars, some of whom had the support of powerful, established male historians. Yet, the field did not yet attain recognition as a distinct body of knowledge, nor did it assume the label "women's history." The creation of women's archives enabled a distinct field on women to coalesce. The efforts of the Radcliffe Seminars on the Role of Women in American History produced the first group of scholars who attempted collectively to demarcate what the field might look like. To borrow from Janet James, they would begin to move beyond Mary Beard's "bulging and ambiguous concept of women in long history," to bring it in line with professional historians' "more formalized views of their discipline."[145] The central goal of the Radcliffe Women's Archives would be most fully realized in these years by the production of *Notable American Women*, which took place over the entire decade of the 1960s. Its publication in 1971 coincided with a new wave of scholarship on women and a dramatic upswing in professional activism by women scholars. But its preparation and the support it garnered from American historians predated and anticipated the nationwide movement for the promotion of women's history that sprang up in the 1970s.

Chapter 5

Producing *Notable American Women, 1955–1971*

In December 1971, Mrs. Emma Weigley received the three-volume reference work *Notable American Women, 1607–1950: A Biographical Dictionary* (*NAW*) as a Christmas present from her husband, Temple University military historian Russell Weigley.[1] By March, Mrs. Weigley had written an enthusiastic letter to one of the dictionary's editors, Edward James, exclaiming, "I find it rather like olives or potato chips—I can't stop at one sketch!"[2] James, obviously pleased, replied that Lyman Butterfield, editor of *The Adams Papers*, had similarly compared reading the sketches to "eating salted peanuts!"[3] The statements of Weigley and Butterfield are indicative of the eagerness with which many scholars had been awaiting *NAW*'s publication since the project's launch in 1958. The central role of the Radcliffe Women's Archives in developing women's history as a field from 1943 included the archive's advisory board's efforts to legitimize and publicize its own work. The publication of *Notable American Women* did just that.[4]

Between 1958 and 1971, *NAW*'s editors and committee of consultants recruited a wide network of scholars to work on the dictionary. *NAW* editors Edward and Janet James (and later Paul S. Boyer) drew on the talents of 698 historians and other scholars who contributed a total of 1,359 biographical articles. Scholars served as consultants on the project to determine who should be included in the final draft of the dictionary.[5] They ultimately chose from a field of 4,000 women submitted for consideration.[6] Supplements were later published in 1980 and again in 2004 to round out the dictionary's coverage of the twentieth century.[7] The work that went into producing *NAW* reveals support and participation from a broad range of scholars, some quite prominent. And their support came at a propitious time; in the 1960s the modern women's movement gained momentum and attracted attention to women's past. This chapter explores how the architects of this major academic achievement, *NAW*, drew on the historical discipline's scholarly networks to legitimize the study of women. These scholars' efforts not only prefigured the women's history movement of the 1970s but also smoothed the way for the new field's acceptance as its practitioners and detractors engaged in polemics in the 1970s over its very legitimacy.

NAW was assembled by harnessing the efforts of hundreds of specialists in diverse aspects of American history. These scholars were men and women, credentialed and non-credentialed historians, archivists, museum directors, literary scholars, political scientists, and graduate students, among others. The scholarly collaboration that began in 1958 had become, by its publication in 1971, a node of activity connecting a far-flung array of scholars interested in the way American women had shaped the nation's past. Moreover, *NAW* linked multiple generations of historians to the cause of building the field. For some, working on *Notable American Women* was their first entrée into the study of American women's history. For others, *NAW* reinforced and validated a prior interest that they had discovered independently in the course of other historical work. Mary Maples Dunn, Joan Jensen, Annette Baxter, Carroll Smith-Rosenberg, Anne Firor Scott, Carl Degler, Gerda Lerner, Helen Lefkowitz Horowitz, and Ruth Bordin are just a few of the scholars who worked as contributors or consultants or on the editorial staff of *NAW*. Later they went on to specialize in American women's history and served in leadership roles in the movement that emerged after 1969.

Notable American Women held a special place in the process of legitimizing the historical study of women. The project illuminates how work done in the 1950s and 1960s was foundational to the field's emergence. *NAW* concretely linked the movement for women's history that emerged after 1969 to the movement for women's archives that preceded it and to individual scholars in multiple subfields across generations. Historians Judith Zinsser and Judith Bennett have acknowledged that the history profession's turn in the 1960s to studying "history from the bottom up" was instrumental in spurring historians in the United States and Europe to look at the history of women. Yet, Zinsser and Bennett share the view that it wasn't until feminism's "second wave" in the early 1970s that historians turned seriously to the study of women. Indeed, in 1993, Zinsser chastised male historians of the 1960s by suggesting that for all they had "accomplished in terms of new methods, new sources and new perspectives, the leaders among these gifted and revolutionary European and United States historians remained traditional in one key respect—they failed to value women's experience equally with men's."[8] Zinsser acknowledged a few sympathetic male allies like David Potter, Herbert Gutman, and Carl Degler. A look behind the scenes of the production of *NAW* suggests, however, there were more than a few male historians in the 1960s who supported the study of women's past.[9] Moreover, some of these historians actively promoted, taught, or completed research in the history of women before 1969.

An Historical Cyclopedia of American Women

The idea for an authoritative and scholarly reference work on women in history had been discussed by Mary Beard, Wilbur K. Jordan, and Arthur M. Schlesinger Sr. as early as 1944.[10] Beard consulted briefly with the publishers of *Encyclopædia Britannica* about improving its representation of women, but the encyclopedia never published any of Beard's suggested entries.[11] Radcliffe's work to create a compendium did not get off the ground until Schlesinger, Alma Lutz, and Elisabeth Anthony Dexter, all members of the Advisory Board of the Women's Archives, took action in 1955.[12] Assigned by the advisory board to investigate the need for such a work, Lutz and Dexter reported favorably on the possibility in 1956, after concluding that women were underrepresented in the *Dictionary of American Biography*.[13] Of more than 14,000 entries in the *Dictionary*, only 664 were about women. In their initial investigation, Lutz and Dexter identified several hundred women whom they thought ought to be included and indicated that their suggested additions did not involve any women who had died after 1920. Nor had the *Dictionary* yet considered women in temperance, the women's club movement, nursing, or medicine. Thus, Lutz, Dexter, and the Advisory Board of the Women's Archives wrote to the Radcliffe Council in early 1957 recommending the production of an authoritative reference work on women in American history. They proposed it be funded by being rolled into the budget as a line item of the Radcliffe Improvement Campaign, a ten-year, $10 million project being launched by the college. The Radcliffe Council quickly voted to fund and house the project. President Jordan sought money from both the Rockefeller Foundation and the Littauer Foundation, but this funding did not materialize.[14] Lutz and Dexter also maintained that *Der Lexicon der Frau* (1953), soon to be published in English in Switzerland, would not offer too much competition, with only 500 entries on American women out of 10,000 total entries.[15] This points to the existence of like-minded projects in Europe during the same time frame.

NAW was not the only publication with which the Radcliffe Women's Archives was involved. In 1956, archive director Elizabeth Borden began collaboration with the A. N. Marquis Company in Chicago to provide research assistance on its serial publication *Who's Who of American Women*. Though Borden was initially enthusiastic about the collaboration, it was clear to the archive's advisory board, especially to Arthur Schlesinger Sr., that the Chicago volume was no substitute for an authoritative scholarly reference work.[16] It was a combination of concern for scholarly legitimacy and wanting to represent the activities of the Radcliffe archive that ultimately prompted the creation of *Notable American Women*. The advisory board wanted a project that would have lasting influence on the field's development, reach a wide audience, and draw in scholarly contributors. *NAW* was designed to provide a frame for the developing field—a starting point for scholars and history students alike interested in the history of American women. It would become an unmistakable signal that women's past was a legitimate field of historical study.

Placed at the editorial helm of *Notable American Women* were historian Edward T. James, editor of supplements 2, 3, and 4 of the *Dictionary of American*

Biography, and his historian wife, Janet Wilson James. Janet James began at *NAW* as assistant editor in 1961 and by 1963 was an associate editor.[17] In 1964 Paul Boyer, then a history PhD candidate at Harvard and part-time worker for *NAW* since the spring of 1963, joined the editorial team as assistant editor. From 1959 to 1971, many librarians, students of library science, and graduate students from Harvard worked on *NAW* as fact-checkers, research assistants, and bibliographers. Historians and other scholars from every region in the United States contributed their expertise, spreading the word about the project throughout the nation's libraries and colleges.[18]

Janet and Edward James were an early dual-career couple. Janet James graduated with a BA from Smith College in 1939, an MA from Bryn Mawr in 1940, and a PhD from Radcliffe in 1954. She directed the Radcliffe Women's Archives from 1965 to 1969. At Radcliffe, the advisor on her dissertation was Arthur M. Schlesinger Sr. The dissertation, "Changing Ideas about Women in the United States, 1775–1825," examined prescriptive literature about women and was published in 1981. Once she earned her PhD, she married Edward James, held temporary appointments at Mills College in California and at Wellesley, and started a family. As she later recalled, "The rest of the decade went into family concerns. Bringing up a son and daughter merged into the creation, during the 1960s, of a reference work, *Notable American Women, 1607–1950*—edited with my husband—and the development of the Arthur and Elizabeth Schlesinger Library on the History of Women in America."[19] In tribute to the Schlesingers, the archive took that name the same year Janet James took over directorship of the library, 1965. *Notable American Women* would, as Edward James's memorialist suggested in 2001, "undergird and stimulate the belated boom in women's history" that began in the 1970s.[20]

Edward James had been the roommate of Arthur Schlesinger Jr. at Harvard College in the late 1930s. He graduated in 1938 and served in the US Navy during World War II. He earned his PhD in history at Harvard in 1954, the same year as Janet Wilson.[21] His appointment as editor of the *Dictionary of American Biography* led Arthur Schlesinger Sr. to invite him to edit *Notable American Women* in 1958. Janet James was soon brought onto the project, first as a consultant. Schlesinger Sr., Janet James's graduate mentor, may have seen the potential for a package deal right from the beginning. By 1963, Janet was the project's associate editor, taking on both editorial and administrative work. Her contributions included authoring a lengthy survey essay explaining the dictionary's contents that provided a scaffold for the burgeoning field.[22] Meanwhile, Edward James returned his attention to the *Dictionary of American Biography*.

After serving as director of the Radcliffe Women's Archives, Janet James moved to a faculty appointment in history at Boston College, where she stayed until her death in 1987. She was the first woman to be appointed full professor at Boston College. In her memorial of James, Kathryn Preyer mentioned the younger women whom James had mentored in the Boston area—Nancy Cott, Susan Ware, Barbara Sicherman, Susan Reverby, and Judith Smith.[23] Prior to her death, James herself reflected on her own path to women's history. "Privately, I had doubts, a real urge to find out about women in the past competing with an uneasy feeling that the subject was out of the mainstream, not one a man would have chosen, and therefore second-class. But Schlesinger's professional eminence and the weight of his personality allowed little doubt. . . . It was decided that I would investigate the antebellum era, building on Elisabeth Dexter's, Mary Benson's, and Julia Spruill's work on women in early America."[24] After only a few weeks of reading and research, she realized that, "at twenty-six, a voyage into the history of women seemed likely not only to produce a dissertation and that important first book but to continue for a scholarly lifetime."[25] Indeed, she was rewarded with a lifetime of pathbreaking scholarly work. She received a Guggenheim Fellowship. At Boston College, she developed the women's studies program, chaired the Women's Affirmative Action Council, and studied women at coeducational institutions, in religion, and at work. She taught courses in women's history at the college, which had only become coeducational the year she arrived.[26] Her career spanned the field's early and transitional epoch from the 1950s to the 1980s.[27]

In November 1958, Arthur Schlesinger Sr. clarified the scholarly nature of the project in a Radcliffe press release. "No pains will be spared to make the 'Cyclopedia' of the same high scholarly and literary quality as the *Dictionary of American Biography* and its distinguished English counterpart, the *Dictionary of National Biography*."[28] In an effort to distinguish *NAW* from *Who's Who of American Women*, Schlesinger added that *Who's Who* was "in no way concerned, as will be the Cyclopedia, with the women who *were* who. . . . Naturally, the publisher [of *Who's Who*] has the sole responsibility for the contents as well as for the financing of their work."[29] This statement stressed the fact that the Radcliffe-directed reference work would not be redundant and did *not* have the financial backing of A. N. Marquis. Concerned that the scholarly legitimacy of the project be indisputable, the *Radcliffe News* reported that the project was designed to "convey a properly balanced picture of the American past" by vastly increasing the number of women notables mentioned, compared with the *Dictionary of American Biography*, and saying that *NAW* would be researched and written by "historians and other qualified scholars in all parts of the country."[30] The name for the "Cyclopedia" was debated. Ultimately, at the suggestion of Henry A. Laughlin, president of Houghton Mifflin, the editors decided to call it *Notable American Women, 1607–1950: A Biographical Dictionary of American Women.* Laughlin had been asked for his opinion by Radcliffe president Wilbur K. Jordan in 1958.[31]

Notable Women, Notable Scholars

The first task that fell to Edward James in 1958 was to set up a system for selecting women to be included in the dictionary. James and the archive's advisory board appointed a Committee of Consultants to draw up lists of possible candidates. These preliminary lists were assessed and modified by experts in relevant subfields of American history. Specialists in the history of women and prominent scholars from other fields served on the Committee of Consultants, which was chaired by Schlesinger. Lester J. Cappon of the Institute of Early American History and Culture served on the committee. Rachel Carson, renowned marine biologist, conservationist, and environmentalist, consulted on women in science. Helen Clapesattle, former head of the University of Minnesota Press, also served, as did Merle Curti of the University of Wisconsin, a former president of the American Historical Association. Historians Elisabeth Anthony Dexter, Eleanor Flexner, and Alma Lutz, as well-known published experts on the history of American women, participated. Historian Constance McLaughlin Green and historian and college president Wilbur K. Jordan each brought their historical expertise to the committee, and Oliver Larkin, a Pulitzer Prize–winning author and art professor at Smith College, also joined. African American historian Elsie Makel Lewis of Howard University was recommended by John Hope Franklin and agreed to work on the committee. Also joining the Committee of Consultants were Annabelle M. Melville, history professor at Bridgewater State Teachers College; Frances Perkins, former Secretary of Labor and Cornell University professor; Ishbel Ross, author of a popular work on women journalists and several historical biographies of women; and William Van Lennep, curator of the Harvard Theatre Collection. Finally, Wellesley's Ola Elizabeth Winslow, Pulitzer Prize–winning biographer of Jonathan Edwards, agreed to serve on the committee.[32]

In 1961, additional scholars were invited to join the committee based on their prominence and their positive response to the overall project.[33] This group included Francis B. Simkins, Louis Filler, William Lichtenwanger, Frederick B. Tolles, and Carl Bridenbaugh. Simkins had coauthored a 1936 study of women in the Confederacy with James Patton.[34] He served as president of the Southern Historical Association in 1953–54. Filler, of Antioch College, was a specialist on antislavery and reform history. Lichtenwanger, who worked at the Library of Congress, specialized in the history of music. Tolles taught at Swarthmore College and was an expert in Quaker history. Carl Bridenbaugh, the colonial historian, served as president of the American Historical Association in 1962. In 1961, Barbara Solomon replaced Elizabeth Borden on the Committee of Consultants since she was the new director of the Radcliffe Women's Archives. Solomon remained on the committee even after she resigned from the directorship of the archive to pursue other opportunities with Harvard.

Each of these historians accepted the invitation to serve on the committee with enthusiasm, and each agreed to write biographical sketches. There is little doubt that they thought the project legitimate, worthy, and interesting. Filler contributed nine sketches; Lichtenwanger, three. Tolles authored five, and Simkins and Bridenbaugh each contributed one. Bridenbaugh began his association with *NAW* in 1959 as a consultant on early America. As his commitment to serving as AHA president impinged on his time and limited his contribution to one sketch, he nevertheless assured Edward James in 1961, "Please remember I am a firm supporter of *Notable American Women* and its editor."[35]

In 1958, in a similar vein, Merle Curti wrote to Wilbur Jordan to accept a position on the Committee of Consultants: "I am very happy to learn about the preparation of an Historical Cyclopedia of American Women. This will be an immensely useful instrument and some day we will wonder how we ever managed to get along without it. My interest in this general field goes back to the time when I was teaching at Smith and encouraged the library to begin building up resources on the role of women in history."[36] A leading American social and intellectual historian, Curti had studied under Frederick Turner and Schlesinger at Harvard. He then taught at Beloit College, Smith College, and Columbia University in the 1930s. In 1942 he moved to the University of Wisconsin. Because Curti was such a distinguished historian—serving as president of the Mississippi Valley Historical Association in 1952 and the American Historical Association in 1954—his support added to *NAW*'s legitimacy in the early stage of the project. Moreover, he trained more than eighty PhDs in his career, and several of them wrote articles for *NAW*, including Roderick Nash and Allen F. Davis. His overall influence was far-ranging; his students John Higham and Richard Hofstadter, for example, achieved renown and went on to train future leaders in the women's history movement like Kathryn Kish Sklar and Linda Kerber.[37] Thus, a web of professional networks and authority at midcentury fostered an acceptance of women as historical subjects. Prominent historians lent their intellectual and professional support. So, while feminist politics were central to the field's development after 1969, from the 1940s until the late 1960s it was professional politics that were crucial.

Historians at every level were enthusiastic about *NAW*. Even when they did not contribute articles, they would evaluate lists of potential sketches that Edward James sent out to specialists in a particular field. An example is Edward James's letter to Clement Eaton, a historian from the University of Kentucky. The two men had spoken at the annual AHA meeting in December 1959, and James wrote to Eaton several months later, reminding him that Eaton had tentatively agreed to write a sketch for *NAW*. In that same letter, he called on Eaton to consult on a list of notable Kentucky women.[38] Eaton declined the offer to write for *NAW* but gladly consulted on the list. Eaton also had his colleagues Thomas D. Clark and Bennett Wall look over the list, and Clark contributed a sketch of his own to the dictionary.[39] Both Clark and Wall were Southern Historical Association Executive Committee members, with Wall being the longtime executive secretary of the SHA. When Eaton returned the list to James, he affirmed, "I think you are undertaking an exceedingly valuable project."[40] This process of professional contact and collegial sharing and referral repeated itself dozens of times over the course of the decade. Edward and Janet James not only worked with their own professional network but also developed new links at the AHA, the SHA, and the MVHA/OAH. News about Radcliffe's work spread among historians.

Who were the historians and other scholars who answered the call to contribute to this academic venture? Of the roughly 700 contributors to *NAW*, almost 300 professional historians held a PhD in history.[41] Nine nationally known non-credentialed historians of women wrote sketches: Eleanor Flexner, Alma Lutz, Elizabeth Schlesinger, Sadie Daniel, Madeleine B. Stern, Ishbel Ross, Anne Lyon Haight, Norma Kidd Green, and Sophie Drinker. Archivists, librarians, museum directors, and curators contributed articles. This included African American archivists Dorothy Porter of Howard University and Jean Blackwell Hutson of the Schomburg Center for Research in Black Culture. The rest of the contributors were specialists with academic credentials in other fields like English, speech, theatre, music, political science, education, the sciences, medicine, religion, and business. A few articles were written by nonspecialists with unique access to family or institutional records.[42] Some 449 men contributed a total of 876 sketches, while 252 women authored a total of 483. These 252 women made up 36 percent of the whole group, a proportion that greatly exceeded the proportion of women historians in the profession in 1970, which stood at about 11 percent.[43] While most authors contributed only 1 biographical sketch, men contributed on average 1.95 articles and women 1.91 articles, indicating there was little difference in the number of articles contributed by sex.

In 1958, when the *NAW* project was initiated, most scholars did not consider the history of women as part of the broad historical tapestry, nor did they necessarily see it as forming a separate historical cloth. The staff at *NAW* commenced their project without much of an outline to guide their selection criteria. Only notable women who had lived between 1607 and 1950 would be considered for the first edition, or volumes 1–3. Which women warranted inclusion in the dictionary? The first list of notables was drawn from the 664 women listed in the *Dictionary of American Biography*. From there, the editors mainly counted on archivists and librarians familiar with the collections at the Radcliffe Women's Archives, the Sophia Smith Collection, and the Library of

Congress to suggest other women to include. An important source of nominees was professional historians who worked in areas of study where women played a prominent part, like social work, nursing, education, missionary work, and reform. Those who could contribute to the list from these fields were easily identified, and their specialized knowledge sped up the selection of notables.

For example, the editors consulted historians and archivists specializing in African American history to ask which African American women ought to be included. Eleanor Flexner and well-known African American scholars John Hope Franklin, E. Franklin Frazier, and Benjamin Quarles were consulted on this field, and they, in turn, referred the editors to African American women scholars and archivists with more specific knowledge of women. Franklin, Quarles, and Flexner wrote sketches on African American women, while Dorothy Porter, Marion Thompson Wright, Elsie Makel Lewis, Sadie Daniel, and Jean Blackwell Hutson consulted and contributed sketches on many others. Of these scholars, only Makel and Wright held a PhD in history. Makel earned her PhD from the University of Chicago in 1946.[44] She taught history at Howard University and was professionally active in the SHA, MVHA, and AHA.[45] In 1940, Marion Thompson Wright was the first Black woman to earn a history PhD in the United States (at Teachers College, Columbia University).[46] The other women had standing in the profession because of work they had done to gather sources in the history of Black women. Porter, for example, worked for years on the National Council of Negro Women's archives project, served as director of the Moorland-Spingarn Research Center, had worked with the Association for the Study of Negro Life and History, published in the *Journal of Negro History and Literature*, and served as archivist of Howard University's Negro Collection.[47] Sadie Daniel taught history at Miner Teachers College and was author of an early book on African American women's history, *Women Builders*. She too worked for the Association for the Study of Negro Life and History for a time.[48] Jean Blackwell Hutson was curator of the Schomburg Collection at the New York Public Library.[49]

The work these women did for *NAW* was some of the first in African American women's history vetted and accepted by mainstream male professors. Historian Pero Dagbovie has suggested that the few Black women scholars with credentials at midcentury were already toiling at the margins within academia and thus did not focus on the history of women.[50] They often were employed at historically Black colleges and, as Black women, were at pains to accommodate more traditional hierarchies of historical significance. This strategy was roughly analogous to that of the white women historians working in women's colleges in the first half of the twentieth century. They also specialized in traditional subfields of history so as to not be even further marginalized within the profession by taking up the topic of women. Dagbovie points out that Black women historians wrote meticulously documented histories to meet the profession's standards. Yet, Lewis and Thompson Wright's collaboration on *NAW* adds a dimension to our understanding of the development of Black women's history, suggesting it began to extend beyond the work of popular history and archivists before the 1970s—when, as we will see, Black women historians began to focus more intensively on the field's development.[51]

The team at *NAW* included content on African American and Native American historical figures at a time in the 1950s and 1960s when doing so was not at all a foregone conclusion. Archival materials on these groups were hard to come by, and scholars knowledgeable enough about the subject matter to write up competent biographical essays were also scarce. Forty-one African American sketches, fifteen Native American sketches, and five Indigenous Hawaiian sketches appeared in volumes 1–3. No Asian American women appeared. Only one verifiably Hispanic woman was featured. Altogether, BIPOC women made up 4 percent of the 1,359 women identified as notable.[52] It was a modest start that was improved upon in subsequent volumes published in 1980 and 2004. Volume 4, edited by Barbara Sicherman and Carol Hurd Green, doubled the representation of women of color to 8 percent. Volume 5, edited by Susan Ware, increased that to 25 percent of entries and brought Evelyn Brooks Higginbotham, Valerie Matsumoto, and Vicki Ruiz onto the advisory committee to represent their fields of African American, Japanese American, and Chicana history.[53]

Non-credentialed historians—generally historians of the women's movement or of specific groups of women—were another important group to make noteworthy nominations for inclusion in *NAW*. The most significant of these were Alma Lutz, Eleanor Flexner, Florence Hazzard, Ishbel Ross, and Elizabeth Schlesinger, all of whom had published popular histories.[54] These non-credentialed scholars consulted and wrote sketches for the project. Flexner alone contributed eleven biographical sketches; Ross authored nine. Most of the others authored one or two.

The question of how to determine which women were to be included in the dictionary came up early in the project's development. In 1959, Dr. Karl de Schweinitz prefaced his list of suggested women social workers with some questions about the meaning of the word "notable." He wrote, "Until I faced your project, I had not realized what a relative word notable is. Three and one half centuries of notability carry for me a different meaning than a span of 50 or 100 years, dating back from 1950. The longer the stretch, the more exacting the definition [need be]. Do you mean notable in their generation though forgotten now or notable as we view the significance of the past for the present? Do you mean notable in one community or notable in the nation or, so notable in a community as to have national influence?"[55] James replied that "important" women of both local and national relevance were being considered for inclusion. Moreover, he explained that a woman could be considered important enough for inclusion based on her prominence during her own time or as seen from the perspective of what her life and work could contribute to a present understanding of the past. James suggested that a local woman of lesser distinction from the South or the West might merit inclusion if her contributions were distinct and could reveal the diversity of women's activities across the nation. A woman social reformer from the South, for example, might be as notable as a nationally known figure by virtue of the hostile climate for social reform in that region and the greater effort and risks that she may have undertaken.[56] James pointed out that an African American woman's accomplishments might warrant inclusion in and of themselves but also as a lesson on the social, racial, economic, and legal barriers she had overcome to achieve them.[57]

The decision about each possible candidate for inclusion was not always clear-cut. Even an experienced scholar of women in American history, such as Elisabeth Anthony Dexter, found that the lists she was asked to consider contained names she didn't know, as well as other marginal figures she thought could be excluded.[58] Eleanor Flexner, author of the influential 1959 work *Century of Struggle*, reviewed potential notables from the ranks of the suffragists, labor women, and African American women. In the case of African American women, Flexner cautioned, "I should explain that I have no knowledge of a large number of these women because my own field of inquiry was definitely limited. Furthermore, in marking those I know A, B, C, I would hope that none of the women in these categories would be omitted since even a C would denote that in my estimation a woman had played a sufficiently important role in the Negro community and its history to justify including her."[59] When Flexner was unfamiliar with a name, she advised James to contact Dorothy Porter, a published author and the custodian of the Howard University Negro Collection.[60] Flexner reported that Porter was "greatly interested" in the Radcliffe project. Indeed, Porter served as a consultant and wrote two biographical sketches for the dictionary.[61]

If the experts on women were occasionally uncertain about inclusion, some male scholars realized that they didn't know much about the field at all. In 1959, labor historian John Hall, in going over the list of nominees, replied, "Boy is my face red! I thought I knew quite a bit about labor history, but your list had me putting down an astonishing number of O's. Even the Crispin gals and the Lowell Mill gals had my head swimming at times. How did you dig them up? Or am I just a dope?"[62] The "O" rating was reserved for figures the rater had absolutely no knowledge of and could not assess.[63] All of these difficulties point to the nascent development of the field in the late 1950s and 1960s. Even when the activities of women had been documented, such as in Caroline Ware's history of Lowell Mill girls, some male experts were struck by their own limited knowledge of women as historical actors.

John Hall's query "How did you dig them up?" was relevant. To be sure, *NAW* staffers drew on their own Radcliffe archives and those at other specialized repositories, like the Sophia Smith Collection. The records of *NAW* reveal, however, that the staff of *NAW* also used a sizable body of published work, much of which was not widely known, recognized, or heralded. *NAW* records show lengthy lists of published scholarship on American women already completed by 1962. One ninety-eight-page list compiled by *NAW* staff contains writings on American women published between 1939 and 1957 drawn largely from local histories, institutional histories, and the histories of academic disciplines and professions.[64] Another ninety-four-page list of works published between 1935 and 1962 was culled from the pages of the *American Historical Review*, indicating there had been widespread interest in the subject during these years.[65] In 1962, Warren F. Kuehl of Mississippi State University sent James a list of thirty-nine PhD dissertations on women in history completed by 1960.[66] Kuehl later contributed sketches on Fanny Fern Phillips Andrews and Lucia True Ames Mead.

John Hall's offhand quip "Or am I just a dope?" suggests that at some level historians were aware of what they did not know. Jack Hexter's famous 1946 quote about history having been unintentionally "mostly stag affairs" may be representative of many male historians' thinking.[67] Yet, by the early 1960s, a sizable minority of historians were willing to entertain the possibility that women, too, had shaped history. The multiplicity of views on the significance of women in history was tied to shifting hierarchies of historical significance in the United States. Greater attention to women's history had been put in motion by writings in progressive, social, and cultural history in the first half of the twentieth century. The endorsement of *NAW* by historians at every level of prominence helped spread the notion that women were legitimate historical subjects. These scholars working collaboratively—lending their names, scholarly efforts, and time to *NAW*—contributed to our understanding of what made a woman *notable* in history.

Intergenerational Links in the Field of US Women's History

Many established and early-career historians, both male and female, welcomed the opportunity to work on *Notable American Women*, heralding the dictionary as long overdue. Some of the women scholars involved became leaders in the Americanist wing of the women's history movement that grew after 1969. Their correspondence with Edward and Janet James left a record not dependent on memory of the field's early days. Still, ex post facto recollections have been key in constructing the narrative of just when the women's history field emerged.[68] Oral histories and reflective essays have mainly suggested that the field emerged only after 1969. And while many said the study of women was either an occasional sidebar to social history or not considered at all before 1969, there were exceptions to this narrative mainly among midcentury feminist non-credentialed scholars and a few professional scholars of both sexes. Understanding the field's trajectory becomes a more complicated process when one examines work on *NAW* from behind the scenes.

Retrospective testimonials and anecdotal accounts of the field's early history generally emphasize themes of exclusion, marginalization, and struggle within a male-dominated profession—and with good reason, as seen in earlier chapters. They describe women historians as not having the clout to shape historical scholarship and having instead to conform to disciplinary standards and subject matter within history's accepted intellectual frameworks. Common causal factors given for the legitimization of women's history within the American academy have been the central role of the modern women's liberation movement and the influence exerted on historians by other twentieth-century movements for social justice. These testimonials may share common tropes, but they are not uniform and rely on memory and are thus sometimes internally and collectively inconsistent. This is because historians trod distinct paths to the study of women's history in the late twentieth century and because the excitement that many women's historians in the 1970s felt about their participation in the movement stage of the field's development has led them to emphasize that phase in the field's development, perhaps unwittingly obscuring the work done within the historical "establishment" in the decades leading up to 1969. These generational perspectives and their central assertions about the roots of women's history remain valid. Indeed, they are the fulcrum upon which this entire history turns. It is the timeline of the women's history phenomenon that needs to be revised. An amended timeline allows us to incorporate work done in the United States between 1920 and 1969, centers work commenced in women's archives and history writing from 1943 forward, and allows us to see change over time more clearly.

In looking backward from the vantage point of the 1990s, many interpreted work on *NAW* as preceding the field's development and not as an integral part of the movement for women's history. But *NAW* was in fact a major achievement of the midcentury movement for women's historical archives. It helped legitimize the study of women within the academy. Any review of the field's creation and struggle for legitimacy must include an analysis of *NAW*'s production. Records left by some of the field's founders can help us date when the field's ground floor was laid out. For example, the careers of Joan Jensen, Carroll Smith-Rosenberg, Anne Firor Scott, Gerda Lerner, Mary Maples Dunn, Barbara

Welter, and Aileen Kraditor spanned fifty years. All but Dunn had published or taught about women in history before 1971. Each had some involvement with *NAW* in the early to mid-1960s. Their connection to the early years of the field reveals the professional roots of American women's history, quite apart from any explanation having to do with the emergence of the women's liberation movement in the late 1960s.

The example of Joan Jensen is illustrative. Jensen was a native of Minnesota who attended college in California in the 1950s, graduating from Pasadena City College before earning her advanced degrees in American military history from UCLA in 1962. She held a series of temporary college teaching positions in California and Arizona and almost dropped out of the historical profession completely before shifting her scholarly focus to American women's history in the 1970s, primarily on rural and farm women in different regions of the country. She won a position on the history faculty at New Mexico State University in 1976, where she taught for nearly two decades, and founded its women's studies program.[69]

In 1959, while still a graduate student at UCLA, Joan Jensen wrote an enthusiastic letter to Edward James after learning of the launch of *Notable American Women*:

> Last semester I had the unfortunate but enlightening experience of attempting some research on the history of American women for Dr. Donald Meyer who teaches Social History and is interested in this field. The lack of material and the uncritical tone of most of the available work forced me in desperation to prepare a paper devoted entirely to the aspects of the history of women that yet need research. Naturally, one of the first problems was the need for an adequate biographical dictionary, which I was happy to read in the AHR [*American Historical Review*] is now being assembled. May I offer my encouragement and cooperation. There is little here on the coast except for the two excellent collections at Scripps and the Huntington. . . . I am delighted that this "New Viewpoint" of Schlesinger which has been neglected for almost thirty years will now receive the criticism and scholarly attention it so badly needs.[70]

Several months later, James replied with "great interest" to Jensen's letter:

> The field of women's history has indeed suffered from scholarly neglect despite Mr. Schlesinger's essay in *New Viewpoints*. . . . I should like to call on you for any nominations you can make of Californians or other women. . . . I should also welcome any suggestions that may occur to you about possible contributors and especially any women on whom you yourself might be interested in writing. . . . I did not know about the

collection on the history of women at the Huntington Library. Does it have a particular custodian? I would be glad to hear about it and also the collection at Scripps. I should be interested some time to read the paper you wrote for Mr. Meyer. I have just had a letter from him, by the way, in which he speaks very well of your work for him.[71]

This reply indicates that in 1959, Edward James himself was still learning about available source material and potential experts on "women's history." Even more critical is Jensen's perspective as an early career historian with an interest in the emerging field already in 1959. The real-time perspective offers insight into the way she later reconstructed the story of her own route to women's history.

In a 2000 interview, Jensen stated that her interest in the history of women, kindled in graduate school by Donald Meyer's course in social history, was not acceptable to the established historians at UCLA, and they would not allow her to pursue the subject as part of her formal study. As a result of this discouragement, Joan Jensen went on to earn her PhD in 1962, completing a dissertation on internal security in the United States during World War I.

> I know that I wasn't the first person to want to do American women's history. Certainly, I wasn't the first one. But I was right at that, at that transition, where I really wanted to do it and the system wouldn't let me. The other thing was that there were no women teaching American history at UCLA at that point. Then, before I graduated, the dictionary of *Notable American Women* project was underway and they had put a little note in one of the historical newsletters saying, if you're interested contact us. So I contacted them [laughter]. This graduate student from out of nowhere saying, you know, I'd love to work on the project. So I think I did four or five little biographical sketches for them . . . [of] these people who are absolutely, totally unknown [laughter]. They apparently didn't have anybody on the West Coast who wanted to do these and so they had assigned them to this graduate student who wanted to do women's history.[72]

Jensen here establishes her early interest in American women's history and her participation in *NAW* at a ground-floor level. But she also clearly found little encouragement to pursue this scholarly interest. To the contrary, she seems to have been actively discouraged and pushed into a more traditional political dissertation topic, internal security during World War I. In the same interview, she creates a distinction between this activity and her later involvement in the field's development. "So, for the first ten years [I taught], I was not [professionally] active until when I came back into the profession. I dropped out for a couple of years. . . . I had to come back because I had to come back and get a job. Women's history was starting. Women's historians were coming into the profession by then. And I just came in with the rest of the women, as though I was just a brand-new [PhD] [laughter]."[73]

She suggests in this interview that before the crest of the women's movement brought many women into the profession, women's history was not being taught or done. And though Jensen worked in several faculty positions from 1962 to 1970, dropping out for a couple of years, in her narrative she links her *rediscovery* of women's history to her discovery of feminism.

> So I really sort of date my feminism from, you know, '69 and '70. But I came back. . . . I was really turned off on the history profession at that point, but I thought, well what else can I do? . . . And then women's history was being taught. The jobs were opening up. I had published, I had not only done those biographical articles, but I had taken the research on two of them and written articles and published them in historical journals. . . . I had a book published. . . . Plus, these other encyclopedic articles and so I was [laughter] qualified to teach at that point. No one was teaching women's history. So, I came back. . . . I volunteered at the feminist bookstore and started reading, started . . . talking to people and they said, well you know, you can be a feminist historian.[74]

Even though Jensen had written a graduate paper on "women's history" in 1959 and had published four sketches in *NAW* and two articles on women in journals between 1959 and 1970, and her professor Donald Meyer was interested in the social history of women, she could become a women's historian only after 1970, when "women's history was starting" as a result of the movement generated by a critical mass of feminist scholars. This movement made it possible for her to continue in the discipline because of the sudden availability of jobs in the field. Jensen's case shows how the professional and political experiences of feminist historians in the 1970s shaped their construction of the field's origins story. She first stepped foot onto her path toward women's history in 1959, but the path to a career devoted to the field was not sufficiently cleared until a decade later. That path was, however, being cleared and widened from the 1950s forward, and those working on *NAW* were the ones doing it.

For Mary Maples Dunn, a leading figure in the women's history movement in the 1970s, *NAW* was her first foray into writing about women as a professional historian. She completed a biographical sketch on Elizabeth Graeme Ferguson in 1963. Dunn had earned a PhD in history at Bryn Mawr College in 1959. She married Richard Dunn, a colonial historian, and in the 1970s she began to focus on colonial women's history. A member of the Berkshire Conference of Women Historians in the early 1960s and its president by 1973, she served as the program chair for the Second Berkshire Conference on the History of Women, which was held at Radcliffe in 1974. In 1968, Edward James again asked Dunn to contribute a sketch, this time on Hanna Penn, someone particularly well known to Dunn, who was a William Penn scholar, but she declined.[75]

Dunn recalled her work with *NAW* and the state of women's history in the 1960s in a 2001 interview.[76] She described joining the Berkshire Conference of Women Historians at the prompting of a Bryn Mawr history professor. She depicted the group as an association that sought to ameliorate the professional isolation many felt when attending professional meetings, feelings that were particularly acute during informal "smokers" where men gathered to smoke, drink, and introduce their more promising graduate students. She reported that the Berkshire Conference mainly existed to provide moral support for women historians and did not have an academic focus. Dunn stated in relation to the Berkshire Conference, "In those days nobody was doing women's history."[77] In this reflection, Dunn appears unaware of the quiet ferment growing across the United States and centered at the Radcliffe Women's Archives. She did not mention her own 1963 contribution to *NAW*, even when she referred in passing to *NAW*'s first edition in 1971.[78] This remark regarding *NAW* followed her comment that "in the seventies, those of us who were working in women's history certainly believed that we were exploring an area which had not been tilled much at all."[79]

Dunn did acknowledge that in the 1960s, "many people who were doing social history in the colonial period were working on things like community studies and so on, where women were part of what they were doing. Not with the same kind of intentionality, but part of it."[80] Intentionality seems to be key to understanding why many historians of women, even those who had done some work in the history of women earlier, often date the field's emergence to 1969 or later. With a few exceptions, social historians who paid some attention to women in history before the women's history movement included women as a part of a much larger historical whole. By 1970, increasing numbers of feminist scholars would come to see this approach as inadequate. Though the new feminist scholars did not consider women in isolation from society, they insisted that the main focus of their scholarship had to be women in society.[81] Yet, the architects of *NAW* at the Radcliffe Women's Archives went about their project with both intentionality and a keen sense of women's integral part in history. The massive thirteen-year undertaking to create an authoritative reference work on women was nothing if not intentional.

The example of Carroll Smith-Rosenberg, who wrote a sketch on Florence Bascom for *NAW* in 1964, reveals the web of professional influence at work on behalf of the history of women by the early 1960s.[82] Smith-Rosenberg earned a PhD in American history from Columbia University in 1968. Her dissertation advisor was Robert Cross, though she later characterized their relationship as distant. Smith-Rosenberg was almost certain that Cross's wife, Barbara—an English professor at Barnard College—had read and commented on her dissertation rather than Robert; she reported being able to recognize Barbara's handwriting in the margins.[83] Still, Smith-Rosenberg benefited from the fact that historians like Cross, William Leuchtenberg, Richard Hofstadter, and David Donaldson were open to working with women graduate students at a time when this was far from routine or expected.[84] Historian Robert Handy of Union Theological Seminary also worked with Smith-Rosenberg on her dissertation. Smith-Rosenberg was well situated at Columbia in the 1960s, one of the most highly regarded history departments in the nation.[85]

Smith-Rosenberg's experience at Columbia overlapped with those of others in its history program or at its women's coordinate, Barnard. This important cohort of early women's historians included Gerda Lerner, Aileen Kraditor, Ann J. Lane, Lois Banner, Dorothy Ross, Barbara Sicherman, William Chafe, Regina Morantz-Sanchez, Carol Berkin, Estelle Freedman, Jacquelyn Hall, Joan Kelly-Gadol, Renate Bridenthal, Bonnie S. Anderson, Mary Nolan, Paula Hyman, Linda Kerber, and Sarah Pomeroy.[86] What this long list illustrates, in combination with those featured in chapters 2–4, is that contrary to the historiographic narrative shared by contemporary women's and gender historians since the 1990s, the impulse to create this field was not limited to half a dozen pioneering scholars prior to the 1970s. Indeed, there were dozens of historians and archivists working toward this goal at midcentury.

Another member of the Columbia history community in the 1960s was Professor Annette Baxter, who taught American history at Barnard College. Baxter wrote three sketches for *NAW* between 1962 and 1967. She taught her course, Women in America, for the first time at Barnard in 1967 after she and Barbara Cross had begun working on it in 1965.[87] In a letter Cross wrote to Baxter, she mentioned that she had shared news of the course with Oscar Handlin of Harvard, who thought it was a good idea. Concerned with the staying power of the course, Cross suggested, "Convincing them it is academically respectable may be easier if we have more 'texts' to offer and I am increasingly enthusiastic about your documents in the history of American women idea. . . . As I see it, the series would bring major intellectual and social-cultural experiences of American people into a new focus, by revealing the shape of those experiences as lived by women." Linda Kerber, a Barnard undergraduate, remembered Baxter's 1967 course, identifying it as one of the earliest on women.[88]

Smith-Rosenberg's 1968 dissertation, "Religion and the Rise of the American City," focused on nineteenth-century female reformers' opposition to prostitution in New York City.[89] Both Rosenberg's and Baxter's articles for *NAW* between 1962 and 1966 suggest their focus on women may have been strengthened by their association with the Radcliffe project.[90] Furthermore, the connections among the Crosses, Baxter, Kerber, and Smith-Rosenberg strongly indicate that support for women's history found fertile ground in the Columbia/Barnard history community as early as 1963. Thus, Harvard and Columbia are two early linked nodes of activity in favor of the legitimization of American women's history.

Barbara Cross authored three biographical sketches for *NAW*; Robert Cross authored two. In 1960 Edward James requested that Robert Cross write on women reformers. In their ensuing exchange of letters between 1960 and 1965, Robert Cross recommended his Columbia students to James. He thought Dorothy Ross, Gerda Lerner, and Carroll Smith-Rosenberg would be likely contributors. In a letter, Cross described Ross as "an unusually capable young woman" studying for her orals. In 1963 he confirmed for James that Gerda Lerner was "an extremely competent woman . . . in her first year of graduate work at Columbia. I am sure she would do a good job for you."[91] And in response to learning that Smith-Rosenberg had agreed to write a sketch for *NAW*, Cross wrote, "I am glad that Carroll Rosenberg has joined your task force. She is a highly competent young lady."[92] It seems clear that Cross willingly recommended those women graduate students who he knew were working in women's history, even if "competent" was the highest praise he could offer. Furthermore, Smith-Rosenberg's scholarly interest in women was accepted within the Columbia history department before the women's history movement and her involvement with it commenced.

Gerda Lerner, too, was in contact with *NAW* in the early 1960s as she completed graduate school at Columbia University. As early as 1963, Edward James contacted Lerner to write a sketch on a prominent suffragist whose papers were in New York City, where Lerner lived. James had initially gotten Lerner's name from Miriam Holden, former suffragist and occasional consultant to the Radcliffe Women's Archive.[93] Holden had allowed Lerner to use her large private collection of materials in connection with Lerner's work on the Grimké sisters.[94] In 1963 Lerner entered the Columbia PhD program with the understanding that she would turn her novel on Angelina and Sarah Grimké into a dissertation.[95]

Lerner declined to write for *NAW* in 1964, citing other commitments and her "present occupation with abolitionist women." But she did offer to be a resource on the topic and later contributed an article to *NAW* on African American educator and abolitionist Sara Mapps Douglass.[96] Sarah and Angelina Grimké, the subjects of her dissertation, had already been assigned to historian Betty Fladeland of Southern Illinois University at Carbondale. Being overbooked in terms of professional and writing commitments was the most common reason scholars gave for declining to contribute to *NAW*. Other common reasons were that they knew too little about the subject or lived too far from archival materials to undertake research for the modest author's fee offered by Radcliffe.[97]

Lerner was unusual in her graduate cohort in that her interest in the history of women predated her entry into college by some years. After coming to the United States in 1939 as a refugee fleeing the Nazi occupation of Austria, she created a new life that included work, marriage, and family as well as activism. She helped found the Los Angeles chapter of the popular front women's organization the Congress of American Women. It was in this group in the late 1940s that Lerner was introduced to the idea of focusing on women in history, leftist feminists, and the American race problem.[98] "I had been a community organizer and peace activist all in between and before I went to Columbia. I was very active in an organization called Congress of American Women. That was a very feminist organization. We did Women's History. And I had already collaborated with Eve Merriam and written a musical which was performed off Broadway, *Singing of Women*, so I was well into Women's History through that. That was long before I ever became an academic."[99]

Lerner's familiarity with American race relations grew when she witnessed attempts to integrate white neighborhoods in New York City in Bedford -Stuyvesant and Knickerbocker Village in the 1950s.[100] These experiences sparked her curiosity about the history of race in America and her ambition to write a novel on abolitionists and women's rights activists Angelina and Sarah Grimké. She set her mind on the genre of historical fiction in 1957 and, wanting her novel to be historically accurate, signed up for part-time classes at the New School for Social Research in 1959. Counselors advised her to register formally so that she could earn credits. She did just that and completed her BA at the New School in 1963. The New School for Social Research had been founded in 1917 by progressive academics, including historian Charles Beard, husband of women's history pioneer Mary Beard.[101] To Lerner's surprise, anthropology professor May Edel suggested Lerner go on to graduate school. And so Lerner, at the age of forty-nine, formally applied to become a graduate student in Columbia's history department. In her interview with the admissions committee, she divulged her interest in "women's history" to a group of men who, she recalled, weren't quite sure what that was.[102]

Gerda Lerner launched her academic career with vigor. She had already completed a great deal of research on her intended dissertation topic while at the New School. There she also offered perhaps one of the first courses in the country on women's history, Great Women in American History, and another titled The Role of Women in American Life and Culture.[103] Lerner gave a series of talks on Pacifica Radio and lectured on the topic of women in American history to women's civic groups. One such talk, "Something to Crow About: Women in American History," was presented to the Bronx River Women's Young

Men's-Young Women's Hebrew Association of America.[104] Lerner completed coursework for the MA by 1965, took her orals, and earned the PhD in 1966.[105] Her first article, "The Grimké Sisters and the Struggle against Race Prejudice" (1963), was published before she earned her PhD.[106] Then in quick succession she published her dissertation (1967) and two readers, *The Woman in American History* (1971), followed by *Black Women in White America: A Documentary History* (1972).[107]

Lerner's leadership in the women's history movement from 1969 forward is renowned.[108] Before that, however, Gerda Lerner—aside from her age and gender—was like any newly minted PhD, preoccupied by building a research agenda and a scholarly network, teaching, and publishing. She taught full-time at Long Island University in Brooklyn and was well regarded there due to her strong publishing record. Her professional contacts included two of her Columbia professors, Eric McKitrick and Carl Degler, who wrote recommendation letters for her for jobs and fellowships.[109] She attended annual meetings of the OAH and AHA during these years, where she befriended Anne Firor Scott, Janet James, Clarke Chambers, and historians of women just entering the profession as graduate students. She participated in Columbia University's by-invitation-only Seminars in American Civilization series starting in 1968. This seminar linked her to active and prominent historians.[110]

Lerner's professional successes by the late 1960s were not enough to eclipse the marginalization she experienced at professional meetings or entirely put to rest her strong sense that her field of specialization was not yet legitimate. She recalled in a colorful anecdote in 1999,

> One of my first memories on the status of things was right after the book was published, and it got very good reviews. . . . I went to a convention, so that must have been maybe the '68 convention, and I asked to speak to the representative of HoughtonMifflin, the textbook representative. I proposed that I do a textbook on women. You know what he did? He burst out laughing, and his flunkies sat there laughing uproariously. It was that funny, "On women? Is there enough to fill a book?" Well, I went away, and I talked to other publishers. Al Young was interested in my doing this. I wanted to do a documentary history of women because by then I had been teaching, and I could see that the documents just weren't available readily.[111]

Chauvinism was clearly still pervasive, and women/women's historians, like Lerner, Scott, and Mary Elizabeth Massey, had to be extremely tough to be able to persist in their work in the face of belittling ridicule and denigrations about women as historical subjects among some historians and publishers—which may be why it took a particularly potent brand of feminist activist historian, and plenty of them working together for institutional change, to fully launch the field. Nevertheless, we can see that there were colleagues and publishers who were interested and supportive of the developing field. Not only did Lerner hold a Columbia PhD and have expansive professional contacts, but her publishing pace and active participation in the OAH and AHA positioned her to become a leader in the women's history movement by 1969.

Anne Firor Scott, too, wrote six articles for *NAW*, a fact that meshes with her view of the centrality of *Notable American Women* in the field's development. The details of Scott's path to women's history from 1958 to 1970 have been recounted already. She was a giant in the field of American women's history for four decades.[112] Scott's professional activism included early work on behalf of women's history. At the December 1966 annual AHA meeting, she chaired a panel on the history of American women. She reported to program chair William Leuchtenberg in January 1967 that the session "New Perspectives on the Woman's Movement in the United States" was received with "lively audience interest" in a room that was perhaps two-thirds full. Two papers were presented. Gerda Lerner's paper was "Changes in the Economic and Social Status of Women, 1800–1840." Scott reported that some of Lerner's assertions were challenged by Edward James and Eleanor Flexner, the commentators for the session. Lerner had defended against the challenges by sharing "a good deal of documentation which had not appeared in the original paper," making it clear that "the paper was on firmer ground than had appeared from her first formulation." David Pivar's paper, "The Role of Women's Rights Leaders in Social Reconstruction, 1876–1900," examined the social purity movement, which Pivar argued had absorbed the women's movement and other progressive causes. James and Flexner totally rejected his thesis and found his evidence unconvincing. Pivar could not effectively meet their objections.[113] In November, in preparation for the conference panel, in fact, Flexner had alerted Scott to her criticism of both papers. Flexner said she found them "rather depressing— though the Lerner paper is a good deal better than the other." She suggested Pivar's paper be rejected and he not be allowed to present it: "I do hate to take anybody's work apart in public as Mr. P's needs to be—that sort of thing should be done in the privacy of a personal conference!"[114] This incident, complete with lively audience response, critical debates over the value of the papers, and the authors' subsequent vigorous defenses, all point to an active interest in the field in late 1966.

Scott reflected on the feeling of being a pioneer in the field of women's history, commenting in an interview on a few important colleagues in her network: "There weren't any [support networks in the early '60s]. Well, there were five of us, you know. There was Barbara Solomon, Janet James, Eleanor Flexner, Gerda Lerner, and me, and that was it. I did have a lot of support from

Julia Spruill before she died. She just kept saying, 'Yes, yes, yes. Do it, do it, do it.' But there was nothing like such as you've got. Right here at UNC you have more graduate student friends than I had in the whole USA in 1970—people who were interested in women's history."[115] Scott also acknowledged the enthusiastic verbal support she received from male colleagues Bernard Bailyn, Fletcher Green, Oscar Handlin, Donald Fleming, and Robert Durden. She recalled how George Frederickson had positively reviewed her groundbreaking *Southern Lady: From Pedestal to Politics, 1830–1930*, thus immeasurably helping her career.[116] She recognized that the James duo were doing "major work" for the field with their *Notable American Women*.[117] Of other pioneers in the 1960s, she recalled,

> I think we pioneers were rather proud of ourselves. . . . I used to room with Barbara Solomon, have breakfast with Gerda Lerner, always talked to Janet James. . . . She was the co-editor of *Notable American Women*. . . . She never got her just deserts. She was a very bright woman. She wrote the first dissertation in women's history, ever, at Harvard. It didn't get published for thirty-seven years, or something like that. . . . Then she was at Boston College where they didn't promote her for years, and years, and years. I always liked to talk to Janet. Eleanor Flexner was a good friend, a quirky old lady, but a good friend. But it was not so much a group as it was one-on-one relationships.[118]

With a powerful and growing "network" of professional colleagues to call on, and who knew to call on her as a specialist in the history of American women, Scott quickly developed both leadership and scholarly abilities. Her links to central institutions in the historical discipline—the history departments at UNC Chapel Hill, Harvard, and Columbia; the MVHA/OAH, the AHA, and the SHA—uniquely positioned her to become a leader and a mentor to many aspiring young historians of women by 1969.

The response to the publication of *Notable American Women* from historians, librarians, and students of American history was overwhelmingly positive. Reviews came out in the most prestigious professional journals: In 1972, Anne Firor Scott wrote a nine-page essay review for the *Journal of Southern History*. Marjorie Gutheim reviewed *NAW* for the *New England Quarterly*. Bell Wiley gave a positive review in *American History Illustrated*. Then in 1973 *NAW* was reviewed in the *American Historical Review* by veteran historian of Southern women Mary Massey; in the *William and Mary Quarterly* by Barbara Welter; and in the *Journal of American History* by Mary Benson. *NAW* was also reviewed in more popular venues, sometimes quite colorfully.[119] Taken together, the reviews heralded *NAW* as long overdue, scholarly, inclusive, authoritative, meticulously researched, well-edited, and a boon to the development of American history generally and American women's history specifically. Eleanor Flexner wrote Edward James in 1973, "Please give my warmest regards to Janet, and bear with me if I tell you again that I think *NAW* was a magnificent work, and I am prouder of having had my little finger in it than of anything I have ever worked on!"[120] This praise, from a scholar some credited with launching the modern field of women's history with her 1959 book, *Century of Struggle*, is a particularly fitting tribute to *Notable American Women*'s influence.[121]

Today, historians of women in the United States rarely acknowledge that the academic field of American women's history has roots much deeper than the work of the feminist scholars of the 1970s.[122] Yet many of them have academic lineages that include those who were involved in the production of *NAW* from 1955 to 1971. A significant array of historians with and without PhDs, archivists, feminists, and librarians created a knowledge base on American women. By uncovering documentary sources, building specialized collections, publishing early monographs, and collaborating on reference works, they provided the groundwork for the field's explosive development in the 1970s and beyond.

In 1975, Carroll Smith-Rosenberg identified the 1950s–1970s as the period of "traditional women's history" and classified *Notable American Women* as the capstone to a women's history acceptable within the "profession's traditional hierarchies of significance," that is, history about publicly and politically active women. Then she characterized her own early work and the work of others in the late 1960s and early 1970s as a departure.[123] Epistemologically speaking, her analysis made sense in 1975 when so much was in flux. Yet, this more nuanced understanding of the field's early historiography was quickly lost to view by the 1980s. It was even distorted by assertions that there had been no women's history field prior to the 1970s. *Notable American Women* was much more than a capstone to an earlier era. *NAW* rescued the field from popularizers and claimed women's history from "amateurs" without dismissing the important work they had done. Indeed, it sought their input. *NAW* used the historical discipline's strict standards to concentrate knowledge about American women with the goal of inspiring new scholarly work. *NAW*'s publication is the point at which "women's history" became a legitimate area of study. It crystallized in three volumes the work done in the field since the 1940s and arguably since the 1920s.

This examination of the production of *Notable American Women* reveals the presence of a wide nexus of historians within the discipline's mainstream who were supportive and even enthusiastic about the new field. Despite the objections of some male scholars in the 1970s and 1980s, the field had powerful allies from several generational cohorts and multiple subfields who were at work building a foundation for the field. Many of the leaders of the movement for women's history forged their skills during the years that *NAW* was being produced. Incontrovertibly, *Notable American Women*'s publication by the Belknap Press at Harvard and the widespread support it garnered from within the historical profession sent a signal that the study of women was a legitimate academic pursuit whose time had come.

Chapter 6

Feminist Historians

Politics, Power, and the History of Women, 1900–1968

> The whole background of women's history should be an essential part of
> every woman's education, and in the postwar revamping of curricula it
> should find a place. Without it, young women today have no backlog of
> self-respect or inspiration to draw upon. Without it, they have no accurate
> estimate of their place in society, or of their great responsibilities.
>
> —Alma Lutz, 1946

To what extent were the scholarly choices of early to mid-twentieth-century historians of women a corollary to their politics? Writing histories of women was
one strategy that women's rights activists used to make the case for American
women's increased participation in politics and public life from the founding of
the republic through the nineteenth century. This was true for those who wrote
in the aftermath of the American Revolution, during the social movements
of the early nineteenth century, and in the years before, during, and after the
formalization of the history profession in the 1880s, when both women and
people of color in the United States intensified their struggles for human and
civil rights.[1] It was also true of the many historians of women featured thus
far in this work. During the first seven decades of the twentieth century, their
scholarly and feminist perspectives were often mutually constitutive.

The first American writers who offered a challenge to traditional male hierarchies of historical significance wrote within the contexts of the American
Revolution's aftermath and the social movements of the early nineteenth century. In the 1780s and 1790s, for instance, Judith Sargent Murray, responding to women's historic, legal, and educational subordination in the young
republic, wrote of the natural rights of women in historical context.[2] In the
nineteenth century, abolitionists and women's rights activists like Lydia Maria
Child, Angelina and Sarah Grimké, Margaret Fuller, and Frederick Douglass
reframed American history to center the fight for human rights. They shone
a light on American history that emphasized the experiences of women and
African Americans in a society that subordinated and disenfranchised both.
From Angelina Grimké's call in 1836 to the Christian women of the South to
look to the historical examples offered by women of the past for inspiration
and moral courage, to Elizabeth Cady Stanton and her 1848 collaborators at

Seneca Falls speaking of the historic and "repeated injuries and usurpations of man against woman," to Douglass asking, "What to the slave is the fourth of July?" in 1852, we learn that human rights activists have long perceived the power of history to influence minds, shape culture, and change unjust laws. Reframing historical narratives, recasting the actors, and identifying origins stories and starting points have been central to legitimizing any assertion of national belonging, rights, and power.[3]

In that vein, in 1876, after thirty years of frustrated and divided activism, the leaders of the National Woman Suffrage Association—Elizabeth Cady Stanton and Susan B. Anthony—began work on their *History of the Woman Suffrage Movement*. This work reflected their foundational belief that "the *history* of mankind is a *history* of repeated injuries and usurpations on the part of man toward women having in direct object the establishment of an absolute tyranny over her," a tyranny of subordinations designed to "destroy her confidence in her own powers, to lessen her self-respect, and to make her willing to lead a dependent and abject life." This line, taken from the 1848 Seneca Falls Declaration of Sentiments and Resolutions, made women central subjects of American history. Here, they demonstrated their understanding that women's erasure from historical accounts was one way tyranny was maintained. By writing their own history, they hoped to ensure that future generations of women would know of those who had struggled before them.

The first four volumes of *History of the Woman Suffrage Movement* were published in 1881, 1882, and 1886 under the editorship of Stanton, Anthony, and Matilda Joslyn Gage. The fifth and sixth volumes were edited by Ida Husted Harper. Published in 1922, the last two volumes emphasized the work of the National American Woman Suffrage Association from 1890 to 1920, during a time when the movement presented a relatively united front in the struggle for women's right to vote. As many historians of the woman suffrage movement have shown, this front was only as unified as the racially segregated, economically unequal, ethnically, and religiously divided nation was.[4] Therefore, the work was flawed in its many exclusions and narrow factional perspectives. It excluded information about rival factions of suffragists. It glossed over the racial biases of Southern white suffragists and the strategic expediency of those willing to compromise with white supremacy to win a woman suffrage amendment to the Constitution. It mostly ignored the suffrage work of women of color. Yet the very act of committing their interpretation of women's history to paper was a radical act of historical validation—an observation made in the work of Lisa Tetrault. It aimed to restore to women their "self-respect" as people, as citizens, and as the subjects of their own history and lives. Other leading suffragists—like Carrie Chapman Catt, Alice Paul, and Maud Wood Park—also worked to preserve and tell of their own pivotal roles in the movement. Most kept records of their individual and collective efforts to secure women the right to vote on equal terms with the men of the country, and they deposited them in archives like the Library of Congress, the Radcliffe Women's Archives, the Sophia Smith Collection, and university and college special collections across the country.[5]

In parallel moves, African American women chroniclers pieced together the fragments of Black women's history in the early twentieth century. These efforts occurred in the context of the Jim Crow era from the 1890s to the 1950s when Black educators and civic activists were conscious of the need to provide African Americans with a positive interpretation of the Black experience in America as one of both accomplishment and struggle against systemic racism.[6] In 1926, for example, Hallie Quinn Brown, a prominent Black educator, reformer, and writer, published *Homespun Heroines and Other Women of Distinction*. Brown, an 1873 graduate with a bachelor of science degree from Wilberforce University in Ohio, worked as a teacher and educator, including at the Tuskegee Institute. She was active through the turn of the twentieth century in the temperance movement, the International Council of Women, and the National Association of Colored Women. Similarly, Sadie Daniel published *Women Builders* in 1931. Her book featured seven Black women whose contributions to the Black community and racial uplift were exceptionally noteworthy. Historian Rayford Logan reviewed Daniel's work positively in the *Journal of Negro History*. His view was that the women featured in the book should be held up as models of activism and that African American schools should assign her work instead of books about Queen Elizabeth I, whom he called a sixteenth-century "flapper" and "Queen of high-jackers." These authors did not necessarily see themselves as writing "women's history." Yet, they nevertheless understood that inspirational examples of civically active Black women of the past fed the souls of contemporary Black women and social activists. Other African American women writers, archivists, and librarians amassed evidence of African American women of the past. Beginning in the 1920s, librarian Dorothy Porter of the Moorland-Spingarn Research Center at Howard University and Ernestine Rose (a white woman), Catharine Latimer, and Jean Blackwell Hutson of New York's Schomburg Center collected papers, data, and testimonies. Zora Neale Hurston recorded Black oral histories for the Federal Writers' Project during the New Deal. They were seeking to correct and augment a record plagued by a dearth of sources. A 1940 bibliographical report composed by Latimer and a report by the Works Progress Administration complained of the paucity of sources on women to be found at the Schomburg Center for Research in Black Culture in New York City. Nevertheless, all of these efforts highlight Black women's participation in the larger New Negro History movement of the early twentieth century and show the emphasis they placed on Black women's centrality to community service and civil rights activism.[7] This early work had profound feminist implications in its valuing of Black female experience and agency within the larger sweep of American history.

Similarly, as we've seen in earlier chapters, suffragists, feminists, female civic activists, and academic feminists began to formalize women's history by establishing archival repositories. Maud Wood Park's donation of National American Woman Suffrage Association and League of Women Voters materials formed the nucleus of Radcliffe's Woman's Rights Collection in 1943. Mary Beard—a former suffragist and progressive historian—left the materials given to her by feminist peace activist Rosika Schwimmer for the defunct World Center for Women's Archives to both the Radcliffe Women's Archives and the Sophia Smith Collection at Smith College. Political scientist Mary Earhart Dillon, the biographer of Frances Willard, donated her own papers about Carrie Chapman Catt to Radcliffe. Catt herself donated her papers to the Library of Congress, as did Mary Church Terrell of the National Association of Colored Women, Alice Paul, and the National Woman's Party.[8]

Many of the first university-trained historians of women had been involved in the woman suffrage movement and other progressive causes from the 1890s to 1920. Lucy Maynard Salmon was a prominent political historian and the first female member of the American Historical Association's executive council. She taught at Vassar College and published pioneering works on domestic service and women's work in 1897 and 1906. Joining the suffrage movement in the 1910s, she served in the National College Equal Suffrage League and on the Executive Advisory Council of the Congressional Union for Woman Suffrage. She carried on this work despite opposition from the president of Vassar. As a professor of American history, Salmon influenced many Vassar women, including Caroline Ware and possibly Alma Lutz. Lutz was a 1912 graduate of Vassar who became a member of the National Woman's Party, wrote pamphlets and news releases for the organization, and authored numerous books in women's history.[9]

As Mary Beard's interest in history, suffrage, and feminism developed, women's history became the frame for her political worldview. While in England with her husband at Ruskin Hall, a free university, from 1898 to 1902, she read the feminist classic *Women and Economics* by American feminist Charlotte Perkins Gilman. She lived across the street from suffragist Emmeline Pankhurst and her daughters and socialized with them regularly. In their company she imbibed their radical form of suffragism and developed a strong interest in working-class women's rights. After her return to the United States and a brief time spent in graduate school at Columbia University, she took a decade to focus on raising her two young children. In due course Beard became active in the American suffrage movement. She joined the Equality League for Self-Supporting Women, the New York Women's Trade Union League, the New York State Woman Suffrage Party, and the Wage Earners' Suffrage League, where she served as editor of its newspaper, *The Woman Voter*. By 1913, Beard left the more conservative New York State Woman Suffrage Party to join the newly created Congressional Union led by Alice Paul and Lucy Burns, both of whom had also been influenced by English suffragists. When she broke with Paul and the National Woman's Party in 1923, it was over the party's single-minded focus on the Equal Rights Amendment, which conflicted with Beard's progressive feminism and its concern for working women.[10] Progressive feminists of the era focused on meeting the material needs of working-class women. They lobbied to pass and preserve legislation that would protect women workers. Equal rights feminists of the National Woman's Party, on the other hand, focused narrowly on passing an equal rights amendment to the Constitution that would eliminate sex-specific labor laws. They believed such an amendment would offer women relief from legal discrimination and give educated and professional women access to political power and equal opportunity. The two goals were incompatible. These political alignments reflected the tensions in the movement between ideological commitment to sexual equality and the fight for economic justice for working people. As feminist organizations struggled to develop platforms and policies that would work across the divides of class and race, feminist historians grappled with those conflicts in their writing.

For Beard, acknowledging and correcting women's exclusion from written history—which implied a subordination and devaluing of women by male writers of history—was radical in and of itself. But after 1923, she was hard-pressed to reconcile the conceptual tension between the mainline equal rights feminist stance that women had historically been oppressed and her view that women had been equal co-makers of civilization with men. As Suzanne Lebsock has suggested, Beard was so determined to prove women were active civilization builders in her *Woman as Force in History* that she grossly understated and even misrepresented the extent to which women's rights had been suppressed within the Anglo-American legal context.[11] The conceptual hurdle facing Beard was the idea that members of an oppressed and exploited group might simultaneously exercise influence and historical agency. Indeed, Beard was charting new historiographic territory with few signposts to help her on her journey.

Beard's suffragist and progressive politics were closely linked to her scholarship. In 1914, she commented on the civics textbook that she and Charles were writing, insisting that "civics concerns the whole community, and women constitute half that community."[12] In 1915, she wrote *Women's Work in Municipalities*, which became a foundational essay on women's political power and the concept of municipal housekeeping in the Progressive Era. As progressive historians, Mary and Charles Beard believed that the history of civilization could be used as an "instrument" *for* civilization and progress.[13] Moreover, when it came to developing the history of women, Mary noticed early on that women were largely absent from history books, and she determined to change that. Mary Beard developed powerful insights on women's increasing participation in the labor force, reform, and politics. She grew to understand the need for "women's history" as part of contemporary women's assertion of their own personhood. In 1943, when responding to an objection to a women's archive and a proposed course in women's history at Smith College, she insisted that developing both would "make women realize that to be 'people' they must be recognized as such and not lost to view."[14] For Mary Beard, recovery of women's part in human history was essential to securing full rights for women as people and citizens; the writing of women's history was a profoundly political act. Beard promoted women's history in the textbooks she wrote with Charles Beard. She worked to establish women's history archives. And she wrote pioneering, if theoretically and organizationally muddled, monographs on the history of women. Beard recognized that the struggle for women's equality rested on women having a firm grasp both of their past and of their place in the current historical moment. This *feminist historicism*, as Beard practiced it, indicted male writers and teachers of history who had omitted women as responsible for the widespread impression that women were not historically significant and deserved neither credit for building society nor a share in power, rights, or privileges. Beard's scholarly and political activities from 1900 to 1958 reveal a broad articulation of the concept of feminist historicism.

Beard's contemporary Elizabeth Bancroft Schlesinger was also a suffragist. After 1920, she belonged to the League of Women Voters and the American Association of University Women. She served on the advisory committee for the Massachusetts Committee for the Equal Rights Amendment through the 1960s. She was married to Arthur Schlesinger Sr., and together they helped found the Radcliffe Women's Archives at Radcliffe College. Elizabeth was active as a volunteer with the archive from 1943 until her death in 1977. She earned her BA from Ohio State University in 1910, and, though she had no formal graduate training in history, she taught high school English and history until her marriage. Civically engaged, notably in the National Woman's Party and the Massachusetts Committee for the Equal Rights Amendment, she wrote and spoke regularly on women's rights and women's history. She published an excerpt from a speech she delivered to the Mother's Study Club of Cambridge in 1942 in *Equal Rights*, the organ of the National Woman's Party. Titled "Is Feminism Old-Fashioned?," she argued it was not. Elizabeth published regularly in newspapers and scholarly journals including the *Boston Globe*, the *New England Quarterly*, *William and Mary Quarterly*, the *New York Historical Society Quarterly*, and *American Heritage*, often engaging the topic of women writers and cultural influencers of the nineteenth century. She reviewed work on African American history. Her early commitment to women's history was recognized when the Radcliffe Women's Archives was renamed in 1965 as the "Arthur and Elizabeth Schlesinger Library on the History of Women in America."[15]

Elizabeth Bancroft Schlesinger held that there was a connection between feminist politics and women's history. In a 1962 review of a biography on Lucy Stone, she wrote that the author "believes that Lucy's fame rests on the single fact that she refused to take her husband's name. This may be true for those indifferent to the history of American women, but for those who care, her name will always recall her contributions to the progress of her sex." Schlesinger then connected Stone's life to women's lives in 1962 and suggested that contemporary women had not yet achieved the goals set out by Lucy Stone, neither in government nor in society. She asked rhetorically, "Have women failed to live up to the expectations of these early pioneers? Are they indifferent to the political power they now possess?"[16] In this rhetorical formulation, Schlesinger revealed her belief that knowledge of women's past struggles is essential to contemporary women's appreciation of their rights and willingness to exercise power.

Another feminist and civic activist, Miriam Young Holden of New York, accumulated one of the largest private collections of women's history sources in the United States. She amassed the collection between 1920 and 1960, eventually donating everything to Princeton University in 1977. Her life is a story of combined interest in women's history and civic engagement. She participated in Mary Beard's efforts on behalf of the World Center for Women's Archives in the 1930s and later served on the Advisory Board of the Women's Archives at Radcliffe. Her political and civic affiliations included the National Woman's Party, the Urban League, the settlement house movement, the Lucy Stone League, the National Women's Trade Union League, the National Association for the Advancement of Colored People, and family planning groups.[17] She herself was not a writer, but her avid interest in collecting shows that she understood the relevance of history to social progress.

This same type of historical consciousness was particularly evident in the work of Alma Lutz. After graduating from Vassar College in 1912, Lutz was active in the suffrage movement, and after 1920 she affiliated with the National Woman's Party—the major group advocating for passage of the Equal Rights Amendment from 1923 to 1972. She was a writer and editor for the party's organ, *Equal Rights*, working on everything from leaflets and pamphlets to major articles on contemporary women's issues. She regularly published in major American newspapers and periodicals, including the *Christian Science Monitor*. Among the half dozen books she wrote, there were four biographies (Elizabeth Cady Stanton, Harriot Stanton Blatch, Susan B. Anthony, and Emma Willard), a book on women in the antislavery movement, and a volume of collected letters of women from the Second World War.[18] Lutz's feminist advocacy and her historical scholarship were intertwined.

In her editorial selections and argumentation on behalf of the Equal Rights Amendment in *Equal Rights*, Lutz countered the arguments of anti-feminist conservative opponents of the ERA. She also confronted the powerful labor feminists in the Women's Bureau of the US Department of Labor, the labor movement, and the consumer movement who emphasized the negative impact the ERA would have on hard-won sex-specific protective laws for women. Lutz made a legal case replete with historical references in favor of the constitutional amendment, particularly after the Fair Labor Standards Act of 1938 established maximum hours and minimum wage standards for men and women and out-lawed child labor.

As the chief publicist for the National Woman's Party, Lutz published a 1935 pamphlet authored by lawyer Rebekah S. Greathouse. Greathouse charted the resistance of the US Supreme Court to women's claims to equal rights. She explained that where women had asserted their rights under the Fifth and Fourteenth Amendments' equal protection and due process clauses, the conservative nature of the Supreme Court (and state courts) during most of US history promulgated rulings based on the original intent of the framers, who neither encompassed nor protected women. American jurisprudence, their rulings suggested, was based on English common-law practice, and the restrictions on women stipulated in *Blackstone's Commentary* of 1765 must, therefore, apply to American women after 1789. As a result, married women suffered legal disabilities that made them wards and dependents of their hus-bands, with none of the constitutional protections enjoyed by male citizens under the Bill of Rights. The ratification of the Fourteenth Amendment in 1868 did nothing to extend rights to women either, Greathouse continued. According to *Bradwell v. Minor* (1869), the court ruled that, regardless of the equal protection clause in the Fourteenth Amendment, Myra Bradwell could not seek admission to the legal profession in Illinois on an equal basis with men. Then, in *Minor v. Happersett* (1875), Virginia Minor of Missouri was denied the right to vote. The Supreme Court ruled that the Constitution did not include voting rights as one of the federally defined "privileges and im-munities of citizens." Greathouse—using these and other cases that allowed for discrimination against women—reminded readers that women had been "forced to depend upon the fluctuating good nature of state legislatures and many of the *ancient discriminations* still remain. The federal Constitution as it stands guarantees to women nothing considered fundamental by men except the right to vote [since 1920] and will guarantee other rights only when an express amendment for the purpose is included therein." Greathouse finished with a historical flourish taken from Bryn Mawr College president M. Carey Thomas: "Forever behind a woman is the mediaeval English common law which places upon her the stigma of inferiority and bondage."[19] For Lutz, following on Greathouse, historical contextualization was essential to feminist argumentation.

In her writings to justify the ERA in *Equal Rights*, Lutz regularly featured the historical context of anti-feminist arguments and the law's codified inequalities. In 1944, for instance, Lutz reminded readers that the anti-feminist opposition used the same arguments every time feminists claimed new rights. Lutz said that the "old argument that the Equal Rights Amendment will destroy our pattern of family life has been dusted off again [and again] by the opposition, and displayed [as a fear tactic], as it was when women first demanded education, when they began to earn money, and when they asked for the vote." She insisted that the claim that equal rights would unsex and deprive women of common-law protective traditions was an oft-repeated rhetorical "trick" designed to influence the "unthinking," which she warned would work if the claims were "glibly repeated often enough."[20] How right she was.

From the 1930s to the 1950s Lutz also worked against the leaders in the AFL-CIO, labor feminists, and legislators who wanted to modify the ERA with the Hayden Rider, which would have created a "grandfather clause" for existing sex-specific labor laws. She and her National Woman's Party colleagues argued that so-called protective legislation limited women's access to higher-paying jobs in industry and was discrimination rather than protection. Lutz pointed out that since the nineteenth century, women had been classed with children by legislators to justify regulating their work hours and terms of employment. Meanwhile, male workers worked under extreme exploitation without protection, but they had the higher wages generally associated with industrial work. Unions dominated by men acquiesced because they feared competition if women joined their workforce. Male workers wanted their privileged access to industrial employment and to prevent the wage reductions associated with a feminized workforce.[21]

Lutz's historical argumentation strategy in the 1960s referenced more recent legal history and again referred to "common law" to explain why judges still did not recognize women as full-fledged "legal entities or persons." She pointed out that the Supreme Court continued to deny women equal protection of the law and due process rights that the Fourteenth Amendment had extended to Black men and later even to corporations. She reminded readers that predominantly male state and federal lawmakers would continue to pass laws that categorically discriminated against women. She pointed to the twenty-six states that had passed or nearly passed Depression era laws barring married women from paid employment.[22] Readers should be reminded that as late as the 2010s, Supreme Court justice Antonin Scalia was arguing publicly that the Constitution, specifically the Fourteenth Amendment, did not guarantee women equality before the law as persons because its authors did not intend to encompass women as persons.[23]

A final example of Lutz's feminist historicism comes from 1946. In a *Christian Science Monitor* article titled "Woman's Hour," Lutz made the case for women's history courses and the inclusion of women's history in textbooks. Emblazoned across the top of the article were portraits of Emma Willard, Lucretia Mott, Susan B. Anthony, Elizabeth Cady Stanton, and Mary Ritter Beard. To each of these history makers, Lutz had a personal connection: She attended the Emma Willard School before heading to Vassar College; she published biographies of both Stanton and Anthony; Mary Beard was her contemporary and former colleague in the National Woman's Party (even if Beard deliberately de-emphasized women's legal, economic, and cultural disabilities while Lutz emphasized them). In the article, Lutz observed with distress that college women knew about the great men of American history but did not know about women. She reported that they registered "a blank" when asked whether they knew who had secured for them the right to an education, property rights, child custody rights, or the vote. Reading indifference into their ignorance, she blamed men's control of written history and women's poor performance as "publicity agents for themselves." Lutz went on to cite the early efforts of Arthur Schlesinger to incorporate the history of women in his courses, and she mentioned Mary Beard's writings and work collecting women's archives. Lutz also credited Goucher College historian Mary W. Williams for her courses on women's contribution to history in the United States and the world. Lutz praised Williams for exerting "her influence to win recognition for women in history" in the American Historical Association. She closed the article with as good an argument for the proliferation of women's history as might be made today.

> The story of the struggle for political and civil rights, not yet fully won, is colorful and inspiring and one with which all women should be familiar. In fact, the whole background of women's history should be an essential part of every woman's education, and in the postwar revamping of curricula it should find a place. Without it, young women today have no backlog of self-respect or inspiration to draw upon. Without it, they have no accurate estimate of their place in society, or of their great responsibilities. Today, as never before, the world needs the best they can give.[24]

This feminist call to action linked knowledge about women's history to women's self-respect. It tied women's ability to engage in informed civic activism to history and to their advancement in the future. Lutz's references to Arthur Schlesinger, Mary W. Williams, and Charles and Mary Beard demonstrate that they, along with feminists of the era, were all creating women's history at intersecting spaces of knowledge production. They were not alone in articulating parallel commitments to scholarship and to civic and feminist ideals.

Elisabeth Anthony Dexter was well-known at midcentury for her books on women in colonial and early America. Unlike Lutz, Beard, or Elizabeth Schlesinger, she had an advanced degree in history. After earning a BA in philosophy from Bates College in 1908 and an AM degree in sociology from Columbia in 1911, she married Robert Dexter in 1914. Even though they had two children, both Robert and Elisabeth attended Clark University, where Elisabeth earned her history PhD in 1923. Her dissertation, *Colonial Women of Affairs*, was published in 1924, and from 1923 to 1927 she taught history and served as head of the history department at Skidmore College. When Robert Dexter took a position in 1927 with the American Unitarian Association in Cambridge, Massachusetts, Elisabeth left her position at Skidmore. She tutored at Radcliffe College for a year. From that point, through World War II, she conducted the research for her second book, *Career Women of America, 1776–1840*, and became involved with the humanitarian work of her husband. In 1940, Robert Dexter was appointed executive director of the Unitarian Universalist Service Committee—a war refugee aid society. The Dexters were stationed in Lisbon, Portugal. Elisabeth worked with the Service Committee from 1941 to 1944 and conducted intelligence work for the Office of Strategic Services. Historian and mother turned spy! From 1944 to 1948, she and Robert represented the Church Peace Union in Europe, a religiously based pacifist organization founded by Andrew Carnegie. Dexter's life as humanitarian, spy, pacifist, and mother left little time for research. Once she had returned to the states after 1948, Dexter was active in the League of Women Voters and the American Association of University Women. She also served on the Radcliffe Women's Archives/Schlesinger Library advisory board periodically from the 1950s until her death in 1972.[25] She prefaced the 1972 reprint edition of *Career Women of America* by saying, "I have tried to give an objective presentation of the facts as I found them, with a minimum of explanation and generalization; but opinions, clearly labeled I trust, have now and then broken through. That these opinions are always justified would be too much to hope."[26] As a scholar trained in the heyday of scientific history, when progressive historians had begun their intellectual ascent and social history was on the horizon, she was concerned that her work appear to be relatively objective.

In both *Career Women of America* and her earlier book, *Colonial Women of Affairs*, Elisabeth Dexter acknowledged that her scholarship served a purpose and had relevance to the modern women's movement. In offering her "small contribution to an understanding of our past," she believed "that the more fully and fairly we achieve this understanding, the better we are equipped to face our future."[27] Moreover, in answer to reviewers who had, to her distress, interpreted the 1924 edition of *Colonial Women of Affairs* as an attack on the modern women's rights movement, she expressed relief that in rereading her own work, she had been assured that these claims were unwarranted. She thought her work might instead encourage the "faint-hearted" by showing them that society survived even when it had publicly active women. Dexter's hope was "that modern women may show as much courage in meeting the problems of the present, and that women and men, together, may go forward."[28] Elisabeth Anthony Dexter was cognizant of the feminist implications of her work and committed to the creation of a usable past.[29]

Other pioneering midcentury historians of women were active in more mainstream women's politics, and some remained active through the 1970s. Caroline Ware, Guion Griffis Johnson, Barbara Miller Solomon, and Anne Firor Scott had commitments ranging from equal rights feminism to progressive feminism to civic feminism. By the 1960s all could be comfortably classified as liberal feminists by virtue of their work on women's issues in women's civic organizations, voluntary associations, and government agencies. Between 1961 and 1972, each served on either the President's Commission on the Status of Women (PCSW), its offshoot, the Interdepartmental Committee and Citizens Advisory Council on the Status of Women, or one of the state commissions on the status of women established by governors.

Caroline Ware, whose academic history was recounted earlier, combined her writing and teaching career with an active political life in civil service and progressive women's organizations. She left Vassar College in 1934 when her husband took a New Deal position in Washington, DC. While teaching part-time at Sarah Lawrence College from 1935 to 1937, she took a position in the National Recovery Administration as a special assistant to the Consumer Advisory Board, a job that evolved into full-time consumer advocacy and led to other appointments in the administration, including the Office of Price Administration; the Council of Economic Advisors; the Department of Health, Education, and Welfare of the Social Security Administration; and the Public Advisory Committee on Trade Negotiations, all from 1943 to 1967. As a New Deal Democrat, Ware's work in consumer advocacy is of special relevance for understanding her brand of feminist politics. Consumer advocacy had grown out of the Progressive Era, when Florence Kelley was a leader in the "white label campaign" of the National Consumers' League to encourage consumers to buy goods produced under safe, fair working conditions. The progressive feminists at the center of consumer advocacy, including those in the Women's Bureau of the US Department of Labor, sought to improve the lives of American women and empower them through education. Ware taught at the Bryn Mawr Summer School for Women Workers and the Vassar College Summer Institute, which provided liberal arts classes for women factory and office workers.[30] Her work in these schools reflected confidence in the emancipatory power of education for the working class—a sentiment common among progressive women.[31]

Ware also joined a wide array of women's civic organizations. She served as social studies chairman of the American Association of University Women and was a member of its legislative committee from 1939 to 1951. From 1953 to 1972, she worked with several national and international organizations of professional social workers and was on the boards or committees of various governmental agencies and civic groups. Some of these were the American Labor Education Service, the National Council of Negro Women, the Inter-American Commission of Women, the Pan-American Union of the Organization of American States, UNESCO, the United Nations, the US Information Service, and the Overseas Education Fund of the League of Women Voters.[32] Ware's résumé in progressive, New Deal era organizations and beyond bridges the decades between the time traditionally understood as the Progressive Era ending in 1920 and the surge in progressive social movements of the 1960s. It demonstrates the ongoing activism of women progressives in American public life, with their work in the field of history offering evidence of their work as public intellectuals.[33]

In 1942, Ware joined the history faculty at Howard University.[34] While there, she became friends with her student Pauli Murray, who audited her course in constitutional history. Murray credited her conversations with Ware as opening her eyes to the parallels between racism and sexism.[35] Ware herself actively supported civil rights, bailing out students arrested for violating Jim Crow laws in Virginia in 1944 and hiring and training Black secretaries for the Office of Price Administration during the war.[36] Ware's intersecting commitments to workers' rights and economic, racial, and gender justice came together when she served on the PCSW. Her politics were characteristic of what Dorothy Sue Cobble has recently labeled "full rights feminism."[37] Active at the same time on the commission were Assistant Secretary of Labor Esther Peterson, Eleanor Roosevelt, and National Council of Negro Women president Dorothy Height. Pauli Murray was appointed to the PCSW by President Kennedy in 1961, and in 1962 she was invited to serve on the commission's Committee on Civil and Political Rights, likely at the recommendation of Ware.[38]

As the only historian on the commission, Ware drafted a preliminary thirty-five-page discussion document titled "Background Memorandum on the Status of Women." When this paper was presented to the PCSW in 1962, it came with a thirty-five-page appendix summarizing Supreme Court and other legal cases related to sex discrimination prepared by Pauli Murray. Murray was on the way to becoming one of the most influential Black feminists and civil rights activists of the era. She pioneered feminist legal theories about the similarities between Jim Crow and what she called Jane Crow, anticipating intersectional theory by thirty years.[39] Murray also had a keen sense of history's illustrative power, writing two autobiographical works. *Proud Shoes* told the story of her family, while *Song in a Weary Throat* was a personal political autobiography.[40] Her personal history demonstrated the intersecting effects of racial and sexual discrimination in her life and their formative impact on her activism.

Ware's document surveyed women's changing status over the prior 100 years of American history. She noted women's growing participation in the workforce and public life and discussed how that had affected their patterns of life. This was Ware's historical bailiwick. She had spent her life examining the impact of industrialization, immigration, and urbanization. Her scholarship had looked at New England industrial women workers in the nineteenth century and immigrant ethnic communities in New York City in the twentieth.[41] Her paper for the PCSW was entirely consistent with her academic training and scholarship, and it spoke to what had drawn her to study women in history.

In the preliminary draft, Ware explained changes over time as they had impacted American women and their families. She focused first on changing patterns of work and life related to advances in industry, technology, residential patterns, and economic consumption. She framed this in the context of modernization, describing the dramatic decline in fertility rates and the rise in life expectancy from 1860 to 1960. With longer lives and smaller families, opportunities had expanded for women. These openings in work and education reached into the lives of both single and married women—with and without children. Ware emphasized that increasingly, even married women with children would have several decades in which they could be workers, civic activists, and community members. Ware suggested that US policy should address this; women over forty-five had become an important resource whose abilities should be developed and put to good use.[42] The job of the President's Commission, as Ware saw it, was to help create the institutions and policies that would facilitate the "equalization process" that had been underway for a hundred years and was, in her view, now possible in modern society.[43]

The Ware memorandum's closing emphasis on the legal disabilities of women under American jurisprudence in some ways paralleled the views of equal rights feminists like Alma Lutz. Ware's feminist historicism, however, was broader. She focused on larger cultural, social, and economic forces acting on women and didn't just remark on the women's rights movement. Her historical perspective influenced policymakers in the Kennedy and Johnson administrations to find ways to help women combine work, family, and civic life. Ware's perspective advanced "women's rights" within a reciprocal framework. The state owed equal protections and opportunities to women, just as women had civic and economic duties and responsibilities to the nation. Ware's influence in providing the historical context and setting the agenda for the work of the PCSW was magnified by the fact that the subsequent fifty state-level commissions had the PCSW as its model.[44]

Historian Guion Griffis Johnson of North Carolina, whose truncated academic career was also featured earlier in this study, engaged in parallel forms of progressive feminism at the state and national level between 1925 and 1972. She belonged to more than two dozen voluntary associations ranging in focus from educational, like the American Association of University Women, to political, like the League of Women Voters. In many, she played a leadership role. The most central to Johnson, though, were those focused on the state of North Carolina and dedicated to social and economic issues. She saw women's groups as a powerful vehicle for social change. Johnson belonged to the North Carolina Federation of Women's Clubs from 1931 to 1986 and served on the North Carolina Council of Women's Organizations from 1950 to 1987. Additional groups she served included the United Church Women (1936–74), the North Carolina Council of World Affairs (1947–73), the Governor's Commission on the Status of Women in North Carolina (1961–65), the American Association for the United Nations (1953–83), the YWCA (1950–68), and a slew of others.

Johnson chose groups that were politically and socially progressive on matters of race and sex equality as well as economic justice, and, like others with this bent, her historical scholarship and her political interests informed each other. She focused on contemporary issues faced by African Americans and women in her writings and speeches, which she generally placed in historical context. Her early interest in feminism was expressed in 1925, when, as a graduate student, she wrote "Feminism and the Economic Independence of Woman."[45] The essay was a term paper written for a UNC Chapel Hill sociology course on the family taught by Jesse Steiner. She won the Chi Omega Sociology Award for the paper, and it was published in the *Journal of Social Forces* in 1925.[46] The essay was not an endorsement of any single type of feminism; Johnson instead offered a survey of the major wings of the women's movement, commenting on the lack of unity among them, and then discussed the centrality of economic independence and birth control to the feminist cause. The article questioned the value of equal rights feminism in providing an adequate solution to the problems faced by working women.[47] She explained that what might work for a professional married woman with hopes of a family might not work so well for a factory worker or a single woman. She closed with the admonition, "It would appear that the [equal rights] feminists have not followed to a logical conclusion some of the theories they advocate." The paper identified Johnson as somewhere between what historians Dorothy Sue Cobble and Landon Storrs have labeled progressive and labor feminists.[48] Further, she recognized the inevitable differences of political opinion among women, explaining, "It is too much to expect that in a group of many millions all should agree upon the method of achieving anything so abstract as the right to be considered capable of intelligence or even that all should be concerned about this right. There has come into existence, therefore, the National League of Women Voters, the National Council of Women in the United States, the American Home Economics Association, the Woman's Party, and many others, each, consciously or unconsciously, seeking to gain prestige for woman as an individual."[49] Thus, as early as 1925 Johnson demonstrated a firm understanding of the size, ubiquity, and diversity of the twentieth-century women's movement in the United States.

Johnson's commitment to Black civil rights would remain central to her thinking throughout her career. In 1958 she wrote "The Changing Status of the Negro" and in 1959 "The Quiet Revolution: Integration in Institutions of Higher Learning." Both appeared in the *Journal of the American Association of University Women.*[50] In each of these essays she made strong statements in favor of integration, backed up by research she and husband Guy Johnson had conducted in the 1930s and 1940s on racial matters in the South. This included her work as a researcher on Gunnar Myrdal's landmark study, *An American Dilemma*, and publications on the ideology of white supremacy.[51] She is also credited with intervening forcefully to prevent the lynching of an African American man falsely accused of rape by a white teenager in Chapel Hill, North Carolina, in 1939.[52] For Guion Griffis Johnson, the study of history was a vehicle to a life of civic activism and a lens through which she could focus her many efforts on behalf of racial, economic, and gender justice. Her career at UNC Chapel Hill's Institute for Research in Social Science took precedence in her life between 1924 and 1944, and she maintained her intellectual ties to the scholarly community there throughout her life. But after 1944 she became one of the most prominent civic activists in the state.

Johnson's reputation as an effective organizer and a liberal grew as she turned toward volunteer work, social justice advocacy, and civic activism. She gave presentations to historical societies and women's groups and at women's colleges, revealing her feminist historicism. Her talks were replete with progressive, anti-racist, and feminist views. She melded her knowledge of the history of women with her research on race inequality and arrived at a progressive position on both women and African Americans in American society.

Johnson's ideas about women as active, working citizens developed more fully during these years. Addressing a graduating class of women at Brenau Academy in 1945, she gave the women a sense of their historical advantage and encouraged them to meet any challenge to their full participation in the workforce of the postwar era. She opened,

It is about a hundred years ago that Thomas Carlyle declared, "The staircase of history resounds to the noise of the wooden shoe of the peasant ascending upward." It might be more accurate to say that the forward steps of time have been made by the women of the world in their struggle for proportionate opportunities for education and intellectual advancement. The measuring stick for any nation is the regard in which it holds its womankind, and that regard, you may be sure, depends upon the honest efforts and the sincerity of women themselves. . . . You are here tonight, educated on the basic assumption that you have the same intellectual capacities as your brothers, and yet . . . less than a century ago . . . education, it was said, would unfit a woman for the responsibilities and duties of married life.[53]

She went on to describe the legal and educational disabilities women faced historically in the United States, something with which she was familiar after researching *Ante-Bellum North Carolina: A Social History*.[54] Yet she also described women's active and varied participation in all walks of life to argue that "today more than ever before in the history of the civilized world, women will have to support, not only themselves but their children and their children's war-maimed fathers." She asked,

Will a humane society penalize these women? Will it prevent their making a decent living simply because they are women wage earners? Yes, it will—unless these wage earners themselves and other women join with them in seeking better standards of work and better work opportunities. . . . As educated women we must think through the problem, and we must not attack it as militant feminists. . . . We must sit down together [with men] and in sympathy and understanding work out the solution. . . . As educated women, we must . . . work hard at the task of being good citizens. . . . You are the builders of this world.[55]

Johnson advocated cross-class collaboration between all economic levels among women to secure equal opportunity, and she suggested women sit down with men in cross-sex collaboration. She negatively invoked "militant feminists" and alluded to intellectual equality between the sexes and the power of educated women.

Johnson adhered to a brand of midcentury feminism that envisioned more than a formal equality based on sameness, as the "militants" of the National Woman's Party had done. Rather, she positioned women as nothing less than the "builders of this [postwar] world." Her view acknowledged that all classes of women would have to work together. During much of Johnson's life, one would have been hard-pressed to label her a feminist at all. But scholars now include a wide spectrum of hyphenated feminists in their histories of feminism, expanding our understanding of American women's activism between the major waves of American feminism.[56] Midcentury activists broadly advocated for women's rights in a wide array of organizations. After 1947, Johnson was highly effective in a host of these groups where she saw no contradiction in women being wives and mothers and civic and political activists.[57] Nowhere in her intellectual work did she limit women. Rather, she suggested, modern women had a responsibility to find ways to combine family, career, community activism, and politics:

> Today more than ever before in the history of man, woman needs to function as the conscience of society. . . . What every woman thinks, what she shows publicly that she wants, is going to determine the cultural pattern of the future. . . . She must speak out on behalf of the underprivileged who have not yet spoken for themselves. . . . She must be willing to work . . . in her political party, in the precinct, in the small chores of public office, and she must not hesitate when qualified to assume the responsibility of high office. . . . She must be informed. . . . She must . . . be willing to state her position, no matter how unpopular it may be. She must put aside the feminist attitude—long outworn—of antagonism toward men and work shoulder to shoulder with men and toward a better world.[58]

In this 1950 talk, Johnson criticized the "feminist attitude," which, at the time, was narrowly identified with the equal rights feminists of the National Woman's Party. She advocated for women as full citizens with full rights and responsibilities—and this in an era notorious for its conservative backslide into prescriptive gender roles. This backslide had been foreshadowed by historian Ferdinand Lundberg and psychiatrist Marynia Farnham in their 1947 book, *Modern Woman: The Lost Sex*, which depicted working mothers as maladjusted, neurotic deviants eroding the social fabric of American life.[59] For Lundberg and Farnham, economically independent women led to dissatisfied husbands and a spike in juvenile delinquency and divorce. Johnson and other professional married women of this era were compelled to contest this narrative. Between 1947 and 1960, Johnson developed and expressed progressive views on race and sex within a multitude of women's organizations; she enjoyed renown as a writer of articles, a researcher, and a public speaker.

By the early 1960s, when she worked on Governor Terry Sanford's newly established Commission on the Status of Women in North Carolina, she was still paying attention to differences between women of distinct races and classes in her speeches. She recognized, for example, that Black women historically had greater levels of employment, proportionally achieved higher levels of education and professional advancement, and had lower rates of marriage and fertility than white women of comparable class. This was due to social, economic, and historical factors that often compelled them to work outside the home and strive for higher education to contribute to their family's survival and their community's uplift.[60]

In her 1964 essay "The Changing Status of Women in the South," she relied heavily on data from the US Department of Labor's Women's Bureau, where many labor feminists had come into influence during the New Deal. These labor feminists were opposed to the Equal Rights Amendment on the grounds that it would invalidate sex-specific protective laws and thus undermine the health, welfare, and safety of working women and children.[61] Johnson's view on women's rights reflected the evolution of the women's movement; by the late 1960s there was consensus that women's needs and rights as workers and professionals were related to their overall equality.[62]

In 1975 Guoin Griffis Johnson came out in favor of the Equal Rights Amendment. In a speech urging the North Carolina Federation of Women's Clubs to "put the federation on the right side of history," she argued that customs in North Carolina, rather than legal precedent, were a more important determinant in the actual behavior of Southern women and men when it came to women's status in society.[63] She provided evidence of such a claim by drawing on her earlier work, especially *Ante-Bellum North Carolina,* In the 1975 speech, she specifically cited property and inheritance laws in which judges, "well enough satisfied with legal and discriminatory practices being followed by the North Carolina court system," continued to rule against widows, insisting they pay inheritance tax on property that their husbands would not have had to pay if their wives had died. She also addressed the impact the ERA would have on protective labor legislation, saying the benefits of the ERA would outweigh any problems—problems that in any case could be resolved by the government's implementation of the proposed law.[64]

Because of Johnson's renown as a civic activist in her home state, historians Jacquelyn Hall and Mary Frederickson conducted a four-part interview with her in 1974 as part of the Southern Oral History Project. These interviews did not address women's history as a field per se. Hall and Frederickson saw Johnson as an interesting historical figure, but they weren't aware of her relevance as a historian who had considered women's activities.[65] Others, too, were unsure where Johnson fit. When Johnson was asked to give a keynote address to the Historical Society of North Carolina in 1978, she warned, "The last time I addressed an evening session before the Society, a sweet lady in the audience observed during the discussion period, 'I think our speaker tonight is too much of a lady to believe a word she has said here tonight!'"[66] What does such a comment even mean, and how does it relate to Johnson as a scholar? The

1978 dinner where Johnson spoke was attended by Jane De Hart Mathews and Mary Frederickson. At the end of the talk, in which Johnson related her professional and activist past, she invited listeners to "judge for yourselves whether I deserve to be called 'a nice southern lady.'" In the context of the changing women's movement of the 1970s, Johnson may have felt that the significance of her career was unrecognizable to younger scholars who entered the profession in a radically different historical context than she herself had.

Both Johnson and Ware were progressive, civic feminists committed to addressing racial and economic inequality, though Ware was a much more prominent one nationally. I borrow the term "civic feminist" from Kathleen Laughlin, who defined such feminists as clubwomen who "believed that women's equality was essential to democracy and national security and considered all forms of public engagement, no matter how modest, as significant exercises in authority and autonomy."[67] In an era before the epistemological framework for women's history as a distinct area of historical study emerged, Johnson and Ware found a way to combine their scholarly interests in women, race/ethnicity, economic justice, and international affairs with political activism. Their work and personal lives were consistent with the contours of women's rising political and professional participation in twentieth-century America. As labor feminists, civic activists, and scholars, their lives reveal that some American women's experiences between 1920 and 1970 were characterized by much more than the feminist backsliding and domesticity that historians have previously associated with the period.[68] They were not alone. Recent examinations of the "long Progressive Era" suggest that the tradition of progressive feminist activism was unbroken between the 1920s and 1940s as women entered politics and civil service work in municipal, state, and national government. The story told here suggests the progressive impulse continued into the 1950s and 1960s and was reflected in the public activities of these women, including their publications on women in history for popular and academic audiences.[69]

Meanwhile, at Radcliffe College and in Harvard's American Civilization Program, Janet Wilson James, Barbara Miller Solomon, and Anne Firor Scott all studied history during the 1940s and 1950s. Solomon and Scott went on to work on the Massachusetts and North Carolina Commissions on the Status of Women, and Scott also served on the PCSW's Citizens' Advisory Council on the Status of Women.

Barbara Miller Solomon, a 1953 PhD from Radcliffe College and director of the Radcliffe Women's Archive from 1960 to 1965, found, like Ware and Johnson, that her commitment to feminism mutually reinforced her commitment to women's history. She was a feminist who understood the reality of women's active participation in civil society throughout history. Her spirited response to a derogatory cartoon about clubwomen in the *Washington Post* in 1962 defended the centrality of clubwomen to American society and heralded them as "an important element in the democratic process of our country." Perhaps feeling compelled to address the criticism of women who fulfilled social roles to the alleged detriment of children and family, she pointed out the many contributions they made in voluntary associations, civic groups, and charity organizations. Countering the theme of the "emancipated but dissatisfied American woman" postulated by Lundberg and Farnham's *Modern Woman: The Lost Sex*, Solomon suggested that such a thesis was based on "the decades between 1920 and 1960 when women were still experimenting with combining marriage and a career." She urged married women not to "allow time for personal dilemmas" but rather to act as "members of a free society" and "take an increasing share in community life."[70] This same theme had come up in Solomon's 1961 address to Wheelock College graduates: "Too much is happening to America and the world to waste human abilities. . . . The image of the American woman has been distorted [since 1920]. . . . The old dilemma is obsolete." She was suggesting that women were well on their way to working out solutions to the so-called dilemma. She was an excellent example of that very solution.[71]

As director of the Radcliffe Women's Archives in 1961, she negotiated the transfer of 1,000 cookery and household management books from Harvard's Widener Library to the archive. The acquisition was widely publicized, including in a three-paragraph write-up in *Newsweek*. The publicity contained a combination of sexism, humor, and acknowledgment of the materials' inherent worth. The *Milwaukee Journal*, the *Boston Sunday Herald*, and Radcliffe's own press mentioned Solomon's physical attributes, as if they were newsworthy. They described her as "slim and youthful at 43 . . . a good example of the modern woman who has managed to combine advanced education and a career with raising a family." Another referred to her as "an attractive blonde, [who] not long ago singlehandedly talked the august corporation of Harvard out of a large number of valuable books." Radcliffe's write-up justified Solomon's return to higher education, assuring readers that the children were "well established in their pattern of life before their mother resumed her studies." Nevertheless, Solomon recognized the inherent value of the collection she had just acquired for the archive. The books were a treasure trove of data about social customs, the work of everyday homemakers, mothers, and wives as cooks, nurses, and transmitters of their culture's values and belief systems.[72]

Solomon easily took her place among key pioneers of her day. When, as the Radcliffe Women's Archives director in 1964, Solomon attended a White House event hosted by Lady Bird Johnson, she fit right in with prominent women in industry, medicine, and politics who had presented talks at the White House. When she reported back to the archive's advisory board, the board mentioned the names of prominent Democratic activists in their discussion, including

India Edwards, Eleanor Poland, Katherine Elkis White, and Women's Bureau official and chief promoter of the PCSW Esther Peterson in the debriefing. Solomon was then appointed to two consecutive state commissions on the status of women in Massachusetts, where she served from 1964 to 1971.[73]

Meanwhile, at Radcliffe, Solomon had met Anne Firor Scott, who would go on to serve on the PCSW Citizens' Advisory Council on the Status of Women and the Governor's Commission on the Status of Women in North Carolina between 1963 and 1968. Anne Firor Scott became a leader in the women's history movement of the 1970s and 1980s. As a college student in the MA program in personnel management at Northwestern in 1943, she had an internship in DC with the National Institute of Public Affairs. Interested in politics, she was assigned to work for Democratic congressman Jerry Voorhis of California.[74] When she returned to Northwestern, Anne changed her major to political science and graduated in August 1944. During her years at Northwestern, she regularly met with political scientist Mary Earhart Dillon, who had published a biography of Frances Willard, leader of the Woman's Christian Temperance Union and one of the most effective political organizers of her era. Under Willard's "Do Everything" rubric, the WCTU created an institutional apparatus whose effectiveness at organizing women was unparalleled at the time.[75] The WCTU successfully worked to ratify the Eighteenth Amendment to the Constitution.[76] After graduating, Anne Firor moved to Washington, DC, to work for the League of Women Voters as a staff writer for the league's *Trends* pamphlets. Anne's "beat" was international affairs. This gave her the opportunity to travel around the country and learn from senior league members. After working with the league for two years, she met and married Andrew Scott. The two moved to Cambridge, Massachusetts, in 1947, where Andrew was entering Harvard's government program. Anne applied to the American civilization program and eventually selected historian Oscar Handlin as her advisor. Scott completed her coursework for the PhD at Radcliffe between 1947 and 1949, during which time she became familiar with the Radcliffe Women's Archives, where she met Janet James and Barbara Solomon. Andrew's work soon took the couple back to DC.[77]

During the 1950s, Anne Scott finished her dissertation on Southern progressives and had three children. In 1950, she returned briefly to work as editor of the *National Voter* for the League of Women Voters. When she left that job, her coworkers gave her a gift of feminist literature, including Simone de Beauvoir's *Second Sex* and Mary Beard's *Woman as Force in History*. She then took a series of temporary teaching positions. By this time, Anne Firor Scott considered herself a "moderately militant feminist," reflecting years later that her experience working in politics and for the League of Women Voters made it possible for her to "see" the women whom she ultimately researched and wrote about in the early 1960s. She later reminisced,

The League certainly affected what I was prepared to see in the past. . . .
When I first went to work for the League we were still getting the letters
from Carrie Chapman Catt telling us what we ought to do. I worked with
. . . Miss Katherine Luddington, . . . who would come sit in my office and
tell me what I ought to be doing. She was very much involved in foreign
policy, and she was well connected. She could call Dean Acheson on
his private line. . . . I met Maude Wood Park . . . So, in that sense I got a
strong impression about suffrage women because these were all strong-
minded [women]. They all were outspoken. They were all articulate, and
you could have no doubt that they were extraordinary. Undoubtedly it
was a very formative experience.[78]

Thus, by Scott's own account, her activism in the League of Women Voters,
which preceded second-wave feminism and the start of the women's history
movement in 1969, had fed her interest in women's history.[79]

By the early 1960s, Scott had moved south with her political scientist husband
and was gaining recognition as a scholar of Southern women's history. In her
academic post at Duke University, where she was hired in 1960, she increasingly
focused on women's history in her teaching and research. North Carolina governor Terry Sanford asked her to serve as the chair of the Governor's Commission on the Status of Women in North Carolina in 1963. Guion Griffis Johnson
was already on a subcommittee for this commission. Scott admired Johnson's
"Report of the Committee on Voluntary Organizations and Expanded Services,"
describing it as exemplary. Scott noted that the North Carolina commission's
final report, "The Many Lives of North Carolina Women, 1964" was modeled
after the *Report of the President's Commission on the Status of Women*, where
historian Caroline Ware held influence. Scott was soon to serve alongside Ware
on the federal Citizens' Advisory Council on the Status of Women (1964–68).[80]
Anne Firor Scott was a liberal feminist from 1944 to 1968; the history she wrote
informed her feminist politics and vice versa.

Women's history was not solely the work of progressive feminists. Conservative women in the South had long been active in shaping the public school curriculum, making sure it included the white supremacist "Lost Cause" narrative
of the Civil War. Conservative women across the nation promoted nationalist
and anti-feminist narratives through patriotic societies like the Daughters of
the American Revolution and the United Daughters of the Confederacy and
through the women's club movement. By midcentury, these conservatives had
decades of experience redbaiting and attacking liberal educators as part of their
culture war against progressive and feminist movements and against any reform
in history and social studies curricula.[81]

Well before the emergence of the New Left, leftist ideology prompted some women historians to explore the power of history on the broader culture. Some, like Eleanor Flexner, Gerda Lerner, and Aileen Kraditor, developed analyses of the interrelated nature of class, race, and sex oppression. This "Red" backstory of modern women's history has been examined in Kate Weigand's *Red Feminism* and in Daniel Horowitz's essay "Feminism, Women's History, and American Social Thought at Midcentury."[82] Of special note in both of these works is Flexner's, Lerner's, and Kraditor's participation in the Congress of American Women, which—like feminist Betty Friedan—they kept secret during the McCarthy era and the Cold War's anti-communist heyday when loyalty oaths were commonplace. Under the pseudonymous byline of Irene Epstein, Flexner wrote articles on women's history for the Communist Party USA's newspaper, *Daily Worker*. Inspired by discussions with Claudia Jones, a Black woman member of the Communist Party USA, and influenced especially by Jones's 1949 article in *Political Affairs*, "An End to the Neglect of the Problems of Negro Women," Flexner's book, *Century of Struggle*, emphasized the activism of women in the abolition, labor, and women's movements of the nineteenth century. The book featured both Black women activists and working-class white women.[83]

In collaboration with former fellow Congress of American Women member Eve Miriam (also a poet), Gerda Lerner wrote the musical *Singing of Women* in the 1950s before starting research on the Grimké sisters, before entering graduate school, and before becoming a professional historian. In her autobiography, *Fireweed*, Lerner later credited her organizing skills and her attention to working-class and Black women to her days in the Congress of American Women and to local left-leaning neighborhood-organizing efforts related to housing discrimination and integration in both Los Angeles and New York City.[84]

Lerner's contemporary Aileen Kraditor joined the Communist Party USA in 1940 and remained a member for eleven years. She was influenced by August Bebel's foundational work, *Woman and Socialism*, and Friedrich Engels's *Origin of the Family, Private Property and the State*. Kraditor graduated from Brooklyn College. She worked in a factory and also as a clerical worker for some years before entering the graduate history program at Columbia University. She finished her dissertation in 1963 and published it in 1965 as *The Ideas of the Woman Suffrage Movement*. Considered a women's history classic, the book examined the strategic, organizational, and ideological divisions within the suffrage movement and offered a critique of the racial and class limitations of the white woman suffrage movement.[85]

Carl Degler, a significant early male supporter of women's history, never formally joined any communist organization, but as a New Jersey college student attending school on the GI Bill in the 1940s he remembered associating with leftist friends who encouraged him to read Marxist literature, including August Bebel. This in turn led to his interest in labor history, African American history, and women's history. A 1952 Columbia history PhD, he was hired to teach at Vassar College, further inspiring him to focus on women in history for his female students. These overlapping emphases on class, race, and sex in his teaching and writing were consistent with the earlier left-wing theorizing of communists, particularly communist women like Mary Inman and Claudia Jones, who developed a theoretical approach to thinking about the imbricated nature and effect of class and sex oppression—and in the case of Jones, racial oppression—that anticipated intersectional theory decades before the term was coined by Kimberlé Crenshaw in 1989.[86] Degler would go on to teach at Columbia and Stanford and became an early male ally of and participant in the women's history movement of the late 1960s and beyond.[87]

Both Weigand and Horowitz leave the reader with the impression that far-left feminists had an outsized role in developing feminist historicism and in anticipating the new women's history of the 1970s. As Weigand demonstrates, they contributed theoretical insights and added terminology like "women's liberation," "male chauvinism," and "consciousness-raising" to the lexicon of second-wave feminism. But feminist historicism was a tool used across the feminist political spectrum over the full course of the twentieth century.[88] Moreover, far-left feminists were not the only ones examining women in social movements. They were not alone in acknowledging Black women's history. Nor did they have a monopoly on understanding the potentially liberatory power of women's history. Women's history, constituting as it does the story of half of humanity, could not and cannot be bounded by any one political ideology.

It is relevant that only some of the feminists fighting for women's history were trained academics with formal careers. Those who were outside of main-stream academic discourse had little to lose in making plain their overt political stand. Their work provided a platform for the history of women and even for the promotion of women's rights in society, but it did not provide academic legitimacy. Credentialed academics, though, lent their authority to women's history and later to the mainstream women's movement. When women, people of color, and those of working-class background began entering the historical profession, especially after midcentury, they began to engage in study of their identified group and to use history as a tool to effect cultural and social change. Nevertheless, these two activities—the political and the scholarly—were often kept in different arenas of their lives.

What is consistent across these arenas and across the political spectrum is that most feminist historians understood that writing history was an inherently political act with power to challenge the status quo or perpetuate it. Writing women's history in the first seven decades of the twentieth century was a way for feminist scholars to grab the proverbial microphone to speak to women's cultural relevance in new and empowering ways. Any particular woman grabbed this microphone in her own way, shaped by her political and academic community. For the suffragists, civic activists, and progressive women of the turn of the century, the central issue was often documenting the history of their own cause. They gathered the primary sources of their own movements' histories and wrote their first drafts. By the 1920s they were joined by credentialed women historians looking to craft narratives legitimized within the ivory tower. These historians produced carefully researched scholarship that did not make overt political arguments. Yet, the subject matter they addressed had political and cultural implications and often ran parallel to their civic and political work outside academia.

Despite many late nineteenth-century American historians' assertions that history was a scientific and objective academic discipline, written history always presents the perspective of the interpreter who selects the topic to explore, the sources to research, and the facts to extract. Facts and data do not have a life or a meaning of their own; they depend on the writer to contextualize them, explain them, and breathe life into them for the broader culture. The stories we tell and the conclusions we draw reflect the personal interests, values, and ideological proclivities of the historian, no matter how firmly rooted in archival evidence. This has political implications; it shapes the culture in which we live. This is equally true for representations of popular and public history. Writing the history of marginalized and subordinated groups was a political act that subverted the power and privilege of the ruling class.

In his lecture "The Historian and His Facts," Edward Hallett Carr said, "The facts speak only when the historian calls on them to speak: it is he who decides which facts to give the floor, and in what order or context."[89] The enormous privilege of producing history was primarily the purview of male scholars during the profession's first 100 years, and history was viewed by most academic historians as a "stag affair."[90] These male historians may have denied intentionality, but intended or not, their androcentric frame of reference served to buttress male cultural and political dominance. The limited access of women, working-class people, and people of color to university training was another mechanism to uphold the hierarchical system.

———————

When people of color, working-class people, and women began the process of writing themselves into history, they understood that they were engaged in a political discourse that could transform society. These efforts started largely outside of academia but gained traction within the progressive and social history approaches to American history. It took academic women longer than feminists, suffragists, far-left feminists, or Black clubwomen and educators to systematically articulate the importance of correcting predominantly (white) male historical narratives. Those women outside academia wrote their histories while they were active in women's civic, social, and political movements; even conservative and anti-feminist club women took an active interest in history and the role of women in history. None were shy about wielding history as a weapon in service to their political commitments. Meanwhile, historians of women in universities did not emphasize their personal politics in their academic writing, because doing so would have made them suspect and illegitimate in the eyes of their more powerful male peers. But claiming historical significance for their female subjects was a profoundly feminist political act. By simply "piling up evidence about women," these historians understood their power to alter the "standards of historical significance." As Joan Scott once wrote, "Women's history critically confronts the politics of existing history and inevitably begins the rewriting of history."[91]

The writing of women's history from 1900 to 1968 is best understood within a feminist historical context. To date, historians have addressed feminist historicism, whether it be in or outside of academia, only in a fragmented manner. But even during the "doldrums" of the twentieth century, across what Nancy Cott called "the Great Divide" between the first and second wave of American feminism, feminist historians were researching and writing.[92] Those who worked between 1920 and 1968 show the diverse ideological roots of women's history.[93] One of the deepest roots is certainly that which grew in the long Progressive Era, from which so many early twentieth-century historians of women drew inspiration.[94] In 1981, historian Janet James suggested that historians of women at Radcliffe in the 1950s were one of the few groups—aside from the National Woman's Party, whose strategies had alienated large segments of civically active progressive women—keeping feminism before the public at midcentury by "promoting women's history, by writing, and by building collections of historical materials."[95] But, the interconnections between historical scholarship about women and feminist political and civic activism examined here shows this sensibility was much broader. Both equal rights feminism and progressive feminism were formative of early writing in the field. Operating in a male-dominated field, feminist historians had to employ scholarly standards in documenting evidence and clarifying arguments; they had to have relative "objectivity" in their work. Yet these women were operating on the belief that history served progressive and feminist racial, sexual, economic, political, and social agendas. As women academics and civic activists, they did their work, as Janet James put it, by presenting themselves as "middle-class women with outside interests" who "were looking for proof that family and career combinations could be had without anything so unladylike as a fight."[96] But a fight was on the horizon, nonetheless. As the modern women's movement advanced, so did the fight to fully legitimize and develop women's history and women as professional historians. This battle would be fully joined in 1969.

Elisabeth Anthony Dexter, portrait taken in relation to her work with the
Unitarian Universalist Service Committee, Holocaust Rescue and Relief, ca. 1939.
© Bachrach Studios. Courtesy Harvard Divinity School, Harvard Libraries.

Barbara Miller Solomon and Arthur M. Schlesinger Sr. socialize at a
Radcliffe College event, circa 1960. Courtesy of Harvard University,
Radcliffe Institute for Advanced Study, Schlesinger Library.

Radcliffe librarians Mary Howard (*seated at left*) and Dorothy Fass pose with Radcliffe Women's Archives director Elizabeth Borden (*standing*) in 1958. Courtesy of Harvard University, Radcliffe Institute for Advanced Study, Schlesinger Library.

Edward James and Janet Wilson James, editors of *Notable American Women*, at work in the Schlesinger Library, 1972. Courtesy of Harvard University, Radcliffe Institute for Advanced Study, Schlesinger Library.

Mary Elizabeth Massey in Winthrop University Library, 1965.
Courtesy of the Louise Pettus Library, Winthrop University Archives.

A. Elizabeth Taylor, circa 1960, at work at Texas Woman's University.
Courtesy of The Woman's Collection, Blagg-Huey Library Special Collections,
Texas Woman's University.

Margaret Storrs Grierson at work in the Sophia Smith Collection, circa 1960s.
Courtesy of Smith College Special Collections.

Elizabeth Bancroft Schlesinger advises Professor Frank Freidel at the
Schlesinger Library in 1967. The photo was printed in the *40th Anniversary
Report* of the Schlesinger Library. Courtesy of Harvard University, Radcliffe
Institute for Advanced Study, Schlesinger Library.

Anne Firor Scott poses for a news editorial with some of her early publications, circa 1971. Courtesy of Duke University Archives.

Professor Albert Sacks, legal scholar Pauli Murray, and Radcliffe's Dr. Mary I. Bunting (*standing, left to right*) pose with Harvard Law Forum guests, feminists Alma Lutz and Betty Friedan. Courtesy Wiki Commons.

Jacquelyn Dowd Hall (*center*) interviews Guy Johnson and Guion Griffis Johnson for the Southern Oral History Project, 1974. Courtesy of Southern Historical Collection, Wilson Library, University of North Carolina at Chapel Hill.

Nell Irvin Painter, Catherine Prelinger, Mary Maples Dunn, and Iris Berger (*left to right*), serving on the Program Committee of the 1976 Big Berkshire Conference. Courtesy of Kathryn Kish Sklar.

Mary Beth Norton (*left*) and Mary Sumner Benson talk at the 1978 Big Berkshire Conference. Courtesy of Mary Beth Norton.

Edith P. Mayo of the Smithsonian Institution at the Alice Paul
Memorial March, Washington, DC, 1977. Wiki Commons.

Muriel Snowden, Margaret Rowley, Marcia Greenlee, Dorothy Porter, Elsie Lewis, Merze Tate, and Yvonne Braithwaite Burke (*left to right*), serving as the advisory board of the Black Women Oral History Project at the Schlesinger Library, July 30, 1976. Courtesy of Harvard University, Radcliffe Institute for Advanced Study, Schlesinger Library.

Ann Gordon, Nancy Schrom Dye, and Mari Jo Buhle (*left to right*) pose for a photo at the 1984 Big Berkshire Conference at Smith College in commemoration of their pathbreaking 1971 *Radical America* essay. Courtesy of Kathryn Kish Sklar.

Participants in the UCLA Teaching Women's History Workshop gather
after dinner in 1979. *Back row, left to right:* Sherna Gluck, Emily Abel,
unidentified, Mary Rothschild, Jane Slaughter, Helen Horowitz.
Front row, left to right: Mary Ryan, Kathryn Kish Sklar, Barbara Epstein,
Patricia Cohen. Courtesy of Kathryn Kish Sklar.

Sixty-three leading scholars attend the Wingspread Conference on Graduate Training in U.S. Women's History, October 1988. Identified from front to back, right to left. *Front row*: C. Karlsen, M. Greenwald, I. W. Scobie, J. Burstyn (white polka-dot shirt), J. Jensen, (?), A. F. Scott (center in culottes w/ dark scarf), J. Walzer Leavitt, L. Gordon, S. Alpern, S. Harley, E. Brooks Higginbotham. *Second row*: J. De Hart, E. Perry, Y. Azize, (?), L. Kerber, N. Cott, J. Hoff-Wilson, S. Evans, (?), S. Ware, (?), R. Rosen, D. Gray White, L. Thatcher Ulrich. *Third row*: E. Freedman, K. Peiss, J. Smith, [gap], A. Swerdlow, A. Kessler-Harris, A. Boylan, M. B. Norton, E. DuBois, L. Año Nuevo Kerr, [gap], T. Adams. *Fourth row*: (?), (?), L. Banner, S. Armitage, L. Rupp (wedged mid-row), R. Terborg-Penn, [gap], K. Kish Sklar, (?), S. Elbert, T. Dublin. *Fifth Row*: R. Rosenberg, V. Ruiz, N. Hewitt, J. Dowd Hall, [gap], P. Cohen, S. Gregory Kohlstedt, W. Chafe, G. Lerner, V. Matsumoto, J. Meyerowitz. *Back Row*: J. Antler (by window in white shirt), S. Michel, (?*), N. Tomes, [gap], (?), M. Rothschild, [gap], (?), [gap], C. Smith-Rosenberg, M. Buhle, (?), B. Stevenson. *Unidentified but present*: C. Aron, L. Grant DePauw, S. Lebsock, R. Morantz-Sanchez, P. Palmer, E. Payne, and S. Stage. *Possibly Joan Jacobs Brumberg, though she was not on the official attendance list. S. Poulsen and other Johnson Foundation staff may also appear in the photograph. (See appendix on p. 343 for list with full names of the participants.)

The conference, held at the Johnson Foundation's Wingspread Conference Center in Racine, Wisconsin, was sponsored by the National Endowment for the Humanities and the Johnson Foundation. Courtesy of the Johnson Foundation at Wingspread.

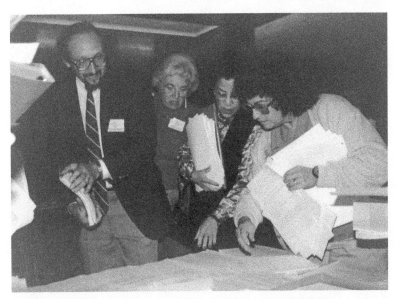

Tom Dublin, Gerda Lerner, Rosalyn Terborg-Penn, and Linda Kerber
(*left to right*) gather syllabi in preparation for a workshop at the
Wingspread Conference on Graduate Training in US Women's History,
October 1988. Courtesy of Kathryn Kish Sklar

Gerda Lerner, Ida Blom of Norway, and Kathryn Kish Sklar (*left to right*) pose
for a photograph at the 1990 Madrid meeting of the International Federation for
Research in Women's History. Courtesy of Kathryn Kish Sklar.

PART III

Founders and Institution Builders

Chapter 7

New Feminist Historians Have Just Begun to Be Heard, 1969–1973

As the Belknap Press of Harvard was putting the finishing touches on *Notable American Women* in the late 1960s and pioneering historians of women were bringing their expertise to bear in public life, forces inside academia were poised for a rapid development of the field of women's history. Among the ranks of professionally active historians who would propel the field forward were many in the early stages of their careers. The work done on *Notable American Women* between 1955 and 1971 showed that the field had garnered some support. But this support was far from universal. Indeed, for many mainstream professionals it hadn't registered a blip. No scholars identified themselves as a "women's historian." History departments did not create job lines in women's history. History majors could not major in women's history. Course offerings on the topic were extremely rare. But this all changed rapidly in the early 1970s in a sweep that must be credited to a new movement for women's history. Participants in that movement shared an interest in improving women's professional status, held an ideological commitment to feminism, and had the common goal of developing and legitimizing the field of women's history.[1]

When women historians organized as a professional force and linked the building of women's history to their goal of improving women's professional status in the 1970s, their movement put in motion a dramatic epistemological shift. Influenced by modern social justice movements including mainstream liberal feminism, civil rights, women's liberation, and the anti-war movement, the activism of these historians was a manifestation of modern feminism inside the academy.[2] Developing women's history in universities was strengthened by concurrent calls to recover women's past in numerous forums, like consciousness-raising groups and feminist media outlets, such as *Ms.* magazine. Here, feminists wanted to recover women's past to bolster and inform their struggle for equality and to develop a fuller understanding of gender inequality's historical underpinnings. As Ruth Rosen points out, it didn't take long for students and faculty involved in the women's liberation movement of the late 1960s to recognize and protest the "patriarchal nature of their educations and the fact that they had learned nothing about women's history, literature, or work."[3] Not only did they engage in attention-grabbing protests, as in 1969 when UC Berkeley graduate students and faculty burned their MA and PhD degrees in front of television cameras, but they also demanded institutional resources be allocated to creating courses and programs about women. The popular interest in the field was a boon to scholars organizing within the profession. But legitimizing women's history within professional societies and in history departments was crucial; if academic legitimacy were achieved, women's history would have staying power, and cultural authority for women would follow. Feminist historians launched this struggle first in mainstream professional institutions and then in newly formed feminist groups, creating a feminist intellectual movement.

Of the historians who organized within the national professional associations from 1969 to 1973 to advance women's history as an academic specialization, the largest number came from the field of US women's history. They benefited from having access to multiple large national professional associations whose major focus was on American history, notably the Organization of American Historians and the Southern Historical Association. However, a sizable number of Europeanists actively worked within the movement to advance women's history every bit as vigorously as the Americanists. Many took on major leadership roles. The result over the next two decades was that US women's history experienced especially intense growth in the quantity of published scholarship, jobs, and courses and in the number of scholars engaged in the field, followed by slower but still impressive gains for scholars of European women's history.[4] These historians combined their professional and epistemological goals. They were manifesting the feminist zeitgeist of the 1970s in their own way; their collective work to build institutions to support the field was an essential element of their success.

Origin Story: The Revolution of 1969

Demands for "women's history" first rang clear in resolutions that feminist historians presented at the annual meetings of the American Historical Association and the Organization of American Historians in December 1969 and March 1970. A movement had been set in motion on September 18, 1969, when Berenice Carroll of the University of Illinois at Urbana sent a letter to peers around the country. Her message stated, "It's clearly time for women in the historical profession to get organized, to oppose discrimination against women in the profession itself and the 'feminine mystique' in historical writing."[5] The "feminine mystique" in historical writing was more than the obvious nod to Betty Friedan's 1963 blockbuster. It referred to the relative absence of women as subjects in historical writing. In the flurry of activity that followed Carroll's letter, the major national historical societies responded to feminist historians by establishing "status of women" committees. Feminist historians also formed their own organizations. The first was the Coordinating Committee on Women in the Historical Profession, established in December 1969.

We've seen that by this time, important scholarly foundations had been built in the field by individual historians and by isolated institutional efforts to create women's archives. Some male "establishment" historians encouraged early pioneers, dabbled in writing women's history, and helped build these women's archives. And all of this occurred during a time full of disadvantages for women historians. But when in the 1970s these older pioneer historians of women were able to take up leadership roles in the new women's history movement, their perseverance paid off. They were joined by a growing number of younger scholars who expanded their vision for the field. The older scholars occupied sometimes uncomfortable, but always crucial, positions as mediators between the male establishment and the new feminist historians. An example comes from Sandi Cooper, who in 1972 was serving as the second chair of the Coordinating Committee on Women in the Historical Profession (CCWHP). That year she wrote to Willie Lee Rose, a historian from the University of Virginia, who had in 1970 been appointed to head up an ad hoc Committee on the Status of Women in the Historical Profession for the AHA. In the letter, Cooper acknowledged the "sardine position" Rose occupied as she mediated between the leading men of the AHA and new feminist historians seeking change. Describing the pressure exerted on Rose by multiple constituencies, Cooper sympathized by observing that Rose was perceived by the male "establishment" as a "rad libber" and by some movement women as an "establishment patsy."[6] Similarly, Anne Firor Scott was identified in pejorative terms in letters between Mary Massey and Bennett Wall in 1971. Wall scorned her connection with the "women's lib faction."[7] Notes from a conversation between Scott and Georgia historian Mollie Camp Davis on March 4, 1971, reveal the irony of Scott's tricky intermediary position. She reportedly told Davis that she was "enjoying being considered 'old-fashioned'" by such activists as Berenice Carroll.[8] This from a historian who had considered herself a "moderately militant feminist" since the 1950s.[9]

Scholars from different generations sometimes looked askance at one another. North Carolina State University historian Doris King wrote her friend Mary Massey upon returning from the 1970 meeting of the AHA, "Missed seeing you at the AHA Meeting in Boston. I was impressed especially by the number of 'women's history' sessions and by the absence from the program of the real scholars in the field. We have an amazing number of 'instant specialists' in all the 'in' fields these days, don't we?"[10] King implied that the pioneer historians of women were being ignored by young historians, whom she identified skeptically in quotation marks as instant women's history specialists. This communication also hints that there was some difference between an older variety of scholarship on women and the newly identified "women's history." As we will see, this intergenerational skepticism was often mutual. What strategies distinguished the "new women's historians" of 1969 and beyond? And how did some midcentury historians of women, notably Anne Firor Scott and Gerda Lerner, bridge this generational difference to become leading lights in the movement?

The answers can be found in the records of the many committees, caucuses, and groups that feminist historians formed between 1969 and 1973 to constitute the women's history movement. Scott's and Lerner's cohort of midcentury feminist scholars and the new feminist historians deployed their networking strategies and built new institutions to advance their scholarly field as part of the broader movement to improve the status of women historians in the profession. Participants in this movement left a rich record of their efforts in the form of archives, oral histories, published literature, and organizational and institutional records.[11] While Judith Zinsser produced an early draft of this story in 1993 that relied heavily on the records of the AHA, a more exhaustive study that draws from a broader array of institutional records and the records left by movement participants is now possible. These records complicate some of Zinsser's grander claims about feminist historians challenging "every aspect of the historian's craft" in the 1970s. We've already seen ample evidence that they were not, as Zinsser claimed, "discovering women's history" for the *first* time.[12] Yet, they did foster an unprecedented and explosive growth in the field of women's history, which only became richer by century's end, giving these scholars academic legitimacy and professional clout. They achieved all of this by applying feminist principles to professional practice—by making the profession more accessible to women and other professionally marginalized groups on the one hand and by challenging androcentrism in historical scholarship on the other.

Berenice Carroll's September 1969 call to end discrimination against women historians and the "'feminine mystique' in historical writing" provoked an eager response from the women to whom she sent the petition.[13] Her actions were inspired by having attended the annual meeting of the American Political Science Association, where a women's caucus had been formed.[14] Carroll's September 18 note announced that she had decided to "take the bull by the horns," write up a petition, and find collaborators. She sent a ready-to-distribute petition and welcomed comments and advice.[15] With this one-page missive, sent to perhaps a dozen historians, Carroll launched a two-pronged movement on behalf of women historians and women's history as a subject. In this she was anticipating a pattern of voluntary professional service and collegial collaboration.

This initiative should be understood within the context of the 1960s, a decade of liberal policy reform and institutional approaches to change, as well as social movements. In 1961, John F. Kennedy had, at the urging of progressive women within the Democratic Party, established the President's Commission on the

Status of Women in his first year in office. The PCSW's goal was to gather data about women's standing in the economy, the workplace, education, and the family. The data was meant to inform and lend authority to the administration's policy recommendations with an eye to helping women balance work and family and allowing them to make a full contribution to society. The PCSW issued reports and created follow-up committees dedicated to more granular studies. It inspired the formation of state-level commissions in all fifty states and passage of gender equity legislation, like the Equal Pay Act of 1963. At both the federal and state levels, the commissions often called on the expertise of women academics, including, as we've seen, historians of women. The commissions, inspired by progressive women activists, were a human rights initiative.[16] The feminist historians pushing for women's history within the formal discipline saw their epistemological project as part of the overall human rights initiatives that gained traction in the 1960s through both mainstream institutions and the social movements of the era. Writing the history of women and other marginalized categories of Americans more fully into American history would place them squarely within the broader culture, marking them as important stakeholders and contributors to American society. First, though, feminist historians had to claim their place within the profession and make their mark on the canon. This would require years of activism within professional institutions and years of scholarly endeavor.

One of the first historians to reply to Carroll's call to action was Gerda Lerner. On October 3, 1969, Lerner replied to Carroll:

> Thank you for thinking of me in connection with your efforts for organizing a women's caucus at the AHA. Count me in. I am enclosing a suggested amendment to your petition. . . . I am also enclosing a separate motion. . . . This one I think is terribly important, because it raises content questions. The society can keep us all happily scurrying around with investigative subcommittees, fact-finding and information gathering, without one single thing changing for decades. But when we start to talk about content, courses for women, courses about *women's history*, fellowships, etc. then we are really dealing with issues demanding immediate attention and CHANGE.[17]

Lerner's motion acknowledged what Arthur Schlesinger Sr., Charles and Mary Beard, David Potter, and others had long pointed out: the neglect of women as subjects in history. Lerner's proposed amendment read:

> Whereas the field of *women's history* is virtually non-existent as a respectable specialty; is not taught on the graduate level, scarcely taught on the undergraduate level and

Whereas women, having for most of our history made up nearly half of the population, so that it cannot be assumed that they have no history worth recording nor that their contributions to general history are so insignificant as not to be worthy the serious attention of historians,

THEREFORE, BE IT RESOLVED,

That the attention of our colleagues be called to the neglect of the *field of women's history* and that efforts be made to stimulate scholarship, research and discussion of topics concerning the past of American women.[18]

Lerner here asserted a new name for the field—*women's history*—and she warned that scholarly neglect of that history would no longer be tolerated. A newly formed "women's caucus" met at the AHA meeting that December and attached Lerner's amendment to the status resolutions the caucus presented. The phrase "the past of American women" was changed to "the history of women" in the final version of the AHA resolution.

Carroll's September letter resulted in the formation of a correspondence network in the intervening months, with twenty-five women constituting themselves as the Coordinating Committee on Women in the Historical Profession. Carroll and Lerner served as cochairs of its steering committee. The CCWHP represented both European and American history and drew members from around the United States. Hilda Smith was to be secretary-treasurer. The steering committee had an equal number of Europeanists and Americanists on it. The Americanists were Lerner, Linda Kerber, Constance Ashton Myers, and Jo Tice Bloom. The Europeanists were Carroll, Smith, Edythe Lutzker, and Sherrin Wyntjes. Indeed, Kerber had already initiated a women's group in California originally called the West Coast Historical Association.[19] She was spurred to start the group by the anxiety she felt in her new home on the West Coast, far away from the Northeastern support group she'd belonged to, the Berkshire Conference of Women Historians. Before Kerber's move, Mary Maples Dunn had advised her to form a similar group on the West Coast.[20] On December 27, 1969, members of the CCWHP met, drew up their statement of purpose, and refined the set of resolutions drafted earlier by Carroll and Lerner. They submitted these at the AHA business meeting the next day. Five of the resolutions dealt with recruiting and retaining women in the profession and with opposing discrimination. The sixth was the one developed by Gerda Lerner in her October 3 letter to Berenice Carroll. It urged the AHA to support research and instruction in women's history.[21] This sixth resolution became a major plank in the program of the national women's history movement at its foundational moment.

While Lerner's was perhaps the most forceful voice advocating the development of women's history within the CCWHP and the AHA in 1969, it was not the only one. She was joined in that first year by a chorus of Americanists, including Kerber, Myers, Mollie Davis, Blanche Wiesen Cook, Ellen DuBois, Carol Bleser and Jane De Hart Mathews. There was a particularly strong cohort of European historians in support of women's history as well: Carroll, Cooper, and Smith were joined by Natalie Zemon Davis, Elisabeth Israels (Perry), and, by 1972, Joan Kelly, Renate Bridenthal, and Karen Offen. Already in 1970, the CCWHP began putting considerable effort into regular bulletins on courses and research-in-progress in women's history. Members sent the bulletins to their emerging national network at the same time that they worked to get women's history papers and panels on conference programs.[22]

Feminist historians' launch of the women's history movement within the established institutions of the historical profession in December 1969 at the annual meeting of the American Historical Association in Washington, DC, took place in the broader context of discontent expressed by radical and New Left historians and by women in all academic disciplines. The 1970s saw the establishment of women's caucuses and committees across academia.[23] But in 1969, when women historians could have joined with the radical New Left scholars, they chose to remain separate to broaden their appeal among members of the AHA.[24] Whether this was in part a corollary to Old Left women historians' fears over red-baiting, the dismissive treatment of women within the male-dominated Old Left, or the scandalously misogynist treatment of women within the New Left isn't known.[25] But given that a primary goal of the women was achieving academic legitimacy for women's history, it makes sense that Lerner would advise her peers not to burden their cause with unnecessary ideological encumbrances.

At the 1969 AHA meeting, the status issue garnered the most institutional support. The CCWHP sponsored a panel discussion on the status of women in the historical profession. This off-the-program panel was hastily organized by Hilda Smith. Despite the haste, it attracted a standing-room-only crowd who listened to panelists Smith, Emiliana Noether, Hanna Holborn Gray, Jo Tice Bloom, and Christopher Lasch.[26] Women's status was the primary concern addressed at the panel, even though Smith and Lasch had both done work in the history of women.[27] The AHA Executive Council reacted on February 21, 1970, by establishing the Ad Hoc Committee on the Status of Women in the Historical Profession and instructing it to conduct a study on women's status in history departments across the country. This committee was headed by Willie Lee Rose, a distinguished Americanist from the University of Virginia, and included Carl Schorske, Page Smith, and Mary Wright.[28] Patricia Aljberg Graham joined the committee in April 1970.[29] The "Rose Report," as this committee's study came to be known, documented a clear pattern of exclusion and discrimination against women in the profession from 1920 forward. It noted a dramatic decline in the numbers of women employed as historians between 1959 and 1969.[30] Between 1920 and 1959, women had never made up more than 16 percent of professional historians. That number dropped to about 9 percent by 1969. Most of the women reflected in that 9 percent were clustered in women's colleges. The status issue would occupy the AHA in its efforts to acknowledge and redress sexual discrimination, and most people in the CCWHP held this as their central concern. Still, about half the group was equally absorbed by the subject of women's history.[31]

Carroll's earliest correspondents included Emiliana Noether, Hilda Smith, and Gerda Lerner—all eager to collaborate with Carroll to form the women's caucus in the AHA.[32] Disagreements over whether to focus on the status question exclusively or to combine this issue with advocacy for women's history emerged early on. Women in the CCWHP from distinct fields of history moved to expand the field to encompass more than just American women, and leaders of the newly formed organization were both Europeanists and Americanists in roughly equal numbers. Notably, Europeanists Smith, Renate Bridenthal, and Donna Boutelle disagreed sharply. Boutelle, the CCWHP's third president, did not want to dilute focus on women's status by focusing on women's history. In the early 1970s this type of opposition may have been simply a strategic matter. Boutelle was not a women's historian, but by 1975 she had changed her mind and backed the CCWHP's advocacy of women's history.[33]

In its first year, the CCWHP set its goals for the next decade of professional activism. Carroll wrote friends in the network on March 1, 1970, "The most urgent business before us right now is organizing activity at forthcoming meetings, and I want to report on the situation and ask help on these now." Efforts to improve women's status focused on getting women elected and appointed to offices and committees within the major historical associations and on securing their participation on the boards of annual program committees and editorial boards. Getting women published in mainstream journals was fundamental. Amid a contraction in the job market in the 1970s, the women emphasized reversing discrimination against women and racial minorities in hiring. Finally, they pushed for women's history across national and geographic fields and demanded that space be given on conference programs and in scholarly journals for new research on women. The CCWHP was instrumental in getting the OAH and AHA to create women's committees. It saw itself as an outside pressure group. From a position independent of AHA and OAH committees, the CCWHP exerted pressure on the mainstream male-dominated profession. Those women historians who operated within the OAH, SHA, and AHA did the same thing from an internal institutional vantage point.[34]

There was an urgency to Carroll's proposals that was determined by the timing of each organization's annual meeting. The AHA met each year in December and the deadline for session proposals was March 1, some nine months earlier. Still, in the fall of 1969, Carroll encouraged women to propose "off the program" sessions to the AHA program committee in the hopes that it might allow these. The OAH 1970 annual meeting was scheduled to convene in Los Angeles on April 16, 1970, and Carroll and the CCWHP submitted strong resolutions and hinted at a possible "off-the-program panel discussion" like the one they organized at AHA '69.[35] They were already planning session proposals for the 1971 OAH meeting.[36] Since the Southern Historical Association met each year in November and the program for SHA '70 was already set, Carroll asked CCWHP charter member Constance Ashton Myers to publicize the CCWHP in the SHA bulletins.[37] Myers, Sandi Cooper, and Mollie Davis set about getting SHA secretary-treasurer Bennett Wall to schedule a room for a women's caucus meeting at the Louisville, Kentucky, gathering. Multiple requests were sent to Wall, causing him to bristle at the duplication of efforts. Wall was irritated by the alleged "abrasiveness" of New Yorker Sandi Cooper, who was not an SHA member and who he claimed called his home at one o'clock in the morning.[38] Mollie Davis of West Georgia College was able to smooth Wall's ruffled feathers. Her correspondence with him showed that the confusion was the result of CCWHP women's unfamiliarity with the procedures and schedules of the various associations. Senior historians such as Wall had not considered that these younger women historians were not yet professionally acculturated. The young women lacked mentoring from senior men in the profession, since it was uncommon for men to mentor women graduate students.

This correspondence reveals a level of defensiveness about maintaining organizational strongholds from one who could be collegial to women scholars. It took skill to liaise between the old guard and movement activists. Davis was able to appeal to him as a fellow Southern historian and his former student.[39] Davis's role in the Southern wing of the women's history movement deserves more recognition as part of the mainstream narrative of the field's trajectory.[40] It helps illustrate how widespread the movement was, beyond the advocacy and eloquence of high-profile leaders like Lerner or Scott or of single organizations like the CCWHP. The women's history movement was large, national in scope, and dependent on regional and local activism. Mollie Davis was active in the OAH, the CCWHP, the SHA, and the AHA. She played an instrumental role in forming the Southern Association for Women Historians. As such, she is a particularly good person to consider when reconstructing the movement's history.

Mollie Davis had attended the annual meeting of the AHA in 1969 in Washington, DC. She missed the first day of CCWHP meetings but, after hearing Constance Myers's enthusiastic account, attended the second day. She recalled meeting a "number of wonderful people" who "decided we would all come back the following year with great gusto and do great things."[41] One person she met that December was Linda Kerber. At the time, Kerber had already been working for nine months to set up the West Coast Historical Association, which became the West Coast Association of Women Historians in 1970.[42] A founding member of the CCWHP, Kerber became very active in the movement and in the aftermath of the December meeting began to publicize and recruit for the organization. At the OAH April 1970 meeting in Los Angeles, Carroll and Kerber's plan was to hold a meeting of the CCWHP, introduce resolutions at the OAH business meeting, and organize an off-the-program session.[43] Kerber agreed to write a newsletter and a bulletin that would identify new research and courses in women's history. The bulletin came out on March 1, 1971.[44] The first newsletter appeared in the spring of 1970 and reported that Kerber and Dorothy Sexter, president of the West Coast group, sponsored a successful "smoker and sherry party" at the Los Angeles conference, where they held a discussion on the problems of women in the historical profession with representatives of the West Coast Historical Association, the Berkshire Conference of Women Historians, and the CCWHP.[45]

When Carroll and Lerner introduced revised CCWHP resolutions at the annual meeting of the OAH in Los Angeles, they were approved without much fanfare. The OAH women's contingent emphasized the content issue in keeping with the organization's institutional focus on American history and left the status issue to the AHA. The OAH had roughly 8,000 members, all Americanists, in its ranks in 1970. They represented by far the most practitioners in any geographic or national field of historical study in the United States. The OAH was positioned to give institutional support to the field of American women's history, and in fact, that field grew more quickly than any other between 1969 and 1990.[46] One measure of this dynamic can be found by doing a simple tally of women's historians listed by field of specialization in 1975, 1980, and 1990 in the AHA's *Directory of History Departments and Organizations in the U.S. and Canada*. The AHA directories for these years show a growing predominance of Americanists in women's history appearing to increase from about two dozen in 1969 to 100 in 1980 and to 338 in 1990. During the same years, the number of listed women's historians specializing in European, Latin American, African, Asian, and other specialties rose from about 58 in 1980 to 100 in 1990. Between 1980 and 1990, historians of American women more than tripled their numbers, while those in all other national/geographic fields nearly doubled theirs. By 1990, roughly three-quarters of all listed historians of women, 338 out of 448, specialized in American history.[47] Much of this was certainly a product of historians' inclination toward the study of their own nation's history. Some of this was surely the result of geographic proximity to local and national archives, which facilitated the research of Americanists. What did the OAH do to support the development of women's history, and why?

On April 17, 1970, Berenice Carroll presented a four-part resolution—streamlined since the AHA meeting in December—to the OAH Executive Board.[48] It highlighted the subject of women's history as follows:

I. Whereas the status of women in the historical profession *and the subject of women's history are matters of concern to the Organization of American Historians*; Be it resolved:
   a. That the OAH provide for equitable representation of women historians in appointive and elective offices, committee assignments, convention panels, and other programs and activities of the OAH; and
   b. That the OAH formally state its opposition to discrimination against women in admissions, grants, awarding of degrees, faculty employment, salary and conditions of employment and consideration for promotion, and that it undertake to receive, solicit, and publicize information relating to specific instances of such discrimination; and
   c. *That the OAH undertake to encourage research and instruction on the history of women in America*; and
   d. That a committee of the OAH be appointed to deal with matters affecting the status of women in the historical profession, and to cooperate with the AHA Committee on the Status of Women, *and that this committee be directed specifically to evaluate and make recommendations concerning the treatment of women in textbooks of American history used in secondary schools, colleges, and universities.*[49]

The vote went in favor of the entire resolution by a wide margin of 180 to 60 votes cast. President David Potter immediately appointed the OAH Committee on the Status of Women in history (OAH-CSW).[50]

This April 17 meeting had been foreshadowed by the events at the AHA's recent annual meeting. Members of the OAH Executive Board hoped to head off the sort of disruptions triggered by the Radical Historians Caucus. On March 6, the executive board met before the annual convention to discuss what to expect of the Radical Historians Caucus, predicting that "strong resolutions might be submitted."[51] President Potter recommended that they give the Radical Historians Caucus a couple of rooms in which members could air their concerns so as to minimize disruption and hear them out. C. Vann Woodward suggested it was "very valuable to keep in touch with the opposition."[52] This defensive view of the radicals as "the opposition" showed that their critique of the profession and its institutions was hitting home. The executive board's decision to give a room to the radicals was preemptive, but perhaps it was also sympathetic. Regarding the women and women's history question, Woodward and Potter were perhaps more sympathetic. Woodward was a sometime friend to women's history and women scholars, and Potter had published a 1962 essay on developing the history of women more fully.[53] There appears to have been no effort to head off the women or characterize them as "the opposition" in that moment. Later, Willie Lee Rose drew attention to Potter's sympathetic stand when she was strategizing with the CCWHP's Sandi Cooper:

> The strongest (absolutely) thing we have ever had going for us as women is the consciousness on the part of large numbers of the best and most influential men in the profession that the treatment of women in the past has indeed been outrageous. . . . They know that positive action is required . . . to secure justice in a practical sense. True they have had to be pushed in many instances, but there were staunch supporters in the highest offices. . . . Men like David Potter, for instance, who did us better service than most of the women can possibly know. He was very quiet, very effective. Without him, my committee might not have gotten that report accepted. Well, he is gone, but I think there are others who feel as he does.[54]

Indeed, the OAH Executive Board from 1969 to 1971 included Thomas D. Clark, Bell I. Wiley, C. Vann Woodward, Ray Billington, and William Leuchtenberg, who were all in line with Potter's attitude toward women and views on women's history. The first four had contributed sketches to *Notable American Women*, and Wiley, Woodward, Billington, and Leuchtenberg had ties to historians of women like Mary Massey and Anne Firor Scott or to others from the Columbia/Barnard circle, including Linda Kerber, Carroll Smith-Rosenberg, Aileen Kraditor, and Gerda Lerner. Mary Massey confided to Mollie Davis in 1972 that Bell Wiley had done more for her professionally than any other person.[55]

The OAH Executive Board's choice as chair of the OAH-CSW in 1970 was Anne Firor Scott of Duke University. John Ezell, Rhoda Dorsey, Nancy Weiss Malkiel, and William Freeling also served. Scott, Ezell, and Dorsey had all contributed biographical sketches to *Notable American Women* in the 1960s. Since the AHA and the American Association of University Professors' "Committee W" had spent considerable resources investigating the status issue, the first year of the OAH-CSW focused on the women's history resolutions. The committee members explained, "All the hearings and surveys come to the same conclusion: there are few women in the profession, particularly at the higher levels, and particularly in the better departments. It did not seem to us necessary to prove that again. . . . We have chosen not to duplicate, but to chart a course for ourselves, and to make our main focus . . . the history of American women."[56]

The initial spate of feminist activism from December 1969 to the spring of 1970 took the historical profession by surprise. In an editorial in the *New York Times Book Review* of July 19, 1970, prominent historian David Donald wrote about an "attempted revolution at the 1969 AHA convention."[57] This was a reference to the newly formed Radical Historians Caucus. The "revolutionaries," as Donald called them, had held off-the-program "counter sessions" and presented resolutions supporting Black civil rights, protesting the Vietnam War, and advocating for class and gender equity within the history profession.[58]

Little more than a month after Donald's comments appeared, Gerda Lerner sent a reply to the paper in response to the letter. She pointed out his "characteristic omission" of the part played by women in the December 1969 "revolution." She admonished Donald, reminding him that "among the groups with 'special grievances and a special sense of urgency' who organized at the convention were not only young radicals . . . but female historians of all ages, philosophies, and degrees of feminism. We met in separate sessions." Some of the women suggested joining with the Radical Historians Caucus, she added, but she advised them not to link their professional goals within the AHA to those of the Radical Caucus. She pointed out that women historians vastly outnumbered radical historians and that they held a wide range of political beliefs. It followed for Lerner that women had broader appeal and a better chance to achieve their goals if they remained organizationally separate.[59] For Lerner, while women historians were deeply concerned with solving the problem of sexual discrimination in the profession, they were also "deeply dissatisfied with the content of history as it is currently written, which assumes blithely that women have no history worth recording." Lerner then predicted, "New feminist historians have just begun to be heard."[60]

In August, Lerner's letter appeared alongside Donald's grudging and dismissive reply. He wrote, "Possibly I ought to have mentioned the discontent among women historians as Gerda Lerner desires, but they have not produced a significant, distinctive body of writing. I sympathize with their movement and hope that . . . five years from now I could point to the stimulating new dimension women historians have added to the study of American history."[61] With this statement Donald defended his oversight while suggesting that existing foundational archives and scholarship focused on women in American history were insignificant and merely marked a starting point for the field. For him, women's history didn't deserve acknowledgment until women produced a significant body of writing of their own. But, of course, the point is that history conferences are supposed to be places where new, cutting-edge scholarship gets peer-reviewed. Lerner and her compatriots were asking for the opportunity to introduce new women's history scholarship into that standard process, not seeking recognition for what had already been produced. They agreed with

Donald that a "distinctive body of writing" about women hadn't yet been produced. In this exchange, Donald implied that the contribution women had to make in the future would be in the area of women's history, essentially ignoring the inequity faced by women historians in program admissions, for example, or in hiring, job retention, and promotion, regardless of their topical specialization.[62] Yet in blurring the issues of women's history and women historians' professional status, he hit on the two distinct goals of the emerging women's history movement. Indeed, disagreement over whether the women's history movement ought to focus on content, status, or both equally would trouble activists through the mid-1970s. Ultimately, for most, the two goals would be equally important and mutually supportive.

In the aftermath of the initial slate of meetings and the exchange between Lerner and Donald, feminist historians got to work within the AHA, OAH, and SHA. Lerner's prediction was about to come true. In 1970 the OAH-CSW drafted a report, submitted for adoption in 1971, which spelled out the organization's plan for fostering equality between men and women in the profession. The plan called for equal opportunity in admissions, recruitment, working conditions, and pay and asked all members of the profession to take responsibility for implementing this principle. It also included recommendations on the availability of part-time work for graduate students of both sexes, with proportionate financial aid and part-time appointments with proportionate benefits. Maternity leave was introduced as an option, as was the abolition of nepotism rules that tended to work against women married to fellow scholars.[63]

The OAH-CSW made plans for research and instruction in women's history in accordance with Resolution C, which had demanded that the OAH encourage and support the development of women's history. It started by establishing an annual $500 cash prize for writing in women's history, for either a book or an article, and it initiated preparations for a special issue of the *Journal of American History* dedicated to new women's history research. To launch the special issue, the CSW proposed that the OAH Executive Board hold a two-day conference for those doing innovative work in women's history, especially economic and social historians. The follow-up on this proposed conference would be a prospectus on research needs, which would be published in the special issue. Finally, the OAH-CSW suggested that the OAH make it a permanent committee so that it could monitor progress for women and women's history. In the final pages of the report, the CSW cited a 1971 study by historians Dolores Barracano Schmidt and Earl R. Schmidt that showed that 99 percent of the textbook market in American history devoted less than 1 percent of its content to women (that is, twenty-six out of twenty-seven college history textbooks). Charles and Mary Beard's *The Rise of American Civilization* devoted only 2 percent of its space to women. According to the Schmidts, a "world without women" in its historical consciousness was a world of socioeconomic oppression of women. The Schmidts marveled at the fact that "until very recently not a single professor protested that historical truth should be so unlike reality" and that "not a single paying customer demanded her money back on the basis that she had paid for a history course and had been sold a male fantasy instead."[64] To begin the work of dispelling this fantasy, the OAH-CSW proposed a panel for the 1972 OAH annual meeting, titled "Where Are the Women?" It also asked the board to undertake the production of a teaching pamphlet on women's history as part of its teaching pamphlet series.[65]

As the OAH worked toward implementing these suggestions over the next decade, much of the work was initiated and orchestrated through the networks of the CCWHP, the outside pressure group. Developing women's history depended on scholars willing to produce original scholarship. The presence of women like Scott, Massey, Lerner, and A. Elizabeth Taylor in the discipline's professional institutions was of immeasurable importance. They could speak with authority on the field's legitimacy and research needs. They could also serve as mentors and advocates for women just learning to navigate history's professional culture.

Though it had been too late for the newly organized pressure groups to propose sessions for the OAH 1970 program in April, they prepared in advance for OAH '71, which was to be held in New Orleans. And by the time the AHA convened in Boston in December 1970, women historians and members of the CCWHP, who had submitted workshop proposals to the AHA in January of 1970, had almost a year to prepare.[66] Three meetings and workshops on women's status and four sessions on women's history were on the AHA program at Boston. Three additional papers on women were included in other sessions. One, coauthored by Linda Gordon, Persis Hunt, Elizabeth Pleck, Marcia Scott, and Rochelle Ziegler (Rochelle Goldberg Ruthchild) was bluntly titled "Sexism in American Historiography." This paper became a chapter in Carroll's *Liberating Women's History*, retitled "Historical Phallacies: Sexism in American Historical Writing." This title was itself adapted by the editor from the authors' first choice: "Up from the Genitals: Sexism in American Historical Writing."[67] On December 30, Eugenia Palmegiano gave a paper, "Feminist Propaganda in the 1850s and 1860s," and Virginia Y. McLaughlin read "Wage-Earning Women in Industrial America."[68]

The women's history sessions were well attended. Anne Firor Scott chaired the session "Feminism: Past, Present and Future."[69] Gerda Lerner, Jo Freeman, and Alice Rossi gave the papers, and William O'Neill commented.[70] "Women's Experience in History: A Teaching Problem" was chaired by Patricia Aljberg Graham. It featured papers and comment by Caroline Bynum, Alan Graebner, and African Americanists Letitia Brown and Winthrop Jordan. The December

29 session, "Why Women's History?," again saw Linda Gordon speaking, along with Juliet Mitchell, Adele Simmons, and Hilda Smith. It was chaired by Berenice Carroll.[71]

Perhaps the most controversial workshop was one sponsored by the CCWHP. Titled "Possibilities and Problems of Research in Women's History," it took place on December 27, 1970, with speakers Janet Giele, Annette Baxter, and Jeannette Cheek.[72] The *CCWHP Newsletter* reported later that the papers were followed by controversy and criticism.[73] The controversy was intense enough to prompt a group to walk out of the session in frustration. Berenice Carroll, in writing about the session, said what surfaced were "some major differences in outlook in the field of women's history."[74] The first of these was the question of "biological differences between men and women" as they related to sex roles and sexual stereotypes and what women's history might reveal about their mutability. The second engaged the relationship between "scholarly discussion and polemical discourse." Presciently, Carroll suggested that "the answers to these questions are far from self-evident, that they are important questions, and that they deserve our serious attention."[75] Indeed, these very questions would remain at the heart of women's history matters into the 1980s when women historians began to use gender as a tool for historical analysis and to increasingly emphasize differences between and among women of diverse backgrounds.

By April 1971, women were already quite a bit more successful at getting women's history onto the program at the OAH. At OAH '71, Anne Scott made her CSW report to the OAH Executive Board. Three women's history sessions were included on the program: "New Perspectives on Women's History," "Mary Ritter Beard," and "Sexuality and Democracy in the Nineteenth Century." At AHA '71 in New York City, six sessions on women's history made the program and included scholarship on the United States, Germany, Russia, Latin America, and China.[76] While Anne Scott, Gerda Lerner, and others were making progress within the OAH and AHA, Mollie Davis of the newly formed Caucus of Women in History made some headway with the program committee of the Southern Historical Association. The SHA was the third largest professional association of historians in the nation with around 6,000 members in 1970. The Caucus of Women in History, renamed the Southern Association for Women Historians in 1976, was one of several large regional hubs established by women historians from 1969 to 1971. Other significant ones were the West Coast Association of Women Historians and the New York Metropolitan Area Group (a branch of the CCWHP). There was considerable overlap in membership between the SHA and the OAH, and many Southern women also played vital roles in the AHA and the CCWHP.

In November 1970, at the Louisville, Kentucky, meeting of the Southern Historical Association, a group of about thirty gathered in a basement room to organize a Southern version of the CCWHP to further the interests of women historians in the South. Mollie Davis and Berenice Carroll took the lead. The two had met at AHA '69, and both attended OAH '70 in Los Angeles, where the CCWHP had inaugurated its exciting work. They corresponded to set the stage for Louisville. Also present at the meeting were Hilda Smith, Charlotte Davis, Rosemary Carroll, and African American colleagues Melerson Guy Dunham and Louise Spears.[77] From the beginning, then, the group comprised both Black and white historians. Dunham was an instructor of history, literature, and social sciences at Alcorn Agricultural and Mechanical College in Mississippi. She earned an MA in history at Indiana University in 1958 at the age of fifty-four and an honorary doctorate from Mississippi Industrial College in 1973. Later she participated in the International Women's Year Conference in Houston as a delegate from Mississippi.[78]

In February, Mollie Davis, then an ABD teaching at West Georgia College, wrote to Carroll to indicate her willingness to become active.[79] The first newsletter of the CCWHP, sent out just before OAH '70, held a brief announcement of a women's meeting intended for the November SHA conference in Louisville.[80] The newsletter solicited papers or ideas for sessions on women's status or on women's history. By summer, Davis and Carroll launched their campaign to get Bennett Wall to provide them with a room at the conference. They were assigned the basement room next to the hotel boiler.[81]

At the meeting itself, Davis later recalled, women were most "furious" over the status issue.[82] Yet, the first newsletter of the Caucus of Women in History reported, "In general, we don't have too much to complain about in regard to the SHA. Since 1935, we have had two women presidents, a number of women on the executive council, three times a woman chaired the nominating committee, and of course at the moment we have a woman vice president."[83] The report from which this information was gleaned indicated that eight women had served on the executive council since 1935, three had served as editorial associates on the *Journal of Southern History*, while another three had served on the journal's board of editors. Moreover, Mary Massey served on the membership committee in 1955 and had been the SHA's program chair in 1962. A. Elizabeth Taylor and Willie Lee Rose served on awards committees in the 1960s.[84] Despite this record being relatively better than the AHA and OAH's, the women nevertheless agreed that a major goal of their group should be to monitor and improve women's professional status in the South.

The caucus also identified a second major goal, which was "the need to get women's history courses into the curriculum of southern schools. We want to put this topic on the agenda for the Houston Colloquium (SHA '71)." The newsletter asked those teaching and doing research in women's history to provide information on their situation, and it requested money and news items for the upcoming issue.[85] Charlotte Davis reported that she would be writing in the next issue on Mollie Davis's activities at the OAH meeting in New Orleans. In 1971, Mollie Davis arranged for the SHA to host two women's history sessions on its program. The first was a colloquium titled "Teaching of Women's History," featuring a panel discussion with Barbara Schnorrenberg, Marsha Marks, and Newt Gingrich of West Georgia College.[86] Mollie Davis later reported that Gingrich actively courted the favor of women in his history department—until he was awarded tenure. A regular session where papers were presented was titled "Right-Wing Extremism and Women in the 1920s." This session included papers by Mollie Davis and J. Stanley Lemons. Dorothy Johnson and Paul Taylor—both of whom had written biographical sketches for *Notable American Women*—offered comment.[87]

Mollie Davis connected with a cohort of established Southern women historians and was able to capitalize on her national ties to build the movement in the South. In the early 1970s she actively corresponded with Berenice Carroll, Constance Ashton Myers, Sandi Cooper, Anne Scott, Willie Lee Rose, and Bennett Wall. By 1971, she was also in touch with Jane De Hart Mathews. De Hart Mathews (now Jane Sherron De Hart) too became an active participant in the women's history movement from 1970 forward.[88] Among Davis's correspondents in these early movement years, only Carroll and Cooper were not Southerners.

In 1970, Jane De Hart Mathews was an adjunct American history professor in the Chapel Hill, North Carolina, area. She finished her PhD at Duke in 1966 but had moved to New Jersey in 1962 for her husband's career. Her husband, Donald Mathews, taught history at Princeton. In 1964, De Hart Mathews took a tenure track job at Douglass College (Rutgers) that helped her assert her identity as a historian in her own right; she resisted being cast in the role of faculty wife.[89] She joined the Berkshire Conference of Women Historians and attended its annual meetings from 1962 until 1968, when she moved back to North Carolina.[90] De Hart Mathews was part of a group along with Sandi Cooper and Margaret Judson, a senior historian in the Douglass history department, that hoped to reverse the decline of the Berkshire Conference by increasing its membership. At Berkshire meetings her cohort included Cooper, Carroll, Kerber, Mary Maples Dunn, Carroll Smith-Rosenberg, Blanche Wiesen Cook, and other younger members who joined the conference in the 1960s.[91] De Hart Mathews formed especially close friendships with Kerber and Cook.[92]

In 1968, when Donald Mathews took a faculty appointment at UNC Chapel Hill, De Hart Mathews returned to North Carolina, giving up her tenure track job.[93] In one year she had a fellowship; in another she taught part-time in the American studies department at Chapel Hill. During this period Anne Scott introduced her to a Chapel Hill dean. When the dean said there were no positions for De Hart Mathews at Chapel Hill, Scott advised her to apply for high school teaching positions, something De Hart Mathews did not see as an option. Rather than becoming another casualty of the gendered history job market, in 1971 De Hart Mathews was hired to fill an opening in American history at UNC Greensboro, formerly North Carolina State Women's College. In that same year, Willie Lee Rose visited Chapel Hill and invited De Hart Mathews to serve on the AHA's Committee on Women Historians (AHA-CWH), which was becoming a permanent committee. She agreed to serve.[94] De Hart Mathews had been a founding member of the CCWHP in December 1969. When she joined the AHA Committee on Women Historians, she began a long period of service in the AHA and OAH on behalf of women and women's history.

Mollie Davis and De Hart Mathews were both present at some of the founding meetings of the CCWHP at AHA '69. They do not appear to have known each other, however, until Davis attended a dinner meeting in New York held by the AHA-CWH just before the meeting of the AHA in December 1971. But Jane De Hart Mathews's name and address appear in a handwritten list of women historians to contact about getting the Caucus of Women in History off the ground, so it is likely Davis knew of her presence at Chapel Hill as early as January 1971.[95] Their professional acquaintance reveals the reach of women's networking efforts in the early 1970s. On January 5, 1971, De Hart Mathews wrote to Davis. Here, she expressed her delight in finally meeting Davis in person and learning about women's activities within the SHA. She committed to working with Davis and with men in the profession, such as Richard Current, with whom she had already met to develop a list of women historians in the South who could be recommended to deliver papers and chair sessions. She closed the letter by asking what else she could do to be of service to the cause of women historians.[96]

As women struggled to strengthen their position in the historical profession, lists of contacts and rosters of colleagues working in similar areas were critical. Notes from telephone conversations between Davis and De Hart Mathews reveal that contacts could lead to jobs, slots on conference programs, or committee appointments. As a result of connecting with Davis in 1971, for example, De Hart Mathews, already well-acquainted with Willie Lee Rose and Anne Scott, made a connection to Bennett Wall. This acquaintance was strengthened by De Hart Mathews's work on the program committee of the SHA that year.[97] The new professional contacts reinforced both women's connections with established historians Willie Lee Rose and Anne Firor Scott as well as Mary Berry and Linda Kerber, who served with De Hart Mathews on the AHA-CWH in 1971. Berry thus became the first African American scholar to serve on the committee. Women historians were now professionally acculturating more quickly by helping one another learn the professional ropes in the national organizations and generating professional opportunities for each other. Prior to this era, women generally lacked the mentoring from professionally active male historians that would facilitate this process. In academic disciplines like history, whom people knew professionally could help them disseminate what they knew historically. Knowing people and how institutions function could help get an individual's paper on a program and thus get scholarship on women or other subjects noticed and vetted. Yet, these women scholars were collaborating in the hopes of improving the status of all women and promoting qualified women scholars in general. They were not merely networking for their own personal professional gain. This reflected a feminist consciousness of, and will to correct, women's collectively low status in the profession. Indeed, by 1975, De Hart Mathews, Suzanne Lebsock, Mary Frances Berry, Carl Degler, and others serving on the AHA-CSW produced the first *Manual for Women (and Other) Historians* in their efforts to demystify the professional culture of historians for women and other historically marginalized groups.[98] The guide went into several editions and is still useful for initiates into the discipline.

For several years, activists in the CCWHP, the West Coast Association of Women Historians, the SHA's Caucus of Women in History, the AHA-CWH, and the OAH-CSW focused on women gaining office in professional associations and securing slots on conference programs. For example, in 1971, at the prompting of the New York Metropolitan Area Group, the CCWHP and the Berkshire Conference together launched a petition to nominate a slate of women for the 1971 AHA elections to the executive council and nominating committee. They nominated Louise Dalby, Emiliana Noether, Gerda Lerner, and Hilda Smith for executive council vacancies and Linda Kerber, Sandi Cooper, and Sister Joel Reed as candidates on the nominating committee. When consulted, Mollie Davis suggested Anne Scott be considered, as hers was one of the most recognizable names among women historians in the country. This suggestion came too late to be put on the ballot, however. In any case, Scott was already serving on the OAH-CSW and would soon accept nomination to the OAH Executive Board.[99] Of the write-in candidates in the petition campaign, only Noether won.

The petition campaign was repeated in 1972 and 1973 with new networks consulting about candidates for available posts. For the 1973 vacancies, AHA administrators proposed running Mary Young as candidate for president against Eugene Genovese, who styled himself an ally of the women's cause. Genovese and Young were in an awkward situation; Young had just been hired at the University of Rochester, where Genovese was chair of the department. Moreover, Mollie Davis, Sandi Cooper, and Jane De Hart Mathews expressed suspicion at Genovese's motives in supporting the movement. They suspected him of creating tensions between women in the AHA who were perceived as establishment and the younger scholars active in the CCWHP who were seen as radicals.[100] They reacted negatively when Genovese lobbied for Young to be taken off the ballot using the argument that she would divide the vote of liberal and progressive historians and guarantee the victory of their more conservative opponent.[101] Young did not, after all, appear on the ballot. Nevertheless, the conservative opponent won anyway.

Though two women's history sessions made it onto AHA programs in 1973 and 1974, the content of program sessions was often cause for a skirmish. A proposal submitted in 1973 by Joan Kelly and Renate Bridenthal for the AHA 1974 program was passed over on the grounds that the AHA frowned on theory- and methodology-focused sessions. The proposed session—"Effects of Women's History on Traditional Conceptions of Historiography"—would have been chaired by Gerda Lerner with papers given by Joan Kelly, Richard Vann, and Renate Bridenthal.[102] Program chair Orest Ranum of Johns Hopkins suggested he might accept the panel if it refocused on "what women did" in the Renaissance rather than on themes of periodization and methodology.[103] Kelly and Bridenthal withdrew the proposal in disgust after being asked repeatedly to modify it beyond their original intent.[104] Ultimately the session appeared on the program of the Second Berkshire Conference on the History of Women held at Radcliffe in 1974, and Kelly later developed the topic in her seminal essay "Did Women Have a Renaissance?" It was later published in Bridenthal and Claudia Koonz's now-classic textbook in European women's history, *Becoming Visible*.[105] Apparently, Robert Cross belatedly gave the OK to Kelly's panel after she had decided to withdraw it. Kelly rejected the offer and replied that she hoped the AHA would redress its "boo boo" and accept more women's history panels in the coming year.[106] Five full sessions on women's history made it onto the AHA program for 1974 out of 109 slots, compared with 1972, when six sessions appeared on the program.[107] That Joan Kelly and Renate Bridenthal presented their work at the Berkshire Conference instead of reshaping it to suit a male program committee was a sign of things to come—the nurturing of separate women's history institutions to advance the field's development and support its practitioners.

When the OAH-CSW made the recommendation in 1971 that a women's history pamphlet be added to the AHA's teaching pamphlet series, it was not the association's highest priority. After two years of repeated urging, Nancy Weiss Malkiel, the new chair of the OAH-CSW, reported in 1973 that the AHA finally agreed to publish the pamphlet.[108] The pamphlet, however, didn't appear until 1981. It was funded by the National Endowment for the Humanities and authored by Gerda Lerner.[109]

Meanwhile, OAH leaders more readily agreed with the goals of more conference panel slots and space for women's history in their journal. They wanted to see a change in the content of history in scholarship and in the classroom. Led by Anne Firor Scott, Gerda Lerner, and the members of the OAH-CSW, the OAH funded major projects and lent support to initiatives to develop American women's history in the 1970s and 1980s. In 1973, though the CSW reported slow progress in getting more women's history panels at annual OAH meetings, it nevertheless could report progress: Women's representation as participants saw a steady increase. The OAH-CSW also made progress on a "List of Research in Progress in the History of Women," which was distributed by the office of the executive secretary and advertised in the AHA's bulletin and the *CCWHP Newsletter*. In addition, four members of the 1972 OAH-CSW had a Rockefeller grant to hold a small conference to explore the idea of developing a graduate program in women's history. The conference focused on the materials and sources needed to start such a program and resulted in the first MA program in women's history in the United States being established at Sarah Lawrence College. The Sarah Lawrence program was under the direction of Gerda Lerner and Joan Kelly. Furthermore, the *Journal of American History* committed to publishing an issue dedicated to women's history once enough quality articles had been submitted. This issue never materialized, despite a flood of scholarship on women. The OAH-CSW also proposed that the OAH encourage the American Revolution Bicentennial Commission to include women and women's history in its planning. This effort was touted in the *Journal of American History*, the AHA's bulletin, and the *CCWHP Newsletter*. Historians were urged to send women's history proposals to the commission.[110]

For its part, the AHA invested time and resources to develop a register of women historians for the purpose of facilitating job opportunities at those history departments committed to correcting the nationwide gender imbalance in hiring. The AHA also created the position of "assistant to the executive secretary for women's status," a job that was filled first by Dorothy Ross and then by Eleanor Straub.[111] After the initial increase from two to six women's history sessions on the program at the annual AHA meetings in 1971 and 1972, some in the CCWHP perceived backsliding when fewer women and women's history panels appeared on conference programs in 1973 and 1974 across all three organizations—the AHA, OAH, and SHA.[112]

Following the lead of the AHA's register of women historians, in 1973 the OAH-CSW urged the printing of a roster of the same type. This roster was published in 1975 with the names of 130 specialists in the history of American women. The roster was organized by state and aimed to make history departments, publishers, television producers, and libraries aware of women's history experts. These entities often called on academics to consult on curriculum and textbook revisions, or to lecture, or to advise libraries on their women's history holdings, for example. Historians were also called to consult on films and public history displays.[113] The AHA roster of women historians had been produced with the singular stated goal of facilitating women's employment.[114] The OAH roster not only promoted the employment of historians of American women but also supported increased visibility for American women's history, demonstrating the OAH's commitment to expanding the women's history content of American history broadly.

The members of the OAH-CSW at the time this roster was proposed in 1973 were Nancy Weiss Malkiel, Clarke Chambers, Ellen DuBois, Gerda Lerner, William O'Neill, Janice Trecker, and Joan Hoff-Wilson. Several of these individuals ended up making major contributions to the development of US women's history beyond their own scholarly contributions through their service to the historical profession. Chambers and Lerner would be instrumental along with Anne Scott in drafting proposals to the National Endowment for the Humanities in 1973 for what would become the Women's History Sources Survey project directed by Chambers and Andrea Hinding at the University of Minnesota's Social Welfare History Archive.[115] Initial plans for this proposal appear in the 1973 OAH-CSW report to the executive board. It resulted in a compendious and invaluable reference work listing archival holdings about women all around the country. Hoff-Wilson served as executive secretary of the OAH from 1981 to 1989.[116] She was appointed by Gerda Lerner in 1981, then the first woman president of the OAH in fifty years. In 1989, Joan Hoff-Wilson took a leading role in establishing the *Journal of Women's History*. By that time, it had become obvious that the field had grown so large and was so productive that mainstream history journals could not accommodate all the good work being produced. Efforts to build the field were often waged one scholar, one grant proposal, one project, and one history department at a time, ultimately engaging many historians in this work. Some of these efforts will be visited later in our story. Some historians stepped into important leadership roles, becoming key brokers for women's history within the discipline's major institutions. This leadership rallied others to the cause, inspiring wider action.

Personalizing Professional Connections/ Mentoring the Next Generation

Just as significant as work done within mainstream professional societies to raise the profile of women's history and raise women's professional status was the fact that these activists worked to bring younger historians of women into the field through direct mentorship and support. The high profile afforded by service on the Committees on the Status of Women of the AHA, OAH, and SHA facilitated connections that led to the fostering of the next generation of leading feminist historians. Two of the scholars who emerged as inspirational leaders of the Americanist wing of this movement were Anne Firor Scott and Gerda Lerner. Both have left ample record of their activities on behalf of women's history and the younger generation of women historians. Their being from an older generation was an important factor in the field's rapid development after 1969. Both mentored and vigorously promoted the scholarship and careers of younger women with whom they established relationships in the early 1970s that endured beyond Scott's and Lerner's retirements. Lerner and Scott were certainly not the only scholars to do this, but for American women's history, they were arguably the most significant.[117] Beyond that, each served as a critical mediator between the mainstream of the historical profession and the women's history movement as it emerged. Their service to their fellow women's historians and the field was in effect a feminist adaptation and modification of the discipline and how it had long worked for male historians and their own protégés. In that same vein, Letitia Woods Brown, a 1966 Howard University history PhD, served as a role model and mentor to up-and-coming African American women historians in the 1970s.

In 1993, *Visible Women: New Essays on American Activism*, a book of collected essays in the field of American women's history, was published to honor Anne Scott.[118] *Visible Women* was edited by Nancy Hewitt and Suzanne Lebsock, themselves members of the 1970s cohort of scholars whose dissertations became landmarks in nineteenth-century American women's history. Hewitt and Lebsock were at the time of the volume's publication faculty members at Duke University and UNC Chapel Hill, respectively, places where Scott had been a powerful presence since the 1960s. The volume was part of a series out of the University of Illinois Press edited by Mari Jo Buhle, Nancy Hewitt, and Jacquelyn Dowd Hall, all scholarly heavyweights in American history by 1993.

Lebsock's path to women's history began in 1970 when her graduate advisor, Willie Lee Rose, encouraged her to study the legal status of women in the South and become an academic.[119] Rose herself was not a historian of women. She had written a respected monograph, *Rehearsal for Reconstruction*. She is remembered in women's history circles for the famous "Rose Report" of 1970, when she was chair of the AHA Ad Hoc Committee on the Status of Women. Rose had invited Lebsock to be the student representative on that committee in 1970–71. Lebsock credited both Rose and Scott with encouraging her on the path to women's history. She acknowledged Scott upon publication of her dissertation in 1984: "From the time it was only an idea for a dissertation, Anne Firor Scott has supported this project in numerous ways. 'Are you writing?' came a postcard. 'If not, why not?'"[120] Similarly, Hewitt, whose path to women's history had begun in 1973 when she took a women's history course at SUNY Brockport, acknowledged Scott when her first book was published in 1984: "The development of this book was aided by many. Anne Firor Scott and Ellen

DuBois read the entire manuscript: I thank them for their incisive criticisms which were generous not only in number but in tone."[121] These comments were typical of praise for Scott, who in the 1970s encouraged young scholars across the nation.[122] She met most of these young women through her involvement with the OAH and the SHA, rather than as their professor, since at Duke, she taught only undergraduate students.

Other contributors to *Visible Women* included a small pantheon of women's history scholars who felt in some way that Scott had played a formative part of their intellectual and professional lives.[123] The tribute essay, "Invincible Woman: Anne Firor Scott," was authored by Nancy Weiss Malkiel, whom Scott recommended to take over as chair of the OAH-CSW in 1973. Weiss Malkiel asserted, "For each of the authors in this volume, Anne Firor Scott has served as an inspiration and guide through her research, her teaching, and her mentorship."[124] Referencing Scott's influential collection of essays in 1984's *Making the Invisible Woman Visible*, she recollected Scott's particular gifts—communicator, teacher, writer—and then referenced her political acumen, generosity to young scholars, and "talent for seizing opportunities and running with them."[125] Rounding out the volume were essays with similar acknowledgments from Darlene Clark Hine and Deborah Gray White, two of the most prominent Black women's historians of the era. Hine and White would themselves go on to mentor many African American historians, turning the specialization into an especially prolific growth field by the end of the century. The enduring effect of Scott's work as a mentor was again celebrated by a similarly stellar and diverse cast of feminist historians in a 2011 volume titled *Writing Women's History: A Tribute to Anne Firor Scott*.[126]

A good way to measure these tributes against the historical record is by examining real-time exchanges between Scott and those she mentored. Scott's correspondence with Mary Rothschild illustrates how women's history networks were fostered through activism in mainstream professional societies in the 1970s and gives a good idea of the spirit of the times. Rothschild came to Scott's attention in February 1971 when she wrote Scott, then the chair of OAH-CSW. Rothschild later described her letter as a "really snotty," "oppressed," "very snippy, mean letter" regarding the upcoming women's history panels at OAH '71 in New Orleans.[127] Nevertheless, Anne Scott kept the letter, and it survives in her papers. Rothschild identified herself as a busy graduate student in American history at the University of Washington in Seattle who was preparing a women's history course titled "Women's Rights and Feminism in America." She added that she was actively trying to get her university to create a women's studies program.[128] "The program for the New Orleans OAH meeting just arrived and, in looking over the sessions, I found several which are of great interest to me as well as, presumably, to other women in the profession.

I am particularly concerned with the two panel discussions, 'New Perspectives on Women's History' and 'Women in the Profession.' As a graduate student, I cannot afford the luxury of a trip to New Orleans and I wondered if you, or anyone on your committee, had entertained the idea of taping those sessions for a later transcription or report?" Rothschild closed the letter by justifying her request, saying, "I am becoming more and more painfully aware of the paucity of material available [in women's history]."[129]

Scott replied on March 11 that taping the sessions was an excellent idea, promising that she would suggest it to the program committee. She surprised Rothschild by adding that she and her husband, Andrew Scott, would be in Seattle in the summer because he had a visiting professorship there.[130] Scott said she looked forward to meeting Rothschild to discuss her course on American women's history. The news sent Rothschild to find Anne Scott's book *The Southern Lady* in the library. She then suggested to her graduate advisor and history department chair, Otis Pease, that he give Anne Scott a visiting appointment.[131] Pease objected based on lack of funding and his ignorance of Scott's scholarship, but Rothschild eventually swayed him, even pronouncing Scott's *Southern Lady* the best thing currently published in women's history.[132] Indeed, in 1972, the University of Washington offered Anne Scott the directorship of its new women's studies program. The letter of inquiry to Scott indicated that Rothschild had continued to push to bring Scott to UW permanently after her summer in Seattle.[133] The Scotts ultimately declined to relocate, but this episode shows that women encouraged and bolstered each other across the generations.

Scott held on to Rothschild's updated 1973 CV in her papers. A look at the CV reveals Rothschild's active role at UW to get a women's history program up and running even as she struggled to complete her dissertation, "Northern Volunteers and the Southern 'Freedom Summers,'" in which she paid attention to the dynamic between women and men, Black and white volunteers. From 1971 to 1972, in addition to developing women's history courses and participating in her school's efforts to create a women's studies program, she was becoming a scholar and teacher. She gave papers on both women's history and women's liberation at conferences and symposia and lectured on women's studies in the local community, where she coordinated a "Rap Group" titled "Woman: Know Thyself." She also worked as a teaching assistant in the history department. She later recalled that she almost gave up writing her dissertation, but Scott would occasionally send notes encouraging and urging her to finish. A year after meeting Scott, Rothschild wrote, "It was lovely to talk to you and I am, as usual, in your debt both for the job information and the recommendation. . . . I would like to send you a longer version of the chapter I've just done on the women volunteers. Someday I'd like to give it as a paper."[134] The exchange between these two historians highlights the advocacy role that Scott and others of her generation played. Letters of recommendation, notes of encouragement, advice and information, reading of works-in-progress—this was all committed service, in this example done for someone outside her home institution and thus unrecognized and uncompensated by Duke.

Yet, Anne Scott too benefited from these exchanges as the young scholars expanded the intellectual and professional community of historians of women. The growing interest in women's history in the 1970s legitimized Scott's own work in the field. Though Scott had received recognition prior to 1970, the "avalanche" of interest in women's history greatly raised her status in the historical profession and at Duke.

> My Duke colleagues suddenly began saying, "Oh, yes. We have a very distinguished historian of women." They'd had me for ten years, and they never noticed until all of a sudden, the rest of the world did. You know what did more for me than anything, professionally? It was having George Frederickson review *The Southern Lady* favorably. A man, a distinguished man, historian at Northwestern University, and then Eric Foner, who didn't understand the book at all, reviewed it very favorably in *The New York Review of Books*. Then the graduate students sat up and took notice. "There must be something to this women's history stuff if you can get reviewed in *The New York Review*."[135]

Rothschild acknowledged that Anne Scott was really important to her.[136] The pattern of mentorship and advocacy repeated itself later in Rothschild's life. She went on to become the director of the women's studies program at Arizona State University after earning her PhD in 1974. Though not so widely known for her publications, she exemplifies a segment of the women's history movement that built programs at universities, hired historians of women and racial minorities, and developed oral history projects.[137] Mary Rothschild was also deeply influenced by Gerda Lerner, though she did not have the same close personal connection to Lerner that she did to Scott.[138] Lerner was a model and mentor for many.

In 1995, Linda Kerber, Alice Kessler-Harris, and Kathryn Kish Sklar published *U.S. History as Women's History: New Feminist Essays* in tribute to Gerda Lerner.[139] This volume, like *Visible Women*, was part of an editorial series with an impressive array of scholars on its editorial board and among its contributors.[140] In the introduction, the editors explained the importance of Lerner to their own lives as historians of women.

> Each of the contributors to this volume found her or his own path to women's history in the years between 1967 and 1972. Trekking through unfamiliar terrain, each of us encountered Gerda Lerner: sometimes it

was through something she had written; sometimes it was at a political meeting; sometimes it was on a scholarly panel. She seemed to be everywhere. Her authoritative voice, with its muted Viennese inflections, cajoled, persuaded, encouraged, and demanded changes in the way we wrote history and in the way the profession treated women. We responded because her words resonated with what we were thinking and because she was radical and brave. She took risks: in the subjects she chose to study, in the research and analytic strategies she adopted, the ways she negotiated the surfaces of the profession. . . . She could hold a room with her formidable presence.[141]

The tribute goes on to emphasize Lerner's professional service, her impact on the field, and her ability to reach beyond a purely academic audience. For instance, she was instrumental in getting Congress to endorse Women's History Week and then Women's History Month. Lerner gave radio talks and public interviews and contributed pieces and interviews to popular magazines like *Ms.*[142]

Inside academia, Lerner mentored younger historians of women and advocated for them professionally. An excellent example of this is her long relationship with Mari Jo Buhle. In 1968, Mari Jo Buhle was a graduate student studying American radical and labor history at the University of Wisconsin–Madison. Her advisor was William O'Neill, the author of the hotly debated monograph on the women's movement *Everyone Was Brave.*[143] In 1968, as O'Neill's teaching assistant, Buhle was allowed to teach her section framed around her interest in women's history. When O'Neill left Wisconsin for Rutgers, Buhle was assigned a new thesis advisor and ran up against other professors who discouraged her. One suggested that the work of socialist women she had highlighted in a seminar paper was a "granfalloon," meaning irrelevant to the socialist movement.[144]

When Mari Jo Buhle's funding ran out at Wisconsin—as did that of her husband, radical historian Paul Buhle—the husband-wife team moved to Somerville, Massachusetts, near Cambridge, to research and write their dissertations. Paul Buhle was the principal editor of the journal *Radical America*. The Buhles' scholarly circles included radical New Left and feminist historians.[145] Mari Jo Buhle's connection to *Radical America* gave her, Ann Gordon, and Nancy Schrom access to publish in it, and in the summer of 1971 they coauthored and published an influential historiographic essay, "Women in American Society."[146] Attention to women's history in *Radical America* had already shown up in the February 1970 issue when a group of women historians, including Buhle, Vilma Sanchez, Selma James, Marlene Dixon, Edith Hoshino Altbach, Gail Paradise Kelly, and Helke Sander, orchestrated a one-issue takeover of the journal to publish a set of essays about women's history and women's liberation.[147]

Buhle first met Gerda Lerner at the annual meeting of the OAH in New Orleans in April 1971. Buhle was on a discussion panel titled "New Perspectives on Women's History" along with Blanche Wiesen Cook, Ellen DuBois, Louise Dalby, Jean Christie, and Robin Morgan.[148] When Buhle spoke about the inadequacy of the "oppression model" of women's history, Gerda Lerner reacted positively. A few months later, Buhle's coauthored article "Women in American Society" came out in *Radical America*. Lerner reached out to her in the fall of 1971, when Buhle was working on her dissertation, "Women in the Socialist Movement in America." Lerner approached Buhle about giving a paper at OAH '72. Lerner's proposed session was "Radicalism and Feminism—A Study in Contrasts." The idea was to feature a paper by Blanche Wiesen Cook on socialist feminist Crystal Eastman and anarchist feminist Emma Goldman and one by Buhle on socialist feminists Kate Richards O'Hare and Rose Pastor Stokes. Though the session did not make the program, it signaled the beginning of a long mentorship.

In November 1971, Buhle wrote Lerner about looking for a job. Lerner replied with several suggestions and asked her for her CV so she could write recommendation letters. Lerner advised Buhle to send publishable portions of her dissertation to Ann Calderwood, who was trying to launch the new journal *Feminist Studies*, adding that Buhle should spread the word about the new journal.[149] Two years later, Gerda Lerner hired Buhle to teach in the new graduate program in women's history at Sarah Lawrence College in Bronxville, New York.[150] Buhle was then teaching part-time at Brown University, and a full-time position was an attractive offer. Buhle stayed only a year at Sarah Lawrence, unhappy with the setting, but managed to finish her dissertation by the end of her stay there. Then she returned to her part-time post at Brown.[151] In 1975, however, the American civilization program at Brown hired Buhle full-time to teach women's and labor history—with a strong endorsement from Gerda Lerner.[152] Lerner continued to support Buhle professionally: reading and promoting her work; writing recommendations for tenure, fellowships, and grants; and sharing course syllabi.[153]

Acknowledging the impact Lerner had on her, Buhle wrote to Lerner after she was awarded the prestigious five-year MacArthur Fellowship in 1991: "I want to use this occasion to thank you again for all the encouragement you've given me over the years, despite the Sarah Lawrence debacle. When I was first starting out in women's history in 1970, you made me believe I had a contribution to make to the field. My pace has obviously slowed under the weight of graduate advising, but I hope now to live up to your first expectations. Thanks for your professional mentoring. Thanks for your friendship. Love, Mari Jo"[154] In living up to those expectations and the model provided by Lerner, Mari Jo Buhle would mentor sixty-two PhDs in American civilization, most in the field of US women's history, over the course of her career at Brown.[155] Her ties to Gerda Lerner certainly helped form her identity, but so did her ties to her own generation of feminist historians. Buhle's connections to Scott and Lerner and to *Radical America* and its cohort reveal the complex and multigenerational roots of the modern field of the new women's history and the way that activism within mainline professional organizations connected these generations. As with earlier iterations of women's history, it was informed by various strands of feminism.

Anne Scott and Gerda Lerner made meaningful interventions on behalf of the emerging generation of feminist historians. They parlayed their individually earned legitimacy to win opportunities for new scholars and successfully combined their experience as political activists with their talent as scholars to help others navigate the historical profession. Scott and Lerner had much in common with the politicized young feminist historians of the 1970s. They had combined their political skills with their professional lives for decades. They could speak to power in muted tones or make demands more assertively. Considered legitimate by the profession, holding tenured positions, they could successfully challenge power structures and traditional hierarchies of historical significance by 1970.

The impact of Lerner and Scott can also be seen on the life and professional trajectory of Ellen DuBois, a young women's historian during the movement's earliest years. In 1971, DuBois was a graduate student at Northwestern University writing a dissertation on the nineteenth-century century women's movement under the direction of Robert Wiebe. From afar, DuBois got critical feedback on her dissertation from both Lerner and Scott as it progressed from conceptual framework to book.

Lerner met DuBois in 1970, and they were on a first-name basis by June 1971. So too were Scott and DuBois. DuBois began to solicit feedback from both Scott and Lerner in late June 1971, after advancing to PhD candidacy at Northwestern.[156] Writing almost identical letters, on June 24 to Scott and on June 26 to Lerner, DuBois related her excitement at finally being able to dig into the archives at the Schlesinger Library in Cambridge. She asked how to cope with the lack of sources in a field that was so new. She wondered, as "all thesis writers" do, how to keep sight of the forest when the compelling details emerging presented the risk of examining the trees too closely. How, she asked, does one define the scope of a project in a sensible way?

The letters mention the many "young feminist historians around the Schlesinger and the conversations we have are equally exciting/frustrating." She inquired whether they could point her to sources on nineteenth-century feminists, and if they could not, could they recommend someone who could?

DuBois was already at the Schlesinger Library, so Lerner suggested that she contact its former director, Janet James. James was, at the time, still serving as coeditor for *Notable American Women*. She also recommended that DuBois reach out to Aileen Kraditor and William O'Neill. Scott suggested she contact Barbara Solomon, dean of Harvard College and former head of the Radcliffe Women's Archives.[157]

Other parallels in Scott's and Lerner's thoughtful responses are striking. Both expressed amusement at so young a historian despairing of not having time to follow all the leads that were popping up in her research. Lerner recommended that she use every detail she unearthed to plan future projects. She urged,

> Make a life plan of projects to do; . . . keep track of great insights and ideas on other subjects as they come; . . . keep track of resources and things to which you want to go back later—but don't try to do it all at once. . . . If it's any consolation I've had four research projects and books mapped out for about six years—not to speak of a long list of biographies of marvelous women which I would like to do and never will get to doing. But at your age, that kind of thing is still in the realm of the possible.[158]

Scott replied to DuBois on August 5,

> I perfectly understand all the leads-you-can't-follow frustration. *Make a note of them, though. Someday* you'll have students looking for topics. . . . Your concern about too much to do can only amuse someone at my stage of life. Look, you're all of what? 23? And you will undoubtedly live to be a 100 if the pollution etc. doesn't get us all—and the basic fact (I learned from Thomas Jefferson) is that if you keep at it enormous amounts of work get done. . . . Given the state of the art . . . the first people have to sketch the maps, (like the first explorers) and the next wave of students need to fill in the details. So, I would cast a large net . . . but leave signposts for the next person.[159]

Each of these senior scholars had faith in Ellen DuBois's future as a professional historian; each envisioned a collective and multigenerational future for the field of women's history. They imagined future historians filling in the details for the map of women's history.

When DuBois asked what they thought about whether nineteenth-century feminists practiced contraception, both older women dismissed DuBois's suggestion that women of that era had forward-thinking sexual ideologies. They responded that she was imposing twentieth-century sexual cultural standards on her nineteenth-century subjects. DuBois's view was that Elizabeth Cady Stanton may have been open to or at least had knowledge of birth control. Not likely, replied both Scott and Lerner. Abstinence, yes; birth control, no. Otherwise, they argued, why did so many feminists have large families, particularly Stanton, who expressed frustration over balancing motherhood with a life of activism and despaired at times of her own fertility?

Both Scott and Lerner continued to shepherd DuBois's thesis, and they promoted opportunities for the young scholar. This included writing recommendation letters for fellowships and jobs. They supported her successful candidacy for a full-time tenure-track job in women's history at SUNY Buffalo in 1974. Moreover, DuBois learned that Scott, as a member of the selection committee, was instrumental in securing a one-year Rockefeller Fellowship that would fund DuBois's work to convert her 1974 dissertation into a book.[160] Lerner consulted with DuBois on several manuscripts through 1979, including when, as an editorial consultant at Schocken Books, Lerner helped get a documentary reader on Stanton and Susan B. Anthony assigned to DuBois.[161] Scott and Lerner's mentorship was a major factor in DuBois's emergence as a scholar. And, just as they had done with Rothschild, Buhle, and DuBois, to varying degrees, Lerner and Scott propelled the intellectual and professional lives of many other women in the 1970s.

These connections made during the formative years of the women's history movement between 1969 and 1973 were later multiplied and expanded when Lerner and Scott made efforts to connect with growing numbers of younger historians. These historians included up-and-coming African American women's historians Darlene Clark Hine, Deborah Gray White, and Nell Irvin Painter starting in the late 1970s. Each of these scholars had contributed to one or both of the "Festschrifts" of Scott and Lerner featured here. Lerner's OAH presidency in 1982 saw her forcefully promoting Black women's history on the annual meeting program. When Scott was elected SHA president in 1988, she made Darlene Clark Hine the chair of the program committee, ensuring strong representation for African American women's history on the program.[162] That this occurred mostly during the women's history movement's second decade is a reflection of how crowded the agenda of feminist historians was in the 1970s, how few Black women's historians there were in the profession still in the 1970s, and the dire need to build interracial bridges within American women's history. One final example of the importance of new women's historians' search for role models, pioneers, and mentors in real time and in the construction of the field's origins story can be seen in the front matter of Deborah Gray White's 2008 *Telling Histories: Black Women Historians in the Ivory Tower*. White acknowledges the encouragement and support she received from Hine, Anne Scott, Nancy Hewitt, Steven Lawson, and Jacquelyn Dowd Hall. But the book was dedicated in tribute to midcentury historians Anna Julia Cooper and Marion Thompson Wright.

Those historians who, between 1969 and 1973, put women's history on the agenda of the major historical associations and framed their scholarship as legitimate historical discourse also confronted the need to improve women's status within the profession's power institutions. Once they created access, it was possible for those developing the field of women's history to push in. The younger scholars were pressing the mostly male arbiters of scholarly legitimacy, but they adopted their new role of professional service with such gusto that they validated their right to influence both the content and the professional culture of the discipline.

Women historians engaged *collectively* with the discipline's mainstream for the first time from 1969 to 1973 to address systemic sex-based inequities. While putting women's status within its institutional structures squarely on the agenda of the profession, they interjected their goal of ending the "feminine mystique" in history to expand the scope of historical studies to encompass women. As women, they were no longer alone in a male-dominated academic world whose structures had marginalized so many women in the past. Recalling the AHA meeting of 1969 and the Rose Report adopted at AHA '70, Linda Kerber related how, for her, the content issue and the status issue were completely interconnected, even though they constituted two distinct goals within the same movement. Regarding the content issue, she said, "I really don't think of myself as a pioneer. I think of Janet James as a pioneer. I think of people who stayed in it [women's history] before there was a feminist wave to carry them as pioneers. I think what I'll take credit for is recognizing that there was a good opportunity for historical work in a subject that had been marginalized. We all talked about it."[163] Then she immediately followed by explaining the impact of hearing the results of the report prepared by Willie Lee Rose and the AHA Ad Hoc Committee on the Status of Women: "They devised an extraordinary report which gave some numbers to the decline of women in the profession so that they could see that the last woman had been appointed at Berkeley in 1920, and the next one in 1969, or something like that. I was at the AHA business meeting when that report was presented. It was stunning. In some ways it was reassuring. It said that if you don't have a job it's not because you're stupid. There's something structural at work here."[164]

The report showed that between 1920 and 1969, the number of full-time tenured female history faculty in coeducational history departments had declined from a high of 16 percent in 1960, to less than 1 percent in 1969. Most tenured female history professors were clustered in women's colleges between 1920 and 1969. The faculty of the leading graduate history programs in the country were 98–99 percent male. National data show that during this time frame, women's rate of earning BA and MA degrees rose steadily. But their attainment of doctoral degrees in all academic disciplines declined from a high of 15 percent in 1920 to 9.6 percent in 1969.[165] Structural and cultural barriers and practices were indeed operating to keep women's presence at the highest level of academia low. The experiences of the pioneering historians featured earlier in this history help explain how.

The status issue burst onto the scene for women historians in 1969. It did much to facilitate the creation of a movement that could advance the study of women. But the earliest efforts to develop the history of women as a legitimate topic of study predated that movement. Earlier efforts to develop the history of women were generally waged at the level of individual scholarly interface. Individuals built the field through their own scholarship and in a handful of specialized archives, and they taught in their own small corners of the profession.

In the national women's history movement that coalesced between 1969 and 1973, the strongest leaders in the US field were Anne Firor Scott and Gerda Lerner. Some older scholars from the Harvard, Columbia, and Chapel Hill cohorts featured earlier in this story also persisted in their work and had deep roots in the progressive tradition in American history. This tradition went all the way back to Arthur Schlesinger Sr., the Beards, the archivists and historians of the Radcliffe Women's Archives, and others who paved the way for what emerged in the 1970s. By 1973, women's historians were gaining considerable professional and intellectual momentum. Seizing on the feminist zeitgeist of the era, the national women's history movement that coalesced between 1969 and 1973 made it possible to envision and work for a broader epistemological shift that would have profound implications for how historians viewed the past. Yet, despite some success in gaining access to professional strongholds and an uptick in the number of academic jobs in women's history, activists in the movement for women's history soon found it necessary to create their own institutional structures, including professional associations, conference groups, and journals to further advance the field.[166]

Chapter 8

Organizing for Women's History, 1973–1987

> The rise and fall of concern for women's history has followed the
> intensity of organized women's movements. Not since 1920, when the
> suffrage movement ended, has there been the interest evident today.
>
> —Mari Jo Buhle, Ann Gordon, and Nancy Schrom, 1971

The initial ferment of feminist historians within the American Historical Association, the Organization of American Historians, and the Southern Historical Association from 1969 to 1973 resulted in a powerful brew to which feminist historians added a proliferating number of institutions that operated independently of the male-dominated mainstream.[1] By 1976, historian Arnita Jones of the National Endowment for the Humanities could describe the institutional framework they created to advocate for the development of women's history as "interlocking networks of new national, local, and regional organizations."[2] These organizations all wanted to improve the status of women historians within academia, but their major focus was to develop the field of women's history. Jones explained that women's history was an important new line of inquiry, closely related to social history.[3] What was more, by 1976, academic employment was in the doldrums, creating a job crisis. Jones suggested that growing student demand for women's history, a corollary of the women's movement, became a way to open new job opportunities for women's historians.

Even as feminist historians ramped up their activities in new organizations and in the AHA and the OAH, the decades-old—but recently revitalized— Berkshire Conference of Women Historians ramped up its activism in the early 1970s, too. In 1971, at the annual meeting of the Berkshire Conference of Women Historians on April 15, women's history appeared on the program for the first time ever, foreshadowing the organization's soon-to-be prominent role in promoting women's history.[4] Sandi Cooper moderated a discussion of Ann Lane's paper, "Women's History as a Topic in American History," and Claudia Koonz, Renate Bridenthal, and Sheila Tobias delivered "Report on a Collective Research Project: Women in the Weimar Republic."[5] The Berkshire group, long the only professional association of women historians in the country, was soon joined by a number of new women's groups. While status of women committees in mainstream associations sought to reform male-dominated professional societies, the women's associations provided an alternate network for women historians and historians of women, both older and newly arrived in the profession. These included the Coordinating Committee on Women in the Historical Profession–Conference Group on Women's History (CCWHP, 1969; CGWH, 1974), the Southern Association for Women Historians (1970), and the West Coast Association of Women Historians (1969), among others.[6] Over the course of the 1970s, these larger national and regional groups were joined by smaller regional groups whose contributions to the women's history movement were significant. Indeed, they indicated the growth of a wide-reaching national movement of feminist historians. They included the New York Metropolitan Area Group (1971), the New England Association of Women Historians (1972), Women Historians of the Midwest (1973), the Upstate New York Women's History Organization (1975), and other small local or interest-specific groups of women historians.[7] In 1977, three historians proposed the establishment of Black Women Historians United. It was renamed the Association of Black Women Historians in 1979.[8]

In the 1970s, operating through new institutions like the Berkshire Conference on the History of Women, the CGWH, and like-minded regional groups, historians of women quickly developed a distinct professional subculture within the discipline, largely modeled on mainstream professional culture but infused with feminist goals. First, they wanted to facilitate and promote a rigorous examination of gender, race, and class in society and women's lives across time and place. Second, they sought to eliminate both sex and race discrimination in the profession.[9] By 1987 they could claim some success with both these goals because they both worked within mainstream professional institutions and created their own separate institutions. These separate institutions were necessary to provide an additional outlet for their energies and a remedy for the limitations of the male mainstream's institutions.

In both the AHA and the OAH, historians of women exerted internal pressure to implement important women's history initiatives.[10] One indicator of the traction they were able to get is that after December 1969, the programs of the Organization of American Historians and the American Historical Association never again omitted women's history as subject matter. But progress in these mainstream institutions was slow. Table 8.1 shows that the AHA and OAH kept pace with one another in terms of the raw number of sessions featuring women's history. But, given the considerably larger size of the AHA program, the OAH gave a relatively greater proportion of its conference time to women's history from 1970 to 1987, an advantage for the field of American women's history.[11]

These numbers suggest that women's history had greater institutional support within the OAH—among American historians—than it did among historians specializing in other geographic and national fields. Despite this relatively greater support, by 1973 it was already clear to a growing cohort of women's

Table 8.1 Program content analysis of the Organization of American Historians and the American Historical Association annual meetings, 1970–1987

	OAH program sessions	AHA program sessions
Year	*No. of sessions with women's history papers/total no. of sessions/percentage*	*No. of sessions with women's history papers/total no. of sessions/percentage*
1970	1 session/40 (3%)	2 sessions/100 (2%)
1971	5 sessions/53 (9%)	6 sessions/129 (5%)
1972	7 sessions/56 (13%)	6 sessions/123 (5%)
1973	3 sessions/59 (5%)	4 sessions/103 (4%)
1974	4 sessions/65 (6%)	11 sessions/109 (10%)
1975	6 sessions/64 (9%)	16 sessions/93 (17%)
1976	4 sessions/83 (5%)	7 sessions/110 (6%)
1977	6 sessions/68 (9%)	7 sessions/98 (7%)
1978	11 sessions/93 (12%)	10 sessions/161 (6%)
1979	14 sessions/97 (14%)	10 sessions/127 (8%)
1980	18 sessions/87 (21%)	15 sessions/125 (12%)
1981	12 sessions/116 (10%)	17 sessions/128 (13%)
1982	19 session/91 (21%)	15 sessions/111 (14%)
1983	17 sessions/88 (19%)	18 sessions/155 (12%)
1984	16 sessions/86 (19%)	12 sessions/127 (9.4%)
1985	18 sessions/104 (17%)	14 sessions/139 (10%)
1986	25 sessions/109 (23%)	20 sessions/123 (16%)
1987	18 sessions/92 (20%)	29 sessions/135 (21%)

Source: Tabulated from annual meeting programs, 1970–87. Programs for all past annual meetings of the American Historical Association can be found on the website of the American Historical Association, at "Past Meetings," www.historians.org/events/annual-meeting, /past-meetings, accessed May 17, 2025. Programs for past annual meetings of the Organization of American Historians can be found in the OAH Records, Ruth Lilly Special Collections and Archives, Indiana University, Purdue University, Indianapolis.

Note: The number of women's history sessions includes sessions on which all papers focused on women's history, sessions with at least one paper featuring women's history, and workshops focused on women's history.

history scholars that the organizational structures of the AHA, OAH, and SHA were insufficient to absorb the scholarly energy of new historians of women coming into the field. The movement to advance women's history sparked a range of responses from male historians, from opposition to indifference to support. But it would be up to women's historians to create their own institutional structures to support and vet women's history scholarship.[12] Key among these separate institutions were the Berkshire Conference on the History of Women (first held in 1973) and the formation of a distinct women's history branch within the CCWHP that took institutional form as the Conference

Group on Women's History between 1973 and 1975. Other regional women's history groups joined these national groups in their emphasis on developing women's history.

The Berkshire Conference on the History of Women was perhaps *the* central institution reflecting the pulse of women's history from 1973 forward. It established a national conference showcasing and vetting new work in all areas of women's history. The first three Berkshire Conferences were held in 1973, 1974, and 1976. In 1978 the schedule regularized, and the conference was held every three years thereafter.[13] From 1974, the Berkshire Conference attracted 1,500 to 2,200 historians to each of its meetings.[14] In fact, attendance rivaled attendance at the annual AHA and OAH meetings.[15] The Berkshire Conference continued to be an integral part of the field's history and a place for discussion, debate, disagreement, and controversies to be aired for decades.

The idea for a major conference focused on the history of women originated in 1971 with Mary Hartman and Lois Banner, at the time both assistant professors at Douglass College, the women's coordinate of Rutgers University in New Jersey. Hartman was a Europeanist; Banner, an Americanist. Hartman had received her MA in 1964 and her PhD in 1969 at Columbia University. Banner earned her MA in European history at Columbia in 1965 and switched to American history for her PhD when her advisor in European history, Shepherd Clough, strongly discouraged her from going for a PhD. Clough complained that she was married and would probably just leave the program when she started a family with her husband, historian James Banner. At that point Lois Banner switched to American history, where Eric McKitrick became her advisor. Banner recalled that the Americanists at Columbia were not openly misogynistic and were relatively open to taking on women students. This implied that the Europeanists *were* misogynistic and that Clough's reluctance to accept her as a student was a product of that misogyny.[16] Banner's husband, James Banner, took work at Princeton University in New Jersey in 1966, which prompted Lois to apply for a job at nearby Douglass College.

Banner and Hartman joined the Douglass history department in 1967 and 1968. They were invited by the department's senior women historians to join the Berkshire Conference of Women Historians (BCWH), which had been founded between 1928 and 1930 as a regional organization for the professional socialization of women historians. There is no indication that the group had ever taken an active interest in the history of women before 1970.[17] According to Banner, she and Hartman were taken to their first annual meeting of the BCWH around 1971. Characterizing herself and Hartman as young and insecure, she felt initially somewhat alienated from the more established historians when they failed to include them in the more informal aspects of the gathering when intimate late-night conversations and drinking transpired. Banner and

Hartman were also acutely conscious of these older scholars' lack of interest in women's history.[18] It was, after all, an organization of women historians, not an organization focused on women's history.

Despite the younger women's impression that the BCWH was not interested in women's history, in 1971 two papers on women's history were presented at the annual meeting. Ann Lane of Douglass College presented a paper on women in American history. Renate Bridenthal, Claudia Koonz, and Sheila Tobias jointly presented research on women in Weimar Germany.[19] Banner and Hartman's assessment of the BCWH's interest in women's history was essentially correct, however. It was only in the mid-1960s that the BCWH began to include scholarly papers at its annual weekend retreat, and that was done at the suggestion of mostly younger BCWH members—Mary Dunn, Berenice Carroll, Sandi Cooper, Linda Kerber, and Jane De Hart Mathews.[20]

Back at Douglass, Hartman and Banner discussed their experience at the BCWH and determined that they would ask the BCWH to sponsor a conference on women's history. They contacted BCWH president Louise Dalby with the idea in 1971. At the April 28–30, 1972, meeting of the BCWH in Lake Minnewaska, New York, the BCWH voted to sponsor the women's history conference.[21] Dalby suggested that either Banner or Hartman become official program chair.[22] They decided to act as cochairs. Though Hartman and Banner's initial expectation was to organize a program with five papers that would attract twenty-five to fifty attendees, word spread quickly throughout the Northeast. By November 1972, Hartman reported to Dalby that they had received some seventy paper proposals.[23] The BCWH advertised the conference in a mailing to its own members, to the CCWHP, and to those in the new AHA job register, thus ensuring national publicity.[24] At this point, thinking that the number of attendees might be much greater than initially anticipated, they planned to print 400 programs.[25]

As news about the conference spread, the overall reaction was, according to Hartman and Banner, "overwhelming."[26] Joining the program committee were Renate Bridenthal, Carroll Smith-Rosenberg, Ann Douglas Wood, Margaret Case, Jessie Lutz, and Claudia Koonz.[27] The conference was titled "Historical Perspectives on Women." The committee endeavored to give a broad representation, across fields, of work in progress in women's history and to construct a program attentive to race and class.[28] The papers chosen for presentation reveal that the "new field" combined the "methods and insights of social history with a heightened awareness of and concern about women"—a product of the vibrant women's liberation movement of the 1970s. The papers strove to place women within their social context rather than "extract them from history."[29]

Lionel Tiger, a controversial Rutgers scholar whose work veered toward what might now be called masculinity studies, was slated to give the keynote address at the conference. Berenice Carroll and other members of the CCWHP, notably Alice Kessler-Harris and Blanche Wiesen Cook, expressed dismay, saying he was a "hostile and bigoted sexist."[30] In response, urged on by members of the BCWH, Hartman and Banner asked women's historian Ann Lane to informally rebut Tiger's views on sex roles and biological determinism. As justification for keeping Tiger on the program, Hartman explained that they were hoping that his paper would provide the opportunity to engage a "public challenge which scholars of women cannot afford to ignore."[31] They were counting on a lively debate and spirited response from feminist historians.

The two-day conference convened on March 2 and 3, 1973. Scholarly conferences often represent the cutting edge in scholarly trends, and this conference did not disappoint. Eleven panels in which forty papers (not including Lionel Tiger's) would be presented and two informal panel discussions were offered to attendees, who ultimately numbered 600. The panels were arranged thematically and were generally composed of three papers from different geographic fields. They featured work on women in social reform, war, the American workforce, the professions, the family, education, religion, and radical movements and on how they were viewed by social scientists and the culture at large in various parts of the world.[32] The final two panels on the program provided moderated discussion of two themes. The first of these, "Three Perspectives on Matriarchy," was moderated by historian Sheila Johanssen and brought together anthropologist Eleanor Burke Leacock, classicist Sarah Pomeroy, and historian Berenice Carroll; the second, "New Perspectives on the History of Women: Teaching and Research," was moderated by historian Jessie Lutz and featured Gail Parker, a historian turned college president, and two sociologists (Jessie Bernard and Suzanne Keller). Other panels also included scholars from disciplines other than history.[33]

A wide range of national specialties was represented on the program. Seventeen research papers focused on US history, with two of these addressing the history of African American women and one addressing Native American women. Two papers offered a comparative look at themes in US, French, and English women's historical experiences. Five papers examined aspects of English women's history. There were two papers on French women and one apiece on German, Chinese, Argentine, and Brazilian women. That there were three papers on American minorities and several focusing on working-class women is noteworthy, since a recurring charge against this generation of scholars has been that they initially construed women's history as the history of middle-class white women. The overall construction of the program reveals an early commitment by women's historians to cross-field presentation of work in broad thematic areas of interest to historians across a range of global geographic regions.[34]

Who participated in this first, institution-launching conference? Some names are familiar due to their longer history working in the field or because they were active in the early women's history initiatives in the AHA, OAH, and SHA. Americanists included Gerda Lerner, Annette Baxter, Barbara Solomon, Barbara Welter, Carroll Smith-Rosenberg, Nancy J. Weiss, Eleanor Straub, and Patricia Aljberg Graham. Some younger Americanists present were Maurine Greenwald, Cynthia Fuchs Epstein, Linda Gordon, Linda Grant DePauw, Paula Fass, Joan Burstyn, Regina Morantz, Blanche Wiesen Cook, Ruth Cowan, and Nancy Cott. Europeanists included Renate Bridenthal, Berenice Carroll, Edythe Lutzker, Judith Walkowitz, Suzanne Wemple, and Joanne MacNamara. Most of these historians would go on to become major scholars in their fields.[35] There were several men on the program, such as Americanists William O'Neill, Philip Greven, and Daniel Scott Smith and Europeanist Peter Stearns.[36] The program was thus inclusive along lines of sex, generation, and field of specialty. While the program content attempted to attend to racial, ethnic, and sexual diversity in its content, racial diversity was not reflected among participants. Of course, the program chairs could choose only from among those proposals and papers that had been sent to them. The absence of women of color participants was a reflection, no doubt, of the ongoing marginalization of women of color within academia. Women of color were not yet linked into emerging women's history networks in 1973, and this would be remedied only slowly and with deliberate action in the coming years.

By all accounts, the conference was a huge success. Historian Lillian Shiman, a member of the newly established New England Association of Women Historians and a staff member of the Radcliffe Institute, highlighted both the responses of her colleagues and her own impressions in a letter to BCWH president Louise Dalby: "Among my acquaintances, the Rutgers conference was a great success. I have heard nothing but good comments on it. Psychologically it was very important for so many women to come together in a conference, to meet and discuss their work as well as to get to know the individuals they have heard of, or who have previously only been a name to them."[37] Early feminist academic conferences were important in generating a sense of professional connectedness and validity. Carroll Smith-Rosenberg later recalled that conferences put her in contact with other scholars, crediting the conferences with making a female academic sphere that created ever larger networks that brought in more people.[38] Soon after the conference, Smith-Rosenberg published an influential essay on women's separate social culture in the nineteenth century, "The Female World of Love and Ritual." Her description of women's history conferences as "making a female academic sphere" illustrates how scholarship and professional activism were entwined in the minds of feminist historians. The way these scholars conceived of their work fused historical interpretation with their goals for improving professional culture and women's professional status.[39]

Similarly, Lois Banner described the atmosphere at the First Berkshire Conference—"Big Berks"—in terms evocative of religious revelation and inspiration. The groundswell of interest in women's history was to her electrifying, dynamic, and like a quasi-religious movement. This characterization of the work of women's history as a movement with a mission was in keeping with her scholarly focus on nineteenth-century American religious history and consonant with the rising tide of feminism sweeping the nation.[40] The impact of the conferences did not diminish in the ensuing two decades. Darlene Clark Hine remembered the importance of the Big Berks conferences in her turn to the study of Black women's history. She described them as "absolutely essential" to her development as a women's historian, credited them with her ability to make contacts with pioneering scholars like Janet James, and described reaction to her work as positive, exciting, and generative of further dialogue.[41]

In the immediate aftermath of the First Big Berks in 1973, Banner and Hartman reported on the conference's success to the members of the BCWH. They mentioned that the program committee had considered eighty proposals and accepted forty. Sixty-seven people were scheduled to speak. Banner and Hartman thought the committee had succeeded in designing a program that was interdisciplinary and cross-cultural. Though panels were structured in a traditional format, audience participation and discussion were strongly encouraged, unlike panels at the OAH and AHA. Banner and Hartman believed that "participants, on the whole, performed superbly. And best of all was the level of discussion and the spirit of the discussion." The two organizers spoke of the need for better funding to offer honoraria to historians traveling from afar and finally that, in hindsight, inviting Lionel Tiger to give the keynote address had been "a bad idea, although we think not because Tiger has ideas repellant to most of us but because his talk was so disappointing. We expected to have someone to 'take on'—Ann Lane deserved this—and we got a mouse."[42]

To anyone considering organizing another such gathering, the two historians warned, "The actual organizing of the conference . . . was a massive task, and we stress this factor to anyone who may be thinking of undertaking such a conference in the future."[43] The emergence of separate women's history associations did not just provide opportunities for professional socialization, nor did they simply promote women's history. They clearly required women historians to do a huge amount of professional service work. Despite Banner and Hartman's warning, Mary Maples Dunn, who was the BCWH's president in 1974 and a history professor at Bryn Mawr College, soon stepped up. This second event was an even greater success and established the conference as a regular feature of the US history profession.[44]

The BCWH decided to hold the 1974 conference at Radcliffe, home of the Schlesinger Library. Dunn had been approached by Radcliffe dean Alberta Arthurs at the First Berkshire Conference at Douglass. When Radcliffe president Matina Horner offered the campus as a conference site, Dunn accepted.[45] In her letter to President Horner, Dunn reassured her, "I realize that Radcliffe is particularly concerned to involve minority women. Our advertisement for program proposals specifically announced our interest in minority women, and I assure you that we will do everything we can to encourage their participation as well as their history."[46]

Serving on the planning committee were Europeanists Louise Dalby, Gwendolyn Evans Jensen, Lillian Shiman, Claudia Koonz, Catherine Prelinger, and Martha Tolpin. The Americanists were Ellen DuBois, Linda Gordon, Patricia King, Sally Kohlstedt, Carroll Smith-Rosenberg, Barbara Rosenkranz, Barbara Sicherman, and Kathryn Kish Sklar. These scholars came from a range of colleges and universities across the nation, from Harvard and other East Coast elite institutions to the University of Michigan to UCLA.[47] This geographically balanced committee met in person at least twice to plan the conference between the fall of 1973 and the spring of 1974 but did most of the planning through correspondence. The work was done on a volunteer basis with no monetary compensation. Dunn applied for and received $5,500 in grant money from the Rockefeller Foundation to cover some conference costs.[48]

The planning committee advertised this second conference more widely than the first, placing ads for proposals in the newsletters of the AHA, the OAH, the CCWHP, and the regional affiliates of the CCWHP. In response, they received several hundred paper and session proposals. A year of work resulted in a program containing forty-five paper sessions, seven workshops, and one panel discussion on the status of women in the historical profession. Twenty-three sessions were on US women's history; sixteen were in European history. Two sessions presented papers on "Third World Women" (Africa, China, Latin America, and India), and three cross-field sessions treated European and American history. One session featured undergraduate research. The workshops addressed research, methodological, and theoretical issues in new areas of study. These were "Workshop on Psychohistory," "Oral History Workshop," "Researching the Black Woman's Experience," "Women in the Growth of Urban and Industrial Economies," "Workshop on Feminism and Class Consciousness among Working Class Women: Some Historical Perspectives," "Workshop on Bisexuality and Homosexuality," and "Women and Poverty: Sources on Poor Relief since 1900."[49]

Of the 110 papers given, 53 were in US history, 39 in European history, 2 in Latin American history, and 1 each on Africa, India, and China. The remaining 13 papers had ambiguous titles that did not indicate a geographical emphasis.

The 4 papers on African American women, 2 on immigrant women, many on working-class women, and several on sex roles and the historical constructions of masculinity and femininity attest to the organizers' efforts to include work on diverse categories of women by 1974. The program featured a full workshop on Black women's history. Participating were Nellie McKay, Elizabeth Pleck, Carol Stack, Andrew Billingsley, Marilyn Greene, Gloria M. White, Cheryl Gilkes, Wendy Puriefoy, and Elizabeth Higginbotham. Higginbotham, Billingsley, White, Stack, Pleck and McKay also appeared on a separate session presenting research in Black women's history. Women's history of the early 1970s had thus already begun trying to advance beyond the descriptive middle-class white women's history it was later characterized as focusing on narrowly.[50] Indeed, Mary Dunn reported, "Emphasis was firmly placed on what we might call a 'new' history of women, getting away from traditional political or biographical approaches. Instead, we wanted to display a variety of new and creative methods for dealing with a challenging historical problem—rediscovering the lives of a long-neglected and often silent majority."[51]

Mary Dunn designed the opening session, "Women's History in Transition." Meant to address progress in the field and how it was changing, Gerda Lerner opened the session, which featured papers by Natalie Zemon Davis and Carroll Smith-Rosenberg. They chronicled past traditions of women's historical writing in both European and American history.[52] Both Davis and Smith-Rosenberg later developed articles based on their papers that were published in *Feminist Studies* in 1975 and 1976.[53] The papers and their articles speak to the connections, gaps, and elisions that occur across scholarly generations—leaving women scholars to reinvent the proverbial wheel of feminist scholarship in each generation. They also hint at the different pace at which women's history developed in the United States and in Europe over the course of the twentieth century.

Carroll Smith-Rosenberg's 1975 analysis of the state of the field in "The New Woman and the New History" acknowledged the tradition of writing about women in US history—a tradition she explained experienced a doldrums from the 1930s through the 1950s but was nevertheless unbroken.[54] Though she mentioned Elisabeth Dexter, Julia Cherry Spruill, Thomas Woody, Mary Earhart Dillon, and Eleanor Flexner, she omitted any reference to the archive-building efforts of Radcliffe and Smith Colleges as part of this tradition. Her interpretation of the origins of "women's history" is nuanced; she knew that her own "transitional" generation of 1960s scholars was not the first. But she criticized earlier histories of women, suggesting that most conformed to what she called the "traditional hierarchies of historical significance"—the public and the political. She identified *Notable American Women* as the capstone to this type of history, arguing it was insufficient in providing a full understanding of women's part in history. Finally, she suggested that the new social history of the 1960s, while providing fertile soil for the study of women, had largely ignored them.[55] Then she pointed toward the intellectual departure she hoped the "new women's historians" would take: the inclusion of the private, sexual, social, cultural, and psychological in historical scholarship.

Natalie Zemon Davis also recognized a centuries-long tradition of scholarship in European women's history, particularly the history of "women worthies." By contrast, though, Davis focused on the works of British historian Alice Clark and French historian Léon Abensour, who published their major works before 1924. In an extended analysis, Davis compared their methods with contemporary methods in the field and made some suggestions for "the best present course" for historians of women. Davis's essay, including her well-developed footnotes, identified no work on women done by European historians working in the United States between 1924 and 1963. With one exception in 1953, she mentioned no work featuring European women that would not be better classified as family or social history.[56] If Davis's footnotes are an accurate reflection, they would suggest that women's history was virtually nonexistent in Europe between 1924 and 1963. A detailed study of historical scholarship on women in Europe during these decades is a field ripe for further study.[57] Any movement for women's history in Europe—like that which emerged in women's archives formation in the 1940s in the United States—would have been severely disrupted by World War II. Consider that Rosika Schwimmer, observing the threat of rising fascism in 1930s Europe, approached Mary Beard and offered her own papers on the international women's peace and feminist movements to start a World Center for Women's Archives in the United States. Moreover, when Rosa Manus and other Dutch feminists founded an international women's archive in Amsterdam in 1936, their efforts were undone during the German occupation of the Netherlands. That archive was sent to Berlin, where much was lost, destroyed, or stolen and never recovered, despite postwar efforts to find and add its items to the International Women's Archives re-established as a repository in the Netherlands in 1947.[58]

While Davis and Smith-Rosenberg acknowledged the older scholarship on women's history, their analyses suggested that, in the fifty years leading to 1970, that scholarship was severely limited. They also implied that before 1970, women's history was marked by a lack of analytical rigor. Furthermore, Davis and Smith-Rosenberg contended that women's history was kept segregated from legitimate academic discourse as defined by men's traditional hierarchies of historical significance—the public and the political—and finally that historians of women had failed to challenge those traditional hierarchies. What's more, they said, European women's history produced almost nothing after Clark and Abensour. Going forward, new women's historians and their academic progeny would tend to emphasize the dismissal that had been constructed by

Davis and Smith-Rosenberg, frequently implying that the field's academic roots only went back to the mid- to late 1960s. But those who entered the profession in the 1960s knew that the history of women was not invented in 1970. New women's historians in the 1970s, however, *did* set out to reframe the parameters of women's history and ramp up its productivity. They wanted to write about race, class, ethnicity, sexuality, and gender and to examine the private and demographic. Historians at the 1973 and 1974 Berkshire Conferences were intent on marking this departure.

In Dunn's final 1974 report to the BCWH, she summarized the overall impact and meaning of the conference. Dunn pointed out that the "new" history presented at the conference displayed original and creative methods for rediscovering the lives of women, moving away from traditional political or biographical approaches.[59] Next, Dunn drew attention to the wide range of attendees. Registration reached 2,000, but many more than that crowded the sessions. Women's historians were the majority of attendees, but feminists, local high school student groups, a delegation from NOW, university students in history, and a group of retired nurses were also present. The accessible location of the conference, on Radcliffe's Cambridge campus, additionally drew members of the public—a sign of the field's vitality and its broad relevance to contemporary women.

The *Harvard Crimson* reported that three "interlocking" groups had attended the conference: "the historians, very professional; the feminists, very political; and the feminist historians."[60] Mary Dunn's final observation in her report highlighted the two distinct generations of historians in attendance. She observed, "We had an 'old girl' group which enjoyed being the 'movers and shakers,' senior historians at a meeting which recognized them as powerful perhaps for the first time; we had another group which was becoming socialized in the profession in a way that we hope was supportive and satisfying. . . . The effect was, we think, a declaration to the profession that the history of women is an important field for research, and teaching, and that without it there can be no true understanding of the past."[61]

Dunn felt gratified that women of her own generation could wield the influence that had eluded them in male-dominated historical societies. She hoped these women would effectively mentor younger women in professional socialization, something Dunn's generation had generally lacked. Finally, through the development of women's history, Dunn said, there was now the opportunity to advance a truer understanding of the past.

An anonymous testimonial from a married, jobless history PhD expressed what was perhaps the crux of the matter for many women at the conference: "I think the Berkshire Conference had a much greater influence on me than I realized. Not so much because it was a woman's conference, but because I met and talked with so many people who had like interests. . . . Other conferences have left me bitter and resentful about being 'outside' academia. Your conference didn't do that."[62] This separate women's history conference was a place where women were not a marginalized "other" being granted a few spots on crowded programs. It was a place where they and their work were mainstream. The Berkshire Conferences would help sustain women's history through the 1970s. It would give it strength and legitimacy, and it would attract people to the rapidly growing field.

In their grant proposal to the Rockefeller Foundation for a third women's history conference, the leaders of the BCWH pointed to the success of the first two conferences, saying they showed a real need for academics to attend to the subject: "These conferences have provided a unique service, because the history of women, a relatively new field of inquiry, needs a public forum through which research can be encouraged and in which ideas, techniques and resources can be discussed and exchanged. Furthermore, the history of women still needs status, and this, the Berkshire Conference can provide, perhaps better than most organizations of women historians." The Berkshire Conference of Women Historians touted its longevity, prestige, and status relative to the newer organizations of women historians (like the CCWHP) to persuade funders that it was ideally suited to sponsor a conference on the history of women. The BCWH also said it could add "status and acceptance of the field (of women's history)" to the larger profession.[63]

In their funding proposal to the Rockefeller Foundation for the 1976 conference—to be held on June 9–11 at Bryn Mawr—leaders of the BCWH indicated that this would be the final round of funding requests to "complete the 'pilot project' we set for ourselves. . . . At its conclusion we will have the kind of information we will need for a decision about whether or not to continue the series." They promised to move forward with further conferences only if registration numbers and program quality remained high in this third meeting. The grant proposal indicated the areas of women's history that would be given more attention at this third convocation, saying the BCWH hoped to include in the program "all the generations of scholars, from the undergraduate to professors emerita, and all the minority groups of women historians." Recognizing the predominance of US women's history at the First and Second Berkshire Conferences, the BCWH proposed that more attention be given to European women's history and the history of minority women. They committed to targeted advertising in the South and West to recruit Black and Chicana women historians in order to ensure greater representation of minority women and their history. They demonstrated a consciousness of the need to proactively make women's history inclusive and to encompass all women's historical experience. These efforts reflected a tradition of self-criticism that was a central feature of the field's development.[64] To help remedy the need for more content on women of color, Nell Irvin Painter, an African American historian, joined the program committee and went to work recruiting both papers and presenters that would diversify the content of the conference and its participants.[65]

The Third Berkshire Conference was another resounding success. Organizationally everything went smoothly, and the Bryn Mawr campus provided an ideal setting. It cannot be said that the program committee achieved all of its objectives regarding the program's composition, however. Even with the heavier representation of Europeanists on the program committee (thirteen of twenty-one), the final program still had 92 of 159 presentations on US women's history. The space allotted to US history had increased from 48 percent to 58 percent.[66] Catherine Prelinger, BCWH president, explained this imbalance by suggesting that there were simply more Americanists doing women's history in the mid-1970s. Though she referred to the predominance of American history on the program as an "over-representation" of the field, she acknowledged it corresponded to the proportional "academic reality" of research in the various fields.[67] This was due, she said, to the practical obstacles to conducting research in European archives, such as travel costs and language barriers. Prelinger also cited the fact that a relatively smaller number of Europeanists in the United States had turned their scholarly gaze to the study of women's history.[68]

The program committee of the Third Big Berks made a concerted effort to recruit African American participants to the conference, though to be sure Black and white historians had presented work on African American women's history at both earlier conferences. Nell Painter invited around sixty Black women historians to submit proposals. Six papers featuring African American women were selected for the program, most given by African American scholars.[69] A full workshop dedicated to oral histories of working-class and minority women was presided over by Letitia Brown, an African American scholar from George Washington University. Despite efforts to recruit Chicana historians from about 100 colleges in the Southwest, only one Chicana graduate student responded. Shirlene Soto gave a paper titled "The Mexican Rural Family."[70]

Nell Painter was highly involved in planning 1978's Fourth Big Berkshire Conference at Mt. Holyoke. She recommended that Eleanor Smith and Rosalyn Terborg-Penn be brought onto the program committee for that conference and saw the first organizational of Black Women Historians United take place there. At the annual meeting of the Association for the Study of Afro-American Life and History in 1976, Painter had suggested the need for an organization to sponsor Black women's history and be a hub for Black women in the profession. Black Women Historians United changed its name to the Association of Black Women Historians (ABWH) in 1979. After 1979, the ABWH promoted inclusion of Black women's history on the program of the Berkshire Conferences but held its own annual meetings alongside the Association for the Study of Afro-American Life and History. According to its constitution, drafted in 1980, the ABWH had a dual and inseparable intellectual and professional commitment to the development of African American history and women's history, and members advocated for their specialty within the women's history subculture and the historical profession at large.[71]

Black women were active in the women's history movement and, in addition to regularly participating in the Big Berks, where they did not always feel acknowledged or respected, organized Black women's history conferences. In 1979, Bettye Collier-Thomas, director of the Bethune Historical Development Project of the National Council of Negro Women, organized the first major scholarly conference on Black women's history to coincide with the dedication of the National Archives for Black Women's History. Funded by an NEH grant, "Black Women: An Historical Perspective" drew 1,500 attendees. They met to learn about new research, develop a national community of scholars, and to strategize for the future. Surveys returned by 600 attendees suggest that 99 percent of participants were women and 95 percent identified as Black. One observer noted that there appeared to be more males and whites in attendance than those who returned surveys, however.[72] Academic respondents surveyed were generally pleased with the quality of panels and presentations, while non-academics reported discontent with the presence of white speakers and the lack of community-based perspectives.

As Black women historians and archivists worked to create their own institutions and produce their own scholarship in Black women's history, they pushed white women's historians and the institutions they had created to recognize and support this work. These white women historians often responded favorably, as for example when the Schlesinger Library launched the Black Women Oral History Project from 1976 to 1978. Initially comprising fifty oral history interviews with Black homemakers, professionals, and civic, community, and business leaders, the project was developed by African American historian Letitia Brown and longtime proponent of Black women's history Dorothy Porter. They recruited other Black women scholars to serve on the advisory board or as interviewers.[73]

Turning our attention back to the Third Berkshire Conference, Catherine Prelinger concluded in her report that "scholarly respectability is no longer a major concern for the field and unquestionably the Berkshire Conference has contributed significantly to this development." The first part of this observation was an overstatement vis-à-vis the larger profession's view of women's history, as there was still a long way to go to secure its acceptance as a legitimate part of mainstream historical study. Nevertheless, Prelinger argued that the conference should be continued because practitioners of women's history needed the opportunity to present and discuss their work. Given the large scholarly output in women's history during these years, her point was well taken. Both the OAH and the AHA made program space for women's history in that first decade after the initial explosion of interest in the field (see table 8.1). However, the field's representation on mainstream annual meeting programs was not stable in this first decade of the movement, ranging from 2 percent of program content to 17 percent per year between 1969 and 1979. Of the twenty annual conference programs designed by OAH and AHA program committees during the decade, women's history made up 10 percent or more of the content on the program only five times. After 1980, though, women's history never made up less than 10 percent of program content, ranging as high as 23 percent by 1986. After the Third Big Berkshire Conference, Prelinger received many letters from conference participants who expected the conferences to become an institution, regardless of what mainstream history associations were willing to do to include women's history on their programs. Based on the success of their "pilot project," the BCWH initiated a fourth conference for 1978 and determined to meet every three years, beginning with the Fifth Big Berks to be held in 1981.[74]

The organizers of subsequent Big Berks Conferences continued to provide a forum whose content and participants were diverse and representative of trends in the burgeoning field. Over the years, from the Second Big Berks in 1974 through 2000, the number of attendees ranged from 1,500 to 2,200. By 1987, the Seventh Big Berks offered a program with an equal number of sessions on Europe and America (sixty-seven each), and it expanded its coverage of other geographic regions as well.[75] Ensuring this successful balance required a logistical approach. In 1978 Sandi Cooper, who chaired the program of the Fourth Berkshire Conference, reported that for every session slot available for American history, five proposals came in, while for every session slot given to European topics, three proposals came in.[76] The thorny question of representative scholarship on racial and ethnic minorities continued to be an issue, and in 1987, Susan Reverby and Dorothy Helly observed that they never seemed able to get enough papers on minority women. The 1987 program did include ten sessions on lesbian history, indicating responsiveness by the so-called old girls to the new scholarship on these topics by younger scholars.[77]

Comparing the thematic titles of the fourth and sixth conferences gives an idea of the rapidly shifting generational understanding of when women's history took hold within the historical profession. The name given to the fourth conference in 1978 was "Celebrating 50 Years of Women Historians and Women's History," in honor of the fifty-year anniversary of "Little Berks" (BCWH). This title implied that both fifty years of scholarship on women and organized professionalism by women historians would be celebrated. While keynote addresses for these two conferences have not survived in the institutional records of the BCWH, the actual subject of the keynote for the fourth conference in 1978 was on the Equal Rights Amendment campaign. It was presented by Jane De Hart (Mathews). Furthermore, commentary and reflections on the 1978 conference suggested that the fiftieth anniversary celebration was focused on the BCWH rather than on the study of women's history.[78] The sixth conference in 1984 was titled "Reassessing our Past: Women's History after 15 Years." The implication was that the modern field of women's history, "our past," went back to 1969. These two titles and subsequent presentations indicate that interpretations about the field's emergence were unclear and conflicting. Yet, these new historians of women were already contemplating the longer historiography of their field.

If the Big Berks was the pulse of women's history scholarship from 1973 forward, it was not the only new national institution created to support the field. The Conference Group on Women's History formed within the Coordinating Committee on Women in the Historical Profession between 1973 and 1975. It came to serve as an information hub that kept women's historians connected in a broad national network, alerting them to job, fellowship, and grant opportunities as well as to women's history initiatives, events, and conferences around the country. It also advocated for women's history as an outside pressure group acting on the AHA, OAH, and SHA. Berenice Carroll first suggested the formation of the CGWH in 1971 when she worried there should be some separation between the "disparate objectives" of the CGWH and the CCWHP.[79] Debate ensued for several years over how to approach this matter. One camp wanted to see the CCWHP maintain its "political focus" on women historians' professional issues rather than "dilute" its energies by taking on women's history too. Most members were supportive of the formation of the CGWH under the institutional arm of the CCWHP. Carroll initially proposed a parallel personnel structure that would allow for a joint dues option. Over the next four years members repeatedly discussed the issue, and Jean Scarpacci and Donna Boutelle heatedly argued that the CCWHP should stick to its primary "political" goals.[80] Eventually, both women came to support the creation of the CGWH. Some, though, wanted a complete separation into two organizations, maintaining that a dual focus exacerbated the prevalent conflation of women historians with women's historians.[81] Renate Bridenthal and Hilda Smith were instrumental in formalizing the CGWH when they called a first organizational meeting of six at the 1974 meeting of the AHA in Chicago. The meeting included Smith, Bridenthal, Peter Vinton-Johansen, Mary Rothschild, and Marlene Wortman.[82]

Ultimately, in 1975 in response to a membership survey, the CCWHP Steering Committee voted to keep the CGWH as an integral part of the organization so that it could continue to serve "as the conscience of the profession" on women's issues while advancing scholarship on women.[83] One structural argument in favor of this continued integration was that it allowed the organization to apply for affiliate status within the AHA. Affiliate status gave the CCWHP greater influence in shaping the programs at AHA annual meetings. Affiliates were required to have a specific scholarly interest, and women's history neatly filled the bill.[84] Karen Offen argued that the majority of the CCWHP membership wanted improvements both for women as professionals and for the field of women's history in general.[85] She did not want to see the group's membership divided, nor presumably their growing influence diluted. The CGWH began with a series of two-hour workshops at the AHA meeting in Atlanta in 1975 focused on teaching, methodology, local and regional history, and unexplored research fields.[86] The group also sponsored a workshop, "Women in the South," with the coordination of Mollie Davis, Gloria Blackwell, Marsha Kass Marks, and Darlene Roth White.[87] And it encouraged the chair of the AHA Committee on Women Historians, Joan Kelly, to convince the AHA to support high school curriculum development initiatives, though funding had not yet been secured for this project. In 1983, the organization established the Joan Kelly Memorial Prize, its first prize in women's history, in commemoration of Kelly's untimely death in 1982.

From the moment it formed in 1969, the CCWHP fostered professional activism among women historians by coordinating activities in conjunction with the women's committees in the AHA and OAH. It continued to advocate for women's representation within the hierarchies of the two organizations, nominating women historians to program committees and seats on prize committees, as well as helping elevate women to the position of OAH executive secretary and nominating them to run for the office of president over the next three decades. The overwhelming majority of the successful women nominees for the office of president in both the OAH and AHA since 1981 have been historians of women and gender, and most have been active members of the CCWHP-CGWH or affiliates over the course of their careers.[88] When Gerda Lerner was elected president of the OAH in 1981, for instance, she nominated Joan Hoff-Wilson of Indiana University at Purdue to the post of executive secretary. Both women had been active in CCWHP. Hoff-Wilson held the position until 1989, which gave her the professional clout to push for American women's history from within the institutional heart of the discipline.

Other CCWHP initiatives focused on professional matters like the gendered tenure clock for men and women, maternity leave, childcare provisions at annual meetings, and sexual harassment within the profession.[89] Such issues affected women scholars, as they did other working women in the broader culture. In keeping with the group's commitment to gender equality within the profession, members joined with the Status of Women Committees in the OAH and AHA to take political action in the late 1970s and early 1980s by launching the Money in Friendly Territories campaign, or "MIFT." This was a nationwide petition drive and economic pressure campaign. Organizers created an escrow account into which members could put their annual dues until both the OAH and AHA agreed to hold annual meetings only in states that voted to ratify the Equal Rights Amendment. This effort was headed up by Barbara Evans Clements and Joanna Zangrando and Robert Zangrando of the University of Akron.[90] The campaign was successful in its efforts to press these organizations to take a stand, even though the ERA ultimately went down to defeat in 1982.[91] As important as attention to these status issues was, the heartbeat of the women's history movement was always the production of new scholarship on women.

The work of women in the CCWHP-CGWH, the OAH-CSW, and the AHA Committee on Women Historians also had international reach. In 1975, when women's representation was deemed too low at the XIV International Congress of Historical Sciences held in San Francisco, August 22–29, Joan Kelly-Gadol and Mary Hamilton of the AHA Committee on Women Historians and Joan Moon of the West Coast Association of Women Historians arranged for Natalie Zemon Davis to give a hastily organized lunchtime talk to the conferees titled "Women's History and Its Uses." The talk was attended by about fifty historians from many countries.[92] Karen Offen, an active member of the CCWHP and proponent of the CGWH, credits this lunchtime intervention with sowing the seeds for the International Federation for Research in Women's History, founded twelve years later in 1987 with a grant from the CCWHP.[93] The American intellectual movement for women's history had begun to reach out to historians overseas. Five years later, in 1980, Barbara Sicherman, E. William Monter, Kathryn Kish Sklar, and Joan Wallach Scott presented a report titled *Recent United States Scholarship on the History of Women* at the XV International Congress of Historical Sciences in Bucharest, Romania.[94] Sklar recalled later that the report's central assertion that sex and gender were central categories of analysis as important as class or race was met with an audible collective gasp.[95] These international developments reveal the close collaboration between Europeanists and Americanists and also their mutual commitment to advance women's history globally, sure in the transformative, consciousness-raising power of that history for all societies.

An important service the CCWHP-CGWH provided to their members was publication of a quarterly newsletter, which kept readers across the nation well-informed of developments relevant to them as historians and as women's historians. Beginning in 1976, the CCWHP-CGWH divided up their quarterly newsletter, with the CCWHP responsible for producing two yearly issues on professional matters and the CGWH two issues on the field of women's history. The newsletters offer a glimpse into the priorities of the women's history movement in which scholarship and teaching formed the central pillars of feminist historians' mandate, while networking and political advocacy provided the brick and mortar. Between 1970 and 1975, the CCWHP put out ten bulletins on new women's history courses and scholarship. The lists were compiled first by Linda Kerber and then by Arnita Jones.[96] According to Jones, the bulletins were possible thanks to the women's historians who filled out surveys on the development of courses on women, including general surveys and more specialized courses in subfields like women's labor history. More and more courses were now feasible because of the scholarly output underway.[97]

The *CGWH Newsletters* published between 1975 and 1981 reveal the concentrated effort of the CGWH to gather and disseminate information on publications, conferences, working groups, and archives in diverse subfields of women's history from all regions of the country. The newsletter posted jobs in women's history and ran a paper-matching service for conference session proposals. It featured a column with the achievements of members, including new appointments, successful grant applications, completion of degrees by graduate students, publication of books, and the awarding of academic prizes. It announced new women's history programs and listed developments in related disciplines. The editors informed members about feminist history initiatives in public history and the women's movement. The CGWH sponsored the publication of Nupur Chaudhuri's *Bibliography of Women's History* that listed 1,046 books and peer-reviewed journal articles produced from 1976 to 1979 alone.[98]

By 1976, the president of each regional group affiliated with the CGWH, from New England to New Mexico, became a representative on the CGWH's executive committee. They regularly sent in notices about their local women's history initiatives. Regional affiliates formed between 1969 and 1976 included the Southern Association for Women Historians, the West Coast Association of Women Historians, Women Historians of the Midwest, the Upstate New York Women's History Organization (UNYWHO), the New York Metropolitan Area Group, the New England Association of Women Historians, the Chicago Area Women's History Conference (CAWHC), the Washington, DC, Area Women Historians, the Chesapeake Bay Area Group of Women Historians, and the Cleveland Area group.[99] The work of these regional affiliates speaks to the widespread reach of the movement and shows that it was fueled by the energy of local and regional activists. By 1976 this was evident. The *CCWHP Newsletter* reported that affiliates organized regional meetings and served as a support network and information exchange. WHOM, the Southern Association for Women Historians, the West Coast Association of Women Historians, and UNYWHO published their own newsletters, sent to mailing lists much larger than their membership lists.[100] Regional groups encompassed history professors, archivists, librarians, graduate students, unemployed PhDs, and historical society workers. Given the regional groups' reach, both geographically and in terms of personnel, it can be argued that for a time, during the 1970s and 1980s, the women's history movement was a social movement as much as it was an intellectual movement within the halls of academia. Regional groups often sponsored public history initiatives, state and local curriculum projects, and women's history initiatives in higher education, some of which will feature later in our story.[101]

In 1976 and 1977, Women Historians of the Midwest jointly sponsored regional women's history initiatives with the Chicago Area Women's History Conference (founded 1971).[102] WHOM, incorporated in 1973, combined an interest in scholarship with public history, archives, and women's history curriculum for K–12 education. Rhoda Gilman, Gretchen Kreuter, Barbara Stuhler, Marjorie Wall Bingham, and Susan Hill Gross were members of WHOM right from the start, though they do not appear to have belonged to the OAH or AHA.[103] WHOM and the CAWHC organized two conferences modeled on the Big Berks, which were each titled "Conference on the History of Women." The publicity committee produced and mailed 30,000 flyers to advertise the two conferences. WHOM and the CAWHC secured funding from General Mills Corporation and the Dayton-Hudson Foundation. St. Catherine's College of St. Paul, Minnesota, offered its campus and support services.[104]

D'Ann Campbell, an Americanist active in the CCWHP, the OAH, WHOM and the CAWHC, reported that the second conference in 1977 had 800 participants from two foreign countries and thirty-nine states. Campbell touted the fifty sessions included on the program. She remarked on their variety, mentioning that the audience showed intense interest and participation. Campbell reported on Joan Scott's keynote address. According to Scott, the dilemma that faced the maturing field was "whether to be critical of a sister's research, and how to structure criticism so that it advances scholarship instead of destroying confidence. . . . Women's history has moved from outcast to marginal to mainstream history. The way to build the scholarly self-confidence of the sisterhood is to develop standards of research and teaching excellence that are beyond question."[105] Scott advanced commitment to high scholarly and teaching standards while invoking feminist sisterhood. Later in 1977, WHOM and the CAWHC held meetings at which members discussed the usefulness of a major OAH initiative being orchestrated by Midwesterners Andrea Hinding and Clarke Chambers—the Women's History Sources Survey project—and heard papers prepared by Joan Scott on French and English women workers and by Blanche Hersh on American feminist abolitionists.[106]

After these two large cosponsored conferences, WHOM focused for the next two years on smaller monthly and annual meetings. These typically had research presentations, discussion of teaching and research, and consultations on applying for grants.[107] WHOM soon brought women's history to the Minneapolis meeting of the National Coordinating Committee for the Promotion of History, an organization it joined in 1978. Inside that organization, members proposed papers and workshops for the group's annual meeting. In 1979, WHOM turned its eye to the American Studies Association, which was set to hold its annual meeting in St. Paul. WHOM members focused their efforts that year on getting Minnesota women's history papers, tours, and movies onto the ASA program.[108]

The Women's History Sources Survey, also based in Minnesota, was a major women's history initiative of national scope and importance. The project had been launched in 1972 after Anne Firor Scott, Gerda Lerner, Janet Wilson James, Clarke Chambers, and Carl Degler organized an OAH session on the need for a guide to women's history sources around the nation. This group of scholars wrote a series of grant proposals that secured $600,000 from the National Endowment for the Humanities between 1975 and 1979.[109] The resulting reference volume, *Women's History Sources: A Guide to Archives and Manuscript Collections in the United States*, became an invaluable research tool for practitioners in the field as it identified holdings in large and small libraries, historical societies, and communities across the country.

By the early 1980s, WHOM was still active, though, as with any organization staffed solely by volunteers, it went through crests and doldrums over the next decade. Members continued to advocate for women's history by reaching beyond scholarly communities—for example, by sponsoring the Upper Midwest Women's History Center for Teachers in 1981. Funded by the 1974 Women's Educational Equity Act, the center held programs and workshops for K–12 teachers on how to integrate women's history into the school curriculum.[110] The center operated from 1980 to 1999, offering an important example of collaboration between academics and archivists, educators and public historians determined to win a broader audience.[111]

Both Midwestern groups, WHOM and the CAWHC, continued to hold regular meetings focused on new scholarship, archives, public history initiatives, and the organization of conferences.[112] In May 1982, WHOM convened its third Conference on the History of Women with keynote speakers Anne Firor Scott and Sara Evans. The event attracted 350 attendees and received a National Endowment for the Humanities grant.[113] The attendance was down from the 1977 conference but nevertheless drew participants from around the country. The smaller size may indicate a leveling of energies in the 1980s after more than a decade of high-octane advances and heady activism. Though WHOM disbanded briefly in 2001, a group of historians immediately revived it under the name Women and Gender Historians of the Midwest that same year.[114]

The Upstate New York Women's History Organization was another active and long-lived regional group that sponsored both women's history conferences and public history initiatives. Established just two years after WHOM, in 1975, it initially focused on creating a scholarly network in upstate New York. By 1979 it claimed over 250 members and could spearhead major campaigns. Patricia Foster Haines, a University of Pennsylvania PhD candidate living in Ithaca, New York, and Judith Wellman of SUNY Oswego were key activists in UNYWHO.[115] In a 1979 CGWH newsletter, Patricia Haines of UNYWHO, reported that between 1974 and 1979, the organization "matured from a loosely knit, semi-organized group of persons sharing interest in women's history and issues affecting women as historians, into a solid organization."[116] Haines noted a membership drawn from an array of cultural institutions. These included faculty from academic history departments, local teachers, librarians, artists, and members of the chamber of commerce and the welfare department.

UNYWHO leaders organized two substantial women's history conferences in 1979. The first took place in March in Rochester, New York, and was modeled on a traditional conference with paper sessions and workshops. It had sixty participants. The second event was the Seneca Falls Women's History Conference, a three-day event sponsored by the Regional Conference of Historical Agencies and the County Historians Association of New York State. Based in the heart of a region known for being a hotbed for the antebellum-era social movements from which the nineteenth-century women's rights movement had emerged so forcefully in the late 1830s, this UNYWHO conference, attended by 350 people, launched a historic project—the establishment of the Seneca Falls Women's Rights National Historical Park by the National Park Service near the site of the former Wesleyan Chapel where the historic Seneca Falls Women's Rights Convention of 1848 had been held. The Wesleyan Chapel itself had fallen into private hands and been at one point converted into a laundromat. UNYWHO collaborated with the Elizabeth Cady Stanton Foundation and the Seneca Falls Consortium to win support for the park's establishment. A smaller organizational conference was held by UNYWHO in Cooperstown, New York, at which member Judith Wellman delivered a paper on Elizabeth Cady Stanton and the group unveiled promotional materials they had designed on behalf of a proposal to restore the Stanton House and create another public history site dedicated to the 1848 women's rights convention. At the time, Stanton's home was owned privately by someone unconnected to Stanton's legacy. Thus, UNYWHO and the local history groups sought to create multiple public history sites in the village long credited with being the birthplace of the American women's rights movement. Their work would ultimately bear fruit as a major public history initiative when Congress approved legislation authorizing the park's building and funding between 1980 and 1983.[117]

In 1977 a group of women historians set in motion plans to found an organization of Black women historians. Eleanor Smith and Rosalyn Terborg-Penn, among others, perceived a need and desire among their peers for such an institution that could serve their professional needs and scholarly interests. They hoped to fill the gaps left by male-dominated and white feminist history organizations. For two years, calling themselves "Black Women Historians United," they gauged the interest of other Black women historians, recruited members, and convened at the meetings of other historical associations such as the Association for the Study of African American Life and History and the Big Berks. By 1979 they were ready to formally establish the organization as the Association of Black Women Historians, which they did at the annual meeting of the Association for the Study of African American Life and History. The first executive board comprised Darlene Clark Hine, Rosalyn Terborg-Penn, Janice Sumler-Lewis, Sharon Harley, Cheryl Johnson(-Odom), Juanita Moore, and Cynthia Neverdon-Morton.[118]

The purpose of the organization was to provide professional opportunities and recognition for Black women scholars and their history broadly. To that design the ABWH established a newsletter called *Truth* (after Sojourner Truth) and took advantage of opportunities to collaborate with mainstream professional societies, particularly the OAH and AHA. An early collaboration with the OAH included signing onto a project initially designed and launched by Gerda Lerner, who in seeking a Black woman historian to codirect the project joined forces with Darlene Clark Hine and secured funding from the Department of Education's Fund for the Improvement of Postsecondary Education in 1980.[119] The ABWH also collaborated with the AHA to add more Black women historians to the third edition of the *American Historical Association Directory of Women Historians* (1981). The first edition of this directory had come out in 1975, a product of efforts initiated by the AHA Committee on Women Historians, headed that year by Joan Wallach Scott and Kathryn Kish Sklar, with members such as Martha Tolpin, Mary Furner, and Rosalyn Terborg-Penn. Also collaborating were leaders within the OAH-CSW, the CCWHP, the Western Association of Women Historians, WHOM, UNYWHO, and the Southern Association for Women Historians. The survey conducted to compile the directory was sent out to 3,000 historians. It received 1,046 responses. Fewer than 100 were members of minority groups.[120]

Like other women's history organizations and committees established in the 1970s with which the ABWH affiliated, such as the CCWHP-CGWH, the ABWH organized conferences to provide a robust forum for the field of Black women's history in its first decade and established dissertation, book, and article prizes named for historic role models and mentors. The first such prize to be established was the Letitia Woods Brown Award in 1983 for most noteworthy book or article on Black women's history. In 1966, Brown had been one of the first women to earn a history PhD at Harvard University. She was fifty-one years old and had been in the program for eighteen years at that point, having moved regularly to follow her husband's career, and taught in historically Black colleges and schools. After that she'd taken a post teaching history at George Washington University in 1971. While she didn't specialize in Black women's history, she consulted on the Black Women Oral History Project at the Schlesinger Library as it geared up to conduct its work, largely completed after her death in 1976.[121]

The academic legitimacy that women's historians gained over the course of the 1970s and 1980s was largely an outgrowth of their scholarly productivity. The support and service provided by women, for women's history, in these organizations helped make recognition of that scholarship possible. Berenice Carroll's 1969 call to address the so-called feminine mystique in historical writing in the historical profession ultimately reverberated far beyond the mainstream of the profession itself. Through new national women's history institutions like the Conference Group on Women's History, the Association of Black Women Historians, and the Big Berks, and through the regional women's history organizations featured in this chapter, these feminist historians harnessed their energies into a vital women's history subculture within the discipline. Yet, the forces that coalesced to promote women's history were not free of internal conflict or dissent. Disagreement over where feminist historians' focus should concentrate could be quite sharp. They frequently centered on the inadequate amount of attention given to women of historically marginalized groups. One particularly pointed disagreement erupted in the wake of the Seventh Berkshire Conference on the History of Women at Wellesley College.

At the opening session of the Seventh Big Berks in 1987, historian Carroll Smith-Rosenberg announced triumphantly, "We have arrived."[122] If, by this, Smith-Rosenberg meant that historians of women had achieved scholarly legitimacy within the historical profession, other historians were already expressing discontent with this view. In response, Antoinette Burton and a graduate student peer, Deborah Rossum, wrote an open letter to conference attendees saying that there was "an amazing (and to some degree) understandable air of triumphalism during the Berkshire's opening session."[123] Yet, they worried, "What does it mean to have arrived, if in doing so we create similarly monolithic, narrowly-visioned structures and become separate from but parallel to the male academic world?" In their criticism of that year's conference, they suggested that the space given to panels presenting scholarship on race, class, and lesbian history had been arranged in such a way as to segregate those subjects. They contended that the now-established women's history leadership had narrowly conceived of women's and gender history as the history of "white, middle-class, and heterosexual" women. The implication of the letter was that the organization of the conference reflected racial, class, and heterosexual biases.

Program cochair Susan Reverby responded.[124] Saying that she recognized the content-related concerns that Burton and Rossum had expressed, she nevertheless insisted that the program committee had done its best to include and incorporate papers on Black women, class, and lesbian history. She explained that the committee had been hobbled in its ability to attract African American scholars that year by the fact that the conference timing had coincided with the National Women's Studies Association's meeting, held that year for the first time at historically Black Spelman College in Atlanta. And because someone had accused Reverby of making "appalling" comments when confronted by complaints about the absence of Black, Native American, Hispanic, and Asian women's history on the program, she stated flatly that they had misreported her statements. She asserted her political credentials:

> As a woman, a Jew, and a political person I would certainly never refer to women of color as "they." Nor would I use such flagrantly stupid and patently untrue terms. I have spent 41 years of my life being "the other" in various situations, and I have never, never used such language. I did say . . . that I thought every black woman historian that existed in the country who could come was here and that we did the best we could. . . . We think we have made progress—not as much as any of us wants, but also of a kind that deserves more than an easy dismissal. You need only compare the Seventh Berks with previous conferences on this.[125]

This exchange might be taken as a sign that, despite tremendous progress, serious generational, political, and epistemological divisions existed among women's historians by 1987. By suggesting that women's historians had not sufficiently addressed race, ethnicity, class, gender, and sexuality, Burton and Rossum touched on a major issue that feminist scholars had grappled with since the early 1970s—historical differences among women. By 1987, however, it would be wrong to think no headway had been made toward this goal. In fact, women's historians paid attention to difference precisely because of their own engagement with American social movements of the New Left, including civil rights, women's liberation, and gay liberation, and because they were committed to reconstructing a full and accurate American historical narrative. This heated exchange might be better understood as an indicator that women's history had reached a stage of sufficient maturity and legitimacy by 1987 that the field was able to withstand serious internal debate and move to incorporate the perspectives of multiple generations of scholars from diverse backgrounds.

Along these lines, a flyer posted at the Seventh Big Berks pointedly asked, "Is this an 'old girls club?' OR . . . is the ONLY *goal of* women's history to achieve academic legitimacy?"[126] This was also not a new question for women's historians. In preparation for the Third Berkshire Conference in 1976, Elizabeth Pleck had made the same point, stating, "I think it is especially important to show that women historians do not replicate the methods of male historians through an old girl network and instead strive to include diverse groups of women."[127] In conferring about the formation of a program committee for the Sixth Berkshire Conference, Ellen DuBois, Judith Walkowitz, and Carol Groneman insisted there should be "representation on the committee from under 35'ers. (We could be accused of ageism!)"[128] Thus, though the 1987 flyer implied that women's history was becoming too establishment, that it was "too white," losing its edge, and increasingly ruled by a powerful "old girl network," these were issues that had been considered since at least 1975. This tradition of constant self-evaluation, reflection on process and representation, and concern with not replicating what women saw as the negative aspects of male historians' traditional professional culture was a major strength of the women's history movement. It kept all generations professionally engaged, discouraged complacency, and did much to propel the field toward legitimacy.

By 1987, several generations of women's historians had already dedicated years to the prospect of achieving academic legitimacy in ways that did not conflict with their feminist politics. They worked first to transform the androcentric, highly gendered professional culture by infiltrating its institutions and implementing change. Their creation of separate women's history organizations was a vital component of that work. While politics often informed and guided their scholarly interests and professional actions, most were conscious that overt politicization of scholarship could hinder the field's advance. Some, like Linda Gordon, took a different approach, asserting a more open acknowledgment of the political underpinnings of the field.[129] Yet in no way did Gordon or her peers reject scholarly standards. Rather, Gordon and other politicized historians were committed to producing historical scholarship according to the discipline's standards. They wrote relevant, usable history, even as they created a more equitable professional culture and opposed the discipline's androcentricity. By the time of the 1987 Big Berks conference, historians of women were well along on the path to establishing their field's hold within the American historical profession. They had reached audiences throughout higher education. They were also reaching beyond the ivory tower, too, to impact the content of K–12 history curriculums and public history. How academics achieved academic and professional legitimacy within their discipline can be understood through looking at their scholarship and their active service in professional organizations. But how they reached broader audiences and furthered historical consciousness about women is a story than can be fully understood only by considering the ferment of activism within classrooms, history departments, large-scale curriculum development projects in higher education, and public history projects.

Chapter 9

Usable Pasts

Feminism, Teaching, and Curriculum Development, 1969–1988

It was 1968, '69. Nothing like women's history had ever been offered
before. Everyone was so grateful, and there was such a spirit. . . . It was
political. It was exciting.

—Mari Jo Buhle, 2000

We were on a crusade. You know, we wanted to reconstruct women's
history. . . . These were not career moves.

—Ellen Carol Dubois, 2001

Teaching and curriculum development were central to achieving the epistemological objectives of the women's history movement. They were at once an
essential corollary to scholarship and a bridge for feminist politics to cross over
into academic discourse in the classroom.[1] In 1971, the Organization of American Historians' Committee on the Status of Women cited a study by Dolores
Barracano Schmidt and Earl Schmidt that documented the dearth of content
about women in American history textbooks.[2] The Schmidts trenchantly observed that students of American history had paid for history courses but had
been sold a "male fantasy" instead. Feminist historians set out in the 1970s to
turn this deficit into a surplus. As the women's history movement was being
launched between 1969 and 1973, older scholars in the Berkshire Conference
of Women Historians showed curiosity about the intentions of the new wom-
en's historians. Chief among the questions was that asked by Viola Barnes as
to whether the younger generation was "interested in scholarship or political
crusades."[3] That the two were fundamentally separate was implied here. One was
a commitment to focusing on knowledge production, and the other was about
"crusading" for women's professional status and access to jobs and leadership
positions. But to neglect the simultaneously emerging crusade on behalf of
scholarship about women's history would fail to capture the excitement of the
era. Indeed, it misses the main point of the movement entirely. This "crusade"
for women's history was led by feminist scholars energized by the modern
feminist movement and committed to attaining scholarly legitimacy within the
discipline. They proved highly successful at achieving their epistemological goal
over the next two decades.[4] The new feminists had another major cultural goal

as well: to reach beyond a purely academic audience. Like those who had gone before them at midcentury, the new women's historians of the late twentieth century thought that women's history had the power to transform the culture if it could illustrate women's wide-ranging participation in the making of society. At midcentury, this had been at the heart of Mary Beard's, Alma Lutz's, Guion Griffis Johnson's, Caroline Ware's and others' historical thinking through the decades as they engaged in individual research in history and applied their historical insights to their political work. For late twentieth-century feminist academic historians whose work would straddle research and teaching, curriculum and program development in higher education was a direct path to achieving that goal.[5]

In the 1970s and 1980s, the demand for courses, instructional materials, and major curriculum reform surged on college campuses across the country. As historians of women designed and taught new courses, they developed a broad conceptualization of "women's history" that gave it the analytical rigor and explanatory power fundamental to challenging the male-centered narrative of traditional history.[6] In response to their male colleagues' question, "What difference does it make to say women participated in history?," women's historians generated a mass of usable curricular materials in addition to their specialized scholarship.[7] And what they contributed had staying power; the theoretical and conceptual framework for understanding the diverse experiences and perspectives of women in the past gradually became part of the mainstream historical narrative in the United States, substantially broadening American history.

Specialized courses in women's history at all levels of collegiate history education became commonplace, as did the integration of women's history into mainstream introductory survey courses. The earliest efforts on this front are documented in the records of the Coordinating Committee on Women in the Historical Profession, which by 1971 had begun to gather data about women's history course offerings across the country in a series of bulletins. These early bulletins were initially put together by Linda Kerber and then expanded in the CCWHP–Conference Group on Women's History newsletters under its various editors. In the first five years of the movement, course offerings in women's history grew from the handful of pre-1969 courses offered at Columbia, Barnard, the New School for Social Research, and the unofficial meetings of the Radcliffe Seminars to dozens of offerings in institutions across the country. In the 1970s, universities and colleges across the United States established courses, job lines, and undergraduate and eventually graduate programs in women's history. These moves were paralleled by attention to women and gender in other academic disciplines and supported by the creation of interdisciplinary women's studies programs.[8]

Because the first CCWHP course bulletins issued between 1971 and 1975 were compiled from surveys returned by CCWHP members, they likely undercount the number of women's history courses around the country. Nevertheless, they reflect the considerable growth in course offerings in the United States, ranging from 38 courses in a single semester in 1971 to 115 in 1973 and 1974. Moreover, the 1974 bulletins identified sixteen graduate history programs where a student could earn a PhD in a traditional field while working with an advisor specializing in women's history. In these years, Gerda Lerner and Joan Kelly established an MA program in women's history at Sarah Lawrence College, and Mary Ryan launched the first PhD program in women's history at the State University of New York at Binghamton. By 1975, activists in the movement put great emphasis on developing graduate education in women's history, understanding that generating more scholars in the field was key to securing a lasting place for women's history in history programs throughout the country over time.[9]

Course and program development came at a time when, inspired by the women's liberation movement, college students demanded women's history courses. The new women's historians recognized that students would continue to enroll in women's history classes only if there were a rich and diversified list of courses; without high enrollment the field might not survive universities' cost analyses. If women's history were to succeed as an epistemological project, it would need to convince the mainstream of the profession of the field's legitimacy and recruit new scholars to undergraduate and graduate study in women's history. Sizable numbers of PhD students were needed to support the development of a distinct new body of knowledge.

The Academic Wing of Women's Liberation: In the Classroom

When in 1975 Linda Gordon wrote in *Feminist Studies*, "It seems to me that we ought to see ourselves forthrightly and unpretentiously as the academic wing of the women's liberation movement," she was simply putting in print what many of her compatriots in the movement were thinking and saying to one another.[10] Much of the energy of the new women's historians and their courage to challenge traditional paradigms surged from their connections to women's liberation and other feminist movements of the era. Liberal feminists of course were those working for reform through institutional and legal policy changes that would equalize education, employment, and social policy for women and men—for example, of the kind represented in the President's Commission on the Status of Women, the Equal Pay Act of 1963, Title VII of the Civil Rights Act of 1964, and Title IX of the Education Amendments

Act of 1972. Women's liberation, on the other hand, focused on exposing and challenging social, cultural, and sexual practices and beliefs that upheld sexual inequality, sometimes but not always within a socialist feminist analytic framework. Women's liberationists coined the term "sexism" and incorporated concern with racism, class inequality, family systems, and sexuality into their work and theory between 1968 and 1975. Both branches of feminism impacted American higher education profoundly, opening the door more widely to female students and leading to a reconsideration of the content of academic disciplines and the gender composition of collegiate faculty. The impact was evident well beyond the discipline of history, and more than eighty interdisciplinary women's studies programs were established around the country between 1969 and 1973.[11]

At the level of individual experiences in conferences, history departments, and classrooms, examples abound of the connection between the new women's history and the feminist politics of the era. Mari Jo Buhle reported that students and professors sometimes felt they were joined in a common feminist cause in pursuit of women's history in the 1970s. She recalled of teaching women's history in these early days, "It was 1968, '69. Nothing like women's history had ever been offered before. Everyone was so grateful, and there was such a spirit. . . . It was political. It was exciting. The commitment was extraordinary."[12]

Similarly, Alice Kessler-Harris reported that teaching in the 1970s was both terrific and "done in the consciousness-raising spirit of the women's movement—a spirit that infused the classroom."[13] The new women's historians entering the profession in the 1970s found that feminist politics, scholarship, and teaching women's history blended seamlessly in the classroom.

For many women, and men, coming into history after 1965, their experiences as social and political activists shaped and energized their professional and intellectual engagement. For some, this was manifested in the sort of history they published or the curricular projects they developed, as, for example, former Black Panther Sharon Harley's work on radical Black women and Rosalyn Terborg-Penn's interest in Black women suffragists.[14] Jacquelyn Dowd Hall's and Sara Evans's work on racially progressive white women in the long civil rights movement are two more examples.[15] For others, as we've seen, the connection manifested itself in organizational activities within mainstream or separate women's history institutions and networks. Still others charted a course to women's history through extra-institutional networks that did not leave much of a record in traditional archives. Oral histories and testimonials are the best route to exploring this feature of the women's history movement.[16]

Feminist historians benefited from extra-institutional networks. One such network emerged in the late 1960s in the Northeast and linked the women's liberation movement to the women's history movement. It included New Left, labor, feminist, and peace historians Mari Jo Buhle, Rosalyn Baxandall, Kathryn Kish Sklar, Ellen DuBois, Susan Reverby, Meredith Tax, Margery Davies, and Gerda Lerner.[17] They studied women of the working class and middle class; those who were politically and culturally influential in the nineteenth and early twentieth centuries; Black and white female abolitionists; domestic economist and inspiration behind the feminization of teaching, Catharine Beecher; and socialists, clerical workers, retail workers, health workers, garment workers, and union organizers.[18] Another overlapping network centered in New York included social, labor, and peace historians such as Baxandall, Lerner, Alice Kessler-Harris, Blanche Wiesen Cook, Renate Bridenthal, Amy Swerdlow, Carole Turbin, Annette Baxter, Sandi Cooper, and Carol Berkin. The work of these historians, both scholarly and institutional, overlapped with that of the national CCWHP, American Historical Association regional affiliates, and the New York Metropolitan Area Group.[19] New Left feminist historians' choice to shift into studying women's history in the late 1960s and early 1970s paralleled New Left women's transition out of the male-dominated New Left. In the New Left, feminists and their concerns and insights were often ignored, denigrated, or outright attacked by male peers. This was, of course, the origins story of the women's liberation movement.[20]

The early research of the Americanists identified above often, if not always, reflected their social, political, and cultural interests or backgrounds. They weren't just interested in constructing women's history because they were feminists. As the daughters and granddaughters of immigrants and the working class, they were interested in researching and writing about working-class, immigrant, and wage-earning women. Thus, Meredith Tax, a member of Bread and Roses, the Committee for Abortion Rights and against Sterilization Abuse, and the Chicago Women's Liberation Union spent ten years working on a book about New York City's largely Jewish immigrant garment workers and their radical unionization before it was published in 1980 as *The Rising of the Women*. Margery Davies wrote a book about women office workers, *Woman's Place Is at the Typewriter*. Blanche Wiesen Cook and Amy Swerdlow were both active in the peace/anti-war movement before they started working on research about feminist socialists and peace activists. Cook shifted her scholarly attention from socialist feminists to writing a biography on Eleanor Roosevelt. Swerdlow wrote a dissertation at Rutgers in the 1970s about the movement she herself had participated in during the 1960s; it was later published as *Women Strike for Peace: Traditional Motherhood and Radical Politics in the 1960s*. Susan Reverby studied women health workers, no doubt influenced by the women's health movement and the publication of *Our Bodies, Ourselves*. She later focused on the medical atrocity committed against African American men during the Tuskegee syphilis study in *Examining Tuskegee*.[21]

Linda Gordon's academic history and her links to women's liberation, the New Left, and emerging networks of feminist historians are illustrative of the dynamics at play in these formative years. A graduate of Swarthmore College, Gordon was encouraged by her history professor, Paul Beik, to apply to Yale for graduate school in 1961. At Yale, she majored in Russian history in a predominantly male program. She observed that she received no mentorship. Because of that and limited access to Soviet archives, her dissertation in Russian history did not progress, and without an intellectual support network or community, she left school for a couple of years, reenrolling in 1967 to finish her PhD. She received her degree in 1970 after completing research in London and Poland.[22] She got a job at the University of Massachusetts in Boston teaching Western civilization just before the academic job market took a serious and sustained nosedive.[23]

Gordon soon became interested in the ideas of the New Left and their emphasis on economic, Marxist interpretations of history. Her introduction to the New Left came through the history department at the University of Massachusetts in Boston, where she co-taught courses with colleagues David Hunt and Peter Weiler. The three coauthored a 1971 essay critiquing a widely assigned textbook, which they circulated but did not publish until 1987. It was titled "History as Indoctrination."[24] Written in the context of the Vietnam War, the essay argued that traditional histories served capitalist and imperialist interests and were thus tools of indoctrination. Feminism entered Gordon's world as well when she met Roxanne Dunbar in 1969.[25] Dunbar, a radical feminist and founder of the group Cell 16, was a persuasive voice on the radical edge of the women's liberation movement. The group, like others in the consciousness-raising mode of women's liberation, encouraged women to analyze their common personal experiences to understand male dominance and women's second-class status. But it also encouraged female separatism from men who did not work actively for women's liberation.[26] By 1970, the professional and political aspects of Gordon's life became increasingly entwined. Her interests shifted to the history of American women, and her core academic peer group expanded to include feminist historians as well as New Left critical thinkers.[27] Gordon was affiliated with the renowned Boston collective Bread and Roses, another consciousness-raising group on the radical, anti-capitalist, anti-imperialist, anti-racist edge of the women's liberation movement.

The feminist historians she was most closely connected to were all Americanists, most of whom were also left-leaning in their politics: Mari Jo Buhle, Nancy Schrom (Dye), Ann Gordon, Ellen DuBois, Kathryn Kish Sklar, and Meredith Tax.[28] In the early 1970s, Gordon and her friends without a Harvard affiliation began to find ways to use the Widener and Schlesinger Libraries at

Harvard, where they studied, for example, books by British historian Alice Clark, who had written about seventeenth-century English working women.[29] Discussions ensued about the library classification systems that obscured the existence of scholarship about women. Mari Jo Buhle recalled that even though Bread and Roses was mostly inactive by the time she arrived in Boston as an all-but-dissertation student, the women's history study group still existed. It became a source of inspiration, friendship, and intellectual stimulation for her.[30] She earned her PhD in 1974 and went on to edit *The Concise History of Woman Suffrage* with husband Paul Buhle before publishing her dissertation, *Women and American Socialism, 1870–1920* in 1981.[31] Before moving to Brown University and launching a very productive graduate teaching career, Buhle had spent a year at Sarah Lawrence, where Gerda Lerner was launching the first MA program in women's history. And before that she was a teaching assistant for William O'Neill at the University of Wisconsin–Madison, where she taught her first women's history class.

Ellen DuBois could also trace her move into women's history to her political interest and involvement in the New Left and women's liberation movements.[32] As a graduate student at Northwestern University in 1968, she became an anti-war, New Left activist in Students for a Democratic Society. She became a draft counselor, helping college-age men get or maintain draft deferments to avoid fighting in the American war in Vietnam. DuBois experienced sexism within the New Left and academia, recalling that she wrote a paper on the Grimké sisters for New Left historian Christopher Lasch, whom she described as an "anti-feminist," and that a professor said she "didn't know how to sit like a lady." By 1969, she helped found a chapter of the Chicago Women's Liberation Union at Northwestern named "The Women's Free School," where she taught women's history for the first time. While at Northwestern, DuBois considered New Left historian Jesse Lemisch her New Left mentor and his wife, well-known feminist Naomi Weisstein, as her feminist mentor.[33] In 1970, while doing dissertation research at the Schlesinger Library in Cambridge, Massachusetts, she connected with Bread and Roses. DuBois reflected on this period of her life and the early women's history movement:

> I was a radical historian at that point [1970]. When I'd go to conventions
> I'd meet with radical historians. I knew I was part of what you would
> call the social history revolution, certainly the women's wing of that. So,
> then I went to Boston and I lived in another commune and went to the
> Schlesinger every day. . . . Our desire to do this history wasn't because we
> thought it was a good career move, or even because what we wanted was
> a spot in the literature. We did it because we were all feminists, and we all

had the same impulses to go back and do our own history. And luckily there were a bunch of us who were being trained as historians and who could do that in a responsible fashion.[34]

Ellen DuBois's well-received 1978 book on the antebellum women's movement, *Feminism and Suffrage: The Emergence of an Independent Women's Movement in America, 1848–1869*, again shows the pattern of parallels between feminist politics and feminist scholarly interests clearly. DuBois earned her PhD in 1975, taught US women's history at the University of Buffalo for sixteen years and then spent the remainder of her teaching career at UCLA, where she was hired to replace Kathryn (Kitty) Sklar. DuBois had boarded with Sklar in Cambridge in 1973, forming part of a tight but fluid network of feminist historians coalescing in the early '70s.[35] From their positions in major universities, this cohort of feminist historians came to exercise considerable influence over collegiate-level history curricula and the direction of new scholarship. Their political roots and scholarly dedication enabled this generation to cultivate a fertile field as educators and writers.

Linda Gordon explained that she met New Yorkers Rosalyn Baxandall and Susan Reverby in Boston, as the women's history group there had a constantly changing membership. These three historians determined to write an anthology of documents about American working women since they were teaching about them and teaching materials were scarce. They carried out research in archives in Boston and New York and published their document-reader, *America's Working Women: A Documentary History, 1600 to the Present*, in 1976.[36] Early teaching texts and anthologies were forged in just this way—by extra-institutional networks of young scholars all over the country. Meanwhile, the individual scholars were also publishing first monographs. These works were disseminated broadly in college classrooms even while they helped build up the ground floor of the rising field on the foundations that had been laid earlier. These young scholars were punching way above their weight.[37] Student excitement for women's history motivated them. Gordon recalled that students at the University of Massachusetts were highly politicized, and many were older, working-class students and others who had dropped out of elite colleges in reaction to conservatism.[38] Students filled the seats; the challenge was to provide curriculum.

At Wheaton College in 1971, Nancy Cott took note of her students' enthusiasm for the subject.[39] Cott, who went on to become a towering figure in American women's history and an influential public intellectual, produced the now-classic anthology of documents *Root of Bitterness: Documents of the Social History of American Women* (1972).[40] In 1970, while a graduate student at Brandeis, she taught two history courses at Wheaton—a twentieth-century

US course and a course in cultural and intellectual history that she made into a women's history course. Her proximity to the Schlesinger Library made it possible to secure archival resources that she could incorporate into her class. At the time, there were no women's history textbooks, but in August 1971 Mari Jo Buhle, Ann Gordon, and Nancy Schrom published their landmark essay in *Radical America*, "Women in American Society: An Historical Contribution."[41] The article was widely assigned by historians developing women's history courses. Cott shaped her first course around this essay and materials she found at the Schlesinger. She explained the significance of these resources:

> Their article was just absolutely foundational for me in understanding a chronology for women's history and analysis. . . . And I was entirely skeptical of other work that had been published in the past in women's history. I assumed it was all partial, that it all took the male point of view, that it was focused on a few great notables or worthies or political actors, that it only told the history of the suffrage movement which I wasn't particularly interested in. . . . I was being enmeshed in that women's liberation outlook of women's consciousness being the most important thing and the way that they share features of womanhood. I was interested in getting at women's own subjectivity and consciousness. And so, I thought primary sources were the only way. And that's when I started haunting the Schlesinger Library—and finding things there. I probably took a lead from the Buhle, Gordon, Schrom pamphlet, but I was also just lucky enough to have these wonderful resources.[42]

Cott's early skepticism of the work of the older generation was clearly shaped by her generational and political perspective. Her skepticism would transform into recognition over the next decade or so.[43]

Ultimately these young scholars came to recognize the important foundation that an earlier generation of scholars had laid for them. Cott told of her growing appreciation of the earlier scholarship she had initially dismissed. In the foreword to the 1986 edition of her widely assigned document reader *Root of Bitterness*, she wrote,

> [In 1971] I distrusted most available accounts of women's lives in history books. . . . Those did not adequately convey to me the richness and variety and change that I was sure inhered in women's social experience and consciousness over time. . . . Most of the existing scholarship on women's history with which I was familiar seemed faulty in one way or another. . . . Flush with the energies of the women's movement and the aim to resurrect women's history, I probably too cavalierly dismissed the efforts of previous historians, on which younger scholars and activists had to build.[44]

Cott's first monograph, *The Bonds of Womanhood* (1977), reflected her under-standing that women's history was rich and varied. In the book, she made careful claims about a specific category of American women—white middle-class New Englanders in the early republic—without generalizing about all American women.[45] In 1991 Cott published *A Woman Making History: Mary Ritter Beard through Her Letters*. Research for this book was eye-opening and raised Cott's awareness of the value of the older generation. She explored letters between Beard, Alma Lutz, Wilbur K. Jordan, Margaret Grierson, Marjorie White, Eliz-abeth Schlesinger, Elizabeth Borden, and Florence Hazzard—all older scholars, librarians, and archivists who worked to advance the history of women, all of whom were connected to the women's archives established at Smith and Radcliffe in the 1940s.[46]

If it took some time for those of the new generation to acknowledge their predecessors, it did not take them long to acknowledge that differences among women had to be written into scholarly narratives and curriculum. It wasn't enough to consider sex-specific commonalities. The inclusion of working-class women, immigrant women, women of color, and African American women in *America's Working Women* and *Root of Bitterness*, for example, illustrates efforts to incorporate diverse groups and perspectives into the field's early frameworks. And of course, Black women's perspectives were the sole focus of Gerda Lerner's hefty 1972 document reader, *Black Women in White America*. To be a white historian focusing on Black history in the 1960s and 1970s was not without risks when we consider the painful, public confrontations that occurred among male historians in these years. Open expressions of Black nationalist historians' disapproval of white male historians who focused on Black history in the 1960s and 1970s sometimes erupted at major history conferences, raising the question of whether white historians should or could write and speak with authority on Black history.[47] This sensibility is one more example of the paral-lels between scholarship and contemporary culture and politics. As the Black Power movement of the late sixties pushed white civil rights activists out of their movement, so some Black scholars pushed white scholars to stay in their own proverbial lane and leave Black history to Black historians. Nevertheless, some white feminist historians in the women's history movement recognized the need to include the topic in their emerging body of work and looked about for Black women's history scholarship and scholars.

Linda Gordon's early forays into the Schlesinger Library were to research her 1976 book *Woman's Body, Woman's Right: A Social History of Birth Control in America*, as well as the reader *America's Working Women*. She too described her early impressions of the Schlesinger Library as being full of nonacademic older women using marginal collections and not doing serious scholarly work. She re-ported that she and the other younger scholars in women's history were arrogant toward them and felt as if their youthful cohort "took over" the Schlesinger and carried out more valuable research.[48] On the other side of the age divide, in 1971, North Carolina State University historian Doris King raised a proverbial eyebrow at the "instant specialists" in women's history who seemed oblivious to the "real scholars in the field."[49]

Yet this early skepticism of older histories and historians also worked to the field's advantage. A cross-generational, vibrant conversation opened in the historiographic divide between the two modes of investigation. New historians of women created a rhetorical starting point for the new, even while the "old" continued. This conversation moved the field toward the prominence documented by Robert Townsend in his 2007 and 2010 statistical analyses of the distribution of areas of specialization in the discipline of history. Townsend revealed that women's history had the greatest growth of any field of historical specialization in the United States between 1975 and 2010. In 1975, about 18 percent of history departments in the United States employed a specialist in women's and gender history. That number itself undoubtedly represented a dramatic increase from just five years before. By 2005, about 80 percent did. In 1975, the proportion of faculty who listed women's and gender history as their topical specialty was about 1 percent—the smallest percentage of any listed specialization. In 2005, women's and gender historians represented 9 percent of historians; social historians made up only a slightly greater proportion. By 2010, women's and gender historians had surpassed social historians as the largest group of specialists among historians in the United States.[50] They accomplished this feat by adopting, adapting, and creating their own feminist versions of key elements of historians' professional culture.

Most of these scholars in the networks of young feminists appeared on the Berkshire Conference's programs at least once between 1973 to 1987 as they built up their women's history professional subculture. But their work also became a regular feature on the annual programs of the OAH, SHA, and AHA. Women historians became reliably active within the mainstream professional culture. Together, the generations of women who had earned PhDs before 1960 and during the 1960s and the new generation of the 1970s developed institutions and extra-institutional networks that adapted to and challenged that professional culture. These challenges sometimes caused controversy and debate. There were even aspersions cast, as for example when male historians responded negatively to the sort of politicization of history found in Linda Gordon's 1976 book about the birth control movement.[51] However painful these controversies were for those targeted, they helped propel the field forward, since they forced a conversation between those favorable to women's history and those less convinced of the field's relevance or who had reservations about the political content of the field.[52] Controversy also inspired a unity among women scholars so that when the legitimacy of one was attacked, the others stepped up in defense.

One example of this dynamic occurred at a labor history conference at SUNY Binghamton in 1974. This was the same year Mary Ryan established the first formal PhD program in women's history in the country at Binghamton. When Alice Kessler-Harris's and Mari Jo Buhle's work on women socialists and labor activists was allegedly "savaged" by the eminent labor historian Melvyn Dubofsky for distorting important matters of class, Blanche Wiesen Cook stood up to him, retorting, "Who do you think you are, the Bobby Riggs of the AHA?"[53] The reference was to Billie Jean King's defeat of retired tennis champion Bobby Riggs in the famous 1973 "Battle of the Sexes" tennis match. Dubofsky—who came late to the talk, disheveled in his tennis clothes after a match—may or may not have intended to "savage" the work of Kessler-Harris and Buhle. He may have wanted to engage it and demand more precision. He later explained that what he was looking for was a comparative analysis of women and men in the same socialist and labor movements.[54] But to Kessler-Harris in 1974, Dubofsky seemed to imply that adding women to labor history made little difference to the field since, according to him, men also sang songs, wrote poetry, and were lonely and alienated while traveling, and those similarities undercut the additive value of women's history in his eyes. The Bobby Riggs rejoinder by Cook suggests that Kessler-Harris weathered the immediate event with some sisterly support. But there were brothers on the scene too. For example, Herbert Gutman encouraged her to submit the essay to *Labor History*. When she protested that it would never get published—considering Dubofsky's comments—he advised her to submit it anyway. It was accepted for publication.[55]

When women's historians broke ranks with the majority view that women's history was important because it created a usable past *for the benefit* of contemporary women, sisterhood could falter. The controversial 1986 court case *EEOC v. Sears, Roebuck*, which addressed sex discrimination in the workplace, is an example. In short, the Equal Employment Opportunity Commission had brought a class action suit against Sears, charging the company with shunting women employees into lower-paying retail jobs and preferring men for high-paying sales commission jobs. Both sides called on the expert testimony of a women's historian to contextualize the history of women's occupational opportunities, choices, and limitations. Rosalind Rosenberg, a mid-career scholar and professor at Barnard College whose research field was women in the social sciences, testified "against women" employees on behalf of Sears. She emphasized that women chose the lower-paying jobs for a variety of personal and familial reasons. The implication was that it was not discrimination on the part of the employer but women's own choices that resulted in their occupational segregation. Rosenberg was strongly criticized by other historians of women,

partly because she was testifying outside of her main area of specialized expertise but mostly because her testimony was to the detriment of women workers. Kessler-Harris, a Hofstra University history professor who specialized in
women's labor history, testified for the EEOC. Her first monograph in women's
history, *Out to Work: A History of Wage-Earning Women in the United States*,
was published in 1982.[56] Thus, she was well-qualified to explain the complex
nexus of factors that limited women's occupational choices and opportunities.
Ultimately, Sears won the case as the EEOC failed to prove discrimination.

A 1986 editorial in the *New York Times* headlined the ensuing trouble in
women's history as a "Bitter Feminist Debate," using a typically negative ad-
jective about feminists.[57] Rosenberg claimed to be a feminist historian and
a supporter of affirmative action, and she had cited Kessler-Harris's work in
women's labor history in her testimony. Kessler-Harris rejoined, "This issue
is purely this—you would not lie in your testimony, but you also would not
say or write something as a historian solely to hurt a group of people, and the
consequences of Rosalind's testimony can be interpreted that way." Kessler-
Harris's view was that Rosenberg was perfectly within her right to testify on
areas of her own expertise but that her testimony on behalf of Sears had misused
Kessler-Harris's scholarship and hurt women workers. Rosenberg's perspective was different. Claiming that her views were not political, she explained,
"Scholars must not subordinate their scholarship to their politics, even if their
scholarship appears to be heading in a politically dangerous direction. If the
scholars allow their politics to drive their scholarship, they will be left with bad
scholarship and misguided public policy." Longtime friend to women's history
and then president of the AHA Carl Degler agreed that Rosenberg had done
right by offering her honest scholarly interpretation on working women, even
though he considered himself "cowardly" for having turned down the chance to
testify on behalf of Sears. Ultimately, Rosenberg remembered the experience as
"personally painful" but a good sign for women's history. She observed, "If we
can't have a controversy like this, we're either engaged in topics that are not of
interest, or the engine of consensus is so strong that dissent is not possible."[58]

The Sears controversy had been foreshadowed in 1978 by a similarly divisive
expression of professional conscience by Andrea Hinding, curator of the Social
Welfare History Archives at the University of Minnesota and codirector of the
Women's History Sources Survey (WHSS) with Clarke Chambers. Hinding had
been censured when she publicly criticized the history profession's decision
to boycott states that hadn't ratified the Equal Rights Amendment. She wrote
an open letter to the *AHA Newsletter* voicing her disapproval of the Money in
Friendly Territories campaign.[59] In this campaign, feminist historians and their
allies had put their annual membership fees in an escrow account to be released
only when the AHA agreed not to hold conferences in states that had not ratified

the Equal Rights Amendment. Hinding's offense was to speak with a *New York Times* reporter about the publication of volumes that had grown out of a five-year research project in the nation's network of libraries and historical societies. Hinding said that the WHSS represented "an incredible record of women's lives showing a full spectrum of achievement" that hadn't "required angry feminists to beat the bushes." Gerda Lerner reacted by reminding Hinding that getting the National Endowment for the Humanities to fund the WHSS had indeed "required at least 3, possibly five 'angry feminists,' beating the bushes for money, grant support and institutional endorsements."[60] Hinding's use of language that labeled feminists as angry, bitter, and humorless undoubtedly irritated many. It was language typically used by conservative detractors of feminism.

Sandi Cooper, Gerda Lerner, Joan Hoff-Wilson, and archivists Andrea Hinding and Elsie Freivogel went on to engage in debate on the role of women historians. None agreed with Hinding's political views, but more importantly, some thought Hinding should not associate the WHSS with an anti-ERA and anti-feminist stance. Others believed that the WHSS and professional organizations should not take a political stance on the ERA at all.[61] Anne Scott intervened to offer her opinion on the matter. She disagreed with Hinding's opinion on the value or appropriateness of an AHA and OAH boycott of states that had not ratified ERA. But neither did she agree with the women's history world closing ranks against Hinding. When Lerner and Hoff-Wilson suggested that Hinding's introduction to the WHSS be approved only if it had oversight from the WHSS Advisory Board, Scott counseled Hoff-Wilson, "When Gerda wrote about Andrea's supposed statement to the *New York Times* my response was that we ought to find out what she really said. . . . Gerda's letter and yours have forced me to pay closer attention to the whole affair. I agree with you that the entire advisory board should approve all introductory materials."[62] Recounting the roots of the WHSS, Scott reminded Hoff-Wilson that the WHSS was the brainchild of Gerda Lerner herself, along with Peter Wood. They had organized a meeting in 1972 with Janet James, Clarke Chambers, and Andrea Hinding, and later the same year the group included Carroll Smith-Rosenberg, Gail Parker, and Herbert Gutman. It was at this point that Hoff-Wilson of the OAH-CSW led a preliminary effort to determine the feasibility of the project and consulted with the National Endowment for the Humanities. The full group, but particularly Lerner, had shaped the NEH proposal until it was accepted. Scott asserted that the historians who had initially discussed the project had the right to consult on its final iteration. Yet, she was mindful of the enormous labor that Hinding and Chambers had contributed.

Scott showed herself to be adept at bridging gaps between political credos and scholarship. She finished her letter to Hoff-Wilson by urging that the indispensability and value of Hinding's work not be overlooked.

One reason the project went forward as well as it did was the willingness, all along, of Clarke Chambers and Andrea to do the actual work, (which no one else was equipped to do) and the excellent reputation of the Social Welfare Archives. Had their skills and their reputation not been available I doubt that NEH would have risked so large a sum of money [$600,000]. ... I think we owe [Andrea] explicit recognition of that fact as part of our asking for clarification of the *New York Times* piece and of assurance that the introduction will be presented to the members of the Board for approval.[63]

Scott confessed that Andrea Hinding might "not represent both legs" of the project—the feminist leg and the technical, professional leg. Hinding later clarified that she was a feminist and that her concern about the Money in Friendly Territories boycott had been over its unintended consequences and limited effectiveness.[64] Scott insisted that completing the WHSS should not be hindered by people's opinion of Hinding, nor should any of the discussions be allowed to reflect negatively on feminism.

Moreover, as Gerda Lerner pointed out in 1970, women's history was not a subject that belonged to followers of any one political credo, feminist or otherwise. If women's history was the history of white, middle-class, immigrant, Black, working-class, liberal, radical, oppressed, feminist, and progressive women, it was also the history of conservative, reactionary, racist, nativist, oppressive, elite, and anti-feminist women. Any serious scholar had to see that. When Lerner echoed Mary Beard in an interview in *Ms.* magazine in 1981 by saying that women had always been and continued to be a force in history, she was expressing perhaps the most radical idea—and yet the simplest—that a women's historian could offer.[65] And women's history had to be encompassed as broadly as possible, leaving room for topical and interpretive diversity.

Mainstreaming US Women's History in Higher Education

Feminist politics, feminist scholarship, and feminist teaching were the baseline integral to the development of the new women's history of the 1970s. After nearly a decade of scholarly development, more long-term and comprehensive efforts to integrate women's history into college history education were possible. Feminist historians in academia saw teaching women's history as an essential corollary to their scholarly efforts to build their field. Moving beyond simply designing their own women's history courses in their own institutions, they worked to create curricular frameworks, lessons, and instructional materials for specialized women's history courses and materials that nonspecialists could use to integrate women into general survey courses in US, European, and world history. To accomplish their vision of incorporating their scholarly insights into history instruction as broadly as possible, they sought funding from national institutions, such as the Department of Education's Fund for the Improvement of Postsecondary Education (FIPSE), the National Endowment for the Humanities, and the OAH.[66]

In 1978 Elizabeth Fox-Genovese spearheaded an early and ambitious curriculum project initially titled "Integrating Women into the Basic History Curriculum."[67] Renamed "Restoring Women to History," the plan was to develop a basic women's history curriculum that could be adopted by college instructors teaching the general survey courses in American, European, and world history. Fox-Genovese, a 1974 Harvard PhD, conceived of "Integrating Women" when she was an assistant professor of French history at the University of Rochester.[68] In 1980, she took a full professorship at SUNY Binghamton, where six years earlier Mary Ryan had established the first graduate program in the country to offer a PhD in women's history. Ryan started that program with little more than departmental permission, a curriculum of her own design, and a brochure.[69] Fox-Genovese's "Integrating Women" idea came in response to a Princeton University report that 70 percent of all college survey courses did not include material on women. Fox-Genovese sought support from the OAH in 1978, reaching out first to the OAH Committee on the Status of Women.

The OAH-CSW, at the time chaired by D'Ann Campbell, agreed to back the plan and brought the idea before the OAH Executive Board in November 1978. Even though the project covered US history surveys, Western civilization surveys, and non-Western surveys in Africa, Asia, and Latin America, Fox-Genovese brought the proposal to the OAH rather than to the AHA. OAH president Arthur Link questioned why this was so in a letter to OAH executive director Joan Hoff-Wilson when the project was at the end of its second grant cycle. He asked, "I wonder why an organization interested exclusively in the history of the United States should be sponsoring projects to promote integration of women's history into survey courses in Western Civilization and Third World women's materials?"[70] Hoff-Wilson's reply reveals certain characteristics of the professional subculture of women's historians. "The field of women's history has created a rather close network of women scholars who work in American and European and Third World fields. . . . In fact, there are a growing number of women who specialize in both American and European women's history because of the necessity of teaching comparative classes. These women tend to belong to both the OAH and the American Historical Association and either organization can benefit from their unique comparative knowledge."[71] Women's historians fostered this dynamic by building institutions that drew together specialists in a wide array of research fields, eventually contributing to the field's major theoretical and conceptual developments—including the rise of gender history in the 1980s, examinations of differences among women and international and transnational women's history in the '90s, and "intersectional" analyses in the early '00s.[72] In 1984, Hoff-Wilson observed that these historians knew each other and held membership in both mainstream national history associations and women's history associations. They were committed to creating a topically broad-ranging history curriculum based on the expansive range of geographic foci that historians of women from different specializations were broaching. The OAH Executive Board unanimously agreed to support the project and signed on as the institutional administrator for a two-year grant from the Department of Education's FIPSE that ran from 1979 through 1980.[73] A second FIPSE grant was approved for 1981–83, and a Lilly Foundation Grant filled a funding gap left by the FIPSE grants.[74]

D'Ann Campbell, a recent UNC Chapel Hill PhD and postdoctoral fellow at the Newberry Library, worked as codirector on the Restoring Women to History project for much of its existence. Her mid-project report explained how it was implemented during its first two years. Twenty target institutions including community colleges, four-year colleges, and research universities were randomly selected to test curriculum packets for both halves of the US history survey and the Western civilization survey. The packets included the work of a dozen scholars who assembled outlines, bibliographies, and primary and secondary materials for use in the classroom. One hundred teachers met in Bloomington, Indiana, in an initial training session. Further workshops at regional and national professional meetings were held for those who would test the packets and publicize the project. In March 1981, the effectiveness of the packets was assessed at a conference, where recommended revisions were drawn up for the second FIPSE grant. Campbell was responsible for organizing and chairing workshops at all the major national and regional conferences on mainstreaming, or integrating material on women into survey courses. Fox-Genovese was to "provide the theoretical justification for our grant," as there were still colleagues unconvinced of women's place in the curriculum.[75]

Fox-Genovese would work closely with the twelve scholars in charge of designing curriculum packets.[76] Carolyn Lougee, E. William Monter, Susan Stuard Mosher, Margaret George, Bonnie Smith, and Richard Stites all worked on the curriculum packets designed for the Western civilization surveys.[77] Sarah Elbert, Joan Gunderson, Sharon Harley, Susan Kleinberg, Elizabeth Pleck, and Harold Woodman made the first round of packets for the United States. Three hundred college instructors received the packets to use in existing survey courses, completely new introductory surveys, or advanced courses they had initiated.[78] After a year of testing, Fox-Genovese could report to FIPSE that the project was a success. The packets had established a network of historians committed to integrating women into the curriculum. They had revitalized the teaching of history more generally.[79]

In Fox-Genovese's application for a second FIPSE grant, modesty was not the operative word. She explained that the project had challenged the very practice of history and illuminated the cultural role played by history in society and political culture: "The network and the materials have, according to all reports, contributed to . . . directing professional attention toward the importance and challenge of including women in the standard curriculum, to focusing collective attention on the problems of integrating political and social history in a narrative form, and to a serious reexamination of the place of history surveys in our political culture as a whole. On the testimony of many participants, integrating women into basic survey courses transforms those courses and revives student interest in them."[80] Women's history integrated social and political history—inculcating average citizens with a new understanding of politics. The new field could be broadly justified for the validating, enriching effect it had on American political culture and on people's sense of connection to that political culture.

Fox-Genovese reported that at the March 1981 conference, Robert Bezucha of Amherst College had suggested that historians "should make no mistake about the revolutionary and subversive implications of the project," claiming that they "were engaged in a feminist, political undertaking—namely the transformation of the received, official version of our past." Fox-Genovese reported the audience was electrified by Bezucha's statement.[81] Fox-Genovese added her own analysis, saying that history evolved as a tool to justify power and those who held it, mainly men, lords, and other elites during the rise of the modern nation-state. Contemporary history was the heir to that version of history, but women's history, she claimed, was a powerful way to interrogate and reshape the narrative. In the process, women's history would contribute to no less than the positive transformation of society.[82] To borrow Audre Lorde's celebrated analogy, whether this process reflected "using the master's tools to dismantle the house" of androcentric history or whether it meant building a new house, the historians of women asserted that their burgeoning field could move society toward gender equity—it could dethrone the male master narrative.[83]

In its penultimate phase in 1983, the project sponsored eight regional conferences to discuss draft curriculum packets. The Southeastern regional conference, for instance, was held at UNC Chapel Hill under the sponsorship of the OAH, the Lilly Foundation, and the UNC history department. Titled "Women's History, Everyone's History," it drew on the talents of professional historians from UNC and other schools in the area. Notably, OAH president for 1983, Anne Firor Scott, and Scott's former student Sara Evans opened the conference. In 1983, Evans was a professor at the University of Minnesota. As an undergraduate at Duke

University in the 1960s, she had become active in the civil rights and women's liberation movements. Her dissertation on the origins of women's liberation, *Personal Politics*, became a classic study in the field. Don Higginbotham, chair of the UNC history department, promoted the conference as an opportunity to begin incorporating the scholarly gains of the "mushrooming field," which, he asserted, challenged traditional interpretations of the past.[84] Thus, the Restoring Women to History project drew deeply on the scholarly network that had been developing for more than two decades, when, for example, we consider that Scott first arrived at Duke in 1961.

The OAH published two compendiums of the curriculum work from the Restoring Women to History project designed for use in the United States. These came out in 1984. Thirteen historians assisted Elizabeth Fox-Genovese in the editing of the two volumes. These included Carl Degler, Sarah Elbert, Joan Gunderson, Richard Jensen, Elizabeth Pleck, Joan Hoff-Wilson, Sharon Harley, Susan J. Kleinberg, and Glenda Riley, among others.[85] The two volumes comprised more than 600 pages of materials that could be readily incorporated into the thematic and chronological units of the traditional college survey course, first contact to the Civil War and the Civil War to the present. The volumes included distinct lesson plans sufficient for twenty-eight weeks of course work. Professors could adopt materials in their entirety or more selectively use them to develop lectures and discussion questions on overarching themes. They contained recommended bibliographic and primary sources to incorporate into instruction. The *Western Civilization I* and *II* counterpart came out the same year and drew on the talents of a similarly well-regarded group of scholars in the European field, including Susan Stuard Mosher and Elisabeth Israels Perry.[86]

In 1984, Fox-Genovese introduced the text *Restoring Women to History: Materials for United States I*, along with a discussion of how to use it in practice. She provided examples of how to place women in context in the traditional narratives of social, political, and intellectual history, making the case for introducing gender into the basic curriculum. She expounded,

> Gender constitutes a good deal more than the stalwarts of the "survey-as-it-always-has-been" want to deal with, and a good deal less than many feminist historians would insist is women's due. By gender, I mean, quite simply, what a society presents as the way to be a man and the way to be a woman—and the proper relations between the two. . . . To introduce gender as one of the essential ways of telling the story of the past will not distort the past. It will leave many of the familiar landmarks of our nation's history in place. But it should revise radically our view of how that past, that history, those landmarks were fashioned; radically revise

what we accept as innate or natural; radically revise how we assess different groups' opportunities to contribute to national development. Above all, it should revise our view of what was necessary and why. And our attitudes toward historical necessity determine our attitudes toward our possibilities for creating a good society.[87]

This formulation of gender as a concept with the capacity to transform not only our understanding of historical development but also contemporary social relationships is simpler and just as powerful as the one Joan Scott famously postulated in her classic 1986 theoretical essay "Gender: A Useful Category of Historical Analysis" because of its accessibility.[88] In contrast to introducing the theoretical mysteries and linguistic methodology of Foucault or Lacan, Fox-Genovese's model teaches the construction of gender through historical examples and thus is highly applicable in the classroom. Fox-Genovese's way was to write *and teach* usable history. She argued that this method could make history socially transformative and restore relevance to the history survey. Here, we have evidence of how gender history grew out of women's history and the field's search for theory.

Scott's now canonical 1986 formulation of gender history grew out of discourse among historians of women in the years before the article's publication. Mary Hartman's opening address at the 1978 Fourth Berkshire Conference claimed that "gender" had already "become established as a major category of analysis."[89] Indeed, gender history had been prefigured by women's historians of the early to mid-1970s. For example, in a series of essays published between 1976 and 1980, Joan Kelly considered the impact of class on perspective and experience. She theorized about "the social relations of the sexes" and the relation of sex and sex roles to property, production, and social change, suggesting that all of these categories needed to be historicized. Her theorizing led her to question the traditional periodization of history. She observed that what marked great changes for men—the scientific and artistic advances of the Renaissance, for example—was often characterized by little change or even a retrogression in women's status. Finally, Kelly questioned historical thinking and feminist theory regarding public versus private, personal experience versus empirical knowledge, and the objective versus the subjective. Kelly's insights challenged male-dominated historical practice and tested ideas of what constituted legitimate evidence, knowledge, and subject matter.[90]

Kelly died of cancer at the age of fifty-four, but feminist historians have discussed, refined, and developed her ideas by regularly teaching and citing her foundational texts. Alice Kessler-Harris, Blanche Wiesen Cook, Claire Cross, Rosalind Pollack Petchesky, and Amy Swerdlow coauthored the introduction to Kelly's posthumously published collected essays, a collection that is still in print today. The early seeds of gender history germinated from years of collaborative work. Part of the power of gender as an analytical tool, as Fox-Genovese explained, was that it "call[ed] attention to men's roles in making history every bit as much as" it added women to the narrative.[91] To that insight, Joan Scott added the idea that gender history would facilitate analyses of gendered relations of power.

In the spring of 1980, the US Department of Education Fund for the Improvement of Postsecondary Education received another women's history proposal. It was an application for a two-year grant "To Promote the History of Black Women and Assist Black Women Scholars in this Field." Gerda Lerner, then president-elect of the Organization of American Historians, submitted this FIPSE proposal. Lerner's scholarship had focused on race and reform in America since she was at Columbia in the early 1960s writing on South Carolina abolitionists Sarah and Angelina Grimké. By 1970, her interests went far beyond the study of white female abolitionists. She turned her attention to the lives and work of Black women in America, presenting papers at national conferences from 1965 to 1973 and publishing essays on the subject in the *Journal of Negro History*.[92] In 1972 she published *Black Women in White America*, the first scholarly documentary history of Black women. In the preface to this volume, she asserted, "Black women have been doubly victimized by scholarly neglect and racist assumptions. Belonging as they do to two groups which have traditionally been treated as inferiors by American society—Blacks and women—they have been doubly invisible."[93] Three of the twelve essays in her classic 1979 anthology, *The Majority Finds Its Past*, were about Black women's history, while a fourth treated antislavery women. The state of Black women's history scholarship in 1980 was that it was in its earliest phase, not sufficiently developed to support large-scale curriculum development. This explains why Lerner's FIPSE proposal would focus on scholarship rather than on curriculum development. One can't have the latter without the former.

Shortly after Lerner submitted the proposal to FIPSE, she invited Rosalyn Terborg-Penn, a Black scholar who studied Black women suffragists and taught at Morgan State University, to be codirector on the project. Terborg-Penn declined.[94] Lerner then invited Darlene Clark Hine, a Black scholar at Purdue University, who agreed to join forces.[95] Hine specialized in American political history and African American history but had only recently shifted to a research focus on Black women's history. The FIPSE proposal had three components. The first was for the OAH to hold several full sessions on Black women's history at its annual meeting in 1982, with papers by Black women scholars. Funds for these scholars and graduate students to attend the conference would be paid by the grant. The second was to establish a communications network of scholars doing work in the field through a series of conferences. Finally, the grant proposed conducting a survey on scholarly research in Black women's history and publishing the findings in a bibliography of secondary and primary sources for teachers and scholars.[96] Mary Frances Berry, historian, law professor, and former assistant secretary for education in the Department of Health, Education, and Welfare, lent her support to the project. She lauded Hine and Lerner as leaders ideally suited to the task and capable scholars.[97] Archivist and scholar Bettye Collier-Thomas of the Mary McLeod Bethune Historical Development Project (National Council of Negro Women) also supported the grant.[98]

Darlene Clark Hine was instrumental in convincing the recently founded Association of Black Women Historians to cosponsor the two-year project. Some ABWH members were wary of a Black women's history project directed by a white woman scholar influential within the OAH, mirroring perhaps the concerns of Black nationalist historians about white scholars' legitimate authority to work in the field. Initially, the steering committee of the ABWH voted against full cosponsorship of the project. Members agreed only to an organizational meeting between the OAH and ABWH to plan the three proposed sessions at the OAH annual meeting in 1982. In this first vote, the ABWH Steering Committee voted against allowing OAH funding of its newsletter. The committee also voted not to organize two of four planned regional conferences and not to seek group affiliation with the OAH.[99]

Lerner and Hine were surprised by the rejection. Hine worked through 1981 to keep the ABWH from withdrawing altogether, expressing frustration over its lingering reluctance. Hine and Lerner came to understand that the issue for the ABWH was protecting its institutional autonomy and not allowing an outside agency to have control of the content of its work. Tensions between Lerner and the ABWH were such that Lerner handed over to Hine the role of primary communicator. Lerner maintained her position as codirector, however, and final decisions were based on full consultation and mutual agreement. Both Hine and Lerner believed that the project's affiliation with the ABWH was of great value; the ABWH was an important network for Black women as professional historians and for the development of Black women's history.[100]

Ultimately, the ABWH and OAH's FIPSE-funded "Black Women's History Project" cooperated fully. In the first year, the ABWH distributed surveys to ascertain current scholarly research in the field. It sent the surveys to historically Black colleges and distributed them at the annual meetings of the Association for the Study of African American Life and History and the OAH and at the Fifth Big Berkshire Conference. Sharon Harley, about to earn her PhD from Howard University and begin a long career as a history professor at the University of Maryland, College Park, took the lead in designing and reporting on the survey. *Truth*, the journal of the ABWH, published a special issue in

December 1981 with the results of the survey. In the spring of 1982, the ABWH Advisory Committee compiled a fifteen-page bibliography. The bibliography demonstrated both that a start had been made in the field and the need for more attention to the field. Four regional conferences were held in 1982 at Oberlin, Spelman, the University of Chicago College Circle, and the Mary McLeod Bethune Museum in DC. These meetings brought together some 150 scholars, teachers, and students working in Black women's history.[101]

Lerner and Hine learned some hard lessons during the implementation of the project. It became clear, for example, that Black women scholars wanted to lead in the development of Black women's history, and much still needed to be done to ensure that took place—despite the recurring calls to attend to race and class within the women's history movement. Yet, Black women historians were only just forming their own national independent professional associations and intellectual networks. In the end, Lerner and Hine's work on this FIPSE-funded, OAH/ABWH-sponsored project was an important intervention that promoted the field of Black women's history and the work of Black women historians in higher education.

Gerda Lerner offered her perspective on the OAH/ABWH FIPSE experience in the final report to the Department of Education:

> As could be expected, a project of this kind, which involved interracial cooperation, could not proceed without problems. From the outset, the motives and intentions of the white co-director were subject to suspicion, constant scrutiny and repeated interpretations. However, some frank and at times hard-hitting discussions and a few necessary organizational adjustments improved the situation. The excellent, trusting and honest collaboration of the two co-directors was never in question and became strengthened by mutual respect and sharing as the project matured. . . . What is to be learned from this, for future inter-racial projects, is that it takes a fairly secure, generous and tough-minded white woman and an equally secure, generous and tough-minded black woman to hold on through the process of overcoming historically conditioned responses in order to do the work that must be done. . . . While inter-racial organizational work is full of pitfalls and difficulties, it can and must be done.[102]

Hine concurred, adding, "It is exceedingly important for leaders of white and black professional organizations to confront problems head on and to work together to achieve satisfactory solutions. Lerner and I were able to build a strong, mutually supportive relationship and refused to lose sight of our major project objectives."[103] Hine too saw the project as a success and thought it resulted in greater recognition in the OAH of Black women and their history. Indeed, this was an accurate assessment. In the 1982 annual meeting program of the OAH, of the nineteen sessions in which work on women featured, eleven sessions were fully devoted to women's history. Five of these sessions were in turn devoted exclusively to Black women's history (see table 8.1). It was no coincidence that this was also the year that Gerda Lerner served as president of the OAH.[104]

Darlene Clark Hine developed another successful women's history project in 1982 called "Black Women in the Middle West." This project, inspired by Shirley Herd of the Indiana branch of the National Council of Negro Women, focused on building a regional history repository for Black women in the Upper Midwest. Hine's 1981 book, *When the Truth Is Told: A History of Black Women's Culture and Community in Indiana, 1875–1950*, had been inspired by Herd, who spent years collecting materials from women's attics across Indiana. Herd encouraged Hine to write a book compiling the material.[105] By 1982, Hine had successfully applied to the National Endowment for the Humanities for funding, and for the duration of this project, the mutually beneficial relationship with Lerner continued. Lerner read and commented on the manuscript Hine produced from the project.[106] Their lifelong professional friendship enriched the field.[107] Hine's public history projects valued the historical experiences of Black women and found accessible avenues to share it. She aimed *When the Truth Is Told* at a lay readership. She resisted collegial advice from Lerner to eliminate laudatory adjectives, assuring Lerner that they were intentional. She left high praise for her subjects in the text.[108] Thus, the educative value of the project and what it could teach African American women (and others) about their experience and contributions to their communities and American history made up the spirit animating the work.

Over the next two decades, Darlene Clark Hine taught at Purdue University mentoring promising Black scholars such as Thavolia Glymph and Pero Dagbovie. She served on committees in the AHA, the OAH, and the Southern Historical Association. In 1988, when Anne Scott was selected president of the SHA, she appointed Hine to be the chair of the SHA's annual program committee. This sort of influential appointment gave those who acquired it tremendous power to shape the direction of historical study and signaled professional legitimacy both for individuals and for topics of study. Scott's presidential address emphasized the need to continue the work done by Lerner, Hine, and the ABWH in advancing the field of Black women's history.[109] The address was titled "The Most Invisible of All." When Hine was later asked how she felt about being a Black woman and a scholar of Black women's history working in "mainstream" women's history, she reported first on the experience of others, saying that other Black women historians reported to her feeling marginalized, aggrieved, and distrustful of mainstream white women historians. She explained that some told her their work was ignored, others reported their work was appropriated, while still others thought that white women refused to incorporate material about Black women into their scholarship.[110] But she characterized her own interface with "mainstream" women's historians much more positively. She acknowledged that her entry into "mainstream women's history" had been facilitated by Gerda Lerner in the early 1980s and that Lerner had introduced her to rising figures in American women's history like Alice Kessler-Harris, Kathryn Kish Sklar, and Linda Kerber. Moreover, when Scott, as president of the SHA, made Black women's history the subject of her presidential address, "The Most Invisible of All," and appointed Hine as chair of the annual program committee of the SHA, Hine was accorded real power to shape the content of the annual meeting, fully incorporating Black women's history into the program.

Contrary to feeling or being marginalized, she was brought right into the center of mainstream American history, and she characterized the working relationships she developed with both Lerner and Scott as "close" and "mutually respectful."[111] Hine found that she and her work benefited from collaboration and mutual support within a broad network of scholars, both Black and white, a situation that benefited the field of women's history, too. In 1989, Hine published *Black Women in White: Racial Conflict and Cooperation in the Nursing Profession, 1890–1950* and a theoretically groundbreaking article in *Signs* titled "Rape and the Inner Lives of Black Women in the Middle West: Preliminary Thoughts on the Culture of Dissemblance."[112] The article came to be incredibly influential in the productive decades that lay ahead for African American women's history.

Race, Black women's history, and Black women historians have played a central role in the development and legitimization of American women's history over the last forty years. Even when Black women were not yet sufficiently incorporated into the field or felt marginalized within the women's history movement, their perspectives and their very presence offered a powerful counterpoint, reminding white historians to consider their subjects from multiple points of view while also working to build inclusivity into their studies and their own ranks. Today, there is broad acknowledgment that Black women's history is an important part of American women's history, and in chapter 10 we will further examine how that came to pass. Indeed, Lois Banner's commentary at the fiftieth anniversary 2023 Berkshire Conference may have in part reflected her acute consciousness of the advances made by African American historians of women over the last fifty years. The sometimes-difficult dialogues and tense collaborations that Black and white women historians forged helped make Black women's history and Black historians of women visible to historians of the United States. In the late 1980s and into the 1990s, this pattern repeated itself, as historians of Chicana and Latina history, Asian American women's history, and Native American women's history gained ground in US history.[113]

The parallelism and interpenetration of politics and cultural struggle in the scholarship of feminist historians resembled what had come before. At midcentury, Guion Griffis Johnson and Caroline Ware had combined their commitments to racial, economic, and social justice with historical scholarship that provided the context to facilitate analysis and problem-solving. A generation later, so too did many younger white and Black historians of women entering the profession in the 1970s. Women who completed dissertations about white women's involvement in racial justice movements in the South were often inspired by their own participation in 1960s civil rights organizing. Jacquelyn Dowd Hall wrote her 1974 dissertation about Jessie Daniel Ames and the quasi-interracial crusade to end lynching in the first half of the twentieth century. It was published as *Revolt against Chivalry* in 1979. Hall came out of the Christian left and had supported Black civil rights while an undergraduate at Southwestern University in Memphis. To the consternation of the school administration, she sent a letter to Dr. Martin Luther King Jr. to ask him to address the school. Hall made a connection between history and activism: "I think that history came to seem to me to go hand in hand with activism. Studying history made you an activist and being an activist, you needed to learn history." In her dissertation, Hall was adept at teasing out the difficulties between white and Black women in the interracial women's committee of the otherwise all-white Association of Southern Women for the Prevention of Lynching. Her analysis attended to the intertwined nature of sexual and racial violence in the South.[114]

Similarly, Sara Evans's dissertation turned first monograph about the roots of women's liberation in the civil rights and New Left movements dealt with the complicated dynamics between white women, Black women, and Black men in grassroots organizations in the 1960s. She had worked as a civil rights organizer in the Methodist Student Movement when she was an undergraduate at Duke University from 1962 to 1966.[115] Both Hall and Evans studied subjects fraught with historical and contemporary racial tension. Despite her movement experience and commitment to human rights, Evans was later criticized for focusing on white women in a movement where Black women had been so organizationally central.[116] Hall's work fared better.

The trajectory of women's history as both a teaching field and a research field has reflected broader trends in American politics and the politics of the American women's movement, both of which have been vexed by conflicted race relations. But women have struggled to find common ground on the incremental scale of marginalization from white to Black, from woman historian to Black woman historian. Participants in the women's history movement rose to meet this challenge as part of their larger political and epistemological project, with some success in the final decade of the twentieth century. This is a storyline to which we will return in the next chapter. Here, we will maintain our focus on the connections between the broad epistemological goals of the women's history movement as they developed from the 1970s and 1980s and the politics of women's history. If the field's practitioners wanted to teach constituencies across class, race, and region, it would have to be attuned to the differences among women as well as to the common ground that women shared across cultural borders. That was clear. This sensibility was reflected in another teaching initiative developed by Kathryn Kish Sklar at UCLA.

In 1977, Sklar, then an associate professor at UCLA, launched the Workshop on Teaching US Women's History. The goal here was collaboration among women's history professors in the Western United States. Sklar, a graduate of Radcliffe College ('65), earned her PhD at the University of Michigan–Ann Arbor in 1969. Her dissertation became an award-winning biography of Catharine Beecher, and her scholarship on Progressive Era women, notably Florence Kelley, made a significant contribution to the literature.[117] Arguably, though, her work as a teacher, mentor, and curriculum innovator has been even more influential. At UCLA (1975–87) and SUNY Binghamton (1988–2012), she trained and mentored thirty-four PhD graduates in US women's history and contributed to creating major women's history institutions.

The Workshop on Teaching US Women's History began in 1977, following a teaching fellowship for Sklar at Yale University in 1975 and an additional year of planning at UCLA. The work was funded by an NEH grant. Sklar wanted to spotlight the teaching of US women's history, reflecting her belief that women's history should fit within the traditional regional and national fields of topical specialization so that historians of women could get jobs and design meaningful courses. More broadly she thought the secret to success for the field of women's history was to make it accessible to undergraduates. As she later reflected, "The vitality of the workshops" stemmed "from the fact that our work comes to life when we communicate it to students in the classroom. The books that we write are very beautiful on their shelves, but there has to be a livingness to the history we write—it has to have meaning for people who are not historians. . . . So, the classroom . . . assumed this larger institutional meaning."[118] Early on at the UCLA workshops, emphasis was placed on creating a general survey course in American women's history. This was in addition to mainstreaming women into traditional US history survey courses. The scholarship in the field was increasingly attentive to the differences among women because of race, class, gender, and sexuality, and these diverse and intersectional perspectives were central to curriculum development from 1978 to 1988. Sklar convened the workshop every year during her tenure at UCLA, welcoming about twenty college professors from the West and Southwest each time. Regular participants included Estelle Freedman, Mary Rothschild, Tom Dublin, and Vicki Ruiz, among others. Rothschild was building the women's studies program at Arizona State University. Dublin and Ruiz specialized in subfields of nineteenth- and twentieth-century labor history. Freedman, who had overlapped in graduate school at Columbia with Dublin, taught at Stanford University. She wrote her first monograph on female prison reformer Miriam van Waters and later co-authored a foundational text in the history of sexuality, *Intimate Matters*, with John D'Emilio.[119] She became embroiled in a harrowing tenure struggle that received national media coverage in 1984 when, despite the history department's unanimous support, the university attempted to oust her. She appealed their denial and won her suit.[120]

The UCLA workshop stressed an egalitarian spirit among participants regardless of their rank or the prestige of their institutions; insights from community college and research institution professors were equally valued.[121] From its inception, the workshop's topical focus was attentive to matters of difference, as reflected in the titles given the workshop from 1979 to 1981: "Commonality and Diversity among Women," "Teaching on the History of Sexuality," "Implementation of Ideas on Third World Women in Our Courses," and "Teaching about 'New Right' Women."[122] The annual workshop was sustained after Sklar left UCLA for SUNY Binghamton in 1988. Ruiz, Rothschild, Carol Srole, and Karen Anderson stepped in to organize the annual event regularly in the 1990s. It continues to this day.[123]

As the women's history movement approached the end of its second decade, Sklar and Gerda Lerner organized in 1988 a conference on graduate training in US women's history at the Johnson Foundation's Wingspread Conference Center in Racine, Wisconsin. The conference was sponsored by the National Endowment for the Humanities and the Johnson Foundation. Sixty-three scholars in US women's history from fifty-seven universities with graduate programs in US women's history attended (see appendix). At the time, there were 202 graduate history programs in the United States with at least one specialist on faculty who could train doctoral candidates in the field. This represented a sea change from pre-movement days. The conference organizers recognized that by 1988, the spectacular growth of scholarship in US women's history had outpaced the average academic's ability to "keep abreast of recent publications in the field." Graduate teachers were now "faced with the task of translating [the field's] dazzling variety of publications into [manageable] curriculum." Additionally, women's historians had forged a narrative by asking critical "questions about the social construction of gender, about the relations between women of different classes and races, about women's access to various forms of power." The conference aimed to foster quality graduate training by consolidating this new narrative into a classroom-ready format usable by those who would shape the field's future.[124]

Gerda Lerner's opening remarks at Wingspread deemed the conference "the Woodstock of women's history" and likened it to a "quilting party" at which the previous fifteen years of work in the field had been akin to women "working on the same quilt in separate places . . . each doing her own piece, but never alone." At Wingspread and beyond, they would piece the quilt together "to reveal the full pattern . . . unfolding it to full view." Nancy Cott, Mari Jo Buhle, and Estelle Freedman oversaw the three workshops held over three days, each of which was followed by a plenary discussion. Linda Kerber gave closing remarks. Participants represented a cross-section of those active in graduate training. Attendees worked at public and private institutions in all regions of the country, and there were several generational cohorts. Eleven historians of color were invited. Nine attended. Four represented the fields of Black women's history; one specialized in Asian American women's history; two specialized in Chicana history; and two specialized in Puerto Rican women's history. Two male women's historians—Tom Dublin and William (Bill) Chafe—attended.[125] Thus, of sixty-three participants, nine were women of color and fifty-four were white, including the two men.

The workshop "The Scope and Content of Women's History Training" focused on training students to use gender as a category of analysis. It was designed to encourage the integration of gender and various kinds of differences in a comparative and interdisciplinary approach to history that questioned the existing structure of the profession, centered as it was on national and regional fields and particular eras. The workshop also discussed mainstreaming, specialized women's history courses, and securing funding for graduate students.

Perhaps the most "lively and emphatic" workshop was the second one, titled "Questions of Difference among Women." This workshop generated "the most concern and energy" among participants. The workshop coordinators reported that women of color offered "open and sharp" criticism of "existing practices in the academy, with the lack of attention given to women of color in writing, research, and teaching, and with general manifestations of racism among feminists." No examples of these "general manifestations of racism" were offered in the report, but many of the white participants agreed, recommitting themselves to "rethinking and redesigning their courses in order to deal creatively with difference." Consensus was reached on the need for a framework that increased opportunities for minority students by celebrating multiple narratives and decentering whiteness as the norm. The third workshop continued the discussion of content and structure of courses and curriculum, adding a focus on mentorship. This workshop addressed faculty welfare issues that affected women more negatively than men, such as sexual harassment, parental leave, domestic partner benefits, childcare, and elder dependent care.[126]

The conference was not without conflict, and "white feminists" were not the only group taken to task. Vicki Ruiz, author of *Cannery Women, Cannery Lives: Mexican Women, Unionization, and the California Food Processing Industry, 1930–1950* (1987), remembered painful, infuriating discussions among women of color about the bifurcated nature of race history in America, in which people of color who were not Black were mostly ignored. This led to considerable discomfort between the Black women at the conference—some of whom insisted all US history was centrally tied to chattel slavery—and the Hispanic and Asian American participants, who argued their existence and histories were erased by this kind of framework. The same might have been suggested by Native American historians, had any been present. In response to these conversations, Ruiz and Ellen DuBois decided to collaborate on what became the classic anthology *Unequal Sisters: A Multicultural Reader in U.S. Women's History.*[127]

The conference ended with expressions of solidarity, optimism, humor, and good feelings. Participants sang songs and presented humorous self-deprecating skits, like Vicki Ruiz's portrayal of a pregnant woman at an academic job interview. Linda Kerber's closing remarks reflected the transformation that had taken place for historians of women between 1969 and 1989. In Kerber's view, the often-solitary pursuit of women's history prior to 1969 was now a collective quest supported by a community of scholars. What's more, it was a pursuit with a powerful political instinct at its heart, one that, in Kerber's view, would transform "our lives, the lives of our students, and the lives of our fellow citizens."[128] The Wingspread Conference had been convened at an inflection point. In the published report of the conference, a sixteen-point action plan was presented. Six points addressed the need for diversity in content, curriculum, and the graduate student body; the rest focused on how to maintain and make further institutional inroads for women and women's history in history departments and professional associations.[129]

The year Sklar organized the Wingspread Conference was the year she moved to SUNY Binghamton with her partner and fellow historian, Tom Dublin. Dublin had completed a prize-winning dissertation at Columbia in 1975 in American women's labor history, published in 1979 as *Women at Work: The Transformation of Work and Community in Lowell, Massachusetts, 1826–1860.*[130] As a feminist historian, he became not just an ally to the women's history movement but an active participant in it well before he met Sklar through his participation in the UCLA teaching workshop.[131]

At Binghamton, Sklar and Dublin taught in their respective subfields of US women's history and continued their separate robust research agendas. But together, they developed key women's history teaching initiatives, including the 1997 digital history project "Women and Social Movements in the United States,

1600 to 2000." The innovative database was to feature "document projects" that could be created by and used to teach students. The National Endowment for the Humanities funded an expansion of the project in 1998, and the database became an online journal in 2003. Responding to the growing international dimension of women's history, Sklar and Dublin launched a second web project in 2007 titled "Women and Social Movements, International, 1840 to the Present," featuring 150,000 pages of primary source material from international women's organizations and scholarly essays. The year 2016 saw the launch of a third database: "Women and Social Movements in Modern Empires since 1820," including 75,000 pages of documents edited by more than forty specialists in women's history. This work created teaching materials for the classroom, a digital research database for scholars, and professional development opportunities for historians at every level of higher education. Undergraduate and graduate students and early career and established scholars could now engage a robust database of primary sources, document projects, scholarly essays, book reviews, and encyclopedic reference material, all of which were available for use in a classroom. Sklar, who had begun her journey into women's history in the late 1960s, certain she would not find any place in the history profession, had instead risen to prominence through scholarship, service, teaching, and institution building. She and Dublin had been inspired by the New Left politics of the era to focus on women in their scholarship at the same time that they were drawn to the traditions of academic history.[132]

Sklar is just one particularly good example of how each of the participants in the women's history movement created nodes of scholarly, professional, and instructional activity and engaged in institution building that firmly established women's history in the United States as a permanent force to be recognized. The Sklar and Dublin partnership underscores the power of sustained scholarly collaboration. When considered in tandem with the fact that together they directed fifty-eight PhD dissertations in American women's history, many of whose authors went on to join the ranks of the American history professoriate, one can begin to grasp how and why the field thrived from the 1980s forward. Many participants in the early women's history movement went on to mentor similarly robust numbers of new women's and gender historians who now teach in the nation's colleges and universities.

––––––––––

The gains made in the field in the 1970s and 1980s were won by embracing and adapting to the professional culture and craft traditions of historians even while critiquing them and innovating. This work demanded inclusion in the mainstream but also the creation of separate women's history institutions. It required professional service, collaborative effort, and work in archives and the classroom. As Darlene Clark Hine once reflected, women's history had succeeded because women's historians had been prolific—they had been "so damned good" at producing scholarship.[133] They had responded vigorously to David Donald's 1970 suggestion that they create a "significant, distinctive body of writing" if they hoped to be recognized and made good on Gerda Lerner's 1970 promise that "new feminist historians have just begun to be heard."[134] Yet, feminist historians also trod extra-institutional paths to women's history that demonstrate the links between the new women's history and modern social movements. They arrived on American campuses when the radical social changes of the 1960s converged at universities in the United States to pose widespread challenges to existing paradigms on race, sex/gender, sexuality, and class in the historical profession.[135]

By the early 1970s, feminist historians were increasingly aware of the demand for courses, curriculum, and scholarship in the new field. Through the 1980s, successes in developing women's history programs assured them that their field would continue to recruit graduate students. The entry of women's historians into mainstream professional culture—their scholarship and professionalism— propelled the field to the fore of the historical profession in the United States. By 1988, when the Wingspread Conference convened to assess graduate training so attendees could chart the future, women's history was well situated indeed for the new phase of expansion, diversification, and institutionalization that was on the horizon. The teaching of women's history to undergraduates and graduates was always at the heart of their mission—coequal with knowledge production for scholarly audiences.

PART IV

Twenty-First-Century Legacies

Chapter 10

The Power and Scope of Women's History

Grappling with Difference during the Long Culture Wars

In July 1990, a feature article in the *Chronicle of Higher Education* claimed in its headline, "Scholars of Women's History Fear the Field Has Lost Its Identity." The article cited several prominent American and English historians in attendance at the Eighth Berkshire Conference. Most apocalyptic of those quoted was English scholar Lyndal Roper, who predicted that "women's history may well dissolve, but that is not bad." Two active participants in the women's history movement in the United States, Judith Bennett and Nancy Hewitt, fretted about the "collapse of old theories," "volatile levels of conflict" among "warring camps" of women's historians, and a "loss of identity" as the field's practitioners challenged one another on diversity, gender, new theoretical approaches, and the political implications of their scholarship. But Bennett and Hewitt also tempered their anxious portrayal, pointing out that debate, disagreement, and new ideas were in fact a sign of the field's vitality. Deborah Gray White of Rutgers was another who assured readers, "We are just beginning to ask many questions in women's history. The field will not disappear." Catherine Hall of the Polytechnic of East London agreed. "Clearly, we are at a very different moment than in the 1970s," she said, "but I don't find that depressing. Feminism has shifted the historical lens, so that we now understand everything differently, in terms of differences between the sexes. Those differences will always be at the heart of every society. The future is ours." In September, Kathryn Kish Sklar and Gerda Lerner replied to the article's negative headline by suggesting that the *Chronicle* should correct its "erroneous impression" of the field's disintegration and instead write about "some aspects of the remarkable progress of women's history in the United States."[1] They insisted, "The field of women's history takes seriously the challenge of diversity in human experience—diversities of ethnicity, race, class, and sexual orientation. It takes seriously the need to develop new historical methods and to reach beyond academia. This makes it a very lively enterprise indeed."[2]

In the final decade of the twentieth century, women's historians in the United States took stock of the advances in their field and noted with pride its growing academic legitimacy. They began to come to terms with the feminist implications of their work and the challenges of creating a usable past for women. Some suggested that feminist history was a glass only half full and that they needed to broaden the scope of women's history.[3] In reality, women's history was overflowing and hard to contain. The "glass half full" image coexisted with an understanding of the power of women's history. The more optimistic believed that women's history could become the new mainstream—a new "riverbed"—in the conceptualization of one scholar.[4] In this narrative, historians could gain an understanding of American history that encompassed women and men, the public and the private, the individual and the structural.[5] The field's vigor, they insisted, was due in large part to women's historians' commitment to understanding diversity in human experience. Attention to differences among women was central to their project.

By this inflection point in 1990, women's historians had created institutions that could sustain and advance their field within the American academy. Even though they had secured legitimacy and relevance within the ranks of the discipline itself, none were complacent about the progress they had made in scholarship, teaching, and public dissemination of knowledge. Yet, conservatives in the broader culture and in academia vigorously rejected increased emphasis on women and multicultural perspectives in the history curriculum. Women's historians and feminist scholars responded to this reactionary criticism by continuing to study racial, ethnic, class, political, and sexual diversity in the content of American women's history. They acknowledged the need to further diversify their own ranks. They understood that they needed to address their field's internal divisions on this front if they were going to effectively meet the external challenges. Within the discipline, they answered to their peers. Outside, the profession was confronted by a determined conservative cultural and political retrenchment against feminism, women's history, and allied social movements and fields of social history. The retrenchment intensified during the Reagan years and continued into the 1990s during the first Bush administration, when conservatives derided historical inquiry into diverse, complex historical realities as "revisionist" and illegitimate. Conflicting values surrounding race, gender, and sexuality were at the center of the culture wars waged by New Right conservatives and progressive coalitions in this era of increasing cultural polarization.

A high-profile manifestation of these conflicts over the content of history was exemplified by the intense controversy over the creation of national history standards that erupted in the 1990s. From 1991 to 1996, conservatives sparred with the social historians and history educators who had been tasked with drafting modern standards for K–12 history education. The experts in the field outlined standards that reflected the state of the art in historical scholarship. Conservatives disapproved and very publicly pressed them to go back to the drawing board. They urged the national history standards designers—all professional historians and teachers—to return to traditional historical foci. That is, they wanted male and political history to predominate in K–12 classrooms rather than see it share curricular space with the insights that a generation of new scholarship on women, ordinary people, and people of diverse ethnic and racial backgrounds had produced.[6] Historians and history educators found themselves in the political crosshairs and had to respond to this challenge. Historians of American women rose to the challenge by continuing to insist on the relevance of teaching the history of the female majority and by doubling down on their commitment to addressing categories of difference thereafter. As ever, they balanced their goals of creating a mass of usable women's history and maintaining scholarly standards. Their success helped them sustain their epistemological gains and expand women's history in the twenty-first century. Gary Nash, one of the major architects of the controversial national history standards, reflected in 1997 that "the human mind seems to require a usable past because historical memory is a key to self-identity."[7] In keeping with this sentiment, like-minded feminist historians in the women's history movement sought—and forged—an inclusive history that spoke to an array of women in the United States and the world. In turn, this offered women a historical foundation for an inclusive, if not unitary, feminist identity.

Nash and his partners on the national history standards project, Charlotte Crabtree and Ross Dunn, made this observation about history and identity in their study of the "history wars" waged over the content of school curriculum during the twentieth century. Their book, *History on Trial*, paid little attention to women's history. Indeed, women's presence in the K–12 curriculum had become a central part of this discussion only in the last quarter of the twentieth century. But historians of women were determined to put women at the center of American historical narratives and public discourse. Neither rigid nor dogmatic, they erected a "big tent"—to borrow from Cornelia H. Dayton and Lisa Levenstein's 2012 discussion of feminist politics and feminist history in the *Journal of American History*—so they could further their epistemological project of recentering American history around women, gender, race, and power from 2000 to 2020.[8] Their "big tent" was expansive enough to encompass scholarship on a diverse cast of female characters from across the racial, ethnic, class, sexual, and ideological spectrum, including right-wing women[9]—an observation that directly counters conservative women's accusations that feminist historians paid little attention to history about conservative and other women who didn't fit their "narrative of oppression."[10] Lost on conservative activists was the fact that women's historians wrote histories that could explain and contextualize women's ideological diversity even as they engaged with the usual markers of diversity.

Undoubtedly, in the 1990s women's history came under increased scrutiny from detractors because of its successes. The field had come far since 1969. Feminist historians had dramatically expanded the scope and quantity of scholarship on women. They had developed new theoretical frameworks. They had made progress toward integrating women into the mainstream content of collegiate instruction in American, world, and Western history. Indeed, their achievements are difficult to definitively quantify. To play on the oft-used "waves" metaphor and borrow from Sara Evans's *Tidal Wave: How Women Changed America at Century's End* (2003), the success and prominence of women's history prompts the question: How does one measure the drops of water in a tsunami?[11]

One measure of the field's growing legitimacy can be found in the rising frequency with which historians of women were elected to high office in the major national historical associations. Before 1980, the American Historical Association and the Organization of American Historians had elected only one woman each to their highest office since their respective founding in 1884 and 1907: Louise Kellogg served as president of the Mississippi Valley Historical Association (the original name of the OAH) in 1930, and Nellie Nielsen served as president of the AHA in 1943. Ella Lonn of Goucher College was elected president of the Southern Historical Association for 1946, followed by Kathryn Abby Hanna in 1953.[12] None of these scholars specialized in the history of women. In the fifty years from 1972 to 2022, however, historians of women have often been elected president, as, for example, Mary Elizabeth Massey's election by the SHA in 1972. Since Gerda Lerner's election to the presidency of the OAH in 1981, twelve historians of women, including four women of color, have achieved that recognition.[13] Since Natalie Zemon Davis's election to the presidency of the AHA in 1987, eleven historians of women and gender and five women with other thematic specializations have been elected to the AHA presidency. Moreover, in the 1970s, each association established a permanent women's committee within its formal institutional structure.[14]

New scholarly prizes and awards also signaled success. In 1983, the AHA and the Coordinating Committee on Women in the Historical Profession established the Joan Kelly Memorial Prize for the best book in women's and gender history.[15] In 1992, the OAH awarded the first Lerner-Scott Prize for the best dissertation in US women's and gender history. In 2010, the OAH established and awarded the first Darlene Clark Hine Prize for best book in African American women's and gender history five years before a book prize in general American women's and gender history was established; and in 2015 the OAH established and awarded the first Mary Nickliss Prize for best book in US women's and/or gender history.[16] Indicative of the central and respected place of race and ethnicity in the study of US women's history, twenty of the thirty winners of the Lerner-Scott Prize have focused on women of color. The Mary Nickliss Prize has had eight recipients, half of whom won for works in African American history. The women's history movement's forward motion is inextricably tied to the recognition that the analytic categories of race and ethnicity have indispensable utility for understanding American history. And if we are considering recognition of women's historians on a broad national cultural scale, eight historians featured in this book have been awarded the National Humanities Medal since 1997: Jacquelyn Dowd Hall (1999), Elizabeth Fox-Genovese (2003), Natalie Zemon Davis (2012), Jill Ker Conway (2012), Anne Firor Scott (2013), Darlene Clark Hine (2013), Vicki Ruiz (2014), and Evelyn Brooks Higginbotham (2014). Three-fourths of these either have been women of color or have made race or women of color a major focus of their work. Each year the president of the United States is allowed to select up to twelve recipients for this honor.

The ranks of history professors swelled in the last three decades of the century generally, even as the predominant research interests of these scholars shifted. By 2000, according to a report issued by Robert Townsend of the AHA, growing numbers of scholars made women's and gender history their topical specialization. The number of women's historians was on an ascendant trajectory, destined to surpass the long-reigning dominant category of social history by 2005.[17] History departments across the nation participated in this trend by offering courses; establishing job lines, minors, and majors; and supporting the development of formal degree programs in women's history. By 1990, in fact, there were 200 history departments offering graduate programs in the field nationwide. There had not been a single such formal program to study women's history in 1970.[18]

Historians of women in the 1990s frequently observed that the amount of scholarship produced since December 1969 was so great that it was impossible to keep up with the field and its many subfields.[19] How might one evaluate this claim? The American Historical Association's second guide to historical literature, published in 1961, is a 962-page tome in which women registered the faintest blip.[20] Neither the table of contents nor the index contained a subject heading for "women." Under United States history entries, only four titles identified works about any woman—one biography each for Mary Baker Eddy, Harriet Beecher Stowe, and Dorothea Dix and an entry for Jane Addams's memoir, *Twenty Years at Hull House*. The results were only slightly better in the modern European field, which listed Ivy Pinchbeck's book on women workers in England and had a fair number of biographical works on queens, empresses, noblewomen, and *salonnières*. This paucity was *not* because scholarship on women did not already exist by 1961. The bibliographies compiled at the Radcliffe Women's Archives and the Sophia Smith Collection prove otherwise. Rather, the absence shows that the AHA compilers placed little value on the history of women.

It wasn't until thirty-four years later, in 1995, that the AHA published its third edition of its *Guide to Historical Literature*. This gap in time is fortuitous because it provides a dramatic picture of sweeping changes in the discipline. Mary Beth Norton and Pamela Gerardi served as editors of the third edition. At 2,027 pages, each section is honeycombed with women's and gender history with numerous entries in the fields of US and European women's history.[21] The subject index for women's history spans ten columns, exclusive of three columns on gender history. Works in sub-specializations were sometimes listed in their topical or geographical field rather than in the women and gender subsections.

The institutional publications of the CCWHP–Conference Group on Women's History also reflected rapid expansion in women's history. The organization began to regularly include bibliographies of recent publications in women's history in their quarterly newsletters and in separate research bulletins from 1971 to 1975. After a four-year gap, in 1979, Nupur Chaudhuri of the CGWH compiled a bibliography of women's history scholarship that had been published between 1976 and 1979, listing 1,046 new scholarly articles and books from a diverse array of topical and geographic fields.[22] This bibliography contained a mere twenty items addressing the topics of race, Black women, Native American women, and Chicanas, perhaps contributing to the drive in the 1980s to address this dearth. Eventually this push yielded numerous works.

In 1981, with funding from the Department of Education's Fund for the Improvement of Postsecondary Education, the newly founded Association of Black Women Historians compiled a fifteen-page bibliography in Black women's history listing works in progress, dissertations, and new publications.[23] Almost a decade later in 1990, Vicki Ruiz and Ellen DuBois published their pathbreaking anthology, *Unequal Sisters: A Multicultural Reader in U.S. Women's History*. The reader featured thirty scholarly essays and four robust bibliographies focused on the major racial and ethnic subfields of American women's history. The bibliographies included 367 entries listing new scholarship published mostly between 1980 and 1990 in Latina and African American, Native American, and Asian American women's history. Ruiz and DuBois opened their textbook with the statement, "Well into its second decade, the field of women's history stands at a crossroads. Growing demands for the recognition of 'difference'—the diversity of women's experiences—can no longer be satisfied by token excursions in the histories of minority women, lesbians, and the working class." Nancy Hewitt contributed the first chapter, a revision of her 1985 historiographic essay "Beyond the Search for Sisterhood." It discussed conceptual frameworks in the field. Hewitt suggested that women's historians had focused too narrowly on middle-class white women and had delineated a distinct women's culture in American society that delimited gender roles for men and women. Framing the state of the field in the mid- to late 1980s as being relatively limited to a major subset of American women—white and middle-class—Hewitt joined women of color who argued that previous approaches had problematically treated white women as raceless, implying that these same historical models could explain women of color's experiences. Women of color (and Hewitt) argued they could not and increasingly called for more attention to be paid to women of color, women of the working class, and sexual minorities.[24] By 2000, *Unequal Sisters* had run into its third edition, offering thirty-nine essays and updated bibliographies.

Paradoxically, the content of *Unequal Sisters* offers strong evidence that by 1990, scholarly work in US women's history went far beyond "tokenism," with attention to difference instead forming a central plank of mainstream women's history discourse.[25] Considering the content of American women's history in longer historical perspective, the seminal essay "Women in American Society," by Mari Jo Buhle, Ann Gordon, and Nancy Schrom, had already helped launch the modern field as early as 1971 with a well-developed discussion on class differences among women of various ethnic groups and a warning against analytic frameworks that ignored race and class or those that focused too narrowly on women's rights movements and organizations.[26] The record suggests that perennial pleas for more attention to race, class, gender, and sexuality were based partly on, as Lise Vogel said in 1991, a "straw woman" argument that the (white) mainstream of the women's history movement lacked interest in women of color, misrepresented them in their scholarship, and distorted women's history by passing off a unified narrative based on middle-class white women as the whole story.[27] Since so many US women's historians had come out of social movements of the 1960s and '70s, they were certainly conscious of the vexed history of relations between white women and women of color and between women of the middle class and those of the working class. That consciousness, combined with the entry of more women of color into the profession from the 1980s forward, shaped the content of women's history in these years and permeated its institutions.

Institution building had been an important aspect of the women's history movement in its first two decades. In 1989, two feminist historians continued this tradition by creating a new institutional landmark. The *Journal of Women's History* (*JWH*) published its first volume in the spring of 1989. It became the journal of record for the field of women's history in the United States. Christie Farnham (later Christie Farnham Pope) of Indiana University was inspired to launch the *JWH* when she pondered why, in a world with a plethora of both topically broad and incredibly specialized academic journals, no academic history journal featuring women existed.[28] She was joined by her colleague Joan Hoff at Indiana. Farnham specialized in antebellum Southern women, while Hoff's work in US women's legal history spanned the eighteenth to late twentieth century.[29] Hoff, for a time going by the hyphenated surname Hoff-Wilson, wielded considerable national influence, since she served as the executive secretary/director of the OAH from 1981 to 1989 and was active in the CCWHP. From its inception, the *JWH* modeled itself on the *American Historical Review* by featuring peer-reviewed original research articles, book reviews, and dialogues related to major debates and departures in the discipline. The journal accepted the importance of gender as a category of analysis but stated that it was most interested in publishing histories of "women qua women" based on empirical research. Further identifying their topical parameters, they asserted that they were "committed to cooperative promotion of scholarship about women in all time periods and geographical areas that is broadly representative of national, racial, ethnic, religious, and sexual groupings. The [journal's] overriding interest is to serve the needs and interests of a wide variety of feminist historians around the world."[30] Anticipating the discipline's turn toward international and transnational history, Farnham and Hoff envisioned the *JWH* as based in the United States but drawing on the expertise and scholarship of historians from around the globe. The journal was especially committed to publishing work that attended to how race, class, gender, and sexuality shaped the histories of women.[31] This reflected scholarly trends in the field. In earlier phases of the field's development, discovering historical commonalities among women had preoccupied historians of women. During the women's history movement, differences among and between women were explored with increasing frequency. In the 1990s, examining differences among women took center stage.

Most historians of women in the United States responded enthusiastically to the new journal. But some scholars expressed reservations that the journal might end up marginalizing the field because only women's historians would read it. Others thought that a similar project being launched in the UK called *Gender and History* would lessen the impact of the *JWH* by making it redundant.[32] They feared that the field could not support two specialized journals dealing with women and gender.[33] It could and does.

Behind the founders' sense that a specialized publishing venue for women's history was overdue was the fact that women's history was still under-represented in mainstream history journals, despite the outpouring of scholarship in the 1980s.[34] In an NEH-funded investigation, Hoff showed that "mainstream" history journals in the United States and abroad had demonstrated their "reluctance . . . to devote any more than ten percent of their articles to women's history" during the 1980s.[35] Her study found that more than 5,500 journal articles in women's history, written between 1980 to 1989, had been published in what she characterized as "obscure journals, state historical society periodicals, or publications which only occasionally carry historical articles."[36]

Hoff contended that this scattershot publication pattern impeded the work of teachers and scholars in the field by hindering access to new work. Furthermore, even if mainstream history journals had been more receptive to women's history, the field of women's history had outstripped both the willingness and the ability of such mainstream journals to absorb the substantial output. The rapidly growing body of scholarship showed no sign of slowing down. It needed a peer-reviewed publication of its own.

If women's history had been nurtured by a political and historical moment favorable to its feminist underpinnings in the 1970s, the journal's establishment during the 1990s took place against an increasingly polarized and reactionary cultural and political backdrop. The kinds of historical topics and perspectives the journal featured were scrutinized by conservatives, even as historians were confronted with postmodern, post-structural theoretical insights portending the end of history as a discipline based primarily on empirical evidence.[37] Theoreticians asked whether history could ever be other than creative and interpretive in nature, and if not, how did that undercut the kinds of truth claims historians made on the basis of empirical evidence?[38] The journal's editors doubled down on their commitment to empirical research and rejected the anxious handwringing over the threat of post-structuralism gripping large swaths of academic historians in the United States at that time. They saw post-structuralism as aiding and abetting the neoconservative attack on so-called political correctness within higher education.[39]

Conservative disdain for "political correctness" expressed itself in many ways in the culture wars of the 1990s, including disdain for refocusing history curriculum on women, people of color, and the themes of inequality and conflict in American history.[40] In the late twentieth century, the conservative reaction to a modernized, expanded curriculum with a more critical view of American history opposed any move away from standard political, patriotic, masculine Anglo-American and Eurocentric perspectives.[41] While controversy over teaching racial inequality received more attention in this debate, in the 1980s and 1990s feminist perspectives came under intense attack as well. According to feminist scholar Ruth Perry, "The attack on the 'politically correct' in the universities" in the 1990s was "an attack on the theory and practice of affirmative action—a legacy of the sixties and seventies—defined as the recruitment to an institution of students and faculty who do not conform to what has always constituted the population of academic institutions: usually white, middle-class, straight, male."[42] And as Peter Novick, Robert Townsend, and William Palmer have demonstrated, the increased presence on campuses of women, people of color, ethnic minorities, and working-class people led academic disciplines like history to refocus their content.[43] "Political correction" depended upon "historical corrections"—corrections that added women, people of color, and the working class into a fuller, more accurate, more inclusive, and evidence-based explanation of the past.

Conservative opponents of this more complex retelling of American history, like anti-feminist icon Phyllis Schlafly and right-wing talk radio host Rush Limbaugh, railed against both multicultural studies and women's studies. They saw historical correction as inherently suspect and ideological in its own way, believing it to be corrosive of national unity and designed to discredit the white male founders and innovators who they thought should be credited as *the* builders of the nation.[44] From the 1970s forward, for example, Schlafly insisted that the progress American women had achieved was due to the capitalist and technological initiative and innovation of male entrepreneurs, rather than to feminist movements for justice, equality, or reproductive health technologies and rights.[45] Of course the two explanations were not mutually exclusive. Schlafly regularly attacked as false and "revisionist" social history that dealt with the working class, ethnic and racial minorities, and sex inequality. She said this history was based in left-wing "victimology" that denied the historic role of Christianity, Anglo-American legal and political traditions, and free enterprise.[46] Rush Limbaugh's book *The Way Things Ought to Be* (1992) channeled and later hyperbolized Ronald Reagan's infamous "Evil Empire" speech of 1983, in which the president admitted his conservative cultural views were dependent upon a "positive view of American history, one that takes pride in our country's accomplishments."[47]

As Limbaugh criticized multiculturalism and feminism in education in the early 1990s, the National Endowment for the Humanities was embroiled in controversy over the content of the newly designed National History Standards drafted and reviewed by hundreds of professional historians and educators. The administration of George H. W. Bush initially approved the writing of these standards in 1989, when the NEH was headed by Reagan appointee Lynne Cheney. Cheney was an influential conservative in her own right who, as wife of Vice President Dick Cheney, would go on to become the Second Lady of the United States in 2001.[48] The standards that were first published in 1994, to no academic historian's surprise, contained content about women and people of color, insights from social history that featured ordinary people, and the story of America's failures and successes.[49] Conservatives were affronted that schoolchildren might learn this fuller history and worried that the new content displaced traditional subject matter. Lynne Cheney observed in a *Wall Street Journal* editorial titled "The End of History" that the standards contained too many mentions of the 1848 Seneca Falls Convention and Harriet Tubman and too few mentions of Ulysses S. Grant, Robert E. Lee, and Thomas Edison.[50] The title also echoed postmodernist doomsayers predicting the death of history as an academic discipline.[51] By 1996, the heated public debate that ensued over what topics ought to be emphasized in the narratives of K–12 history education resulted in a dramatically pared down and revised edition of the National History Standards.

In the revised 1996 edition, women's representation, which had been relatively low to begin with in 1994, was further reduced by the total elimination of the teaching examples. The teaching examples had been the main focus of conservative criticism. Hoff and Farnham, in their final year at the editorial helm of the *JWH*, featured a series of essays analyzing and discussing these changes. The data presented show that, while scholarship and teaching of women's history at the collegiate level had advanced significantly, women's history was still poorly represented in K–12 history education; across the fields of American, Western, and world history; and across historical eras. Barbara Moss's analysis, for example, showed that women featured in only 5.9 percent of the suggested teaching examples offered across the major topical and chronological standards identified in 1994. Moreover, within that 5.9 percent, women of European descent predominated. When the teaching examples were dropped, so were most references to women and their part in history, severely reducing the likelihood that social studies educators would include women's history in their history lessons, since one can't teach what one doesn't know, nor something that has never even registered in one's consciousness.[52] Joan Scott, who was by 1997 a towering intellectual figure in French women's and gender history, offered her perspective as a participant in the National History Standards revision process that produced the heavily redacted 1996 edition. She acknowledged it was true that the number of references to specific women had been dramatically reduced by elimination of the teaching examples. But she suggested the bigger concern of historians of women and gender should be to work toward a more thoroughgoing reconceptualization of how to incorporate women and gender into mainline historical narratives—particularly political historical narratives that were emphasized in K–12 education curricula—before making recommendations in future revisions of the standards.[53]

The disciplinary debates over postmodernism and the controversy over national history standards provide the wider intellectual and political backdrop against which Hoff and Farnham founded the *Journal of Women's History*. The debates help explain and validate Hoff and Farnham's fear that post-structuralism—when combined with neoconservatism—would threaten the epistemological goals of the women's history movement and the *JWH*, the main goal of which was to incorporate more women into scholarship and curriculum. That the *JWH* was able to flourish despite these swirling controversies is a testament to the staying power of women's history in the historical discipline and to its impact on the broader culture.[54]

The content and structure of the *JWH* during its first eight years closely reflected the original aims of the editors to make the *JWH* the journal of record

Table 10.1 Content analysis of the *Journal of Women's History*, volumes 1–8, 1989–1996 (Farnham and Hoff years)

Geographic/national/topical field	No. of articles	Percentage of total content
United States (African American, Asian American, Latina, Native American)	87 (24)[a]	34%
Europe	85	33%
Asia	29	11%
Comparative/international/empire	28	11%
Historiographic/theory/methodology/professional[b]	30	n/a
Bibliographies[b]	25	n/a
Latin America	11	4%
Africa	6	2%
Sexuality	6	2%
Canada & Australia	2	1%
Total	254	

[a]Number of articles about women of color.
[b]This category is excluded from the total.

for the *international* field of women's history. Hoff's connection to a large international network allowed her to solicit and attract submissions from well-known and emerging scholars around the world.[55] Under Farnham and Hoff, the journal featured sections that were modeled after traditional academic journals but reflected feminist sensibilities. Each issue had three to five scholarly articles based on new empirical research; there was also a book reviews section. The journal featured historiography, with articles that delineated the connection between women's history, feminist activism, and the history of feminism, as reflected by the regular section "International Trends in Women's History and Feminism." The inaugural issue featured Mary Beth Norton's reflections on her experience with the newly emerging women's history of China. Another set of essays discussed developments in women's history in France and pondered the compatibility of French theories and methods with US approaches. This "International Trends" feature recurred in the first eight volumes under various titles. During the early years, the editors published thematic and geographically framed bibliographies for the field's practitioners, since the amount of scholarship was overwhelming.

Analysis of the journal's first eight volumes (1989–96) shows that it gave roughly equal coverage to American and European content. In US women's history, 24 of the 87 articles, or 28 percent, focused on women of color. Comparative and international content and work on Asia, Latin America, and Africa made up about one-third of the contents. Farnham and Hoff were keenly interested in incorporating work from around the world. Six special issues were published with specific geographic foci. Since Africa, Asia, the Middle East, and Latin America did not typically receive as much scholarly attention as the United States, France, Great Britain, and Germany, guest editors were invited to put together issues focused on these regions.[56] Hoff and Farnham arranged special issues on Eastern Europe, Ireland, and China from 1994 to 1996. A special double issue was dedicated to Irish women's history in 1995.[57] The special issue on China came out in 1996, one year after the United Nations Fourth Conference on Women was held in Beijing. There, when First Lady Hillary Rodham Clinton famously declared that "women's rights are human rights and human rights are women's rights," she was echoing past feminists.[58] As early as 1869, Elizabeth Cady Stanton had invoked the language of human rights in her fight for women's rights.[59] And in 1948, Eleanor Roosevelt oversaw the adoption of the United Nations Universal Declaration of Human Rights, a document on which she and other women had worked to ensure women's inclusion.[60] In general, the JWH special issues tended to consider women in their isolated geographic location rather than generating a comparative frame of analysis. But this work represented a necessary stage in the development of international women's history in that it provided the national studies and data essential to the comparative international scholarship yet to be written.

Even if Hoff and Farnham were committed to internationalizing the JWH, the number of articles submitted by international scholars tended to be low.[61] A similar dynamic existed for the Berkshire Conferences. Scholars outside of the United States found it difficult to attend the Big Berks for financial, visa, and professional reasons, and lack of English often made it difficult for them to present work.[62] The first and only Big Berkshire Conference held outside of the United States to date convened in 2014 in English-speaking Toronto, Canada, though efforts were made to draw in Indigenous and French-speaking Canadian scholars. Despite these logistical challenges, the American women's history movement was internationalizing its own perspectives by 1989 and becoming aware of parallel developments in other parts of the world. Historians of women and gender in other nations organized their own institutions, and in 1987, the International Federation for Research in Women's History was formed by Karen Offen of the United States, Ida Blom of Norway, and Ruth Roach-Pierson of Canada.[63] The *Journal of Women's History*'s original international vision meant that the editors pursued international material despite challenges. Editors succeeding Farnham and Hoff did the same.[64]

The *JWH*'s original mission also stirred debate centered on the best approach to doing women's history. All agreed that innovative empirical research was key to the practice of history, but different opinions arose on whether the field should remain identified with feminist approaches. Discussions ensued on the benefits and drawbacks of a gender history approach, and some wondered how different national historiographies of women could enrich and strengthen the field worldwide and reflect the global scope of women's history.

Though women's historians of Hoff and Farnham's generation were indelibly marked by the professional, feminist, and scholarly activism of the 1970s, they came of professional age in the 1980s.[65] The Reagan '80s represented a period of reaction against the women's movement.[66] When, in the late 1980s and the 1990s, postmodernism, post-structuralism, and the linguistic turn in its gendered permutations gained ascendency, these new approaches were perceived as a threat that could depoliticize or take the feminist teeth out of the field. The textual relativism of post-structuralism seemed to make history too abstract and inaccessible to be politically relevant.[67] It made historical texts the central objects of analysis in ways that were disconcerting to historians who had devoted their intellectual energies to surfacing women's very existence and experiences and who had emphasized their agency and subjecthood. The *JWH*, despite claims in its opening editorial to "espouse no particular ideological or methodological approach," was a feminist academic project of global scope that favored work based on empirical research. Richard Evans, writing in *In Defense of History* (1997), notes that the theoretical concerns over the "post-structural threat" were embedded in debates within the larger historical discipline in the United States at the end of the twentieth century.[68] He argued that, despite postmodernist and conservative prognostications of the downfall and destabilization of history as a discipline, most historians kept on doing critical work based on research in the historical record. The concerns of post-structural theorists were simply too far removed from what historians actually do to warrant the anxiety they produced.[69] This perspective was certainly reflected in the work of the *JWH* editors.

The first eight volumes revealed its feminist underpinnings. Feminist or anti-feminist quotes regularly graced the journal's title page to drive home the connections between recording and analyzing women's past and achieving feminist progress in the present. The quotes ranged from the ironic to the outrageous to the commemorative. For example, the first issue of volume 1 quoted Oscar Wilde—"Anybody can make history. Only a great man can write it"—while a later issue quoted an 1853 newspaper as saying, "All these women reformers are either old maids, or divorced wives, and as homely as sin." In 1991, the editor of the Phi Beta Kappa journal *The American Scholar* was quoted on the *JWH* title page in "yet another sexist quote" as writing, "The feminists roll on, perpetually angry, making perfectly comprehensible the joke about the couple in their West Side Manhattan apartment, who, having been twice robbed, determined to protect themselves, he wanting to get a revolver, she a pit bull, and so they agree to compromise and instead get a feminist."[70] Some issues were dedicated to feminist greats upon their deaths, like Audre Lorde and Barbara Jordan.[71] The quotes kicking off each issue reminded readers of the connections between feminism and women's history.[72] This journalistic device was dropped in 1997, but the feminist logo featuring a globe encircled by the symbol for woman was retained until 2008.

Christie Farnham's last "Editor's Note" in volume 8 made clear her reservations about the dangers of allowing gender analysis and analyses of difference to erase the centrality of women and feminism to women's history.[73] "If there is one lesson feminists learned in the eighties, it was that we are a very diverse group. Appreciation of this diversity should be celebrated, but it must not become the impetus by which feminism recedes out of focus in favor of a murky mélange of gender, race, class, age, sexuality, and imperialist/colonialist positions."[74] This was Farnham's plea—that scholarship on difference must expand the field in ways that were consistent with feminism. She and Hoff later identified the tension between women's and gender history as one of the central issues that had contributed to a depoliticization of the field.[75] Yet they understood that the *JWH* was not immune to natural cycles of discourse within the academy and *should* reflect the developing field.[76] If Hoff, Farnham, and others were leery of gender's power to destabilize the category "woman," proponents of gender as a central category of analysis thought it was a powerful strategy for exposing gendered relations of power between men, women, and those with nonbinary gender identities. Furthermore, they wanted to deconstruct ideas around gender identity and sexuality that worked to uphold heteronormativity and male dominance in all its manifestations.[77]

Farnham and Hoff saw the *JWH* as integral to institutionalizing the field. They did not share the opinion that institutionalizing the field caused it to lose its radical edge—for example, when feminist scholars became career academics, executives in professional associations, and journal editors.[78] They remembered too well what it was like before the *JWH*, the CCWHP-CGWH, the Big Berks, or the women's committees of the OAH, AHA, and SHA. For them, institutionalization was empowering and stabilizing, and it secured the future of the field and the positions of its practitioners.[79] Farnham and Hoff had created the journal to anchor women's history within the shifting currents of historiography in the United States. And they had nudged the field along to national and global legitimacy.

In the fall of 1996, the *JWH* moved to Ohio State University, where Leila Rupp and a new team of editors shaped its direction and content for the next eight years. Rupp was a founding member of the *JWH* editorial board whose own scholarship on the United States and Germany was comparative and international in its focus.[80] When she took over the editorship of the journal, she had been teaching women's history at Ohio State for years and was approaching publication of her third book.[81] She was joined by a team of four associate editors at Ohio State.[82] A 1976 PhD graduate of Bryn Mawr College, Rupp had a long association with the women's history movement and had been mentored by Mary Maples Dunn and Barbara Miller Lane in the heady days when the women's history movement generated so much enthusiasm for the work.[83] Steeped in the women's liberation movement, her interest in women's history was a corollary to that.[84] Rupp challenged dominant narrative frameworks in the history of feminism that centered on feminist "waves" and women in particular national contexts. Her work on the continuity of the American women's movement between the so-called first and second waves and the transnational aspects of the women's movement were on the cutting edge of American women's history in the 1980s and 1990s.[85] Committed to challenging heterosexism in scholarship, Rupp shifted to histories of same-sex sexuality in the late '90s.[86] Alongside scholars such as Carroll Smith-Rosenberg, Estelle Freedman, and John D'Emilio, she authored her own pathbreaking work in the history of sexuality.[87] Each of these scholarly interests would be reflected in the pages of the journal from 1997 to 2004.

As editor, Rupp hosted dialogues featuring the work of pioneers, foremothers, and paradigm shifters as she expanded the journal's coverage of international history and the history of sexuality.[88] She was eager to increase "communications across traditional lines of geographically and chronologically defined fields" and to attend to understudied areas. The first two guest-edited special issues under her leadership were on sexuality and religious fundamentalism.[89]

In 1998 Rupp stated plainly that the *JWH* followed in the feminist tradition of women's history: "Born from the women's movement . . . women's history has always made connections to the present."[90] Indeed, much of the content of the journal during her tenure connected to contemporary political issues either explicitly or implicitly. Rupp introduced new sections devoted to theory, teaching, and historiography, including a multigenerational dialogue series, "Women's History in the New Millennium." Historiographic issues took on an international perspective. For example, a series of retrospectives on women's history classics included discussions of the impact of Barbara Welter's "Cult of True Womanhood" and Carroll Smith-Rosenberg's "Female World of Love and Ritual."[91] The journal featured dialogues about paradigm-shifting scholarship such as *A Midwife's Tale*, by Laurel Thatcher Ulrich, and Adrienne Rich's "Compulsory Heterosexuality," hoping to illuminate their impact on different national historiographies around the world.[92]

Rupp also looked to future generations. The 2003 multi-issue dialogue series "Women's History in the New Millennium" included the panel discussion "Considering the State of U.S. Women's History." It featured several generations of scholars discussing the state of the field with an eye toward future scholarly

Table 10.2 Content analysis of the *Journal of Women's History*, volumes 9–15, 1997–2004 (Rupp years)

Geographic/national/topical fields	No. of articles	Percentage of total content
United States (# of articles about African American, Native American, Latina, and Asian American history)	158 (38)[a]	36%
Europe (# of European articles about Premodern Europe)	101 (9)	23%
Comparative/international/transnational/empire	63	14%
Sexuality	40	9%
Asia (including the Middle East)	40	9%
Methodology, theory, professional, teaching[b]	35	n/a
Latin America and the Caribbean	22	5%
Africa	12	3%
Australia	5	1%
Canada	2	.04%
Total	443	

[a]Number of articles about women of color.
[b]This category is excluded from the total.

pursuits.[93] In 2001 the *JWH* began to sponsor a women's history prize for best essay by a high school student that went with the National History Day program. Building a bridge to the future, Rupp brought graduate assistants onto the editorial team, in the tradition of Hoff and Farnham. Stephanie Gilmore, managing editor for the *JWH*, for example, remembers that Rupp fostered a democratic spirit of mutual respect for younger team members, entrusting them with editorial processes and consulting them on editorial decisions.[94] This was in keeping with the spirit of feminist historians of the 1970s who worked both to mentor graduate students and to eliminate the profession's traditions of nepotism, hierarchy, and competition by creating a more supportive and demystified work culture.[95]

By the end of Leila Rupp's term as editor, she had expanded the number of articles in the history of sexuality and on international, transnational, and comparative history. Though table 10.2 suggests that much of this growth had come at the expense of publishing work on European women's history, in fact much of this work focused on the dialectical exchanges between Europeans and colonial subjects. Rupp's editorship promoted reflection on the international state of the field, intergenerational dialogue, and moving the field toward the creation of its own historiography.[96]

Tables 10.1 and 10.2 show that the content of the *JWH* from 1989 to 2004 increasingly focused on women of color, women from around the world, the

Table 10.3. Content analysis of the *Journal of Women's History*, volumes 16–22, 2005–2010 (Burton and Allman years)

Geographic/national/topical field	No. of articles	Percentage of total content
Comparative/international/transnational/empire	91	27%
United States (African American, Native American, Latina, Asian American)	82 (20)[a]	25%
Europe	60	18%
Asia	36	11%
Latin America	18	5%
Africa	10	3%
Sexuality	24	7%
Theory, methodology, professional, historiographic[b]	19	n/a
Canada	6	2%
Australia, New Zealand	5	2%
Total	332	

[a]Number of articles about women of color.
[b]This category is excluded from the total.

history of sexuality, and the vibrant theoretical debates going on in the field. Within the journal's coverage of US women's history, which continued to predominate in its pages through the turn of the century, dialogues about difference, including class, race, sexuality, and gender, were central. In spring 2005, the *JWH* editorship passed to Antoinette Burton and Jean Allman of the University of Illinois Urbana-Champaign (see table 10.3). This too reflected the editorial board's desire to diversify and internationalize women's history at the *JWH*, as Burton specialized in the history of British imperialism and Allman was an Africanist.

The history of this flagship American journal and the evolving focus of the field from 1990 forward shows that the dynamic growth of women's history can be attributed not to a narrow focus on middle-class white women but rather to its practitioners' approach to surfacing and developing histories of diverse women and to understanding these women's changing places in societies and cultures around the world. Within US women's history, attention to diversity had been on the scholarly agenda since the 1970s with particularly strong emphasis on class differences in the modern field's first two decades.[97] During the 1980s, considerations of gender and race as historically contingent cultural constructs that impacted women's lives increasingly moved to the center. Participating in this process, African American women historians moved the treatment of Black women's history forward in productive ways to the benefit of the field writ large. Their work has been central to the emergence of what might now be called intersectional analyses of history. This development was a product of two key features of the women's history movement. First, feminist historians of all racial and ethnic backgrounds tended to share a philosophical commitment to incorporating the full array of American diversity into the narratives of American history in an inclusive, broad-ranging way. This was done in tandem with the construction of other subfields of American history, like Black history and Chicana/o history.[98] As with feminist historians, the commitment often originated with these scholars' exposure to the social and economic justice movements of the 1960s and 1970s. Second, the construction of these fields of historical inquiry also simply reflected the realities detected in the actual historical record as historians went about their investigations and identified archival collections that historians had hitherto overlooked, while also gathering oral histories and documenting oral traditions.

Reliance on empirical research in the historical record is the sine qua non of academic legitimacy in the discipline of history. Women's history is no different from traditional areas of historical study focused on men in this regard, which is why the archives-building work begun at midcentury by women was so critical a step in creating a foundation for women's history. But women's history derived its relevance, resonance, and electricity from the feminist politics of the last quarter of the twentieth century. Dynamic tensions along the cultural fault lines of race, sex, and ideology generated that energy but also generated opposition to these new histories. The dual political and scholarly commitments reflected in American women's history, African American history, and African American women's history were fraught, to be sure. This was not because women's or Black history was more politically motivated or prone to bias than more traditional areas of historical study. Rather, these areas of study were subject to criticism because women's history, Black history, and Black women's history were so very relevant to contemporary political and cultural fault lines; lines that became increasingly unstable during the 1970s as conservative Americans rejected the progressive racial and sexual equality policies designed by liberal Democrats in power and the values promoted in the streets by New Left activists in the 1960s. These New Left and liberal values were reflected in the new social history that emerged from this era.[99] Placing value on the history of working people, women, and people of color by simply acknowledging and studying their existence and refusing to accept their irrelevance was a radical and culturally transformative act. If it were not, it wouldn't have been resisted so fiercely. While conservatives have effectively harnessed cultural fears about threats to the traditional family and sexual and gender norms and destabilized racial hierarchies, liberals have struggled to forge and maintain a unified but racially and ideologically diverse coalition.

The historical lenses through which we understand our culture have always figured in the processes by which certain groups retain cultural authority and power and other groups reach for the same.

The historical and political stakes are remarkably high indeed. Since 1989, conservatives have effectively eroded and reversed major liberal policy advances achieved in the 1960s and 1970s. For example, the Supreme Court took the teeth out of the oversight mechanisms of the Voting Rights Act of 1965 in its 2013 ruling in *Shelby v. Holder*, making it easier for states to implement racially disparate barriers to voting rights. In 1989 and 1992, SCOTUS rulings on abortion rights incrementally but substantially restricted women's access to safe, medical abortion services by allowing states the discretion to impose more and more restrictions on service providers.[100] The 2022 SCOTUS ruling in *Dobbs v. Jackson Women's Health Organization* has now definitively overturned the nearly fifty-year precedent established by *Roe v. Wade* (1973), which had provided federal protection for abortion rights. Women in roughly half the states in the union now effectively have no access, or extremely limited access, to abortion services. Those seeking or providing abortions are subject to heavy criminal penalties, including fines and jailtime. It remains to be seen whether the legal reasoning overthrown by *Dobbs* will be extended to challenge the rulings that legalized birth control for the nation's married women in 1965 (*Griswold v. Connecticut*) and their single sisters in 1972 (*Eisenstadt v. Baird*). Will the constitutional right to same-sex marriage established by *Obergefell v. Hodges* (2015) be overturned next? If so, Republicans will have succeeded in ushering in a new era of sexual, marital, and reproductive ultra-conservatism. Already, the ultra-conservative SCOTUS has put in extreme jeopardy the voting rights of racial and ethnic minorities and the health, lives, and self-determination of women of childbearing age across the country by ceding legislative and regulatory control of these issues back to the states. We are experiencing a political and historical "Groundhog Day" that requires a reexamination of the same historic struggles engaged by our mothers, grandmothers, and great-grandmothers. This makes understanding women's history, BIPOC (women's) history, and opposition to teaching them more important than ever. If academic and public historians aren't mindful and active, their voices will be drowned out by conservative voices intent on recapturing historical narratives for traditionally dominant cultural and political stakeholders along the lines of what the governor of Florida and his followers have done with their Stop WOKE Act in 2022. These same efforts were reflected in the Trump administration's "1776 Report," a set of guidelines for rewriting American history curricula put out in the waning days of his first administration in 2021.[101]

The conservative strategy of deflection in which the perpetrator of a transgression accuses their rivals of the same transgression is certainly a well-rehearsed hallmark of the New Right. So is rhetorical script-flipping, in which a term considered by liberals to be positive is turned into a negative, a victimizer into a victim. Before he was awarded the Presidential Medal of Freedom by Donald Trump in 2020, millions of Americans listened to Rush Limbaugh on AM radio for three decades. He wrote and spoke about the "way things ought to be" in the 1990s.[102] Central to his message were attacks on multiculturalism in education, women's studies, "political correctness," and feminism. He coined the term "Feminazi"—a conflation of feminism, or equality for men and women, with Nazism, the authoritarian, misogynistic, and racist doctrine of the Holocaust.[103] This sort of discourse spoke to a strain of white male perceptions of loss of relative privilege and power over women and people of color in American society after the crests of the Black civil rights movement and modern women's movement. Limbaugh was an effective culture warrior. His take on history was but one weapon in his armory. He and his listeners wanted to restore androcentric and Eurocentric history to their central place of honor in the history curriculum. Limbaugh was not being particularly original in his use of history. Nash, Crabtree, and Dunn showed in *History on Trial* that political conflict over the content and focus of American history had long been a major front in the battle for the minds and political loyalties of Americans.[104]

The cultural challenges that historians of women and people of color faced in the 1990s as they worked to expand their fields have yet to be resolved. The recent hysteria over "critical race theory" and its conflation with typical instruction of Black history and the history of white supremacy is just more of the same. Control over history education and the content of formal narratives of American history holds great cultural force and therefore political power. Women, like people of color, had been categorically excluded from mainstream historical narratives until the recent past, and their presence in history was hard-won. Conservative attempts to return to traditional exclusionary modes of history posed (and poses) an existential threat to women and people of color because to deny the historical relevance of an entire category of people, to disappear them from history curricula, fundamentally demeans and dehumanizes them. The simultaneous conservative assault on multicultural and women's history in the 1990s probably strengthened feminist historians' resolve to focus on women of color from the 1990s forward, since historically, women of color had suffered under the weight of racism and sexism and their historical experiences seemed likely to have explanatory power. This dual sense of peril and power, past and present, continues to energize the work of women's history today.

Thus, within communities of feminist historians, race has long loomed large and complicated women's ability to shape and work toward collective epistemological goals. As demonstrated by Gloria Hull, Patricia Bell-Scott, and Barbara Smith in the classic anthology *All the Women Are White, All the*

Blacks Are Men, but Some of Us Are Brave and by Winifred Breines in *The Trouble between Us: An Uneasy History of White and Black Women in the Feminist Movement*, working through criticisms of mainstream white feminism(s) has been essential to establishing feminism's political relevance to a broader array of American women.[105] Black and white feminist historians and social scientists have demanded attention to difference, with women of color and white women historians often engaged in challenging, sometimes painful, but ultimately constructive dialogue.

A common criticism of women's history beginning in the late 1980s was that the modern field's founding "mothers" had narrowly focused on the history of middle-class white women and feminists. Critics cited influential early articles and monographs like Barbara Welter's essay on the prescriptive bourgeois ideology of the "cult of true womanhood," Kitty Sklar's biography of Catharine Beecher, Nancy Cott's *Bonds of Womanhood*, and Ellen DuBois's *Feminism and Suffrage* for their narrow focus on middle-class white women.[106] At the 1987 Big Berks, women sparred over whether the conference had included historians and histories of women of color and lesbians. In 1988, the Wingspread Conference heard Latina, Chicana, and Black and Asian American women's historians call for more attention to their histories.[107] And in 1989, Evelyn Brooks Higginbotham's essay "Beyond the Sound of Silence: Afro-American Women in History" argued that both women's history and Afro-American history had "suffered from the weakness of omission," in which Black history failed to address gender and women and women's history failed to adequately address race.[108] Higginbotham made the case that Black women's history was a field of study in its own right but was also integral to a full understanding of American history. Indeed, few mainstream scholarly publications or presses published work by or about Black women before 1980.[109]

In the vanguard in 1972, Pantheon Books published Gerda Lerner's seminal document reader, *Black Women in White America*. Here, she characteristically wrote that both Black people and women in America had been denied their place in the "body of American history" because that history had primarily been written by white male historians. Acknowledging the Black historians (in the Black history movement) who had worked to arouse "pride in a legitimate past, enhancing self-respect, and providing heroes with whom black people can identify," she linked the writing of Black history to serving the needs of Black people, culture, and politics. Women's history, Lerner argued, had suffered from the same sort of neglect and could fill the same needs for women. Lerner stated that Black women had been "doubly invisible"—the records of their past ignored, and their significance denied. Lerner's recommendation was for women and Black people—and Black women—"to define themselves autonomously and to interpret their past, their present, and their future." She also suggested that white historians who studied Black history needed to do better to consider Black viewpoints. The document reader format of *Black Women in White America* allowed Black viewpoints and voices to predominate.[110] As more Black women entered the historical profession in the 1980s, Lerner followed her own advice and quietly made her exit from specializing in Black women's history.[111] Her decision may have been influenced by the tense collaborations that had unfolded between her and members of the Association of Black Women Historians on the Department of Education's Fund for the Improvement of Postsecondary Education project to promote Black women's history and historians between 1980 and 1982.

From the late 1970s forward, other white women published on race with some success and acceptance, often focusing on the difficult relations between white and Black women reformers; on white women's work either fighting or upholding white supremacy in the Jim Crow South, the civil rights movement, and the suffrage movement; or on the impact of race on determining white and Black women's relative experiences of marginalization and privilege within society. The work has been widely accepted and vetted, has been seen as carefully researched, and is acknowledged by Black scholars in the field.[112] Notable examples from this body of scholarship included Jacquelyn Dowd Hall's *Revolt against Chivalry*, Jacqueline Jones's *Labor of Love/Labor of Sorrow*, Glenda Elizabeth Gilmore's *Gender and Jim Crow*, Michelle Newman's *White Women's Rights*, and Danielle McGuire's *At the Dark End of the Street*. From the mid-1980s, as Black women's historians entered the profession in growing numbers, they had pressed "mainstream" (read "white") women's historians to engage with and recognize their work. That these historians were now "mainstream" was itself a testament to progress.[113]

In fact, the academic world had made strides in giving recognition to African American history already. In the 1950s, 1960s, and 1970s, prominent white male scholars like Kenneth Stampp, Eugene Genovese, Herbert Gutman, George Frederickson, Leon Litwack, and Stanley Elkins joined Black historians and sociologists working in the tradition of W. E. B. Du Bois and Carter G. Woodson. Men like E. Franklin Frazier, John Hope Franklin, and John Blassingame, for instance, focused on Black history, including the Black family. None, however, offered sustained attention to the experiences and perspectives of Black women.[114] According to Angela Davis, few cut through the stereotypes promulgated about Black women as either promiscuous or domineering.[115] In this context, Black women entering academia in the 1970s found themselves marginalized within the fields of Black history and Black studies by Black men, while white feminist scholars, meanwhile, were building women's history. Thus, in 1982, Mary Frances Berry's foreword to *All the Women Are White, All the Blacks Are Men, but Some of Us Are Brave* stated that had it not been for pioneers like Gerda Lerner and Rosalyn Terborg-Penn, there would have been little scholarship on Black women's historical experiences.[116]

Black women's historians of the 1970s were faced with the challenging prospect of carving out intellectual space and a scholarly community of their own that could exist within the broader ivory tower. They had to prove themselves as scholars, and they had to insist that Black women's history was a legitimate area of inquiry that they were qualified to write. In *Telling Histories: Black Women Historians in the Ivory Tower*, Deborah Gray White and other Black women scholars wrote about navigating history careers at the intersections of race, class, and gender in America. They detailed their experiences with marginalization in the historical profession, in Black studies, and in the women's history movement. For example, Rosalyn Terborg-Penn recalled studying at both Howard University and Morgan State University in the 1970s, where she received mixed messages about the viability of her investigating Black woman suffragists and reformers. One professor denigrated her topic as "Mickey Mouse" and urged her to focus on male reformers. Others, like Benjamin Quarles, John Henrik Clarke, and Dorothy Porter, were more encouraging. When Terborg-Penn presented her early work at academic conferences, including the Big Berks, she observed that "several of my white feminist socialist colleagues in women's history challenged the argument in my dissertation that white women discriminated against Black women seeking to join the nineteenth-century women's movement." She reported that some argued that patriarchy meant white women didn't participate in white supremacy or bear equal responsibility with white men for institutional racism. Meanwhile, at Black academic conferences like that of the Association for the Study of African American Life and History, Black male scholars criticized her work for its inherent feminism, and "some men came to sessions where papers on Black women were being presented just to criticize the authors." She recalled that "the prevailing attitude among many Black men who attended [Association for the Study of African American Life and History] conferences was sexist. Many of them argued that women's history was feminism and distracted us from the struggle to legitimize Black studies."[117] Feminism, these men argued, ran counter to Black nationalism, and women's studies and women's history competed with Black studies programs for scarce institutional resources. In response to their common experiences of sexism vis-à-vis Black history and racism vis-à-vis American and American women's history, Black women's historians organized professionally on their own behalf between 1978 and 1980, forming the Association of Black Women Historians and choosing to make the Association for the Study of African American Life and History its home affiliation.[118]

Deborah Gray White completed her pioneering dissertation on Black women in slavery in 1978 after years of reportedly being discouraged by professors, peers, and students in the Black studies program at the University of Illinois Chicago Circle. Ultimately, W. W. Norton published the dissertation as *Ar'n't I A Woman?* in 1985. In the years after completing the dissertation, though, White's manuscript was repeatedly rejected by publishers who claimed it was poorly researched because it was based on oral histories and narratives of enslaved women rather than on traditional archival records. It was only after Anne Firor Scott and Jacquelyn Dowd Hall told Norton that the dissertation was the "best thing written on women's slavery" that the book saw the light of day.[119] Indeed, by the 1980s, the mostly white leaders of the women's history movement often sought out and promoted work by Black women scholars.

Younger Black women entering the history discipline in the 1970s had, like white women and other women of color, benefited from the gains made by the Black civil rights movement, which opened access to higher education and employment to African Americans, women, and ethnic minorities from 1964 forward thanks to Title VII of the Civil Rights Act of 1964. The act barred discrimination in employment, public accommodations, and federally funded programs on grounds of race, sex, or national origin and established the Equal Employment Opportunity Commission to address discrimination claims. The movements out of which this and other civil rights legislation grew were movements in which many women historians, including Black women historians, had personally participated. Black women of this generation were often drawn to the study of Black history as a corollary to their commitments to the ongoing civil rights movement—Sharon Harley and Rosalyn Terborg-Penn are two notable examples of this dynamic. Harley stated that her "research reclaiming for historical memory the lives of African American women became a site of resistance, a place for me to confront and condemn, intellectually and politically, the racial and gender oppression of women of color."[120] In 1974, Harley and Terborg-Penn began collaboration on an influential collection of scholarly essays authored by African American historians. They worked from what they called a "Black nationalist feminist perspective," showing that "racism was the primary obstacle in the way of African American women's achievements." The essays exclusively featured Black scholars, including one male scholar. Neither the front matter of the 1978 original edition nor the 1997 reprint acknowledged work done by white scholars in Black women's history. But in 1997 the editors acknowledged that "over time, Women's History developed in many stages, and Black Women's History *became* an accepted wing of the theoretical as well as the subject matter of the field." More thoroughgoing analytic attention to race, class, and gender facilitated the growth of Black women's history in the 1980s and '90s.[121]

Black women scholars often found that their dual commitments to Black history and to the history of women created conflicts of interest. As Deborah Gray

White has suggested, Black women's historians occupied a doubly demanding place between two vibrant, growing fields of historical inquiry and between two paradigm-shifting intellectual movements.[122] They found themselves having to assert the coequal importance of race with class, gender, and sexuality as categories of analysis while still pressing for more space for Black women scholars within the movement and the academy.[123] As a result, from 1978 forward, Black women's historians produced some of the most consequential scholarship in the field of US women's history. Black women were also challenged to include other racial and ethnic minorities in their concept of who was a woman of color. The existence of pan-African perspectives and "Third World" feminist alliances within women's liberation also challenged the dominance of a white feminist paradigm. This was all an integral part of how, according to Linda Gordon, feminist historians contributed to the necessary if "painful transformation" in American history that forced scholars to be cognizant of race and gender.[124]

Indeed, the growth and development of a racially, ethnically, sexually inclusive American women's history prefigured—and perhaps helped lay the groundwork for—contemporary iterations of feminism as manifested, for example, in the Women's March on Washington and Me Too movements. Rebecca Traister points out in *Good and Mad* (2018) that these new movements are led by a multiracial coalition of feminists acutely conscious of the limitations of any feminism that is less than intersectional. The term "intersectional" dates to Kimberlé Crenshaw's 1989 academic article "Demarginalizing the Intersection of Race and Sex."[125] Popular feminist slogans to emerge in the second decade of the twenty-first century have been Flavia Dzodan's "My feminism will be intersectional, or it will be bullshit!" and "If your feminism isn't intersectional, it isn't feminism."[126] The ideological richness of contemporary feminism owes a debt to the struggles of late twentieth-century academic feminists, and Black women historians have been central to these developments in the historical discipline.[127]

Works of history written by philosopher Angela Davis (1981) or Black feminist bell hooks (1981 and 1989) are perhaps more broadly read than the work of historians. But their work is contemporaneous with what was being done in history.[128] Bettye Collier-Thomas, Sharon Harley, and Rosalyn Terborg-Penn, for instance, did pathbreaking foundational work in archives and scholarship in the 1970s, followed closely by the work of Paula Giddings, Deborah Gray White, Darlene Clark Hine, and Nell Painter in the early to mid-1980s. Harley and Terborg-Penn collaborated to come out with *The Afro-American Woman: Struggles and Images* in 1978. Giddings published *When and Where I Enter* in 1984. Terborg-Penn completed her dissertation about Black woman suffragists in 1978; it was published belatedly in 1998.[129] Deborah Gray White defended her dissertation on enslaved women in 1978; it was published as the pathbreaking

Ar'n't I a Woman in 1985. Darlene Clark Hine published *Black Women in the Middle West: A Source Guide* (1984), *Black Women in White: Racial Conflict and Cooperation in the Nursing Profession, 1890–1950* (1989), *Hine Sight: Black Women and the Re-Construction of American History* (1994), and (with Kathleen Thompson) the textbook *A Shining Thread of Hope* (1998). Prominent Black woman scholars whose primary research focus was not women and gender also ventured into women's history, as with Nell Painter, who published *Sojourner Truth: A Life, a Symbol* in 1996 and Mary Berry, who published *Why ERA Failed* (1986), *The Politics of Parenthood: Child Care, Women's Rights, and the Myth of the Good Mother* (1993), and *My Face Is Black Is True: Callie House and the Struggle for Ex-Slave Reparations* (2006).[130]

The formation of the Association of Black Women Historians in 1979 provided a community of mutual support and served as a bridge between the "mainstream" Black history movement and the "mainstream" women's history movement.[131] That bridge helped Black women historians build a self-sustaining scholarly community that could continue to press white women historians to consider race as an essential category of analysis for American women's history. The enduring effects of this pressure were reflected in the centennial commemorations of the ratification of the Nineteenth Amendment in 2020. Historians' commemorations focused on the activism of women of color and scrutinized their exclusion from white suffrage organizations. These discussions included work on Latina, Asian American, and Native American woman suffragists and the amendment's limited impact on these groups. The centennial, in fact, became a referendum on the limits of *white suffragism* and, by extension, *white feminism*.[132]

By the 1990s, a more diverse array of women of color scholars existed, among them Vicki Ruiz, Deena González, Cynthia Orozco, Regina Morantz-Sanchez, Clara Sue Kidwell, Louise Año Nuevo Kerr, Judy Yung, and Valerie Matsumoto. They pushed for expanded attention to women of color, insisting that it must include Indigenous, Latinx, Asian American, and other racial and ethnic groups of women.[133] Many of these scholars had active connections to various ethnic studies movements and departments and their movement corollaries outside of academia. In the 1980s, when most were either finishing doctoral programs or in the early stages of their careers, they found welcome in the women's history movement, whose leaders, white and Black, believed that inclusion of diverse voices and histories was essential to the intellectual legitimacy of American women's history. Moreover, dialogue between Black and white women's historians had made clear that it was unacceptable for white women to be *the* dominant scholarly voices regarding the history of women of color, even when they produced solid work in the field.

As demonstrated in *Telling Histories: Black Women Historians in the Ivory Tower*, Black women's experience in the discipline of history and in the ivory tower is particularly representative of the ways race and gender combine to differentiate and compound the challenges faced by women of different backgrounds—even those engaged in common feminist causes. These scholars sought acceptance and respect in multiple national academic communities—the historical profession, the Black history movement, and the women's history movement. These communities made sometimes conflicting but always compounded demands upon them, even as Black women's historians sought to make an impact on the larger culture and the lives of contemporary Black women. Deborah Gray White in her 2007 essay "'Matter Out of Place': *Ar'n't I a Woman?* Black Female Scholars and the Academy" argued that Black women scholars were often treated as "out of place" in various academic communities and felt the weight of "carrying their race and gender" with them into every professional setting. This had, in her view, a negative effect on their workload, well-being, careers, and longevity. She cited the untimely deaths of Black women scholars and referred to Constance Carroll's study showing that in 1968, 91 percent of PhDs conferred by historically Black colleges and universities went to men; there was an extreme scarcity of Black female PhDs as late as 1982 (only 3 percent in 1982). As an underrepresented minority in academia, they were forced to assert their existential legitimacy in academia as women, as African Americans, and as scholars who studied Black women. They had to fight to secure the legitimacy of Black history and to prove themselves as scholars. They had to walk the path between celebratory advocacy and the need to uphold the standards of the academic historical tradition.[134] Institutional resources were (are) finite and subject to competition. They were on the razor's edge, expected to privilege the "Black part" of their history over the "women part" and to support Black history and Black studies over women's history and women's studies. Nevertheless, they persisted, knowing their work mattered, and brought recognition to African American women's history. They explained that they were "in fact in the right place" and where they were "supposed to be." But White maintained that this had created "too heavy a load."[135]

Black women's historians' prominence within American women's history is apparent today. The 2020 annual meeting of Little Berks—that once all-white, New England history association founded circa 1930—featured the work of Euro-American, Indigenous, Latinx, African American and Asian American women and focused on the connections between contemporary events, feminist politics, and US women's history.[136] The program cochairs of the 2020 Big Berks were both Black women specializing in Black women's history—Martha S. Jones of Johns Hopkins University and Tiya Miles of Harvard University.[137] The 2020–23 copresidents of the Coordinating Council of Women in History (formerly the CCWHP-CGWH) were both African American women scholars—Crystal Feimster of Yale University and Rachel Jean-Baptiste of UC

Davis.[138] The last thirty years of annual meeting programs for the OAH and the AHA further confirm the growing leadership, acceptance, and prominence of women and women of color within the field of US women's history. Indeed, the women's and gender history content of the 2024 OAH annual meeting program would suggest that BIPOC women's history currently accounts for much of the scholarly momentum in the field. Further evidence of this trend is that the OAH, which currently offers three annual monetary prizes in American women's history, has regularly recognized scholarship by and about Black women since 1990 with over two-thirds of the winning submissions focused substantively or totally on women of color.[139]

If in the 1970s, historians of women had sought to understand the impact of race on women of color, class on women of the laboring classes, and gender and sexuality on an undifferentiated category of women, by the 1980s this no longer sufficed. Most historians of women adopted approaches to analyzing women's pasts that recognized the simultaneous workings of multiple elements of identity on women in the past. In other words, multiple elements of social location and identity including, but not limited to, race, class, gender, and sexuality bore upon women's historical experiences simultaneously in any given historical context. This theoretical direction was consistent with the kind of intersectional theory introduced in a different disciplinary context by legal scholar Kimberlé Crenshaw in 1989.[140] However, historians did not adopt the term "intersectional" in their writing in the late twentieth century, since they had been developing their own theoretical approaches to understanding the race, class, and gender triad well before 1989.

Instead, by 1992, despite broader cultural concerns over too much attention to diversity "fragmenting" US history, a new consensus regarding mutually imbricated, compounded, serial effects of all of these factors on historical subjects was firmly in place in American women's history.[141] Elsa Barkley Brown acknowledged that women's historians had addressed difference in terms of race, class, gender, and sexuality. But she also suggested this was not enough. The next step was to consider "the relational nature of those differences" by examining, for example, the way that white women's lives existed as they did only in relation to the lives of women of color. At the "risk of over-simplifying," she offered the example of Black women's greater labor force participation and middle-class white women who had domestic servants and thus the ability to engage in voluntarism as factors that distinguished them from each other.[142] Similarly, by 1992, Nancy Hewitt suggested that it wasn't enough to study elements of social location separately. She argued that historians needed to investigate how multiple factors of identity and experience melded together to create "compounded differences." Once fused, those elements become inseparable, something altogether distinct, like a chemical compound.[143] Historians too borrowed from feminist sociologists, political scientists, and philosophers as they reached for theoretical approaches that would be constructive and fruitful, rather than de(con)structive and divisive.[144] They were determined to remain focused on real lives and real structures and systems and to evaluate empirical evidence about diverse groups of women. These strategies created an indisputable place for women's history in the US field and helped historians weather the winds of post-structuralism and postmodernism by remaining rooted in empirical research.[145]

Of course, race is just one particularly salient category of analysis that historians of American women have vigorously examined. The histories of working women of diverse ethnic, racial, and class backgrounds and in a wide array of industries and professions is prolific and wide ranging. Thomas Dublin, Ava Baron, Alice Kessler-Harris, Maurine Greenwald, Ruth Milkman, Dolores Janiewski, Dorothy Sue Cobble, Rosalind Rosenberg, and Margaret Rossiter are just a few of the many scholars who have examined the work lives of American women in specific industries and professions of the nineteenth and twentieth centuries.[146] There are many fine histories of women's working-class culture and involvement in American labor movements offered by the likes of Susan Porter Benson, Kathy Peiss, Nan Enstad, and Annelise Orleck.[147] Scholars who have traced women's political efforts to transform how the US government addressed women's place in the shifting political economy of America include Kathryn Kish Sklar, Dorothy Sue Cobble, Landon Storrs, Cynthia Harrison, and Elisabeth Israels Perry.[148] Examinations of the mobilizations of both conservative and radical women now form part of the field's canon.[149] Historians of women, gender, and sexuality, including Estelle Freedman, John D'Emilio, Leila Rupp, Lillian Faderman, and Finn Enke, have been instrumental in moving the histories of LGBTQ women into American academic historical discourse.[150] For more than fifty years, scholars have thoroughly tilled and cultivated many other subfields of American women's history. They address so many arenas and avenues of women's lives that they could occupy an avid reader for a lifetime.

The insights of the women's history movement, taken in tandem with efforts to develop the histories of other categories of historically marginalized and disenfranchised Americans, have transformed the narratives of American history. This accumulation of new historical knowledge has been so profound and has such radical potential that it has continued to provoke conservative reaction. Silencing inclusive, critical histories in public schools has become a central plank of conservative political platforms. They have committed to re-sanitizing the narratives of American history.[151] Yet, in an era marked by the inability to control or stem the flow of information, it is unlikely they will be successful in this censorial mission. American historians' long decades of work surfacing how race, class, gender, and other markers of difference have figured in women's history, working people's histories, ethnic and sexual minority history, and Black history have paid off for current generations—both for scholars and students. A more diverse array of Americans can, if they so choose, now see themselves reflected in their American history lessons. In 1971, history textbooks and curricula presented America's past within a very narrow national political framework in which great men of European ancestry—mostly Anglo-American—dominated. Today, educators develop textbooks and curricula honeycombed with the intersecting stories of men, women, immigrants, entrepreneurs, and workers and the stories of people of of European, African, Asian, Indigenous, and Latinx ancestry. The great scholarly ferment of the women's history movement during the late twentieth century, among other scholarly shifts in American history, made this possible. Diverse feminist historians put their proto-intersectional feminism into professional practice in the late twentieth century. In doing so, they were attempting to create feminist, anti-racist intellectual and professional environments through dialogue and allyship. What they wrought collectively was radical epistemological and institutional change.

Chapter 11

Women's History in the Public Eye in an Era of Polarized Politics, 1972–2000

In September 1972, before Richard Nixon's reelection, the Smithsonian Institution's National Museum of American History (NMAH) opened an exhibit titled *The Right to Vote*.[1] This exhibit was designed to mark the 1971 ratification of the Twenty-Sixth Amendment to the US Constitution that lowered the voting age to eighteen. Edith Mayo, recently appointed to a post in the Political History Division, was assigned to the project.[2] As curatorial assistant, she gathered materials for the exhibit from the campaigns of Nixon, George McGovern, and Shirley Chisolm. But her vision was broad and stretched beyond traditional political campaigns. Despite the disapproval of the museum's director, Daniel Boorstin,[3] she sought out materials that would highlight historic struggles to expand American democracy. Indian rights activists of the Menominee nation who had launched a get out the Indian vote campaign for 1972 and Black civil rights activist John Lewis of the Voter Education Project responded enthusiastically. Lewis donated materials and his organization funded an exhibit catalog—something the museum was unwilling to do. The exhibit featured material on woman suffrage, too. Overall, under Mayo's guidance, the exhibit reflected the diverse voting rights groups who spoke out, organized, marched, picketed, went on hunger strikes, and were ridiculed, assaulted, and jailed for their efforts before achieving their goals over the course of the twentieth century.[4]

The exhibit was due to run until the beginning of February 1973. It was closed early, before Nixon's second inauguration on January 20, 1973. According to Mayo, Nixon's inaugural committee deemed it "too controversial for good Republicans to see" and demanded its closure. Mayo explained:

> That, of course, was the election where the Committee to Reelect the President was doing all of its nefarious deeds [for example, the Watergate break-ins]. . . . The people from CREEP [Committee to Re-Elect the President] bodily migrated into the inaugural committee. When they came to sort of "case the place" for the inaugural ball and inaugural festivities, which they had had a tradition of holding at the [National Museum of American History], and the Air and Space Museum, and the Kennedy Center, . . . and saw this "Right to Vote" show they just about freaked out, and went to the assistant director, and said that this show was

too controversial for good Republicans to see, and they closed it during the inaugural week, and it remained closed until the end of January when it came down. . . . They physically closed the exhibition. I was called into the assistant director's office and told if I went to the *Washington Post* I would lose my job. . . . They [members of Nixon's inaugural committee] were appalled by sights of women picketing in front of the White House, and Blacks on the march at Selma, and Indians voting! . . . If it hadn't been so personally frustrating and traumatic for me it would have been a hoot . . . , but at the time it was pretty scary. . . . Even my conservative colleagues thought it was a bit much to close the show. . . . It was exactly like being on [Nixon's] Enemies List. I felt I'd really arrived.[5]

Mayo understood the negative reaction to the exhibit as an indication that the content hit home by challenging traditional conservative conceptions of whose history mattered.

Conservative Republicans in the ascendant "New Right" took American history seriously, as both a reflection and a shaper of American culture. This example of their censure of the new social and political histories of women and people of color attests to how these histories undercut the ability of the Right to appeal to American voters through uncritical renderings of the nation's past. Prior to the 1960s, traditional history narratives, including those featured in museums, were replete with American exceptionalism and focused on white male founders, leaders, and mavericks. They typically ignored America's diversity, paradoxes and inequalities and the conflicts that featured prominently in much of the cutting-edge scholarship by the 1970s. To recenter history on women and marginalized racial, ethnic, sexual, and economic groups was, as Mayo perceived, a challenge to the powerful white men who had dominated the nation and its history since its founding. Mayo found her work at the Smithsonian to be in the political crosshairs of an increasingly polarized public discourse on American history and identity.

Mayo became a museum professional in the wake of the civil rights movement and at the height of the women's liberation movement. She was eager to design historical exhibits featuring the contributions of women and people of color to American political history. But as a federal employee in the nation's premier museum, she faced censure by political operatives opposed to presenting knowledge as it was being recast by women and minorities. Mayo claimed that she felt she had "really arrived," when the Nixon inaugural committee targeted the content of her show. She knew she had created a political impact strong enough to provoke opposition; her work incorporating women and people of color mattered. Indeed, this episode foreshadowed history's place in the culture wars of the late twentieth century. Over the next two decades,

Reagan Republicans of the New Right would make controlling or taking back the dominant historical narrative, defunding education, and starving agencies that supported social science research a key part of their political and cultural agenda.[6] For them, the social, progressive, and radical history produced over the course of the twentieth century was biased, too critical of America, too divisive, and unpatriotic.[7] They moved to defund and dissolve the National Endowment for the Humanities and to defund the National Archives. They persistently attacked American educators in schools, colleges, and universities and attempted to restrict public access to the National Archives. These efforts continue to this day.

Meanwhile, Mayo's work on the 1972 *Right to Vote* exhibit indicated that the women's history movement too was aiming to do more than shift gendered paradigms within the historical profession. Mayo's work was part of a broader effort to disseminate the insights gained by scholars in academia. Women's historians saw public history, secondary education, and legal and educational consultancy as promising arenas for expanding and transforming Americans' appreciation of women's place in history and society. And they were not alone. The women's history field emerged at a moment when the nation's historians, social studies educators, archivists, and museum professionals felt threatened by conservative censorship and contempt. In 1976, partly in response to Republicans' moves to delegitimize, privatize, and even eliminate government institutions that preserved and made accessible the nation's historical records and sites, historians created the National Coordinating Committee for the Promotion of History (later the National Coalition for History). The organization hired a full-time specialist to lobby Congress and the White House on issues of importance to history professionals.[8]

Public historians and feminist historians joined forces. Efforts to raise the public's awareness of American women's history flourished after 1970 in museums, national parks, K–12 curricular reforms, the mass media, and the emerging digital realm. It was an all-hands-on-deck effort that profoundly impacted the broader culture and informed public policy.

Women's History/Public History—
Museums and the National Park Service

After the controversy over *The Right to Vote* exhibit, Edith Mayo continued a long career with the Smithsonian. Her work on the porcelain place settings used at the White House over several presidential administrations was innovative; she interpreted First Ladies' activities within the informal social elements of DC's political culture. She endeavored to integrate women's history into the museum's programs generally. In her day-to-day work, Mayo initiated projects that featured new approaches to women's history emerging throughout the country. She highlighted women in all areas of life, not only those in traditional politics. Hers was a definition of "political" that included less-formal relations of power.[9]

In the early 1980s, Mayo conceptualized an exhibit, *From Parlor to Politics*, focusing on women's reform movements in the Progressive Era. To create enthusiasm, Mayo planned an event focused on Eleanor Roosevelt. Her life's work as a progressive Democrat spanned women's reform from the Progressive Era through 1961, when she served on the President's Commission on the Status of Women. Collaborating with Smithsonian colleagues Howard Morrison and Shirley Cherkasky to celebrate the hundredth birth anniversary of Roosevelt in 1984, Mayo created a small exhibit called *Eleanor Roosevelt: First Person Singular*.[10] The team designed a walking tour of Washington, DC, and presented a lecture series in which actress Jean Stapleton, known for the television series *All in the Family*, played Roosevelt. Meanwhile, Mayo organized a conference for scholars on the history of the New Deal that included William Chafe, Robert and Joanna Zangrando, and Blanche Wiesen Cook. The conference showcased former New Dealers Esther Peterson and Pauli Murray, both of whom had been progressive feminist civil rights activists at the center of American political developments during the middle decades of the twentieth century.[11] Because the Smithsonian did not provide any funding for these events, Peterson, a former Democratic lobbyist and architect of John F. Kennedy's President's Commission on the Status of Women, helped Mayo secure funding from Congress.[12]

The success of the Eleanor Roosevelt events bolstered Mayo's ambitions to realize the full exhibit she had envisioned earlier, *From Parlor to Politics: Women and Reform in America, 1890–1925*. Roger Kennedy, then director of the NMAH, approved the project but initially indicated that the museum had no funds to support it. Mayo set about securing funds, including a grant from the American Historical Association. The project held such promise that upwards of thirty specialists in New Deal, Progressive Era, and women's history agreed to be consultants. This groundswell of support led to a successful application to the Rockefeller Foundation for a grant of $100,000. At that point, the Smithsonian relented and funded the project with a $350,000 grant from its Special Exhibits Fund.[13] Focused on women's reform organizations ranging from temperance groups, women's clubs, and settlement house workers, to labor unions, Black and Jewish women's civic associations, and public health initiatives launched by women, the exhibit opened in 1990 and remained open until 2004. It became one of the longest-running temporary exhibits in the history of the Smithsonian.[14]

Mayo then shifted her focus to an exhibit reconceptualizing the way the museum had addressed the history of First Ladies. Moving beyond a presentation of their ceremonial roles and restoration of the First Ladies' gown collection, Mayo proposed "politicizing" the exhibit to show how each woman had been instrumental in her husband's administration. When featured in this light, Lou Henry Hoover, Edith Roosevelt, Eleanor Roosevelt, and Mamie Eisenhower stood out as taking active and at times transformative roles in American politics. The exhibit opened in 1992.

Over the next three years, Mayo laid the groundwork for a seventy-fifth anniversary celebration of the ratification of the Nineteenth Amendment. It would not be the first time the museum commemorated the event. The year before Mayo joined the Smithsonian, Keith Melder, author of a 1963 dissertation on the nineteenth-century women's movement and curator in political history at the museum, had created a woman suffrage exhibit in honor of the fiftieth anniversary of the ratification of the Nineteenth Amendment in 1970.[15] In 1995, Mayo pitched the idea of a seventy-fifth anniversary program commemorating the success of the suffrage movement. Mayo recalled that she went to the NMAH's new director, Spencer Crew, asking him to green-light funds for an exhibit and a scholarly conference on the single largest extension of voting rights in the country's history.[16] Crew was the first African American appointed to head the NMAH. Mayo appealed to Crew by pointing out that the date was "a huge political anniversary." Crew's response, according to Mayo, was to question the need for the exhibit and conference. In a 2001 interview conducted by Mary Rothschild, Mayo described her rejoinder to Crew: "'If this were the 75th anniversary of the Emancipation Proclamation, would we even be having this discussion?' which he thought was a really nasty thing to say. I'm not sure I meant it quite as nasty as it came out, but it's sort of like, 'Yoo-hoo, we have this huge political anniversary here. We are the Political History Division. We are the nation's museum. We ought to be doing something.'"[17] Crew never did authorize the exhibit, but Mayo used about $10,000 from a discretionary account that she controlled earmarked for lectures, tours, speaking engagements, and travel to organize the conference.

With her proposal rejected by the Smithsonian's top leadership, she instead collaborated with the National Museum of Women in the Arts, which had incorporated in 1981 but took until 1987 to open its doors in DC.[18] This museum provided personnel and publicity for the conference, which was ultimately held in the NMAH auditorium. Mayo had no support from the Smithsonian on this initiative, but the conference, nevertheless, attracted a lively audience. CSPAN agreed to give national publicity to the conference by recording and broadcasting it, and even though representatives of the Smithsonian administration tried to eject the CSPAN crew from the NMAH auditorium, their efforts failed, and the cameras rolled.[19] The conference also counted on the participation of prominent scholars in the field. When it opened on August 25, 1995, Edith

Mayo introduced Ellen DuBois as the keynote speaker. DuBois was a foremost scholar in American feminism and woman suffrage. Joining her on the panel were Marjorie Spruill Wheeler and Rosalyn Terborg-Penn, among others. As the conference took place, Wheeler announced to the audience that a note had just arrived from Bill Clinton's White House proclaiming August 26, 1995, to be Women's Equality Day.[20]

Mayo had a significant impact on the content of the nation's premier history museum during her tenure. Yet even after nearly twenty-five years at the museum, when American women's history was well integrated into academic scholarship and discourse, Mayo still found herself defending the relevance and legitimacy of women's history at the Smithsonian. Public history remained an active front in the battle for women's history. After Mayo retired in 1995, she continued to publish and lecture on women's history, primarily focused on the impact of First Ladies on American politics.[21] And she continued consulting broadly on public history projects about women.[22]

Meanwhile, Heather Huyck came to exercise some influence over the content of exhibits at the National Park Service during a decades-long career spent actively integrating women into NPS sites.[23] She originally took a job as a seasonal park worker for the NPS in 1971, and by 1980 she was a content specialist in women's history in the NPS—the only person in that position. A course at Carleton College had awakened her interest in women's history. Then, as a graduate student at the University of Minnesota, she had been a field-worker on the Women's History Sources Survey, the project that generated the reference work promoted by the Organization of American Historians' Committee on the Status of Women and managed by Clarke Chambers and Andrea Hinding.[24] Huyck had a special fondness for historic landmarks and parks, having visited many in her childhood, which is why she chose to work in public history.[25] While at the NPS, she developed an understanding of how to make women's history a part of the nation's public history. Beginning in the late 1970s, Huyck participated in public history sessions, workshops, and conferences at OAH meetings and at the Southwest Institute for Research on Women in Tucson. She trained public historians as interpreters at the NPS training center in Harpers Ferry, Virginia. In 1981, the NPS sent her to Seneca Falls, New York, the site credited as the birthplace of the American women's rights movement, to consult on the early planning and development of the Women's Rights National Historical Park.[26]

The concept for the park had originated with local history groups, including the Seneca Falls Consortium and the Elizabeth Cady Stanton Foundation, and with scholars active in the Upstate New York Women's History Organization in 1979. These groups lobbied Congress to establish the park in Seneca Falls.[27] Congress approved the legislation for the site in December 1980 but by 1982 still had not appropriated funds to build it or its programs.[28] UNYWHO and the Seneca Falls Consortium mounted an intense lobbying campaign in support of adequate congressional appropriations for the park. In their efforts to raise money to purchase and renovate the Elizabeth Cady Stanton House and the Wesleyan Chapel, where the famous Declaration of Sentiments and Resolutions had been read in 1848, the Elizabeth Cady Stanton Foundation attracted a star-studded cast to its Honorary Trustees Board. These included star of the *M*A*S*H* TV series Alan Alda, feminist artist Judy Chicago, feminist activists Betty Friedan and Gloria Steinem, congresswoman Shirley Chisholm, presidential advisor Linda Johnson Robb, anthropologist Ashley Montague, and feminist theorist Adrienne Rich.[29] The new National Park Service superintendent warned that unless the Seneca Falls project could draw national attention to the prospective park, it would go the way of other federal programs for women, "archival oblivion."[30] In 1982, UNYWHO and the Seneca Falls Consortium mounted a major conference and festival in the village of Seneca Falls to give shape to the plans. Alan Alda attended the opening ceremony, bringing added national media attention to the event. The response from every corner of the women's history movement was overwhelmingly positive.

A central figure in the initiatives for the Seneca Falls park was Judith Wellman, who from 1981 to 1983 served as the chair of the OAH Committee on the Status of Women. She was also a founder of UNYWHO. Her institutional connections helped her garner support from other academic women's historians for this event.[31] She'd been appointed to the OAH-CSW by Gerda Lerner, who along with Anne Firor Scott and Joan Hoff-Wilson were at the conference and collectively represented the OAH as current or former officers of that association. Heather Huyck represented the National Park Service; Patricia Miller King attended as director of the Schlesinger Library. Assistance was rendered from afar by the AHA's Noralee Frankel and the Smithsonian Institution's Anita Rapone and Edith Mayo. Betty Morgan of National Women's History Week and Bettye Collier-Thomas of the Bethune Museum and the National Archives for Black Women's History also participated.[32] A dozen more leading scholars attended.[33] Thus, this major public history initiative had the support of many individual scholars as well as more formal history institutions.

The Elizabeth Cady Stanton Foundation claimed success when on July 19, 1983, the 135th anniversary of the reading of the Declaration of Sentiments and Resolutions, Congress appropriated a half-million dollars for the Women's Rights National Historical Park. New York senators Daniel Patrick Moynihan and Alfonse D'Amato drafted the appropriations bill. The Women's Rights National Historical Park is still in operation to this day.[34] Eventually both the Stanton House and site of the Wesleyan Chapel were purchased, restored, and put into operation as public history sites by the National Park Service. The NPS also acquired the Mary Anne M'Clintock House and the Hunt House in nearby Waterloo, New York, where two of the fomenters of the 1848 convention lived and planned their historic deeds.[35]

Public historians and regional women's history groups, like UNYWHO, an affiliate of the national Conference Group on Women's History, reached beyond the ivory tower and national historical associations. By the early 1980s, these groups were bringing programs to schoolchildren, as with Minnesota's Teaching Women's History Center, and to the public, as with the Women's Rights National Historical Park of the National Park Service. Scholars like Judith Wellman, for example, who was active across multiple professional associations, advanced women's history in both the public and academic spheres. Academic work had public applications, and regional work had national ramifications. For Heather Huyck, who saw women's history as a transformative and consciousness-raising force, the Women's Rights National Historical Park was an exemplary outcome, reflecting her broader vision.

> I was trying both to get park units to understand they had women's history and to get more park units focused on women's history. . . . We had a joke for a long time that there was one site where there was no women's history. We thought it was Alcatraz, but then we found out that the wardens' families lived there and the prisoners' families visited. . . . So we always talked about the "Alcatraz principle"—that the only question is, "How hard do you want to look [for women] and how do you interpret it?," not, "Were there women?"[36]

Huyck's consultation on Seneca Falls, which she saw as a "landmark theme study in women's history," was part of her larger intellectual project of integrating women into the interpretation of America's historic places everywhere. She knew that women had a presence in all national monuments and parks.[37] In 2001 she remarked,

> The park system is now 383 units . . . everything from Constitution Gardens in DC to Yellowstone to Alcatraz. . . . There's women's history all over the place. . . . The basic understanding I've always had was you had this national system of delivery, to put it into marketing terms. You have a built-in audience. We get [millions of] visitors a year, and you have quality [resources]. A more recent director of the Park Service said it was a huge campus, but what I've seen is it was an amazing set of resources and delivery to willing audiences "of who we are and where we came from." If there's a piece that's core to me it's *that*. Then the piece that's right there in terms of my own background in women's history is to tell the "whole story" at each and every one of these sites. So more recently I

did a piece on women and the Civil War, and I said those battlefields were people's farmyards. All the horrific stories of your dining room being taken over for surgery and the stories of the women who hid out in the caves of Vicksburg . . . and it's a . . . civil war. It's a domestic war and what does that mean? So, I'm much more conscious now of being able to say by using a feminist approach, by looking at the whole story and the women's history, you get a totally different interpretation of what happened.[38]

Huyck's insight was that women's history, when presented through the National Park Service, could reach millions of Americans who had scarce opportunity to study in a university. The tens of millions of park visitors each year represented an audience who would find in the parks an integrated view of women in history.[39] This meant introducing women's stories into existing sites as well as creating sites dedicated solely to women. Women's historians—even as they struggled for legitimacy within academia—were keenly aware of the need to introduce their grand epistemological project to the broader public.[40]

Meanwhile, academic women's history got a good deal of mainstream publicity in the 1970s and 1980s. William Chafe's 1972 book, *The American Woman: Her Changing Social, Economic and Political Roles, 1920–1970*, was an early account of American women in the first fifty years after the suffrage amendment.[41] The work had been Chafe's doctoral dissertation at Columbia University, where he worked under William Leuchtenberg.[42] Chafe credited his interest in women's history to his immersion in New Left activism at Columbia and to the women's liberation movement overall, including encounters with "very radical feminist students" and discussions in his own home on the division of household labor.[43] Duke University hired Chafe in 1971 with the support of Anne Firor Scott, who proclaimed after his job interview, waving her fists in the air, "We're going to have the best one-two punch in American women's history in the country. We'll be training the best women's historians in the country."[44] Chafe was one of a handful of men researching and teaching women's history and active in the women's history movement in the 1970s. He, along with Carl Degler, who edited a book on Charlotte Perkins Gilman among his other publications on race and gender, and Thomas Dublin, whose classic study on women in the textile industry, *Women at Work: The Transformation of Work and Community in Lowell, Massachusetts, 1826–1860*, won the Bancroft Prize in 1980, worked in the little-known tradition of male allies in the historical profession.[45] Gerda Lerner had taken Degler's course at Columbia in the early 1960s when he was a visiting professor. Degler, president of the AHA in 1986, collaborated with Lerner and Anne Firor Scott in both the OAH and AHA.[46]

In the 1970s, mainstream media outlets frequently called on Chafe to talk about his work in women's history. Chafe recalled, "I was on talk shows with major feminist figures on the radio. I was on Studs Turkel in Chicago. I was on a number of TV shows in Boston, New York, Philadelphia and Chicago, Cleveland. So, I was doing a whole lot of that stuff. So, there was a lot of attention being given to the book, far more than one would ever have dreamed was possible for a first book by someone who at that point had just turned thirty."[47] Chafe's work was the subject of news articles in North Carolina, Los Angeles, and Chicago after his book was published. A *Winston-Salem Journal* article from 1973 titled "History's Tide Runs with the Feminists: What's Happened to Women? Historian's Book Tells All" captured the public's interest.[48] The *New York Times* published occasional editorials on the field, wrote reviews of new scholarship, and reported on controversies arising in the women's history subculture.

Ms. magazine also gave women's history considerable visibility in the 1970s and early 1980s. Gerda Lerner was interviewed on the importance of women's history in 1981, and Barbara Haber, curator of books and manuscripts at the Schlesinger Library, was named the "Arbiter of Women's History" in 1982.[49] *Ms.* featured the launch of annual Women's History Week celebrations, which was initially a state-level effort in California in the early 1970s led by Molly Murphy McGregor. In 1979 McGregor created the nonprofit National Women's History Project that developed and distributed K–12 curriculum packets throughout the country with an eye to forming a Women's History Week with national reach. By 1982, it had garnered congressional support, and since then the month of March has been officially designated as Women's History Month each year.[50] When Joan Jacobs Brumberg went on a book tour and appeared on *The Oprah Winfrey Show* in 1998 to talk about her book *The Body Project*, she again strengthened the interface between academic historians and the public.[51] Brumberg suggested that women's history produced in universities should be made more accessible to the public.[52]

The impact of the women's history movement in the United States—of the relationship between the public and the academic women's historians of the 1970s and 1980s—was described by Kathryn Kish Sklar and Gerda Lerner in 1989 when they observed, "During the past twenty years a new field of history has captured the imagination of professional historians and the reading public. At a time when many criticize the profession for losing touch with a wider readership, the field of women's history has won that readership. Lovers of history and writers of history both realize that the inclusion of female experience vastly expands, invigorates, and complicates the scope of historical inquiry."[53] This statement stands in contrast to Judith Zinsser's treatment of public history initiatives. Zinsser acknowledged there was a "Popular Feminist Initiative" that paralleled the more academic movement she herself was part of.[54] She recognized Gerda Lerner and a handful of academic historians involved in

Women's History Week and their relationship to McGregor's nonacademic National Women's History Project. Yet she characterized popular grassroots initiatives, like the National Women's History Project, as separate from rather than connected to academic initiatives.[55] Still, there were clear and strong connections between popular women's history initiatives and scholarly ones. Working collectively from the 1970s to the 1990s, scholars built a field and a professional subculture characterized by cooperation among various types of history makers. For this work to have staying power and legitimacy, it had to be anchored by vetted, responsible scholarship that could survive changing political winds or the ebb and flow of popular interest.

Historians of women were also at the helm of the National Coordinating Committee for the Promotion of History (NCCPH) from 1976 to 2000. The NCCPH was incorporated in 1976 as a nonprofit lobbying group representing history professionals, including historians, educators, archivists, preservationists, and museum professionals. The AHA and OAH provided initial funding. By the early 1980s, other organizations, such as the Society of American Archivists, the American Political Science Association, and the American Library Association, joined in supporting the NCCPH.[56] The organization relied on a single hired lobbyist who worked out of an office in Washington, DC, made available rent-free in the AHA headquarters. Overall, the NCCPH advocated for the history profession with legislative and regulatory bodies.[57] The organization's first mission was to address the crisis in the history job market by promoting alternate careers for historians in public history and government. Arnita Jones was director for the initial launch of the organization, followed by public historian Page Putnam Miller, who was director and chief lobbyist from 1980 to 2000.[58] Jones and Miller regularly reported on their activities in the pages of the newsletters of the AHA, the OAH, and the Coordinating Committee on Women in the Historical Profession–Conference Group on Women's History.[59]

The NCCPH was centrally concerned with government records preservation and access, as these things were necessary to the work of history professionals. The history of records preservation and access is partisan in nature. The National Archives had been established as an independent agency in 1934 under Franklin D. Roosevelt's Democratic New Deal. Then in 1949, the Republican-controlled 80th Congress attached the National Archives to the General Services Administration—an office that oversees building maintenance and office supplies.[60] In 1967, the Freedom of Information Act became law under the Democratic supermajority that resulted from Lyndon B. Johnson's landslide victory in 1964.[61] The law was meant to ensure the people's access to government records, as a means of keeping government accountable. When the Reagan administration proposed cutting in half the funding for the National Endowment for the Humanities and promised to use an executive order to limit access to historical documents rescued from oblivion by the 1967 Freedom of Information Act, the NCCPH immediately knew this would impact historians' ability to do their work.[62] Archivists and historians began to advocate to make the National Archives an independent agency, free of partisan politics. In 1985, the 99th Congress again made the National Archives an independent agency. At the time, Democrats securely controlled the House, while Republicans maintained a narrow majority in the Senate.

Page Putnam Miller described her work as a lobbyist for the NCCPH. It included "pounding the halls of Congress, and knowing the legislative aides, and testifying at hearings, and showing up for mark-ups [for appropriations bills]. ... The other half [was] working with your constituency. My constituency were university professors, public historians, and archivists."[63] Miller was dedicated to pushing policy issues through the halls of Congress that were important to the work of historians writ large. She worked on funding appropriations for the NEH, for example, but also on agency appointments, confirmation hearings, and changing regulatory policies. Miller's work was buffeted by political winds. The New Right Republicans of the Newt Gingrich era proposed their "Contract with America" that included in its emphasis on small government the elimination of the Department of Education and a stripping away of the social safety net created by liberal Democratic administrations. Progressive women had been active in the construction of the safety net created by the Roosevelt administration in the 1930s and revitalized by the Johnson administration in the 1960s. Thus, conservatives' reaction against progressive feminism, which they saw as both "anti-family" and communistic, went hand in hand with their antipathy to women's history, which they saw as the work of "bitter" feminists.[64]

At the NCCPH, Miller did not have a mandate to promote women's history, as this was not the central thrust of the organization. Nevertheless, she promoted the field when she could, and her work aligned with the goals of the women's history movement on several important overlapping projects. As professional historians, those who wrote on women in history had interests aligned with the profession at large. They advocated for education, research funding, and records access and preservation. Miller, as head of the NCCHP, championed these issues. Additionally, Miller worked with others, including OAH executive director and *Journal of Women's History* founder Joan Hoff and the NPS's Heather Huyck, to increase women's representation in public history sites.[65] A major initiative undertaken by Miller was to increase the number of registered history landmarks that featured women while pushing the National Park Service to develop some into interpretive sites. Miller also worked to include more well-rounded interpretations of women's role in NPS exhibits that were already in place but not specifically designed to highlight women. Miller's third major concern centered on the thematic framework of the NPS, which she thought should incorporate more of the recent scholarship in social history and women's history.[66]

Recognizing the urgent necessity to rethink and reshape US historic landmarks to feature women's history, Miller collaborated with public and academic historians to develop studies that would encourage the selection and development of more women's history landmark sites by the National Park Service. Building on earlier studies that had noted the invisibility of women in landmarks and sites, Miller brought the fields of public and women's history together.[67] The first important step in this process was the preparation of thematic studies that would provide the essential historical context and analysis to inform decisions about which sites should be nominated for landmark status and potentially developed into park sites.[68] Miller recruited seven prominent historians to contribute to the volume *Reclaiming the Past*, which ultimately spotlighted homes and businesses of women including Clara Barton, Susan B. Anthony, Madame C. J. Walker, and Zora Neale Hurston, as well as major sites of significance to women's history like the Wesleyan Chapel in Seneca Falls, Hull House in Chicago, and the Triangle Shirtwaist Factory in New York City. Miller's introduction to the volume pointed out that only 5 percent of the nation's historical landmarks, parks, and sites featured women's history, and she insisted that a corrective was necessary. Principally, Miller and the contributors to this volume wanted the public to connect to the exciting developments in the new women's history of the late twentieth century.[69] Historical structures and landmarks could make these developments visible to the general public in ways that scholarly monographs and organizing within the profession could not. They were capturing the attention of new audiences.

As specific sites were nominated for landmark status, NPS reviewers' concerns over each building's physical and historical integrity were raised, as were political concerns.[70] Sites connected to Emma Goldman, early twentieth-century anarchist feminist, for example, and Molly (Mary) Dewson, prominent Democrat and New Dealer, were rejected out of hand. The group in charge of choosing sites to add to the register of sites for development vetoed a Goldman site because she was an anarchist; Dewson was rejected because a reviewer thought she sounded "like a lesbian."[71] Thus, reviewers imposed their cultural and political biases on a feminist history project initially conceived to be more inclusive.

In 1990, the Democratic 101st Congress passed Public Law 101–628, Section 1209, mandating that the NPS update and revise its interpretive framework. Miller worked again with Huyck. The original framework—created in 1936 when historical interpretation focused on American progress and the achievements of political and military leaders—sorely lacked insights from scholarship developed after World War II.[72] In Miller's analysis, the 1936 framework had a rigidly conceived set of thirty-five thematic areas in which to categorize and interpret historic properties. After 1990, the NPS called on historians, archaeologists, and anthropologists to create a dynamic model for interpreting material culture that could convey the connectedness of people in action, both in groups and as individuals.[73] The final framework, adopted in 1994, included eight themes: "Peopling Places," "Creating Social Institutions and Movements," "Expressing Cultural Values," "Shaping the Political Landscape," "Developing the American Economy," "Expanding Science and Technology," "Transforming the Environment," and "Changing Role of the United States in the World Community."[74] Another result of these efforts was the publication of a series of pamphlets explaining the new NPS interpretive framework and its application to various subfields of American history. In the pamphlets, Miller and collaborators focused on integrating labor history, Black history, Chicano history, and women's history. The first booklet in the series was called *Exploring Our Common Past: Interpreting Women's History in the National Park Service.*[75]

Miller retired from the NCCPH in 2000. In a 2001 interview, she suggested,

> [Women's history] struck a chord. It was a part of the past that people really wanted to know about. . . . If you're just a fly on the wall and you hear people going through house museums, you'll hear "Oh, my grandmother had one of those," or "Do you remember such and such[?]" . . . There's a kind of way in which [to] connect with your own past through this, but I think that women's history has had a sophistication about looking at a more comprehensive and authentic way of viewing the past. Previously the past had been observed in such a narrow way, through upper-class male leaders basically. So, to really open it up, it was exciting to think of a new way of viewing the past. . . . U.S. history has changed as a result of women's history. Even if you look at the recent textbooks, and that's really the final test. You start out in new scholarship with monographs, but it's when those monographs get into college texts and then when they get into high school texts you know you've really made a change.[76]

This reference to high school texts reminds us that women's historians in the late twentieth century focused on building the scholarly foundations upon which to base public history and curricular materials for both collegiate and K–12 education. Yet, the decentralized nature of public K–12 education in America meant that this effort had far less success than it enjoyed at the university level. Ultimately, professionally trained historians don't control the content of K–12 history education. Moreover, the public controversy over national history standards that consumed the National Endowment for the Humanities from 1991 to 1996 highlighted the power of conservative opposition to the new scholarly historical perspectives.

Lynne Cheney, a George H. W. Bush appointee to head the National Endowment for the Humanities (1986–93) and wife of Dick Cheney, vice president under George W. Bush, decried the "dark and gloomy" portrait of American history in the national history standards. As chair of the NEH, she had initially approved the drafting of national history standards but later lobbied the US Senate to reject the standards once she saw that they included heavy doses of Black, social, and women's history that exposed various areas of oppression, inequality, and struggle. At her urging, the standards were voted down in a 99–1 vote in the Senate and were never formally adopted.[77] Condemning "narratives of victimization," whether of working-class people, people of color, or American women, Cheney (and Phyllis Schlafly) insisted that writing on systemic inequality, as had taken place from the 1970s through the 1990s throughout academia, was essentially left-wing propaganda biased against America, Western civilization, and white male historical figures. Conservative academics joined the chorus. Allan Bloom published *The Closing of the American Mind* in 1987 to discredit the new social history. Leaving New Left intellectual orthodoxy unchallenged, Bloom argued, was detrimental to critical thinking.[78] From the late 1980s, conservative public intellectuals repeatedly insisted that patriotic history was under assault from the New Left and, if ignored, would make young people "hate their country."[79] And cultural conservatives active since the 1990s have continued to decry what they see as the corrosive, divisive effect of "political correctness," including revised and expanded historical analyses that emphasize inequality and unequal power relations between economic classes, different ethnic and racial groups, and women and men. Loud cries for a history curriculum designed around narratives of American exceptionalism and America's great leaders came into the spotlight as the conservative organizing principle for public K–12 history education in the 1990s. This remains hotly contested—and is far from settled.[80] Indeed, the flames have been rekindled by politicians like Ron DeSantis of Florida rallying cultural conservatives to "Stop Woke Education." But the hypocrisy of these complaints should be obvious to anyone familiar with American historiography, since had it not been for the social history of the 1960s and 1970s sweeping into academic history, the engine of consensus represented by the traditionalist "consensus school" of history with its emphasis on powerful white men, dominant through the 1950s, would have continued to reign unchallenged itself, standing as a singular politically correct, orthodox, conservative version of American history that in essence disappeared the majority of Americans.[81] Moreover, most of the scholarship on working people, women, and people of color was positive in its approach, surfacing these people's existence and agency and their refusal to be "victimized" or disappeared from the annals of history. It was far from "dark and gloomy."

Scholars in the women's history movement persisted in presenting new research and offering their fresh interpretations. In tandem, Heather Huyck, Edith Mayo, and Page Putnam Miller wove working people, people of color, and women into the American historical narrative as presented in the Smithsonian Institution's NMAH and the National Park Service. In doing so, they joined university-based academic historians in raising the profile of diverse women in American history and culture.

Feminist Historians as Public Intellectuals: Policy, the Courts, and Public Discourse, 1978–2000

In keeping with the historical philosophy that women's history needs feminism and feminism needs women's history, late twentieth-century historians of women have at times ventured beyond the ivory tower and formal public history sites to impact the broader society. As public intellectuals and expert witnesses, feminist historians have brought their expertise to bear on public opinion and public policy. They have interfaced with all branches of the federal government, including the presidency, Congress, and the Supreme Court. They have attempted to shape history as it unfolds by offering non-historians analyses that rest upon the increasingly rich body of scholarship produced in the academy.

An early example of feminist historians' direct efforts to influence public policy was seen in their active support for the ratification of the Equal Rights Amendment. Passed by Congress in 1972, it was sent out for ratification by the states with a ten-year time limit—a requirement not stipulated in the Constitution. The ERA quickly generated both widespread support from feminists and opposition from conservatives. Feminist historians came out strongly in favor, and it became the subject of the keynote address at the Fourth Big Berkshire Conference on the History of Women in 1978.[82] Soon after, members of the CCWHP, OAH, and AHA created the Money in Friendly Territory initiative to support the ratification movement. The initiative pressured the OAH and AHA to boycott states that hadn't yet ratified the ERA by refusing to hold their large annual conventions in those states. Money in Friendly Territory participants secured pledges from 1,000 historians promising to put their annual membership fees in an escrow account until the two organizations agreed to support the boycott.[83] Ultimately, both the OAH and the AHA agreed to the boycott. In Illinois, historians participated in a pro-ERA march of 30,000–50,000 on May 10, 1980.[84] In 1982, Kitty Sklar sent out a letter as chair of the AHA Committee on Women Historians asking the major national and regional women's history groups around the country, including the CCWHP, the Association of Black Women Historians, and Washington Women Historians, to sponsor a planned AHA session on the "fate of the ERA" featuring Jane De Hart Mathews, Mary F. Berry, and Joan Scott, among others. The letter also solicited funds to support bringing feminist activists to a reception following the panel. Most of these organizations sent along their support.[85]

Feminist historians also reached out to non-historian feminist activists. They disseminated their scholarly work among feminist organizations and independent feminist media outlets then proliferating around the country. Quarterly newsletters of the CCWHP and CGWH of the mid-1970s through the 1990s reported much of this work. In July 1979, Gerda Lerner, Alice Kessler-Harris, and Amy Swerdlow hosted the Summer Institute in Women's History for Leaders of National Women's Organizations at Sarah Lawrence College. The institute was designed to provide the organizers with the space and time to develop ideas about how to "bring women's history into the work of their organizations" and raise awareness of the need to preserve organizational records. Forty-five women leaders representing thirty-seven national women's organizations attended the seventeen-day institute. Lerner likened the experience to a full semester course with three intense seminars. Topics ranged from "Women, Lifecycles, and Family Roles" and "Women in the Economy" to "Women in Community and Political Life." Participating groups included the National Council of Negro Women, Church Women United, the Coalition of Labor Union Women, Comisión Feminíl Mexicana, the National Coalition against Domestic Violence, the National Gay Task Force, the National Women's Political Caucus, and the Girl Scouts, USA, among others.[86]

The Summer Institute also pressed participants to lobby for a national Women's History Week to be celebrated the second week in March each year. This project and action plan were developed by Molly Murphy McGregor of California. Participants were encouraged to write to their governors, to President Carter, and to their congresspersons. Representative Barbara Mikulski supported a resolution in the House, and by 1980 Senator Orrin Hatch agreed to sponsor S.J. Res. 211 in the Senate to establish Women's History Week.[87] The work of the institute garnered national media attention in December 1979, when *Ms.* ran a four-page feature by Lerner and Barbara Omolade, a Black women's historian at the College of New Rochelle.[88] Omolade, a staff member of the Women's Action Alliance and a sponsor of the institute, served as the project's administrative coordinator. The *Ms.* article promoted Women's History Week "kits" produced by the Sonoma County Commission on the Status of Women to be used for local celebrations. Molly McGregor would go on to form the National Women's History Project. Meanwhile, Berenice Carroll urged feminist historians to work with feminist theorists and activists to publish in other radical feminist media outlets, for example, *off our backs*, a feminist magazine.[89]

These examples are evidence that feminist historians in the women's history movement did not see their work as only academic or as merely adjacent to the women's movement but rather as an integral part of it—or as Linda Gordon asserted, "as the academic wing of the women's liberation movement."[90] Yet this happy marriage between feminist activism and women's history scholarship was often fraught. Gordon understood very well the benefits and risks of combining feminist politics with scholarship. Her blockbuster 1976 work on the American birth control movement, *Woman's Body, Woman's Right*, had garnered both widespread acclaim and harsh criticism from within the ranks of historians.[91] Perhaps this was to be expected, given its publication in the early days of the women's history movement when feminist historians were still battling for acceptance in the discipline against a sometimes-recalcitrant, male-dominated profession. It was also to be expected given the centrality and controversiality of women's bodily and reproductive autonomy to the twentieth-century women's movement. Cultural conservatives had long opposed the legalization of birth control as immoral and anti-family. For example, Margaret Sanger, the recognized leader of the twentieth-century birth control movement in the United States who was arrested in 1917 for distributing information on contraception and opening a birth control clinic, has been a favorite target of both conservatives and pronatalist activists ever since. Her legacy continues to be maligned and misconstrued to this day. Her objective to legalize and expand access to contraception was largely achieved by the end of her life in 1966. In the year before her death, the Planned Parenthood Federation of America, an organization she had founded, and the American Civil Liberties Union secured the first in a series of victories for reproductive health rights when the Supreme Court ruled in 1965 on the legality of contraception for married women (*Griswold v. Connecticut*). This was followed in 1972 by *Eisenstadt v. Baird*, which legalized birth control for single women. Constitutional protection for access to abortion was extended by the court in *Roe v. Wade* in 1973.[92] These victories were won in the waning days of the liberal Warren Court.

That Gordon and other feminist historians of the 1970s were interested in studying the history of the birth control and other radical feminist movements reflected the entwined nature of scholarship and politics. As we've seen, this connection gave the women's history movement its energy but also provoked questions about its objectivity and legitimacy. And though the new women's historians of the women's history movement went far beyond studying the history of feminist activism and fully embraced the scholarly standards of the historical profession, the fact that most were avowed feminists raised the suspicion of conservatives, who either ignored or rejected the new scholarship.

This suspicion was a major catalyst for the rise of organized reactionary conservatism of Republican women like Phyllis Schlafly, Beverly LaHaye, and Connie Marshner.[93] Both the scholarship and reader reaction to it was influenced by politics. But this should not be seen as delegitimizing.

In twentieth-century US historiography, there has always been a detectable parallelism between scholarly research interests and political leanings. This is true of traditional, progressive, consensus, and new social history. Indeed, New Left history, feminist history, and Black history were intended as antidotes to white male elites' dominance of history. They were meant to correct an inherent bias and imbalance in traditional historical scholarship that had long masqueraded as "objective" history. In the historical study of women, this parallelism took several tacks. Just as liberal feminists worked through the courts and other branches of the government to secure expanded rights for women, women's historians worked through mainstream history institutions to open their peers' eyes to women's history. Radical feminists of the women's liberation movement challenged traditional gender constructs and heteronormative standards in society, while radical feminist historians wrote about radical feminists of the past and developed gender history, the history of sexuality, and LGBTQ history. There was a certain parallelism between feminist politics, the research foci of the new women's history, and even the professional strategies these diverse feminist historians developed. Therefore, the negative reaction of conservative women like Phyllis Schlafly to women's history from the 1970s forward should, likewise, be understood as parallel to their ideological response to feminism. That response entailed a doubling down on the preservation of traditional gender roles within the heteronormative family. These conservatives railed against abortion. They associated birth control with sexual libertinism/ sexual revolution—not women's emancipation. They believed equal rights for women threatened the protections and privileges they considered traditional perks for women inside male-headed families. And conservatives understood feminist advances in women's history and reproductive and other rights to be a corollary of liberal democratic politics and progressive perspectives. Therefore, they rejected the new women's history and labeled it as ideologically suspect. This all shows how using women's history as a tool for achieving feminist goals could have unintended consequences. Anti-feminist forces, too, could use women's history to further their political goals. Anti-feminists could offer their own historical interpretations and could cite feminist historical scholarship to indict the "liberal bias" of academia.[94] It doesn't seem to matter to conservatives that women's history and feminist historical scholarship is based on decades of carefully vetted empirical research and analysis.

The possibility that feminist history might be used to the detriment of women was made manifest in 1985 when two feminist historians were recruited to testify on opposing sides in a federal class action lawsuit brought by the Equal Employment Opportunity Commission against Sears, Roebuck, as first mentioned in chapter 9. Sears was accused of sexual discrimination in hiring and promotion practices in violation of Title VII of the Civil Rights Act of 1964. Though Sears attempted to implement policies in compliance with this legislation, lawyers for the EEOC argued that statistical discrepancies between men and women in the hiring and in the promotion of women to higher-paying commission sales and management jobs demonstrated systemic discrimination within the company.

Feminist historians were by this time effectively showing that such practices existed and had long been a concern of organized women's movements going back to the 1840s. American women had increasingly participated in the paid workforce since the Industrial Revolution. But equal opportunity and equal pay for equal work had long eluded them. Women workers were generally understood to be dependents, wives, and mothers first and workers and income earners second. They were said to have different motivations for working and needed different protections within the workplace because of their biological differences and their social role within the family. Occupational sex segregation was standard in American society. Lines of work that became feminized were downgraded in terms of status and pay. The historical record also showed that women were often eager to work in higher-paying "men's" occupations when the opportunity presented itself.[95]

In the *Sears* case, lawyers defending Sears effectively used the expert witness testimony of Rosalind Rosenberg to suggest that women's choices and preferences, as well as cultural constructs surrounding gender roles, were the reasons that men monopolized high-commission sales and management jobs within Sears, and not deliberate discrimination carried out by the corporation. Historian Alice Kessler-Harris acted as chief witness for the EEOC. Her testimony proved to be a nuanced accounting of a wide array of women's paid employment in all sectors of the economy set within diverse historical contexts. Yet, it did not convince the court. Rosenberg's testimony, which selectively quoted Kessler-Harris's own work, helped Sears win the case, to the detriment of women workers at Sears. It created reason to doubt that sex discrimination was 100 percent to blame for occupational segregation and pay inequality. At the heart of the dispute, which the *New York Times* billed as a "Bitter Feminist Debate," was the tension and danger inherent in combining scholarship and political advocacy. Rosenberg argued that women's history scholarship should not be utilized to bolster political positions. If that were done, she reasoned, it would delegitimize women's history in the eyes of the public and among scholars; it would be used to make bad public policy. Kessler-Harris agreed with this point but argued that Rosenberg's testimony had distorted her own scholarship and that women's historians had an ethical responsibility neither to misrepresent history nor to testify in a way that would harm living American women, which she maintained Rosenberg's testimony had done. Most feminist historians agreed with Kessler-Harris.[96] Joining her, the CCWHP issued a resolution passed at the annual AHA meeting in New York in December 1985 that stated, "We believe as feminist scholars we have a responsibility not to allow our scholarship to be used against the interests of women struggling for equity in our society."[97] The next month the Supreme Court ruled in favor of Sears.[98] If we frame the intentions of feminist historians more positively here, these scholars intended their work to buttress and support women in their ongoing struggles for justice, equal rights, equal opportunities, and their fair share of power.

Clarence Thomas headed the EEOC between 1982 and 1990 and so was at its helm during the *Sears* case. He'd been appointed by Ronald Reagan to replace Black feminist lawyer Eleanor Holmes Norton in 1981. As a staunch conservative, Thomas was known to be hostile to the EEOC's use of statistics to prove discrimination, class action suits, and affirmative action. In 1990, Thomas was nominated to the US Supreme Court, the second African American man to ascend to the highest court in the land. He was confirmed in 1991, in a controversial Senate hearing in which he was accused of the sexual harassment of Anita Hill, a young Black woman attorney on his staff during his tenure as chairman of the EEOC.[99] In 1991, when Hill's allegations of sexual harassment were made public against her wishes, she was called to testify at Thomas's confirmation hearings, where she was discounted and challenged by the all-male, all-white Senate judiciary committee, chaired by Senator Joe Biden. To deflect focus from his alleged misconduct, Thomas accused the committee and Hill of engaging in a "high-tech lynching" of a Black man. It was a gross misuse of one of the darkest chapters in American history.[100]

Feminist historians—many with expertise in the entwined history of race, gender, actual lynching, and sex, were collectively appalled by Thomas's confirmation and his distortion of history. Ahead of the hearings, the fall issue of the *CCWHP Newsletter* featured a strong statement against Thomas's confirmation from CCWHP copresidents Nancy Hewitt and Margaret (Peg) Strobel.

> We think that white women find it easier to oppose Thomas than do African American women. We have seen little equivocation in the opposition expressed by women's organizations with largely white memberships. However, among African Americans who are not pleased with Thomas's nomination, the decision to oppose him is not made easily. The NAACP for example, deliberated long before opposing him. . . . Indeed, we feel many white women would feel the same ambivalence

about a conservative female nominee. As co-presidents of an organization comprised overwhelmingly of white members that hopes to be a comfortable place for people of color, we do not wish to alienate potential or existing members by speaking as an organization (as opposed to urging our members to speak individually). . . . We urge you to contact people who will vote on the nomination. Do so immediately.[101]

Hewitt and Strobel collapsed categories like white women/white feminists and African American women/African American feminists. They made assumptions about likely positions these groups would take, forgetting that sizable percentages of white women were not feminists and likely did support Thomas's nomination because they were conservatives. They did not, however, make assumptions about what Black feminist scholars thought. The Hewitt–Strobel statement demonstrated caution and humility with regard to respecting the difficult position Black feminist historians occupied.

African American women's historians were less hesitant. They quickly formulated statements opposing the Thomas nomination in the face of broader Black ambivalence about standing against him.[102] They organized a *New York Times* full-page ad, "African American Women in Defense of Ourselves."[103] Historians Elsa Barkley Brown and Barbara Ransby were joined by sociologist Deborah King in drafting the statement. They raised money to pay for the ad and gathered over 1,600 signatories among Black women academics. The ad conveyed both outrage and hurt. It exposed the long American historical tradition of sexual abuse endured by African American women in the workplace from slavery to the present, clearly linking this tradition to the disrespectful treatment of Anita Hill in the EEOC, during the confirmation hearings, and in the court of public opinion. Taking aim at Thomas's misrepresentation of the history of lynching, the ad said that Black women would speak for themselves about their collective historical experiences. The statement declared,

As women of African descent, we are deeply troubled by the recent nomination, confirmation, and seating of Clarence Thomas as an Associate Justice of the U.S. Supreme Court. . . . Further, the consolidation of a conservative majority on the Supreme Court seriously endangers the rights of all women, poor and working-class people, and the elderly. The seating of Clarence Thomas is an affront not only to African American women and men, but to all people concerned with social justice. . . . We are particularly outraged by the racist and sexist treatment of Professor Anita Hill, an African American woman who was maligned and castigated for daring to speak publicly of her own experience of sexual abuse.[104]

While Black feminists were speaking as scholars, women, and African Americans, they were also concerned with the impact Thomas and a conservative majority seated on the Supreme Court would have on social justice for all Americans. They feared that the treatment of Hill would have a chilling effect on other women's willingness to speak out on sexual abuse.

Exposing the combined effects of racism and sexism on historical experience and speaking as women of African descent, they further asserted,

> Clarence Thomas outrageously manipulated the legacy of lynching in order to shelter himself from Anita Hill's allegations. To deflect attention away from the painful reality of sexual abuse in African American women's lives, he trivialized and misrepresented this painful part of African American people's history. This country, which has a long history of racism and sexism, has never taken the sexual abuse of Black women seriously. Throughout U.S. history Black women have been stereotyped as immoral, insatiable, and perverse; the initiators of all sexual contacts—abusive or otherwise. The common assumption in legal proceedings, as well as in the larger society, is that Black women cannot be raped or otherwise sexually abused. As Anita Hill's experience demonstrates, Black women who speak on these matters are not likely to be believed. In 1991, we cannot tolerate this type of dismissal of any one Black woman's experience, or this attack upon our collective character, without protest, outrage, and resistance. . . . We pledge ourselves to continue to speak out in defense of one another, in defense of the African American community, and against those who are hostile to social justice no matter what color they are. No one will speak for us but ourselves.[105]

Their final sentence, "No one will speak for us but ourselves," announced their intention to be *the* authorized scholarly voices on their own personal, painful, and political history.[106]

After the *Sears* case and the Thomas hearings, feminist historians became wary of serving as expert witnesses. They realized all too well that courtroom argumentation, as opposed to scholarly discourse, had a different function in society with high stakes for living women.[107] In history, the presentation of evidence is characterized by nuance, conflict, irony, and the acknowledgment of contradictory evidence. Not so in court. To testify or not to testify? That decision would impact perceptions about the relevance of history, its academic legitimacy, and its place in our broader political culture. After 1985, feminist historians and their allies continued to attempt to serve as expert informants in the courts to the benefit of women and others, with mixed results. The amicus curiae briefs prepared by historians for *Webster v. Reproductive Health Services*

(1989) helped defend but ultimately weaken *Roe v. Wade*, while their brief for *Obergefell v. Hodges* (2015) helped expand marriage rights to gay Americans.

During the twentieth century, historians rarely stepped into the judicial arena. They were uncomfortable serving as advocates, fearing that advocacy was not in keeping with their scholarly traditions and might "distort their work."[108] For example, the NAACP, in preparing for *Brown v. Board of Education* in 1954, hoped that historians might lend weight to the lawyers' assertion that the authors of the Thirteenth, Fourteenth, and Fifteenth Amendments had *originally* intended them to bar racial segregation. When the historians could offer no unambiguous line of evidence, the lawyers relied instead on material, psychological, and social scientific evidence to win their case.[109] Between 1954 and 1973, however, as civil liberties and human rights for people of color and women were inscribed into federal law by liberal courts and administrations, the New Right went on the offensive against these gains. In this polarized political context, historians occasionally stepped up to lend their expertise to the courts as "amici" or friends of the court during the 1980s and 1990s.[110]

In the late 1980s, historians intervened to protect reproductive health rights established by the Supreme Court's 1973 ruling in *Roe v. Wade*. Attorney Sylvia A. Law worked in consultation with some 400 historians in 1989 to file an amicus brief in a case that, if successful, would erode women's access to abortion services. Most notable among the historians were James C. Mohr and Estelle B. Freedman. Mohr was the author of a respected monograph on the history of abortion policy in the United States.[111] Freedman was a pioneer in the history of sexuality and female prison reform.[112] She had garnered national media attention and support from the national women's history community in the mid-1980s when she successfully challenged Stanford University after it denied her tenure, even though the Stanford history department had recommended she be awarded tenure.[113]

In the *Webster* case, the court was asked to rule on the constitutionality of restrictive regulations imposed by the State of Missouri. Also at stake was the entire *Roe v. Wade* decision establishing the constitutional right to abortion during the first and into the second trimester of pregnancy based on Ninth Amendment privacy rights and Fourteenth Amendment equal protection rights. Missouri's legislature passed a law in 1986 asserting that life begins at conception and requiring viability tests starting at twenty weeks. The law also prohibited the use of public funds and public employees for any abortion procedure done for reasons other than to save the mother's life and made it illegal to counsel women on abortion.[114] The lawyers for the State of Missouri planned to rely on the original intent of the framers of the Constitution and on "history and tradition" regarding the legality and morality of abortion. They claimed that the predominant legal view in America from the late eighteenth to early nineteenth century was opposition to abortion.

Experts in the history of abortion, contraception, and sexuality in America joined the opposition. Their amicus brief showed that abortion was broadly tolerated in America into the nineteenth century before "quickening," the point at which a mother could feel the fetus move. The historians pointed out that abortion prior to "quickening" became illegal in the mid-nineteenth century only when the male-dominated medical profession combined forces with "social purity" reformers to control the sexual and reproductive behavior of women and men. The doctors and moralists sought to keep sex and reproduction confined within the bonds of marriage. In this they hoped to reverse a decline in fertility that was occurring, especially among white middle-class Protestants. Historians showed that concern with fetal life became central to the anti-abortion cause only in the late twentieth century. The insistence on this chronology was significant. It revealed that there was no deep-seated cultural or legal tradition litigating against abortion at the nation's founding.[115] This stance garnered broad agreement within the historical profession, in stark contrast to the scholarly disagreements on display in the *Sears* trial just a few years earlier.[116] Historians in the *Webster* brief stuck to summarizing and explicating historical facts. They gave the lawyers expert contextualization but left them free to craft arguments that were not bound by professional historians' standards.[117]

The Supreme Court's conservative majority ruled 5–4 on behalf of the State of Missouri. The decision upheld *Roe*'s central reasoning but allowed the restrictions, thus paving the way for any state to place similar restrictions on abortion access. Again, historians wondered about the wisdom of participating in legal advocacy. Freedman asked, "Given the outcome of the case, I wonder in retrospect about the usefulness of historical arguments and historians' briefs—are we, in fact, the 'kiss of death'?"[118] Mohr asked whether historians' academic legitimacy could be questioned if they acted as expert advocates. He inquired whether "their credibility as open-minded observers" could be maintained.[119] He reflected that if it weren't for the chilling effect it might have on young historians, historians would be well-advised "to never write a sentence that you would not be willing to have read aloud in the Supreme Court of the United States, with the quality of life and the civil rights of millions of people potentially at issue."[120] This echoed Alice Kessler-Harris's concerns in the aftermath of the *Sears* case. She worried that her own scholarship had been distorted and weaponized against women and warned that historians had to be truthful and accurate in their testimony even as they took care "to not say anything that would hurt women."[121]

Nancy Cott and other historians later authored more successful amicus briefs that expanded gay rights. The first, spearheaded by Cott and George Chauncy, among others, was for *Lawrence v. Texas* (2003), which overturned the *Bowers v. Hardwick* (1986) ruling that permitted the criminalization of same-sex sodomy.[122] Then in 2015, historians, including Estelle Freedman and Linda Kerber, prepared a brief on the same-sex marriage case *Obergefell v. Hodges*. This brief drew heavily on Cott's book *Public Vows: A History of Marriage and the Nation* (2000).[123] The book emphasized that marriage was a public institution that had taken many forms in service to the state, morphing in response to economic, social, and cultural changes. The majority opinion of the Supreme Court, which ultimately legalized same-sex marriage, relied heavily on Cott's *Public Vows*.

The reproductive, human, and civil rights of women and LGBTQ Americans continue to be political footballs for the American Right. For now, access to contraception and gay marriage rights remain protected by court rulings, as well as by recent federal legislation passed by the Democratic Congress in 2022. Access to safe, medical abortion, however, is no longer a guaranteed protection. In 2022, the Supreme Court's 6–3 conservative supermajority ruling in *Dobbs v. Jackson Women's Health Organization* stripped away abortion rights and threw women back to the era before *Roe*, when states could criminalize the procedure. Despite historians' efforts to recapitulate and update their analysis in the amicus brief prepared for the *Webster* case in 1989, Justice Samuel Alito, writing for the majority in 2022, essentially dismissed them.[124] This should not be read as a total negation of the historians' contributions. Amicus briefs become part of the official historical record, and the arguments made create a chain of evidence unequivocally placing American historians on the side of defending women's liberty and human and civil rights. Yet it is evidence that the Supreme Court of 2022 concerns itself neither with long-established legal precedents nor with historical facts as carefully presented by experienced, trained historians.

American Women's History in the Public Eye at Millennium's End

In 1998, Hillary Clinton participated in the 150th Anniversary Celebration of the Seneca Falls, New York, Women's Rights Convention. As a featured speaker at the sesquicentennial and as First Lady of the United States, her presence signaled a recognition of the significance and legitimacy of US women's history in the eyes of the nation. Her speech on July 16, 1998, declared,

> We must tell and retell, learn and relearn, these women's stories, and we must make it our personal mission, in our everyday lives, to pass these stories on to our daughters and sons. Because we cannot—we must not—ever forget that the rights and opportunities we enjoy as women today were not just bestowed upon us by some benevolent ruler. They

were fought for, agonized over, marched for, jailed for and even died for by brave and persistent women and men who came before. . . . That is one of the great joys and beauties of the American experiment. We are always striving to build and move toward a more perfect union, that we on every occasion keep faith with our founding ideas and translate them into reality.[125]

Clinton understood the relevance of American women's history—of American women's long struggle for inclusion in a more perfect union. She understood that this history placed cultural value on women and could serve to maintain and advance their rights and opportunities.

The sesquicentennial celebration coincided with the Clinton administration's issuance of Executive Order 13090 to establish the President's Commission on the Celebration of Women in American History. The commission was tasked with making recommendations on how best to recognize and celebrate women's contributions to the nation's development. Chairing the commission were Ann Lewis, the former White House director of communications, and Beth Newburger of the General Services Administration. The commission was rounded out by a diverse group of civic, business, and academic leaders, including Dr. Johnetta Cole of Spelman College; Dr. Barbara Goldsmith, a social historian; LaDonna Harris, a Native American feminist and civic activist; Gloria T. Johnson of the Coalition of Labor Union Women; Dr. Elaine Kim of UC Berkeley; and Dr. Ellen Ochoa of NASA, among others. Page Putnam Miller of the NCCPH testified before the commission.[126] The commission called for input from local, state, and federal agencies and organizations. Representatives of the military and major civic, business, religious, and feminist groups participated. Librarians, archivists, public historians, and academic historians joined the commission as speakers and consultants. From public history, Molly Murphy McGregor of the National Women's History Project, Karen Strasser of the National Museum of Women's History, Edith Mayo of the Smithsonian, and Marsha Semmel of the Women of the West Museum stand out. From academia, about two dozen professional historians consulted. They represented the subfields of American women's political, labor, religious, military, and art history. Well-represented were experts in African American, Asian American, Native American, and Latinx history. The discipline's major institutions, too, were represented by Cynthia Harrison of the OAH and Barbara Woods of the Association of Black Women Historians. Stalwarts of the mainstream women's history movement consulted, including Mary Ryan, Lynn Weiner, and Estelle Freedman.[127]

Over the course of a year, the commission held conferences around the country, strategically including sites that would encompass women from all major ethnic and racial backgrounds. They started in Canandaigua, New York, where Susan B. Anthony was put on trial in 1872 for voting illegally in nearby Rochester. They convened in Atlanta at the Martin Luther King, Jr. National Historical Park, where Coretta Scott King linked the parallel struggles for Black and women's civil rights. In Albuquerque, at a museum exhibit on Hispanic women at work, LaDonna Harris and Molly Murphy McGregor emphasized the need for inclusiveness and diversity. In DC, the meeting took place in the State Department's East Auditorium. Archivists from a range of institutions advised the commission of the need to change the way records about and by women were cataloged to increase their visibility. They were joined by Congresswomen Pat Schroeder and Louise Slaughter, in addition to nationally recognized feminists Betty Friedan and Eleanor Smeal of NOW.[128]

In March 1999, the commission issued its report alongside recommendations of local, regional, and national scope. National recommendations included developing traveling exhibits and a "National Women's History Umbrella Website"; designating a formal women's history site in the nation's capital; encouraging federal agencies and buildings to commemorate women's work in government with events and more permanent physical installations; exploring ways in which the Department of Education might develop new curricular materials in American women's history; and actively surfacing and featuring the National Archives' and Library of Congress's holdings on women via the World Wide Web and in print publications.[129] Local and state history recommendations focused on identifying and developing historic markers, sites, history trails, and inclusive heritage celebrations; honoring the work of women's organizations and voluntarism; establishing local and statewide women's history initiatives focused on suffrage and other topics; and developing and improving access to local archives.[130] Many of these recommendations have since come to fruition. Much of this work, too, had already been pioneered by participants in the women's history movement without the advice or support of the federal government. This shows that feminist historians were in the vanguard on the frontiers of historical knowledge in the late twentieth century.

Notably absent from the national recommendations was reference to creating a permanent dedicated women's history building at the Smithsonian Institution. In fact, it wouldn't be until 2020 that Congress passed legislation authorizing this undertaking.[131] Upon learning of the legislation, James Grossman and Mary Lindemann of the AHA wrote Senator Susan Collins of Maine in support. They reminded Congress that the museum would be wise to "draw upon the vast scholarship on American women, which has expanded substantially over the last half-century." They also reminded the senator that "the history of American women is, in part, a history of incomplete citizenship, a reminder of how the impairment of any citizen's rights impoverishes the very essence of democracy."[132]

On May 16, 1999, two months after the President's Commission on the Celebration of Women in American History submitted its final report, and just four months after the White House held the Fifth Millennium Evening event that featured talks by historians Natalie Zemon Davis and Martin Marty,[133] the *New York Times Magazine* ran an issue titled "Women: The Shadow Story of the Millennium." It contained a series of articles by more than a dozen public intellectuals reflecting on the approaching end to the millennium. Just two historians, Davis and Jill Ker Conway, contributed to the issue. They focused on the broad sweep of historical change for (Western) women over the last thousand years—no small task in a five-page article! Writing as veterans of the late twentieth-century women's history movement, they first observed the masculine state of history writing during those thousand years: "For all their drama and insight, traditional histories of the last thousand years fall short. Written mostly by men, they introduced women into the standard parade of wars, revolutions, monarchs, and parliaments only at moments like their ascension to inherited thrones or religious authority. In the 19th century, most male historians compounded the problem by making women's history sound as though women had only then begun making headway. Women's history has more to it than that."[134] They wrote with authority as historians of women working in the United States because they—and hundreds of others—had just spent six decades establishing archives and institutions, conducting research, writing books, establishing women's history programs, and teaching thousands of young people, all while engaging in feminist activism. These historians had fundamentally transformed the discipline of history. They were successful in pushing the gendered historical paradigm toward more inclusive content and broader ranging perspectives. The work begun by Mary Beard, Arthur and Elizabeth Schlesinger, Alma Lutz, Dorothy Porter, Barbara Solomon, Janet James, Mary Massey, and others at midcentury was systematically pursued by the mass of feminist historians who entered the historical profession in the 1960s and beyond. Together, these generations of scholars established the centrality of women to nearly every area of American history. They made strides in disseminating their work to the public through media and public history initiatives. The integration of this knowledge in public school curricula still needs attention and is still resisted—sometimes passively, other times fiercely. Nevertheless, American women's historians have solidified and vigorously expanded the gains made over the last seventy years and more. They have offered students of history a powerful reconceptualization of American history recentered around the female majority. The seeds planted in the vineyard of American women's history by earlier generations continue to bear fruit as new scholars cultivate them and plant new varieties in adjacent fields.

Appendix

List of Attendees at the 1988 Wingspread Conference on Graduate Training in US Women's History

List of attendees at the Wingspread Conference on Graduate Training in US Women's History, sponsored by the National Endowment for the Humanities and the Johnson Foundation and held at the Johnson Foundation's Wingspread Conference Center, Racine, Wisconsin, 1988 (see illustration on p. 182).

Tom Adams of the National Endowment
    for the Humanities
Susan Poulsen of the Johnson Foundation
Sarah Alpern
Karen S. Anderson
Louise Año Nuevo Kerr
Joyce Antler
Susan Armitage
Cindy S. Aron
Yamila Azize
Lois Banner
Anne Boylan
Mari Jo Buhle
Joan Burstyn
William Chafe
Lee Chambers-Schiller
Patricia Cohen
Nancy Cott
Jane De Hart
Linda Grant DePauw
Thomas L. Dublin
Ellen C. DuBois
Sarah Elbert
Sara M. Evans
Estelle Freedman
Linda Gordon
Maurine Greenwald
Jacquelyn Dowd Hall
Sharon Harley
Nancy Hewitt
Evelyn Brooks Higginbotham
Joan Hoff-Wilson
Joan Jensen
Carol F. Karlsen

Linda K. Kerber
Alice Kessler-Harris
Sally Gregory Kohlstedt
Judith Walzer Leavitt
Suzanne Lebsock
Gerda Lerner
Valerie Matsumoto
Joanne Meyerowitz
Sonya Michel
Regina Morantz-Sanchez
Mary Beth Norton
Phyllis Palmer
Elizabeth A. Payne
Kathy Peiss
Elisabeth Perry
Ruth Rosen
Rosalind Rosenberg
Mary Rothschild
Vicki Ruiz
Leila Rupp
Mary Ryan
Ingrid Winther Scobie
Anne F. Scott
Kathryn Kish Sklar
Judith Smith
Carroll Smith-Rosenberg
Sarah Stage
Brenda Stevenson
Amy Swerdlow
Rosalyn Terborg-Penn
Nancy Tomes
Laurel Thatcher Ulrich
Susan Ware
Deborah Gray White

Notes

GLP 1950–95	Gerda Lerner Papers, 1950–1995, MC 75-37-96-M8, Schlesinger Library on the History of Women in America, Radcliffe Institute for Advanced Study, Harvard University, Cambridge, MA
JAH	*Journal of American History*
JWH	*Journal of Women's History*
JWH OHP	Twenty-Fifth Anniversary *Journal of Women's History* Oral History Project
JWH Records	Records of the *Journal of Women's History*, Sophia Smith Collection, Smith College, Northampton, MA
KKS Papers	Kathryn Kish Sklar Papers, Sophia Smith Collection, Smith College, Northampton, MA
LUSWHOHP	Living US Women's History Oral History Project, SSC-MS-00423, Sophia Smith Collection, Smith College, Northampton, MA
MEM Papers	Mary Elizabeth Massey Papers, MS 20, Louise Pettus Archives, Winthrop University, Rock Hill, SC
MRB Papers	Mary Ritter Beard Papers, Sophia Smith Collection, Smith College, Northampton, MA
MSG Papers	Margaret Storrs Grierson Papers, Sophia Smith Collection, Smith College, Northampton, MA
NAW Records	Records of *Notable American Women, 1607–1950*, 1958–1973, MC 230, Schlesinger Library on the History of Women in America, Radcliffe Institute for Advanced Study, Harvard University, Cambridge, MA
OAH Records	Records of the Organization of American Historians, MSS 27, Ruth Lilly Special Collections and Archives, University Library, Indiana University, Indianapolis
RG XXXII Records	Records of the Radcliffe Seminars on Women, 1950–1985 (inclusive), 1950–59 (bulk), Schlesinger Library on the History of Women in America, Radcliffe Institute for Advanced Study, Harvard University, Cambridge, MA
SAWH Records	Southern Association for Women Historians Records, MS 4152, Southern Historical Collection, Wilson Library, University of North Carolina at Chapel Hill
SCA	Smith College Archives, Smith College Collections, Smith College, Northampton, MA
SHA Records	Records of the Southern Historical Association, MC 4030, Southern Historical Collection, Wilson Library, University of North Carolina at Chapel Hill
SHC	Southern Historical Collection, Wilson Library, University of North Carolina at Chapel Hill
SL	Schlesinger Library on the History of American Women, Radcliffe Institute for Advanced Study, Harvard University, Cambridge, MA
SOHP	Southern Oral History Project, Southern Historical Collection, Wilson Library, University of North Carolina at Chapel Hill
SSC	Sophia Smith Collection, Smith College, Northampton, MA

Introduction

1. Anne Firor Scott to Barbara Miller Solomon, December 7, 1971, Chronological Correspondence files, box 1, AFS Papers.

2. The epigraphs repeatedly express the view that women's history had been largely ignored prior to 1970. The quotes are from Lerner, *Woman in American History*, 5; Harley and Terborg-Penn, *Afro-American Woman*, ix; and Mary Beth Norton, "Is Clio a Feminist? The New History," *New York Times*, April 13, 1986, BR1 (here Norton dates the field's start to 1971).

3. Crenshaw, "Demarginalizing the Intersection of Race and Sex."

4. Bloch, *Historian's Craft*, xxi, vii.

5. The subtitle was added in 1953 by the publisher. Bloch had died at the hands of Nazi captors during World War II, and the book was published posthumously.

6. Jack H. Hexter, review of *Woman as Force in History*, by Mary Beard, *New York Times Book Review*, March 17, 1946, 5.

7. Hexter, *On Historians*, front matter. Hexter does graciously acknowledge his wife, two female research assistants, and his female editorial team in the acknowledgments, however.

8. Kate Asaphine Everest Levi Papers, 1833–1850, 1891–1893, Wisconsin Historical Society Archives, Madison; Hesseltine and Kaplan, "Women Doctors of Philosophy in History," 254. Levi's 1893 dissertation was "German Immigration to Wisconsin."

9. Joan Wallach Scott, "American Women Historians, 1884–1984," in Scott, *Gender and the Politics of History*, 178–98; Goggin, "Challenging Sexual Discrimination"; "List of Dissertations in the History of American Women Based on Warren F. Kuehl, 'List of Doctoral Dissertations in History Completed in American Universities1960,'" folder 140, *NAW* Records; White, *Telling Histories*; Dagbovie, "Black Women Historians"; Dagbovie, "Black Women."

10. Gordon, "Race, Gender, and Painful Changes."

11. Tetrault, *Myth of Seneca Falls*; Murphy, *Citizenship and the Origins of Women's History*.

12. Robert B. Townsend, "What's in a Label? Changing Patterns of Faculty Specialization since 1975," *Perspectives* 45, no. 1 (2007): 12–14, www.historians.org/perspectives/issues/2007 /0701/0701new1.cfm 2/8/2008; Robert B. Townsend, "The Rise and Decline of History Specializations over the Last Forty Years," *Perspectives on History*, December 2015, www.historians .org/perspectives-article/the-rise-and-decline-of-history-specializations-over-the-past-40 -years-december-2015/.

13. A. Scott, "On Seeing and Not Seeing."

14. J. Johnson, "'Drill into Us . . . the Rebel Tradition'"; Erickson, "'We Want No Teachers.'"

15. Nash et al., *History on Trial*.

16. In 2022, American Historical Association (AHA) president James Sweet named many of these same sites of cultural controversy in a column in *Perspectives on History*. Here, he fretted over the threat that "presentism" in historical scholarship posed to historians' legitimacy in the eyes of the public. His column received mostly negative responses from other historians. He was pressed by the AHA to issue an apology for having caused racial harm to his peers by implying that Black history was identity politics and for fueling the flames of right-wing reaction against "woke" history. He apologized and tried to clarify that wasn't what he'd meant or intended. Responding to Sweet's remarks was Joan Wallach Scott, a leading light in the development of gender history and specialist in French women's history. She observed in the *Chronicle of Higher Education* that "history is always about politics" and warned that "the line between a politically engaged critical history and a dogmatic reading of the past is

not easy to distinguish." Moreover, she reminded readers that fields like women's and gender history and Black history emerged in response to their virtual absence from traditional history writing done largely by elite white men. She warned that ideologues on both the right and the left represented a more serious threat to honest academic history discourse and that we shouldn't lose sight of that. She insisted that it was possible to write responsible, politically engaged history of relevance without allowing dogma to overtake scholarship. Priya Satia too reminded readers in the AHA's *Perspectives on History* that history has always been political. She pointedly observed that Sweet's focus on the 1619 Project perpetuated the misconception that somehow history focused exclusively on traditional holders of power and privilege was not political or not also rooted in "identity politics." Moreover, she observed his examples of identitarian, presentist history were not drawn from the work of fellow historians but rather from the work of journalists. She posed the rhetorical question, "Who are these historians who have betrayed their disciplinary duty?" James H. Sweet, "Is History History? Identity Politics and Teleologies of the Present," *Perspectives on History*, August 2022. Sweet's apology after an immediate outcry against some of his observations can be found at www.historians .org/research-and-publications/perspectives-on-history/september-2022/is-history-history -identity-politics-and-teleologies-of-the-present, alongside Priya Satia, "'The Presentist Trap' Response to Sweet, 'Is History History?,'" *Perspectives on History*, September 2022; and Joan W. Scott, "History Is Always about Politics: What the Recent Debates over Presentism Get Wrong," *Chronicle of Higher Education* online, August 24, 2022, https://www.chronicle.com /article/history-is-always-about-politics.

17. Schmidt and Schmidt, "Invisible Woman," 54; Lerner, *Majority Finds Its Past*.

18. A. Schlesinger, *New Viewpoints in American History*.

19. Des Jardins, *Women and the Historical Enterprise*, 52–91.

20. Rossiter, *Women Scientists in America: Struggles and Strategies*; Rossiter, *Women Scientists in America: Before Affirmative Action*; Des Jardins, *Madame Curie Complex*. Des Jardins looks at women's strategies and impact in science over the first eighty years or so of the twentieth century. Her work on the middle period of the century, 1941–62, emphasizes women scientists' strategies for fitting into the professional cultures of different science disciplines during a period she calls the age of heroic science. She identifies a pervasive cult of masculinity within the hard sciences that could not comfortably accommodate the image of the woman scientist. Rossiter studies the impact of social and political shifts during World War II and the Cold War on women in science, demonstrating they were essentially squeezed out of the science pipeline. A similar, if not identical, dynamic existed in the discipline of history.

21. Rosenberg, *Beyond Separate Spheres*; Rosenberg, *Changing the Subject*.

22. Glazer and Slater, *Unequal Colleagues*.

23. B. Smith, *Gender of History*; Iggers, *Historiography in the Twentieth Century*.

24. Iggers, *Historiography in the Twentieth Century*.

25. Novick, *That Noble Dream*, 232–33.

26. Dagbovie, "Black Women Historians," 252. Dagbovie observes that this double-edged sword was more complicated for Black women historians. To be Black, a woman, and a historian who wrote about Black women was a triple threat to one's scholarly legitimacy, and thus credentialed Black women scholars through midcentury studied more traditional political history.

27. Townsend, *History's Babel*.

28. Palmer, *From Gentleman's Club to Professional Body*.

29. Des Jardins, *Women and the Historical Enterprise*.

30. Tetrault, *Myth of Seneca Falls*.

31. Zinsser, *History and Feminism*, 3; see also Goggin, "Challenging Sexual Discrimination"; J. Scott, "American Women Historians, 1884–1984," 178–98; and Alberti, *Gender and the Historian*.

32. Zinsser, *History and Feminism*, 3.

33. Bloor and Dawson, "Understanding Professional Culture."

34. Bloch, *Historian's Craft*, 1–19.

35. Iggers, *Historiography in the Twentieth Century*; Bloch, *Historian's Craft*; Rampolla, *A Pocket Guide to Writing History*; Storey, *Writing History: A Guide for Students*.

36. Bloor and Dawson, "Understanding Professional Culture."

37. Boor and Dawson, "Understanding Professional Culture," 276.

38. The Mississippi Valley Historical Association changed its name in 1965 to the Organization of American Historians to reflect that the organization's field of emphasis had shifted from regional history to American history.

39. Novick, *That Noble Dream*, 491–510.

40. Higham, *History*.

41. Sklar interview by Gustafson, LUSWHOHP, 47–48 and 62–64.

42. Iggers, *Historiography in the Twentieth Century*.

43. E. James et al., *Notable American Women*.

44. The Berkshire Conference on the History of Women (Gender/s, and Sexuality/ies) was first held in 1973 at Douglass College in New Jersey and was repeated in 1974 (Radcliffe) and 1976 (Bryn Mawr). In 1978 it became a triennial academic conference that has regularly drawn well over a thousand registered participants from around the United States and the world each time it has convened. It came to be called the "Big Berks" to distinguish it from its institutional sponsor, the much older and smaller Berkshire Conference *of* Women Historians, or the "Little Berks." The Big Berks has been an institution in the field ever since, a place where feminist historians from around the world gather to network, present new work in the field, reflect on the state of the field, and plot new directions. But the 2023 meeting of the conference, its fiftieth anniversary, was rocked by ugly controversy over allegedly racist, ethnocentric, and homophobic public comments made by a scholar on a plenary session at the conference. The comments were made after a distinguished African American historian had spoken on Black women's absence from the Little Berks in its first few decades of existence and their exclusion from the historical profession prior to the 1970s. Without going into unsavory detail about the comments, the strong reaction against them from conference attendees, or the response of conference organizers, suffice it to say that many were left stunned, hurt, and outraged. Many openly rejected the sentiments, disavowing them. Others saw the moment as indicative of broader maladies plaguing the discipline of women's history and needing redress. An official apology was published by the Little Berks a month later, acknowledging racial harm had been caused. How are we as historians to make sense of this moment in the discipline of women's history without a comprehensive historiography of our own? Executive Board, Berkshire Conference of Women Historians, "Statement on Racism and the Berks," July 5, 2023, https://berksconference.org/news/statement-on-racism-and-the-berks; 2023 Little Berks Conference Schedule, October 13–15, 2023, Hyatt Lodge in Oak Bridge, Chicago, Berkshire Conference of Women Historians, accessed June 13, 2025, https://berksconference.org/little-berks/past-annual-meetings/2023-little-berks/2023-little-berks-schedule.

45. Antoinette Burton and Deborah J. Rossum to Dear Friends, "An Open Letter to Participants," July 1, 1987, folder 12, box 34, BCWH Records.

46. Boris and Chaudhuri, *Voices of Women Historians*; Schulz and Turner, *Clio's Southern Sisters*; White, *Telling Histories*; Gillespie and Clinton, *Taking Off the White Gloves*.

47. The project was conceived by historians Kathryn Kish Sklar and Mary Rothschild and developed by these two historians in conjunction with Sherrill Redmon of the Sophia Smith Collection. Originally, it was titled "Living US Women's History: Voices from the Field, 1960–2000." It was funded and supported by the American Association of University Women, Arizona State University, the Arizona Humanities Council, the Arizona Historical Society, and the Center for the Historical Study of Women and Gender at SUNY Binghamton. It will be cited as LUSWHOHP throughout the book.

48. Goggin, "Challenging Sexual Discrimination."

49. The records of the Berkshire Conference at the Schlesinger Library contain records dat-
ing back to 1930. However, Margaret Judson's professional autobiography claims she attended the second meeting of the group in 1929 or 1930, which would date the organization's foun-
dation to 1928 or 1929. The organization celebrated its fiftieth anniversary in 1978, supporting Judson's claim. The name of this group underwent several changes, from Lakeville Historical Conference to Berkshire Historical Conference to Berkshire Conference of Women Historians. It is not synonymous with the later Berkshire Conference on the History of Women, which was established as a regular academic conference in 1973. Judson, *Breaking the Barrier*; "Meeting Minutes, May 13, 1978," box 11, folder 11.9, BCWH Records.

50. Dagbovie, "Black Women Historians," 252; Des Jardins, *Women and the Historical Enterprise*; Novick, *That Noble Dream*; Cott, *Grounding of Modern Feminism*, 230–33.

51. For example, the creation of the job register of the AHA resulted from efforts of women and allied historians to counter the nepotistic "old boy network" system of getting a job. In general, women historians were central to efforts in the 1970s and 1980s to demystify the professional practices necessary to succeed in history. They were also behind the creation of the AHA Committee on Women Historians' 1975 *Manual for Women (and Other) Historians*. Originally prepared by Suzanne Lebsock, Mary Frances Berry, Carl Degler, Mary Jane Hamilton, Joan Kelly, Linda Kerber, Jane De Hart Mathews, Emiliana Noether, and Marie Perinbam, it went into several editions before the close of the century. Gustafson, *Becoming a Historian*, was its final iteration by 2000.

52. Echols, *Daring to Be Bad*, 139–202; Gordon, "Socialist View of Women's Studies." Many of the interviews in LUSWHOHP discuss the link between feminist politics and feminist history in the 1970s. The interviews with Linda Gordon, Sara Evans, Kathryn Kish Sklar, Mari Jo Buhle, Alice Kessler-Harris, Ellen DuBois, Thomas Dublin, and Lois Banner are particularly relevant to this point.

53. The women's history movement of the 1970s had most of the major characteristics of a social movement, including collective behavior, extra-institutionality, multicentered networks, and the willingness to disrupt order within history's professional institutions. But I think a social movement should also be required to reach a relatively broad segment of society, so I apply the term "social movement" only to the period after 1970. See Gerlach and Hine, *People, Power, Change*; Morris and Mueller, *Frontiers in Social Movement Theory*; and Roth and Horan, Introduction to *What Are Social Movements?*

Chapter 1

1. Mary Beth Norton, "Is Clio a Feminist? The New History," *New York Times*, April 13, 1986, BR1. Here Norton dates the field's start to 1971. The 1971 "bibliography" to which she referred was already quite a bit longer than one page, as chapters 2 through 5 will demonstrate. Historian William O'Neill replied testily to Norton's statements about the field's post-1970 roots by writing in to the *New York Times* with this rejoinder: "Lest readers imagine that Mary Beth Norton arose from a vacuum allow me to set the record straight . . ." He then listed a dozen scholars who had published quality histories about American women between 1959 and 1969 before closing with the following statement about the works: "All predate, in conception at least, the new feminist movement. They constitute a remarkable body of scholarship all the same." William O'Neill, "Clio, Feminist or Not," *New York Times*, May 11, 1986, BR37; Gerda Lerner and Kathryn Kish Sklar, *Graduate Training in U.S. Women's History: A Conference Report*, folder 4, box 30, KKS Papers; Boylan, "Textbooks in U.S. Women's History"; Kerber et al., *U.S. History as Women's History*; Alice Kessler-Harris, "Do We Still Need Women's History?," *Chronicle of Higher Education*, December 7, 2007, B6–B7.

2. Lasser, "Century of Struggle."

3. A. Scott, *Unheard Voices*; Lebsock, "In Retrospect"; DuBois, "Politics and Culture in Women's History"; Sicherman, "Review Essay." In the 2003 roundtable discussion in Cott et al., "Considering the State of U.S. Women's History," Nancy Cott dates the "contemporary field" of women's history to "30 years ago," Ellen DuBois categorizes herself as part of the "first generation" of women's historians, and Gerda Lerner says, "We have had thirty years . . . of modern history writing on women." In Kessler-Harris, "Do We Still Need Women's History?," B6, Kessler-Harris states, "When I entered the profession in the late 1960s there was no such field as women's history, and only a few enterprising souls were willing to explore the arena." Boylan, "Textbooks in U.S. Women's History"; Rupp, review of *Toward an Intellectual History of Women* and *Why History Matters: Life and Thought*, 322. In Karen J. Winkler, "Scholars of Women's History Fear the Field Has Lost Its Identity," *Chronicle of Higher Education*, July 5, 1990, A4, Winkler reported, "In the late 1960s and 1970s feminist politics helped turn the attention of scholars to the subject of women's history."

4. Vogel, "Telling Tales." An example of the viewpoint arguing opposite Vogel's observation was Hewitt, "Beyond the Search for Sisterhood." Hewitt viewed the women's history of the 1970s as primarily middle-class, white, and Northeastern in its orientation. That's certainly an accurate description of her own first monograph based on a dissertation she began in the 1970s, *Women's Activism and Social Change: Rochester, New York, 1822–1872*. I will offer evidence over the next several hundred pages showing this was a belief, strategy, and rhetorical stance, perhaps not always entirely deliberate, used by scholars who wanted to push women's history further in terms of analysis of race, class, sexuality, and regional histories of women. It was good for the field but not an accurate representation of the state of the field throughout the 1970s.

5. The women's history movement is defined here as the organized, collective efforts of historians to improve the status of women in the historical profession and to promote and legitimize the study of women in history.

6. Lerner, "Women among the Professors of History," 6, 10, 12, 13; A. Scott interviews by Rothschild and Glusman, LUSWHOHP, combined transcripts, 62.

7. Rossi and Calderwood, *Academic Women on the Move*; Briscoe, "Phenomena of the Seventies." Briscoe wrote primarily about women in the sciences, but women in the humanities and social sciences also formed these caucuses and committees from 1969 to 1978.

8. Carroll et al., *History of the Coordinating Committee*; Arnita Jones, "Women Historians and Women's History: An Organizational Guide," *Women's Studies Newsletter*, September 1976, 11, folder 1, box 15, OAH Records.

9. Smith-Rosenberg, "New Woman and the New History."

10. Buhle et al., "Women in American Society," 3.

11. For example, in 1991 Nancy Cott published a documentary history of Mary Beard's life and in 1986 recalled she had "too cavalierly dismissed the work of an earlier generation of historians." Cott, foreword to *Root of Bitterness* (1986 ed.), xiii; Cott, *Woman Making History*.

12. Lerner, *Fireweed*, 254.

13. Weigand, *Red Feminism*, 47–48.

14. Lerner, *Fireweed*; Weigand, *Red Feminism*, 1–2.

15. Lerner, "Autobiographical Note" in *Majority Finds Its Past*; Weigand, *Red Feminism*, 109. Weigand points out that Lerner's interest in the history of women, Black women, and abolitionists was first sparked through her membership in the communist Congress of American Women.

16. Lerner, *Fireweed*, chaps. 16–19.

17. "Great Women in American History," "The Role of Women in American Life and Culture," and "The Role of Women in American Culture," Course Bulletins, New School for Social Research, folder 13 "Publicity for Courses Offered by Gerda Lerner on Women's History, 1962–1964," series 1, GLP 1950–95; Nancy Seely, "A Scholar Sheds New Light on Woman's Role in History," *New York Post*, September 17, 1962, 30.

18. Lerner, *Woman in American History*, 5; the quote is from Lerner, "Autobiographical Note," xiv, xix–xx; Lerner interview by Rothschild, LUSWHOHP; Lerner, "Women among the Professors of History."

19. She studied under William Leuchtenberg, who suggested the topic to her, and Robert Cross; Kraditor, *Ideas of the Woman Suffrage Movement, 1890–1920* (1981), viii.

20. Annette Baxter to Barbara Cross and Cross to Baxter, 1965-1967, folder 24, box 10, and "History 41, [History] 42 1965-1967" and "History 61, [History] 62 1967-1968," Course Descriptions, folders 8–12, box 40, Annette Kar Baxter Papers, 1905–1984, SSC.

21. Lerner interview by Rothschild, LUSWHOHP, 8–9. At least many archives believed they didn't have materials on women.

22. Lerner, *Fireweed*, 2.

23. Folder 13 "Publicity for Courses Offered by Gerda Lerner on Women's History, 1962–1964," carton 1, GLP 1950–95.

24. Louise Phelps Kellogg held the office of the OAH presidency for 1930-31. The OAH at the time still retained its original name of Mississippi Valley Historical Association. The name change was made in 1965.

25. Lerner interview by Rothschild, LUSWHOHP, 10–11.

26. Gerda Lerner to Joan Hoff-Wilson, [partially dated letter, 1982], folder "Gerda Lerner, 1980–1987 (1)," box 18, OAH Records. Lerner admonished Hoff-Wilson for an unseemly outburst at Al Young at the annual meeting of the OAH in 1982.

27. Lerner, "New Approaches to the Study of Women in American History" and "Placing

Women in History: Definitions and Challenges," reprinted from 1969 and 1975 in Lerner, *Majority Finds Its Past.*

28. Lerner, *Teaching Women's History.*

29. A more detailed professional biography of Anne Firor Scott appears in chapter 2.

30. A. Scott, *Unheard Voices.*

31. A. Scott interviews by Rothschild and Glusman, LUSWHOHP, 62.

32. Massey's *Bonnet Brigades* was published as part of Allan Nevins's Impact Series to wide acclaim and recognition, while her earlier two books dealing with the Civil War in the South (*Ersatz in the Confederacy* and *Refugee Life during the Civil War*) also focused mostly on women, the home front, and social history. These works were published in 1952 and 1964, respectively, and had helped establish her scholarly reputation in the South. A. Elizabeth Taylor was the recognized scholar of woman suffrage in the South after 1947; her dissertation and eighteen articles on the subject established her as a respected scholar in Southern history. Until very recently their names and success stories have not appeared in most published accounts of the field's origins and development. Taylor's pioneer work was recognized by the Southern Association for Women Historians in 1993, when the organization named a prize after her. These two historians' careers are highlighted fully in chapter 3

33. A. Scott interviews by Rothschild and Glusman, LUSWHOHP, 60, 62; A. Scott interview by Constance Schulz in Schulz and Turner, *Clio's Southern Sisters,* 40–41; the quotes are from the latter interview.

34. The phrase, "hierarchies of historical significance," is from Smith-Rosenberg, "New Woman and the New History"; Kerber interview by Wiesiger, LUSWHOHP, 28. Kerber names Janet James as a "pioneer" who stayed in women's history "before there was a feminist wave to carry them forward." Other tellings of the origins of women's history date the emergence of the field in 1968 or 1969. For example, see Berkin and Norton, *Women of America,* 3; and Buhle et al., "Women in American Society," the latter of which gives extensive bibliographic notes yet still places the field's origins in the late 1960s. On pages 1–2, Berkin and Norton jump from 1920 to Mary Beard and then to the modern women's movement of the 1960s to explain the field's roots. Lerner and Sklar, *Graduate Training in U.S. Women's History,* 1, KKS Papers, date the start of the field in 1969.

35. Henry, "Promoting Historical Consciousness"; Collier-Thomas, "Towards Black Feminism," 43–66.

36. Zinsser, *History and Feminism,* 24.

37. Lerner interview by Rothschild, LUSWHOHP, 9–10.

38. Zinsser, *History and Feminism,* 119; Tilly, "Gender, Women's History, and Social History."

39. Kessler-Harris interview by Gustafson, LUSWHOHP, 44; Dubofsky, "City Kid's View."

40. Melvyn Dubofsky, "Gertrude Barnum," in E. James et al., *Notable American Women,* vol. 1; Melvyn Dubofsky to Edward James, 1961, folder "Du" 37, box 6, *NAW* Records.

41. A. Scott, *Women in American Life.*

42. Lerner, *Woman in American History.*

43. Lerner, *Black Women in White America.*

44. Bennett Wall to Mollie Davis, June 27, 1972, folder "Bennett Wall, 1972," box 4, SAWH Records.

45. Bennett Wall to June K. Burton, October 28, 1983, folder "Correspondence May 1983–December 1983," series D, subseries 1, Ad Hoc Committee on the Status of Women in the SHA, SHA Records.

46. Mary Massey to Grady McWhiney, December 17, 1970, folder 9-90, box 9, MEM Papers; Mary Massey to Bennett Wall, January 6, 1971, folder 493, "Secretary Treasurer: 1970–1971, Vice President, M. E. Massey," SHA Records; the second letter noted here is in the files of the SHA secretary-treasurer (Ben Wall), leading me to deduce that the handwritten notes in the margins of Massey's letter referring to Anne Scott as "nuts" were written by Ben Wall rather than Massey.

47. Massey to Wall, January 6, 1971, SHA Records.

48. John Hope Franklin, "Remarks Introducing Mary Elizabeth Massey as President of the Southern Historical Association" at the annual meeting of the SHA, November 16, 1972, folder 120-123, box 12, MEM Papers.

49. Schmidt and Schmidt, "Invisible Woman," reprinted from a 1971 essay and OAH conference paper in Carroll, *Liberating Women's History*, 54.

50. Lerner, *Majority Finds Its Past*, xxv, 3–14, 145–59; Lerner, *Living with History*, 46; Lerner interview by Rothschild, LUSWHOHP.

51. Smith-Rosenberg, "New Woman and the New History"; Buhle et al., "Women in American Society."

52. See note 3 above.

53. Carroll, "Mary Beard's Woman as Force in History," 26–42; Lane, *Mary Ritter Beard*; Turoff, *Mary Beard as Force in History*; Lebsock, "In Retrospect"; Rupp, "Eleanor Flexner's Century of Struggle"; B. Smith, "Seeing Mary Beard"; Cott, *Woman Making History*. One of the most recent and comprehensive textbooks in US women's history echoes the title of Beard's 1933 *America through Women's Eyes* quite intentionally to herald her as the founding influence in the field. The textbook published in 2005 harkens to the forty-year history of scholarship in American women's history, thus dating the field's origins to 1965; see DuBois and Dumenil, *Through Women's Eyes*.

54. By midcentury historians of women, I refer to scholars with a history PhD who were professionally active between roughly 1930 and 1969, after the earliest wave of scholarship on women in history began but before the emergence of the women's history movement in 1969.

55. Doris King to Mary Massey, February 11, 1971, Incoming Correspondence Files, folder 9-92, box 9, MEM Papers.

56. Gordon interview by Gustafson, LUSWHOHP, 48.

57. Lerner, "Autobiographical Note," xix. Lerner recalls telling the graduate admissions committee to which she spoke at Columbia in 1963, "I want . . . to complete the work begun by Mary Beard." Mentioning Mary Beard as the field's foremother while eliding work done by professional historians in the field between 1945 and 1960 has become commonplace.

58. A somewhat dismissive recognition of male scholars' attempts at writing women's history in the early 1960s is found in the seminal essay by Buhle et al., "Women in American Society." See also Lebsock, "In Retrospect," 324–39; Rupp, "Eleanor Flexner's Century of Struggle: Women's History and the Women's Movement"; and B. Smith, "Seeing Mary Beard." Most historians of women also are aware of the seminal publications of Barbara Welter and Aileen Kraditor in 1965 and 1966, but these historians have not been written about, historicized, or added to the pantheon of pioneer historians of women, like Beard, Spruill, and Flexner. This may be because they have not wanted to be interviewed, grouped, or identified with the generation of scholars who became active on behalf of the field after 1969. In 2002, Barbara Welter curtly rejected an offer to be part of a major oral history project funded by the National Endowment for the Humanities about historians of US women; Barbara Welter to Kathryn

Kish Sklar, July 5, 2002, KKS Papers (unprocessed at this date). Kraditor also succinctly declined the offer to be interviewed for the project in 2002. Kraditor and Welter belonged to an intermediate generation of women's history scholars who, perhaps, did not identify with the feminist historians who emerged to lead the field after 1969.

59. Tomás, introduction to "The Women's History Movement"; Boris and Chaudhuri, *Voices of Women Historians*; Schulz and Turner, *Clio's Southern Sisters*; White, *Telling Histories*; Gillespie and Clinton, *Taking Off the White Gloves*.

60. Buhle et al., "Women in American Society," 3.

61. Meyerowitz, *Not June Cleaver*; Scharf and Jensen, *Decades of Discontent*; Rupp and Taylor, *Survival in the Doldrums*; Laughlin and Castledine, *Breaking the Wave*.

Chapter 2

1. A. Taylor interview by Pamela Dean, November 5, 1992, in Schulz and Turner, *Clio's Southern Sisters*, 27.

2. Table 318.10, "Degrees conferred by postsecondary institutions, by level of degree and sex of student: Selected years, 1869–70 through 2025–26," National Center for Education Statistics, *Digest of Education Statistics*, accessed December 22, 2023, https://nces.ed.gov/programs/digest/d15/tables/dt15_318.10.asp.

3. A. Scott, *Unheard Voices*, 57; Hesseltine and Kaplan, "Women Doctors of Philosophy in History."

4. Palmer, *From Gentleman's Club to Professional Body*.

5. Edward Hallet Carr, Jack Hexter, and Marc Bloch, for example.

6. Rose et al., "Report of the American Historical Association Ad Hoc Committee"; A. Scott, *Unheard Voices*. Scott features Virginia Gearhart, Guion Griffis Johnson, Marjorie Mendenhall, Eleanor Boatright, and Julia Cherry Spruill, who all married and thus had their career options limited. Mary Elizabeth Massey and A. Elizabeth Taylor, not included in the book, remained single and had careers in women's colleges.

7. A. Scott interview by Rothschild, LUSWHOHP, 11–14; Mrs. Andrew M. Scott to Professor Richard Watson, Chairman, Dept. of History, March 1, 1963, folder "Business Correspondence, 1963," box 1, AFS Papers.

8. Guion Griffis Johnson, "Some Reflections on Research and Writing in Social History," folder 1392, series 12.1, GGJ Papers, 3, 9; Guion Griffis Johnson interview by Mary Frederickson, May 28, 1974, transcript, 17–18, Collection 04007, SOHP. The historian she overheard was J. G. de Rouhlac Hamilton according to Thuesen, "Taking the Vows of Southern Liberalism," 291; Rosalyn Terborg-Penn, "Being and Thinking outside the Box: A Black Woman's Experience in Academia," in White, *Telling Histories*, 77; Lerner, "Women among the Professors of History," 5; Banner interview by Rothschild, LUSWHOHP; Kessler-Harris, "Long Road from Home," 68

9. Joan Wallach Scott, "American Women Historians, 1884–1984," in *Gender and the Politics of History*; Goggin, "Challenging Sexual Discrimination"; Rose et al., "Report of the American Historical Association Ad Hoc Committee," 9; Hesseltine and Kaplan, "Women Doctors of Philosophy in History."

10. Kathryn Kish Sklar and Joan Scott, "Summary Report of the Committee on Women Historians, 1980," American Historical Association, accessed May 4, 2025, www.historians.org/resource/committee-on-women-historians-1980-summary-report; Carla Hesse, "AHA Issues Report on the Status and Hiring of Women and Minority Historians in Academia,"

March 1, 1996, 4–5, www.historians.org/perspectives-article/aha-issues-report-on-the-status
-and-hiring-of-women-and-minority-historians-in-academia/.

11. Lundberg and Farnham, *Modern Woman*; Friedan, *Feminine Mystique*.

12. Malkiel, *"Keep the Damned Women Out."* The title is a quote from a male Dartmouth alumnus opposed to turning Dartmouth College into a coeducational school.

13. A. Scott, *Unheard Voices*, 47–59.

14. Higham, "Cult of American Consensus."

15. Novick, *That Noble Dream*, 240–49, 332–60, 415–38; Higham, *History*.

16. Novick, *That Noble Dream*; B. Smith, *Gender of History*; Dagbovie, "Black Women Historians"; Palmer, *From Gentleman's Club to Professional Body*; Townsend, *History's Babel*.

17. Levine, *Degrees of Equality*, 23–24, 67–68; Cott, *Grounding of Modern Feminism*, 117–42.

18. Cott, *Grounding of Modern Feminism*, 231. Cott cites a woman historian, Ella Lonn, on this point. Lonn, "Academic Status of Women on University Faculties." Lonn taught at Goucher College and was the first woman president of the Southern Historical Association. She held that post in 1946.

19. Adams, *Woman Professional Workers*, 19, 28–29, as cited in Cott, *Grounding of Modern Feminism*, 230.

20. Becker, "Annual Address"; Novick, *That Noble Dream*, 231–33, 491–93.

21. Helton, *Scattered and Fugitive Things*; Snyder, *Making Black History*.

22. Cott, *Grounding of Modern Feminism*, 145–211.

23. Ross, *Ladies of the Press*. Ross also authored popular historical biographies of several presidents' wives including Mary Todd Lincoln, Varina Davis, Grace Coolidge, and Edith Wilson; Ross, *Child of Destiny*, is a history of Elizabeth Blackwell. Ross authored a half dozen other books on notable historical American women and contributed nine sketches to and sat on the advisory board for E. James et al., *Notable American Women*. Florence Woolsey Hazzard Papers, 1940–1950, MS 76, SSC; Florence Woolsey Hazzard Papers, MC H431, MC 99-M124, MC 315, SL; Sophie Hutchinson Drinker Papers, 1935–1966, MS 181, SSC; Sophie Hutchinson Drinker Papers Ms 84-M96, SL; Drinker, *Music and Women* (some of her later work focused on colonial women); Flexner, *Century of Struggle*; Fitzpatrick, foreword to reprint of *Century of Struggle*, xxi–xxii; Des Jardins, *Women and the Historical Enterprise*, 121, 124, 135–37, 153, 175.

24. Eleanor Flexner, Florence Woolsey Hazzard, Sophie Hutchinson Drinker, and Elizabeth Bancroft Schlesinger are scholars who do not fit either category here since none held more than an MA, yet each was known for doing excellent scholarship on women in history. The Daughters of the American Revolution, Confederate Daughters of America, and Colonial Dames Societies are examples of groups categorized as "ancestor worshippers" and historical preservationists.

25. Savage, *Merze Tate*.

26. Dagbovie, "Black Women Historians."

27. Bonnie Smith, Jacqueline Goggin, Joan Scott, and Julie Des Jardins all make similar arguments about women's professional marginalization during the period in which history professionalized between the late nineteenth century and mid-twentieth century. Des Jardins, *Women and the Historical Enterprise*; Goggin, "Challenging Sexual Discrimination"; J. Scott, "American Women Historians, 1884–1984," 178–98; B. Smith, *Gender of History*.

28. Glazer and Slater, *Unequal Colleagues*, 44–69.

29. Another class of professional historian working on the subject of women in history consisted of scholar wives. These women had either an MA or a PhD in history but also had

academic or professional husbands whose careers circumscribed those of their spouses. Until the 1960s, it was quite difficult for a scholar wife to have a traditional professorial career in academia. Marriage could be a powerful handicap to the woman professional, regardless of her qualifications. Des Jardins, *Madame Curie Complex*; Rosenberg, *Changing the Subject*.

30. M. Benson, *Women in Eighteenth-Century America*.

31. Mary Sumner Benson Papers, MS 0878, Mount Holyoke Archives and Special Collections, Mount Holyoke College, South Hadley, MA.

32. "Elisabeth Anthony Dexter," *Who's Who of American Women: Volume I (1958–1959)* (Chicago: A. N. Marquis Company, 1958), 332. Copy in folder "Correspondence EAD to MSG, 1945–1965," EAD Papers.

33. Dexter, *Colonial Women of Affairs*; Dexter, *Career Women of America*. Both were reissued in 1972 by Augustus M. Kelley Publishers, Clifton, NJ. Dexter appears to have been the progenitor of the "golden colonial era for women" interpretation that was later much debated by specialists in women's history.

34. Finding aid, EAD Papers. These civic organizations were the Church Peace Union of New York City, the Rhode Island World Affairs Council, and the Unitarian Universalist Service Committee for which she served as the European director. The Dexters worked in Lisbon providing relief to war refugees. Robert Dexter also worked for the World Affairs Council. From 1945 to 1948, Elisabeth Dexter was a representative, with her husband, of the Church Peace Union, stationed in New York, London, and Geneva.

35. Elisabeth Anthony Dexter to Margaret Grierson, November 18, 1960, and November 20, 1961, folder "EAD to MSG—Correspondence 1945–1965," EAD Papers.

36. EAD Papers; "Elisabeth Anthony Dexter," *Who's Who of American Women*, 332; E. James et al., *Notable American Women*, front matter. Dexter also served on the Committee of Consultants for *Notable American Women*.

37. Dexter, *Career Women of America* (1972), vii–viii.

38. Schlesinger, *New Viewpoints in American History*, 158.

39. Fitzpatrick, "Caroline F. Ware and the Cultural Approach to History," 173–76.

40. E. James et al., *Notable American Women*; Goggin "Challenging Sexual Discrimination"; Salmon, *Domestic Service*; Salmon, *Progress in the Household*.

41. L. Brown, *Apostle of Democracy*.

42. L. B. Merk, "Massachusetts and the Woman Suffrage Movement" (PhD diss., 1956) RG XXXII, MC 326; Freidel, "Frederick Merk"; Rodman, "Frederick Merk, Teacher and Scholar." Merk became her advisor in 1930. They became engaged in 1931. She earned her MA before they married and had two children. Lois Merk returned to graduate study to earn her PhD in the 1950s and worked under the guidance of Schlesinger. She collaborated on four of Frederick Merk's five major books on westward expansion in the 1960s after earning her PhD in 1961. It seems likely that as a college history professor herself and as his domestic and intellectual partner she rendered assistance to Frederick Merk from the late 1930s to 1961 as well and that they had a strong scholarly partnership.

43. Dublin, "Caroline Farrar Ware," 657–59.

44. Ware, *Early New England Cotton Manufacture*; Fitzpatrick, "Caroline F. Ware and the Cultural Approach to History"; Dublin, "Caroline Farrar Ware," 657–59.

45. Ware, *Greenwich Village*.

46. Council for Research in the Social Sciences Records, 1922–1968, UA#127, Rare Book and Manuscript Library, Columbia University, New York, finding aid—Mary Dublin, "Study of

Sterility," 1933, folder 9, box 10, UA#127; Mirra Komarovsky, "A Sociological Study of Voluntary Associations," 1934–1941, folder 12, box 10; John Seward and Georgene H. Seward, "Psychological Effects of Ovarian Hormone Injections in Women during Menopause," 1937–1938, folder 17, box 12; Ruth Bunzel, "A Study of Family Life in the Pueblo of Zuni," 1939–1954, folder 27, box 12; Edmund Brunner, Lyman Bryson, and Irving Lorge, "Marital Ideas of a Lower Middle Class Population," 1939–1954, folder 28, box 12; William J. Goode, "Adjustment after Divorce," 1952–1954, folder 52, box 13; Chilton Williamson, "Suffrage Issue in American History," 1952–1954, folder 53, box 13; Herman Ausuble, "Mrs. Besant and the Late Victorians," 1953–1954, folder 4, box 15; Robert K. Webb, "Harriet Martineau and Her Relationship to English Radicalism," 1955–1958, folder 21, box 15; Elizabeth Baker, "Technology and Women's Work, 1800–1960," 1962–1964, folder 19, box 17; finding aid accessed October 20, 2011, www.columbia.edu/cu/libraries/inside/projects/findingaids/scans/pdfs/Council_Research_SocialSciences.pdf.

47. Council for Research in the Social Sciences Records, 1922–1968, UA#127, Rare Book and Manuscript Library, Columbia University, finding aid; see note 37 for examples.

48. Dublin, "Caroline Farrar Ware," 658.

49. Mayeri, *Reasoning from Race*.

50. Ware, *Cultural Approach to History*.

51. Dublin, "Caroline Farrar Ware," 658.

52. Dublin, "Caroline Farrar Ware," 658.

53. Rosenberg, *Changing the Subject*, 131, 112–19.

54. This uncle by marriage was American historian Ralph Varney Harlow. Harlow had authored a biography of abolitionist Gerrit Smith. A. Scott, "Chance or Choice?," 46; "Anne Firor Scott," in Schulz and Turner, *Clio's Southern Sisters*, 30–37, 38; Guide to the John William Firor Papers, 1860–1986, Duke University Archives, Duke University, Durham, NC/, accessed October 3, 2011, http://library.duke.edu/digitalcollections/rbmscl/firor/inv.

55. A. Scott interview by Rothschild, LUSWHOHP, 4; Schulz and Turner, *Clio's Southern Sisters*, 37.

56. Anne Scott email to Jennifer Tomás, September 25, 2011, re: Mary Earhart Dillon, in author's possession. Scott confirmed she knew Dillon at the time and spoke with her "quite a bit." From 1944 to 1947, Dillon was looking for a home for a sizable collection of women's rights materials she had gathered up during her research; A. Scott, "Chance or Choice?," 50.

57. A. Scott, *Anecdotes of My Years as a LWV Staffer*

58. Interview with Anne Firor Scott, in Schulz and Turner, *Clio's Southern Sisters*, 35, 45; A. Scott interviews by Rothschild and Glusman, LUSWHOHP, 4–5.

59. A. Scott interviews by Rothschild and Glusman, LUSWHOHP, 24, 7. Scott also wrote about the impact of the league on her understanding of women in history in "Historian's Odyssey," xiv.

60. Interview with A. Scott in Schulz and Turner, *Clio's Southern Sisters*, 37–39; A. Scott interviews by Rothschild and Glusman, LUSWHOHP, 11.

61. A. Scott interviews by Rothschild and Glusman, LUSWHOHP, 5–6; A. Scott, "Chance or Choice?," 52–53. She had been working under Benjamin Wright, but he left Harvard for an appointment as the president of Smith College just after she passed her oral exams.

62. A. Scott interviews by Rothschild and Glusman, LUSWHOHP, 6. Solomon worked under Oscar Handlin and earned a Radcliffe PhD in history in 1953. James worked under Arthur Schlesinger Sr. and earned her history PhD in 1954. Scott was present in Cambridge

in the doctoral program at Radcliffe from 1946 to 1954. Solomon and Scott shared Oscar Handlin as an advisor.

63. A. Scott interviews by Rothschild and Glusman, LUSWHOHP, 9.

64. A. Scott, *Making the Invisible Woman Visible*, xix; Freeman, "Search for Political Woman," 5; L. Young, *In the Public Interest*; L. Young, *Understanding Politics*; L. Young, "Women's Place in American Politics."

65. A. Scott interviews by Rothschild and Glusman, LUSWHOHP, 11–14. We know from Guion Griffis Johnson's history that the Chapel Hill history department had had at least one woman in the department, briefly; Mrs. Andrew M. Scott to Professor Richard Watson, Chairman, Dept. of History, March 1, 1963, folder "Business Correspondence, 1963," box 1, AFS Papers.

66. A. Scott interviews by Rothschild and Glusman, LUSWHOHP, 21; A. Scott, "'New Woman' in the New South."

67. A. Scott, *Making the Invisible Woman Visible*, xx; A. Scott, *Southern Lady*.

68. Fitzpatrick, foreword to *Century of Struggle*, xxi.

69. A. Scott interviews by Rothschild and Glusman, LUSWHOHP, 61. Those Scott lists specifically here were Bernard Bailyn, Donald Fleming, Robert Durden, Fletcher Green, and of course Oscar Handlin. In general Scott says men in her department at Duke were supportive, as were people at Harvard.

70. Anne Firor Scott, folders "Business Correspondence, 1963–1973," box 1, AFS Papers.

71. Alan Simpson to Mr. And Mrs. Scott, January 27, 1966, folder "Business Correspondence, 1966," box 1, AFS Papers.

72. Goggin, "Challenging Sexual Discrimination"; BCWH Records contain records dating back to 1930. Margaret Judson's professional autobiography dates the organization's foundation to 1928. The fact that the organization celebrated its fiftieth anniversary in 1978 supports Judson's timeline. Judson, *Breaking the Barrier*; "Meeting Minutes, May 13, 1978," folder 11.9, box 11, BCWH Records.

73. Goggin, "Challenging Sexual Discrimination"; J. Scott, "American Women Historians, 1884–1984"; Judson, *Breaking the Barrier*; Viola Barnes and Elizabeth Kimball, interview by Ann Lane, Mary Maples Dunn, and Mary Hartman, November 17, 1976, folder 1.3, "BCWH, Histories, 1976," BCWH Records.

74. White, *Telling Histories*, 12.

75. Savage, *Merze Tate*.

76. Dagbovie, "Black Women Historians," 252; Dagbovie, "Black Women."

77. Goggin, "Challenging Sexual Discrimination,"; J. Scott, "American Women Historians, 1884–1984"; Judson, *Breaking the Barrier*; Barnes and Kimball interview by Lane, Dunn, and Hartman, November 17, 1976, BCWH Records.

Chapter 3

1. Bleser, "Three Women Presidents of the Southern Historical Association," 101–2.

2. Cott, *Grounding of Modern Feminism*, 229–31; Lonn, "Academic Status of Women," 10.

3. Kirkendall, *Organization of American Historians*.

4. Astin, *Woman Doctorate in America*, 67–70.

5. A. Scott, *Unheard Voices*.

6. J. Spruill, *Women's Life and Work*. This classic was originally published by the University of North Carolina Press in 1938. A. Scott, *Unheard Voices*, 33–38.

7. J. Spruill, *Women's Life and Work*.

8. J. Spruill, *Women's Life and Work*, preface. Spruill also acknowledged the assistance of Katherine Jocher, the assistant director of the Institute for Research in Social Science, her husband, and several archivists, men and women.

9. *Historical Register of Harvard University, 1636–1936* (Cambridge, MA: Harvard University Press, 1937). Corydon Spruill was invited to serve as an instructor and tutor in economics at Harvard in 1929–30. Julia Cherry Spruill accompanied him, and thus her presence at Harvard predated the development of the Women's Archives at Radcliffe, though it was fortunate that she met Beard and Schlesinger, who almost certainly had begun a conversation about women's archives and the role of women in history by then.

10. Membership Lists for the 1940s, 1950s, and 1960s, folder 1063–1064, subseries 9.10, Historical Society of North Carolina, 1948–1967, GGJ Papers. The number of women members in the society in 1948 was six, eleven in 1956, ten in 1963, and fourteen in 1967. Nannie Tillie was a business historian known for her history of the R. J. Reynolds tobacco company. She was a history professor at East Texas State College. Sarah Lemmon was a UNC Chapel Hill PhD (ca. 1952) and a historian of World War I employed at Meredith College in the 1950s. She later moved to North Carolina State University. Mattie Russell earned the PhD from Duke University in 1956. Russell was curator of Manuscripts at Duke's University Library from 1952 until her retirement sometime in the late 1960s.

11. A. Scott, introduction to *Unheard Voices*, 16.

12. A. Scott, introduction to *Unheard Voices*, 6–11, 14–16, 17–20, 20–26. Mendenhall, "Southern Women of a Lost Generation." Mendenhall wrote critical reviews of Mary Beard's *Woman as Force in History* among other works, such as a biography on Varina Davis. Her dissertation was not on women's history.

13. GGJ Papers; A. Scott, *Unheard Voices*, 38–46; Guion Griffis Johnson interview by Mary Frederickson, May 28, 1974, transcript, Collection 04007, SOHP.

14. Thuesen, "Taking the Vows of Southern Liberalism," 285.

15. Thuesen, "Making Southern History."

16. Guion Griffis Johnson, "Some Reflections on Research and Writing in Social History," talk given to the Historical Society of North Carolina, March 30, 1979, folder 1392, Document Case 125, Series 12.2, GGJ Papers, 3, 9; G. G. Johnson interview by Frederickson, May 28, 1974, 16, 17–18, SOHP. The historian she overheard was J. G. de Rouhlac Hamilton.

17. G. G. Johnson, *History of the South Carolina Sea Islands*.

18. G. G. Johnson interview by Frederickson, May 28, 1974, SOHP.

19. G. G. Johnson, *Ante-Bellum North Carolina*, viii.

20. G. G. Johnson, *Ante-Bellum North Carolina*.

21. G. G. Johnson, *History of the South Carolina Sea Islands*; Johnson and Johnson, *Research in Service to Society*.

22. Alex Mathews Arnett, review of *Ante-Bellum North Carolina*, by Guion Griffis Johnson, in *Journal of Southern History* 4, no. 2 (1938): 229–31; Avery Craven, "A Social History," in *Social Forces* 16, no. 3 (1938): 431–32; Ralph B. Flanders, review in *Pennsylvania Magazine of History and Biography* 64, no. 1 (1940): 132–36; Howard E. Jensen, review in *American Sociological Review* 5, no. 6 (1940): 980; Myrtle R. Phillips, review in *Journal of Negro Education* 10, no. 1 (1941): 84–85; Ulrich B. Phillips, review in *Mississippi Valley Historical Review* 17, no. 4 (1931):

623–24; Charles C. Tansill, review in *Annals of the American Academy of Political and Social Science* 197 (May 1938): 266–67; review (no author noted) in *Georgia Historical Quarterly* 16, no. 4 (1932): 321–22.

23. Johnson, "Some Reflections on Research and Writing," GGJ Papers.

24. G. G. Johnson interview by Frederickson, May 28, 1974, 14, SOHP.

25. Myrdal, *American Dilemma.*

26. Gunnar Myrdal to Dr. Frederick Keppel, Carnegie Corporation, April 28, 1939, and Myrdal to Guion Griffis Johnson, May 3, 1939, Chronological Correspondence files, Guy Benton Johnson Papers, MC 3826, SHC.

27. Guion Johnson to Gunnar Myrdal, June 30, 1939; Myrdal to Guion Johnson, June 15, 1939; Guion Johnson to Myrdal, July 7, 1939; Rowena S. Hadsell-Saeger to Guy and Guion Johnson, all in Chronological Correspondence files, Guy Benton Johnson Papers, SHC.

28. G. G. Johnson interview by Frederickson, May 28, 1974, 40, SOHP; Myrdal, *American Dilemma*, xi. While Guy Johnson is listed as a regular staff member along with Richard Sterner, Ralph Bunche, Paul Norgren, Dorothy Thomas, and Doxey Wilkerson, Guion Johnson is listed along with thirty other persons as "outside the staff" "who undertook various research tasks."

29. G. G. Johnson interview by Frederickson, May 28, 1974, 46, SOHP. Johnson had taken umbrage at the uneven quality of research and writing done by the other researchers on the project, and she also seems to have been wary of others getting credit for her more thorough work, which she offered as a partial explanation for why she didn't want Myrdal to publish her work.

30. G. G. Johnson, "Ideology of White Supremacy"; G. G. Johnson, "Southern Paternalism toward the Negro."

31. G. G. Johnson, "Southern Paternalism toward the Negro."

32. Guion Griffis Johnson interview by Jacquelyn Dowd Hall, August 19, 1974, transcript, 13, SOHP, Collection 04007.

33. Chapel Hill was not unique in its treatment of liberals and women academics with connections to progressive organizations. From 1944 to 1960, most institutions of higher education were faced with the prospect of rooting out or investigating alleged communists and fellow travelers. Schrecker, *No Ivory Tower.* Schrecker does not highlight UNC Chapel Hill, but the citation is offered as a general reference to the climate in universities during the Cold War. Levine, *Degrees of Equality*, 67–82; Thuesen, "Taking the Vows of Southern Liberalism." Thuesen also examines this period of political controversies in Guy Johnson's career.

34. G. G. Johnson interview by Frederickson, May 17, 1974, SOHP; G. G. Johnson interview by Hall, August 19, 1974, 10–11, SOHP.

35. The number of members was raised to seventy-five in the 1960s to accommodate growing numbers in the historical profession.

36. G. G. Johnson interview by Frederickson, May 28, 1974, 34, SOHP.

37. G. G. Johnson interview by Hall, August 19, 1974, 18–24, SOHP. She and Julia Cherry Spruill were cut from the institute's staff since they were married women who had husbands to support them financially. The institute staff who remained took 10 percent pay cuts, while faculty and staff at Chapel Hill took 33 percent pay cuts.

38. G. G. Johnson, "Southern Paternalism toward the Negro"; G. G. Johnson, "Impact of War upon the Negro." Johnson also authored a dozen or more reviews in peer-reviewed journals in the 1930s and 1940s .

39. G. G. Johnson interview by Frederickson, May 28, 1974, 30–31, 20–22, SOHP.

40. G. G. Johnson interview by Frederickson, May 28, 1974, 19, SOHP.

41. G. G. Johnson interview by Frederickson, May 28, 1974, SOHP.

42. Green, *Essays in Southern History*.

43. Ware, preface to *Greenwich Village*; Johnson and Johnson, *Research in Service to Society*.

44. See sources in chapter 2, n. 46.

45. Council for Research in the Social Sciences Records, 1922–1968, UA#127, Rare Book and Manuscript Library, Columbia University, finding aid; see note 44.

46. Des Jardins, *Madame Curie Complex*.

47. By the 1960s some women historians, including some of the historians of women examined in this chapter, were finding ways to have history careers and families. The most common solution was to marry supportive academic men. But it was not easy to make a dual career work. Usually, it was the married woman academic who made professional compromises in deference to a spouse's career. If she were lucky, the dual career academic wife could get a foot in the door at a neighboring college or as an occasional lecturer in her husband's institution.

48. Schulz and Turner, *Clio's Southern Sisters*, 3–5.

49. Johnson and Johnson, *Research in Service to Society*.

50. Johnson and Johnson, *Research in Service to Society*; Broschart, "Research in the Service of Society"; Thuesen, "Making Southern History."

51. Johnson and Johnson, *Research in Service to Society*.

52. Taylor earned the MA at Chapel Hill before moving on to Vanderbilt to complete her PhD.

53. A. Elizabeth Taylor interview by Pamela Dean, November 5, 1992, in Schulz and Turner, *Clio's Southern Sisters*, 23–24.

54. Twelve Southerners, *I'll Take My Stand*; Johnson and Johnson, *Research in Service to Society*, 161–225; E. Shapiro, "Southern Agrarians."

55. Suzanne Lebsock, "Woman Suffrage and White Supremacy: A Virginia Case Study," in Hewitt and Lebsock, *Visible Women*, 62–100; Terborg-Penn, *African American Women*; Newman, *White Women's Rights*.

56. Schulz and Turner, *Clio's Southern Sisters*, 23.

57. A. Taylor, "Lifelong Interest," 2–11; A. Taylor interview by Dean, in Schulz and Turner, *Clio's Southern Sisters*, 21–29.

58. Folders 1–5, AET Papers.

59. A. Taylor, "Lifelong Interest," 7.

60. A. Taylor interview by Dean, in Schulz and Turner, *Clio's Southern Sisters*, 25.

61. The Organization of American Historians was named the Mississippi Valley Historical Association until 1965. Taylor was a member from the 1940s through the end of her life in 1992.

62. A. Elizabeth Taylor to Mary Elizabeth Massey, May 6, 1963, folder 52, box 6, MEM Papers.

63. Taylor, "A Lifelong Interest," 9.

64. A. Taylor to Massey, May 6, 1963, folder 52, box 6, MEM Papers.

65. Folders 1–5, AET Papers; Executive Council Meeting Minutes, SHA Records.

66. Folders 1–5, AET Papers.

67. A. Taylor to Massey, February 8, 1965, folder 52, box 6, MEM Papers.

68. A. Taylor to Massey, May 6, 1963, folder 52, box 6, MEM Papers.

69. A. Taylor, "Origin of the Woman Suffrage Movement in Georgia"; A. Taylor, "Woman Suffrage Movement in Texas"; A. Taylor, "Woman Suffrage Movement in Mississippi"; A. Taylor, "Woman Suffrage Movement in Florida"; A. Taylor, *Woman Suffrage Movement in Tennessee*; Texas Woman's University News Bureau Notice that Taylor gave one of four comments at a

1966 OAH session titled "The Crusade for Woman Suffrage," April 19, 1966, folder 3 "Clippings," AET Papers, MSS 332c; "Dr. Taylor Reads Research Paper at Meeting," *Alum Bulletin* 170-820, November 15, 1969, folder 3 "Clippings," AET Papers, MSS 332c. In total, Taylor published nineteen articles in journals and history magazines from 1941 to 1980, according to a list in her papers titled "Publications by A. Elizabeth Taylor." Biographical file for A. Elizabeth Taylor, AET Papers. Also listed is a forthcoming entry on Miriam Ferguson that appeared in Sicherman and Green, *Notable American Women*, 230–32.

70. Antoinette Elizabeth Taylor to Mollie Davis, undated, folder "List of Women for Committees, SHA, 1972 for 1974," box 5, SAWH Records.

71. A. Taylor interview by Dean, in Schulz and Turner, *Clio's Southern Sisters*, 27.

72. A. Taylor, "Woman Suffrage Movement in Mississippi."

73. A. Taylor, "Woman Suffrage Movement in Texas," 208.

74. A. Taylor, review of *Susan B. Anthony*; A. Taylor, review of *The Ideas of the Woman Suffrage Movement*; A. Taylor, review of *The Right to Be People* and *The Puritan Ethic and Woman Suffrage*; A. Taylor, review of *The Woman Citizen*; A. Taylor review of *Revolt against Chivalry*.

75. A. Taylor interview by Dean, in Schulz and Turner, *Clio's Southern Sisters*, 26.

76. Mary Massey to Bennett Wall, January 6, 1971, folder 493 "Secretary Treasurer: 1970–1971, Vice President, M. E. Massey," SHA Records.

77. Betty Fladeland to Betty Brandon, October 2, 1983, untitled folder, box 3, SAWH Records (this collection was unprocessed when this research was conducted); Andrea Hahn, "Colleagues Remember Betty Fladeland as a Pioneer," *SIU News*, April 1, 2008, https://news.siu.edu/2008/04/040108amh8068.php.

78. "Dr. Taylor named VP of SAWH," December 1, 1976, *Lass-O*, 1, 3, folder 3, Biographical File for A. Elizabeth Taylor, AET Papers, MSS 332c.

79. "Dr. Taylor named VP of SAWH," December 1, 1976, AET Papers.

80. Heath, "Mary Elizabeth Massey."

81. Mary Elizabeth Massey, "Curriculum Vita" and "Application for Grant, Social Sciences Research Council," 1962, folder 1-2, box 1, MEM Papers.

82. Bennett Wall to Mary Massey, 1961, Incoming Correspondence, folder 56, box 6, MEM Papers; Link and Patrick, *Writing Southern History*.

83. Arthur Link to Mary Massey, July 8, 1961, and October 1, 1962, "Letter to the contributors to the Green volume," all folder 36, box 4, MEM Papers. Massey was hesitant to join the project but after some cajoling by Link, she agreed; Link later suggested to other contributors that Massey's chapter be used as a model since it was particularly lucid and provided good coverage.

84. Rembert W. Patrick to Mary Elizabeth Massey, January 3, 1962, and Link to Massey, July 8, 1961, both in Incoming l Correspondence files, folder 36, box 4, MEM Papers.

85. Mary Elizabeth Massey, "Curriculum Vita," "Application for Grant, Social Sciences Research Council," and "Application for Grant, Guggenheim 1962," folder 1-2, box 1, MEM Papers.

86. Allan Nevins to Mary Elizabeth Massey, September 27, 1962, folder 44, box 4, MEM Papers.

87. C. Vann Woodward to Mary Elizabeth Massey, July 31, 1963, Incoming Correspondence Files, folder 58, box 6, MEM Papers.

88. Massey to Nevins, October 15, 1962, Outgoing Correspondence, folder 3-9, box 1, MEM Papers.

89. Wall to Massey, partially dated letter, 1963, Incoming Correspondence Files, folder 10-58, box 6, MEM Papers.

90. Bell Wiley to Mary Massey, October 11, 1962, Incoming Correspondence Files, folder 57-58, box 6, MEM Papers.

91. Massey to Wiley, November 28, 1962, Outgoing Correspondence Files, folder 3-9, box 1, MEM Papers.

92. Bell Wiley, "Suggestions for Centennial Observances" speech delivered before the Civil War Centennial Commission National Assembly in Richmond, VA, April 17, 1959, Incoming Correspondence Files, folder 57-58, box 6, MEM Papers. The speech was printed in the March 1960 issue of *United Daughters of the Confederacy Magazine*, but Wiley forwarded a reprinted copy to Massey in 1962, suggesting she follow some of the leads he offered.

93. Mary Massey to Major General U. S. Grant III, Chairman Civil War Centennial Commission, April 23, 1958, Outgoing Correspondence Files, folder 3-9, box 1, MEM Papers; Wiley to Massey, June 13, 1962, Incoming Correspondence Files, folder 57, box 6, MEM Papers. James Patton had served as executive secretary to the Southern Historical Association just prior to Bennett Wall's thirty-year tenure; "Francis Butler Simkins," *South Carolina Encyclopedia*, accessed January 18, 2021, www.scencyclopedia.org/sce/entries/simkins-francis-butler/. Simkins was a 1928 PhD graduate of Columbia University.

94. Mary Massey to Elizabeth Dwight Cole, 1955, Outgoing Correspondence Files, folder 3-9, box 1, MEM Papers.

95. Mary Elizabeth Massey to Congressman Fred Schwengel, September 27, 1961, Outgoing Correspondence Files, folder 3-9, box 1, MEM Papers. Schwengel was on the Committee on Criteria and Recognition for the Civil War Centennial Commission.

96. Massey to Schwengel, September 27, 1961, MEM Papers.

97. Mary Elizabeth Massey to William E. Rooney, October 23, 1958, folder 3-9, box 1, MEM Papers.

98. Heath, "Mary Elizabeth Massey."

99. A. Taylor interview by Dean, in Schulz and Turner, *Clio's Southern Sisters*, 27.

100. Mary Massey to Grady McWhiney, December 17, 1970, Outgoing Correspondence Files, folder 57, box 6, MEM Papers.

101. Wiley to Massey, November 25, 1970, Incoming Correspondence Files, folder 57-58, box 6, MEM Papers.

102. Massey to Wall, January 6, 1971, folder 493 " Secretary Treasurer: 1970–1971, Vice President, M. E. Massey," SHA Records.

103. Wall to Massey, and Massey to Wall, 1970–1971, folder 463 "1970–1971: Annual meeting of the women's caucus," SHA Records. See chapter 7 for an elaboration on Davis's involvement in the Coordinating Committee on Women in the Historical Profession and the Caucus of Women in History of the SHA in the early 1970s.

104. A. Taylor interview by Dean, in Schulz and Turner, *Clio's Southern Sisters*, 27.

105. Massey to Wiley, February 2, 1972, Outgoing Correspondence Files, folder 3-6, box, 1, MEM Papers; A. Taylor, interview by Dean, November 5, 1992, in Schulz and Turner, *Clio's Southern Sisters*, 27; Bleser, "Three Women Presidents of the Southern Historical Association."

106. Doris King to Mary Massey, February 11, 1971, Incoming Correspondence Files, folder 9-92, box 9, MEM Papers; Bleser, "Three Women Presidents of the Southern Historical Association."

107. John Hope Franklin, "Remarks Introducing Mary Elizabeth Massey as President of the Southern Historical Association" at the annual meeting of the SHA, November 16, 1972, folder

120-123, box 12, MEM Papers. Franklin sent Massey a copy of this introduction and signed it, "For Mary Elizabeth—Love and best wishes. John Hope Franklin." These affirmations of affection, respect, and goodwill from her male colleagues are a constant in her correspondence. A. Elizabeth Taylor's retrospective observation of the esteem and affection in which they held her is undeniably accurate.

108. Owsley, *Plain Folk of the Old South*.

109. G. G. Johnson interview by Frederickson, May 17, 1974, SOHP; G. G. Johnson interview by Hall, August 19, 1974, SOHP; Thuesen, "Making Southern History."

Chapter 4

1. Tetrault, *Myth of Seneca Falls*; Des Jardins, *Women and the Historical Enterprise*, chaps. 4 and 5 consider African American women's history work in detail.

2. I have found the terms "women's history" and "woman's history" used as early as 1944, though much more frequent ways to refer to the field before the 1970s were "women in history," "the role of women in history," or "the history of women." The point is relevant because practitioners in the field didn't claim the title "women's history" until 1969.

3. Typically, the history of women's archives at midcentury and the story of women's history's emergence are treated separately in historiographic literature with little effort to connect work begun in the 1940s, with the intensified and broad-ranging efforts of women's historians after 1969 to develop and legitimize the field. Des Jardins's *Women and the Historical Enterprise in America* is a case in point. Des Jardins's closing chapter focuses on Beard's disenchantment with Radcliffe's approach to collecting and to women's history. But Beard's views on the best course for women's collecting and her negative reaction to Radcliffe's design should not be allowed to substitute for a deep description and analysis of the founding of these two pillars of the field's foundation. Radcliffe's focus was not as narrow as Beard thought it was, nor were the archivists at Radcliffe as unfriendly to encouraging use of its collections as Beard claimed (Des Jardins, chap. 8). Moreover, the Radcliffe archive, located as it was in the heart of Cambridge, was highly accessible to historians and graduate students. It had the support of Radcliffe administrators and key Harvard history faculty members.

4. Cott, *Woman Making History*; Des Jardins, *Women and the Historical Enterprise*; Lane, *Mary Ritter Beard*; Hildenbrand, *Women's Collections*.

5. Cott, *Woman Making History*, 4–15; Rosenberg, *Changing the Subject*, 112–13, 116–19.

6. Beard, *Women's Work in Municipalities*.

7. The jointly authored textbooks were Beard and Beard, *History of the United States* (1921); *The Rise of American Civilization*, 2 vols. (1927); *America in Midpassage*, 2 vols. (1939); *The American Spirit* (1942); and *A Basic History of the United States* (1944).

8. Cott, "Two Beards."

9. Mendenhall, "Review of *On Understanding Women* by Mary R. Beard"; Bruce, "Review of M. R. Beard, *Through Women's Eyes*"; Jack H. Hexter, review of *Woman as Force in History*, by Mary Beard, *New York Times Book Review*, March 17, 1946, 5.

10. Degler, "'Woman as Force in History' by Mary Beard."

11. Schwimmer's instincts were spot-on, and her fears were well-founded given the Nazis' propensity for book burning and looting archives and museums during World War II.

12. Lubelski, "'Kicking Off the Women's 'Archives Party.'"

13. Cott, *Woman Making History*, 181–82.

14. Mary Beard to the Board of the World Center for Women's Archives, June 26, 1940, as reprinted in Cott, *Woman Making History*, 210–11.

15. Relph, "World Center for Women's Archives"; Cott, *Woman Making History*; Des Jardins, *Women and the Historical Enterprise*; Lane, *Mary Ritter Beard*.

16. Snyder, *Making Black History*; J. Johnson, "'Drill into Us . . . the Rebel Tradition'"; Des Jardins, *Women and the Historical Enterprise*, chap. 4.

17. Helton, *Scattered and Fugitive Things*; Tomás, "Better Homes."

18. Henry, "Promoting Historical Consciousness"; Collier-Thomas, "Towards Black Feminism," 43–66.

19. Cott, *Woman Making History*, 195–99.

20. Cott, *Woman Making History*, 195–99; Collier-Thomas, "Towards Black Feminism," 43–66.

21. Collier-Thomas, "Towards Black Feminism," 43–66.

22. Collier-Thomas, "Towards Black Feminism," 55–57.

23. Henry, "Promoting Historical Consciousness"; Collier-Thomas, "Towards Black Feminism," 43–66. The Bethune Museum and the National Archives for Black Women's History was recognized as a National Historical Site by the National Park Service in 1982. Its archives, consisting of sixty-seven manuscript collections, have since been moved off-site to Landover, MD. The NPS website for the entire National Archives for Black Women's History has indicated that since 2020 or longer, it is not accepting research requests for this location, www.nps.gov /mamc/learn/historyculture/mamc_nabwh.htm. A 2024 email to the contact provided on the NPS webpage for the National Archives for Black Women's History confirmed that no access is available; Mike Antionini of the NPS email to Jennifer Tomás, June 17, 2024.

24. For example, Mary Church Terrell had donated her papers to the Library of Congress in the 1940s, and the Schlesinger Library on the History of Women in America had completed a large Black Women Oral History Project under direction of Letitia Woods Brown in 1978.

25. Rosenberg, *Changing the Subject*, 112–13, 116–19; Cott, *Woman Making History*, 39–40.

26. Though it was President Ada Comstock's earlier efforts that yielded the Maud Wood Park donation initially.

27. Cott, *Woman Making History*, 247–49.

28. Anke Voss Hubbard, "'No Documents, No History': Mary Ritter Beard and the Early History of Women's Archives," p. 2, file 3, box 1, series 1, RG 42, MSG Papers. Hubbard suggests that efforts to create women's collections emerged partly out of the passage of the National Archives Act of 1934, but her essay focuses primarily on Smith College as the institution that "made the greatest commitment to support a women's archive on its campus."

29. Grierson herself held a PhD in philosophy.

30. The distinctions I make about the point at which the Smith College Archives, the Collection of Women Writers, and the women's collection later named the Sophia Smith Collection came into being are worthy of clarification in and of themselves but also because they help clarify a point of contestation and rivalry that Grierson and Mary Beard raised throughout the 1940s about which collection came first and which took a better approach to women's collecting, Sophia Smith or the Radcliffe Women's Archives.

31. Nina F. Browne to President Neilson, June 13, 1921, folder "History of the College Archives—Nina Browne," box 30, collection 10.9, Smith College Histories, SCA.

32. Margaret Storrs Grierson, *Friends of the Smith College Library, Annual Reports 1–10, 1942–1952*, SCA.

33. Grierson, *Friends Annual Report, March 1, 1943*, 9, SCA.

34. Grierson, *Friends Annual Report, March 1, 1943*, 9, SCA.

35. Mary Beard to Margaret Grierson, April 11, 1943, folder "Series II, Correspondence, Margaret Grierson, 1941–1945," box 1, MRB Papers. There is no correspondence between the two for the years 1941 or 1942, though the folder is labeled 1941–1945. This is the first letter between the two that appears in the collection.

36. Beard to Grierson, April 11, 1943, MRB Papers.

37. Beard to Grierson, June 1, 1943, folder "Series II, Correspondence, Margaret Grierson, 1941–1945," box 1, MRB Papers.

38. Margaret Grierson to Nina Browne, July 10, 1943, file 21 "Correspondence to Nina Browne," box 1, series 3, MSG Papers.

39. Grierson to Browne, July 10, 1943, MSG Papers (italics added).

40. Grierson to Browne, August 31, 1943, file 21, box 1, series 3, MSG Papers.

41. Grierson to Browne, February 25, 1944, file 21, box 1, series 3, MSG Papers.

42. Grierson to Browne, April 15, 1944, file 21, box 1, series 3, MSG Papers. This consisted of some of Beard's own papers and commitments from Dorothy Kenyon and Florence Kitchelt to leave papers with Smith.

43. Grierson to Browne, June 5, 1944, file 21, box 1, series 3, MSG Papers.

44. Ada Louise Comstock to Mrs. Blackall, Mrs. Chronkhite, Mrs. Hill, and Mrs. Hinckley, September 30, 1942, "Substance of conversation with Mrs. Maud Wood Park and Mrs. Stantial," folder 1 "Correspondence with EBB, Mrs. Stantial, and Mrs. Park; Radcliffe Women's Archives Founding 1942–1970," AESL Records.

45. Merle Curti to Wilbur Jordan, September 30, 1958, folder Cr 33, box 5, *NAW* Records. Curti, a graduate of Harvard's history department, claims to have suggested building a women's collection at Smith when he taught there in the 1930s. Arthur Schlesinger Sr. was Curti's graduate advisor. Curti earned his PhD under Schlesinger in 1927. Merle Eugene Curti Papers, 1908–2000, finding aid, p. 2, Wisconsin Historical Society, Madison.

46. Des Jardins, *Women and the Historical Enterprise*, chap. 6, "Remembering Organized Feminism," treats feminists' effort to preserve and write their own histories through the gathering and donating of manuscripts and the writing of popular histories.

47. Grierson to Browne, June 20, 1944, file 21, box 1, series 3, MSG Papers. The Northwestern collection undoubtedly refers to the effort of political scientist Mary Earhart Dillon to place materials she had collected from Carrie Chapman Catt and other women activists during her work on a biography of Frances Willard. These materials eventually went to Radcliffe in 1948 since she could not convince Northwestern's library, nor any other, to take them. The California reference is probably to efforts by the Huntington Library to build up its holdings on women, although Grierson might be referring to some parallel effort within the University of California system.

48. Grierson to Browne, June 20, 1944, MSG Papers.

49. Grierson to Browne, January 30, 1945, file 21, box 1, series 3, MSG Papers.

50. Margaret Storrs Grierson, "The Present Situation at Radcliffe," 1, report dated November 1950, 1, folder SSC, box 30-31, collection 10.9, Smith College Histories, SCA, 1.

51. Grierson, "Present Situation at Radcliffe," 1, SCA.

52. Grierson, "Present Situation at Radcliffe," 2, SCA.

53. Grierson held a PhD in philosophy.

54. Grierson, "Present Situation at Radcliffe," 4, SCA (italics added).

55. Grierson, "Present Situation at Radcliffe," 4, SCA.

56. Grierson, "Present Situation at Radcliffe," 3, SCA.

57. Bennett, *History Matters*, offers a polemical presentation of many of these themes.

58. File 21, "Correspondence with Nina Browne, 1942–1950," series 3, MSG Papers.

59. Grierson to Browne, January 30, 1945, MSG Papers.

60. Mary Beard to the *Daily Bulletin*, November 23, 1944, folder 30 "Beard, Jordan, Hinckley Correspondence re: The Women's Archives," Mary Beard Papers, MC A-9, SL; "Plan for Advanced Research Fellowships for Women," undated, folder 21, Mary Beard Papers, MC A-9, SL.

61. Mary Beard to Margaret Grierson, June 22, 1944, series 2: Correspondence, Outgoing, Grierson, Margaret, 1941–1945, Mary Beard Papers, SL.

62. Grierson, "Present Situation at Radcliffe," 4, SCA.

63. Hague, "'Never . . . Another Season of Silence,'" 14–15.

64. Beard to Grierson, June 1943, "Addenda," folder "Series II, Correspondence, Margaret Grierson, 1941–1945," box 1, MRB Papers. Also see correspondence in MSG Papers, 1951–1956. Beard died in 1958, so the lapse in correspondence after 1956 was probably due to her advanced age at that point.

65. Hague, "'Never . . . Another Season of Silence,'" 11–12.

66. Margaret Storrs Grierson to Barbara K. Turoff, October 16, 1979, Beard Papers Donor File, SCA, as cited in Hague, "'Never . . . Another Season of Silence,'" 15.

67. Margaret Grierson to Mr. Jackson Martindell, Publisher, October 31, 1959, file 1 "Correspondence, General, 1922–1972," series 3, RG 42, MSG Papers.

68. Hague, "'Never . . . Another Season of Silence,'" 22.

69. A. Schlesinger, *New Viewpoints in American History*.

70. A. Schlesinger, *New Viewpoints in American History*, 158. Des Jardins amply illustrates this stage in the development of popular women's history within the context of her study on women as writers of history in the nineteenth and early twentieth centuries. Though Des Jardins does not focus only on writers of women's history, she provides ample documentation of women writing about women in history as part of their regional, ethnic, racial, social, cultural, labor, and movement histories up through 1940. Des Jardins juxtaposes these popular histories against the context of the gendering of professional, "scientific" history as masculine. The amateur historian/history was thus framed by professional historians as inherently "feminine" and lesser than the professional historian/history. Des Jardins qualifies this analysis by recognizing that progressive historians advocated for "liberal" histories that recognized the importance of recovering the histories of minorities, women, and common people.

71. L. Brown, *Apostle of Democracy*.

72. J. James, "Recollections of a Veteran in Women's History," vi. This 1981 preface was added to the first press of James's 1954 dissertation.

73. J. James, "Recollections of a Veteran in Women's History," vi.

74. Schlesinger Library/Collections as of April 12, 2021, www.radcliffe.harvard.edu /schlesinger-library/collections; Smith College Libraries Repositories Access Web Page, accessed April 13, 2021, https://findingaids.smith.edu/repositories. This number does not include collections in the Smith College Archives, which total 477 manuscript collections.

75. Julie Des Jardins deals effectively with this correlation between the history of women, women historians, and women's politics for the period 1880–1945. Des Jardins, *Women and the Historical Enterprise*.

76. Alma Lutz, "Facts the Historians Missed," *Independent Woman*, April 1954, 125–26, folder "Women's Archives Publicity #1, 1946–1959," box 1, series 4, AESL Records.

77. Hildenbrand, *Women's Collections*.

78. Hildenbrand, *Women's Collections*, 125–26.

79. Lutz, "Facts the Historians Missed," April 1954, AESL Records.

80. Lutz, *Created Equal*; Lutz, *Susan B. Anthony*; Lutz, *With Love, Jane*; Lutz, *Emma Willard*; Lutz, *Crusade for Freedom*.

81. ALP.

82. James's husband, Edward James, and historian Paul Boyer came to the Women's Archives in 1959 to work on the first ever scholarly encyclopedia of women in American history, *Notable American Women* (1971). Janet James would join this massive project as associate editor, steering it to completion in 1971 and making an invaluable contribution to the field's development in the process. Work on *Notable American Women* in the 1960s will be the major focus of chapter 5 because it was instrumental in building the field and broad support for it.

83. Edna Stantial to Maud Wood Park, July 9, 1943, and Mrs. Hinckley to Edna Stantial, July 19, 1943, folder 1 "Correspondence with Mrs. Stantial and Mrs. Park," box 1, series 1, AESL Records; Georgiana Ames Hinckley, "Report of the Librarian," Radcliffe College Report, Reports of the Officers, 1942–1943, pp. 48–49, accessed February 1, 2021, https://iiif.lib.harvard.edu/manifests/view/drs:427973187$49i.

84. Comstock to Blackall, Chronkhite, Hill, and Hinckley, September 30, 1942, AESL Records.

85. Finding aid, Mary Earhart Dillon Collection, 1863–1955, SL. When Dillon's plan fell through at Northwestern, the college asked her to remove from storage the archival materials she'd collected from Carrie Chapman Catt and other women activists, so Dillon donated the materials to Radcliffe in 1948; Dillon, *Frances Willard*.

86. Comstock to Blackall, Chronkhite, Hill, and Hinckley, September 30, 1942, AESL Records.

87. Ada Comstock Notestein, President, [to sponsors], July 8, 1943, folder 1 "Correspondence with Mrs. Stantial and Mrs. Park," box 1, series 1, AESL Records.

88. Oscar Handlin encouraged Anne Firor Scott's early work on Southern women progressives in the late 1950s and early 1960s, and Arthur Schlesinger encouraged Julia Cherry Spruill and Eleanor Flexner in the 1930s and 1950s, respectively. At Columbia in the early to mid-1960s, Aileen Kraditor, Carroll Smith-Rosenberg, and Gerda Lerner completed dissertations on women's topics under the direction of Robert Cross, William Leuchtenberg, and Eric McKitrick.

89. Scanlon and Cosner, "Natalie Zemon Davis," in *American Women Historians*, 53–55.

90. N. Davis, "Life of Learning," 12.

91. Des Jardins, *Women and the Historical Enterprise*, 244–51.

92. By 1948, relations between Beard and Radcliffe Women's Archives staff were cool but cordial. Radcliffe archivist Mary Howard attended Beard's talk "Understanding Woman by Knowing Her in History" at a meeting of the Friends of the Smith College Library in May of that year. Howard reported that she made many contacts and gained much valuable information. Mary Howard, "The Women's Archive: Report for the Year 1947–1948," folder "Women's Archives: General," box 1, series 1, AESL Records. Beard was still corresponding with President Jordan in the late 1940s as well, though often to testily disagree on some point of interpretive

historical framework for understanding women in history. Mary Beard to Wilbur Jordan, April 4, 1947, folder 30 "Beard, Jordan, Hinckley Correspondence Re: The Women's Archives," Mary Beard Papers, MC A-9, SL.

93. Des Jardins, *Women and the Historical Enterprise*, 256–57.

94. These portraits are less detailed than was the case for my Southern subjects because of the availability of records. In the case of Schlesinger, Ullian, Lutz, Dexter, Merk, and even Beard, only small collections of papers have been left behind for historians to interpret. Barbara Solomon and Janet James left extensive records at the Schlesinger Library, but those have restrictions on them, making them inaccessible to researchers.

95. Comstock to Blackall, Chronkhite, Hill, and Hinckley, September 30, 1942, AESL Records.

96. Des Jardins, *Women and the Historical Enterprise*, chap. 6, "Remembering Organized Feminism."

97. "Women's Exclusion from AMG Deplored at Radcliffe Parley," *Boston Herald*, August 27, 1943; Woman's Rights Collection: Partial Publicity; *Radcliffe News*, August 20, 1943, 1; *Radcliffe News*, August 27, 1943, 1, all from folder 8 "Publicity," box 1, series 1, AESL Records.

98. "Career Girls' Freedom Result of an Evolution of Woman's Rights Accelerated by 19th Century Suffragette Movement," *Radcliffe News*, August 27, 1943, folder 8 "Woman's Rights Collection, Partial Publicity," box 1, series 1, AESL Records.

99. "Ada Louise Comstock Notestein form letter, July 8, 1942," folder 1 "Correspondence with Mrs. Stantial and Mrs. Park," box 1, series 1, AESL Records.

100. "Career Girls' Freedom Result of an Evolution of Woman's Rights Accelerated by 19th Century Suffragette Movement," *Radcliffe News*, August 27, 1943, folder 8, box 1, series 1, AESL Records.

101. Mrs. Georgiana Ames Hinckley to Maud Park, June 12, 1945, folder 1 "Woman's Rights Collection—Correspondence with E. Stantial, Mrs. Park—Mrs. Hinckley," box 1, series 1, AESL Records. Abigail Adams had written that famous line in 1776.

102. Hinckley to Park, June 25, 1946, folder 2 "Woman's Rights Collection at Radcliffe College, corr. with E. L. Stantial and Mrs. Park to Mrs. Hinckley," box 1, series 1, AESL Records.

103. See chapter 2, note 42, above.

104. L. Merk, "Massachusetts and the Woman Suffrage Movement," frames 4–5, RG XXXII.

105. L. Merk, "Massachusetts and the Woman Suffrage Movement," RG XXXII.

106. "From the Council minutes of September 7, 1943," folder 2 "Woman's Rights Collection at Radcliffe College, corr. with E. L. Stantial and Mrs. Park to Mrs. Hinckley," box 1, series 1, AESL Records.

107. Marjorie Sprague to Miss Howard, from the Office of the President, Radcliffe College, October 20, 1948, folder 2 "Woman's Rights Collection at Radcliffe College, corr. with E. L. Stantial and Mrs. Park to Mrs. Hinckley," box 1, series 1, AESL Records.

108. Wilbur K. Jordan to Mrs. Carr V. Van Anda, September 20, 1944, folder 3 "U–V," box 2, series 1, AESL Records.

109. "All About Women!," *Worcester Sunday Telegram*, September 29, 1957, 7–8; and Gordon Simpson, "Radcliffe Archives Holds Record of Women's Role in World's Work," unidentified newspaper clipping, June 18, 1957, both in folder 1 "Women's Archives Publicity #1," box 1, series 4, AESL Records; Mann, *Yankee Reformers*; Tharp, *Until Victory*.

110. Notable exceptions of work developed first in the seminar and then published are E. Schlesinger, "Fanny Fern"; Merk, "Boston's Historic Public School Crisis"; Lutz, "Early

American Women Historians"; Lutz, "Hannah Adams"; Lutz, "Susan B. Anthony for the Working Woman"; Lutz, "Susan B. Anthony and John Brown"; and Lutz, *Susan B. Anthony*.

111. "Papers presented at the Radcliffe Seminar on American women, 1951–1952 and 1952–1953," box 1A, 1v, and 2v, series 1, RG XXXII.

112. (Weeks 1–12, 1951–1952) "Group Discussion, Seminar on Women," RG XXXII, MC 326.

113. Elizabeth Borden, "Report on the Seminar, 'The Role of the American Woman':(an experimental workshop conducted during the winter 1951–1952 by Elizabeth Borden, director Radcliffe Seminars and Archives)," folder "Role of Women—Correspondence," box 3, series 1, RG XXXII; "[week] 11. Group discussion—Seminar on Women, May 26, 1952," folder "Role of Women—Minutes, 1951–1952," box 3, series 1, RG XXXII.

114. Frieda Silbert Ullian Papers, 1950–1971 SC 89, Radcliffe College Archives, SL; Frieda Silbert Ullian was a Radcliffe alumna who had earned her BA (1921), MA (1935), and PhD (1938) from Radcliffe. The latter two degrees were in economics. She had also earned an EdM from the Harvard School of Education. Ullian was married to Hyman Ullian in 1924, thus completing two of her advanced degrees after she had commenced marriage and family life. She worked as a research fellow at Radcliffe, economist in the US Bureau of Labor Statistics, and economics tutor at Radcliffe and was a member of the economics department at Simmons College in Boston. As an active alumna she served as an officer on many Radcliffe committees, associations, and boards. In addition to being a participant in the Seminars on Women and trying her hand at historical scholarship, she also belonged to a number of voluntarist/civic groups. She served as chair of the Massachusetts Board of Higher Education in 1965 and president of the Massachusetts State Division of the American Association of University Women, among other organizations. She was a member of the American Association of University Professors and the American Economic Association.

115. "Group Discussion—Seminar on Women," week 12, June 4, 1952, folder "Minutes, 1951–1952," RG XXXII.

116. Elizabeth Borden, "Report on an Informal Seminar Known as the 'Workshop on Women,' 1952–1953," folder "Annual Reports, 1950–1954," box 4, series 1, RG XXXII.

117. "Seminar on American Women" course outlines Fall 1951 and Spring 1952, and "Reading List for Seminar on American Women, January–May 1952," folder "Role of Women—General," box 3, series 1, RG XXXII.

118. Borden, "Report on an Informal Seminar Known as the 'Workshop on Women,' 1952–1953," RG XXXII.

119. Folder "General," box 3, series 1, RG XXXII.

120. Of these guest speakers, two were prominent historians. Helen Maud Cam was a medievalist and the first female faculty member of the Harvard history department (appointed in 1948). Cecilia Kenyon was a respected if under-recognized scholar of the American Revolution who held a faculty position at Smith College. Her work was posthumously hailed as formative for the subfield in Elkins et al., *Men of Little Faith*.

121. Radcliffe College Seminar on Women, Records, 1951–1959: A Finding Aid for MC 326 and the papers therein.

122. "Lois Merk, 89, Taught History at Radcliffe," *Boston Globe*, obituaries, October 3, 1992.

123. Elisabeth Dexter to Margaret Grierson, November 20, 1961, folder "EAD to MSG—Correspondence 1945–1965," EAD Papers.

124. "Seminar on American Women" course outlines Fall 1951 and Spring 1952, and "Reading List for Seminar on American Women, January–May 1952," RG XXXII. Lutz, Schlesinger, and

Merk did manage to publish essays based largely on research conducted during the seminars. See note 110.

125. Ware, "Barbara Miller Solomon."

126. Solomon, *Ancestors and Immigrants*; Solomon, *Pioneers in Service*.

127. Barbara Miller Solomon, biographical synopsis for her speech given at Wheelock College, "The Dilemma of Educated Women," undated, *Wheelock Newsletter*, 4–7, folder 1 "Women's Archives Publicity #2," box 1, series 4, AESL Records; Handlin, "Memoirs."

128. Handlin, "Memoirs," 202.

129. Ulrich, *Yards and Gates*. Of particular relevance are essays and vignettes on pages 215–89 that chronicle various stages of Radcliffe's integration with Harvard. Radcliffe students never had their own faculty and attended sex-segregated classes given by Harvard professors until 1943. In 1943, classes were integrated in part in response to low male enrollments caused by the war and because Radcliffe president Ada Comstock had waged a long campaign for such an integration. Full integration of dormitories and other facilities, like libraries, did not begin until the late 1960s, though. Andrew Mandel's essay in Ulrich's volume, "Feminism and Femininity in Almost Equal Balance," describes how Radcliffe women coped with the integration, retaining feminine demeanor and appearances and developing other behavioral strategies in order to gain acceptance by Harvard men and a place in sex-integrated classrooms.

130. "Byerly Bailiwick," undated article in unidentified Radcliffe publication, ca. 1961, folder "Women's Archives Publicity #2, 1960–1962," box 1, series 4, AESL Records.

131. Barbara Miller Solomon Papers, 1953–1975, SL, collection closed; authorized descendant unresponsive to requests for access to the collection in 2022. Finding aid indicates she was appointed in 1964 to Governor Endicott Peabody's Special Committee on the Status of Women. In 1971 she was appointed to the Massachusetts Commission on the Status of Women by Governor Francis W. Sargent.

132. Harvard University, Radcliffe College press release for Friday morning papers of May 21, 1965, folder "Clippings and Releases: Women's Archives Publicity #3," box 1, series 4, AESL Records; Ware, "Barbara Miller Solomon." .

133. Ware, "Barbara Miller Solomon." \

134. Barbara Miller Solomon, Recollections Sound Recording, Schlesinger T-1, [CD 41], SL.

135. All news clippings cited in this section come from folder "Clippings and Releases: Women's Archives Publicity #3," box 1, series 4, AESL Records.

136. Vera Glaser, "First Lady Rewards the 'Doers,'" *Evening Bulletin* (Philadelphia), July 6, 1964.

137. "First Lady Hostess," *Evening Star* (Washington, DC), February 19, 1964.

138. Stanlee Miller, "Preserve Those Scribbles! You Might Be Famous," *Washington Daily News*, February 20, 1964, 54.

139. Isabelle Shelton, "Women Doers are Told History Needs Records," *Evening Star*, February 20, 1964.

140. Solomon, Recollections Sound Recording, Schlesinger T-1, [CD 41], SL.

141. Solomon, Recollections Sound Recording, Schlesinger T-1, SL.

142. Solomon, Recollections Sound Recording, Schlesinger T-1, SL.

143. Solomon, Recollections Sound Recording, Schlesinger T-1, SL.

144. Anne Firor Scott to Barbara Miller Solomon, December 7, 1971, Chronological Correspondence files, box 1, AFS Papers.

145. J. James, "Recollections of a Veteran in Women's History," xxv.

Chapter 5

1. In 1971 the set sold for a retail price of $75. The equivalent value today would be roughly $400. I mention this lest we think that Professor Weigley bought his wife the volumes on a lark.

2. Mrs. Emma Weigley to Edward James, March 10, 1972, folder 105, box 19, series 1, *NAW Records*.

3. E. James to Weigley, March 21, 1972, folder 105, *NAW* Records.

4. E. James et al., *Notable American Women*, 3 vols.

5. Figures drawn from the author's own database of contributors and the Publicity and Reviews file in folders 104 and 105, box 19, series 1, *NAW* Records.

6. These numbers are drawn from the Publicity and Reviews files, folders 103 and 104, box 19, series 1, *NAW* Records.

7. Sicherman and Green, *Notable American Women*; Ware, *Notable American Women*.

8. Zinsser, *History and Feminism*, 22; Bennett, *History Matters*. Both of these provocative books date the field's emergence in the United States to the 1970s. Seeing the development of women's history as a corollary to the women's movement, they emphasize the struggle of women and women's historians to achieve legitimacy as professional scholars and focus, in part, on the resistance that many male historians offered to the field of women's history.

9. Zinsser, *History and Feminism*, 24.

10. Mary Beard had attempted to get Britannica interested in improving its coverage on women. Her papers at the Schlesinger Library show that she shared her ideas about doing this with Jordan and that Jordan was already hopeful of producing a historical encyclopedia on American women as early as 1944. Mary Beard to Wilbur K. Jordan, January 20, 1944, and Jordan to Beard, January 29, 1944, folder 30 "Beard, Jordan, Hinckley Correspondence," Mary Beard Papers, A-9, SL.

11. Cott, *Woman Making History*, 221–51.

12. Edward T. James and Janet Wilson James, preface to E. James et al. *Notable American Women*, 1:ix.

13. Schuyler and James, *Dictionary of American Biography*. Supplements 3, 4, and 5 were also edited by James.

14. Wilbur K. Jordan, "Application to the Lucius N. Littauer Foundation, Inc. for a Grant to Assist with the Financing of a Biographical Dictionary of American Women," May 1959, and Wilbur K. Jordan, "Application to the Rockefeller Foundation for a Grant to Assist with the Financing of a Biographical Dictionary of American Women," May 1959, folder 2 "A. M. Schlesinger Correspondence," box 1, *NAW* Records.

15. Alma Lutz and Elizabeth Anthony Dexter, "To the Advisory Board of the Radcliffe Women's Archives," 1956, folder 1 "Prospectus and Early Correspondence of NAW," box 1, *NAW* Records; Keckeis, *Lexicon of Women in Two Volumes*, vols. 1–2.

16. Arthur M. Schlesinger, Chairman, Advisory Board, Women's Archives, "Cyclopedia of American Women," *Radcliffe Quarterly*, November 1958, 27, folder 1 "Women's Archives Publicity #1," box 1, series 4, AESL Records.

17. Edward T. James to Committee of Consultants, January 1966, folder 5 "Descriptive Brochure and Researcher Forms," box 1, *NAW* Records; Edward T. James to Mary Bunting, June 12, 1964, Bunting to Janet Wilson James, September 14, 1961, and Edward T. James to Bunting, July 25, 1961, folder 17, box 2, *NAW* Records.

18. Janet Wilson James evaluation of bio-bibliographies, folder 8, box 1, *NAW* Records.

19. J. James, "Recollections of a Veteran in Women's History," viii.

20. A. Schlesinger Jr., "In Memoriam."

21. A. Schlesinger Jr., "In Memoriam."

22. J. James, introduction to E. James et al., *Notable American Women*, 1:xvii–xlx; A. Scott, "Making the Invisible Women Visible: An Essay Review."

23. Preyer, "Janet Wilson James."

24. J. James, "Recollections of a Veteran in Women's History," vi. This 1981 introduction was added to the first press of James's 1954 dissertation.

25. J. James, "Recollections of a Veteran in Women's History," vii.

26. Preyer, "Janet Wilson James," 175–76.

27. The Janet Wilson James Papers are housed at the Schlesinger Library.

28. A. Schlesinger, "Cyclopedia of American Women," AESL Records.

29. A. Schlesinger, "Cyclopedia of American Women," AESL Records.

30. "Council Approves Archives Project," *Radcliffe News*, February 22, 1957, folder 1 "Press Releases and Clippings, Publicity Files, 1946–1959," box 1, series 4, AESL Records.

31. "From the Office of the President," October 2, 1958, to Mr. James, folder 1 "Prospectus and Early Correspondence of NAW," box 1, *NAW* Records; Lovell Thompson, "Henry Alexander Laughlin."

32. List of the original Committee of Consultants, folder 4 "Committee of Consultants," box 1, *NAW* Records.

33. Edward T. James to Arthur M. Schlesinger, May 8, 1961, folder 1 "Prospectus and Early correspondence of NAW," box 1, *NAW* Records.

34. Simkins and Patton, *Women of the Confederacy*; SHA Records. Patton had also served a term as Southern Historical Association president.

35. Carl Bridenbaugh to Edward James, April 30, 1961, folder "BR Z8," box 4, *NAW* Records.

36. Merle Curti to Wilbur Jordan, September 30, 1958, folder "Cr 33," box 5, *NAW* Records. That Curti, a graduate of Harvard's history department, claims to have suggested building a women's collection at Smith when he taught there in the 1930s is interesting in light of Margaret Grierson's assertion in 1947 that the Radcliffe Women's Archives "scheme" had been instigated by the suggestion of a Smith College professor. See chapter 4 for the reference; Arthur Schlesinger Sr. was Curti's graduate advisor. After earning his PhD under Schlesinger Sr., in 1927 Curti taught at Smith College from 1927 to 1937. Merle Eugene Curti Papers, 1908–2000, finding aid, p. 2, Wisconsin Historical Society, Madison.

37. Higham was also a mentor to Mary Beth Norton when she was an undergraduate at Michigan University. Norton interview by Barnes, LUSWHOHP, 12–13. Richard Hofstadter, Linda Kerber's dissertation advisor, taught at Columbia University and was a mentor along with William Leuchtenberg and Robert and Barbara Cross to Caroll Smith-Rosenberg, Aileen Kraditor, and Gerda Lerner.

38. Edward James to Professor Clement Eaton, March 7, 1960, folder E, box 6, *NAW* Records.

39. E. James et al., *Notable American Women*, "Georgia Madden Martin," 2:502–4.

40. Eaton to E. James, March 16, 1960, folder E, box 6, *NAW* Records.

41. I identified the professionals by cross-referencing my list with the 1967 membership list of the OAH and the 1975 edition of the *Guide to Departments of History* and by referencing correspondence files in *NAW* Records. This number should be considered a low estimate. I did not attempt to verify the credentials of any contributor I did not immediately recognize who did not appear in either the OAH or AHA list or whose name fell alphabetically in the

second half of the alphabet. I did not have the chance to systematically examine the *NAW* correspondence for those people.

42. This data on contributors is derived from a database of my own creation, which was compiled from the 1971 edition of *Notable American Women* and then cross-referenced with the *Guide to History Departments* (1975), and the 1967 membership list for the Organization of American Historians. I also searched for individual contributors' names in the JSTOR database of academic journals for clues to the discipline the contributors belonged to and their institutional affiliation and academic credentials.

43. Rose et al., "Report of the American Historical Association Ad Hoc Committee." This report came to be called the "Rose Report." It surveyed the major history departments in the United States and revealed the low representation of women in these departments from 1920 until 1969 and a particularly stark decline in their representation in history departments between 1959 and 1969.

44. Dagbovie, "Black Women Historians," 254.

45. Dagbovie, "Black Women Historians," 254.

46. Dagbovie, "Black Women Historians," 252.

47. Jean Blackwell Hutson to Edward James, October 19, 1960, folder "Hu," box 8, *NAW* Records.

48. Eleanor Flexner to Edward James, September 16, 1959, folder F, *NAW* Records; Daniel, *Women Builders*; Des Jardins, *Women and the Historical Enterprise*, 135–37, 153, 175.

49. Hutson to E. James, October 19, 1960, *NAW* Records.

50. Dagbovie, "Black Women Historians," 252.

51. It will in the future be interesting to look at the papers of these scholars for evidence of their teaching women's history as a sign of precursors to the modern field of Black women's history. Did they teach any of the later leading historians of Black women? Julie Des Jardins has given us a fairly thorough account of the activities of Black women archivists, history educators, researchers, and popular authors for the first half of the twentieth century. Des Jardins, *Women and the Historical Enterprise*, 118–76; White, *Telling Histories*.

52. E. James et al., *Notable American Women*, vol. 3, index.

53. Volume 4 added entries for women who died between 1951 and 1975. Published under the editorial direction of Barbara Sicherman and Carol Hurd Green in 1980, it made progress toward improving representation of women from racial and ethnic minority groups, making a deliberate effort to consult representatives of Black, Indigenous, Asian American, and Hispanic American organizations and scholars from those groups. Representation of women of color doubled to about 8 percent (35 of 442 entries), with Black women comprising the largest number. In 2004, volume 5 of *Notable American Women* was published under the editorial direction of Susan Ware. Her efforts reflected directions the field of American women's history took in the 1980s and 1990s and her generation's commitment to diversifying scholarship in American women's history. Volume 5's contents were dramatically more racially and ethnically diverse, with approximately 25 percent of the subjects being Black, Indigenous, Hispanic, and Asian American. The main editors of volumes 1 through 5 were white, but every team had one or more BIPOC editorial consultants.

54. Correspondence files, *NAW* Records; E. James et al., *Notable American Women*.

55. Karl de Schweinitz to Edward James, November 11, 1959, folder "De," box 5, *NAW* Records.

56. E. James to de Schweinitz, November 19, 1959, folder "De," box 5, *NAW* Records.

57. Horace Bond to Edward T. James, February 18, 1960, folder "Bo," box 4; E. Franklin

Frazier to E. James, September 25, 1961, folder "Fr," box 7; John Hope Franklin to E. James, October 8, 1958, and July 4, 1958, folder "Fr," box 7; Hutson to E. James, October 19, 1960, all in *NAW* Records. Adelaide Hill and Schomburg Center archivist Dorothy Porter also consulted on the inclusion of Black women.

58. Elizabeth Anthony Dexter to Edward James, February 17, 1960, "De," *NAW* Records.

59. Eleanor Flexner to Edward James, June 29, 1959, folder "Fi," box 6, *NAW* Records.

60. Flexner to E. James, January 16, 1959, *NAW* Records.

61. E. James et al., *Notable American Women*. Porter wrote the entries for Maria Louise Baldwin and Sarah Parker Redmond.

62. John P. Hall to Edward James, November 30, 1959, folder "Ha," box 7, *NAW* Records.

63. The rating system asked consultants to give those women who they had no doubt should be included an "A," figures they thought should probably be included got a "B," borderline cases received a "C," and the rest received a "D" or even an "F" if the consultant felt strongly enough about their lack of historical significance.

64. "List of Writings in American History," 1958, folder 138, *NAW* Records. The list is also sometimes titled "Women in Writings on American History."

65. "American Historical Review," folder 137, *NAW* Records.

66. Warren F. Kuehl, "List of Doctoral Dissertations in History Completed by 1960," folder 140, *NAW* Records.

67. Jack H. Hexter, review of *Woman as Force in History*, by Mary Beard, *New York Times Book Review*, March 17, 1946, 5; Bonnie Smith quotes Hexter in her illuminating study *Gender of History*, 3; Bennett, *History Matters*, 18–19. Bennett quotes Hexter as a lead into her assertion that "in the 1970s feminist historians in the United States and elsewhere built the practice of women's history while working within a largely male profession, most of whose members were either non-feminists or anti-feminists. In this hostile environment, feminists demanded not just that the profession accommodate women more fully, but also that women's history be integrated into mainstream history." A statement as strong as this dismisses the efforts of men and women historians active on behalf of women's history in the profession in the fifteen or so years prior to 1970. Zinsser, *History and Feminism*, 34. Zinsser referenced the Hexter quote in her discussion of Mary Beard and her lack of acceptance as a legitimate scholar.

68. See the interviews in LUSWHOHP.

69. Jensen interview by Barnes, LUSWHOHP.

70. Joan Jensen to Edward James, June 4, 1959, folder J, box 9, *NAW* Records.

71. E. James to Jensen, September 11, 1959, folder J, box 9, *NAW* Records. Ray Billington, a former history professor at Northwestern until ca. 1959, was the director of the Huntington Library by 1962. Billington had encouraged Mary Massey's work *Bonnet Brigades* and authored two sketches for *Notable American Women*.

72. Jensen interview by Barnes, LUSWHOHP, 7.

73. Jensen interview by Barnes, LUSWHOHP, 7–8.

74. Jensen interview by Barnes, LUSWHOHP, 17. Jensen authored the biographical sketches in *Notable American Women* for Charlotte Amanda Black Brown, Cloe Annette Buckel, Ellen Beach Yaw, and Caroline Seymour Severance. Jensen, "After Slavery"; Jensen, "Annette Abbott Adams."

75. Mary Dunn to Edward James, July 8, 1968, Folder "Du," Box 6, *NAW* Records.

76. Dunn interview by Rothschild, LUSWHOHP, 26–27.

77. Dunn interview by Rothschild, LUSWHOHP, 26–27.

78. Dunn interview by Rothschild, LUSWHOHP, 38.

79. Dunn interview by Rothschild, LUSWHOHP, 34.

80. Dunn interview by Rothschild, LUSWHOHP, 26–27, 34, 36, 38.

81. Hartman and Banner, *Clio's Consciousness Raised*, vii–viii.

82. "Florence Bascom," folder "Florence Bascom," box 27, *NAW* Records.

83. Smith-Rosenberg interview by Rothschild, LUSWHOHP, 24, 34.

84. Smith-Rosenberg interview by Rothschild, LUSWHOHP, 19–20.

85. Palmer, *From Gentleman's Club to Professional Body*.

86. Smith-Rosenberg interview by Rothschild, LUSWHOHP, 27; Rosenberg, *Changing the Subject*, 232.

87. Barbara Cross to Annette Baxter, June 17, 1966, series 5, Barnard College, History Department, Classes, Hist 41, 42 "Women in America" General 1965–1966, Annette Kar Baxter Papers, 1905–1984, SSC.

88. B. Cross to Baxter, June 17, 1966, SSC. Linda Kerber also reported in her LUSWHOHP interview that Annette Baxter was an influential teacher for her in her undergraduate years at Barnard. Kerber interview by Weisiger, LUSWHOHP, 12, 29.

89. Smith-Rosenberg, *Religion and the Rise of the American City*.

90. Annette Baxter correspondence with Edward James, 1962–66, folder "B Z4," box 3, *NAW* Records.

91. Robert Cross to Edward James, January 25, 1961, folder "Cr," box 5, *NAW* Records; E. James to R. Cross, November 14, 1963, folder "Cr," box 5, *NAW* Records.

92. R. Cross to E. James, January 25, 1961, *NAW* Records.

93. E. James to R. Cross, November 14, 1963, folder "Cr," box 5, *NAW* Records.

94. Lerner interview by Rothschild, LUSWHOHP, 7.

95. E. James to R. Cross, November 14, 1963, and R. Cross to E. James, November 20, 1963, folder "Cr," box 5, *NAW* Records.

96. Gerda Lerner to Edward James, January 1, 1964, folder "Li 61," box 10, *NAW* Records; E. James et al., *Notable American Women*, 1:511–12.

97. The honorarium ranged from $12 to $36 depending on the length of the article. The fee today would be approximately equivalent to $84 to $252. If the writer already had resources on hand about the subject, this was probably fair, but if the writer needed to undertake any new research, the fee was indeed modest.

98. Lerner interview by Rothschild, LUSWHOHP, 47; Horowitz, *Betty Friedan*, 213; Weigand, *Red Feminism*, 1–2, 62; Lerner, *Fireweed*.

99. Lerner interview by Rothschild, LUSWHOHP, 12.

100. Lerner interview by Rothschild, LUSWHOHP, 4.

101. Rosenberg, *Changing the Subject*, 131.

102. Lerner interview by Rothschild, LUSWHOHP, 5–6; Lerner, *Fireweed*.

103. Folder 13 "Publicity for Courses Offered by Gerda Lerner on Women's History, 1962–1964," series 1, GLP 1950–95.

104. Folder 13 "Publicity for Courses Offered by Gerda Lerner on Women's History, 1962–1964," GLP 1950–95.

105. Gerda Lerner, Curriculum Vitae (Short Form), folder "Resumes," carton 1, GLP 1950–95.

106. Lerner, "Grimké Sisters."

107. Lerner, *Woman in American History*; Lerner, *Black Women in White America*.

108. As exemplified by the naming of the Organization of American Historians' Lerner-Scott Prize for the best dissertation in US women's history, first awarded in 1992, https://www.oah .org/awards/dissertation-awards/lerner-scott-prize/.

109. Erick McKitrick to Gerda Lerner, October 6, 1967; Carl Degler to Gerda Lerner, March 25, 1965; and Degler to Lerner, October 20, 1969, folder 26, carton 1, GLP 1950–1995.

110. "American Civilization Seminar, 1968–1979," folder 18, GLP 1950–95.

111. Lerner interview by Rothschild, LUSWHOHP, 11–12. Apparently these company representatives did not agree with others in the publishing house about women in history, as Houghton-Mifflin published a document reader on American women by Anne Firor Scott in 1970. A. Scott, *Women in American Life*.

112. Correspondence folders, box 1, AFS Papers; Anne Firor Scott Papers, 1963–2002, finding aid, https://archives.lib.duke.edu/catalog/uaafs; Neil Genzlinger, "Anne Firor Scott, Scholar of Women's History, Dies at 97," *New York Times*, February 13, 2019, www.nytimes.com/2019 /02/13/obituaries/anne-firor-scott-dead.html.

113. Anne Firor Scott to William Leuchtenberg, January 6, 1972, Business Correspondence folders, Chronological, AFS Papers.

114. Eleanor Flexner to Anne Firor Scott, November 21, 1966, Business Correspondence files, Chronological, AFS Papers.

115. A. Scott interviews by Glusman and Rothschild, LUSWHOHP, 19, 60.

116. A. Scott interviews by Glusman and Rothschild, LUSWHOHP, 19, 60; A. Scott, *Southern Lady*; Frederickson, "Review of *The Southern Lady*."

117. A. Scott interviews by Glusman and Rothschild, LUSWHOHP, 17; A. Scott, "Making the Invisible Women Visible."

118. A. Scott interviews by Glusman and Rothschild, LUSWHOHP, 60.

119. M. Benson, review of *Notable American Women: 1607–1950*; Gutheim, "*Notable American Women*"; Massey, "*Notable American Women*"; A. Scott, "Making the Invisible Women Visible"; Welter, "Review of *Notable American Women, 1607–1950*."

120. Flexner to E. James, January 29, 1973, folder 105, "Reactions from Readers," box 19, *NAW* Records.

121. Dubois, "Foremothers I."

122. For reference to the major textbook introductions and historiographic statements supporting this assertion, see chapter 1.

123. Smith-Rosenberg, "New Woman and the New History," 186, 188–189.

Chapter 6

1. Murphy, *Citizenship and the Origins of Women's History*; Tetrault, *Myth of Seneca Falls*.

2. Judith Sargent Murray, "On the Equality of the Sexes," 1790, National Humanities Center, accessed July 20, 2022, http://nationalhumanitiescenter.org/pds/livingrev/equality/text5 /sargent.pdf.

3. A. Grimké, *Appeal to the Christian Women of the South*; S. Grimké, *Letters on the Equality of the Sexes*; Child, *Biographies of Madame de Stael and Madame Roland*; Fuller, *Woman in the Nineteenth Century*; Stanton et al., *History of Woman Suffrage*, vols. 1–3; Anthony and Harper, *History of Woman Suffrage*, vol. 4; Harper, *History of Woman Suffrage*, vol. 5; Tetrault, *Myth of Seneca Falls*.

4. This point has been made by many historians of the woman suffrage movement in the United States, including, as early as 1965, Kraditor, *Ideas of the Woman Suffrage Movement*; Terborg-Penn, *African American Women*; Newman, *White Women's Rights*; and Sneider, *Suffragists in an Imperial Age*.

5. Buhle and Buhle, *Concise History of Woman Suffrage*, 10.

6. McCluskey, *Forgotten Sisterhood*; Daniel, *Women Builders*; H. Brown, *Homespun Heroines*.

7. Dagbovie, "Black Women Historians," 252; Des Jardins, *Women and the Historical Enterprise*, 170–72; J. Johnson, "'Drill into Us . . . the Rebel Tradition'"; Logan, review of *Women Builders*; Snyder, *Making Black History*; Helton, *Scattered and Fugitive Things*.

8. Finding aid, Mary Earhart Dillon Collection, 1863–1955, SL. When Dillon's plan fell through at Northwestern, the college asked her to remove from storage the archival materials she'd collected from Carrie Chapman Catt and other women activists, so Dillon donated the materials to Radcliffe in 1948. Dillon, *Frances Willard*; Ada Louise Comstock to Mrs. Blackall, Mrs. Chronkhite, Mrs. Hill, and Mrs. Hinckley, September 30, 1942, "Substance of conversation with Mrs. Maud Wood Park and Mrs. Stantial," folder 1 "Correspondence with EBB, Mrs. Stantial, and Mrs. Park; Radcliffe Women's Archives Founding 1942–1970," AESL Records; Mary Beard to the Board of the World Center for Women's Archives, June 26, 1940, as reprinted in Cott, *Woman Making History*, 210–11.

9. Salmon, *History of the Appointing Power of the President*; "Lucy Maynard Salmon," *Vassar College Encyclopedia*, accessed January 13, 2011, http://vcencyclopedia.vassar.edu/faculty/prominent-faculty/lucy-maynard-salmon.html accessed; L. Brown, *Apostle of Democracy*; Salmon, *Domestic Service*; Salmon, *Progress in the Household*; Woman Suffrage Papers, folder 23, box 5, Lucy Maynard Salmon Papers, Vassar College Archives and Special Collections Library, Poughkeepsie, NY.

10. Lebsock, "In Retrospect"; Cott, *Woman Making History*, 10–30; DuBois, *Harriot Stanton Blatch*.

11. Lebsock, "In Retrospect," 328–32.

12. Cott, *Woman Making History*, 15.

13. Cott, *Woman Making History*, 10; Baker, "Domestication of Politics."

14. Mary Beard to Margaret Grierson, April 11, 1943, folder 1 "Series II, Correspondence, Margaret Grierson, 1941–1945," box 1, MRB Papers.

15. "Writings, etc., Published Book Reviews by EBS, 1938-1970," folder 23, box 2, Papers of Elizabeth Bancroft Schlesinger, MC 894; John C. Devlin, "Elizabeth Bancroft Schlesinger, Feminist and Historian's Widow," *New York Times*, June 2, 1977, 34, www.nytimes.com/1977/06/02/archives/long-island-opinion-elizabeth-bancroft-schlesinger-feminist-and.html.

16. Papers of Elizabeth Bancroft Schlesinger, MC 894, box 2, folders 8–14 and 25–32, SL; E. B. Schlesinger, "Review of *Morning Star: A Biography of Lucy Stone, 1818–1893*, by E. R. Hays," *New England Quarterly* 35, no. 1 (1962): 117–19; E. Schlesinger, "Two Early Harvard Wives"; E. Schlesinger, "Proper Bostonians"; E. Schlesinger, "Cotton Mather and His Children"; E. Schlesinger, "Nineteenth-Century Woman's Dilemma"; E. Schlesinger, "Review of Ray Billington.'" She authored about two dozen reviews of works in the fields of women's, Black, immigrant, and social history for scholarly journals from the 1950s through the 1970s.

17. Miriam Y. Holden Collection, 1676–1993 (bulk 1930), Series 3: Activities, 1895–1983, Manuscripts Division, Department of Special Collections, Princeton University Library.

18. Alma Lutz Papers, 1912–1971, Vassar College Archives and Special Collections Library, Poughkeepsie, NY; ALP.

19. Rebekah S. Greathouse, LLB, *Constitutional Rights of Women*, National Woman's Party pamphlet, edited by Alma Lutz, printed June 1935, "Woman's Rights" #1871, ALP.

20. Alma Lutz, "A Feminist Thinks It Over," *Equal Rights*, December 1944, 88, folder "Miscellaneous Pamphlets and Writings," ALP.

21. Alma Lutz, "Protective Legislation for Women: Yesterday and Today," leaflet reprinted from *Equal Rights*, ca. 1933–40 (reference to retrogressive policies of Germany and Italy suggest this was published in the interwar period), folder "Protective Legislation," ALP; Alma Lutz, "Hits AFL-CIO Opposition for Equal Rights," letter to the editor, *Boston Sunday Herald*, July 13, 1958, folder "Miscellaneous Pamphlets and Writings," ALP.

22. Alma Lutz, "Equal Rights for Women," *New York Herald Tribune*, May 27, 1962, folder "Miscellaneous Pamphlets and Writings," ALP.

23. Ruthann Robson, "Justice Scalia's Legacy on Gender Equality: No Need to Remember the Ladies," Oxford Human Rights Hub, March 21, 2016, https://ohrh.law.ox.ac.uk/justice-scalias -legacy-on-gender-equality-no-need-to-remember-the-ladies/; Marcia Greenberger, "Justice Scalia's Legal Approach Hurt Women," *USA Today*, February 21, 2016, www.usatoday.com/story /opinion/2016/02/21/scalia-women-discrimination-rights-damage-column/80549952 /; Max Fisher, "Scalia Says Constitution Doesn't Protect Women from Gender Discrimination," *The Atlantic*, January 4, 2011, www.theatlantic.com/politics/archive/2011/01/scalia-says-constitution -doesn-t-protect-women-from-gender-discrimination/342789; Adam Cohen, "Justice Scalia Mouths Off on Sex Discrimination," *Time*, September 22, 2010, http://content.time.com/time /nation/article/0,8599,2020667,00.html.

24. Alma Lutz, "Woman's Hour: Present Generation Encouraged to Study Those Who Stood for Suffrage and Enlightenment," *Christian Science Monitor*, August 24, 1946, 3, folder "Writings," ALP.

25. EAD Papers; "Elisabeth Anthony Dexter," *Who's Who of American Women: Volume I (1958–1959)* (Chicago: A. N. Marquis Company, 1958), 332; E. James et al., *Notable American Women*. Dexter also served on the Committee of Consultants for *Notable American Women*.

26. Dexter, *Career Women of America* (1972), vii–viii.

27. Dexter, *Career Women of America* (1972), viii.

28. Dexter, *Colonial Women of Affairs* (1972), ix.

29. Papers of Elizabeth Bancroft Schlesinger, MC 894; see also chapters 3 and 4 of this book. EAD Papers; Robert Cloutman and Elisabeth Anthony Dexter Papers, MS 2005.029, Brown University Archives, Providence, RI.

30. A. Scott, *Pauli Murray and Caroline Ware*, 2–3; finding aid for the Papers of Caroline Farrar Ware, 1924–1990, Biographical Sketch, CV, Franklin Delano Roosevelt Presidential Library, Hyde Park, NY.

31. Frederickson and Kornbluh, *Sisterhood and Solidarity*; Sklar et al., *Social Justice Feminists*; Sklar, *Florence Kelley*; Laughlin, *Women's Work and Public Policy*; finding aid for the Papers of Caroline Farrar Ware, 1924–1990, Biographical Sketch, CV, Franklin Delano Roosevelt Presidential Library.

32. Finding aid for the Papers of Caroline Farrar Ware, 1924–1990, Biographical Sketch, CV, Franklin Delano Roosevelt Presidential Library.

33. Sklar et al., "'Long Progressive Era.'"

34. Dublin, "Caroline Farrar Ware," 658.

35. A. Scott, *Pauli Murray and Caroline Ware*.

36. Murray, *Song in a Weary Throat*, 198–200; Ware, "Interview with Caroline F. Ware—Women in the Federal Government Project," January 1982, Black Women Oral History Project, SL.

37. Cobble, *For the Many*.

38. Murray, *Song in a Weary Throat*, 347–48; *American Women: Report of the President's Commission on the Status of Women*, 78.

39. A. Scott, *Pauli Murray and Caroline Ware*; Mayeri, *Reasoning from Race*; Bell-Scott, *Firebrand and the First Lady*; Rosenberg, *Jane Crow*.

40. Murray, *Song in a Weary Throat*; Murray, *Proud Shoes*.

41. Caroline Farrar Ware, "Preliminary Draft for Discussion: Background Memorandum on the Status of Women," President's Commission on the Status of Women, pp. 24–29, microfilm, reel 3, frames 57–12b, Women and Social Movements in the United States, 1607 to 2000, Database, Alexander Street Press, retrieved March 23, 2021; Ware, *Early New England Cotton Manufacture*; Ware, *Greenwich Village*; Ware, *Cultural Approach to History*.

42. Ware, "Preliminary Draft for Discussion," 24–29.

43. Ware, "Preliminary Draft for Discussion," 13–20, 29–30.

44. Blain and Sklar, "How Did the President's Commission . . . . Address Issues Related to Race, 1963–1980?"; Cobble, "Labor Feminist Origins"; Harrison, "State Commissions and Economic Security for Women"; Laughlin, "How Did State Commissions on the Status of Women Overcome Historic Antagonisms?"; Spruill, "Conservative Challenge to Feminist Influence."

45. G. G. Johnson, "Feminism and the Economic Independence of Woman."

46. G. G. Johnson, "Some Reflections on Research and Writing in Social History," talk given to the Historical Society of North Carolina, March 30, 1979, 14, folder 1392, series 12.2, GGJ Papers; Johnson, "Feminism and the Economic Independence of Woman," 612–16.

47. G. G. Johnson, "Feminism and the Economic Independence of Woman," 613.

48. Cobble, *Other Women's Movement*; Cobble, *Sex of Class*; Storrs, *Civilizing Capitalism*.

49. G. G. Johnson, "Feminism and the Economic Independence of Woman," 613.

50. G. G. Johnson, "Changing Status of the Negro"; G. G. Johnson, "Quiet Revolution." Johnson seems to have been part of the progressive racial agenda of the American Association of University Women that Susan Levine identifies in *Degrees of Equality*. North Carolina had a particularly active state branch of the AAUW, judging by the number of examples Levine pulls from the state.

51. Myrdal, *An American Dilemma*, xi; Guion Griffis Johnson interview by Mary Frederickson, May 28, 1974, transcript, 40–46, Collection 04007, SOHP; G. G. Johnson, "Ideology of White Supremacy"; G. G. Johnson, "Southern Paternalism toward the Negro."

52. Gilmore, "From Jim Crow to Jane Crow," 142–43.

53. Guion Griffis Johnson, "The Educated Woman Faces the Post War World," talk given to Brenau Academy graduating class, May 1945, folder 1345, GGJ Papers.

54. G. G. Johnson, *Ante-Bellum North Carolina*.

55. G. G. Johnson, "The Educated Woman Faces the Post War World," GGJ Papers.

56. Cobble, *Other Women's Movement*; Storrs, *Civilizing Capitalism*.

57. Guion Griffis Johnson, "The Family in a Democratic Society," talk, Cooperative Extension Work in Agriculture and Home Economics, State of Virginia, July 30, 1952, folder 1352, GGJ Papers.

58. Guion Griffis Johnson, "The Role of Women in Today's World," talk, October 18, 1950, folder 1351, GGJ Papers.

59. Meyerowitz, *Not June Cleaver*. To be a feminist, activist, scholar, wife, and mother and remain "feminine" was a challenge that many women at midcentury rose to creatively; Lundberg and Farnham, *Modern Woman*.

60. Guion Griffis Johnson, "Brief Introductory Remarks at 15th Annual Coed Weekend, N.C. College at Durham, March 13, 1964," folder 1371, GGJ Papers; Guion Griffis Johnson, "The Changing Role of the North Carolina Woman, October 28, 1964," folder 1373, GGJ Papers; G. G. Johnson et al., *Governor's Commission on the Status of Women in North Carolina*. On the history of Black women's employment and education rates—as a product of their need to help support families and engage in racial uplift—see J. Jones, *Labor of Love*; and Hine and Thompson, *Shining Thread of Hope*.

61. Cobble, *Other Women's Movement*; Storrs, *Civilizing Capitalism*.

62. Moon and Sklar, *How Did Florence Kitchelt Bring Together Social Feminists*.

63. Guion Griffis Johnson, "Let's Put the Federation on the Right Side of History: A Statement in Support of the ERA Resolution," presented at the North Carolina Federation of Women's Clubs, 1975 convention, folder 1388, GGJ Papers.

64. G. G. Johnson, "Changing Status of Women in the South," 418–36; G. G. Johnson, "Let's Put the Federation on the Right Side of History," GGJ Papers.

65. Hall interview by Glusman, LUSWHOHP.

66. Guion Griffis Johnson to Robert M. Calhoun, Department of History, University of North Carolina at Greensboro, November 2, 1978, folder "General Files, 1979–1985," GGJ Papers; G. G. Johnson, "Some Reflections on Research and Writing in Social History," GGJ Papers. This unidentified critic of Johnson's scholarly credentials in the early 1970s may have come from the younger generation of women historians. In the 1970s, it seems this would be the much more likely case than anything else. Unfortunately, the paper has not survived. Southern Historical Collection staff looked in several likely places, but they could not locate Johnson's paper so that I could get some context. It is teasing but inadequate evidence for the generational differences argument that runs through chapters 1–3. Her May 28, 1974, SOHP interview with Mary Frederickson suggests she gave the address in question only "several years" before 1974, and Johnson indicates that the talk was drawn from her work on Southern paternalism toward the Negro on page 32 of the interview transcript.

67. Laughlin and Castledine, *Breaking the Wave*, 12. I draw the term "civic feminist" from Laughlin and Castledine, *Breaking the Wave*, 11–24. Laughlin uses the term "civic feminists" to describe the generation of women's rights activists working between the waves. She defines them on page 12 thusly: "They believed that women's equality was essential to democracy and national security and considered all forms of public engagement, no matter how modest, as significant exercises in authority and autonomy. Civic feminists linked the suffrage movement and the modern women's movement . . . making claims for women's rights as essential to the public interest . . . and unapologetically claiming power and authority in public life in great numbers."

68. Meyerowitz, *Not June Cleaver*.

69. Sklar et al., "'Long Progressive Era.'"

70. "Cartoonists Draw Clubwomen's Fire," *Washington Post*, Saturday, April 14, 1962, A12.

71. Barbara Miller Solomon, "The Dilemma of Educated Women," undated printing of speech given on June 4, 1961, at Wheelock College Commencement, *Wheelock Newsletter*, 4–7, folder "Women's Archives Publicity #2, 1960–1962—Speeches by B. Solomon," AESL.

72. Barbara Miller Solomon, Recollections Sound Recording, Schlesinger T-1, [CD 41], SL; "Take One Duck's Head," *Newsweek*, July 24, 1961, copy in folder "Women's Archives Publicity #2, 1960–1962—Speeches by B. Solomon," *AESL Records; "Historian Traces Woman's Role: Mrs. Peter Solomon Is Head of Archives," *Milwaukee Journal*, May 1, 1962, copy in folder "Women's Archives Publicity #2, 1960–1962—Speeches by B. Solomon," AESL Records; "Vivid Collection of 'Cookery': Radcliffe Strips Harvard of Books," *Boston Sunday Herald*, July 16, 1961, sec. 4, p. 9; Handlin, "Memoirs."

73. Handlin, "Memoirs."

74. Voorhis held his Twelfth Congressional District of California seat for five consecutive terms between 1936 and 1946 and was a strong supporter of the New Deal. Bullock, *Jerry Voorhis*; "Voorhis, Horace Jeremiah (Jerry)," Biographical Directory of the United States Congress, accessed March 31, 2021, https://bioguide.congress.gov.

75. Anne Firor Scott email to Jennifer E. Tomás, September 25, 2011, re: Mary Earhart Dillon, in author's possession.

76. Bordin, *Woman and Temperance*; Paulson, *Women's Suffrage and Prohibition*.

77. A. Scott interviews by Rothschild and Glusman, LUSWHOHP, 1–10, 22–23, 41; A. Scott email to Tomás, September 25, 2011; A. Scott, *Anecdotes of My Years as a LWV Staffer*.

78. A. Scott interviews by Rothschild and Glusman, LUSWHOHP, 1–10, 22–23, 56; A. Scott email to Tomás, September 25, 2011; A. Scott, *Anecdotes of My Years as a LWV Staffer*.

79. A. Scott, *Making the Invisible Woman Visible*, xvi–xviii; A. Scott interviews by Rothschild and Glusman, LUSWHOHP, 22–23, 56.

80. A. Scott interview by Constance Schulz in Schulz and Turner, *Clio's Southern Sisters*, 40–41; Anne Firor Scott is listed as the former chairman of the Governor's Commission on the Status of Women, North Carolina, in "Report on Progress in 1965 on the Status of Women," Second Annual Report of Interdepartmental Committee and Citizens' Advisory Council on the Status of Women, December 1965, US Department of Labor, Women's Bureau (Washington, DC: Citizens' Advisory Council on the Status of Women, 1965); North Carolina Governor's Commission on the Status of Women, "The Many Lives of North Carolina Women," 1964, North Carolina Digital Collections, accessed June 17, 2025, https://digital.ncdcr.gov/documents/detail/5740445?item=5741699; G. G. Johnson et al., *Governor's Commission on the Status of Women in North Carolina*.

81. J. Johnson, "'Drill into Us . . . the Rebel Tradition'"; Bailey, "Textbooks of the 'Lost Cause'"; Erickson, "'We Want No Teachers'"; Apple and Oliver, "Becoming Right"; Storrs "Attacking the Washington 'Femmocracy.'"

82. Weigand, *Red Feminism*; Horowitz, "Feminism, Women's History, and American Social Thought," 191–209.

83. Weigand, *Red Feminism*, 101.

84. Weigand, *Red Feminism*, 142–54; Lerner, *Fireweed*, 253–61.

85. Kraditor, *Ideas of the Woman Suffrage Movement*.

86. Weigand cites Claudia Jones, "An End to the Neglect of the Problems of Negro Woman," *Political Affairs* 28 (1949): 51–67, in *Red Feminism*, 184; Crenshaw, "Demarginalizing the Intersection of Race and Sex"; Crenshaw, "Mapping the Margins."

87. Weigand, *Red Feminism*, chaps. 2, 4, and 5; Horowitz, "Feminism, Women's History, and American Social Thought," 193.

88. Weigand, *Red Feminism*; Horowitz, "Feminism, Women's History, and American Social Thought," 191–209; Tom[á]s, "Flexner, Eleanor (04 October 1908–25 March 1995)."

89. Carr, *What Is History?*, 9.

90. Jack H. Hexter, review of *Woman as Force in History*, by Mary Beard, *New York Times Book Review*, March 17, 1946, 5.

91. J. Scott, *Gender and the Politics of History*, 21, 27.

92. Nancy Cott, "Across the Great Divide: Women in Politics before and after 1920," in Wheeler, *One Woman, One Vote*, 353–73; Cobble, *Other Women's Movement*; Storrs, *Civilizing Capitalism*; Rupp and Taylor, *Survival in the Doldrums*.

93. Alma Lutz to Massachusetts Committee for the Equal Rights Amendment, January 21, 1964, folder 1-9 "Alma Lutz: Miscellaneous Pamphlets and Writings," ALP. These women's names appeared on the organizational letterhead.

94. Sklar et al., "'Long Progressive Era.'" Beard, Johnson, Ware, and the Schlesingers are the most obvious progressive historians of women.

95. J. James, "Recollections of a Veteran in Women's History," xv.

96. J. James, "Recollections of a Veteran in Women's History," xxviii.

Chapter 7

1. The women's history movement of the 1970s had all the major characteristics of a social movement, including collective behavior, extra-institutionality, multicentered networks, and the willingness to disrupt order within history's professional institutions. See Gerlach and Hine, *People, Power, Change*; Morris and Mueller, *Frontiers in Social Movement Theory*; and Roth and Horan, Introduction to *What Are Social Movements?*

2. Sara Evans, *Personal Politics*; Tomás, "Introduction to 'The Women's History Movement.'"

3. Rosen, *World Split Open*, 205–6.

4. *Directory of History Departments and Organizations*; *Guide to Departments of History* (1980). The figures represent a fair barometer of the growth of women's history faculty but do not represent all history departments in the United States. The number of US women's historians rose from 100 to 338 between 1980 and 1990, while the number of historians of women in all other specialty areas (i.e., Europe, Latin America, Africa, medicine) rose from 58 to 100. Historians of US women more than tripled in number over the period. Those in all other fields combined didn't quite double their numbers.

5. Berenice Carroll to Gerda Lerner, September 18, 1969, folder "Coordinating Committee on Women in the H. P. CCWHP, 1969–," carton 1, CCWHP Records. Carroll was a historian of Germany who had earned her PhD at Brown University in 1960 and taken a job teaching in the political science department at the University of Illinois at Urbana.

6. Sandi Cooper to Willie Lee Rose, May 10, 1972, and Rose to Cooper, May 6, 1972, folder "AHA Nominations," carton 3, CCWHP Records. Rose was not a historian of women, but I later offer evidence to show that she was supportive of the "new" field.

7. Mary Massey to Bennett Wall, January 6, 1971, folder 493 "Secretary Treasurer: 1970–1971, Vice President, M. E. Massey," SHA Records.

8. "Conversation with Anne Firor Scott, 3-4-71," notes in Mollie Davis files, folder "Preparation for 1971 AHA Meeting," box 4/5, SAWH Records.

9. A. Scott interviews by Rothschild and Glusman, LUSWHOHP, 1–10, 22–23, 56; Anne Firor Scott email to Jennifer E. Tomás, September 25, 2011, re: Mary Earhart Dillon; A. Scott, *Anecdotes of My Years as a LWV Staffer*; Schulz and Turner, *Clio's Southern Sisters*.

10. Doris King to Mary Massey, February 11, 1971, Incoming Correspondence Files, folder 9-92, box 9, MEM Papers.

11. Boris and Chaudhuri, *Voices of Women Historians*; Carroll et al., *History of the Coordinating Committee*; Schulz and Turner, *Clio's Southern Sisters*; LUSWHOHP; White, *Telling Histories*. These are some of the most important collections of essays, interviews, and institutional history pamphlets in this reflective vein that address the earliest days of the women's history movement.

12. Zinsser, *History and Feminism*, 3.

13. Berenice Carroll, Curriculum Vitae, folder "Coordinating Committee on Women in the H. P. CCWHP, 1969–," carton 1, CCWHP Records.

14. Briscoe, "Phenomena of the Seventies."

15. Carroll to Lerner, September 18, 1969, CCWHP Records.

16. Harrison, *On Account of Sex*; Hartmann, *Other Feminists*; A. Scott, *Pauli Murray and Caroline Ware*; Mayeri, *Reasoning from Race*; Bell-Scott, *Firebrand and the First Lady*; Rosenberg, *Jane Crow*.

17. Gerda Lerner to Berenice Carroll, October 3, 1969, folder "Coordinating Committee on Women in the H. P. CCWHP, 1969–," carton 1, CCWHP Records (italics added).

18. Lerner to Carroll, October 3, 1969, CCWHP Records (italics added).

19. *West Coast Historical Association: An Organization of Women Historians, Newsletter* 1, no. 1 (n.d.); *West Coast Association of Women in History, Newsletter* 1, no. 2 (October 28, 1970), available online at wawh.org; Jo Tice Bloom obituary, *Reed Magazine*, June 18, 2019, www.reed.edu/reed-magazine/in-memoriam/obituaries/2019/jo-tice-bloom-1955.html; "Edith Lutzker Dead; Medical Historian, 87," *New York Times*, August 23, 1991, D17, www.nytimes.com/1991/08/23/obituaries/edythe-lutzker-dead-medical-historian-87.html; Kerber interview by Weisiger, LUSWHOHP. Hilda Smith studied British feminism and was a graduate student from the University of Chicago. Linda Kerber was a 1968 graduate of Columbia's doctoral program. Constance Ashton Myers was at Augusta College in Georgia. Jo Tice Bloom taught at Bowie State College. Edythe Lutzker specialized in the history of science and medicine. Sherrin Wyntjes specialized in Dutch history. Constance Ashton Myers, interview by Kathleen Hanna, June 11, 1977, 1977 International Women's Year Oral History Collection https://digital.library.sc.edu/exhibits/iwy/south-carolina-interviews/constance-myers.

20. Kerber interview by Weisiger, LUSWHOHP, 30.

21. Lerner to Carroll, October 3, 1969, CCWHP Records.

22. Linda Kerber to Berenice Carroll, n.d., folder "Coordinating Committee on Women in the H. P. CCWHP, 1969–," carton 1, CCWHP Records; *CCWHP Newsletters*, vols. 1–2. Linda Kerber, *Courses in Women's History and Related Fields, Bulletin #1*, March 1, 1971; Linda Kerber, *Courses in Women's History and Related Fields, Bulletin #2*, October 1, 1971; Linda Kerber, *Current Research on the History of Women, Bulletins 1–4* were issued between March 1, 1971, and March 1, 1972. Nupur Chaudhuri took over the production of the bulletin in 1975. Copies of Kerber bulletins in author's possession.

23. Briscoe, "Phenomena of the Seventies." Women in the humanities and social sciences also formed these caucuses and committees from 1969 to 1978.

24. Lerner to Carroll, October 3, 1969, CCWHP Records; Lerner interview by Rothschild, LUSWHOHP, 17.

25. Weigand, *Red Feminism*; Echols, *Daring to Be Bad*; Rosen, *World Split Open*.

26. Hilda Smith, "CCWHP: The First Decade," in Carroll et al., *History of the Coordinating Committee* (1994), 9. Noether was president of the Berkshire Conference and a historian of Italy. Hanna Holborn Gray was a 1957 graduate of Harvard who specialized in the Renaissance and Reformation.

27. Smith, while still a graduate student, wrote her dissertation on seventeenth-century English feminism. Christopher Lasch edited a book about Jane Addams. During the 1960s he authored five biographical sketches for *Notable American Women*. H. Smith, "Regionalism, Feminism, and Class," 34; Lasch, *Social Thought of Jane Addams*; E. James et al., *Notable American Women*, vols. 1 and 3. Lasch authored the biographical sketches for Rachel G. Foster Avery, Alva Belmont, Sophonisba Breckenridge, Mary Ware Dennett, and Rachelle Slobodinsky Yarros.

28. Schorske was a Europeanist. Smith was an Americanist and author of *Daughters of the Promised Land: Women in American History*. Mary Wright was probably the distinguished Chinese historian of Yale University. Wright was diagnosed with lung cancer in late 1969 and was thus replaced by Patricia Albjerg Graham.

29. Graham specialized in the history of American women in education.

30. Rose et al., "Report of the American Historical Association Ad Hoc Committee."

31. CCWHP Membership Survey, 1970, folder "Membership Surveys," carton 1, CCWHP Records.

32. Noether taught at the University of Connecticut.

33. Correspondence between Renate Bridenthal, Karen Offen, Hilda Smith, and Donna Boutelle, 1973–1975, folder 2, carton 3, CCWHP Records (accession #77-M82/80-M111). The debate over creating an affiliated specialized institutional women's history arm within the CCWHP or separating it from the CCWHP continued into 1978. Hilda Smith, "Statement in Support of Separating CCWHP and the Conference Group in Women's History," and Karen Offen, "Statement Opposing Total Separation of CGWH from CCWHP," *CCWHP Newsletter*, December 1978, 9–13. Copy in author's possession.

34. Berenice Carroll to Dear Friends, March 1, 1970, folder "Coordinating Committee on Women in the H. P. CCWHP, 1969–," carton 1, CCWHP Records; *CCWHP Newsletter* 1, no. 2, folder "CCWHP Newsletters," box 4/5, SAWH Records.

35. Carroll to Dear Friends, March 1, 1970, 2, CCWHP Records.

36. Carroll to Dear Friends, March 1, 1970, 1, CCWHP Records.

37. Carroll to Dear Friends, March 1, 1970, CCWHP Records.

38. Bennett Wall to Mollie Davis, June 27, 1972, folder "Bennett Wall, 1972," box 4, SAWH Records.

39. Mollie Davis to Connie Myers, October 20, 1971, folder "Connie Myers, 1971, re: founding of Caucus, etc.," carton 1, SAWH Records.

40. Zinsser's study centers on national leaders and organizations—the AHA and the CCWHP.

41. Mollie Davis interview by Pamela Dean, in Schulz and Turner, *Clio's Southern Sisters*, 64.

42. *West Coast Historical Association, Newsletter* 1, no. 1 (n.d.); *West Coast Association of Women in History, Newsletter* 1, no. 2 (October 28, 1970), available online at wawh.org; Kerber interview by Weisiger, LUSWHOHP, 30. Also active in the effort to set up the West Coast group was historian Grace Larsen. Essington, "Changing the Historical Profession in the 1960s, 1970s, and 1980s: The Coordinating Committee on Women in the Historical Profession and Western Association of Women Historians," paper delivered to the Organization of American

Historians, Milwaukee, April 21, 2012; In 1980, the West Coast group took the name, "Western Association of Women Historians," https://wawh.org/wawh-history.

43. Carroll to Dear Friends, March 1, 1970, 2, CCWHP Records.

44. Carroll to Dear Friends, March 1, 1970, 4, CCWHP Records; *Courses in Women's History and Related Field, Bulletin #1*, March 1, 1971, CCWHP (CCWHP mailing, in author's possession).

45. *CCWHP Newsletter* 1, no. 1 (Spring 1970): 1, folder "CCWHP Newsletter," box 5, SAWH Records.

46. "Membership Reports," folder 30 "Membership Committee Reports, 1954, 1957, 1966–1979," box 10, OAH Records. The AHA did not begin publishing these directories until 1975, so I don't have figures for 1969.

47. *Directory of History Departments and Organizations*; Guide to Departments of History (1975). These directories do not represent or list all historians in the United States, and I offer these figures only as a rough estimate of the growth experienced in women's history relative to particular fields. The actual number of women's historians was undoubtedly much higher in all fields since Joyce Allen Justice's 1975 *AHA Directory of Women Historians* listed 205 historians of US women and 121 historians of women in other fields of geographic specialization. Also, attendance at the Second Berkshire Conference on the History of Women held at Radcliffe in 1974 exceeded 2,000, suggesting much higher numbers already by that year.

48. "Minutes of the Business Meeting of the Organization of American Historians, April 17, 1970," *Journal of American History* 57, no. 2 (1970): 516–28, 520–21.

49. "Minutes of the Business Meeting of the Organization of American Historians, April 17, 1970," 520 (italics added).

50. "Executive Board Minutes," November 1970, folder 18, box 1, and "Executive Board Minutes, April 1971," folder 19, box 1, OAH Records.

51. Executive Board Meeting Minutes, Saturday, March 6, 1970, 10:00 a.m., Chicago O'Hare Airport, folder 18, box 1, OAH Records.

52. Executive Board Meeting Minutes, March 6, 1970, OAH Records.

53. D. Potter, "American Women and the American Character."

54. Willie Lee Rose to Sandi Cooper, February 10, 1973, folder "Corr. 1972–1974," carton 1, CCWHP Records.

55. Mary Elizabeth Massey to Mollie Camp Davis, February 9, 1972, folder "Ill-fated proposal sent to Grady McWhiney (not pro-woman)," box 4/5, SAWH Records. The conflict prompted, among other things, the creation of the AHA Survival Kit for Women When Jane De Hart Matthews and Mary Frances Berry were on the AHA Committee on the Status of Women."

56. Anne Firor Scott (chairman), John Ezell, Rhoda Dorsey, William Freeling, and Nancy Weiss, "Report of the Committee on the Status of Women to the Organization of American Historians," submitted April 14, 1971, at OAH Executive Board Meeting, New Orleans, according to the Executive Board Minutes Agenda, April 1971, folder 19, box 1, OAH Records.

57. David Donald, "Radical Historians on the Move: Radical Historians," *New York Times*, July 19, 1970, p. 190.

58. Gerda Lerner, "How Women and Their Organizations Changed the Profession of History," in Carroll et al., *History of the Coordinating Committee*, 46.

59. Gerda Lerner to Berenice Carroll, December 3, 1969, folder "CCWHP 1969–," carton 1, CCWHP Records; Gerda Lerner, "Letter to the Editor re: David Donald," *New York Times*, July 27, 1970; original draft of Gerda Lerner letter to the *New York Times Book Review*, folder

"CCWHP 1969–," carton 1, CCWHP Records (accession 77-M82/M11, unprocessed manuscript collection).

60. Gerda Lerner, "Letter to the Editor, Re: David Donald," *New York Times*, August 30, 1970, 282, folder "CCWHP, 1969–," carton 1, CCWHP Records.

61. David Donald, "Mr. Donald Replies," *New York Times*, August 30, 1970, www.nytimes.com/1970/08/30/archives/radical-historians.html; *CCWHP Newsletter* 2, no. 1, supplement, sec. 10, p. 4, folder "CCWHP Newsletters, Vol. II," box 4, SAWH Records.

62. Rose et al., "Report of the American Historical Association Ad Hoc Committee."

63. "Executive Board Minutes, April 1971," 7, OAH Records.

64. A. Scott et al., OAH-CSW Report, April 14, 1971, 4, folder "OAH 1971 New Orleans," box 5, SAWH Records. The report was later reworked by Schmidt and Schmidt and published as "The Invisible Woman: The Historian as Professional Magician," in Carroll, *Liberating Women's History*.

65. A. Scott et al., OAH-CSW Report, 5, SAWH Records.

66. *CCWHP Newsletter* 1, no. 1; Carroll to Dear Friends, March 1, 1970, both in CCWHP Records.

67. Draft of table of contents for *Liberating Women's History*, folder "Coordinating Committee on Women in the H. P. CCWHP, 1969–," carton 1, CCWHP Records. Gordon was then a Russian historian, not yet focusing on American women. Ziegler was also a historian of Russia. Hunt and Pleck were Americanists. Carroll, *Liberating Women's History*, 55–92.

68. "Meetings of Interest to CCWHP at AHA Convention," folder "1970 Boston AHA, resolutions, our push," box 5, SAWH Records.

69. *CCWHP Newsletter* 2, no. 1, p. 2, box 5, SAWH Records.

70. Gerda Lerner to Anne Firor Scott, June 6, 1970, Business Correspondence folders, box 1, AFS Papers.

71. "Meetings of Interest to CCWHP at AHA Convention," SAWH Records.

72. Giele and Cheek were affiliated with the Schlesinger Library. Annette Baxter was an American history professor at Barnard.

73. *CCWHP Newsletter* 2, no. 1, p. 3, SAWH Records (newsletter supplement included a summary of these criticisms by Tasha Tennenbaum, but I don't have the complete supplement with Tennenbaum's criticisms).

74. *CCWHP Newsletter* 2, no. 1, supplement, sec. 10, p. 12, SAWH Records.

75. *CCWHP Newsletter* 2, no. 1, supplement, sec. 10, p. 12, SAWH Records.

76. *CCWHP Newsletter* (volume not indicated), "Convention Information, December 1971," folder "CCWHP Business Meeting, NY AHA 1971," box 4, SAWH Records.

77. Davis interview by Dean and Rosemary Carroll interview by Constance Schulz, in Schulz and Turner, *Clio's Southern Sisters*, 60–74, 87–100.

78. Melerson Guy Dunham, interview by Mollie Camp Davis, November 18–21, 1977, 1977 International Women's Year Oral History Collection, https://digital.library.sc.edu/exhibits/iwy/national-interviews/melerson-guy-dunham/.

79. Mollie Davis to Berenice Carroll, February 18, 1970, folder "CCWHP Newsletter (I)," box 5, SAWH Records.

80. *CCWHP Newsletter* 1, no. 1, p. 2, folder "CCWHP Newsletter (I)," box 5, SAWH Records.

81. Davis interview by Dean, in Schulz and Turner, *Clio's Southern Sisters*, 66; *CCWHP Newsletter* 6, no. 2, p. 3, folder "CCWHP Newsletter (I)," box 5, SAWH Records.

82. Davis interview by Dean, in Schulz and Turner, *Clio's Southern Sisters*, 66.

83. *Caucus of Women in History, Newsletter* 1 (April 1971), folder "CWH, 1st 3 Newsletters, Vol. I, Apr., Nov., Dec. 1971," box 4, SAWH Records.

84. Wall, "Southern Historical Association, 1935–1970."

85. *Caucus of Women in History, Newsletter* 1 (April 1971), SAWH Records.

86. Schnorrenberg was teaching at UNC Chapel Hill and Marks was at Alabama A&M. At the time, Gingrich was an untenured history professor at West Georgia College.

87. *CCWHP Newsletter* 2, no. 2 (December 1971), p. 8, folder "CCWHP Newsletters, Vol. II," box 4, SAWH Records; correspondence in box 5 also discusses the session proposals.

88. Jane De Hart Mathews Correspondence in boxes 4 and 5, SAWH Records; Jane De Hart Mathews to Mollie Davis, January 5, 1971, folder "Southern Caucus of Women in History Steering Committee, 1972," box 5, SAWH Records.

89. De Hart Mathews worked briefly at Educational Testing Services and then taught full-time at Douglass College during these years. She also published her first book while at Princeton.

90. De Hart Mathews attended a pivotal meeting of the Berkshire Conference of Women Historians in 1970, whose history I chronicle more generally in chapter 8, at which this younger group met and discussed professional matters. In this group were Kerber, Carroll Smith-Rosenberg, Blanche Cook, and Sandi Cooper. De Hart reported to the author in an email that this meeting served as something of a "consciousness-raising group for underemployed recent PhDs—all of us feminists." She and Cook roomed together discussing, among other things, their "hero" Willie Lee Rose. De Hart remembered they discussed also her job market travails while in North Carolina. Her alma mater, Duke, didn't hire its own alumni. UNC Greensboro wouldn't hire commuters. Chapel Hill enforced nepotism rules, so since Donald Mathews was on the history faculty there, it wouldn't consider hiring her. North Carolina State University had offered the excuse that it already had a woman and she was terrible so they didn't want another. Another source detailing this 1970 meeting is in De Hart, "Celebrating and Becoming Blanche Wiesen Cook."

91. De Hart interview by Rothschild, LUSWHOHP, 43. All of these historians' names appear on the meeting attendance sheets of the Berkshire Conference of Women Historians during these years.

92. De Hart interview by Rothschild, LUSWHOHP, 43.

93. De Hart interview by Rothschild, LUSWHOHP, 20–21. De Hart completed a project for the Rockefeller Foundation and the American Council for the Arts and lectured part-time in the American studies program at UNC Chapel Hill between 1968 and 1970.

94. Carroll et al., *History of the Coordinating Committee*, appendix A; *CCWHP Newsletter* 2, no. 2 (December 1971), p. 6, SAWH Records. This issue lists De Hart Mathews as a member of the new standing Committee on the Status of Women of the AHA, giving UNC Chapel Hill as her institutional affiliation in 1971, so the meeting with Willie Lee Rose must have occurred earlier in 1971 rather than in 1972 as her oral history interview suggests.

95. Mollie Davis notes, folder "Notes of January 1971, phone calls, and other notes," box 5, SAWH Records.

96. De Hart Mathews to Davis, January 5, 1971, SAWH Records.

97. In connection with her program committee work and AHA activism, De Hart Mathews conceived the idea that the AHA should create a handbook for women historians in the early 1970s. This work was taken up by Maureen Murphy Nutting, with the first two editions coming out in 1975 and 1979. In 1991 the third edition appeared. Gustafson, *Becoming a Historian*.

98. Gustafson, *Becoming a Historian*, vii–viii.

99. Mollie Davis to Sandi Cooper, March 6, 1971, folder "Southern Women, Schnorrenberg," carton 1, CCWHP Records.

100. De Hart interview by Rothschild, LUSWHOHP, 23.

101. Folder "AHA Nominations—Misc Correspondence," carton 3, CCWHP Records. The BCWH Records and SAWH Records contain ample duplication of this correspondence, indicating it was indeed a major area of concern for the women in the groups, who expressed considerable irritation with Genovese.

102. Joan Kelly, "Proposal for AHA Panel for December 1974"; Joan Kelly to Donna Boutelle, April 29, 1974; and Boutelle to Kelly, May 3, 1974, all in folder "CCWHP Purpose Statement," carton 1, CCWHP Records.

103. Tamara Hareven to Robert Cross, February 8, 1974; Joan Kelly-Gadol to Robert Cross, February 25, 1974; and Orest Ranum to Joan Kelly-Gadol, April 3, 1974, all in folder "CCWHP Purpose Statement," carton 1, CCWHP Records.

104. Joan Kelly-Gadol to Donna Boutelle, May 8, 1974, folder "CCWHP Purpose Statement," carton 1, CCWHP Records.

105. Bridenthal and Koonz, *Becoming Visible*.

106. Kelly-Gadol to Boutelle, June 3, 1974, folder "CCWHP Purpose Statement," carton 1, CCWHP Records.

107. Program of the Annual AHA Meeting, 1972, www.historians.org/wp-content/uploads/2024/05/1972-Annual-Meeting-Program.pdf; Program of the Annual AHA Meeting, 1974, www.historians.org/wp-content/uploads/2024/05/1974-Annual-Meeting-Program.pdf.

108. Nancy Weiss, Committee on the Status of Women, Report to the Executive Board, April 1973, p. 2, folder "Executive Board Minutes, April 1973," folder 19, box 1, OAH Records.

109. Lerner, *Teaching Women's History*.

110. Weiss, Committee on the Status of Women, Report to the Executive Board, April 1973, p. 2, OAH Records.

111. Justice, *AHA Directory of Women Historians*, lists Ross's field as US intellectual history and Straub's as US social and women's history.

112. D'Ann Campbell, "We Are Losing Ground," *CCWHP Newsletter* 6, no. 1 (February 1975): 4. Campbell calculated that in 1974, the number of women on SHA and OAH programs was only 6 percent, and that number represented a 4–5 percent drop from 1973. She said the AHA numbers were little better. Program data for the AHA and OAH show that 1973 and 1974 also saw a drop in women's history sessions from six and four, respectively, in 1972 to three and two in 1973 but then a rise to eleven and four in 1974. After 1974 the number of women's history sessions making the annual programs of the AHA and OAH began a slow, steady rise.

113. Nancy Weiss, Committee on the Status of Women, Report to the Executive Board, April 1975, folder 25 "Executive Board Minutes, April 1975"; *OAH Roster of Historians of Women*, 1975 (OAH Committee on the Status of Women, 1975), copy in author's possession.

114. Justice, *AHA Directory of Women Historians*.

115. Hinding, preface to *Women's History Sources*, ix; Mason, "'Grand Manuscripts Search.'"

116. *Conference Group on Women's History Newsletter* 6, no. 2 (August 1981): 8.

117. For instance, Mary Dunn and Joan Jensen are two scholars who entered the profession before 1969 who have mentored many historians of women and provided important professional service to the discipline.

118. Hewitt and Lebsock, *Visible Women*.

119. Lebsock, acknowledgments in *Free Women of Petersburg*, ix–xi.

120. Lebsock, acknowledgments in *Free Women of Petersburg*, ix–xi.

121. Hewitt, *Women's Activism and Social Change*, 10.

122. Chronological Correspondence files, box 1, AFS Papers.

123. They were Ellen DuBois, LeeAnn Whites, William Chafe, Sara Evans, Mari Jo Buhle, Jacquelyn Hall, Darlene Clark Hine, Deborah Gray White, Marion Roydhouse, Mary Frederickson, Dolores Janiewski, Linda Kerber, and Nancy Weiss Malkiel.

124. Malkiel, "Invincible Woman," 381.

125. Malkiel, "Invincible Woman," 381.

126. Payne, *Writing Women's History*.

127. A. Scott interviews by Rothschild and Glusman, LUSWHOHP, 17.

128. Mary [Rothschild] Aickin to Professor Scott, February 25, 1971, Business Correspondence, AFS Papers.

129. Aickin to Scott, February 25, 1971, AFS Papers.

130. A. Scott interviews by Rothschild and Glusman, LUSWHOHP, 17.

131. A. Scott interviews by Rothschild and Glusman, LUSWHOHP, 18.

132. That Rothschild accomplished this feat of university and departmental politicking in 1971 is remarkable given the fact that she was still a graduate student.

133. Aldon D. Bell, Associate Dean, to Professor Anne Firor Scott, December 6, 1972, folder "Correspondence, Fall 1972," AFS Papers.

134. Mary Rothschild to Anne Scott, November 28, 1972, folder "Professiorial Correspondence, Fall 1972," AFS Papers.

135. A. Scott interviews by Rothschild and Glusman, LUSWHOHP, 19.

136. Mary Rothschild email to Jennifer Tomás, August 28, 2011; Rothschild interview by Barnes, LUSWHOHP, 124.

137. See LUSWHOHP.

138. Rothschild interview by Barnes, LUSWHOHP, 124.

139. Kerber et al., *U.S. History as Women's History*.

140. These included Nancy Cott, Linda Gordon, Nell Irvin Painter, Estelle Freedman, Judith Walzer Leavitt, William Chafe, Jane De Hart, Barbara Sicherman, Joyce Antler, Amy Swerdlow, Ruth Rosen, and Darlene Clark Hine.

141. Kerber et al., *U.S. History as Women's History*, 3.

142. Catharine R. Stimpson, "Gerda Lerner on the Future of Our Past," *Ms.*, September 1981, 51; National Women's History Week Materials, folder 189 "Women's History Week (national): Correspondence, lobbying, publicity, 1979–1987," series 4, GLP 1950–95; Mary E. Fiorenza, "On Women and History: An Interview with Gerda Lerner," *L & S Magazine*, Spring 1987, 17–19; Nancy Seely, "Scholar Sheds New Light on Woman's Role in History," *New York Post*, September 17, 1962, 8; listing for radio lecture by Lerner, "Forgotten Women in American History, 9–9:30," on Radio (WBAI-FM), in *New York Times*, July 15, 1963. Other examples abound.

143. O'Neill, *Everyone Was Brave*. He had another monograph out on the women's movement too.

144. Buhle interview by Barnes, LUSWHOHP, 16. "Granfalloon" is a reference to a Kurt Vonnegut book meaning something that didn't really exist.

145. Buhle et al., "Women in American Society"; Buhle interview by Barnes, LUSWHOHP, 17, 29, 31, 38.

146. Buhle interview by Barnes, LUSWHOHP, 17; Buhle et al., "Women in American Society."

147. *Radical America* 4, no. 2 (1970); the volume was edited by Edith Hoshino Altbach and contained articles by Mari Jo Buhle, Altbach, Helke Sander, Vilma Sanchez, Marlene Dixon, Gail Paradise Kelly, and Selma James.

148. Program of the 64th Annual Meeting of the Organization of American Historians, New Orleans, 1971, 23, OAH Records (copy in author's possession). Buhle related her memory of this first meeting with Gerda Lerner to me in an email dated April 30, 2012.

149. Gerda Lerner to Mari Jo Buhle, October 11, 1971; Buhle to Lerner, November 13, 1971; Lerner to Buhle, November 22, 1971; Lerner to Buhle, December 14, 1971, all in folder 2.16 "Mari Jo Buhle, 1971–1992, n.d.," box 2, GLP 498.

150. Lerner and Buhle correspondence, 1973, folder 2.16, "Mari Jo Buhle, 1971–1992, n.d.," box 2, GLP 498; Buhle interview by Barnes, LUSWHOHP, 17.

151. Buhle interview by Barnes, LUSWHOHP, 17.

152. Gerda Lerner to William G. McLoughlin, American Civilization Program, Brown University, January 6, 1975, folder 2.16 "Mari Jo Buhle, 1971–1992, n.d.," box 2, GLP 498.

153. Folder 2.16, "Mari Jo Buhle, 1971–1992, n.d.," GLP 498.

154. Mari Jo Buhle to Gerda Lerner, June 16, 1991, folder 2.16, "Mari Jo Buhle, 1971–1992, n.d.," GLP 498.

155. "Mari Jo Buhle, Emerita," faculty profile at Brown history department website, accessed April 26, 2012, www.brown.edu/Departments/History/people/facultypage.php?id=10077.

156. Ellen DuBois to Gerda Lerner, June 26, 1971, folder "Ellen DuBois Correspondence, 1971–1985," GLP 498; Ellen DuBois to Anne Firor Scott, June 24, 1971, folder "Professional Correspondence, Summer 1971," AFS Papers. DuBois explained in an email to me dated April 26, 2012, that she met Anne Scott in Chicago, where both had been invited to talk on a radio show. DuBois met Lerner at an OAH meeting when she rushed up to her to hand her an article she had published in a women's liberation journal on the Grimké sisters.

157. DuBois/Lerner correspondence, folder "Ellen DuBois, 1970–1986," GLP 498; DuBois/Scott correspondence in folder "Professional Correspondence, Summer 1971," AFS Papers.

158. Lerner to DuBois, September 8, 1971, folder "Ellen DuBois, 1970–1986," GLP 498.

159. A. Scott to DuBois, August 5, 1971, "Correspondence, Summer 1971," AFS Papers.

160. DuBois interview by Barnes, LUSWHOHP, 26; Dubois, *Feminism and Suffrage*.

161. Lerner to DuBois, November 4, 1977; DuBois to Lerner, April 4, 1978; DuBois to Lerner, March 6, 1978; Lerner to DuBois, March 4, 1979; DuBois to Eva Glaser, president of Schocken Books, September 16, 1979, all in folder 29 "Correspondence, Ellen DuBois, 1970, 1986," GLP 498.

162. Folders 1367 "Anne Firor Scott," and 1514–1516 "Darlene Clark Hine, 1988– 1989," SHA Records; Hine interview by Rothschild, LUSWHOHP, 37–42, 68; Darlene Clark Hine and Gerda Lerner, "Final Report on OAH/ABWH Project on Black Women's History," folder 140 "Proposal 1980," series 3, GLP 1950–95; *Organization of American Historians 1982 Program* (Arlington Heights: Harlan Davidson, 1982).

163. Kerber interview by Weisiger, LUSWHOHP, 30; Rose et al, "Report of the American Historical Association Ad Hoc Committee."

164. Kerber interview by Weisiger, LUSWHOHP, 30; Rose et al., "Report of the American Historical Association Ad Hoc Committee."

165. Table 318.10, "Degrees conferred by postsecondary institutions, by level of degree and sex of student: Selected years, 1869–70 through 2025–26," *Digest of Education Statistics*, National

Center for Education Statistics, accessed December 12, 2023, https://nces.ed.gov/programs /digest/d15/tables/dt15_318.10.asp.

166. The *Journal of Women's History* and *Gender and History* both officially launched in 1989. Before that, women's history appeared either in mainstream history journals or in interdisciplinary feminist journals like *Signs* and *Feminist Studies*, which were established in 1975 and 1972, respectively.

Chapter 8

1. The source of the epigraph is Buhle et al., "Women in American Society," 3.

2. Arnita Jones, "Women Historians and Women's History: An Organizational Guide," *Women's Studies Newsletter*, September 1976, 11, folder 1, box 15, OAH Records. Jones held a PhD in modern European history from Emory College. J. Anthony Lukas, "Historians' Conference: The Radical Need for Jobs," *New York Times*, March 12, 1972, SM38.

3. A. Jones, "Women Historians and Women's History: An Organizational Guide," 11, OAH Records.

4. Berkshire Conference of Women Historians, Annual Meeting Program, May 14–16, 1971, folder 11.7 "Business Meetings, 1970–1971," box 11, BCWH Records.

5. Berkshire Conference of Women Historians, Annual Meeting Program, May 14–16, 1971, BCWH Records. Cooper taught at Richmond College; Koonz listed Southampton College of Long Island University as her professional affiliation. Bridenthal had earned her PhD in history from Columbia in 1970. In 1971 she was teaching at Brooklyn College of CUNY. Tobias listed Wesleyan University as her professional affiliation.

6. The Southern Association for Women Historians formed out of the Caucus of Women in History, which was established in November 1970 at the annual meeting of the Southern Historical Association in Louisville, Kentucky. The Southern group was renamed the Southern Association for Women Historians in 1976. The West Coast Association of Women Historians predated the CCWHP by half a year.; it later became the Western Association of Women Historians. During its first year it went by the name of West Coast Historical Conference and was associated with the Pacific Coast Branch of the AHA. Linda Kerber and Grace Larsen were the founders of the group.

7. A. Jones, "Women Historians and Women's History: An Organizational Guide," 11, OAH Records.

8. Rosalyn Terborg-Penn, "A History of the Association of Black Women Historians, 1977–1981," ca. 1981, folder 144 "Correspondence with Darlene Hine," series 3, GLP 1950–95; the historians were Eleanor Smith, Nell Painter, and Rosalyn Terborg-Penn.

9. *Manual for Women (and Other) Historians* was first produced by the AHA Committee on Women Historians in 1975 and prepared by Suzanne Lebsock, Mary Frances Berry, Carl Degler, Mary Jane Hamilton, Joan Kelly, Linda Kerber, Jane De Hart Mathews, Emiliana P. Noether, and Marie Perinbam. The second edition was produced in 1979 by the OAH-CWH, which included Joan Scott, Rosalyn Terborg-Penn, Mary O. Furner, Martha Toplin, Judith Babbitts, and Sydney James. The 1991 edition was largely the work Melanie Gustafson and was titled *Becoming a Historian: A Survival Manual for Women and Men*.

10. Some of these were identified in chapter 7. I will add to the list of OAH-sponsored women's history activities in this chapter.

11. Data compiled from the annual meeting programs of the Organization of American Historians and the American Historical Association. Robert Townsend kindly supplied me with scans of the programs and the data from unscannable programs (1971 and 1972). The rapid development of gender history and the history of sexuality complicates the categorization of a session under the category of "women's history." Where the title of a session uses the term "gender," "family," "sexuality," "sex," or "reproduction," I have classified that session as women's history if the session had at least one paper that dealt substantively with "women," a woman, or a group or institution consisting of women. Papers or sessions that were clearly about masculinity, male homosexuality, or male prescriptions or perceptions about women were not considered "women's history" sessions/papers. Similarly, in sessions that had titles that made no reference to gender, women, sexuality, etc. but included at least one paper substantively about women, a woman, or a group or institution representing or comprising women, I added that session to the session count. I included full paper sessions, workshops, and panel discussions in this count to give a good overall measure of conference time allotted to the field. I did not include conference time allotted to the issue of the contemporary status of women in the historical profession. Six of these sessions were one-hour workshops held in the same time slot, making it necessary for women's historians to choose between them. This arrangement was a bit stingy.

12. The conference is best categorized or placed as part of the institutional/organizational structures that practitioners of the field created to support their development. The Big Berks came to be intimately connected to and representative of the values and interests of the BCWH, just as the annual meetings of AHA and OAH reflected the intellectual trends and values those organizations held dear.

13. The 2020 "Big" Berkshire Conference, scheduled to take place at Johns Hopkins University, did not meet in person because of the COVID-19 pandemic. A typically robust conference had been fully planned, and organizers hosted a scaled-back virtual conference; see https://berksconference.org/big-berks/2020-berkshire-conference/.

14. Registration was limited to 1,500 at the Mount Holyoke Big Berks in 1978. Sandi Cooper, Final Committee Report on the Fourth Berkshire Conference on the History of Women, 1974, folder 21.2 "4th Big Berks: Program committee, Reports, 1978," box 21, BCWH Records.

15. Zinsser, *History and Feminism*, 94. Zinsser doesn't cite AHA or OAH records for attendance numbers, nor does she cite BCWH records. For the First, Second, Third, and Fourth Big Berks, I compiled data from the conference reports.

16. Banner interview by Rothschild, LUSWHOHP, 13, 9.

17. Banner interview by Rothschild, LUSWHOHP, 13, 9; Stanley Pargellis to Dorothy Ganfield Fowler, March 6 and March 19, 1942; Fowler to Pargellis, March 18 and March 23, 1942, folder 4, box 1, BCWH Records (MC 267). I searched the records of the early Berkshire Conference in vain for evidence of members' advocacy or interest in the history of women prior to 1970. The only time this was evinced was in 1942 when AHA program chair Stanley Pargellis asked whether they could help put together a panel on the effect of great crises on the status of women. After some quick scrambling in their files, they suggested papers from three scholars—Pearl Kibre, Wilhelmine Williams, and Mary Sumner Benson. But when Pargellis protested that these women's research interests did not meet his design, they dropped the matter.

18. Banner interview by Rothschild, LUSWHOHP, 28. The story is corroborated in Smith-Rosenberg interview by Rothschild, LUSWHOHP, 60.

19. Berkshire Conference of Women Historians, Annual Meeting Program, May 14–16, 1971, BCWH Records.

20. Member Lists and Reports, folder "Early Officer Files, 1950–1959, 1990," BCWH Records.

21. Louise Dalby to Members of the Berkshire Conference, n.d.; Lois Banner, Mary S. Hartman, and Jessie Lutz to Dalby, March 28, 1972; Dalby to Banner, April 12, 1972, all in folder 2.5 "President's Correspondence: Louise Dalby, 1971–1973," box 2, BCWH Records.

22. Dalby to Banner, April 12, 1972, BCWH Records.

23. Banner interview by Rothschild, LUSWHOHP, 28.

24. Lois Banner and Mary S. Hartman to Members of the Berkshire Conference, 1973 Conference Report, n.d., folder 13.6, box 2, BCWH Records.

25. Hartman to Dalby, November 15, 1972, folder 2.5 "President's Correspondence: Louise Dalby, 1971–73," box 2, BCWH Records.

26. Banner and Hartman to Members of the Berkshire Conference, 1973 Conference Report, n.d., BCWH Records.

27. Mary Hartman to Berenice Carroll, January 22, 1973, folder 2.6 "President's Correspondence: Louise Dalby, 1971–1973," box 2, BCWH Records.

28. Banner interview by Rothschild, LUSWHOHP, 29.

29. Hartman and Banner, *Clio's Consciousness Raised*, vii.

30. Hartman to Carroll, January 22, 1973, BCWH Records; Carroll to Hartman and Banner, January 17, 1973, folder 2.6 "President's Correspondence: Louise Dalby, 1971–1973," box 2, BCWH Records; Blanche Wiesen Cook and Alice Kessler-Harris to Banner and Hartman, January 30, 1970, folder 2.6 "President's Correspondence: Louise Dalby, 1971–1973," box 2, BCWH Records.

31. Hartman to Carroll, January 22, 1973, BCWH Records.

32. Panel titles were "Women in Movements for Social Reform," "Women and War," "Women and Work in the United States," "Women and Power in the Family," "Women and Education," "Women in Religion," "Women and the Family in the United States," "Women in Radical Movements," "Women Viewed by the Social Scientists," "Image and Reality: Middle and Working Class Women in England," "Stereotypes, Sex Roles and Practices," and "Women in the Professions"; conference program, "Historical Perspectives on Women," presented by the Berkshire Conference of Women Historians and Rutgers College, March 2–3, 1973, folder 13.6, box 13, BCWH Records.

33. Conference program, "Historical Perspectives on Women," BCWH Records; Bernard, *Academic Women*.

34. Conference program, "Historical Perspectives on Women," BCWH Records.

35. Conference program, "Historical Perspectives on Women," BCWH Records. Linda Gordon earned a PhD in Russian history, but her research focus shifted to American women in 1970.

36. O'Neill, *Everyone Was Brave*. These men specialized in, respectively, Progressive Era history, American demographic history, and social and family history.

37. Lillian Shiman to Louise Dalby, April 20, 1973, folder 2.6 "President's Correspondence: Louise Dalby, 1971–1973," box 2, BCWH Records.

38. Smith-Rosenberg interview by Rothschild, LUSWHOHP, 65.

39. Smith-Rosenberg, "Female World of Love and Ritual."

40. Banner interview by Rothschild, LUSWHOHP, 31.

41. Hine interview by Rothschild, LUSWHOHP, 69–70.

42. Banner and Hartman to Members of the Berkshire Conference, 1973 Conference Report, n.d., p. 3, BCWH Records.

43. Banner and Hartman to Members of the Berkshire Conference, 1973 Conference Report, n.d., p. 3, BCWH Records.

44. A. L. Macrakis, Chairman Regis College, Department of History, to Mary Dunn, May 30, 1973, folder 14.1, box 14, BCWH Records; program of the Second Berkshire Conference on the History of Women, sponsored by Radcliffe College, October 26–27, 1974, folder "Materials for Report—2nd Conference, 1974–1975," BCWH Records (MC 83–M212).

45. Mary Maples Dunn to President Matina Horner, February 6, 1974, folder 14.1, box 14, BCWH Records; Mary Maples Dunn, "First Draft, Committee Report, Second Berkshire Conference on the History of Women, Radcliffe College, October 1974," folder 14.8 "2nd Big Berks: Financials & Rockefeller Foundation Correspondence," box 14, BCWH Records.

46. Dunn, "First Draft, Committee Report, Second Berkshire Conference," BCWH Records.

47. Program of the Second Berkshire Conference on the History of Women, October 26–27, 1974, BCWH Records. Other schools and institutions represented on the committee were the University of Pennsylvania, Yale, SUNY Buffalo, the University of Massachusetts–Boston, College of the Holy Cross, Nichols College, University of New Haven, the Schlesinger Library, and the Radcliffe Institute. Fields verified in Justice, *AHA Directory of Women Historians*.

48. Dunn, "First Draft, Committee Report, Second Berkshire Conference," BCWH Records; Summary of Costs and Grant Money, "Grant GA HUM 7433 for Berkshire Conference of Women Historians," May 30, 1975, folder 14.8, "2nd Big Berks: Financials & Rockefeller Foundation Correspondence," box 14, BCWH Records.

49. Program of the Second Berkshire Conference on the History of Women, October 26–27, 1974, BCWH Records; "Committee Report, Second Berkshire Conference on the History of Women, Radcliffe College, October 1974," folder 14.8, "2nd Big Berks: Financials & Rockefeller Foundation Correspondence," box 14, BCWH Records.

50. Program of the Second Berkshire Conference on the History of Women, October 26–27, 1974, BCWH Records. The notion that women's history had been overly focused on white middle-class women was commonplace from the mid-1980s forward. For an example and discussion of whether this characterization was accurate, see Hewitt, "Beyond the Search for Sisterhood," 299–321. The Hewitt essay was first published in 1985 and was revised and reprinted in Ruiz and DuBois, *Unequal Sisters* in 1990. See also Vogel, "Telling Tales."

51. Dunn, "First Draft, Committee Report, Second Berkshire Conference on the History of Women," p. 4, BCWH Records.

52. Mary Maples Dunn to Natalie Zemon Davis, March 28, 1974, folder 14.1 "2nd Big Berks: General Corresp., Mary Dunn," BCWH Records; program of the Second Berkshire Conference on the History of Women, October 26–27, 1974, BCWH Records.

53. Smith-Rosenberg, "New Woman and the New History," 185–98; N. Davis, "'Women's History' in Transition," 83–103.

54. Smith-Rosenberg, "New Woman and the New History," 185–98.

55. Smith-Rosenberg, "New Woman and the New History," 189.

56. N. Davis, "'Women's History' in Transition."

57. Worthy of note here is that French author Simone de Beauvoir's essential feminist tract, *The Second Sex*, was published in 1953. It featured an anthropological analysis of women's secondary place in all societies as man's "other."

58. De Haan and Mevis, "IAV/IIAV's Archival Policies," 23–43.

59. Mary Dunn, "Committee Report, Second Berkshire Conference on the History of Women, Radcliffe College, October 1974," folder "Materials for Report," BCWH Records (MC 82–M212).

60. Dunn, "Committee Report, 1974," 4–5, BCWH Records.

61. Dunn, "Committee Report, 1974," 5, BCWH Records.

62. "Unsolicited Testimonial from a PhD," n.d., folder "Materials for final report—2nd Berkshire Conference, 1974–1975," BCWH Records (MC 82–M212).

63. BCWH Committee, "A Proposal from the Berkshire Conference of Women Historians," n.d., folder "Materials for final report—2nd Berkshire Conference, 1974–1975," BCWH Records (MC 82–M212).

64. BCWH Committee, "A Proposal from the Berkshire Conference of Women Historians," BCWH Records.

65. "Berkshire Conference of Women Historians, 3rd BB; 1976 (4 folders)," Nell Irvin Painter Papers, DUA.

66. Program of the Third Berkshire Conference on the History of Women sponsored by Bryn Mawr College, June 9–11, 1976, folder 15.1, box 15, BCWH Records; author tally. Papers in European history included many on England, Germany, and France and a few on themes from Greek and Roman antiquity.

67. Catherine M. Prelinger, President, report, Third Berkshire Conference on the History of Women, folder 17.10 "3rd conf. report—extra copies," box 17, BCWH Records.

68. I refer here to the nationality of the historians, of course, not to their field of specialization.

69. Tullia Hamilton, "The National Association of Colored Women, 1896–1920"; Dennis C. Dickerson, "Black Women in the Mill Towns of Pennsylvania, 1920–1945"; Rosalyn Terborg-Penn, "Black Women and the Rationale for Woman Suffrage"; Marli Weiner, "The Working Lives of Slave Women"; Tahi Mottl, "Women as Movement Leaders: Boston's School Movement of the 1960s and 1970s"; and William Chafe, "Sex and Race: The Analogy of Social Control," Program of the Third Berkshire Conference on the History of Women, 1976, BCWH Records.

70. Program of the Third Berkshire Conference, 1976, folder "Comments of 3rd Berkshire Conference 1975–1977," box 15, BCWH Records.

71. Rosalyn Terborg-Penn, "A History of the Association of Black Women Historians, 1977–1981," ca. 1981, folder 144 "Correspondence with Darlene Hine," series 3, GLP 1950–95; revised ABWH Constitution, 1980, folder "Association of Black Women Historians—1980," Nell Irvin Painter Papers, DUA.

72. Nupur Chauduri, "Conference Report on Black Women: An Historical Perspective," held November 12 and 13, 1979, at the Mary McLeod Bethune Memorial Center, *Conference Group on Women's History Newsletter* 5, no. 3 (July 1980): 19–20.

73. Patricia Miller King, "Report of the Schlesinger Library 1976–1978," 1979, 11–15, AESL Records.

74. Prelinger, report, Third Berkshire Conference on the History of Women, 10, BCWH Records.

75. Dorothy Helly and Susan Reverby, Report on the 7th Berkshire Conference, folder 39.13 "Reports," box 39, BCWH Records.

76. Sandi Cooper to Mary Hartman, July 13, 1978, folder 2.12 "BCWH Presidents Corresp., Mary Hartman, 1978," box 2, BCWH Records.

77. Helly and Reverby, Report on the 7th Berkshire Conference, BCWH Records.

78. D'Ann Campbell, "The Fourth Berkshire Conference on the History of Women," *CGWH Newsletter* 4, no. 1 (October 1978): 3; Frances Richardson Keller, "Impressions, Perspectives and Reflections, Fourth Berkshire Conference on the History of Women," *CGWH Newsletter* 4, no. 1 (October 1978): 4–5.

79. Berenice Carroll to members of the Steering Committee and Nominating Committee of CCWHP, other interested parties, Re: Future of CCWHP, New Officers, October 26, 1971, folder "Misc. for files," carton 2, CCWHP Records.

80. *CCWHP Newsletter* 6, no. 1 (February 1975): 4. Copies of original newsletters in author's possession. Microfilm of *CCWHP Newsletters* available at the Schlesinger Library.

81. Hilda Smith, "Letter to the Editor," *CCWHP Newsletter* 9, no. 2 (June 1978): 17; Hilda Smith, "Statement in Support of Separating CCWHP and the Conference Group in Women's History," *CCWHP Newsletter* (December 1978): 9–11.

82. *CCWHP Newsletter* 1, no. 2 (May 1975): 8.

83. Boris and Chaudhuri, *Voices of Women Historians*, xi–xiv. CCWHP Records suggest a heated debate over this issue transpired; "News from Atlanta: CCWHP Business Meeting," and "Conference Group in Women's History," *CCWHP Newsletter* 7, no. 1, 4–5.

84. *CCWHP Newsletter* 11, no. 1 (February 1975): 4.

85. Karen Offen to Members of the CCWHP Steering Committee, December 14, 1975, folder "Misc. for files," carton 2, CCWHP Records. She held to this position three years later, as shown in Karen Offen, "Statement Opposing Total Separation of CGWH from CCWHP," *CCWHP Newsletter* (December 1978), 11–13.

86. *CCWHP Newsletter* 6, no. 2 (May 1975): 15a.

87. *CCWHP Newsletter* 6, no. 3 (October 1975): 4.

88. Historians of women and gender who were elected OAH president from 1981 to 2025 included Gerda Lerner, Anne Firor Scott, Mary Frances Berry, Linda Kerber, Darlene Clark Hine, Jacquelyn Dowd Hall, Vicki Ruiz, Nell Irvin Painter, Elaine Tyler May, Alice Kessler-Harris, Nancy Cott, Joanne Meyerowitz. Those elected AHA president from 1987 to 2025 included Natalie Zemon Davis, Louise Tilly, Caroline Walker Bynum, Lynn Hunt, Linda Kerber, Barbara Weinstein, Gabrielle M. Spiegel, Laurel Thatcher Ulrich, Mary Beth Norton, Jacqueline Jones, and Thavolia Glymph. Eight women who did not specialize in women's history were also elected to these honorific offices.

89. Carroll et al., *History of the Coordinating Committee*.

90. "ERA Petition," *CCWHP Newsletter* 8, no. 3, 13; copies of the many petitions gathered in the OAH Records and the CCWHP Records.

91. Carroll et al, *History of the Coordinating Committee*; Boris and Chaudhuri, *Voices of Women Historians*.

92. Karen Offen, "Twenty Years after the Beginning: Presentation by Dr. Karen Offen," 2007, available at www.ifrwh.com/id38.html; "1975/76 Report of the Committee on Women Historians to CCWHP," *CCWHP Newsletter* 7, no. 1 (March 1976): 11.

93. Offen, "Twenty Years after the Beginning."

94. Sicherman et al., *Recent United States Scholarship on the History of Women*.

95. Personal conversation with Kathryn Kish Sklar, March 4, 2012. In the 1980 Bucharest report (Sicherman et al., *Recent United States Scholarship on the History of Women*), she and the coauthors cite the work of Joan Kelly-Gadol, using the phrase "social relations of the sexes" on page 11 and the term "gender" on page 27.

96. Arnita Jones, *CCWHP Research Bulletin #10*, 1975.

97. Arnita Jones, *CCWHP Research Bulletin #8*, 1974.

98. Chaudhuri, *Bibliography of Women's History*, in author's possession. Chaudhuri was editor of the *CGWH Newsletter* from 1976 to 1980 before serving as treasurer and secretary from 1982 to 1988; Carroll et al., *History of the Coordinating Committee*, appendix C.

99. A. Jones, "Women Historians and Women's History: An Organizational Guide," OAH Records. The list is also derived from the *CCWHP Newsletters* for 1976 to 1979. A couple more short-lived regional groups made brief appearances on the list of affiliated groups. The Association of Black Women Historians did not become an affiliate of the CCWHP-CGWH in the 1980s. As of June 1983, it was listed not as an "Affiliated Organization" but rather under "Other Important Associations for Networking," along with the OAH-CSW, the AHA's Committee on Women Historians, the Upper Midwest Women's History Center for Teachers, the National Coordinating Committee on the Promotion of History, and the Special Assistant on Women and Minorities at the AHA (Noralee Frankel). *CGWH Newsletter* 14, no. 2 (June 1983): 2–3.

100. *CGWH Newsletter* 2, no. 1 (December 1977): 19.

101. The final chapter of the book will consider the public history initiatives of local, regional, national, public, and academic historians.

102. *CGWH Newsletter* 2, no. 2 (March 1977): 3.

103. Manuscripts Collection, Women Historians of the Midwest Organizational Records, Minnesota Historical Society, St. Paul, accessed January 23, 2012, www2.mnhs.org/library/findaids/00419.xml.

104. *CGWH Newsletter* 2, no. 2 (March 1977): 3.

105. *CGWH Newsletter* 3, no. 1 (December 1977): 10–11.

106. *CCWHP Newsletter* 3, no. 3 (October 1977): 8.

107. *CGWH Newsletter* 4, no. 3 (May 1979): 7–8; *CGWH Newsletter*, December 1981, 32.

108. *CGWH Newsletter* 4, no. 3 (May 1979): 7–8.

109. Andrea Hinding, preface to Hinding et al., *Women's History Sources*, ix.

110. *CGWH Newsletter*, December 1981, 32.

111. Manuscripts Collection, Upper Midwest Women's History Center Organizational Records, Minnesota Historical Society, St. Paul, accessed January 23, 2012, www.mnhs.org/library/findaids/00734.xml.

112. *CGWH Newsletter* 5, no. 2 (February 1980): 8; *CGWH Newsletter*, December 1981, 18.

113. *CGWH Newsletter*, June 1982, 19.

114. Inventory of Women Historians of the Midwest Organizational Records, Minnesota Historical Society, WHOM Collection at Monmouth College Archives finding aid, accessed January 23, 2012, department.monm.edu/archives/WHOM2.htm (webpage no longer available; copy of inventory in author's possession).

115. Patricia Haines, "Report for 1979: Upstate New York Women's History Conference," *CGWH Newsletter* 5, no. 2 (February 1980): 9–10. Haines's residence and university affiliation were found in Nutting, *American Historical Association Directory of Women Historians*, 21.

116. Haines, "Report for 1979: Upstate New York Women's History Conference," 9–10.

117. *Elizabeth Cady Stanton Foundation Newsletter*, January 1980, 1, box 3, SAWH Records; Patricia Foster Haines, "Report on the Opening of the Women's Rights National Historical Park, July 1982," *CGWH Newsletter* 13, no. 4 (December 1982): 16–17.

118. Sumler-Edmond, "Association of Black Women Historians"; Rosalyn Terborg-Penn, "Association of Black Women Historians," in Mjagkij, *Organizing Black America*.

119. Gerda Lerner to Richard Kirkendall, March 30, 1980, folder 145 "Outside Correspondence, 1980–1982"; Gerda Lerner, Project Proposal, 1980, folder 140 "Proposal 1980"; Rosalyn Terborg-Penn (National Co-Director, ABWH) to Gerda Lerner, January 29, 1980, folder 145 "Outside Correspondence, 1980–1982"; folder 144 "Correspondence with Darlene Hine," series 3, GLP 1950–95; Darlene Clark Hine and Gerda Lerner, "Final Report on OAH/ABWH Project on Black Women's History," folder 140 "Proposal 1980," series 3, GLP 1950–95.

120. Nutting, *American Historical Association Directory of Women Historians*, front matter; Sumler-Edmond, "Association of Black Women Historians"; Terborg-Penn, "Association of Black Women Historians."

121. Scanlon and Cosner, *American Women Historians*, 31.

122. Antoinette Burton and Deborah J. Rossum to Dear Friends, "An Open Letter to Participants," July 1, 1987, folder 12, box 34, BCWH Records.

123. Burton and Rossum, "An Open Letter to Participants," July 1, 1987, BCWH Records.

124. Susan Reverby to Antoinette Burton and Deborah Rossum, October 26, 1987, folder 12, box 34, BCWH Records. Reverby was an early participant in the women's history movement of the 1970s, a scholar who focused on American working-class women, and a faculty member at Wellesley, where the Seventh Berkshire Conference on the History of Women was held in 1987. Cochairing the program with Reverby was Dorothy O. Helly, who directed the women's studies program at Hunter College. Both Burton and Rossum specialize in British history.

125. Reverby to Burton and Rossum, October 26, 1987, BCWH Records.

126. "Does This Conference Smack of Elitism?," flyer from the Seventh Berkshire Conference on the History of Women, 1987, folder 12, box 34, BCWH Records.

127. Elizabeth Pleck to Catherine Prelinger, November 8, 1975, folder 17.2 "3rd Berkshire Conference, Program Cmte," box 17, BCWH Records. Pleck was an assistant professor of American history at the University of Michigan in 1975.

128. Carol Groneman to Mary Beth Norton, March 19, 1982, folder 27.1 "6th Big Berks Program Cmte Correspondence," box 17, BCWH Records.

129. Gordon, "Socialist View of Women's Studies," 565; Gordon was speaking about the political origins of women's studies as a discipline and working from her perspective on the discipline of history. Her argument was also made from the frame of socialist feminism.

Chapter 9

1. The quotes in the epigraph are from Buhle interview by Barnes, LUSWHOHP, 23, 53; and DuBois interview by Barnes, LUSWHOHP, 22.

2. Anne Firor Scott (chairman), John Ezell, Rhoda Dorsey, William Freeling, and Nancy Weiss, "Report of the Committee on the Status of Women to the Organization of American Historians," submitted April 14, 1971, at OAH Executive Board Meeting, New Orleans, according to the Executive Board Minutes Agenda, April 1971, folder 19, box 1, OAH Records; Schmidt and Schmidt, "Invisible Woman."

3. Viola Barnes to Emiliana Noether, May 11, 1969, folder 2.4 "President's Correspondence: Emiliana P. Noether, 1969–1971," box 2, BCWH Records.

4. Chaudhuri, *Bibliography of Women's History*; Joan Hoff, introduction to Fischer, *Journal of Women's History*, 9–37; BCWH Records. I am measuring success here by sheer mass quantity of published scholarship.

5. I will focus on two curriculum development projects, but there were many others, such as one funded by the National Endowment for the Humanities and the Woodrow Wilson Foundation in 1981 and another sponsored by the New York Council for the Humanities in 1995. Berkin et al., *Woman's Place Is in the History Books*; Groce, *American Women's Lives*, copy in box 5, Sara Evans Papers, DUA; *Readings and Resources for Institute on Las Mujeres*, sponsored by a Ford Foundation–funded project, "Incorporating Feminist Scholarship concerning Gender and Cultural Diversity into the Curriculum," conference held at St. Cloud State University, Minnesota, February 16 and 17, 1990, box 5, Sara Evans Papers, DUA. The annual UCLA Workshop on Teaching US Women's History was founded in 1978 by Kathryn Kish Sklar. It drew scholars from the West and Southwest each year and received a start-up grant from the National Endowment for the Humanities; Sklar interview by Gustafson, LUSWHOHP, 96; Sklar, "Women's Studies Movement," 130.

6. Lerner, *Majority Finds Its Past*; Lerner, *Why History Matters*; Lerner, *Teaching Women's History*.

7. Zinsser, *History and Feminism*, 119.

8. Howe, *Politics of Women's Studies*.

9. Linda Kerber, *Courses in Women's History and Related Fields, Bulletin #1*, March 1, 1971, CCWHP Records; Linda Kerber, *Courses in Women's History and Related Fields, Bulletin #2*, October 1, 1971, CCWHP Records; Linda Kerber, *Courses in Women's History and Related Fields, Bulletin #3*, March 15, 1972, CCWHP Records; Linda Kerber, *Courses in Women's History and Related Fields, Bulletin #6*, May 1, 1973, CCWHP Records; *CCWHP Research Bulletin #7*, Fall 1974; *CCWHP Research Bulletin #8*, 1974; *CCWHP Newsletter: A Special Edition for Graduate Students*, March 1975; Zinsser, *History and Feminism*, 77–84; Ryan interview by Rothschild, LUSWHOHP, 24–25.

10. Gordon, "Socialist View of Women's Studies," 565.

11. DuBois and Dumenil, *Through Women's Eyes*, 5th ed., 647–49.

12. Buhle interview by Barnes, LUSWHOHP, 23, 53.

13. Kessler-Harris interview by Gustafson, LUSWHOHP, 32–33.

14. White, *Telling Histories*, 72–84 and 101–34.

15. Hall, *Revolt against Chivalry*; Sara Evans, *Personal Politics*.

16. See LUSWHOHP.

17. Gordon interview by Gustafson, LUSWHOHP, 77–78; Gordon, *Woman's Body*, v–vi.

18. S. Benson, *Counter Cultures*; Buhle, *Women and American Socialism*; DuBois, *Feminism and Suffrage*; Sklar, *Catharine Beecher*.

19. Kessler-Harris interview by Gustafson, LUSWHOHP, 29, 34, 46; Turbin, *Working Women of Collar City*; Carol Berkin specialized in colonial and Revolutionary era history, though she didn't publish a monograph in women's history until 2006. The work of other scholars listed here has been identified elsewhere.

20. Echols, *Daring to Be Bad*.

21. Reverby, *Ordered to Care*; Reverby, *Examining Tuskegee*; Baxandall, *Words on Fire*; Davies, *Woman's Place Is at the Typewriter*; Tax, *Rising of the Women*; Swerdlow, *Women Strike for Peace*; Priscilla Murolo, "Amy Swerdlow: Activist, Scholar, Teacher," 2012, Jewish Women's Archive, https://jwa.org/weremember/swerdlow-amy.

22. Gordon interview by Gustafson, LUSWHOHP, 1–4, 12–13, 25, 27.

23. J. Anthony Lukas, "Historians' Conference: The Radical Need for Jobs," *New York Times*, March 12, 1972, p. SM38.

24. Gordon interview by Gustafson, LUSWHOHP, 33; Gordon et al., "History as Indoctrination."

25. Gordon interview by Gustafson, LUSWHOHP, 35.

26. Echols, *Daring to Be Bad*, 158.

27. Gordon interview by Gustafson, LUSWHOHP, 35; Buhle interview by Barnes, LUSWHOHP, 30–31.

28. Gordon interview by Gustafson, LUSWHOHP, 38.

29. Clark, *Working Life of Women*.

30. Buhle interview by Barnes, LUSWHOHP, 31.

31. Buhle and Buhle, *Concise History of Woman Suffrage*; Buhle, *Women and American Socialism*.

32. DuBois interview by Barnes, LUSWHOHP; DuBois, *Feminism and Suffrage*.

33. Weisstein became a figure of national recognition as a woman academic and feminist cultural critic. Leila McNeill, "This Feminist Psychologist Turned Rock Star Led a Full Life of Resistance," *Smithsonian Magazine*, April 7, 2017, www.smithsonianmag.com/science-nature /feminist-psychologist-turned-rock-star-led-multifaceted-life-resistance-180962814/.

34. DuBois interview by Barnes, LUSWHOHP, 17–20.

35. Sklar interview by Gustafson, LUSWHOHP, 77.

36. Gordon interview by Gustafson, LUSWHOHP, 40.

37. For example, Kathryn Kish Sklar taught at Ann Arbor, Michigan, from 1969 to 1974 before taking a professorship at UCLA in 1974. She moved to SUNY Binghamton in 1989. Linda Gordon moved from Boston to Madison, Wisconsin, in 1984. Ellen DuBois moved from SUNY Buffalo to UCLA in 1989. Cott, Tax, Baxandall, Reverby, and Buhle remained in the Northeast. Sklar, "Women's Studies Movement," 130–41; Sklar interview by Gustafson, LUSWHOHP.

38. Gordon interview by Gustafson, LUSWHOHP, 45.

39. Cott interview by Gustafson, LUSWHOHP, 24.

40. Cott, *Root of Bitterness*.

41. Buhle et al., "Women in American Society."

42. Cott interview by Gustafson, LUSWHOHP, 23–24; Buhle et al., "Women in American Society."

43. Cott interview by Gustafson, LUSWHOHP, 24.

44. Cott, foreword to *Root of Bitterness* (1986 ed.), xiii.

45. Cott, *Bonds of Womanhood*.

46. Cott, *Woman Making History*. When I met Nancy Cott in 2009, while I was completing the research for the dissertation upon which this book is based, she pointed out that the massive portrait of history professor and Radcliffe president Wilbur K. Jordan that now hangs in the reading room at the Schlesinger Library was moved there at her suggestion because Jordan had been so instrumental to the archive's establishment from 1943 to 1960.

47. Novick, *That Noble Dream*, 472–91.

48. Gordon interview by Gustafson, LUSWHOHP, 48.

49. Doris King to Mary Massey, February 11, 1971, Incoming Correspondence Files, folder 9-92, box 9, MEM Papers.

50. Robert Townsend, "What's in a Label? Changing Patterns of Faculty Specialization since 1975," *Perspectives* 45, no. 1 (2007), www.historians.org/perspectives/issues/2007/0701 /0701new1.cfm 2/8/2008; Robert B. Townsend, "Decline of the West or the Rise of the Rest?

Data from 2010 Shows Rebalancing of Field Coverage in Departments" *Perspectives on History*, September 2011, 34–37.

51. See reviews by Shorter; D. Kennedy; and Lemons. Gordon, *Woman's Body*; Fox-Genovese, "Comment on the Reviews of *Woman's Body, Woman's Right*."

52. Gordon interview by Gustafson, LUSWHOHP, 53. Gordon admitted that the excoriation of her 1976 book by a few male historians was quite hurtful but that she pretended she didn't care. The community of feminist scholars she had supporting her helped her through it.

53. Kessler-Harris, "Long Road from Home"; Kessler-Harris interview by Gustafson, LUSWHOHP, 44; the conference was held at SUNY Binghamton, September 21–22, 1974.

54. Dubofsky, "City Kid's View," 76.

55. Kessler-Harris, "Organizing the Unorganizable."

56. Kessler-Harris, *Out to Work*.

57. Samuel G. Freedman, "Of History and Politics: Bitter Feminist Debate," *New York Times*, June 6, 1986, B1.

58. Freedman, "Of History and Politics," B1; Alice Kessler-Harris to Jennifer Tomás, April 29, 2012 (in author's possession). Both the Kessler-Harris quotes and the Rosalind Rosenberg quotes are from "Of History and Politics."

59. Elsie Freivogel to My Colleagues on the WHSS Advisory Board, September 21, 1978; Andrea Hinding to Richard Kirkendall, September 13 and 19, 1978; Andrea Hinding, "The Statement in Opposition," *AHA Newsletter*, March 1974, all in folder 3 "Committee on the Status of Women 1978–1979, 2," box 15, OAH Records.

60. Gerda Lerner to Andrea Hinding, August 15, 1978, folder 3 "Committee on the Status of Women 1978–1979, 2," box 15, OAH Records.

61. OAH file on this matter, folder 3 "Committee on the Status of Women 1978–1979, 2," box 15, OAH Records.

62. Anne Firor Scott to Joan Hoff-Wilson, September 18, 1978, Chronological Business Correspondence files, Fall 1978, AFS Papers.

63. A. Scott to Hoff-Wilson, September 18, 1978, AFS Papers.

64. Andrea Hinding, interview by Clarke A. Chambers, October 14, 1994, 6–10, University of Minnesota, https://conservancy.umn.edu/bitstream/handle/11299/49811/1/hindingAndrea.pdf.

65. Catharine R. Stimpson, "Gerda Lerner on the Future of Our Past," *Ms.*, September 1981, 51.

66. Aside from those I feature here, there were many others; see note 5 in this chapter.

67. Box 70 and 71, OAH Records.

68. Elizabeth Fox-Genovese Papers, SHC; Ryan interview by Rothschild, LUSWHOHP, 18–21, 24–25. The program was started in 1974 or 1975, according to Ryan. Elizabeth Fox-Genovese CV in folder 22 "Grant Proposal, 1980," box 70, OAH Records.

69. Ryan interview by Rothschild, LUSWHOHP, 18–21, 24–25.

70. Arthur S. Link to Dr. Joan Hoff-Wilson, January 3, 1984, folder 14 "Arthur Link (OAH President) 1984–1987," box 19, OAH Records.

71. Hoff-Wilson to Link, January 23, 1984, folder 14 "Arthur Link (OAH President) 1984–1987," box 19, OAH Records.

72. While I do not pursue this point further in this chapter, it is nonetheless an important observation that deserves further analysis. Later, I touch on the development of gender history, intersectionality, and transnational women's history developed in the 1990s and beyond. I see the cross-field nature of the women's history subculture as foreshadowing transnational history.

73. D'Ann Campbell, "A Brief History of the Organization of American Historians Project to Integrate Material on Women into History Survey Courses," 1, ca. 1981, folder 14 "Restoring Women to History Correspondence, 1981–1984," box 70, OAH Records.

74. Campbell, "Brief History," 1, OAH Records.

75. Campbell, "Brief History," 1, OAH Records.

76. Campbell, "Brief History," 2, OAH Records.

77. Campbell, "Brief History," 2, OAH Records.

78. Elizabeth Fox-Genovese, Organization of American Historians, Grant Proposal to FIPSE, 1980, "Integrating Women's Experience and Perceptions into the Basic Curriculum," 2–3, folder 22, box 70, OAH Records.

79. Fox-Genovese, OAH Grant Proposal to FIPSE, 3.

80. Fox-Genovese, OAH Grant Proposal to FIPSE, 3.

81. Elizabeth Fox-Genovese, "Writing Women into History," essay prepared for the OAH-FIPSE Conference on Integrating Material on Women into the History Survey Courses, March 23, 1981, folder 12 "Restoring Women to History; Conference, 1980–1981," box 71, OAH Records.

82. Fox-Genovese, "Writing Women into History," 4, 10, 16, OAH Records.

83. Lorde, *Sister Outsider* (2007), 110–14.

84. R. Don Higginbotham to Dear Friends, January 24, 1983, folder 14, box 71, OAH Records; Sara Evans, *Personal Politics*. Evans's acknowledgments tell of her early involvement in women's liberation in Chicago 1967, her experience in a few civil rights marches and anti-war activism, and the importance of having had Anne Scott as role model and teacher when she was an undergraduate at Duke in 1963.

85. Fox-Genovese et al., *Restoring Women to History: United States I* and *Restoring Women to History: United States II*, folders 6 and 13, box 71, OAH Records. Also participating were Deborah Hoskins, Douglas Deal, Mary Tachau, and Harold Woodman. Mary Tachau worked in the AHA's Teaching Division. Harold Woodman specialized in African American and New South era history at Purdue.

86. Fox-Genovese et al., *Restoring Women to History: United States I* and *United States II*.

87. Fox-Genovese et al., *Restoring Women to History: United States 1*, 4–5.

88. J. Scott, "Gender."

89. "Mary Hartman Opening Address to the Fourth Berkshire Conference on the History of Women," folder 17.11, BCWH Records.

90. Kelly, *Women, History, and Theory*, xiii. Kelly was a 1963 PhD graduate of Columbia University and a professor in the CUNY system from 1956 until 1971, when she moved over to Sarah Lawrence College. There, Gerda Lerner was in the process of creating the first MA program in women's history in the country at Sarah Lawrence. She asked Kelly to join the program and think about women's history in relation to her own field and about courses or lectures she might develop. Demurring at first, Kelly was convinced by a four-hour phone call in which Lerner insisted there were "almost infinite possibilities that lay ahead of me in women's history." What followed was the profoundly destabilizing realization that everything she thought she knew about the Renaissance was "utterly questionable" when looked at from the vantage point of women.

91. Fox-Genovese et al., *Restoring Women to History: United States I*, 5; Des Jardins, "Women's and Gender History," 136–58. Des Jardins points out that women's history and gender history complemented one another and coexisted, gender history largely growing out of women's history. Yet she underscores her explanation of the development of gender history with Joan

Scott's canonical 1986 essay in the *American Historical Review*, typically underscoring that work as close to the beginning rather than at some point in the middle of that analytic category's emergence.

92. Lerner, *Majority Finds Its Past*, 63, 83, 94.

93. Lerner, *Black Women in White America*, xviii.

94. Gerda Lerner to Richard Kirkendall, March 30, 1980, folder 145 "Outside Correspondence, 1980–1982," series 3, GLP 1950–95.

95. Hine interview by Rothschild, LUSWHOHP. Thavolia Glymph and Kate Whittenstein were her first two women's history students; Darlene Clark Hine is now a distinguished historian of African American women's history. Among her many publications are *Hine Sight*; *Black Women in White*; and *Black Victory*. This last book is a new edition of her 1975 dissertation, which was originally published in 1979; Hine has also published widely in scholarly journals and edited and coedited a number of volumes.

96. Gerda Lerner, Project Proposal, 1980, folder 140 "Proposal 1980," series 3, GLP 1950–95.

97. Mary Berry to Richard Kirkendall, April 4, 1980, folder 145 "Outside Correspondence, 1980–1982," series 3, GLP 1950–95.

98. Bettye Collier-Thomas to Gerda Lerner, May 29, 1980, folder 145 "Outside Correspondence, 1980–1982," series 3, GLP 1950–95.

99. Rosalyn Terborg-Penn (National Co-Director, ABWH) to Gerda Lerner, January 29, 1980, folder 145 "Outside Correspondence, 1980–1982," series 3, GLP 1950–95.

100. Folder 144, "Correspondence with Darlene Hine, 1981–1982," series 3, GLP 1950–95.

101. Darlene Clark Hine and Gerda Lerner, "Final Report on OAH/ABWH Project on Black Women's History," folder 140 "Proposal 1980," series 3, GLP 1950–95.

102. "Part E. Problems, Gerda Lerner's Perspective," in Hine and Lerner, "Final Report on OAH/ABWH Project on Black Women's History," GLP 1950–95.

103. "Part E. Problems, Darlene Clark Hine's Perspective," in Hine and Lerner, "Final Report on OAH/ABWH Project on Black Women's History," GLP 1950–95.

104. "Part E. Problems, Darlene Clark Hine's Perspective," 17. Table 8.1 shows figures for all sessions with a women's history component to number nineteen, but the 1982 OAH Program shows that there were in fact eleven full women's history sessions on the program that year.

105. Darlene Clark Hine, "Proposal for A Planning Grant: Black Women in the Mid-Western States: Indiana, Illinois, Ohio, Michigan and Wisconsin: An Historical Study and Exhibition," folder 139 "FIPSE Proposal by DH, 1982," series 3, GLP 1950–95.

106. Hine interview by Rothschild, LUSWHOHP, 37–42, 68.

107. Hine interview by Rothschild, LUSWHOHP, 39.

108. Darlene Clark Hine to Gerda Lerner, May 6, 1981, folder 144 " Correspondence with Darlene Hine, 1980–1982," series 3, GLP 1950–95.

109. Folders 1367 "Anne Firor Scott," and 1514–1516 "Darlene Clark Hine, 1988– 1989," SHA Records; Hine interview by Rothschild, LUSWHOHP, 39.

110. Hine interview by Rothschild, LUSWHOHP, 68.

111. Hine interview by Rothschild, LUSWHOHP, 69.

112. Hine, *Black Women in White*; Hine, "Rape and the Inner Lives of Black Women."

113. Ruiz and DuBois, *Unequal Sisters* (1990). Nancy Hewitt's essay in the third edition (2000) of *Unequal Sisters*, "Beyond the Search for Sisterhood," acknowledged that her earlier essay of that title, published in 1984, had unfairly criticized earlier generations of women's historians for ignoring the ethnic, racial, and class diversity inherent in American women's

history. Nevertheless, this practice of critiquing earlier scholarship for being insufficient, even when that criticism was not entirely fair, prompted historians to do more and better history. This pattern replicated the intergenerational dynamic between new women's historians of the 1970s and the "old" women's historians. The overall effect of these critiques was to the great benefit of the larger field as it spurred historians to do more and better work incorporating all women into the American historical tapestry.

114. Hall, *Revolt against Chivalry*. The dissertation was completed in 1974; Hall interview by Glusman, LUSWHOHP, 15, 21–22. This interview is closed to researchers, but I obtained permission from Jacquelyn Dowd Hall to read and quote portions of it.

115. Evans interview by Weisiger, LUSWHOHP, 4–6.

116. Robnett, *How Long?*, 9, 115–37.

117. Sklar, *Catharine Beecher*; Sklar, *Florence Kelly*.

118. Sklar interview by Gustafson, LUSWHOHP, 94–95; UCLA Workshop on Teaching U.S. Women's History, KKS Papers; Workshop on Teaching Women's History, Manuscript Collection, LSC.0431, UCLA Special Collections, Charles E. Young Research Library, Los Angeles.

119. Rothschild interview by Barnes; Dublin interview by Gustafson; Ruiz interview by Rothschild; and Freedman interview by Rothschild, all in LUSWHOHP; Freedman, *Their Sisters' Keepers*.

120. Freedman, "Women's Networks"; Walter Goodman, "Women's Studies: The Debate Continues," *New York Times Magazine*, April 22, 1984, 39; Kathryn Kish Sklar, Temma Kaplan, and Joyce Appleby to Donald P. Kennedy, President, Stanford University, April 28, 1983, KKS Papers; "Support Committee for Estelle Freedman," letter requesting letters of support for Freedman be sent to the provost's office at Stanford, in addition to money to fund her legal challenge to the tenure denial, KKS Papers.

121. Kathryn Kish Sklar to Jen Tomás, undated, ca. 2012, in author's possession.

122. UCLA Teaching Workshop Document Index, to be Published in Women and Social Movements Database. Contains correspondence, agenda topics, and participant and organizer names.

123. "Participants List for the UCLA Teaching U.S. Women's History Workshop, 1978–1991"; and Nan Yamane, "Inventory of [UCLA] Teaching Women's History Workshop, 1978–2020, 'February 2021: Documents Thread,'" in author's possession.

124. Gerda Lerner and Kathryn Kish Sklar, *Graduate Training in U.S. Women's History: A Conference Report*, folder 4, box 30, KKS Papers.

125. Lerner and Sklar, *Graduate Training in U.S. Women's History*, 11–15, 18–23, KKS Papers.

126. Lerner and Sklar, *Graduate Training in U.S. Women's History*, 11–15, 18–23, KKS Papers.

127. Ruiz interview by Rothschild, LUSWHOHP, 81–82; Ruiz and DuBois, *Unequal Sisters*; Lerner and Sklar, *Graduate Training in U.S. Women's History*, 11–15, 18–23, KKS Papers.

128. Lerner and Sklar, *Graduate Training in U.S. Women's History*, 22–23, KKS Papers.

129. Lerner and Sklar, *Graduate Training in U.S. Women's History*, 47–48; for an example of some of the criticism of feminists, see Terborg-Penn interview by Rothschild, LUSWHOHP, 50. Terborg-Penn attended Wingspread in 1988.

130. Dublin, *Women at Work*.

131. Dublin interview by Gustafson, LUSWHOHP; Dublin, *Women at Work*.

132. Sklar interview by Gustafson, LUSWHOHP, 94–112; UCLA Workshop on Teaching U.S. Women's History, KKS Papers; Workshop on Teaching Women's History, Manuscript Collection 431, UCLA Special Collections; list of dissertations directed by Kathryn Kish

Sklar, 2021, in author's possession; Sklar, *Catharine Beecher*; "History of the *WASM* Web Site," accessed February 23, 2021, https://search.alexanderstreet.com/wass/about#history; Kathryn Kish Sklar and Thomas Dublin, eds., "About Women and Social Movements International—1840 to Present," accessed February 23, 2021, https://search.alexanderstreet.com/wasi. The Women and Social Movements Database is subscribed to by 500 libraries and is managed by Alexander Street Press. Since Sklar and Dublin retired, it has gone to a rotating system of editors. In 2022, Judy Tzu-Chun Wu and Rebecca Jo Plant, both of the University of California, held that position.

133. Hine interview by Rothschild, LUSWHOHP, 72.

134. David Donald, "Mr. Donald Replies," *New York Times*, August 30, 1970, www.nytimes.com/1970/08/30/archives/radical-historians.html; Gerda Lerner, "Letter to the Editor," *New York Times*, August 30, 1970; original draft of Gerda Lerner letter to the *New York Times Book Review*, folder "CCWHP 1969–," carton 1, CCWHP Records (accession 77-M82/M11, unprocessed manuscript collection); *CCWHP Newsletter* 2, no. 1, supplement, sec. 10, p. 4, folder "CCWHP Newsletters, Vol. II," box 4, SAWH Records.

135. Palmer, *From Gentleman's Club to Professional Body*, 251–60; Novick, *That Noble Dream*, 415–629.

Chapter 10

1. Karen J. Winkler, "Scholars of Women's History Fear the Field Has Lost Its Identity," *Chronicle of Higher Education*, July 5, 1990, A4, A6; Kathryn Kish Sklar and Gerda Lerner, "Article Misrepresented Women's History," *Chronicle of Higher Education*, September 5, 1990, B7.

2. Sklar and Lerner, "Article Misrepresented Women's History," B7.

3. Zinsser, *History and Feminism*.

4. Sklar suggested the new riverbed concept. Sklar and Lerner, "Article Misrepresented Women's History"; Cott et al., "Considering the State of U.S. Women's History."

5. Cott et al., "Considering the State of U.S. Women's History."

6. Nash et al., *History on Trial*, chaps. 7, 8, 9.

7. Nash et al., *History on Trial*, 8.

8. Dayton and Levenstein, "Big Tent"; Gidlow, *Obama, Clinton, Palin*. Public feminist intellectuals and activists need a historical basis upon which to build their arguments and theories, even when they are not historians. See hooks, *Ain't I a Woman*; Faludi, *Backlash*; and Traister, *Good and Mad*.

9. Klatch, *Women of the New Right*; Nielsen, *Un-American Womanhood*; K. Kennedy, *Disloyal Mothers*; Erickson, "'We Want No Teachers'"; Thurner, "Better Citizens without the Ballot," 203–20; McGirr, *Suburban Warriors*; Critchlow, *Phyllis Schlafly*; Delegard, *Battling Miss Bolsheviki*; Blee, "Women in the 1920s Ku Klux Klan Movement"; Blee and Deutsch, *Women of the Right*; Nickerson, "Moral Mothers and Goldwater Girls"; Spruill, *Divided We Stand*.

10. For example, see the *Phyllis Schlafly Report* and the *Eagle Forum* for this constant drumbeat on the failings of women's history as feminist history. *Phyllis Schlafly Report*, February 1972, offers an early presentation of conservative historical interpretation dismissing newer interpretations of women's history emphasizing women's diverse historical experiences, perspectives, and agency as protagonists of their own lives. In Schlafly's conservative vision of history, women owed their well-being and any progress they enjoyed to men, their

technological innovations, and their support as husbands and breadwinners. Schlafly frequently attacked "liberal" and "radical" interpretations of history in her newsletters thereafter. Phyllis Schlafly, "Teaching History: Fact or Fiction?," *Phyllis Schlafly Report*, August 2003; Schlafly, "What's Happened to Public School Curriculum?," *Phyllis Schlafly Report*, November 2010; "Call Your Representatives—No Women's Museum on the Mall," *Eagle Forum*, May 5, 2014, https://eagleforum.org/publications/alerts/2014-archives/call-your-representatives-no -womens-museum-on-the-mall.html. "College Student Alert: Beware of One-Party Classroom," *Phyllis Schlafly Report*, April 2009, is one example that presents this perspective; more recently, the *Eagle Forum* published "'Honest History': Don't Fall for the Scam" on July 28, 2019, in reference to "critical race theory" and adjacent controversies over the content of American history courses.

11. Sara Evans, *Tidal Wave*.

12. Bleser, "Tokens of Affection."

13. Additionally, there have been more than half a dozen women elected to these honorific offices during these years who did not specialize in women's history.

14. "List of Presidential Addresses by Year," American Historical Association, accessed July 31, 2022, www.historians.org/about-aha-and-membership/aha-history-and-archives /presidential-addresses/by-year; "Past Officers," Organization of American Historians, accessed July 31, 2022, www.oah.org/about/past-officers/#presidents.

15. Joan Kelly Memorial Prize, AHA website, accessed July 31, 2022, www.historians.org /awards-and-grants/awards-and-prizes/joan-kelly-memorial-prize.

16. "Lerner-Scott Prize Winners," 1992–2022, Organization of American Historians, www .oah.org/awards/awards-for-graduate-students-and-recent-graduates/lerner-scott-prize/. In 1992 the OAH awarded the first Lerner-Scott Prize for the best dissertation in US women's and gender history after two years of fundraising to fund the award; "Darlene Clark Hine Prize Winners," 2010 to 2021, Organization of American Historians, www.oah.org/awards/book -awards/darlene-clark-hine-award/winners/; "Mary Nickless Prize in U.S. Women's and/or Gender History," Organization of American Historians, www.oah.org/awards/book-awards /mary-nickliss-prize, all accessed July 31, 2022.

17. Robert B. Townsend, "Decline of the West or the Rise of the Rest? Data from 2010 Shows Rebalancing of Field Coverage in Departments," *Perspectives on History*, September 2011, 36.

18. Gerda Lerner and Kathryn Kish Sklar, *Graduate Training in U.S. Women's History: A Conference Report*, folder 4, box 30, KKS Papers.

19. Joan Hoff and Christie Farnham, "Statement of Purpose of the *Journal of Women's History*," *Journal of Women's History* 1, no. 1 (1989): 6.

20. G. Howe, *American Historical Association's Guide to Historical Literature*.

21. Norton and Gerardi, *American Historical Association's Guide to Historical Literature*.

22. Chaudhuri, *Bibliography of Women's History*.

23. Darlene Clark Hine and Gerda Lerner, "Final Report on OAH/ABWH Project on Black Women's History," folder 140 "Proposal 1980," series 3, GLP 1950–95. The report itself was prepared in 1982.

24. Hewitt, "Beyond the Search for Sisterhood," 299–321. Between 1985 and 2000, Hewitt revised her initial assessment of the limited focus of American women's historians, acknowledging that she had failed to sufficiently recognize scholarship on working-class and ethnically and racially diverse groups of women. In 2000 she published a corrective to her 1985 essay,

titled simply "Beyond the Search for Sisterhood: American Women's History in the 1990s," in Ruiz and DuBois, *Unequal Sisters* (2000), 1–19.

25. Ruiz and DuBois, *Unequal Sisters* (2000), 447–62.

26. Buhle et al., "Women in American Society."

27. Vogel, "Telling Tales."

28. Christie Farnham, "Draft Statement of Purpose of the *Journal of Women's History*," October 27, 1987, folder "Founder," box 1, *JWH* Records; Hoff and Farnham, "Statement of Purpose," 6–10; Farnham Pope and Hoff, interview by Tomás, April 12, 2013, segment 1, *JWH* OHP; Christie Farnham to Mitch Allen, February 25, 1988, folder "Initial Organizational Plans for JWH," box 1, *JWH* Records; Farnham to John Gallman of Indiana University Press, March 11, 1988, folder "Initial Organizational Plans for JWH," box 1, *JWH* Records.

29. Hoff, *Law, Gender, and Injustice*.

30. Hoff and Farnham, "Statement of Purpose," 8–9, *JWH* Records.

31. Farnham, "Draft Statement of Purpose," *JWH* Records; Farnham and Hoff, "Statement of Purpose," 6–10, *JWH* Records.

32. *Gender and History* 1, no. 1 (1989).

33. See correspondence in folders "Complaints about JWH" and "Initial Organizational Plans," box 1, *JWH* Records.

34. Norton and Gerardi, *American Historical Association's Guide to Historical Literature*; Robert Townsend, "What's in a Label? Changing Patterns of Faculty Specialization since 1975," *Perspectives* 45, no. 1 (2007), accessed February 8, 2008, www.historians.org/perspectives /issues/2007/0701/0701new1.cfm.

35. Joan Hoff, "Introduction: An Overview of Women's History in the United States," in Fischer, *Journal of Women's History*, 9.

36. Hoff, "Introduction," in Fischer, *Journal of Women's History*, 9.

37. Stone, "History and Post-Modernism"; Spiegel, "History and Post-Modernism"; Appleby et al., *Telling the Truth about History*; Richard Evans, *In Defense of History*, 7–12.

38. Jenkins, *Postmodern History Reader*.

39. Hoff and Farnham both address the topic of post-structuralism in Fischer, *Journal of Women's History*. Farnham Pope and Hoff, interview by Tomás, April 12, 2013, segment 1, *JWH* OHP; Farnham to Allen, February 25, 1988, *JWH* Records; Farnham to Gallman of Indiana University Press, March 11, 1988, *JWH* Records.

40. Nash et al., *History on Trial*, 1–24.

41. Kat Chow, "'Politically Correct': The Phrase Has Gone from Wisdom to Weapon," *Code Switch*, NPR, December 14, 2016, www.npr.org/sections/codeswitch/2016/12/14/505324427 /politically-correct-the-phrase-has-gone-from-wisdom-to-weapon; Perry, "Historically Correct." Allan Bloom's 1987 *Closing of the American Mind* offers a good example of conservative views on changes in the content of American history. See also Lindy West, "Political Correctness Does Not Hinder Free Speech, It Expands It," *The Guardian*, November 15, 2015, www.theguardian.com/commentisfree/2015/nov/15/political-correctness-free-speech-racism -misogyny-university-yale-missouri, on "political correctness" and "identity politics" and dropping the terms in favor of what they actually stand for in liberal minds, which is civil rights.

42. Perry, "Historically Correct," 15-16.

43. Novick, *That Noble Dream*; Townsend, *History's Babel*; Palmer, *From Gentleman's Club to Professional Body*.

44. Limbaugh, *Way Things Ought to Be*, 204–7.

45. *Phyllis Schlafly Report*, February 1972; Nash et al., *History on Trial*, 218–19. Schlafly regularly pilloried feminists as angry radicals and feminist and social history as left-wing distortions of America's great past in her *Eagle Forum*.

46. Phyllis Schlafly, "What's Wrong with Equal Rights for Women?," *Phyllis Schlafly Report*, February 1972; Schlafly, "Teaching History: Fact or Fiction?"; Schlafly, "What's Happened to Public School Curriculum?"; "Call Your Representatives—No Women's Museum on the Mall."

47. Ronald Reagan, "Evil Empire," speech before the Annual Convention of the National Association of Evangelicals, March 8, 1983, Ronald Reagan Presidential Library and Museum website, www.reaganlibrary.gov/archives/speech/remarks-annual-convention-national -association-evangelicals-orlando-fl.

48. Nash et al., *History on Trial*, 188–222.

49. Nash and Crabtree, *National Standards*; national history standards books were published in Western and world history as well that year; revised version of the standards is available at UCLA History: Public History Initiative, accessed May 12, 2024, https://phi.history.ucla .edu/nchs/history-standards/.

50. Lynn Cheney, "The End of History," *Wall Street Journal* via American Enterprise Institute, October 24, 1994.

51. Evans, *In Defense of History*, 4.

52. *JWH* 9, no. 3 (1997): 140–76. In a section in this issue, Christie Farnham, Barbara Moss, Virginia Wilson, Helga Harriman, Joan Hoff, and Joan Scott contributed comments discussing and evaluating the treatment of women's history in the *National History Standards*."

53. Joan Scott, "Comment on 'Women's History and the National History Standards,'" *JWH* 9, no. 3 (1997): 172–76.

54. Christie Farnham, *JWH* 8, no. 2 (1996). Farnham and five other prominent scholars participated in a dialogue the following year, when Leila Rupp was serving her first year as *JWH* editor; *JWH* 9, no. 3 (1997).

55. Farnham Pope and Hoff, interview by Tomás, April 12, 2013, segment 0303 and 0300, *JWH* OHP.

56. *JWH* 1, no. 2 (1989); and 2, no. 1 (1990). Cheryl Johnson-Odim and Margaret Strobel were the guest editors of these volumes. In some ways the international and comparative focus of the *JWH* anticipated the turn to transnational history. Ian Tyrrell dates the emergence of "transnational history" to the early 1990s efforts of historians in the United States to consider history from perspectives not dependent on the nation-state and to place the field of American history in a more global context. He defines as the history of "the movement of peoples, ideas, technologies, and institutions across national boundaries." "What Is Transnational History?," January 2007, Ian Tyrrell website, accessed February 2, 2014, http:// iantyrrell.wordpress.com/what-is-transnational-history/. He credits the development of the concept to himself, Akira Iriye, David Thelen, and Thomas Bender but acknowledges that it grew out of older twentieth-century historiographic traditions in comparative, international, immigration, and global history.

57. *JWH* 5, no. 3 (1994); 6, no. 4 (1995); 7, no. 1 (1995); 8, no. 4 (1997).

58. Hillary Rodham Clinton, "Remarks to the U.N. 4th World Conference on Women Plenary Session," September 5, 1995, Beijing, American Rhetoric Top 100 Speeches, www .americanrhetoric.com/speeches/hillaryclintonbeijingspeech.htm.

59. Elizabeth Cady Stanton, "Address to the National Woman Suffrage Association Convention," Washington, DC, January 19, 1869, in Buhle and Buhle, *Concise History of Woman Suffrage*, 249–56.

60. Eleanor Roosevelt, "The Struggle for Human Rights," speech delivered September 28, 1948, in Paris, France, Eleanor Roosevelt Papers Project, Columbian College of Arts and Sciences, https://erpapers.columbian.gwu.edu/struggle-human-rights-1948.

61. In reaching for their international goals, Farnham and Hoff found themselves constrained by several factors. There were far fewer numbers of submissions from certain regions of the globe and premodern periods. The fact that this was an English-language publication and that translation was expensive for the journal but also cumbersome for contributors who did not write in English presented another challenge. Moreover, academics from other countries might not see the professional utility of publishing work in a North American English-language journal if that journal was not recognized by scholars in their home country. These troubles did not abate when Leila Rupp served as editor from 1997 to 2004, nor later when Antoinette Burton and Jean Allman were at the journal's editorial helm from 2005 to 2010. Continental and national divisions and professional expediencies often thwarted their best intentions.

62. See chapter 8 of this book.

63. "About the Federation," IFRWH website, accessed October 1, 2022, www.ifrwh.com /about-the-federation.

64. Farnham Pope and Hoff interview by Tomás, April 12, 2013, *JWH* OHP.

65. Farnham Pope and Hoff interview by Tomás, April 12, 2013, segment 0303 and 0300, *JWH* OHP.

66. Faludi, *Backlash*.

67. Gordon, "Socialist View of Women's Studies," 565; Fischer, *Journal of Women's History*.

68. Evans, *In Defense of History*, 4.

69. Evans, *In Defense of History*, 3–12.

70. *JWH* 1, no. 1 (1989); 3, no. 3 (1991); 3, no. 2 (1991).

71. The "Passages" column on the current *JWH* website is reminiscent of this journal tradition.

72. *JWH* 1, no. 1 (1989); 3, no. 3 (1992); 3, no. 2 (1991); 5, no. 1 (1993); 8, no. 1 (1996). Leila Rupp dropped the use of these quotes in 1997.

73. Christie Farnham, "Editor's Note: Male Bashing, or What's in a Name? Feminism in the United States Today," *JWH* 8, no. 2 (1996): 6–9.

74. Farnham, "Editor's Note," 9.

75. Farnham Pope and Hoff interview by Tomás, April 12, 2013, segment 0303 and 0304, *JWH* OHP; Bock, "Women's History and Gender History."

76. Farnham Pope and Hoff interview by Tomás, April 12, 2013, segment 0303, *JWH* OHP.

77. J. Scott, *Feminism and History*.

78. Jennifer Tomás, "The Women's History Movement in the U.S." (PhD diss., UMI, 2012), 351–55; J. Scott, "Feminism's History"; Karen J. Winkler, "Scholars of Women's History Fear the Field Has Lost Its Identity," *Chronicle of Higher Education*, July 5, 1990.

79. Farnham Pope and Hoff interview by Tomás, April 12, 2013, segment 0303, *JWH* OHP.

80. Rupp interview by Berkery, May 31, 2013, segment sdv-0311, *JWH* OHP; *JWH* 1, no. 1 (1989).

81. Rupp, *Mobilizing Women for War*; Rupp and Taylor, *Survival in the Doldrums*; Rupp, *Worlds of Women*.

82. The associate editors were Susan Hartmann, Stephanie Shaw, Claire Robertson, and Birgitte Søland, who specialized in American, African American, African, and European women's history, respectively. Donna Guy, a Latin Americanist, served as coeditor between 2003 and 2005, when Rupp left Ohio State.

83. At Bryn Mawr, where Rupp completed her BA in 1972 and her PhD in 1976, she studied with two women historians who helped shape her perspectives and interests. The first was Barbara Miller Lane, who was in German history. Lane did not study women's history but was supportive of Rupp's interests. The second was Mary Maples Dunn, who specialized in colonial America. Dunn taught Rupp her first women's history course in 1971. At the time that Rupp was attending Bryn Mawr, Dunn was a very recent convert to women's history who was actively involved in the decades-old Berkshire Conference of Women Historians. She served as its president in 1974. Instrumental in organizing the historic second Berkshire Conference on the History of Women at Radcliffe in 1974, Dunn brought the third Berkshire Conference on the History of Women to Bryn Mawr College in 1976. Rupp presented papers at both the 1974 and 1976 "Big Berks" and organized the book exhibit for the Third Big Berks at Bryn Mawr in 1976 Thus, as a graduate student at Bryn Mawr from 1974 to 1976, Rupp was thoroughly immersed in the emerging women's history movement. In 1976 Rupp went on the job market. This task was complicated by the comparative nature of her dissertation and the fact that most jobs then, as now, were designed around national areas of specialization. Rupp was hired on a one-year appointment to fill in for Carroll Smith-Rosenberg at the University of Pennsylvania. From there she took a job in the newly developing women's studies department at Ohio State University in 1977 with a joint appointment in history. She was a particularly attractive candidate for that position because of the comparative nature of her scholarly focus and her openness to the interdisciplinary field of women's studies. She taught European history, American history, and women's studies at Ohio State.

84. Rupp interview by Weisiger, LUSWHOHP, 6–7; Rupp interview by Berkery, May 31, 2013, *JWH* OHP.

85. Rupp, *Mobilizing Women for War*; Rupp and Taylor, *Survival in the Doldrums*; Rupp, *Worlds of Women*; Scharf and Jensen, *Decades of Discontent*. This is just one anthology of scholarship that had begun to make departures toward reframing the chronology of American women's history.

86. Rupp, *Desired Past*; Rupp, *Sapphistries*.

87. D'Emilio and Freedman, *Intimate Matters*. The book went into its third edition in 2012. Smith-Rosenberg, "Female World of Love and Ritual"; C. Potter, "Female Academic's World of Love and Ritual." Potter's essay was a revision of a talk presented at the annual meeting of the OAH in 2015.

88. *JWH* 11, nos. 1 (1999) and 2 (1999); 16, no. 4 (2004).

89. "Sexing Women's History," ed. Joanne Meyerowitz and Gail Hershatter, special issue, *JWH* 9, no. 4 (1998); "Women and Twentieth-Century Religious Politics: Beyond Fundamentalism," ed. Nikki R. Keddie and Jasamin Rostam-Kolayi, special issue, *JWH* 10, no. 4 (1999).

90. Leila Rupp, "Editor's Note," *JWH* 10, no. 3 (1998): 6.

91. "Women's History in the New Millenium: Carroll Smith-Rosenberg's 'The Female World of Love and Ritual' after Twenty-Five Years," *JWH* 12, no. 3 (2000): 7–38; "Women's History in

the New Millenium: A Retrospective Analysis of Barbara Welter's 'Cult of True Womanhood, 1820–1860,'" *JWH* 14, no. 2 (2002): 149–73.

92. "Dialogue: Paradigm Shift Books: *A Midwife's Tale* by Laurel Thatcher Ulrich," *JWH* 14, no. 1 (2002): 133–82; "Women's History in the New Millenium: Adrienne Rich's 'Compulsory Heterosexuality and Lesbian Existence'—A Retrospective," *JWH* 15, no. 3 (2003): 9–89.

93. Cott et al., "Considering the State of U.S. Women's History," *JWH* 15, no. 1 (2003); 15, nos. 2, 3, and 4, continued this discussion in print as "Women's History in the New Millenium."

94. Gilmore interview by Berkery, May 31, 2013, segment 01, *JWH* OHP.

95. Similar concerns were reflected earlier in Antoinette Burton and Deborah J. Rossum to Dear Friends, "An Open Letter to Participants," July 1, 1987, folder 12, box 34, BCWH Records. Gustafson's *Becoming A Historian* was initially conceived as a survival guide for women; it evolved and is still in print as *Becoming a Historian: A Survival Manual*. Gustafson served as the graduate student representative on the AHA's Committee on the Status of Women in the early 1990s.

96. Leila Rupp, "Editor's Note," *JWH* 16, no. 4 (1998).

97. Baxandall and Gordon with Reverby, *America's Working Women*; Dublin, *Women at Work*; Tentler, *Wage-Earning Women*; Kessler-Harris, *Out to Work*; Janiewski, *Sisterhood Denied*; Milkman, *Gender at Work*; Gluck, *Rosie the Riveter Revisited*.

98. See, for example, Snyder, *Making Black History*; and Acuña, *Making of Chicana/o Studies*.

99. H. Johnson, *Sleepwalking Through History*; Hardisty, *Mobilizing Resentment*; Ferguson and Rogers, *Right Turn*; Liebman and Wuthnow, *New Christian Right*; Critchlow, *Phyllis Schlafly*; Nickerson, "Moral Mothers and Goldwater Girls"; Spruill, *Divided We Stand*.

100. Webster v. Reproductive Health Services, 492 US 490 (1989); Planned Parenthood of Southeastern Pa. v. Casey, 505 U.S. 833 (1992).

101. Olivia Waxman, "Trump's Threat to Pull Funding from Schools over How They Teach Slavery Is Part of a Long History of Politicizing American History Classes," *Time*, September 17, 2020, https://time.com/5889051/history-curriculum-politics/; "The 1776 Report," The President's Advisory 1776 Commission, January 2021, accessed October 1, 2022, https://trumpwhitehouse.archives.gov/wp-content/uploads/2021/01/The-Presidents-Advisory-1776-Commission-Final-Report.pdf.

102. Limbaugh, *Way Things Ought to Be*.

103. Monica Hesse, "Rush Limbaugh Had a Lot to Say about Feminism. Women Learned Not to Care," *Washington Post*, February 19, 2021, www.washingtonpost.com/lifestyle/style/rush-limbaugh-feminism-feminazis/2021/02/19/3a00f852-7202-11eb-85fa-e0ccb3660358_story.html; Alexa Mikail, "How Rush Limbaugh Turned Feminism into an Urgent Threat to the Republican Party," *The 19th**, February 18, 2021, https://19thnews.org/2021/02/rush-limbaugh-feminism/. The article also appeared in *USA Today*, February 19, 2021, www.usatoday.com/story/news/nation/2021/02/19/rush-limbaugh-feminism-how-talk-radio-host-made-political-threat/4497407001/.

104. Nash et al., *History on Trial*; Laats, *Other School Reformers*.

105. Hull et al., *All the Women Are White*; Breines, *Trouble between Us*.

106. Hewitt, "Beyond the Search for Sisterhood"; Vogel, "Telling Tales," 94–96.

107. Burton and Rossum to Dear Friends, "An Open Letter to Participants," July 1, 1987, BCWH Records; Susan Reverby to Antoinette Burton and Deborah Rossum, October 26, 1987, folder 12, box 34, BCWH Records; Lerner and Sklar, *Graduate Training in U.S. Women's History*, KKS Papers.

108. Higginbotham, "Beyond the Sound of Silence."

109. Henry, "Promoting Historical Consciousness." Sadie Daniel St. Clair and Hallie Q. Brown published the most notable popular works in the history of Black women. Elsie Malkiel Lewis had collaborated with the producers of *Notable American Women* in the 1950s and 1960s, helping to ensure the inclusion of biographical sketches on Black women in that work.

110. Lerner, *Black Women in White America*, xvii–xxxiii.

111. "Part E. Problems, Gerda Lerner's Perspective" and "Part E. Darlene Clark Hine's Perspective," in Hine and Lerner, "Final Report on OAH/ABWH Project on Black Women's History," GLP 1950–95.

112. Black scholars who offered favorable blurbs or reviews on the back covers of the following works include Nell Irvin Painter (for Elizabeth Fox-Genovese); Toni Morrison, Nathan I. Huggins, and Henry Louis Gates (for Jacqueline Jones); Darlene Clark Hine (for Hall's second edition); Hazel Carby (for Michelle Newman); and John Hope Franklin and Barbara Ransby (for Anne Firor Scott's 2006 collection of letters between Pauli Murray and Caroline Ware).

113. See also Fox-Genovese, *Within the Plantation Household*; and Bederman, *Manliness and Civilization*. On the second point see Hine, *Hine Sight*; and Hine, "Black Women's History."

114. Higginbotham, "Beyond the Sound of Silence," 51.

115. A. Davis, *Women, Race, and Class*, 1–3.

116. Mary Frances Berry, foreword to Hull et al., *All the Women Are White*, xv.

117. Rosalyn Terborg-Penn, "Being and Thinking Outside the Box," in White, *Telling Histories*, 79.

118. Terborg-Penn, "Being and Thinking Outside the Box," in White, *Telling Histories*, 72–84.

119. Deborah Gray White, "My History in History," in White, *Telling Histories*, 85–100.

120. White, *Telling Histories*, 17, 72–84, 101–34; Harley, "Reclaiming Public Voice," 189.

121. Harley and Terborg-Penn, "Introduction to the 1997 Edition," *Afro-American Woman* (italics added).

122. White, *Telling Histories*, 19; White, "'Matter Out of Place,'" 5–12.

123. Darlene Clark Hine and Gerda Lerner, "Final Report on OAH/ABWH Project on Black Women's History," folder 140 "Proposal 1980," series 3, GLP 1950–95; OAH Committee reports, OAH Records, box 14 and 15; Lerner and Sklar, *Graduate Training in U.S. Women's History*.

124. Ruiz and DuBois, *Unequal Sisters* (2000); Baxandall and Gordon, *Dear Sisters*; Lerner and Sklar, *Graduate Training in U.S. Women's History*; Gordon, "Race, Gender, and Painful Changes," B4.

125. Crenshaw, "Demarginalizing the Intersection of Race and Sex."

126. Aja Romano, "This Feminist's Most Famous Quote Has Been Sold All Over the Internet. She Hasn't Seen a Cent," *Vox*, August 12, 2016, www.vox.com/2016/8/12/12406648/flavia -dzodan-my-feminism-will-be-intersectional-merchandise.

127. Traister, *Good and Mad*.

128. A. Davis, *Women, Race, and Class*; hooks, *Ain't I A Woman*; hooks, *Talking Back*.

129. "Biography of Rosalyn Terborg-Penn," The History Makers: The Digital Repository for the Black Experience, accessed May 1, 2022, www.thehistorymakers.org/biography/rosalyn -terborg-penn-38; Terborg-Penn interview by Rothschild, LUSWHOHP; White, *Telling Histories*; White interview by Gustafson, LUSWHOHP.

130. Giddings, *When and Where I Enter*; White, *Ar'n't I a Woman?*; Black Women in the Middle West Project Records, 1932–1986, M#530, Indiana Historical Society, Indianapolis,

https://indianahistory.org/wp-content/uploads/black-women-in-the-middle-west-project
-records.pdf.

131. Sumler-Edmond. "Association of Black Women Historians"; Rosalyn Terborg-Penn, "Association of Black Women Historians," in Mjagkij, *Organizing Black America*.

132. "Voting Matters: Gender, Citizenship, and the Long Nineteenth Amendment," six-part webinar series, 2020, Radcliffe Institute for Advanced Study at Harvard University, accessed August 8, 2022, www.radcliffe.harvard.edu/events-and-exhibitions/series/voting-matters -gender-citizenship-and-the-long-19th-amendment.

133. Transcripts of LUSWHOHP interviews with the following historians were consulted as follows: Gonzalez interview by Barnes, 8, 16–17, 44–45; Ruiz interview by Rothschild, 18, 22–23, 44, 97, 115–16; Kidwell interview by Barnes, 18, 21, 30–31, 56; Matsumoto interview by Barnes, 26, 37, 49; Yung interview by Rothschild, 15, 28, 30–35, 38, 45, 89. Acuña, *Making of Chicana/o Studies*. The content of *CCWHP Newsletters*, Big Berks conference programs, and the 1990 exchange in the *Chronicle of Higher Education* cited at the start of this chapter all support this assertion.

134. White, "'Matter Out of Place,'" 7.

135. White, "'Matter Out of Place'"; White, *Too Heavy A Load*.

136. "Little Berks Virtual Conference, 2020" program, accessed May 14, 2025, https:// berksconference.org/little-berks/little-berks-2020/.

137. Program of the Eighteenth Berkshire Conference on the History of Women, Genders and Sexuality, Johns Hopkins University, Baltimore, MD, May 28–31, 2020, https:// berksconference.org/big-berks/2020-berkshire-conference/. The conference was held virtually due to the COVID-19 pandemic.

138. "CCWH Executive Board," 2019 to 2024, CCWH, accessed June 9, 2024, https://theccwh .org/about-the-ccwh/executive-board/.

139. See note 16 in this chapter.

140. Crenshaw, "Demarginalizing the Intersection of Race and Sex."

141. A. Shapiro, *Feminists Revision History*; J. Scott, *Feminism and History*; I. Young, "Gender as Seriality"; Hewitt, "Compounding Difference."

142. E. Brown, "What Has Happened Here?," 298–300.

143. Hewitt, "Compounding Difference."

144. Joan Hoff-Wilson and Farnham, "Editors' Note and Acknowledgments: Histories about the End of Everything," *JWH* 1, no. 3 (1990): 6–11.

145. Hoff-Wilson and Farnham, "Editors' Note and Acknowledgments," 6–11.

146. Most authors cited here have published multiple volumes in women's labor history. I am citing only their debut publication in the subfield and authored during the years of the women's history movement from 1969 to 2010: Baxandall and Gordon with Reverby, *America's Working Women*; Dublin, *Women at Work*; Tentler, *Wage-Earning Women*; Kessler-Harris, *Out to Work*; Janiewski, *Sisterhood Denied*; Milkman, *Gender at Work*; Gluck, *Rosie the Riveter Revisited*; Greenwald, *Women, War, and Work*; Cobble, *Dishing It Out*; Baron, *Work Engendered*. Most imaginable categories of America's working women have at least one and often multiple scholarly monographs of their own, including domestic workers; factory workers; textile workers; sex workers; houseworkers; enslaved women; clerical, retail, agricultural, cannery, and food service workers; and professionals of every imaginable category—doctors, nurses, lawyers, professors, scientists, civil servants. If you can think of a category of female

worker, it has probably been the focus of a dissertation, a scholarly article, a monograph, or multiple monographs.

147. To identify just a few significant titles in the history of women's labor activism and working-class culture published during the women's history movement: Tax, *Rising of the Women*; S. Benson, *Counter Cultures*; Peiss, *Cheap Amusements*; Boydston, *Home and Work*; Enstad, *Ladies of Labor*; Orleck, *Common Sense and a Little Fire*.

148. The history of women in American political economy, emerging in tandem with the history of progressive reform during the women's history movement, is particularly well-developed. Just a few significant titles in this field include Sklar, *Florence Kelley*; Kessler-Harris, *In Pursuit of Equity*; Boris, *Home to Work*; Storrs, *Civilizing Capitalism*; Laughlin, *Women's Work and Public Policy*; and Cobble, *Other Women's Movement*.

149. Klatch, *Women of the New Right*; Nielsen, *Un-American Womanhood*; K. Kennedy, *Disloyal Mothers*; Erickson, "'We Want No Teachers'"; Thurner, "Better Citizens without the Ballot," 203–20; McGirr, *Suburban Warriors*; Critchlow, *Phyllis Schlafly*; Delegard, *Battling Miss Bolsheviki*; Blee, "Women in the 1920s Ku Klux Klan Movement"; Blee and Deutsch, *Women of the Right*.

150. D'Emilio and Freedman, *Intimate Matters*; Enke, *Finding the Movement*; Rupp, *Sapphistries*; Faderman, *Odd Girls and Twilight Lovers*.

151. "Youngkin Administration Scraps Education Materials It Deemed 'Divisive,'" *Richmond Times Dispatch*, February 25, 2022, https://richmond.com/news/state-and-regional/govt-and -politics/youngkin-administration-scraps-education-policy-materials-it-deemed-divisive /article_a8eb71ca-bd7a-5925–9bb0-c46a8b8a077b.html; "The 1776 Report," President's Advisory 1776 Commission, January 2021; Trevor Hughes, "History Curriculum, Books Were Written by and for White People. What about Kids of Color?," *USA Today*, September 12, 2021, www.usatoday.com/story/news/education/2021/09/12/history-curriculum-textbooks-critical -race-theory/5513019001/?gnt-cfr=1; Barbara Rodriguez, "Republican State Lawmakers Want to Punish Schools That Teach the 1619 Project," *USA Today*, February 10, 2021, www.usatoday .com/story/news/education/2021/02/10/slavery-and-history-states-threaten-funding-schools -teach-1619-project/4454195001/. A Google search of the phrase "school board culture wars" returned the following hits among many others on October 9, 2022: "Republicans Running on Race See Gains in School Board Elections," *USA Today*, October 8, 2022; "Attacks on Teachers 'Never Been as Bad as Right Now,'" *USA Today*, August 30, 2022; "School Board Races Show Mixed Result for Critical Race Theory," *USA Today*, November 3, 2021; John Nichols, "The School Board Culture War: Republicans Are Pushing National Wedge Issues to the Local Level but Smart Progressives Are Beating Them," *The Nation*, May 20, 2022, www.thenation .com/article/society/the-school-board-culture-war/ accessed 10/0/2021.

Chapter 11

1. Mayo interview by Rothschild, LUSWHOHP, 29–31, 40–42.

2. Mayo interview by Rothschild, LUSWHOHP, 29–31C.

3. John Y. Cole, "In Memoriam, Daniel J. Boorstin, 1914–2004," September 2004, *Perspectives on History*, September 2004, www.historians.org/research-and-publications/perspectives-on -history/september-2004/in-memoriam-daniel-j-boorstin.

4. Mayo interview by Rothschild, LUSWHOHP, 42.

5. Mayo interview by Rothschild, LUSWHOHP, 42–45.

6. Dan Bauman and Brock Read, "A Brief History of GOP Attempts to Kill the Education Dept.," *Chronicle of Higher Education*, June 21, 2018, www.chronicle.com/article/a-brief-history -of-gop-attempts-to-kill-the-education-dept/; Laats, *Other School Reformers*.

7. Limbaugh, *Way Things Ought to Be*, 204–7. Phyllis Schlafly, "What's Wrong with Equal Rights for Women?," *Phyllis Schlafly Report*, February 1972, offers an early presentation of conservative historical interpretation dismissing newer interpretations of women's history that emphasize women's active role in fighting for their rights and advancements. In Schlafly's conservative vision of history, women owed their well-being and any progress they enjoyed to men, their technological innovations, and their support as husbands and breadwinners. Schlafly frequently attacked "liberal" and "radical" interpretations of history in her newsletters thereafter. Phyllis Schlafly, "Teaching History: Fact or Fiction?," *Phyllis Schlafly Report*, August 2003; Schlafly, "What's Happened to Public School Curriculum?," *Phyllis Schlafly Report*, November 2010; "Call Your Representatives—No Women's Museum on the Mall," *Eagle Forum*, May 5, 2014, https://eagleforum.org/publications/alerts/2014-archives/call-your -representatives-no-womens-museum-on-the-mall.html; Ronald Reagan, Republican National Convention Acceptance Speech, July 17, 1980, Ronald Reagan Presidential Library and Museum website, www.reaganlibrary.gov/archives/speech/republican-national-convention -acceptance-speech-1980; Ronald Reagan "Evil Empire" speech before the Annual Convention of the National Association of Evangelicals, March 8, 1983, Ronald Reagan Presidential Library and Museum website, www.reaganlibrary.gov/archives/speech/remarks-annual-convention -national-association-evangelicals-orlando-fl.

8. Arnita Jones, "National Coordinating Committee"; "Who We Are," National Coalition for History, accessed August 5, 2021, https://historycoalition.org/who-we-are/. The National Coalition for History was renamed as such in 2002. Prior to that it was, as founded in 1976, the National Coordinating Committee for the Promotion of History. Its first two executive directors were women's historians, Arnita Jones and Page Putnam Miller, who, combined, headed the organization for twenty years. Bruce Craig, "NCCPH Strategic Plan (2002–2005)," May 7, 2002, www.h-net.org/~nch/StrategicPlan.html.

9. Mayo, "Women's History and Public History."

10. *Eleanor Roosevelt: First Person Singular*, Smithsonian National Museum of American History, September 13, 1984, to May 5, 1985, accessed May 14, 2025, www.si.edu/exhibitions /eleanor-roosevelt-first-person-singular%3Aevent-exhib-3391.

11. Hall, "Long Civil Rights Movement," 1233–63; Sklar et al., "'Long Progressive Era.'"

12. Mayo interview by Rothschild, LUSWHOHP, 62–63.

13. Mayo interview by Rothschild, LUSWHOHP, 64–65; Harrison, *On Account of Sex*.

14. Mayo interview by Rothschild, LUSWHOHP, 66–67; *From Parlor to Politics: Women and Reform in America, 1890–1925*, Smithsonian American Women's History Museum, June 28, 1990–August 28, 2004, accessed May 14, 2025, https://womenshistory.si.edu/exhibitions /parlor-politics-women-reform-america-1890–1925:event-exhib-4071; Tyler-McGraw, "Parlor to Politics."

15. Kathryn Schneider Smith, "Keith Eugene Melder, 1932–2017," *Washington History* 30, no. 1 (2018): 67–68; Melder, *Beginnings of Sisterhood*.

16. "Spencer Crew Biography," American Historical Association, Jobs and Development, accessed May 14, 2025, www.historians.org/jobs-and-professional-development/career-resources /careers-for-students-of-history/historians-in-museums/spencer-crew. Crew was appointed in 1994.

17. Mayo interview by Rothschild, LUSWHOHP, 90–91.

18. "About the National Museum of Women in the Arts," National Museum of Women in the Arts, accessed May 14, 2025, https://nmwa.org/about/.

19. Mayo interview by Rothschild, LUSWHOHP, 92–93.

20. Ellen DuBois, "Keynote Address at the 19th Amendment 75th Anniversary, Forum on Women's Suffrage," CSPAN video recording, August 25, 1995, available at www.c-span .org/video/?67044-1/19th-amendment-75th-anniversary. DuBois's keynote was followed by a talk by conference moderator Marjorie Spruill Wheeler, a specialist in the history of the woman suffrage movement in the South, CSPAN video recording, August 25, 1995, available at www.c-span.org/video/?66846-1/womens-suffrage-movement-75th-anniversary. The letter's arrival is recorded at 34:00. Three other speakers participated in the morning session, Robert Cooney, Alice Sheppard, and Lisa Baumgartner. Baumgartner was a trained historian who was then working as press secretary for New York representative Carolyn Maloney. Baumgartner highlighted both suffrage strategies and the connections between women's history scholarship and feminist political activism.

21. Mayo, *Smithsonian Book of the First Ladies*; Mayo, "Teaching the First Ladies Using Material Culture"; Mayo and Graddy, *First Ladies*.

22. Mayo interview by Rothschild, LUSWHOHP, 94–100.

23. Huyck, "Twenty-Five Years of Public History"; Huyck, *Doing Women's History*; Huyck, *Women's History*.

24. Huyck interview by Rothschild, LUSWHOHP, 48. Huyck held advanced degrees in cultural anthropology (MA, 1978) and American history (1981, PhD) from the University of Minnesota; Hinding, *Women's History Sources*, front matter.

25. Huyck interview by Rothschild, LUSWHOHP, 1.

26. Huyck interview by Rothschild, LUSWHOHP, 48. SIROW stands for Southwest Institute for Research on Women. This was a major public history initiative in which both academic and public historians participated in the late 1970s.

27. *Elizabeth Cady Stanton Foundation Newsletter*, January 1980, 1, in box 3, SAWH Records.

28. Patricia Foster Haines, "Report on the Opening of the Women's Rights National Historical Park, July 1982," *CGWH Newsletter* 13, no. 4 (1982): 16–17.

29. Lucille Povero, Elizabeth Cady Stanton Foundation, to Dear Friends, n.d., box 3, SAWH Records.

30. Haines, "Report on the Opening of the Women's Rights National Historical Park, July 1982," 16–17. ·

31. Folder 4, "CSW Correspondence, 1980–1981," box 15; folder 14, "Seneca Falls, 1981–1982," and folder 15, "Seneca Falls, 1982," box 54, OAH Records.

32. Haines, "Report on the Opening of the Women's Rights National Historical Park, July 1982," 16–17; see also folder 14 "Seneca Falls, 1981–1982," box 54, OAH Records, for specific citations.

33. Haines, "Report on the Opening of the Women's Rights National Historical Park, July 1982," 16–17. The star-studded list of scholars included Mary Beth Norton, Elizabeth Fox-Genovese, Ellen DuBois, Suzanne Lebsock, Joan Jacobs Brumberg, Kitty Sklar, Thomas Dublin, Winnifred Wandersee, Carroll Smith-Rosenberg, Sally Gregory Kohlstedt, Sara Evans, Lois Scharf, D'Ann Campbell, and others.

34. As an undergraduate student in 1998, working toward a BA in history and secondary education in nearby Ithaca, NY, I attended the 150th Anniversary event with my aunt and

four-year-old daughter. First Lady Hillary Clinton gave a rousing speech. This was the year that I first became a student of American women's history, after taking two American history survey courses at the local community college in which women were only minimally integrated into the curriculum. I wrote a paper on the Seneca Falls Declaration of Sentiments and Resolutions in one class and a paper on Emma Goldman in the other.

35. "Women's Rights in Seneca Falls: Women's Rights National Historical Park," National Park Service, last updated March 29, 2023, www.nps.gov/places/womensrights.htm.

36. Huyck interview by Rothschild, LUSWHOHP, 49–50.

37. Huyck interview by Rothschild, LUSWHOHP, 48.

38. Huyck interview by Rothschild, LUSWHOHP, 51.

39. Annual Reports of the National Park Service indicate that its historical sites and parks locations have welcomed roughly 28–29 million visitors each year: https://irma.nps.gov/STATS /SSRSReports/National%20Reports/Annual%20Visitation%20Summary%20Report%20 (1979%20-%20Last%20Calendar%20Year (accessed July 15, 2022; site no longer available).

40. Heather Huyck pointed out, in reaction to reading this passage, that the National Council for Public History was of particular importance to women's historians doing public history in this period.

41. Chafe, *American Woman*.

42. Chafe interview by Glusman, LUSWHOHP, 30–31.

43. Chafe interview by Glusman, LUSWHOHP, 27–30, 33–36.

44. A. Scott interview by Rothschild, LUSWHOHP, 14. The quote is from Mary Rothschild, who remembered this from a dinner conversation she'd had with Scott the year Chafe was hired. Chafe's hire date is verified by his CV in Duke University Archives' Associated Press folder for him.

45. Dublin interview by Gustafson, LUSWHOHP, 30–50; Dublin, *Women at Work*.

46. Degler interview by Rothschild, LUSWHOHP, 38–39, 50. The papers of Anne Firor Scott at Duke University and those of Gerda Lerner at the Schlesinger Library contain professional correspondence with Degler beginning in 1966 for Lerner and 1968 for Scott; Degler was also a collaborator on the Women's History Sources Survey. Hinding, preface to *Women's History Sources*, ix.

47. Chafe interview by Glusman, LUSWHOHP, 48.

48. *Winston-Salem Journal* (NC), March 6, 1973, A7, news clipping in William Chafe, Associated Press clippings file, DUA.

49. Catharine Stimpson, "Gerda Lerner on the Future of Our Past," *Ms.*, September 1981, 51; Christina Robb, "Barbara Haber: Arbiter of Women's History," *Ms.*, September 1982, 10–13.

50. Public Law No. 97-28, 97th Congress, Joint Resolution Designating the Week Beginning March 7, 1982, as "Women's History Week," Legislative History—S.J. Res. 28, *Congressional Record*, vol. 127 (1981); folder 189, "Women's History Week (National): Correspondence, lobbying, publicity, 1979–1987," GLP 1950–95.

51. Brumberg interview by Rothschild, LUSWHOHP, 37–38, 88–89; Brumberg, *Body Project*. Brumberg also appeared on the *Today Show* in an interview with Katie Couric about her book *Fasting Girls*.

52. Brumberg interview by Rothschild, LUSWHOHP, 89.

53. Lerner and Sklar, *Graduate Training in U.S. Women's History*, 7.

54. Zinsser, *History and Feminism*, 127–41.

55. Zinsser, *History and Feminism*, 127.

56. Miller interview by Rothschild, LUSWHOHP, 44; "Who We Are," National Coalition for History; Jones, "National Coordinating Committee: Programs and Possibilities."

57. "Who We Are," National Coalition for History.

58. Miller interview by Rothschild, LUSWHOHP, 41–42.

59. *CCWHP-CGWH Newsletters* from 1976 to 2000 contain regular reports from the NCCPH.

60. Miller interview by Rothschild, LUSWHOHP, 44–45; General Records of the General Services Administration, finding aid, accessed July 5, 2024, www.archives.gov/research/guide -fed-records/groups/269.html, suggests the GSA took over the National Archives in December 1949. This was the result of legislation passed by the Republican-controlled 80th Congress; see "National Archives History and Mission," National Archives, accessed July 5, 2024, www .archives.gov/about/history/about/history/history-and-mission.

61. Nash et al., *History on Trial*; Bauman and Read, "Brief History of GOP Attempts to Kill the Education Dept."

62. Horowitz and Miller, "Freedom of Information Act."

63. Miller interview by Rothschild, LUSWHOHP, 45.

64. See, for example, feminist interpretations of history and Schlafly's years of railing against bitter feminists in note 7 in this chapter.

65. Miller interview by Rothschild, LUSWHOHP, 62, 68. Others, for example, were Sara Evans and Lynn Weiner.

66. Miller interview by Rothschild, LUSWHOHP, 73.

67. Tinling and Ruffner-Russell, "Famous and Forgotten Women"; Tinling, *Women Remembered*; Roth, "Feminine Marks on the Landscape"; Dubrow, "Restoring a Female Presence."

68. Miller, *Reclaiming the Past*, 21.

69. Miller, *Reclaiming the Past*. Contributors were Joan Hoff, Barbara Howe, Barbara Melosh, Gail Dubrow, Helen Lefkowitz Horowitz, Jean Soderlund, and Lynn Weiner. Miller interview by Rothschild, LUSWHOHP, 65–66.

70. Miller interview by Rothschild, LUSWHOHP, 62–65.

71. Miller interview by Rothschild, LUSWHOHP, 62–66.

72. "History in the National Parks Service: Themes and Concepts, Preamble, Overview, and New Framework," National Park Service, last updated February 13, 2025, www.nps.gov /subjects/nationalhistoriclandmarks/nhl-thematic-framework.htm.

73. Miller interview by Rothschild, LUSWHOHP, 73–74.

74. "History in the National Parks Service: Themes and Concepts, Preamble, Overview, and New Framework."

75. Miller interview by Rothschild, LUSWHOHP, 71–72; Miller et al., *Exploring Our Common Past*; Miller et al., *Exploring a Common Past*.

76. Miller interview by Rothschild, LUSWHOHP, 76–77.

77. Lynne V. Cheney, "The End of History," *Wall Street Journal*, October 10, 1994; National Center for History in Schools, accessed June 14, 2022, https://phi.history.ucla.edu/nchs/history -standards/; Nash and Crabtree, *National Standards for United States History*; National Center for History in the Schools, *National Standards for World History: Exploring Paths to the Present* (Los Angeles: The Center, 1994); National Council for the Social Studies, *Expectations of Excellence: Curriculum Standards for Social Studies* (Washington, DC: NCSS, 1994); Gary B. Nash, "The History Children Should Study," *Chronicle of Higher Education*, April 21, 1995, A60; Gary B. Nash, "The Great Multicultural Debate," *Contention* 1, no. 3 (1992): 1–28; Ross

Dunn, "Communications: The Debate over National History Standards," *The Historian* 57, no. 2 (1995): 449–64; Ross Dunn, "History Standards and Culture Wars," *Social Education* 59, no. 1 (1995): 5–7.

78. Bloom, *Closing of the American Mind*.

79. "College Student Alert: Beware of One-Party Classroom," *Phyllis Schlafly Report*, April 2009, is one example that presents this perspective; see also citations in note 7 in this chapter. More recently, the *Eagle Forum* published "'Honest' History? Don't Fall for the Scam," on July 28, 2021, in reference to "critical race theory" and adjacent controversies over the content of American history courses (https://eagleforum.org/publications/insights/honest-history-dont -fall-for-the-scam.html).

80. Perry, "Historically Correct"; Belz, "National Standards for United States History: The Limits of Liberal Orthodoxy," *Continuity*, Spring 1995, 59–71; Cheney, "End of History"; Nash and Crabtree, *National Standards for United States History*; National Center for History in the Schools, *National Standards for World History*; National Council for the Social Studies, *Expectations of Excellence*; Nash, "Great Multicultural Debate," 1–28; Nash, "History Children Should Study"; Ross Dunn, "Communications"; Ross Dunn, "History Standards and Culture Wars"; Kat Chow, "'Politically Correct': The Phrase Has Gone from Wisdom to Weapon," *Codeswitch*, NPR, December 14, 2016, www.npr.org/sections/codeswitch/2016 /12/14/505324427/politically-correct-the-phrase-has-gone-from-wisdom-to-weapon; Olivia Waxman, "Trump's Threat to Pull Funding From Schools over How They Teach Slavery Is Part of a Long History of Politicizing American History Classes," *Time*, September 17, 2020; David Warren Saxe, "The National History Standards: Time for Common Sense," *Social Education* 60, n. 1 (1996).

81. Higham, *History*; Novick, *That Noble Dream*.

82. D'Ann Campbell, "The Fourth Berkshire Conference on the History of Women," *CGWH Newsletter* 4, no. 1 (October 1978): 3; Frances Richardson Keller, "Impressions, Perspectives and Reflections, Fourth Berkshire Conference on the History of Women," *CGWH Newsletter* 4, no. 1 (October 1978): 4–5.

83. "ERA Petition," *CCWHP Newsletter* 8, no. 3, 13; copies of the many petitions gathered abound in the OAH Records and the CCWHP housed respectively at the Ruth Lilly Special Collections and Archives, University Library, Indiana University, and at the Schlesinger Library. Hilda Smith "The First Decade," in Carroll et al., *History of the Coordinating Committee*, 17–18; Boris and Chaudhuri, *Voices of Women Historians*.

84. "We Were There," *CGWH Newsletter* 5, no. 3 (July 1980): 2.

85. Kathryn Kish Sklar, AHA Committee on Women, to Rosalyn Terborg-Penn, October 31, 1982, folder "Association of Black Women Historians," Nell Irvin Painter Papers, DUA.

86. Gerda Lerner, "Report on the Summer Institute in Women's History for Leaders of National Women's Organizations," *CGWH Newsletter* 5, no. 2 (February 1980): 15–16; other groups who participated were the Women's Equity Action League and the American Association of University Women.

87. "CCWHP Annual Meeting Notes," *CGWH Newsletter* 5, no. 1 (February 1981): 11.

88. Gerda Lerner, "Lost from the 'Official' Record," *Ms.*, December 1979, 109–10; Barbara Omolade, "Finding Ourselves—and Each Other," *Ms.*, December 1979, 110–12.

89. Berenice Carroll, "Feminism and the Professions: 10 years Later," *CGWH Newsletter* 5, no. 3 (July 1980): 5.

90. Gordon, "Socialist View of Women's Studies," 565.

91. Gordon, *Woman's Body*; Shorter, review of *Woman's Body*; D. Kennedy, review of *Woman's Body*; Lemons, review of *Woman's Body*; Fox-Genovese, "Comment on the Reviews of *Woman's Body, Woman's Right*."

92. Tone, *Controlling Reproduction*; Petchesky, *Abortion and Woman's Choice*.

93. Faludi, *Backlash*, chaps. 9, 10, and 14.

94. See Schlafly, Limbaugh, Bloom, Nash, and others as previously cited in the chapter.

95. Baxandall and Gordon with Reverby, *America's Working Women*; Dublin, *Women at Work*; Tentler, *Wage-Earning Women*; Kessler-Harris, *Out to Work*; Janiewski, *Sisterhood Denied*; Milkman, *Gender at Work*; Gluck, *Rosie the Riveter Revisited*; Greenwald, *Women, War, and Work*; Cobble, *Dishing it Out*; Baron, *Work Engendered*. These are some of the major titles completed or in the works at the time of the trial.

96. Hall and Cooper, "Women's History Goes to Trial"; Milkman, "Women's History and the Sears Case"; Rosenberg, "Women's History and EEOC v. Sears, 'Disparity or Discrimination?'"; Kessler-Harris "Women's History and EEOC v. Sears, 'Differences and Inequality?'"; Samuel G. Freedman, "Of History and Politics: Bitter Feminist Debate," *New York Times*, June 6, 1986, B1; J. Scott, "The Sears Case," chap. 8 in *Gender and the Politics of History*, 167–77.

97. Milkman, "Women's History and the Sears Case," 392; Phyllis Stock, "From the Editor," *CGWH Newsletter* (October 1985); Nupur Chaudhuri, "CCWHP-CGWH: The Second Decade," in Carroll et al., *History of the Coordinating Committee*, 21–42; also, appendix B, "Resolutions Passed at 1985 Business Meeting," in Carroll et al., *History of the Coordinating Committee*, is of interest.

98. EEOC v. Sears, Roebuck & Co., 628 F. Supp. 1264 (N.D. Ill. 1986), https://law.justia.com /cases/federal/district-courts/FSupp/628/1264/2595936/.

99. Jellison, "History in the Courtroom"; Milkman, "Women's History and the Sears Case," 377.

100. Hill and Jordan, *Race, Gender and Power in America*, ix–xxix; H. Davis, "High-Tech Lynching"; Geneva Smitherman as cited in Margaret Russell, "Retracing the Watershed," *Women's Review of Books* 13, no. 6 (1996): 5–6. From *Ms.*, January/February 1992: Rochelle Sharp, "Sexual Harassment: Capitol Hill's Worst Kept Secret" (28–31); Anita Hill, "The Nature of the Beast" (32–33), and Patricia Williams, Barbara Smith, Rebecca Walker, Marcia Ann Gillespie, and Eleanor Holmes Norton, "Forum: Refusing to be Silenced" (34–45).

101. Nancy Hewitt and Margaret Strobel, "Urgent and Timely from the CCWHP-CGWH Presidents regarding the Clarence Thomas Nomination to the Supreme Court," *CCWHP Newsletter* 22, no. 3 (September/October 1991): 5–6.

102. On Black scholars' views and Black views generally, see, for example, Boyd, "Collard Greens"; and H. Davis, "High-Tech Lynching."

103. Elsa Barkley Brown, Deborah King, and Barbara Ransby, "African American Women in Defense of Ourselves," *New York Times*, November 18, 1991.

104. Brown et al., "African American Women in Defense of Ourselves."

105. Brown et al., "African American Women in Defense of Ourselves"; Hall, *Revolt against Chivalry*; McGuire, *At the Dark End of the Street*; J. Jones, *Labor of Love*.

106. Smitherman, *African American Women Speak Out*. In the 1993 edition of *Revolt against Chivalry*, Jacquelyn Dowd Hall, a white anti-racist, feminist scholar, did offer an analysis of the Thomas hearings, Thomas's historical distortions, and the abuse of Anita Hill in the new introduction to her classic work on white and Black women's work to end lynching.

107. Freedman, "Historical Interpretation," 1; Hall and Cooper, "Women's History Goes to Trial."

108. Erman and Perl-Rosenthal, "Historians' Amicus Briefs," 9.

109. Erman and Perl-Rosenthal, "Historians' Amicus Briefs."

110. On efforts to roll back Black civil rights, for example, see Alexander, *New Jim Crow*; on parallel efforts to roll back women's rights, see Faludi, *Backlash*.

111. Mohr, *Abortion in America*.

112. Freedman, *Their Sisters' Keepers*; Freedman et al., *Lesbian Issue*; Freedman, *Maternal Justice*; Freedman, *No Turning Back*; D'Emilio and Freedman, *Intimate Matters*.

113. Walter Goodman, "Women's Studies: The Debate Continues," *New York Times Magazine*, April 22, 1986, 29; Freedman, "Women's Networks"; Kathryn Kish Sklar, Temma Kaplan, and Joyce Appleby of UCLA Department of History to President Donald P. Kennedy of Stanford University, April 28, 1983 (copy in author's possession); Request for Funds for the Support Committee for Estelle Freedman, ca. January 1983, signed by Stanford faculty Barbara Babcock, Carl Jacklin, Barrie Thorne, Barbara Gelpi, Mary Felstiner, Albert Camarillo, Anne Mellor, Myra Strober, Marilyn Yalom, Mary Pratt, and John Felstiner (copy in author's possession from the files of Kathryn Kish Sklar, who sent twenty-five dollars to the support committee).

114. Webster v. Reproductive Health Services, 492 US 490 (1989), www.oyez.org/cases/1988/88-605.

115. Spillenger et al., "Brief of 281 American Historians."

116. E. Freedman, "Historical Interpretation."

117. Mohr, "Historically Based Legal Briefs"; Law, "Conversations between Historians and Lawyers."

118. E. Freedman, "Historical Interpretation," 27.

119. Erman and Perl-Rosenthal, "Historians' Amicus Briefs," 10; Mohr, "Historically Based Legal Briefs," 25.

120. Mohr, "Historically Based Legal Briefs," 25–26.

121. Alice Kessler-Harris as quoted in Samuel G. Freedman, "Of History and Politics: Bitter Feminist Debate," *New York Times*, June 6, 1986, B1. See also Kessler-Harris, "'Differences and Inequality?'"

122. Brief of Professors of History George Chauncy, Nancy F. Cott, John D'Emilio, Estelle B. Freedman, Thomas C. Hold, John Howard, Lynn Hunt, Mark D. Jordan, Elizabeth Lapovsky Kennedy, and Linda P. Kerber as Amici Curiae in Support of Petitioners, No. 02-102, *Lawrence*, 539 US 558 (2003) at 567–68, 571.

123. Cott, *Public Vows*.

124. No. 19-1392, Brief for Amici Curiae American Historical Association and Organization of American Historians in support of respondents, in Thomas E. Dobbs, State Health Officer of the Mississippi Department of Health, et al. v. Jackson Women's Health Organization, et al., www.supremecourt.gov/DocketPDF/19/19-1392/192957/20210920133840569_19-1392%20bsac%20Historians.pdf; Jennifer Schuessler, "The Fight over Abortion History," *New York Times*, May 4, 2022. Historians continue to try to provide relevant historical context and analysis, as with Ziegler et al., *On the Threshold of a Post-Roe Era?*

125. Front matter of the *President's Commission on the Celebration of Women in American History*, March 1, 1999, https://govinfo.library.unt.edu/whc/whcreport.pdf.

126. Miller interview by Rothschild, LUSWHOHP, 47; *President's Commission on the Celebration of Women in American History*.

127. *President's Commission on the Celebration of Women in American History.*

128. *President's Commission on the Celebration of Women in American History.*

129. *President's Commission on the Celebration of Women in American History,* 12–17.

130. *President's Commission on the Celebration of Women in American History,* 6–11.

131. HR 1980, Smithsonian Women's History Act, February 12, 2020, Congress.gov, www.congress.gov/bill/116th-congress/house-bill/1980/text; James Grossman and Mary Lindemann of the American Historical Association to The Honorable Susan Collins, United States Senate, September 17, 2020, accessed November 20, 2022, historians.org.

132. Grossman and Lindemann to Collins, United States Senate, September 17, 2020.

133. "The Meaning of the Millenium: The Fifth Millenium Evening at the White House," hosted by William J. Clinton and Hillary Clinton, January 25, 1999, https://clintonwhitehouse4.archives.gov/Initiatives/Millennium/mill_eve5.html.

134. Natalie Zemon Davis and Jill Ker Conway, "The Rest of the Story: Understanding the Millenium Requires Looking Past the Male Milestones of Traditional History to See the Shape of Women's Lives," *New York Times Magazine,* May 16, 1999, sec. 6, 81.

Bibliography

Primary Sources

Archives and Manuscript Collections

Brown University Archives, Providence, RI
  Robert Cloutman and Elisabeth Anthony Dexter Papers, MS 2005.029
Duke University Archives, Durham, NC
  William Chafe, Associated Press clippings file
  Sara Evans Papers, 1960–2000
  Nell Irvin Painter Papers, 1793–2006
  Anne Firor Scott Papers, 1963–2000
Franklin Delano Roosevelt Presidential Library, Hyde Park, NY
  Papers of Caroline Farrar Ware, 1924–1990
Indiana Historical Society, Indianapolis
  Black Women in the Middle West Project Records, 1932–1986, M#530
Library of Congress, Washington, DC
  American Historical Association Records
  Mary Church Terrell Papers
Louise Pettus Archives, Winthrop University, Rock Hill, SC
  Mary Elizabeth Massey Papers, MS 20
Manuscripts Division, Department of Special Collections, Princeton University Library,
      Princeton, NJ
  Miriam Y. Holden Collection, 1676–1993, Series 3: Activities, 1895–1983
Minnesota Historical Society, St. Paul
  Upper Midwest Women's History Center Organizational Records
  Women Historians of the Midwest Organizational Records
Mount Holyoke Archives and Special Collections, Mount Holyoke College,
      South Hadley, MA
  Mary Sumner Benson Papers, MS 0878
Rare Book and Manuscript Library, Columbia University, New York, NY
  Council for Research in the Social Sciences Records, 1922–1968, UA#127
Ruth Lilly Special Collections and Archives, University Library, Indiana University,
      Indianapolis
  Records of the Organization of American Historians, Mss 27
Schlesinger Library on the History of Women in America, Radcliffe Institute for
      Advanced Study, Harvard University, Cambridge, MA
  Mary Beard Papers
  Ada Louise Comstock Papers
  Mary Earhart Dillon Collection, 1863–1955

Sophie Hutchinson Drinker Papers
Ellen Carol DuBois Papers
Eleanor Flexner Papers
Florence Woolsey Hazzard Papers
Janet Wilson James Papers
Gerda Lerner Papers, 1941–2001, MC 498
Gerda Lerner Papers, 1950–1995, MC 75-37-96-M8
Alma Lutz Papers
Papers of Elizabeth Bancroft Schlesinger, MC 894
Radcliffe College Archives
    Frieda Silbert Ullian Papers, 1950–1971 (SC 89)
Records of the Arthur and Elizabeth Schlesinger Library on the History of Women in
        America, 1942–2022, RG XVIII
Records of the Berkshire Conference of Women Historians (MC 606); inclusive of the
        Records of the Berkshire Conference on the History of Women (formerly identified
        as MC 83–M212; and MC 267, the records of the BCWH, 1930–1960s)
Records of the Black Women Oral History Project
Records of the Coordinating Committee on Women in the Historical Profession–
        Conference Group on Women's History, 1966–2009, MC 692 (inclusive of
        accessions #77-M82/80-M111, accessed before the collection was processed)
Records of *Notable American Women, 1607–1950*, 1958–1973, MC 230
Records of the Radcliffe College Seminars on Women, 1950–1985 (inclusive), 1950–59
        (bulk), RG XXXII
Barbara Miller Solomon Papers, 1953–1975, Finding Aid
Smith College Special Collections, Northampton, MA
    Smith College Archives
    Sophia Smith Collection of Women's History
        Annette Kar Baxter Papers, 1905–1984
        Mary Ritter Beard Papers
        Elisabeth Anthony Dexter Papers, 1837–1950, MS 47
        Sophie Hutchinson Drinker Papers, 1935–1966
        Constance McLaughlin Green Papers, 1954–1959
        Margaret Storrs Grierson Papers
        Florence Woolsey Hazzard Papers, 1940–1950, MS 76
        Alma Lutz Papers, 1871–1974, MS 96
        Records of the *Journal of Women's History*, MS-00489
        Kathryn Kish Sklar Papers
Southern Historical Collection, Wilson Library, University of North Carolina at
        Chapel Hill
    Elizabeth Fox-Genovese Papers
    Guion Griffis Johnson Papers, MC 4546
    Guy Benton Johnson Papers, MC 3826
    William Leuchtenberg Papers
    North Carolina Historical Society Records
    Southern Association for Women Historians Records, MS 4152
    Southern Historical Association Records, MC 4030

Southern Oral History Project
Southern Oral History Project Research Files (Series G, H.11)
UCLA Special Collections, Charles E. Young Research Library, Los Angeles, CA
  Workshop on Teaching Women's History, Manuscript Collection LSC.0431
Vassar College Archives and Special Collections Library, Poughkeepsie, NY
  Alma Lutz Papers, 1912–1971
  Lucy Maynard Salmon Papers
Wisconsin Historical Society, Madison
  Merle Eugene Curti Papers, 1908–2000, Finding Aid
  Kate Asaphine Everest Levi Papers, 1833–1850, 1891–1893, Finding Aid
The Woman's Collection, Texas Woman's University, Denton
  Antoinette Elizabeth Taylor Papers

Online Databases and Archives

The Shalvi/Hyman Encyclopedia of Jewish Women. Jewish Women's Archive. https://jwa
  .org/.
Women and Social Movements, International, 1840 to Present. Alexander Street Press
  Database. https://alexanderstreet.com/products/women-and-social-movements
  -international-1840-present.
Women and Social Movements in the United States, 1600 to 2000. Alexander Street Press
  Database. https://documents.alexanderstreet.com/womhist.

Periodicals

Boston Sunday Herald
Christian Science Monitor
Eagle Forum
Milwaukee Journal
Ms.
The Nation
Newsweek
New York Post
New York Times

Phyllis Schlafly Report
Richmond Times Dispatch
Smithsonian Magazine
Society
Time
USA Today
Wall Street Journal
Washington Post

Oral History Transcripts, Video, and Sound Recordings

Schlesinger Library on the History of Women in America, Radcliffe Institute for Advanced
    Study, Harvard University, Cambridge, MA
  Barnes, Viola, and Elizabeth Kimball. Interview by Ann Lane, Mary Maples Dunn, and
      Mary Hartman, November 17, 1976, Folder 1.3, "BCWH, Histories, 1976," MC 606.
  Recollections Sound Recording, Schlesinger T-1, 1964 (Barbara Miller Solomon on the
      Woman's Archive to Lady Bird Johnson at White House), and Oral History with
      Barbara Miller Solomon, Schlesinger RA A/5684 2007-T7.
  Ware, Susan. "Interview with Caroline F. Ware—Women in the Federal Government
      Project," January 1982, supplement to the Black Women Oral History Project.

Sophia Smith Collection, Smith College, Northampton, MA

    Living US Women's History Oral History Project, SSC-MS-00423 (transcriptions)

        Anderson, Karen. Interview by Mary L. Rothschild, January 14–15, 2001.

        Año Nuevo Kerr, Louise. Interview by Melynn Glusman, April 16–17, 2001.

        Antler, Joyce. Interview by Melanie Gustafson, November 15, 2000.

        Banner, Lois. Interview by Mary L. Rothschild, April 26, 2001.

        Brumberg, Joan Jacobs. Interview by Mary L. Rothschild, May 29–30, 2001.

        Buhle, Mari Jo. Interview by Claudine Barnes, December 28, 2000.

        Chafe, William. Interview by Melynn Glusman, May 21, 2001.

        Cott, Nancy. Interview by Melanie Gustafson, November 7–8, 2000.

        Degler, Carl. Interview by Mary L. Rothschild, December 6, 2001.

        De Hart, Jane. Interview by Mary L. Rothschild, August 9–10, 2001.

        Dublin, Thomas. Interview by Melanie Gustafson, November 6, 2001.

        DuBois, Ellen C. Interview by Claudine Barnes, February 19, 2001.

        Dunn, Mary Maples. Interview by Mary L. Rothschild, May 16, 2001.

        Evans, Sara. Interview by Marsha Weisiger, December 13–14, 2001.

        Freedman, Estelle. Interview by Mary L. Rothschild, October 16–17, 2000; April 20, 2001.

        Gluck, Sherna. Interview by Mary L. Rothschild, September 3, 2004.

        González, Deena. Interview by Claudine Barnes, February 21, 2001.

        Gordon, Linda. Interview by Melanie Gustafson, October 15–16, 2000.

        Hall, Jacquelyn Dowd. Interview by Melynn Glusman, March 19; April 26; May 2, 3, and 10, 2002.

        Hewitt, Nancy. Interview by Mary L. Rothschild, June 5, 8, 2004.

        Hine, Darlene Clark. Interview by Mary L. Rothschild, October 28, 2001.

        Horowitz, Helen Lefkowitz. Interview by Mary L. Rothschild, May 16–17, 2001.

        Huyck, Heather. Interview by Mary L. Rothschild, March 10–11, 2001.

        Jensen, Joan. Interview by Claudine Barnes, November 17–18, 2000.

        Kerber, Linda. Interview by Marsha Weisiger, December 28–29, 2000.

        Kessler-Harris, Alice. Interview by Melanie Gustafson, November 9–10, 2000.

        Kidwell, Clara Sue. Interview by Claudine Barnes, February 17, 2001.

        Leavitt, Judith Walzer. Interview by Marsha Weisiger, January 3–4, 2001.

        Lerner, Gerda. Interview by Mary L. Rothschild, June 6, 1999; April 23, 2001.

        Matsumoto, Valerie. Interview by Claudine Barnes, February 23, 2001.

        Mayo, Edith P. Interview by Mary L. Rothschild, May 20–21, 2001.

        Miller, Page Putnam. Interview by Mary L. Rothschild, March 6–7, 2001.

        Norton, Mary Beth. Interview by Claudine Barnes, February 2001.

        Perdue, Theda. Interview by Melynn Glusman, April 3, 6, 2001.

        Rosen, Ruth. Interview by Mary L. Rothschild, April 20, 2001.

        Rothschild, Mary L. Interview by Claudine Barnes, July 13–14, 2001.

        Ruiz, Vicki L. Interview by Mary Rothschild, March 28–29, 2005.

        Rupp, Leila J. Interview by Marsha Weisiger, November 16, 2000.

        Ryan, Mary. Interview by Mary L. Rothschild, October 18, 2000.

        Scott, Anne Firor. Interview by Mary L. Rothschild, March 21–22, 2000; and Scott, Anne Firor. Interview by Melynn Glusman, May 13, 2001. (combined in single transcript)

Sklar, Kathryn Kish. Interview by Melanie Gustafson, March 5, 2000.

Smith-Rosenberg, Carroll. Interview by Mary L. Rothschild, November 8, 2001.

Terborg-Penn, Rosalyn. Interview by Mary L. Rothschild, March 13, 16, 2001.

Ulrich, Laurel Thatcher. Interview by Claudine Barnes, January 4, 2001.

Ware, Susan. Interview by Melanie Gustafson, September 26–27, 2009.

White, Deborah Gray. Interview by Melanie Gustafson, October 16, 2000.

Wiesen-Cook, Blanche. Interview by Mary Rothschild, October 16, 2001.

Yung, Judy. Interview by Mary Rothschild, April 18–19, 2001.

Twenty-Fifth Anniversary *Journal of Women's History* Oral History Project. Video recordings in author's possession. (To be deposited with Records of the *Journal of Women's History*, MS-00489.)

Burton, Antoinette, and Jean Allman. Interview by Jennifer Tomás, October 6, 2013.

Gilmore, Stephanie. Interview by Mary Berkery, May 31, 2013.

Pope, Christie Farnham, and Joan Hoff. Interview by Jennifer Tomás, April 12, 2013.

Rupp, Leila J. Interview by Mary Berkery, May 31, 2013.

Published Primary Sources

INSTITUTIONAL AND GOVERNMENT PUBLICATIONS

American Women: Report of the President's Commission on the Status of Women, 1963. Washington, DC: US Government Printing Office, 1963.

Chaudhuri, Nupur. *Bibliography of Women's History: 1976–1979.* Manhattan, KS: Conference Group on Women's History, 1979.

Directory of History Departments and Organizations in the United States and Canada, 1990–91. Washington, DC: American Historical Association Institutional Services, 1990

Guide to Departments of History, 1975–76. Washington, DC: American Historical Association Institutional Services, 1975.

Guide to Departments of History, 1980–81. Washington, DC: American Historical Association Institutional Services, 1980.

Gustafson, Melanie, ed. *Becoming a Historian: A Survival Manual for Women and Men.* Washington, DC: AHA Committee on Women Historians, 1991.

Howe, George F., ed. *The American Historical Association's Guide to Historical Literature.* 2nd ed. New York: Macmillan, 1961.

Justice, Joyce Allen. *AHA Directory of Women Historians.* Washington, DC: AHA Institutional Services, 1975.

Lerner, Gerda. *Teaching Women's History.* Washington, DC: American Historical Association, 1981.

Miller, Page Putnam, Gail Lee Dubrow, Sara Evans, Danyelle Nelson, Dwight Pithcaithley, and Sandy Weber. *Exploring Our Common Past: Interpreting Women's History in the National Park Service.* Washington, DC: National Park Service, 1996. Copy accessible at http://npshistory.com/publications/interpretation/womens-history-1996.pdf.

Miller, Page Putnam, et al. *Exploring a Common Past: Researching and Interpreting Women's History for Historic Sites.* 2nd ed. Washington, DC: National Park Service, 2003. https://npshistory.com/publications/interpretation/womens-history.pdf.

Norton, Mary Beth, and Pamela Gerardi, eds. *The American Historical Association's Guide to Historical Literature, Third Edition in Two Volumes.* New York: Oxford University Press, 1995.

Nutting, Maureen Murphy. *American Historical Association Directory of Women Historians*. 3rd ed. Washington, DC: AHA Institutional Service, 1981.

Rose, Willie Lee, Patricia Aljberg Graham, Hanna Grey, Carl Schorske, and Page Smith. "Report of the American Historical Association Ad Hoc Committee on the Status of Women." Washington, D.C.: American Historical Association, 1970.

Sicherman, Barbara, E. William Monter, Kathryn Kish Sklar, and Joan Wallach Scott. *Recent United States Scholarship on the History of Women: A Report Presented at the XV International Congress of Historical Sciences, Bucharest, Romania, 1980*. Washington, DC: American Historical Association, 1980.

BOOKS AND BOOK CHAPTERS

Adams, Elizabeth Kemper. *Woman Professional Workers*. New York: Macmillan, 1921.

Anthony, Susan B., and Ida Husted Harper. *History of Woman Suffrage*. Vol. 4. Indianapolis: Hollenbeck Press, 1902.

Astin, Helen. *The Woman Doctorate in America: Origins, Career and Family*. New York: Russell Sage Foundation, 1969.

Banner, James, Jr., and John R. Gillis. *Becoming Historians*. Chicago: University of Chicago Press, 2009.

Baxandall, Rosalyn. *Words on Fire: The Life and Writings of Elizabeth Gurley Flynn*. New Brunswick: Rutgers University Press, 1987.

Beard, Charles A., and Mary Ritter. *America in Midpassage*. 2 vols. New York: Macmillan, 1939.

Beard, Charles A., and Mary Ritter Beard. *The American Spirit: A Study of the Idea of Civilization in the United States*. New York: Macmillan, 1942.

Beard, Charles A., and Mary Ritter Beard. *A Basic History of the United States*. New York: Doubleday, 1944.

Beard, Charles A., and Mary Ritter. *The Rise of American Civilization*. 2 vols. New York: Macmillan, 1927.

Beard, Mary Ritter. *America through Women's Eyes*. New York: Macmillan, 1933.

Beard, Mary Ritter. *History of the United States*. New York: Macmillan, 1921.

Beard, Mary Ritter. *On Understanding Women*. New York: Longmans, Green, 1931.

Beard, Mary Ritter. *Woman as Force in History*. New York: Macmillan, 1946.

Beard, Mary Ritter. *Women's Work in Municipalities*. New York: National Municipal League, 1915.

Bederman, Gail. *Manliness and Civilization*. Chicago: University of Chicago Press, 1995.

Benson, Mary Sumner. *Women in Eighteenth-Century America*. New York: Columbia University Press, 1935.

Benson, Susan Porter. *Counter Cultures: Saleswomen, Managers, and Customers in American Department Stores, 1890–1940*. Champaign: University of Illinois Press, 1986.

Berkeley, Ellen Perry, and Matilda McQuaid, eds. *Architecture: A Place for Women*. Washington, DC: Smithsonian Institution Press, 1989.

Berkin, Carol, Linda Kerber, Lois Banner, Sara Evans, and Anne Firor Scott. *Woman's Place Is in the History Books, HER STORY: 1620–1980; A Curriculum Guide for American History Teachers*. Princeton, NJ: Woodrow Wilson National Fellowship Foundation, 1981.

Berkin, Carol, and Mary Beth Norton. *Women of America: A History*. Boston: Houghton Mifflin, 1979.

Bernard, Jessie. *Academic Women.* University Park: University of Pennsylvania Press, 1964.

Berry, Mary Frances. *My Face Is Black Is True: Callie House and the Struggle for Ex-Slave Reparations.* New York: Vintage Books, 2006.

Berry, Mary Frances. *The Politics of Parenthood: Child Care, Women's Rights, and the Myth of the Good Mother.* New York: Penguin Books, 1993.

Berry, Mary Frances. *Why ERA Failed.* Bloomington: Indiana University Press, 1986.

Bleser, Carol. "Tokens of Affection: The First Three Women Presidents of the Southern Historical Association." In *Taking Off the White Gloves: Southern Women and Women Historians,* edited by Michele Gillespie and Catherine Clinton. Columbia: University of Missouri Press, 1998.

Bloch, Marc. *The Historian's Craft.* New York: Vintage Books, 1953.

Bloom, Allan. *The Closing of the American Mind.* New York: Touchstone/Simon and Schuster, 1987.

Boles, John B., ed. *Shapers of Southern History: Autobiographical Reflections.* Athens: University of Georgia Press, 2004.

Boris, Eileen. *Home to Work: Motherhood and the Politics of Industrial Homework in the United States.* New York: Cambridge University Press, 1994.

Boris, Eileen, and Nupur Chaudhuri, eds. *Voices of Women Historians: The Personal, the Political, the Professional.* Bloomington: Indiana University Press, 1999.

Boydston, Jeanne. *Home and Work: Housework, Wages, and the Ideology of Labor in the Early Republic.* New York: Oxford University Press, 1990.

Bridenthal, Renate, and Claudia Koonz, eds. *Becoming Visible: Women in European History.* Boston: Houghton Mifflin, 1977.

Brown, Hallie Quinn. *Homespun Heroines and Other Women of Distinction.* Xenia, OH: Aldine, 1926.

Brown, Louise Fargo. *Apostle of Democracy: The Life of Lucy Maynard Salmon.* New York: Harper and Brothers, 1943.

Brumberg, Joan Jacobs. *The Body Project.* New York: Vintage Books, 1997.

Brumberg, Joan Jacobs. *Fasting Girls.* New York: Vintage Books, 2000.

Buhle, Mari Jo. *Women and American Socialism, 1870–1920.* Urbana: University of Illinois Press, 1981.

Buhle, Mari Jo, and Paul Buhle, eds. *The Concise History of Woman Suffrage.* Chicago: University of Illinois Press, 1978.

Carr, Edward Hallet. *What Is History?* New York: Vintage Books, 1961.

Carroll, Berenice, ed. *Liberating Women's History: Theoretical and Critical Essays.* Urbana: University of Illinois Press, 1976.

Carroll, Berenice. "Mary Beard's Woman as Force in History." In *Liberating Women's History: Theoretical and Critical Essays,* edited by Berenice Carroll. Urbana: University of Illinois Press, 1976.

Chafe, William. *The American Woman: Her Changing Social, Economic and Political Roles, 1920–1970.* New York: Oxford University Press, 1972.

Child, Lydia Maria. *The Biographies of Madame de Stael and Madame Roland.* Boston: Carter and Hendee, 1832.

Clark, Alice. *Working Life of Women in the Seventeenth Century.* London: Routledge, 1919.

Cook, Blanche Wiesen. *Crystal Eastman on Women and Revolution.* New York: Oxford University Press, 1981.

Cook, Blanche Wiesen. *Eleanor Roosevelt*. Vol. 1, *The Early Years, 1884–1933*. New York: Penguin, 1993.

Cook, Blanche Wiesen. *Eleanor Roosevelt*. Vol. 2, *The Defining Years, 1933–1938*. New York: Penguin Random House, 1999.

Cook, Blanche Wiesen. *Eleanor Roosevelt*. Vol. 3, *The War Years and Beyond, 1939–1962*. New York: Penguin Random House, 2016.

Cott, Nancy. *The Bonds of Womanhood: "Woman's Sphere" in New England, 1780–1835*. New Haven, CT: Yale University Press, 1977.

Cott, Nancy, ed. Foreword to *Root of Bitterness: Documents of the Social History of American Women*. Boston: Northeastern University Press, 1986.

Cott, Nancy. *The Grounding of Modern Feminism*. New Haven, CT: Yale University Press, 1987.

Cott, Nancy. *Public Vows: A History of Marriage and the Nation*. Cambridge, MA: Harvard University Press, 2000.

Cott, Nancy, ed. *Root of Bitterness: Documents of the Social History of American Women*. New York: Dutton, 1972.

Cott, Nancy. *A Woman Making History: Mary Ritter Beard through Her Letters*. New Haven, CT: Yale University Press, 1991.

Daniel, Sadie Iola. *Women Builders*. Washington, DC: Associated Publishers, 1931.

Davies, Margery. *Woman's Place Is at the Typewriter: Office Work and Office Workers, 1870–1930*. Philadelphia: Temple University Press, 1982.

Davis, Angela. *Women, Race, and Class*. New York: Random House, 1981.

De Haan, Francisca, and Annette Mevis. "The IAV/IIAV's Archival Policies and Practice: Seventy Years of Collecting, Receiving, and Refusing Women's Archives, 1935–2005." In *Traveling Heritages: New Perspectives on Collecting, Preserving and Sharing Women's History*, edited by Saskia E. Wieringa. Amsterdam: Aksant Academic Publishers, 2008.

D'Emilio, John B., and Estelle B. Freedman. *Intimate Matters: A History of Sexuality in America*. Chicago: University of Chicago Press, 1988.

Dexter, Elisabeth Anthony. *Career Women of America, 1776–1840*. Boston: Houghton Mifflin, 1950.

Dexter, Elisabeth Anthony. *Career Women of American, 1776–1840*. Clifton, NJ: Augustus M. Kelleyr, 1972.

Dexter, Elisabeth Anthony. *Colonial Women of Affairs*. 2nd ed. Boston: Houghton Mifflin, 1931.

Dexter, Elisabeth Anthony. *Colonial Women of Affairs*. Clifton, N.J.: Augustus M. Kelley, Publisher, 1972.

Dillon, Mary Earhart. *Frances Willard: From Prayers to Politics*. Chicago: University of Chicago Press, 1944.

Drinker, Sophie Hutchinson. *Music and Women: The Story of Women in Their Relation to Music*. New York: Coward-McCann, 1948.

Dublin, Thomas. *Women at Work: The Transformation of Work and Community in Lowell, Massachusetts, 1826–1860*. New York: Columbia University Press, 1979.

DuBois, Ellen. *Feminism and Suffrage: The Emergence of an Independent Women's Movement in America, 1848–1869*. Ithaca, NY: Cornell University Press, 1978.

DuBois, Ellen. *Harriot Stanton Blatch and the Winning of Woman Suffrage*. New Haven, CT: Yale University Press, 1997.

Dubrow, Gail Lee. "Restoring a Female Presence: New Goals in Historic Preservation." In *Architecture: A Place for Women*, edited by Ellen Perry Berkeley and Matilda McQuaid. Washington, DC: Smithsonian Institution Press, 1989.

Enstad, Nan. *Ladies of Labor, Girls of Adventure: Working Women, Popular Culture, and Labor Politics at the Turn of the Twentieth Century*. New York: Columbia University Press, 1999.

Evans, Sara. *Personal Politics: The Roots of Women's Liberation in the Civil Rights Movement and the New Left*. New York: Vintage Books, 1979.

Evans, Sara. *Tidal Wave: How Women Changed America at Century's End*. New York: Free Press, 2003.

Faderman, Lillian. *Odd Girls and Twilight Lovers: A History of Lesbian Life in Twentieth Century America*. New York: Columbia University Press, 2012.

Faludi, Susan. *Backlash: The Undeclared War against American Women*. New York: Anchor Books by Doubleday, 1991.

Fischer, Gayle, comp. *Journal of Women's History: Guide to Periodical Literature*. Bloomington: Indiana University Press, 1992.

Flexner, Eleanor. *Century of Struggle: The Woman's Rights Movement in the United States*. Cambridge: Belknap Press of Harvard University Press, 1959.

Freedman, Estelle B. *Maternal Justice: Miriam Van Waters and the Female Reform Tradition in America*. Chicago: University of Chicago Press, 1996.

Freedman, Estelle B. *No Turning Back: The History of Feminism and the Future of Women*. New York: Ballantine Books, 2002.

Freedman, Estelle B. *Their Sisters' Keepers: Women's Prison Reform in America*. Ann Arbor: University of Michigan Press, 1981.

Freedman, Estelle, Barbara C. Gelpi, Susan L. Johnson, and Kathleen M. Weston, eds. *The Lesbian Issue: Essays from Signs*. Chicago: University of Chicago Press, 1985.

Friedan, Betty. *The Feminine Mystique*. New York: W. W. Norton, 1963.

Fox-Genovese, Elizabeth. *Within the Plantation Household: Black and White Women of the Old South*. Chapel Hill: University of North Carolina Press, 1988.

Fox-Genovese, Elizabeth, et al., eds. *Restoring Women to History: Materials for United States I*. Bloomington: Organization of American Historians, 1984.

Fox-Genovese, Elizabeth, et al., eds. *Restoring Women to History: Materials for United States II*. Bloomington: Organization of American Historians, 1984.

Fox-Genovese, Elizabeth, et al., eds. *Restoring Women to History: Materials for Western Civilization I*. Bloomington: Organization of American Historians, 1983.

Fox-Genovese, Elizabeth, et al., eds. *Restoring Women to History: Materials for Western Civilization II*. Bloomington: Organization of American Historians, 1983.

Fuller, Margaret. *Woman in the Nineteenth Century*. New York: Greeley and McElrath, 1845.

Giddings, Paula. *When and Where I Enter: The Impact of Black Women on Race and Sex in America*. New York: William Morrow, 1984.

Gidlow, Liette, ed. *Obama, Clinton, Palin: Making History in Election 2008*. Urbana: University of Illinois Press, 2011.

Gilmore, Glenda Elizabeth. *Gender and Jim Crow*. Chapel Hill: University of North Carolina Press, 1996.

Gluck, Sherna Berger. *Rosie the Riveter Revisited: Women, War and Social Change*. New York: Twayne, 1987.

González, Deena J. *Refusing the Favor: The Spanish Mexican Women of Santa Fe, 1820–1880.* New York: Oxford University Press, 1999.

Gordon, Linda. *Dorothea Lange: A Life beyond Limits.* New York: W. W. Norton, 2010.

Gordon, Linda. *The Great Arizona Orphan Abduction.* Cambridge, MA: Harvard University Press, 2001.

Gordon, Linda. *Heroes of Their Own Lives: The Politics and History of Family Violence, Boston 1880–1960.* New York: Viking, 1988.

Gordon, Linda. *The Moral Property of Women: A History of Birth Control Politics in America.* Champaign: University of Illinois Press, 2007.

Gordon, Linda. *Woman's Body, Woman's Right: A Social History of Birth Control in America.* New York: Grossman Press, 1976.

Green, Fletcher, ed. *Essays in Southern History.* Chapel Hill: University of North Carolina Press, 1949.

Greenwald, Maurine Weiner. *Women, War, and Work: The Impact of World War I on Women Workers in the United States.* Ithaca, NY: Cornell University Press, 1990.

Grimké, Angelina. *Appeal to the Christian Women of the South.* New York: New York Anti-Slavery Society, 1836.

Grimké, Sara. *Letters on the Equality of the Sexes and the Condition of Woman.* Boston: Isaac Knapp, 1838.

Groce, Nancy. *American Women's Lives: 1995 Humanities Teacher Institute, Anthology, July 8–16, 1995.* Albany: New York Council for the Humanities, 1995.

Hall, Jacquelyn Dowd. *Revolt against Chivalry: Jessie Daniel Ames and the Women's Campaign against Lynching.* New York: Columbia University Press, 1979.

Hall, Jacquelyn Dowd, James Leloudis, Robert Korstad, Mary Murphy, Lu Ann Jones, and Christopher B. Daly. *Like a Family: The Making of a Southern Cotton Mill World.* New York: W. W. Norton, 1987.

Harley, Sharon. "Reclaiming Public Voice and the Study of Black Women's Work." In *Gender, Families, and Close Relationships: Feminist Research Journeys*, edited by Donna L. Sollie and Leigh A. Leslie. Thousand Oaks: SAGE, 1994.

Harley, Sharon, and Rosalyn Terborg-Penn, eds. *The Afro-American Woman: Struggles and Images.* Baltimore: Black Classics Press, 1997. Originally published in 1978.

Harper, Ida Husted, ed. *History of Woman Suffrage.* Vol. 5. New York: J. J. Little and Ives for the National American Woman Suffrage Association, 1922.

Hartman, Mary S., and Lois W. Banner, eds. *Clio's Consciousness Raised: New Perspectives on the History of Women.* New York: Harper and Row, 1974.

Hewitt, Nancy. "Beyond the Search for Sisterhood." In *Unequal Sisters: A Multicultural Reader in U.S. Women's History.* 3rd ed., edited by Vicky L. Ruiz and Ellen Carol DuBois. New York: Rutledge, 2000.

Hewitt, Nancy. *Southern Discomfort: Women's Activism in Tampa, Florida, 1880s–1920s.* Urbana: University of Illinois Press, 2001.

Hewitt, Nancy. *Women's Activism and Social Change: Rochester, New York, 1822–1872.* Ithaca, NY: Cornell University Press, 1984.

Hewitt, Nancy A., and Suzanne Lebsock, eds. *Visible Women: New Essays on American Activism.* Urbana: University of Illinois Press, 1993.

Hexter, Jack H. *On Historians: Reappraisals of Some of the Masters of Modern History.* Cambridge, MA: Harvard University Press, 1979.

Hinding, Andrea, Ames Sheldon, Clarke A. Chambers, and Suzanna Moody, eds. *Women's History Sources: A Guide to Archives and Manuscript Collections in the United States*. New York: R. R. Bowker, 1979.

Hine, Darlene Clark. *Black Victory: The Rise and Fall of the White Primary in Texas.* Columbia: University of Missouri Press, 2003.

Hine, Darlene Clark. *Black Women in White: Racial Conflict and Cooperation in the Nursing Profession, 1890–1950*. Indianapolis: Indiana University Press, 1989.

Hine, Darlene Clark. *Hine Sight: Black Women and the Re-Construction of American History*. Indianapolis: Indiana University Press, 1994.

Hine, Darlene Clark. *When the Truth Is Told: A History of Black Women's Culture and Community in Indiana, 1875–1950*. Indianapolis: National Council of Negro Women, Indianapolis Section, 1981.

Hine, Darlene Clark, and David Barry Gaspar, eds. *More Than Chattel: Black Women and Slavery in the Americas*. Indianapolis: Indiana University Press, 1996.

Hine, Darlene Clark, and Earnestine Jenkins, eds. *A Question of Manhood: A Reader in U.S. Black Men's History and Masculinity*. Indianapolis: Indiana University Press, 1999.

Hine, Darlene Clark, Rosalyn Terborg-Penn, and Elsa Barkley Brown, eds. *Black Women in America: An Historical Encyclopedia*. Bloomington: Indiana University Press, 1994.

Hoff, Joan. *Law, Gender, and Injustice: A Legal History of U.S. Women*. New York: New York University Press, 1991.

hooks, bell. *Ain't I a Woman: Black Women and Feminism*. Boston: South End Press, 1981.

hooks, bell. *Talking Back: Thinking Feminist, Thinking Black*. Boston: South End Press, 1989.

Hull, Gloria T., Patricia Bell-Scott, and Barbara Smith, eds. *All the Women Are White, All the Blacks Are Men, but Some of Us Are Brave*. New York: Feminist Press of CUNY, 1982.

Huyck, Heather. *Doing Women's History: A Handbook for Interpretation at Museums and Historic Sites*. New York: Rowman and Littlefield, 2020.

Huyck, Heather. *Women's History: Sites and Resources*. 2nd ed. Champaign: University of Illinois Press, 2010.

James, Edward T., Janet Wilson James, and Paul S. Boyer, eds. *Notable American Women, 1607–1950: A Biographical Dictionary*. 3 vols. Cambridge, MA: Belknap Press of Harvard University Press, 1971.

James, Janet Wilson. Introduction to *Notable American Women, 1607–1950: A Biographical Dictionary*, edited by Edward James, Janet Wilson James, and Paul S. Boyer. 3 vols. Cambridge, MA: Belknap Press of Harvard University, 1971.

James, Janet Wilson. "Recollections of a Veteran in Women's History." In *Changing Ideas about Women in the United States, 1776–1825*. New York: Garland, 1981.

Janiewski, Dolores. *Sisterhood Denied: Race, Gender, and Class in a New South Community*. Philadelphia: Temple University Press, 1985.

Jensen, Joan M. *Loosening the Bonds: Mid-Atlantic Farm Women, 1750–1850*. New Haven, CT: Yale University Press, 1988.

Johnson, Guion Griffis. *Ante-Bellum North Carolina: A Social History*. Chapel Hill: University of North Carolina Press, 1937.

Johnson, Guion Griffis. "The Changing Status of Women in the South." In *Continuity and Change in the South*, edited by John C. McKinney. Durham, NC: Duke University Press, 1964.

Johnson, Guion Griffis. *A History of the South Carolina Sea Islands with Special Reference to St. Helena, South Carolina*. Chapel Hill: University of North Carolina Press, 1930.

Johnson, Guion Griffis. "The Ideology of White Supremacy." In *Essays in Southern History*, edited by Fletcher Green. Chapel Hill: University of North Carolina Press, 1949.

Johnson, Guion Griffis, et al. *Governor's Commission on the Status of Women in North Carolina: Report of the Committee on Voluntary Organizations and Expanded Services*. Raleigh: North Carolina Commission on the Status of Women, 1964.

Johnson, Guy Benton, and Guion Griffis Johnson. *Research in Service to Society: The First Fifty Years of the Institute for Research in Social Science at the University of North Carolina*. Chapel Hill: University of North Carolina Press, 1980.

Jones, Jacqueline. *Labor of Love/Labor of Sorrow: Black Women, Work, and the Family, from Slavery to the Present*. New York: Basic Books, 1985.

Judson, Margaret. *Breaking the Barrier: A Professional Autobiography By A Woman Educator and Historian Before the Women's Movement*. New Brunswick, NJ: Rutgers, State University of New Jersey, 1984.

Keckeis, Gustav. *The Lexicon of Women in Two Volumes*. Vol. 1, *A–H*. Zurich: Encyclios Verlag, 1953.

Keckeis, Gustav. *The Lexicon of Women in Two Volumes*. Vol. 2, *I–Z*. Zurich: Encyclios Verlag, 1954.

Kelly, Joan. *Women, History, and Theory: The Essays of Joan Kelly*. Chicago: University of Chicago Press, 1984.

Kerber, Linda. *No Constitutional Right to Be Ladies: Women and the Obligations of Citizenship*. New York: Hill and Wang, 1998.

Kerber, Linda. *Toward an Intellectual History of Women: Essays by Linda Kerber*. Chapel Hill: University of North Carolina Press, 1997.

Kerber, Linda. *Women of the Republic: Intellect and Ideology in Revolutionary America*. Chapel Hill: University of North Carolina Press, 1980.

Kerber, Linda, Alice Kessler-Harris, and Kathryn Kish Sklar, eds. *U.S. History as Women's History: New Feminist Essays*. Chapel Hill: University of North Carolina Press, 1995.

Kessler-Harris, Alice. *In Pursuit of Equity: Men, Women, and the Pursuit of Economic Citizenship in 20th Century America*. New York: Oxford University Press, 2003.

Kessler-Harris, Alice. *Out to Work: A History of Wage-Earning Women in the United States*. New York: Oxford University Press, 1982.

Kraditor, Aileen S. *The Ideas of the Woman Suffrage Movement, 1890–1920*. New York: Columbia University Press, 1965.

Kraditor, Aileen S. *The Ideas of the Woman Suffrage Movement, 1890–1920*. New York: W. W. Norton, 1981.

Lane, Ann J. *Mary Ritter Beard: A Sourcebook*. New York: Schocken Books, 1977.

Lasch, Christopher. "Rachel G. Foster Avery," "Alva Belmont," "Sophonisba Breckenridge," "Mary Ware Dennett," and "Rachelle Slobodinsky Yarros," entries in *Notable American Women, 1607–1950: A Biographical Dictionary*, vols. 1–3, edited by Edward T. James, Janet Wilson James, and Paul S. Boyer. Cambridge, MA: Belknap Press of Harvard University, 1971.

Lasch, Christopher, ed. *The Social Thought of Jane Addams*. Indianapolis: Bobbs-Merrill, 1965.

Leavitt, Judith Walzer. *Brought to Bed: Childbearing in America, 1750–1950*. New York: Oxford University Press, 1986.

Lebsock, Suzanne. *The Free Women of Petersburg: Status and Culture in a Southern Town, 1784–1860*. New York: W. W. Norton, 1984.

Lerner, Gerda. *Black Women in White America: A Documentary History*. New York: Pantheon Books, 1972.

Lerner, Gerda. *Fireweed: A Political Autobiography*. Philadelphia: Temple University Press, 2002.

Lerner, Gerda. *Living with History/Making Social Change*. Chapel Hill: University of North Carolina Press, 2009.

Lerner, Gerda. *The Majority Finds Its Past: Placing Women in History*. New York: Oxford University Press, 1979.

Lerner, Gerda. *Teaching Women's History*. Washington, DC: American Historical Association, 1981.

Lerner, Gerda. *Why History Matters: Life and Thought*. New York: Oxford University Press, 1997.

Lerner, Gerda. *The Woman in American History*. Menlo Park, CA: Addison-Wesley, 1971.

Lerner, Gerda. "Women among the Professors of History." In *Voices of Women Historians: The Personal, the Political, the Professional*, edited by Eileen Boris and Nupur Chaudhuri. Bloomington: Indiana University Press, 1999.

Limbaugh, Rush. *The Way Things Ought to Be*. New York: Pocket Books, 1992.

Link, Arthur Stanley, and Rembert Wallace Patrick, eds. *Writing Southern History: Essays in Historiography in Honor of Fletcher M. Green*. Baton Rouge: Louisiana State University Press, 1966.

Lorde, Audre. *Sister Outsider: Essays and Speeches*. Berkeley, CA: Crossing Press, 1984.

Lorde, Audre. *Sister Outsider: Essays and Speeches*. Toronto: Crossing Press, 2007.

Lundberg, Ferdinand, and Marynia Farnham. *Modern Woman: The Lost Sex*. New York: Harper and Brothers, 1947.

Lutz, Alma. *Created Equal: A Biography of Elizabeth Cady Stanton, 1815–1902*. New York: Octagon Books, 1940.

Lutz, Alma. *Crusade for Freedom: Women of the Anti-Slavery Movement*. Boston: Beacon Press, 1968.

Lutz, Alma. *Emma Willard: Pioneer Educator of American Women*. Boston: Beacon Press, 1964.

Lutz, Alma. *Susan B. Anthony: Rebel, Crusader, Humanitarian*. Boston: Beacon Press, 1959.

Lutz, Alma. *With Love, Jane: Letters from American Women on the War Front*. New York: John Day, 1945.

Malkiel, Nancy Weiss. "Invincible Woman: Anne Firor Scott." In *Visible Women: New Essays on American Activism*, edited by Nancy A. Hewitt and Suzanne Lebsock. Urbana: University of Illinois Press, 1993.

Mason, Kären M. "'A Grand Manuscripts Search': The Women's History Sources Survey at the University of Minnesota, 1975–1979." In *Perspectives on Women's Archives*, edited by Tanya Zanish-Belcher and Anke Voss. Chicago: Society of American Archivists, 2013.

Massey, Mary Elizabeth. *Bonnet Brigades: American Women and the Civil War*. New York: Alfred A. Knopf, 1966.

Massey, Mary Elizabeth. *Ersatz in the Confederacy*. Columbia: University of South Carolina Press, 1952.

Massey, Mary Elizabeth. *Refugee Life in the Confederacy*. Baton Rouge: Louisiana State University Press, 1964.

Matsumoto, Valerie. *Farming the Homeplace: A Japanese American Community in California, 1919–1982*. Ithaca, NY: Cornell University Press, 1993.

Mayo, Edith P. *The Smithsonian Book of the First Ladies*. New York: Henry Holt, 1996.

Mayo, Edith P., and Lisa Kathleen Graddy. *First Ladies: Political Role and Public Image*. London: Scala Publishers, 2004.

McGuire, Danielle. *At the Dark End of the Street: Black Women, Rape, and Resistance—A New History of the Civil Rights Movement from Rosa Parks to the Rise of Black Power*. New York: Vintage Books, 2010.

Melder, Keith. *Beginnings of Sisterhood: The American Women's Rights Movement, 1800–1850*. New York: Schocken Books, 1977.

Milkman, Ruth. *Gender at Work: The Dynamics of Job Segregation by Sex during World War II*. Chicago: University of Illinois Press, 1987.

Miller, Page Putnam, ed. *Reclaiming the Past: Landmarks of Women's History*. Indianapolis: Indiana University Press, 1992.

Murray, Pauli. *Proud Shoes: The Story of an American Family*. Boston: Beacon Press, 1999. Originally published in 1956.

Murray, Pauli. *Song in a Weary Throat: An American Pilgrimage*. New York: Harper and Row, 1987.

Myrdal, Gunnar. *An American Dilemma: The Negro Problem and Modern Democracy*. New York: Harper and Brothers, 1944.

Nash, Gary B., and Charlotte Crabtree. *National Standards for United States History: Exploring the American Experience*. Los Angeles: National Center for History in the Schools, 1994. Rev. ed., 1996.

Nash, Gary B., Charlotte Crabtree, and Ross E. Dunn. *History on Trial: Culture Wars and the Teaching of the Past*. New York: Vintage Books, 1997.

O'Neill, William. *Everyone Was Brave: A History of Feminism in America*. New York: Quadrangle/The New York Times Book Co., 1969.

Orleck, Annelise. *Common Sense and a Little Fire: Women and Working-Class Politics in the United States, 1900–1965*. Chapel Hill: University of North Carolina Press, 1995.

Owsley, Frank. *Plain Folk of the Old South*. Baton Rouge: Louisiana State University Press, 1949.

Painter, Nell Irvin. *Sojourner Truth: A Life, a Symbol*. New York: W. W. Norton, 1996.

Payne, Elizabeth Anne, ed. *Writing Women's History: A Tribute to Anne Firor Scott*. Jackson: University Press of Mississippi, 2011.

Peiss, Kathy. *Cheap Amusements: Working Women and Leisure in Turn-of-the-Century New York*. Philadelphia: Temple University Press, 1986.

Petchesky, Rosalind Pollack. *Abortion and Woman's Choice: The State, Sexuality, and Reproductive Freedom*. Boston: Northeastern University Press, 1990.

Pivar, David. *Purity Crusade: Sexual Morality and Social Control, 1868–1900*. New York: Greenwood Press, 1973.

Reverby, Susan. *Examining Tuskegee: The Infamous Syphilis Study and Its Legacy*. Chapel Hill: University of North Carolina Press, 2009.

Reverby, Susan. *Ordered to Care: The Dilemma of American Nursing*. New York: Cambridge University Press, 1987.

Rosen, Ruth. *The Lost Sisterhood: Prostitution in America, 1900–1918*. Baltimore: Johns Hopkins University Press, 1982.

Rosen, Ruth. *The World Split Open: How the Modern Women's Movement Changed America*. New York: Viking Penguin, 2000.

Ross, Ishbel. *Child of Destiny: The Life Story of the First Woman Doctor*. New York: Harper and Brothers, 1949.

Ross, Ishbel. *Ladies of the Press: The Story of Women in Journalism by an Insider*. New York: Harper and Row, 1936.

Rossi, Alice, and Anne Calderwood, eds. *Academic Women on the Move*. New York: Russell Sage Foundation, 1974.

Ruiz, Vicki L. *Cannery Women, Cannery Lives: Mexican Women, Unionization, and the California Food Processing Industry, 1930–1950*. Albuquerque: University of New Mexico Press, 1987.

Rupp, Leila J. *A Desired Past: A Short History of Same-Sex Love in America*. Chicago: University of Chicago Press, 1999.

Rupp, Leila J. *Mobilizing Women for War: German and American Propaganda, 1939–1945*. Princeton, NJ: Princeton University Press, 1978.

Rupp, Leila J. *Sapphistries: A Global History of Love between Women*. New York: New York University Press, 2009.

Rupp, Leila J. *Worlds of Women: The Making of an International Women's Movement*. Princeton, NJ: Princeton University Press, 1997.

Rupp, Leila J., and Verta Taylor. *Survival in the Doldrums: The American Women's Rights Movement, 1945 to the 1960s*. New York: Oxford University Press, 1990.

Rutland, Robert Allen, ed. *Clio's Favorites: Leading Historians of the United States, 1945–2000*. Columbia: University of Missouri Press, 2000.

Salmon, Lucy Maynard. *Domestic Service*. New York: Macmillan, 1897.

Salmon, Lucy Maynard. *History of the Appointing Power of the President*. New York: G. P. Putnam and Sons, 1886.

Salmon, Lucy Maynard. *Progress in the Household*. Boston: Houghton Mifflin, 1906.

Scharf, Lois, and Joan M. Jensen, eds. *Decades of Discontent: The Women's Movement, 1920–1940*. Boston: Northeastern University Press, 1983.

Schlesinger, Arthur M.. *New Viewpoints in American History*. New York: Macmillan, 1922.

Schmidt, Dolores Barracano, and Earl Robert Schmidt. "The Invisible Woman: The Historian as Professional Magician." In *Liberating Women's History: Theoretical and Critical Essays*, edited by Berenice Carroll. Urbana: University of Illinois Press, 1976.

Schulz, Constance B., and Elizabeth Hayes Turner, eds. *Clio's Southern Sisters: Interviews with Leaders of the Southern Association for Women Historians*. Columbia: University of Missouri Press, 2004.

Schuyler, Robert Livingston, and Edward James, eds. *Dictionary of American Biography: XXII, Supplement Two*. New York: Charles Scribner's, 1958.

Scott, Anne Firor. "Chance or Choice?" In *Shapers of Southern History: Autobiographical Reflections*, edited by John B. Boles. Athens: University of Georgia Press, 2004.

Scott, Anne Firor. "A Historian's Odyssey." In *Making the Invisible Woman Visible*. Urbana: University of Illinois Press, 1984.

Scott, Anne Firor. Interview by Constance Schulz in *Clio's Southern Sisters: Interviews with Leaders of the Southern Association for Women Historians*, edited by Constance B. Schulz and Elizabeth Hayes Turner. Columbia: University of Missouri Press, 2004.

Scott, Anne Firor. *Making the Invisible Woman Visible*. Urbana: University of Illinois Press, 1984.

Scott, Anne Firor, ed. *Pauli Murray and Caroline Ware: Forty Years of Letters in Black and White*. Chapel Hill: University of North Carolina Press, 2006.

Scott, Anne Firor. *The Southern Lady: From Pedestal to Politics, 1830–1930*. Chicago: University of Chicago Press, 1970.

Scott, Anne Firor. *Women in American Life: Selected Readings*. Boston: Houghton Mifflin, 1970.

Scott, Joan Wallach, ed. *Feminism and History*. New York: Oxford University Press, 1996.

Scott, Joan Wallach. *Gender and the Politics of History*. New York: Columbia University Press, 1988.

Shapiro, Ann-Louise, ed. *Feminists Revision History*. New Brunswick, NJ: Rutgers University Press, 1994.

Sicherman, Barbara, and Carol Hurd Green, eds. *Notable American Women: The Modern Period*. Cambridge, MA: Belknap Press of Harvard University Press, 1980.

Simkins, Francis, and James Patton. *The Women of the Confederacy*. Richmond, VA: Garret and Massie, 1936.

Sklar, Kathryn Kish. *Catharine Beecher: A Study in American Domesticity*. New York: W. W. Norton, 1976.

Sklar, Kathryn Kish. *Florence Kelley and the Nation's Work: The Rise of Women's Political Culture, 1830–1900*. New Haven, CT: Yale University Press, 1995.

Sklar, Kathryn Kish. "The Women's Studies Movement: 1972." In *The Politics of Women's Studies: Testimony from 30 Founding Mothers*, edited by Florence Howe. New York: Feminist Press, 2000.

Sklar, Kathryn Kish, Anja Schüler, and Susan Strasser, eds. *Social Justice Feminists in the United States and Germany: A Dialogue in Documents, 1885–1933*. Ithaca, NY: Cornell University Press, 1998.

Smith, Hilda. "Regionalism, Feminism, and Class: The Making of a Feminist Historian." In *Voices of Women Historians: The Personal, the Political, the Professional*, edited by Eileen Boris and Nupur Chaudhuri. Bloomington: Indiana University Press, 1999.

Smith, Page. *Daughters of the Promised Land: Women in American History*. Boston: Little Brown, 1970.

Smith-Rosenberg, Carroll. *Religion and the Rise of the American City: New York City Mission Movement, 1812–1870*. Ithaca, NY: Cornell University Press, 1972.

Solomon, Barbara Miller. *Ancestors and Immigrants: A Changing New England Tradition*. Cambridge, MA: Harvard University Press, 1956.

Solomon, Barbara Miller. *In the Company of Educated Women*. New Haven, CT: Yale University Press, 1985.

Solomon, Barbara Miller. *Pioneers in Service: A History of the Associated Jewish Philanthropies of Boston*. Boston: Jewish Philanthropies of Boston, 1956.

Spruill, Julia Cherry. *Women's Life and Work in the Southern Colonies*. New York: W. W. Norton, 1972. Originally published in 1938.

Stanton, Elizabeth Cady, Susan B. Anthony, and Matilda Joslyn Gage, eds. *History of Woman Suffrage*. Vol. 1, *1848–1861*. New York: Fowler and Wells, 1881.

Stanton, Elizabeth Cady, Susan B. Anthony, and Matilda Joslyn Gage, eds. *History of Woman Suffrage*. Vol. 2, *1861–1876*. New York: Fowler and Wells, 1882.

Stanton, Elizabeth Cady, Susan B. Anthony, and Matilda Joslyn Gage, eds. *History of Woman Suffrage*. Vol. 3, *1876–1885*. Rochester: Susan B. Anthony, 1886.

Swerdlow, Amy. *Women Strike for Peace: Traditional Motherhood and Radical Politics in the 1960s*. Chicago: University of Chicago Press, 1993.

Taylor, A. Elizabeth. Interview by Pamela Dean, November 5, in *Clio's Southern Sisters: Interviews with Leaders of the Southern Association for Women Historians*, edited by Constance B. Schulz and Elizabeth Hayes Turner. Columbia: University of Missouri Press, 2004.

Taylor, A. Elizabeth. "A Lifelong Interest." In *Citizens at Last: The Woman Suffrage Movement in Texas*, edited by Ruthe Winegarten and Judith N. McArthur. Austin: Ellen C. Temple, 1987.

Taylor, A. Elizabeth. "Miriam Ferguson." In *Notable American Women: The Modern Period*, edited by Barbara Sicherman and Carol Hurd Green. Cambridge, MA: Belknap Press of Harvard University Press, 1980.

Taylor, A. Elizabeth. *The Woman Suffrage Movement in Tennessee*. New York: Bookman Associates, 1957.

Tax, Meredith. *The Rising of the Women: Feminist Solidarity and Class Conflict, 1880–1917*. New York: Monthly Review Press, 1980.

Tentler, Leslie Woodcock. *Wage-Earning Women: Industrial Work and Family Life in the United States, 1900–1930*. New York: Oxford University Press, 1979.

Terborg-Penn, Rosalyn. *African American Women in the Struggle for the Vote, 1850–1920*. Indianapolis: Indiana University Press, 1998.

Thompson, Lovell. "Henry Alexander Laughlin," *Proceedings of the Massachusetts Historical Society*, 3rd ser., 90 (1978): 117–19.

Thurner, Manuela. "Better Citizens without the Ballot: American Anti-Suffrage Women and Their Rationale in the Progressive Era." In *One Woman, One Vote: Rediscovering the Woman Suffrage Movement*, edited by Marjorie Spruill Wheeler. Troutdale, OR: New Sage Press, 1995.

Tinling, Marion. *Women Remembered: A Guide to Landmarks of Women's History*. New York: Greenwood Press, 1986.

Traister, Rebecca. *Good and Mad: The Revolutionary Power of Women's Anger*. New York: Simon and Schuster, 2018.

Turoff, Barbara. *Mary Beard as Force in History*. Dayton, OH: Wright State University, 1979.

Ulrich, Laurel Thatcher. *Good Wives: Image and Reality in the Lives of Women of Northern New England, 1650–1750*. New York: Knopf, 1982.

Ulrich, Laurel Thatcher. *A Midwife's Tale: The Life of Martha Ballard Based on Her Diary, 1785–1812*. New York: Knopf, 1990.

Ware, Caroline F., ed. *The Cultural Approach to History*. New York: Columbia University Press, 1940.

Ware, Caroline F. *The Early New England Cotton Manufacture: A Study in Industrial Beginnings*. Boston: Houghton Mifflin, 1931.

Ware, Caroline F. *Greenwich Village, 1920–1930: A Comment on American Civilization in the Post-War Years*. New York: Columbia University Press, 1935.

Ware, Susan, ed. *Notable American Women: A Biographical Dictionary, Completing the Twentieth Century*. Cambridge, MA: Belknap Press of Harvard University, 2004.

Welter, Barbara. *Dimity Convictions: American Women in the Nineteenth Century*. Athens: Ohio University Press, 1976.

White, Deborah Gray. *Ar'n't I a Woman? Female Slaves in the Plantation South*. New York: W. W. Norton, 1985.

White, Deborah Gray, ed. *Telling Histories: Black Women Historians in the Ivory Tower*. Chapel Hill: University of North Carolina Press, 2008.

White, Deborah Gray. *Too Heavy a Load: Black Women in Defense of Themselves*. New York: W. W. Norton, 1999.

Young, Louise M. *In the Public Interest: A History of the League of Women Voters, 1920–1970*. Westport, CT: Greenwood Press, 1989.

Young, Louise M. *Understanding Politics: A Practical Guide for Women*. New York: Pellegrini and Cudahy, 1950.

ARTICLES AND BOOK REVIEWS

Banner, Lois. "On Writing Women's History." *Journal of Interdisciplinary History* 2, no. 2 (1971): 347.

Becker, Carl. "Annual Address of the President of the American Historical Association." Minneapolis, December 29, 1931. *American Historical Review* 37, no. 2 (1932): 221–36.

Benson, Mary. Review of *Notable American Women, 1607–1950: A Biographical Dictionary*, edited by Edward James, Janet Wilson James, and Paul S. Boyer. *Journal of American History* 59, no. 4 (1973): 972–73.

Bleser, Carol, ed. "The Three Women Presidents of the Southern Historical Association: Ella Lonn, Kathryn Abby Hanna, and Mary Elizabeth Massey." *Southern Studies* (Summer 1981): 101–21.

Bock, Gisela. "Women's History and Gender History: Aspects of an International Debate." *Gender and History* 1, no. 1 (1989): 7–30.

Boyd, Melba Joyce. "Collard Greens, Clarence Thomas, and the High-Tech Rape of Anita Hill." *Black Scholar* 22, no. 1/2 (1991/1992): 25–27.

Boylan, Ann M. "Textbooks in U.S. Women's History." *Feminist Studies* 18, no. 2 (1992): 351–61.

Briscoe, Anne M. "Phenomena of the Seventies: The Women's Caucuses." *Signs* 4, no. 1 (1978): 152–58.

Brown, Elsa Barkley. "What Has Happened Here?" *Feminist Studies* 18, no. 2 (Summer 1992): 295–312, 298–300.

Bruce, Kathleen. "Review of M. R. Beard, *Through Women's Eyes*." *Mississippi Valley Historical Review* 20, no. 4 (1934): 592–93.

Buhle, Mari Jo, Ann Gordon, and Nancy Schrom. "Women in American Society: An Historical Contribution." *Radical America* 5, no. 4 (July–August 1971): 3–66.

Cott, Nancy, Gerda Lerner, Kathryn Kish Sklar, Ellen DuBois, and Nancy Hewitt. "Considering the State of U.S. Women's History." *Journal of Women's History* 15, no. 1 (2003): 145–63.

Davis, Henry Vance. "The High-Tech Lynching and the High-Tech Overseer: Thoughts from the Anita Hill/Clarence Thomas Affair." *Black Scholar* 22, no. 1/2 (1991/1992): 27–29.

Davis, Natalie Zemon. "A Life of Learning." Charles Homer Haskins Lecture for 1997. ACLS Annual Meeting in Philadelphia, PA, May 2, 1997. American Council of Learned Societies, Occasional Paper No. 39. https://www.acls.org/wp-content/uploads/2021/11/Occasional_Paper_039_1997_Natalie_Zemon_Davis.pdf.

Davis, Natalie Zemon. "'Women's History' in Transition: The European Case." *Feminist Studies* 3, no. 3/4 (1976): 83–103.

Dayton, Cornelia H., and Lisa Levenstein. "The Big Tent of U.S. Women's and Gender History: A State of the Field." *Journal of American History* 99, no. 3 (2012): 797–817.

Degler, Carl N. "'Woman as Force in History' by Mary Beard." *Daedalus* 103, no. 1 (1974): 67–73.

De Hart, Jane. "Celebrating and Becoming Blanche Wiesen Cook." *Meridians* 10, no. 2 (2010): 68–73.

Dubofsky, Melvyn. "A City Kid's View of Working-Class History: An Interview with Melvyn Dubofsky." Interview by David Palmer. *Labor History: Studies in Working Class History of the Americas* 7, no. 2 (2010): 53–81.

DuBois, Ellen. "Foremothers I: Eleanor Flexner and the History of American Feminism." *Gender and History* 3, no. 1 (1991): 81–90.

DuBois, Ellen. "Politics and Culture in Women's History." *Feminist Studies* 6, no. 1 (1980): 28.

Frederickson, George M. "Review of *The Southern Lady: From Pedestal to Politics, 1830–1930*. Chicago: Chicago University Press, 1970 by Anne Firor Scott." *American Historical Review* 76, no. 4 (1971): 1223–24.

Freedman, Estelle. "Historical Interpretation and Legal Advocacy: Rethinking the Webster Amicus Brief." *Public Historian* 12, no. 3 (1990): 27–32.

Freedman, Estelle. "Women's Networks and Women's Loyalties: Reflections on a Tenure Case." *Frontiers* 8, no. 3 (1986): 50–54.

Fox-Genovese, Elizabeth. "Comment on the Reviews of *Woman's Body, Woman's Right*." *Signs* 4, no. 4 (1979): 804–8.

Gordon, Linda. "Race, Gender, and Painful Changes in Field of American History." *Chronicle of Higher Education*, July 11, 1997. www.chronicle.com/article/race-gender-and-painful-changes-in-field-of-american-history/.

Gordon, Linda. "A Socialist View of Women's Studies: A Reply to Editorial, Volume 1, Number 1." *Signs* 1, no. 2 (1975): 559–66.

Gordon, Linda, David Hunt, and Peter Weiler. "History as Indoctrination: A Critique of Colton and Palmer's *History of the Modern World*." *History Teacher* 21, no. 1 (1987): 53–103.

Gutheim, Marjorie. "*Notable American Women: 1607–1950: A Biographical Dictionary* by James, James, and Boyer." *New England Quarterly* 45, no. 2 (1972): 281–83.

Hall, Jacquelyn Dowd. "Disorderly Women: Gender and Labor Militancy in the Appalachian South." *Journal of American History* 73, no. 2 (1986): 354–82.

Hall, Jacquelyn Dowd. "The Long Civil Rights Movement and the Political Uses of the Past." *Journal of American History* 1, no. 94 (2005): 1233–63.

Hesseltine, William B., and Louis Kaplan. "Women Doctors of Philosophy in History." *Journal of Higher Education* 14, no. 5 (1943): 254–59.

Hewitt, Nancy. "Beyond the Search For Sisterhood." *Social History* 10, no. 3 (1985): 299–321.

Hewitt, Nancy. "Compounding Difference." *Feminist Studies* 18, no. 2 (1992): 313–26.

Higginbotham, Evelyn Brooks. "Beyond the Sound of Silence: Afro-American Women in History." *Gender and History* 1, no.1 (1989): 50–67.

Higham, John. "The Cult of American Consensus: Homogenizing Our History." *Commentary* 27, no. 2 (1959): 93–100.

Hine, Darlene Clark. "Black Women's History, White Women's History: The Juncture of Race and Class." *Journal of Women's History* 4, no. 2 (1992): 125–33.

Hine, Darlene Clark. "Rape and the Inner Lives of Black Women in the Middle West: Preliminary Thoughts on the Culture of Dissemblance." *Signs* 14, no. 4 (1989).

Horowitz, Paul, and Page Putnam Miller. "The Freedom of Information Act: Federal Policy and the Writing of Contemporary History." *Public Historian* 4, no. 4 (1982): 87–96.

Huyck, Heather. "Twenty-Five Years of Public History: Perspectives from a Primary Document." *Public Historian* 21, no. 3 (1999): 29–38.

Jellison, Katherine. "History in the Courtroom: The Sears Case in Perspective." *Public Historian* 9, no. 4 (1987): 9–1.

Jensen, Joan. "After Slavery: Caroline Severance in Los Angeles." *Southern California Quarterly* 48 (June 1966): 175–86.

Jensen, Joan. "Annette Abbott Adams." *Pacific Historical Review* 35 (1966): 185–201.

Johnson, Guion Griffis. "The Changing Status of the Negro." *Journal of the American Association of University Women* 53 (1958): 217–20.

Johnson, Guion Griffis. "Feminism and the Economic Independence of Woman." *Journal of Social Forces* 3, no. 4 (1925): 612–16.

Johnson, Guion Griffis. "The Impact of War upon the Negro." *Journal of Negro Education* 10, no. 3 (1941): 596–611.

Johnson, Guion Griffis. "The Quiet Revolution: Integration in Institutions of Higher Learning." *Journal of the American Association of University Women* (Ithaca, NY: Empire Express, 1959): 133–36.

Johnson, Guion Griffis. "Southern Paternalism toward the Negro, 1870–1914." *Journal of Southern History* 23, no. 4 (1957): 483–509.

Jones, Arnita "National Coordinating Committee: Programs and Possibilities." *Public Historian* 1, no. 1 (1978): 49–60.

Kennedy, David. Review of *Woman's Body, Woman's Right*, by Linda Gordon. *Journal of American History* 64, no. 3 (1977): 823–24.

Kerber, Linda "History Practice: Conditions for Work for Women Historians in the Twenty-First Century, Risking Our Dreams." *Journal of Women's History* 18, no. 1 (2006): 122.

Kessler-Harris, Alice. "'Differences and Inequality?' Interview by David Tell." *Society*, September/October 1987, 4–16.

Kessler-Harris, Alice. "Long Road from Home: An Interview with Alice Kessler-Harris." Interview by Melanie Gustafson. *Labor: Studies in Working-Class History of the Americas* 3 (Spring 2006): 59–86.

Kessler-Harris, Alice. "Organizing the Unorganizable: Three Jewish Women and Their Trade Union." *Labor History* 17 (Winter 1976): 5–23.

Lasser, Carol. "Century of Struggle, Decades of Revision: A Retrospective on Eleanor Flexner's Suffrage History." *Reviews in American History* (June 1987): 344–54.

Law, Sylvia A. "Conversations between Historians and Lawyers." *Public Historian* 12, no. 3 (1990): 11–17.

Lebsock, Suzanne. "In Retrospect: Reading Mary Beard." *Reviews in American History* 17, no. 2 (1989): 321–39.

Lemons, J. Stanley. Review of *Woman's Body, Woman's Right*, by Linda Gordon. *American Historical Review* 82, no. 4 (1977): 1095.

Lerner, Gerda. "The Grimké Sisters and the Struggle against Racial Prejudice." *Journal of Negro History* 48, no. 4 (1963): 277–91.

Lerner, Gerda. "New Approaches to the Study of Women in American History." *Journal of Social History* 3, no. 1 (1969): 53–62. Later published in Lerner, *The Majority Finds Its Past*.

Lerner, Gerda. "Placing Women in History: Definitions and Challenges." *Feminist Studies* 3, nos. 1–2 (1975): 5–14. Later published in Lerner, *The Majority Finds Its Past*.

Logan, Rayford W. Review of *Women Builders*, by Sadie Iola Daniel. *Journal of Negro History* 17, no. 2 (1932): 234–35.

Lonn, Ella. "Academic Status of Women on University Faculties." *Journal of the American Association of University Women* 17 (January 1924): 8–10.

Lubelski, Sarah. "Kicking Off the Women's 'Archives Party': The World Center for Women's Archives and the Foundations of Feminist Historiography and Women's Archives." *Archivaria* 78 (Fall 2014): 95–113.

Lutz, Alma. "Early American Women Historians." *Boston Public Library Quarterly* 8, no. 2 (1956): 85–99.

Lutz, Alma. "Hannah Adams, an American Bluestocking." *New England Galaxy* 12, no. 4 (1971): 29–34.

Lutz, Alma. "Susan B. Anthony and John Brown." *Rochester History* 15, no. 3 (1953): 1–16.

Lutz, Alma. "Susan B. Anthony for the Working Woman." *Boston Public Library Quarterly* 11, no. 1 (1959): 33–43.

Massey, Mary Elizabeth. "*Notable American Women, 1607–1950: A Biographical Dictionary*. Volume 1, *A–F*; Volume 2, *G–O*; Volume 3, *P–Z*, by Edward T. James, Janet W. James, and Paul S. Boyer." *American Historical Review* 78, no. 1 (1973): 144–45.

Mayo, Edith P. "Teaching the First Ladies Using Material Culture." *OAH Magazine of History* 15, no. 3 (2001): 22–25.

Mayo, Edith P. "Women's History and Public History: The Museum Connection." *Public Historian* 5, no. 2 (1983): 63–73.

Mendenhall, Marjorie. "Review of *On Understanding Women* by Mary R. Beard." *North Carolina Historical Review* 9, no. 4 (1932): 397–99. www.jstor.org/stable/23515218.

Mendenhall, Marjorie Stratford. "Southern Women of a Lost Generation." *South Atlantic Quarterly* 33 (1934): 334–53.

Merk, Lois Bannister. "Boston's Historic Public School Crisis." *New England Quarterly* 31, no. 2 (1958): 172–99.

Mohr, James. "Historically Based Legal Briefs: Observations of a Participant in the Webster Process." *Public Historian* 12, no. 3 (1990): 25–26.

Perry, Ruth. "Historically Correct." *Women's Review of Books* 9, no. 5 (1992): 15–16.

Potter, David. "American Women and the American Character." *Stetson University Bulletin* 62 (January 1962): 1–22.

Rosenberg, Rosalind. "Women's History and EEOC v. Sears, 'Disparity or Discrimination?' Interview by David Tell." *Society*, September/October 1987, 4–16.

Roth, Darlene. "Feminine Marks on the Landscape: An Atlanta Inventory." *Journal of American Culture* 3 (Winter 1980): 680–85.

Rupp, Leila J. "Eleanor Flexner's Century of Struggle: Women's History and the Women's Movement." *NWSA Journal* 4, no. 2 (1992): 157–69.

Rupp, Leila J. Review of *Toward an Intellectual History of Women* (1997), by Linda Kerber, and *Why History Matters: Life and Thought* (1997), by Gerda Lerner, in *Signs* 26, no. 1 (2000): 322.

Schlesinger, Elizabeth Bancroft. "Cotton Mather and His Children." *William and Mary Quarterly* 10, no. 2 (1953): 181–89.

Schlesinger, Elizabeth Bancroft. "Fanny Fern: Our Grandmothers' Mentor." *New York Historical Society Quarterly* 38, no. 4(October 1954): 501–19.

Schlesinger, Elizabeth Bancroft. "The Nineteenth-Century Woman's Dilemma and Jennie June." *New York History* 42, no. 4 (1961): 365–79.

Schlesinger, Elizabeth Bancroft. "Proper Bostonians as Seen by Fanny Fern." *New England Quarterly* 27, no. 1 (1954): 97–102.

Schlesinger, Elizabeth Bancroft. "Review of Ray Billington, 'The Journal of Charlotte Forten.'" *New England Quarterly* 26, no. 3 (1953): 409–11.

Schlesinger, Elizabeth Bancroft. "Two Early Harvard Wives: Eliza Farrar and Eliza Follen." *New England Quarterly* 38, no. 2 (1965): 147–67.

Scott, Anne Firor. *Anecdotes of My Years as a LWV Staffer*. Alexandria, VA: Alexander Street Press, 2008. https://search.alexanderstreet.com/view/work/bibliographic_entity| bibliographic_details|2605122.

Scott, Anne Firor. "Making the Invisible Women Visible: An Essay Review." *Journal of Southern History* 38, no. 4 (1972): 629–38.

Scott, Anne Firor. "The 'New Woman' in the New South." *South Atlantic Quarterly* 61, no. 4 (1962): 473–83.

Scott, Anne Firor. "On Seeing and Not Seeing: A Case of Historical Invisibility." Presidential Address to the Organization of American Historians, April 5, 1984. *Journal of American History* 71, no. 1 (1984): 7–21.

Scott, Joan. "Feminism's History." *Journal of Women's History* 16, no. 2 (2004): 10–27.

Scott, Joan. "Gender: A Useful Category of Historical Analysis." *American Historical Review* 91, no. 5 (1986): 1053–75.

Shorter, Edward. Review of *Woman's Body, Woman's Right*, by Linda Gordon. *Journal of Social History* 11, no. 2 (Winter 1977): 269–74.

Sicherman, Barbara. "Review Essay: American History." *Signs* 1, no. 2 (1975): 461–85.

Smith, Bonnie. "Seeing Mary Beard." *Feminist Studies* 10, no. 3 (1984): 399–416.

Smith-Rosenberg, Carroll. "Female World of Love and Ritual: Relations between Nineteenth Century American Women." *Signs* 1, no. 1 (1975): 1–29.

Smith-Rosenberg, Carroll. "The New Woman and the New History." *Feminist Studies* 3, no. 1 (1975): 185–98.

Spiegel, Gabrielle. "History and Post-Modernism." *Past and Present* 135 (1992): 194–208.

Spillenger, Clyde, Carson E. Larson, and Sylvia A. Law. "Brief of 281 American Historians as Amici Curiae Supporting Appellees." *Public Historian* 12, no. 3 (1990): 57–75.

Stone, Lawrence. "History and Post-Modernism." *Past and Present* 131 (1991): 217–18.

Taylor, A. Elizabeth. "The Origin of the Woman Suffrage Movement in Georgia." *Georgia Historical Quarterly* 28 (1944): 63–80.

Taylor, A. Elizabeth. Review of *The Ideas of the Woman Suffrage Movement*, by Aileen Kraditor. *Journal of American History* 52, no. 4 (1966): 855–56.

Taylor, A. Elizabeth. Review of *Revolt against Chivalry*, by Jacquelyn Dowd Hall. *Journal of American History* 66, no. 4 (1980): 991–92.

Taylor, A. Elizabeth. Review of *The Right to Be People*, by Mildred Adams, and *The Puritan Ethic and Woman Suffrage*, by Alan P. Grimes. *Journal of Southern History* 34, no. 1 (1968): 153–54.

Taylor, A. Elizabeth. Review of *Susan B. Anthony: Rebel, Crusader, Humanitarian*, by Alma Lutz. *Mississippi Valley Historical Review* 46, no. 2 (1959): 322–24.

Taylor, A. Elizabeth. Review of *The Woman Citizen*, by J. Stanley Lemons. *Journal of Southern History* 39, no. 4 (1973): 620–21.

Taylor, A. Elizabeth. "The Woman Suffrage Movement in Florida." *Florida Historical Quarterly* 36 (1957): 42–60.

Taylor, A. Elizabeth. "The Woman Suffrage Movement in Mississippi, 1890–1920." *Journal of Mississippi History* 30, no. 1 (1968): 1–34.

Taylor, A. Elizabeth. "The Woman Suffrage Movement in Texas." *Journal of Southern History* 17, no. 2 (1951): 194–215.

Taylor, Ula. "The Historical Evolution of Black Feminist Theory and Praxis." *Journal of Black Studies* 29, no. 2 (1998): 234–53.

Tilly, Louise. "Gender, Women's History, and Social History." *Social Science History* 13, no. 4 (1989): 439–62.

Tyler-McGraw, Marie. "Parlor to Politics: Women and Reform, 1890–1925." *Journal of American History* 78, no. 1 (1991): 260–64.

Vogel, Lise. "Telling Tales: Historians of Our Own Lives." *Journal of Women's History* 2, no. 3 (1991): 89–101.

Wall, Bennett H. "The Southern Historical Association, 1935–1970: A Compilation of Officers and Other Data." *Journal of Southern History* 36, no. 3 (1970): 388–99.

Welter, Barbara. "The Cult of True Womanhood: 1820–1860." *American Quarterly* 18, no. 2 (1966): 151–74.

Welter, Barbara. "Review of *Notable American Women, 1607–1950: A Biographical Dictionary* by Edward T. James; Janet Wilson James; Paul S. Boyer." *William and Mary Quarterly*, 3rd ser., 30, no. 3 (1973): 518–22.

White, Deborah Gray. "'Matter Out of Place': *Ar'n't I a Woman?* Black Female Scholars and the Academy." *Journal of African American History* 92, no. 1 (2007): 5–14.

Young, Iris Marion. "Gender as Seriality: Thinking about Women as a Social Collective." *Signs* 19, no. 3 (1994): 713–38.

Young, Louise. "Women's Place in American Politics: The Historical Perspective." *Journal of Politics* 38, no. 3 (1976): 300–320.

Secondary Sources

Books, Articles, and Reviews

Acuña, Rodolfo. *The Making of Chicana/o Studies: In the Trenches of Academe*. New Brunswick, NJ: Rutgers University Press, 2011.

Alberti, Johanna. *Gender and the Historian*. Harlow, Eng.: Pearson Education, 2002.

Alexander, Michelle. *The New Jim Crow: Mass Incarceration in the Age of Color Blindness*. New York: New Press, 2010.

Apple, Michael, and Anita Oliver. "Becoming Right: Education and the Formation of

Conservative Movements." In *Sociology of Education: Emerging Perspectives*, edited by Carlos Torres and Theodore Mitchell. Albany: SUNY Press, 1998.

Appleby, Joyce, Lynn Hunt, and Margaret Jacobs. *Telling the Truth about History*. New York: W. W. Norton, 1994.

Bailey, Fred Arthur. "The Textbooks of the 'Lost Cause': Censorship and the Creation of Southern State Histories." *Georgia Historical Quarterly* 75, no. 3 (1991): 507–33.

Baker, Paula. "The Domestication of Politics: Women and American Political Society, 1780–1920." *American Historical Review* 89, no. 3 (1984): 620–47.

Baron, Ava. *Work Engendered: Toward a New History of American Labor*. Ithaca, NY: Cornell University Press, 1991.

Bell-Scott, Patricia. *The Firebrand and the First Lady: Portrait of a Friendship: Pauli Murray, Eleanor Roosevelt, and the Struggle for Social Justice*. New York: Vintage Books, 2017.

Bennett, Judith. *History Matters: Patriarchy and the Challenge of Feminism*. Philadelphia: University of Pennsylvania Press, 2006.

Berlin, Jean V. "Introduction to the Bison Book Edition." In *Women in the Civil War*, by Mary Elizabeth Massey. Lincoln: University of Nebraska Press, 1994.

Berube, Margery S., et al. *The American Heritage Dictionary, Second College Edition*. Boston: Houghton Mifflin, 1985.

Blain, Keisha N., and Kathryn Kish Sklar. *How Did the President's Commission on the Status of Women and Subsequent State and Local Commissions Address Issues Related to Race, 1963–1980?* Alexandria, VA: Alexander Street Press, 2010. https://search.alexanderstreet .com/view/work/bibliographic_entity|bibliographic_details|2613206.

Blee, Kathleen. "Women in the 1920s Ku Klux Klan Movement." *Feminist Studies* 17, no. 1 (1991): 57–77.

Blee, Kathleen. *Women of the Klan: Racism and Gender in the 1920s*. Berkeley: University of California Press, 1991.

Blee, Kathleen, and Sandra McGee Deutsch, eds. *Women of the Right: Comparisons and Interplay across Borders*. University Park: University of Pennsylvania Press, 2012.

Bloor, Geoffrey, and Patrick Dawson. "Understanding Professional Culture in Organizational Context." *Organization Studies* 15, no. 2 (1992): 275–95.

Bordin, Ruth. *Woman and Temperance: The Quest for Power and Liberty, 1873–1900*. Philadelphia: Temple University Press, 1981.

Breines, Winifred. *The Trouble between Us: An Uneasy History of White and Black Women in the Feminist Movement*. New York: Oxford University Press, 2006.

Broschart, Kay. "Research in the Service of Society: Women at the Institute for Research in Social Science." *American Sociologist* 33, no. 3 (2002): 92–106.

Brown, Kathleen M. *Good Wives, Nasty Wenches, and Anxious Patriarchs: Race, Gender, and Power in Colonial Virginia*. Chapel Hill: University of North Carolina Press, 1996.

Bullock, Paul. *Jerry Voorhis: The Idealist as Politician*. New York: Vantage Press, 1978.

Carroll, Berenice, Nupur Chaudhuri, Gerda Lerner, and Hilda Smith. *A History of the Coordinating Committee on Women in the Historical Profession–Conference Group on Women's History*. Brooklyn: CCWHP-CGWH, 1994.

Case, Sarah. "The Historical Ideology of Mildred Lewis Rutherford: A Confederate Historian's New South Creed." *Journal of Southern History* 68, no. 3 (2002): 599–628.

Chaudhuri, Nupur, Sherry J. Katz, and Mary Elizabeth Perry, eds. *Contesting Archives: Finding Women in the Archives*. Chicago: University of Illinois Press, 2010.

Cobble, Dorothy Sue. *Dishing It Out: Waitresses and Their Unions in the Twentieth Century*. Chicago: University of Illinois Press, 1991.

Cobble, Dorothy Sue. *For the Many: American Feminisms and the Global Fight for Democratic Equality*. Princeton, NJ: Princeton University Press, 2021.

Cobble, Dorothy Sue. *The Labor Feminist Origins of the U.S. Commissions on the Status of Women*. Alexandria, VA: Alexander Street Press, 2009. https://search.alexanderstreet .com/view/work/bibliographic_entity|bibliographic_details|2605189.

Cobble, Dorothy Sue. *The Other Women's Movement: Workplace Justice and Social Rights in Modern America*. Princeton, NJ: Princeton University Press, 2004.

Cobble, Dorothy Sue, ed. *The Sex of Class: Women Transforming American Labor*. Ithaca, NY: Cornell University Press, 2007.

Collier-Thomas, Bettye. "Towards Black Feminism: The Creation of the Bethune Museum-Archives." In *Women's Collections: Libraries, Archives, and Consciousness*, edited by Suzanne Hildenbrand. New York: Haworth Press, 1986.

Cott, Nancy. "Two Beards: Co-Authorship and Concept of Civilization." *American Quarterly* 42, no. 2 (1990): 274–300.

Crenshaw, Kimberlé Williams. "Demarginalizing the Intersection of Race and Sex: A Black Feminist Critique of Antidiscrimination Doctrine, Feminist Theory and Antiracist Politics." *University of Chicago Legal Forum*, no. 1 (1989): 139–67.

Crenshaw, Kimberlé Williams. "Mapping the Margins: Intersectionality, Identity Politics, and Violence against Women of Color." *Stanford Law Review* 43, no. 6 (1991): 1241–99.

Critchlow, Donald. *Phyllis Schlafly and Grassroots Conservatism: A Woman's Crusade*. Princeton, NJ: Princeton University Press, 2005.

Dagbovie, Pero Gaglo. "Black Women, Carter G. Woodson, and the Association for the Study of Negro Life and History, 1915–1950." *Journal of African American History* 88, no. 1 (2003): 21–41.

Dagbovie, Pero Gaglo. "Black Women Historians, from the Late 19th Century to the Dawning of the Civil Rights Movement." *Journal of African American History* 89, no. 3, (2004): 252.

Delap, Lucy. *Feminisms: A Global History*. Chicago: University of Chicago Press, 2020.

Delegard, Kirsten Marie. *Battling Miss Bolsheviki: The Origins of Female Conservativism in the United States*. Philadelphia: Pennsylvania University Press, 2012.

Des Jardins, Julie. *The Madame Curie Complex: The Hidden History of Women in Science*. New York: Feminist Press, 2010.

Des Jardins, Julie. *Women and the Historical Enterprise in America: Gender, Race, and the Politics of Memory, 1880–1945*. Chapel Hill: University of North Carolina Press, 2003.

Des Jardins, Julie. "Women's and Gender History." In *The Oxford History of Historical Writing: Historical Writing since 1945*. Vol. 5, edited by Axel Schneider and Daniel Woolf. London: Oxford University Press, 2011.

Dublin, Thomas. "Caroline Farrar Ware." In *American National Biography*. Vol. 22, edited by John A. Garraty and Mark C. Carnes. New York: Oxford University Press, 1999.

Echols, Alice. *Daring to Be Bad: Radical Feminism in America, 1969–1975*. Minneapolis: University of Minnesota Press, 1989.

Elkins, Stanley, Eric McKitrick, and Leo Weinstein, eds. *Men of Little Faith: Selected Writings of Cecilia Kenyon*. Boston: University of Massachusetts Press, 2002.

Enke, Finn. *Finding the Movement: Sexuality, Contested Space, and Feminist Activism*. Durham, NC: Duke University Press, 2007.

Erickson, Christine K. "'We Want No Teachers Who Say There Are Two Sides to Every Question': Conservative Women and Education in the 1930s." *History of Education Quarterly* 46, no. 4 (2006): 487–502.

Erman, Sam, and Nathan Perl-Rosenthal. "Historians' Amicus Briefs: Practice and Prospect." In *The Oxford Handbook of Legal History*, edited by Markus Dubber and Christopher Tomlin. Cambridge: Oxford University Press, 2021.

Evans, Richard J. *In Defense of History*. New York: W.W. Norton, 1990.

Ferguson Thomas, and Joel Rogers. *Right Turn: The Decline of the Democrats and the Future of American Politics*. New York: Hill and Wang, 1986.

Fitzpatrick, Ellen. "Caroline F. Ware and the Cultural Approach to History." *American Quarterly* 43, no. 2 (1991): 173–98.

Fitzpatrick, Ellen. Foreword to reprint of *Century of Struggle: The Woman's Rights Movement in the United States, Enlarged Edition*, by Eleanor Flexner. Cambridge, MA: Belknap Press of Harvard University Press, 1996.

Frederickson, Mary, and Joyce L. Kornbluh, eds. *Sisterhood and Solidarity: Workers' Education for Women, 1914–1984*. Philadelphia: Temple University Press, 1984.

Freeman, Jo. "The Search for Political Woman." JoFreeman.com. Accessed September 26, 2011. www.jofreeman.com/academicwomen/polwoman.htm.

Freidel, Frank. "Frederick Merk." *Proceedings of the Massachusetts Historical Society*, 3rd ser., 89 (1977): 181–83.

Gerlach, Luther P., and Virginia H. Hine. *People, Power, Change: Movements for Social Transformation*. Indianapolis: Bobbs-Merrill, 1970.

Gillespie, Michele, and Catherine Clinton, eds. *Taking Off the White Gloves: Southern Women and Women Historians*. Columbia: University of Missouri Press, 1998.

Gilmore, Glenda Elizabeth. "From Jim Crow to Jane Crow or, How Anne Scott and Pauli Murray Found Each Other." In *Writing Women's History: A Tribute to Anne Firor Scott*, edited by Elizabeth Anne Payne. Jackson: University Press of Mississippi, 2011.

Glazer, Penina Migdal, and Miriam Slater. *Unequal Colleagues: The Entrance of Women into the Professions, 1890–1940*. New Brunswick: Rutgers University Press, 1987.

Goggin, Jacqueline. "Challenging Sexual Discrimination in the Historical Profession: Women Historians and the American Historical Association, 1890-1940." *American Historical Review* 97, no. 3 (1992): 769–802.

Hague, Amy. "'Never . . . Another Season of Silence': Laying the Foundation of the Sophia Smith Collection, 1942–1965." In *Revealing Women's Life Stories: Papers from the Fiftieth Anniversary Celebration of the Sophia Smith Collection, September 1992*. Williamsburg, MA: Allethaire Press, 1995.

Hall, Jacquelyn Dowd, and Sandi E. Cooper. "Women's History Goes to Trial: EEOC v. Sears Roebuck and Company, Preface by the Board of Editors." *Signs* 11, no. 4 (1986): 751–79.

Handlin, Mary. "Memoirs: Barbara Miller Solomon." *Proceedings of the Massachusetts Historical Society*, 3rd ser., 104 (1992): 201–6.

Hardisty, Jean. *Mobilizing Resentment: Conservative Resurgence from the John Birch Society to the Promise Keepers*. Boston: Beacon Press, 1999.

Harrison, Cynthia. *On Account of Sex: The Politics of Women's Issues, 1945–1968*. Berkeley: University of California Press, 1988.

Harrison, Cynthia. *State Commissions and Economic Security for Women*. Alexandria, VA: Alexander Street Press, 2009.

Hartmann, Susan. *The Other Feminists: Activists in the Liberal Establishment*. New Haven, CT: Yale University Press, 1998.

Heath, Frederick M. "Mary Elizabeth Massey." In "The Three Women Presidents of the Southern Historical Association: Ella Lonn, Kathryn Abby Hanna, and Mary Elizabeth Massey." Edited by Carol Bleser. *Southern Studies* 20 (Summer 1981): 116–21.

Helton, Laura E. *Scattered and Fugitive Things: How Black Collectors Created Archives and Remade History*. New York: Columbia University Press, 2024.

Henry, Linda J. "Promoting Historical Consciousness: The Early Archives Committee of the National Council of Negro Women." *Signs* 7, no. 1 (1981): 251–59.

Higham, John. *History: The Development of Historical Studies in the United States*. Englewood Cliffs, NJ: Prentice-Hall, 1965.

Hildenbrand, Suzanne, ed. *Women's Collections: Libraries, Archives, and Consciousness*. New York: Haworth Press, 1986.

Hill, Anita Faye, and Emma Coleman Jordan, eds. *Race, Gender and Power in America: The Legacy of the Hill–Thomas Hearings*. New York: Oxford University Press, 1995.

Horowitz, Daniel. *Betty Friedan and the Making of the Feminine Mystique*. Amherst: University of Massachusetts Press, 1989.

Horowitz, Daniel. "Feminism, Women's History, and American Social Thought at Midcentury." In *American Capitalism: Social Thought and Political Economy in the Twentieth Century*, edited by Nelson Lichtenstein. Philadelphia: University of Pennsylvania Press, 2007.

Howe, Florence, ed. *The Politics of Women's Studies: Testimony from 30 Founding Mothers*. New York: Feminist Press, 2000.

Iggers, George. *Historiography in the Twentieth Century: From Scientific Objectivity to the Postmodern Challenge*. Middleton, CT: Wesleyan University Press, 1997.

Jenkins, Keith, ed. *The Postmodern History Reader*. New York: Routledge, 1997.

Johnson, Haynes. *Sleepwalking through History: America in the Reagan Years*. New York: Anchor Books, 1991.

Johnson, Joan Marie. "'Drill into Us . . . the Rebel Tradition': The Contest over Southern Identity in Black and White Women's Clubs, South Carolina, 1898–1930." *Journal of Southern History* 66, no. 3 (2000): 525–62.

Kennedy, Kathleen. *Disloyal Mothers and Scurrilous Citizens: Women and Subversion during World War I*. Bloomington: Indiana University Press, 1999.

Kirkendall, Richard, ed. *The Organization of American Historians and the Writing and Teaching of American History*. New York: Oxford University Press, 2011.

Klatch, Rebecca E. *Women of the New Right*. Philadelphia: Temple University Press, 1987.

Laats, Adam. *The Other School Reformers: Conservative Activism in American Education*. Cambridge, MA: Harvard University Press, 2015.

Laughlin, Kathleen. *How Did State Commissions on the Status of Women Overcome Historic Antagonisms between Equal Rights and Labor Feminists to Create a New Feminist Mainstream, 1963–1973?* Binghamton: State University of New York, 2005. https://search.alexanderstreet.com/view/work/bibliographic_entity|web_collection|2495532.

Laughlin, Kathleen. *Women's Work and Public Policy: A History of the Women's Bureau, U.S. Department of Labor, 1945–1965*. Boston: Northeastern University Press, 2000.

Laughlin, Kathleen, and Jacqueline Castledine, eds. *Breaking the Wave: Women, Their Organizations, and Feminism, 1945–1985*. New York: Routledge Press, 2011.

Levine, Susan. *Degrees of Equality: The AAUW and the Challenge of Twentieth Century Feminism*. Philadelphia: Temple University Press, 1995.

Liebman, Robert C., and Robert Wuthnow. *The New Christian Right: Mobilization and Legitimation*. New York: Aldine Publishing, 1983.

Malkiel, Nancy Weiss. *"Keep the Damned Women Out": The Struggle for Coeducation*. Princeton, NJ: Princeton University Press, 2016.

Mann, Arthur. *Yankee Reformers in the Urban Age*. Cambridge, MA: Harvard University Press, 1954.

Mayeri, Serena. *Reasoning from Race: Feminism, Law, and the Civil Rights Revolution*. Cambridge, MA: Harvard University Press, 2014.

McCluskey, Audrey Thomas. *A Forgotten Sisterhood: Pioneering Black Women Educators in the Jim Crow South*. New York: Rowman and Littlefield, 2014.

McGirr, Lisa. *Suburban Warriors: The Origins of the New American Right*. Princeton, NJ: Princeton University Press, 2001.

Meyerowitz, Joanne, ed. *Not June Cleaver: Women and Gender in Postwar America, 1945–1960*. Philadelphia: Temple University Press, 1994.

Milkman, Ruth. "Women's History and the Sears Case." *Feminist Studies* 12, no. 2 (1986): 375–95.

Mjagkij, Nina, ed. *Organizing Black America: An Encyclopedia of African American Associations*. New York: Routledge, 2001.

Mohr, James. *Abortion in America: The Origins and Evolution of National Policy, 1800–1900*. New York: Oxford University Press, 1978.

Moon, Danelle, and Kathryn Kish Sklar. *How Did Florence Kitchelt Bring Together Social Feminists and Equal Rights Feminists to Reconfigure the Campaign for the ERA in the 1940s and 50s?* Alexandria, VA: Alexander Street, 2010. https://search.alexanderstreet.com/view/work/bibliographic_entity|web_collection|2499186.

Morris, Aldon D., and Carol McClurg Mueller, eds. *Frontiers in Social Movement Theory*. New Haven, CT: Yale University Press, 1992.

Murphy, Teresa Ann. *Citizenship and the Origins of Women's History in the United States*. Philadelphia: University of Pennsylvania Press, 2013.

Newman, Michelle. *White Women's Rights: The Racial Origins of Feminism in the United States*. New York: Oxford University Press, 1999.

Nickerson, Michelle. "Moral Mothers and Goldwater Girls: Women and Grassroots Conservatism in the American Sunbelt." In *The Conservative Sixties*, edited by David Farber and Jeff Roche. New York: Peter Lang, 2003.

Nielsen, Kim. *Un-American Womanhood: Antiradicalism, Antifeminism, and the First Red Scare*. Columbus: Ohio State University Press, 2001.

Novick, Peter. *That Noble Dream: The "Objectivity Question" and the American Historical Profession*. New York: Cambridge University Press, 1988.

Palmer, William. *Engagement with the Past: The Lives and Works of the World War II Generation of Historians*. Lexington: University Press of Kentucky, 2001.

Palmer, William. *From Gentleman's Club to Professional Body: The Evolution of the History Department in the United States, 1940–1980*. Charleston, SC: Book Surge Publishing, 2008.

Paulson, Ross Evans. *Women's Suffrage and Prohibition: A Comparative Study of Equality and Social Control*. Glenview, IL: Scott, Foresman and Company, 1973.

Potter, Claire. "The Female Academic's World of Love and Ritual: Women's History and Radical Feminism." OutHistory.com, June 4, 2015. https://outhistory.org/blog/the-female -academics-world-of-love-and-ritual-womens-history-and-radical-feminism/.

Preyer, Kathryn. "Janet Wilson James." *Proceedings of the Massachusetts Historical Society*, 3rd ser., 99 (1987): 174–77.

Rampolla, Mary Lynn. *A Pocket Guide to Writing History*. Boston: Bedford/St. Martin's, 1998.

Relph, Anne Kimbell. "The World Center for Women's Archives, 1935–1940." *Signs* 4, no. 3 (1979): 597–603.

Robnett, Belinda. *How Long? How Long? African American Women in the Struggle for Civil Rights*. New York: Oxford University Press, 1997.

Rodman, Paul. "Frederick Merk, Teacher and Scholar: A Tribute." *Western Historical Quarterly* 9, no. 2 (1978): 141–48.

Rosenberg, Rosalind. *Beyond Separate Spheres: Intellectual Roots of Modern Feminism*. New Haven, CT: Yale University Press, 1982.

Rosenberg, Rosalind. *Changing the Subject: How the Women of Columbia Shaped the Way We Think about Sex and Politics*. New York: Columbia University Press, 2004.

Rosenberg, Rosalind. *Jane Crow: The Life of Pauli Murray*. New York: Oxford University Press, 2020.

Rossi, Alice, and Anne Calderwood, eds. *Academic Women on the Move*. New York: Russell Sage Foundation, 1974.

Rossiter, Margaret. *Women Scientists in America: Before Affirmative Action, 1940–1971*. Baltimore: Johns Hopkins University Press, 1995.

Rossiter, Margaret. *Women Scientists in America: Struggles and Strategies to 1940*. Baltimore: Johns Hopkins University Press, 1982.

Roth, Benita, and Marian Horan. Introduction to *What Are Social Movements and What Is Gendered about Women's Participation in Social Movements? A Sociological Perspective*." Binghamton: State University of New York, 2001. https://documents.alexanderstreet.com /c/1000636376.

Savage, Barbara. *Merze Tate: The Global Odyssey of a Black Woman Scholar*. New Haven, CT: Yale University Press, 2023.

Scanlon, Jennifer, and Sharon Cosner. *American Women Historians, 1700s–1990s: A Biographical Dictionary*. Westport, CT: Greenwood Press, 1996.

Schlesinger, Arthur M., Jr. "In Memoriam: Edward T. James." *Perspectives on History*, October 2001. www.historians.org/perspectives/issues/2001/0110/0110inm2.cfm.

Schrecker, Ellen W. *No Ivory Tower: McCarthyism and the Universities*. New York: Oxford University Press, 1986.

Scott, Anne Firor, ed. *Pauli Murray and Caroline Ware: Forty Years of Letters in Black and White*. Chapel Hill: University of North Carolina Press, 2006.

Scott, Anne Firor, ed. *Unheard Voices: The First Historians of Southern Women*. Charlottesville: University of Virginia Press, 1993.

Shapiro, Edward. "The Southern Agrarians: H. L. Mencken and the Quest for Southern Identity." *American Studies* 13, no. 2 (1972): 75–92.

Sklar, Kathryn Kish, Christopher Capozzola, Liette Gidlow, Melanie Gustafson, Annelise Orleck, Kim Cary Warren, and Mason Williams. "'The Long Progressive Era':

A Roundtable on *After the Vote: Feminist Politics in La Guardia's New York* by Elisabeth Israels Perry." *Journal of the Gilded Age and Progressive Era* 20, no. 3 (2021): 430–60.

Smith, Bonnie G. *The Gender of History: Men, Women and Historical Practice.* Cambridge, MA: Harvard University Press, 1998.

Smitherman, Geneva, ed. *African American Women Speak Out on Anita Hill–Clarence Thomas.* Detroit: Wayne State University Press, 1995.

Sneider, Allison. *Suffragists in an Imperial Age: U.S. Expansion and the Woman Question, 1870–1920.* New York: Oxford University Press, 2008.

Snyder, Jeffrey Aaron. *Making Black History: The Color Line, Culture, and Race in the Age of Jim Crow.* Atlanta: University of Georgia Press, 2018.

Spruill, Marjorie J. *The Conservative Challenge to Feminist Influence on State Commissions on the Status of Women.* Alexandria, VA: Alexander Street Press, 2009. https://search .alexanderstreet.com/view/work/bibliographic_entity|bibliographic_details|2605192.

Spruill, Marjorie J. *Divided We Stand: The Battle over Women's Rights and Family Values That Polarized America.* New York: Bloomsbury, 2017.

Storrs, Landon R. Y. "Attacking the Washington 'Femmocracy': Antifeminism in the Cold War Campaign against 'Communists in Government.'" *Feminist Studies* 33, no. 1 (2007): 118–52.

Storrs, Landon R. Y. *Civilizing Capitalism: The National Consumers' League, Women's Activism and Labor Standards in the New Deal Era.* Chapel Hill: University of North Carolina Press, 2000.

Storey, William Kelleher. *Writing History: A Guide for Students.* New York: Oxford University Press, 1996.

Sumler-Edmond, Janice. "Association of Black Women Historians, Inc." In *Black Women in America: An Historical Encyclopedia*, edited by Darlene Clark Hine, Rosalyn Terborg-Penn, and Elsa Barkley Brown. Bloomington: Indiana University Press, 1994.

Tetrault, Lisa. *The Myth of Seneca Falls: Memory and the Women's Suffrage Movement, 1848–1898.* Chapel Hill: University of North Carolina Press, 2014.

Tharp, Louise Hall. *Until Victory: Horace Mann and Mary Peabody.* Boston: Little Brown, 1953.

Thuesen, Sarah Caroline. "Making Southern History: Guion Griffis Johnson's Ante-Bellum North Carolina." Available online at Documenting the American South, accessed February 2, 2010. http://docsouth.unc.edu/nc/johnson/support1.html.

Thuesen, Sarah Caroline. "Taking the Vows of Southern Liberalism: Guion and Guy Johnson and the Evolution of an Intellectual Partnership." *North Carolina Historical Review* 74, no. 3 (1997): 284–324.

Tomás, Jennifer. "Better Homes, Better Schools, Better Churches, and a Better Country: The International Council of Women of the Darker Races." Alexandria, VA: Alexander Street, 2012. https://search-alexanderstreet-com.ezpvcc.vccs.edu/view/work /bibliographic_entity|bibliographic_details|2476953.

Tom[á]s, Jennifer. "Flexner, Eleanor (04 October 1908–25 March 1995)." *American National Biography.* April 1, 2015. www.anb.org/view/10.1093/anb/9780198606697.001.0001/anb -9780198606697-e-1401184.

Tomás, Jennifer. *Introduction: The Women's History Movement as Viewed through the "Living U.S. Women's History Oral History Project."* Alexandria, VA: Alexander Street,

2019. https://search.alexanderstreet.com/view/work/bibliographic_entity|bibliographic
_details|4037308.

Townsend, Robert B. *History's Babel: Scholarship, Professionalization, and the Historical
Enterprise in the United States, 1880–1940*. Chicago: University of Chicago Press, 2013.

Turbin, Carole. *Working Women of Collar City: Gender, Class, and Community in Troy,
1864–1886*. Champaign: University of Illinois Press, 1994.

Twelve Southerners. *I'll Take My Stand: The South and the Agrarian Traditions*. New York:
Harper and Brothers, 1930.

Ulrich, Laurel Thatcher. *Well-Behaved Women Seldom Make History*. New York: Alfred A.
Knopf, 2007.

Ulrich, Laurel Thatcher, ed. *Yards and Gates: Gender in Harvard and Radcliffe History*. New
York: Palgrave Macmillan, 2004.

Ware, Susan. "Barbara Miller Solomon, 1919–1992." *The Jewish Women's Archive: Jewish
Women; A Comprehensive Historical Encyclopedia*. Accessed January 13, 2011. http://jwa
.org/encyclopedia/article/solomon-barbara-miller.

Ware, Susan. *Beyond Suffrage: Women and the New Deal*. Cambridge, MA: Harvard
University Press, 1981.

Ware, Susan. *Why They Marched: Untold Stories of the Women Who Fought for the Right to
Vote*. Cambridge, MA: Belknap Press of Harvard University Press, 2020.

Weigand, Kate. *Red Feminism: American Communism and the Making of Women's
Liberation*. Baltimore: Johns Hopkins University Press, 2001.

Wheeler, Marjorie Spruill. *New Women of the New South: The Leaders of the Woman
Suffrage Movement in the Southern States*. New York: Oxford University Press, 1993.

Wheeler, Marjorie Spruill, ed. *One Woman, One Vote: Rediscovering the Woman Suffrage
Movement*. Troutdale, OR: New Sage Press, 1995.

Wieringa, Saskia E., ed. *Traveling Heritages: New Perspectives on Collecting, Preserving and
Sharing Women's History*. Amsterdam: Aksant Academic Publishers, 2008.

Ziegler, Mary, Rickie Solinger, and Karissa Haugeberg. *On the Threshold of a Post-Roe Era?
The Past and Future of Abortion Rights in the United States*. Edited by Rebecca Jo Plant.
Alexandria, VA: Alexander Street Press, 2022. https://search.alexanderstreet.com/view
/work/bibliographic_entity%7Cbibliographic_details%7C5233362.

Zinsser, Judith P. *History and Feminism: A Glass Half Full*. New York: Twayne, 1993.

Major Undergraduate Teaching Texts in US Women's History

Baxandall, Rosalyn, and Linda Gordon, eds. *Dear Sisters: Dispatches from the Women's
Liberation Movement*. New York: Basic Books, 2000.

Baxandall, Rosalyn, Linda Gordon, eds., with Susan Reverby. *America's Working Women:
A Documentary History, 1600 to the Present*. New York: Vintage Books, 1976.

Berkin, Carol, and Mary Beth Norton. *Women of America: A History*. Boston: Houghton
Mifflin, 1979.

Burton, Antoinette. *Gender History: A Very Short Introduction*. New York: Oxford
University Press, 2024.

Cott, Nancy F., ed. *No Small Courage: A History of Women in the United States*. New York:
Oxford University Press, 2000.

Cott, Nancy F., and Elizabeth H. Pleck, eds. *A Heritage of Her Own: Toward a New Social History of American Women*. New York: Touchstone/Simon and Schuster, 1979.

DuBois, Ellen Carol, and Lynn Dumenil. *Through Women's Eyes: American History with Documents*. Boston: Bedford/St. Martin's, 2009; 5th ed., 2019.

Evans, Sara M. *Born for Liberty: A History of Women in America*. New York: Free Press, 1989.

Hine, Darlene Clark, and Kathleen Thompson. *A Shining Thread of Hope: The History of Black Women in America*. New York: Broadway Books, 1998.

Kerber, Linda, and Jane De Hart Mathews. *Women's America: Refocusing the Past*. New York: Oxford University Press, 1982.

Kerber, Linda, Jane Sherron De Hart, Cornelia Hughes-Dayton, and Judy Tzu-Chun Wu. *Women's America: Refocusing the Past*. 8th ed. New York: Oxford University Press, 2016.

Lerner, Gerda. *The Female Experience: An American Documentary*. Indianapolis: Bobbs-Merrill, 1977.

Norton, Mary Beth, and Ruth M. Alexander, eds. *Major Problems in American Women's History*. Lexington, MA: D. C. Heath and Company, 1989.

Norton, Mary Beth, and Ruth M. Alexander, eds. *Major Problems in American Women's History*. Boston, MA: Cengage Learning, 2013.

Ruiz, Vicki L., and Ellen Carol DuBois, eds. *Unequal Sisters: A Multicultural Reader in U.S. Women's History*. 1st ed. New York: Routledge, 1990.

Ruiz, Vicki L., and Ellen Carol DuBois, eds. *Unequal Sisters: A Multicultural Reader in U.S. Women's History*. 4th ed. New York: Routledge, 2007.

Ryan, Mary P. *Womanhood in America from Colonial Times to the Present*. 2nd ed. New York: New Viewpoints, 1975.

Tone, Andrea. *Controlling Reproduction: An American History*. Wilmington: Scholarly Resources Books, 1997.

Ware, Susan. *American Women's History: A Very Short Introduction*. New York: Oxford University Press, 2015.

Index

Chicago Women's Liberation Union, 253, 255

Chicana history, 124, 233–34, 273, 277, 301, 304

Civil Rights Act of 1964, 24, 251, 307, 33

Civil War Centennial Commission, 77–78

Clarke, John Henrik, 306

Clinton, Hillary, 295, 339, 410n58, 418n34, 424n133

Cobble, Dorothy Sue, 152, 154, 312

Cole, Johnetta, 340

Collier-Thomas, Bettye, 87, 235, 270, 308, 320

Columbia Council for Research in the Social Sciences, 50, 68

Comstock, Ada, 89, 93, 101–2, 104, 109–10

Congress of American Women, 26, 134, 163, 352n15

Connor, R. D. W., 60, 62, 66

consensus school, 43, 81, 261, 328, 332

conservatism: and attacks on feminism, 325, 332, 407n10; and attacks on the Institute for Research in Social Science, 66, 69; and attacks on work of historians, 284–85, 291–93, 296, 302–3, 312, 328, 407n10, 416n7; and consensus history, 43; courts and, 147, 302, 335–36, 338–39; of New York State Woman Suffrage Party, 144; 1950s and, 157; 1970s and, 301; 1980s and, 328; 1990s and, 284, 291, 302, 328; and opposition to ERA, 147, 329; and opposition to reproductive rights, 331–32; and public history, 314–16; and redbaiting, 162; of Clarence Thomas, 334–36; at Vanderbilt, 70; and World Center for Women's Archives board, 87

Cook, Blanche Wiesen: and conference on New Deal History, 317; and First Berkshire Conference on the History of Women, 226–27, 389n90; networks of, 193, 204, 253; at 1974 SUNY Binghamton labor conference, 260; and OAH, 215; peace activism of, 253; publications of, 268

Cooper, Anna Julia, 5, 218

Cooper, Sandi: and AHA, 193, 206; and Berkshire Conference of Women

Historians, 204, 221, 225, 236; career of, 393n5; and ERA, 262; networks of, 204, 253, 389n90; and Willie Lee Rose, 189, 198; and SHA, 32, 195; and need to balance Big Berks program content, 236

Coordinating Committee on Women in the Historical Profession (CCWHP): and AHA, 193–95, 206–7, 238, 330, 334; and *AHA Directory of Women Historians*, 244; and Berkshire Conferences on the History of Women, 225–26, 229; and CCWHP-CGWH, 237–38; co-chairs of, 189, 192; and ERA support, 330; focus of, 192, 194, 206; founding of, 189, 192, 205, 223–24; international reach of, 239; and Joan Kelly Memorial Prize, 286; and Money in Friendly Territory, 329; and the OAH, 194, 196, 201–2, 208, 238; publications of, 196, 239–40, 251; and *Sears* case, 333–34; and SHA, 32, 79, 203; and generational tensions, 189; and Clarence Thomas, 334–35

Coordinating Committee on Women in the Historical Profession—Conference Group on Women's History (CCWHP-CGWH): and AHA, 238–39; and *Bibliography of Women's History*, 240, 288; founding of, 237–39, 243; focuses on women's history, 222, 245, 250; international reach of, 239; newsletter of, 239–40, 250, 324, 330; and OAH, 238; and regional groups, 240–41; research bulletins of, 250, 288. *See also* Coordinating Council of Women in History

Coordinating Council of Women in History, 310

Cott, Nancy, *182*; career of, 256–57; and First Berkshire Conference on the History of Women, 227; mentored by Janet W. James, 119; and *Lawrence v. Texas*, 338–39; publications of, 256, 258, 352n11; and Wingspread Conference, 277, 343; and women's historiography, 44, 166, 257, 351n3

craft traditions of historians, 4, 8, 10, 12–13, 18, 28, 35, 279

Crenshaw, Kimberlé, 4, 164, 308, 311
Cross, Barbara, 26, 132–33
Cross, Robert, 131–32, 207, 369n87
"Cult of True Womanhood" (Welter article), 298, 304
Curti, Merle, xiii, 14, 93, 120–21, 367n45, 374n36

Dagbovie, Pero, 45, 81, 123, 272, 328n26
Dalby, Louise, 206, 215, 225, 227, 229
Daniel St. Clair, Sadie, 45, 122–23, 142, 413n109
Davis, Angela, 305, 308
Davis, Mollie Camp: and AHA, 206; and Caucus of Women in History (SHA), 202–3; and CCWHP, 195–96, 205; and CCWHP-CGWH, 238; and women's history, 204; networks of, 193, 204; and Anne Firor Scott, 189; and SHA, 79, 195; and Southern Association for Women Historians, 195
Davis, Natalie Zemon: awarded National Humanities Medal, 287; education of, 102–3; networks of, 193; at 1975 AHA meeting, 239; presents at Second Berkshire Conference on the History of Women, 230–31; as president of AHA, 286, 398n88; speaks at White House, 342; and European women's historiography, 231–32
Degler, Carl: Gerda Lerner and, 135, 419n46; and Manual for Women (and Other) Historians, 206, 350n51, 393n9; and Notable American Women, 116; origin of interest in women's history, 163–64; and Restoring Women to History project, 267; Anne Firor Scott and, 55, 419n46; and Sears case, 261; teaching career of, 164; and women's historiography, 31; women's history publications of, 30, 322; and Women's History Sources, 242
De Hart, Jane Sherron: and AHA Committee on the Status of Women, 205–6; and Berkshire Conference of Women Historians, 225, 389n90; and Berkshire Conference on the History of Women, 237;

career of, 204–5, 389n89; and CCWHP, 193, 205; and Mollie Davis, 204–5; and Guion Griffis Johnson, 158–59; and Manual for Women (and Other) Historians, 350n51, 389n97; presents at AHA, 330; and Wingspread Conference, 343
Des Jardins, Julie: on emergence of gender history, 404–5n91; on women archivists, 81, 103, 375n51; on women historians, 10–12, 356n27, 368n70; on women in science, 9, 248n20
Dexter, Elisabeth Anthony, 169; background of, 150; dissertation of, 5; education of, 47, 150; and Notable American Women, 125; and objectivity, 48; work for OSS, 150; publications of, 47, 150–51; and Radcliffe Women's Archives, 47, 111, 117; and Radcliffe Seminar on Women, 107–9, 111; teaching career of, 47, 81; and women's historiography, 30, 230
Dictionary of American Biography, 117–19, 122
Dillon, Mary Earhart, 52, 102, 143, 161, 230, 367n47
Drinker, Sophie Hutchinson, 122, 356n24
Dublin, Thomas, 182, 183; career of, 278–79, 312; publications of, 322; and UCLA Teaching U.S. Women's History Workshops, 275–76; and Wingspread Conference, 277; and Women and Social Movements website, 278–79, 406–7n132
DuBois, Ellen, 182; and AHA, 193; and Berkshire Conferences on the History of Women, 229, 247, 278; coedits Unequal Sisters, 278, 288; early career of, 256, 402n37; politics of, 254–55; mentored by Gerda Lerner and Anne Firor Scott, 216–18; and National Museum of Women's History, 319; and OAH, 215; and OAH-CSW, 209; publications of, 218, 256, 354n53, 379n10; and Wingspread Conference, 343
Dunn, Mary Maples, 177; and Berkshire Conferences on the History of Women, 131, 204, 225, 228–29, 232; and focus of early women's history, 230, 232; as mentor

229; career of, 402n37; education of, 254, 395n35; on politics and history, 247, 251, 308, 331; networks of, 254, 256; presents at AHA, 201–2; publications, 258, 331; at Wingspread Conference, 343

Governor's Commission on the Status of Women in North Carolina, 154, 157, 161–62

Graham, Patricia Aljberg, 193, 201, 227, 386n29

Gray, Virginia Gearhart, 5, 60–62, 68, 81

Greathouse, Rebekah S., 147–48

Green, Fletcher: career of, 63; and Historical Society of North Carolina, 61, 66; and Guion Griffis Johnson, 66–68, 75; and Mary Massey, 69–71, 75, 77; and Anne Firor Scott, 54, 137, 359n69; supports some women's historians, 102; and A. Elizabeth Taylor, 69–71, 75

Greenwald, Maurine, 182, 227, 312, 343

Grierson, Margaret Storrs, 174; and Mary Beard, 89, 91–92, 97, 103; and Elisabeth Anthony Dexter, 47; and Radcliffe Seminars on Women, 108; and Radcliffe Women's Archives, 92–97; and Sophia Smith Collection, 47, 89–92, 98, 100, 103, 108, 174

Gutman, Herbert, 116, 260, 262, 305

Hall, Jacquelyn Dowd, 177, 182; awarded National Humanities Medal, 287; background of, 274; and Guion Griffis Johnson, 158–59; networks of, 132; publications of, 210, 274; serves as OAH president, 398n88; supports Deborah Gray White, 218, 307; and Wingspread Conference, 343; on Anita Hill, 422n106

Handlin, Oscar: and Anne Firor Scott, 3, 28, 46, 53–55, 137, 161, 359n69, 369n88; and Barbara M. Solomon, 3, 101–2, 109, 358n62; supports women's history course at Barnard, 132

Harley, Sharon, 182; and Association of Black Women Historians, 244; and Black Women's History Project, 270; and civil rights movement, 307; research focus of,

252; and Wingspread Conference, 343; and women's history curriculum development, 265, 267

Harris, LaDonna, 340–41

Hartman, Mary, 224–26, 228

Hazzard, Florence Woolsey, 124, 258, 356n24

Height, Dorothy, 152

Helly, Dorothy, 236, 400n24

Hewitt, Nancy, 182; career of, 210; on state of women's history, 283; on Clarence Thomas nomination, 334–35; publications of, 210, 288; and Anne Firor Scott, 210–11; supports Deborah Gray White, 218; writings about difference, 289, 311, 351n4

Higginbotham, Evelyn Brooks, 124, 182, 230, 287, 304, 343

Higham, John, xiii, 14, 121, 374n37

Hill, Anita, 334, 336

Hinckley, Georgiana, 93, 101, 104–6

Hinding, Andrea, 209, 241, 261–63, 319. See also *Women's History Sources*

Hine, Darlene Clark: and Association of Black Women Historians, 244; awarded National Humanities Medal, 287; and Berkshire Conferences on the History of Women, 228; and Black Women in the Middle West project, 273; chairs SHA program committee, 218, 273; and FIPSE grant to develop Black women's history, 269–72; Gerda Lerner and, 244, 269–72; as mentor, 211, 218, 272; OAH establishes Darlene Clark Hine prize, 286; publications of, 211, 218, 273, 309, 405n95; serves as OAH president, 398n88

Historical Society of North Carolina, 61, 66, 158

history in politics: battle over National History Standards, 284–85, 292, 293, 327, 420n77 ; confederate monuments, xi, 7; conservative history as indoctrination, 254; and culture wars, xii, 7, 17, 283–84, 291, 315, 416n151, 420n77; filiopietistic societies efforts to control K–12 history curriculum, 7, 11, 78, 162; historians as

Jordan, Wilbur Kitchener: appoints Elizabeth Borden director of Radcliffe Women's Archives, 106; and establishment of Radcliffe Women's Archives, 89, 101–3, 105, 402n46; and *Notable American Women*, 116–17, 119–21, 373n10; and scope of Woman's Rights Collection, 106; and women's historiography, 96, 258

Journal of Women's History (JWH), 209, 289–90, 293–300, 325

K–12 curriculum: and Black women's history, 12, 44; and culture wars, 284–85, 292–93, 328; National Women's History Project and, 323; and public history, 316; women's absence from before 1970s, 7; and women's history, 241–42, 247, 285, 293, 327

Kellogg, Louise Phelps, 27, 286, 352n24

Kelly, Joan: chairs AHA Committee on Women Historians, 238–39; cofounds first MA program in women's history, 27, 208, 251; and "Did Women Have a Renaissance?," 207; and Fourth Berkshire Conference on the History of Women, 268; impact of on women's history, 268–69, 398n95; and *Manual for Women (and Other) Historians*, 350n51, 393n9; networks of, 132, 193; and *Radical America*, 214. *See also* Joan Kelly Memorial Prize

Kelly-Gadol, Joan. *See* Kelly, Joan

Kerber, Linda, *182*, *183*; and AHA Committee on Women Historians, 205; and Berkshire Conference of Women Historians, 204, 225; and CCWHP, 192–93, 196, 240, 250; education of, 121, 133, 385n19; and *Notable American Women*, 198; and *Obergefell v. Hodges*, 339; publications of, 209; serves as OAH president, 398n88; and Wingspread Conference, 277, 343; on women's history pioneers, 132, 219

Kerr, Louise Año Nuevo, 309, 343

Kessler-Harris, Alice, *182*, feminism of, 252; network of, 253; publications of, 213, 260,

268–69, 312; and *Sears* case, 261, 333–34, 343; serves as OAH president, 398n88; and Summer Institute in Women's History for Leaders of National Women's Organizations, 330; and women's historiography, 31, 351n3; work criticized by male historians, 31, 225–26, 260

Kidwell, Clara Sue, 309

King, Deborah, 340

King, Doris, 71, 79, 189, 259

Kohlstedt, Sally Gregory, *182*, 229, 343, 418n33

Koonz, Claudia, 221, 225, 229

Kraditor, Aileen: background of, 163; education of, 163, 369n88, 374n37; politics of, 163; networks of, 132, 198, 217; publications of, 26; and women's historiography, 28, 30, 127–28, 354–55n58

Lane, Ann J., 132, 225–26, 228

Lane, Barbara Miller, 298

Lasch, Christopher, 193, 255, 386n27

Latimer, Catharine, 142

Laughlin, Kathleen, 159, 382n67

League of Women Voters: Elisabeth Anthony Dexter and, 150; Guion Griffis Johnson and, 154–55; Maud Wood Park and, 89, 93; Radcliffe Women's Archive and, 102, 143; Elizabeth Schlesinger and, 145; Anne Firor Scott and, 28, 53, 161–62; Caroline Ware and, 152

Lebsock, Suzanne, 44, 206, 210, 343

Lerner, Gerda, *182*, *183*; and AHA, 207; background, 25–26; and Berkshire Conference of Women Historians, 227, 230; and Black women's history, 244, 269–72, 304–6; and CCWHP, 191–96; cofounds first MA program in women's history, 208, 251, 255; and Congress of American Women, 163; early career of, 28, 41, 134–36, 322, 369n88; and exchange with David Donald, 199–200; and impact of women's history, 323; as mentor of younger women, 201, 210, 213–18, 273, 404n90; and *Notable American Women*,

women's history curriculum development, 341

National Archives for Black Women's History: creation of, 86, 88; hosts conferences, 235, 271; mentioned, 15, 30, 320

National Association for the Advancement of Colored People (NAACP), 146, 334, 337

National College Equal Suffrage League, 143

National Coordinating Committee for the Promotion of History (NCCPH): focus of, 324–25; founding of, 316, 324; Page Putnam Miller and, 325, 327; renaming of, 417n8; Women Historians of the Midwest and, 242; women's history and, 327

National Council of Negro Women (NCNW): and Black Women in the Midwest project, 272; and Black women's history archives, 30, 83, 86–88; and civil rights movement, 88; and curriculum development, 88; Dorothy Height and, 152; and Mary McLeod Bethune Historical Development Project, 235, 270; Dorothy Porter and, 87; and Summer Institute in Women's History for Leaders of National Women's Organizations, 330; Sue Bailey Thurman and, 87–88; Caroline Ware and, 152

National Endowment for the Humanities (NEH): and attacks from New Right, 316, 324–25, 327–28; Lynne Cheney and, 328; funds AHA teaching pamphlet on women's history, 207; funds "Black Women in Historical Perspective" conference, 235; funds "Black Women in the Middle West," 272; funds Restoring Women to History project, 264; funds survey of women's history journal articles, 290; funds Wingspread Conference, 182, 276, 343; funds Women and Social Movements website, 279; funds Women's Historians of the Midwest conference, 242; funds women's history oral history project, 354n58; funds *Women's History Sources*, 209, 242, 262–63; funds Workshop on Teaching Women's History, 275,

401n5; Page Putnam Miller and, 325; and National History Standards, 292

National Museum of American History (NMAH), 314, 317–18, 329. *See also* Edith Mayo

National Park Service (NPS), 243, 316, 319–22, 325–27, 329, 366n23

National Woman's Party: alienates progressive women, 166; archives of, 100, 104, 143; Mary Beard and, 84, 144, 149; equal rights feminism of, 144, 156–57; Miriam Y. Holden and, 146; Alma Lutz and, 100–101, 143, 146–49; opposition to protective labor legislation, 148; Elizabeth B. Schlesinger and, 145

National Women's History Project, 323–24, 330, 340

Native American women's history: and *Bibliography of Women's History*, 288; and centennial commemorations of ratification of Nineteenth Amendment, 309; development of, 273; and First Berkshire Conference on the History of Women, 226; and *Journal of Women's History*, 294, 299–300; *Notable American Women* and, 124; and President's Commission on the Celebration of Women in American History, 340; and Seventh Berkshire Conference on the History of Women, 246; and *Unequal Sisters*, 288; and Wingspread Conference, 278

Nevins, Allan, 76–77

New Deal, 50, 142, 151–52, 158, 317, 324

New England Association of Women Historians, 222, 227, 240

New Left: conservative backlash against, 328; and development of women's history, 24, 193, 214, 246, 252–55, 274, 279, 322, 332; and midcentury women's historians, 163; misogyny of, 193, 253, 255; and new social history, 301

new social history, 12, 43, 230, 315, 328, 332

New York Metropolitan Area Group, 202, 206, 222, 240, 253

New York State Woman Suffrage Party, 143–44

Conference on the History of Women, 230; and Third Berkshire Conference on the History of Women, 247, 267

Porter, Dorothy, *180*; and Black women's history, 234; and Black women's history archives, 86–87; and Howard University Negro Collection, 125; and Moorland-Spingarn Research Center, 87, 142; and *Notable American Women*, 122–23, 125, 376n57, 376n61; and Rosalyn Terborg-Penn, 306

Postmodern threat, 14, 291–93, 296, 312, 409n38

Potter, David, 31, 116, 191, 197–98

Prelinger, Catherine, *177*, 229, 234–36

President's Commission on the Celebration of Women in American History (Clinton White House), 340, 342

President's Commission on the Status of Women (PCSW): findings of, 24; goals of, 191; liberal feminists and, 251; impact of, 191; Pauli Murray and, 50; origin of, 20, 190; Esther Peterson and, 161, 317; Eleanor Roosevelt and, 317; Anne Firor Scott and, 161; Caroline Ware and, 50, 15, 152–53, 162. *See also* Governor's Commission on the Status of Women in North Carolina; Massachusetts Commission on the Status of Women; Sonoma County Commission on the Status of Women

Progressive Era: Mary Beard's publications during, 144; *From Parlor to Politics* exhibit and, 317; Florence Kelley and, 151; and objectivist history, 42; historians study, 159, 166, 275

progressive feminism: conservative backlash against, 325; and early twentieth-century women's historians, 165; Guion Johnson and, 155, 157, 159; Pauli Murray and, 317; National Woman's Party and, 166; Esther Peterson and, 317; and PCSW, 190–91; Caroline Ware and, 159

progressive history: Charles Beard and, 84–85, 134; Mary Beard and, 85, 143–44; and development of women's history, 16, 42–43, 46, 60, 81, 89, 126; Elisabeth Anthony

Dexter and, 48, 150; New Right backlash against, 316; Arthur Schlesinger Sr. and, 9, 89; Caroline Ware and, 51

Quarles, Benjamin, 123, 306

Radcliffe Women's Archives: Elizabeth Borden and, 106–8; Elisabeth A. Dexter and, 47, 117, 150; early years of, 94–95, 101–2; founding of, 145, 374n36; Margaret S. Grierson and, 93–95, 98, 366n30; Miriam Y. Holden and, 146; Alma Lutz and, 101, 117; and *Notable American Women*, 115, 117–26, 131, 369n82; Rosika Schwimmer and, 143; Anne Firor Scott and, 53, 161; and Radcliffe Seminars on Women, 30, 103, 105, 107–8; size of, 100, 106; Barbara M. Solomon and, 109–13, 160. *See also* Arthur and Elizabeth Schlesinger Library on the History of Women in America; Comstock, Ada; James, Edward T.; James, Janet Wilson; Jordan, Wilbur Kitchener; Schlesinger, Arthur, Sr; Schlesinger, Elizabeth Bancroft

Radical America (journal), 35, 180, 214–16, 257

Radical Historians Caucus, 197, 199

Ransby, Barbara, 335

Restoring Women to History project: D'Ann Campbell and, 265; Elizabeth Fox-Genovese and, 264–67; OAH and global scope of, 264–65, 267

Reverby, Susan: background of, 400n124; and Berkshire Conferences on the History of Women, 236, 246, 400n124; mentored by Janet W. James, 119; networks of, 253, 256; publications of, 256; research focus of, 253

Right to Vote exhibit, 314, 316

Rockefeller Foundation, 68–69, 117, 229, 233, 317

Roosevelt, Eleanor, 87, 152, 295, 317–18

Rose, Willie Lee: acknowledges supportive male colleagues, 198; career of, 189, 210; and Caucus of Women in History (SHA), 203; and CCWHP, 189, 193;

of Women, 151; and Barbara M. Solomon, 112–13; and Women Historians of the Midwest, 242

Scott, Joan: and *AHA Directory of Women Historians*, 244; and ERA, 330; and *Manual for Women (and Other) Historians*, 393n9; and marginalization of women in early history profession, 356n27; and National History Standards, 293, 410n52; and Organization of American Historians, 241; on political nature of historical writing, 166, 347–48n16; and *Recent United States Scholarship on the History of Women*, 239; and Women Historians of the Midwest, 241; writes "Gender: A Useful Category of Analysis," 268–69

Sears case. See *EEOC v. Sears, Roebuck* (1986)

Seneca Falls Consortium, 243, 319–20

Seneca Falls Women's History Conference, 243

Seneca Falls Women's Rights Convention: and conservative attacks on women's history curriculum, 292, 321; critiques of US society at, 140–41; 150th anniversary celebration of, 339; and *Reclaiming the Past*, 326; and women's history origins stories, 15, 103. *See also* Stanton, Elizabeth Cady

SHA Committee on the Status of Women, 32

Sicherman, Barbara, 119, 124, 132, 229, 239, 375n53

Signs (journal), 273, 393n166

Simkins, Francis B., 77–78, 120–21, 364n92

Sklar, Kathryn Kish, *177, 181, 183*; career of, 275, 278, 402n37; chairs AHA Committee on Women Historians, 329–30; coauthors *Recent United States Scholarship on the History of Women*, 239; coedits *U.S. History as Women's History*, 213; and development of US women's history, 14, 275, 283, 323; education of, 14, 121, 275; politics of, 254–55, 279; and Living US Women's History Oral History Project, 350n47;

networks of, 254–56, 273; publications of, 275, 380n31, 406n117, research focus of, 312; and Second Berkshire Conference on the History of Women, 229; and Wingspread Conference, 182, 276, 343; and UCLA Workshop on Teaching US Women's History, 275–76, 401n5; and Women and Social Movements websites, 278–79, 406–7n132

Smith, Barbara, 303

Smith, Bonnie, 10, 265, 356n27

Smith, Eleanor, 234, 244, 393n8

Smith, Hilda, 192–94, 202–3, 206, 237, 385n19

Smith College Archives (SCA), 89–90, 92, 366n30

Smith-Rosenberg, Carroll: and Berkshire Conference of Women Historians, 204, 389n90; education of, 26, 131–32, 369n88, 374n37; and First Berkshire Conference on the History of Women, 225, 227; networks of, 198, 204, 389n90; and *Notable American Women*, 116, 131, 133, 138, 230; and Second Berkshire Conference on the History of Women, 229–30; publications of, 227, 230–32; and Wingspread Conference, 343; women's history origins stories, 230–31; and *Women's History Sources*, 262; writes on the history of sexuality, 298

Social Welfare History Archives, 209, 261, 263

Solomon, Barbara Miller, *170*; background of, 110; civic activism of, 151; as part of cohort of pioneers, 136–37; deanship at Harvard, 217; education of, 101–2, 159, 358n62; feminism of, 151, 159; and First Berkshire Conference on the History of Women, 227; and Massachusetts Commission on the Status of Women, 159, 161; speaks at White House, 110; and *Notable American Women*, 120–21; and Radcliffe Women's Archives, 109–11, 113, 160; teaching career of, 111

Sonoma County Commission on the Status of Women, 330

Ullian, Frieda Silbert, 107–8, 370n94, 371n114

Ulrich, Laurel Thatcher, 298, 343, 398n88

Unequal Sisters: A Multicultural Reader in U.S. Women's History, 278, 288–89

Upstate New York Women's History Organization (UNYWHO), 222, 240, 243–44, 319–21

US history curriculum: amateur women historians and, 11; conservatives shape in the South, 162; and culture wars, 7, 284–85, 291, 303, 328; Smith college faculty opposes introducing women into, 97; women's absence from before 1970s, 7. *See also* K–12 curriculum; women's history curriculum development

Wall, Bennett: Mollie Davis and, 204; and discomfort with feminist historians, 32, 79, 189, 195, 203, 353n46; Mary Massey and, 73–75, 77, 79–80; Jane De Hart Mathews and, 205; and *Notable American Women*, 122; Anne Firor Scott and, 79, 189; and SHA, 32, 72; A. Elizabeth Taylor and, 72

Ware, Caroline: career of, 50–51, 68, 81, 151, 152; civic activism of, 152; education of, 49, 143; feminism of, 151, 159; methodology of, 274; and New Deal, 151; and PCSW, 152–54, 162; publications of, 49–51; and women's history origins stories, 30

Ware, Susan, 110, 119, *182*, 124, 343, 375n53

Wellman, Judith, 243, 320–21

Welter, Barbara, 30, 128, 137, 227, 354n58; scholarship of, 298

Wesley, Dorothy Porter. *See* Porter, Dorothy

West Coast Association of Women Historians, 296, 202, 206, 222, 239–40

White, Deborah Gray: and Berkshire Conferences on the History of Women, 218; professional obstacles Black women faced in history, 41, 57, 306; publications of, 211, 218, 306–10; and Wingspread Conference, 343

Wiley, Bell I., 61, 102, 137; supports of Mary Massey, 77, 79, 198

Williams, Mary Wilhelmine, 100, 149, 394n17

Wingspread Conference on Graduate Training in US Women's History, *182*, 276–78, 280, 304, 343

Woman's Rights Collection, 92–94, 103, 105–6, 143

"Women in American Society" (Buhle, Gordon, and Schrom article), 25, 215, 221, 257, 289, 353n34

Women and Social Movements websites, 278–79, 406–7n132

Women Historians of the Midwest (WHOM), 222, 240–44; revived as Women and Gender Historians of the Midwest, 242

Women's Bureau, 112, 147, 151, 158, 161

women's history curriculum development: AHA Committee on the Status of Women and, 249; Black history and, 12, 88; CCWHP and, 241, 250; CCWHP-CGWH and, 238; conservatives oppose, 284–85, 291, 303, 328; and demand for women's history, 250, 256; *Journal of Women's History* and, 293; National Women's History Project and, 323; and need for inclusivity, 258; Radcliffe Seminars on Women and, 107–8; and Restoring Women to History project, 264–68; SHA Caucus of Women in History and, 203; Kathryn Kish Sklar and, 275–76, 278–79; Wingspread Conference and, 276–78; Women Historians of the Midwest and, 241–42. *See also* K–12 curriculum; US history curriculum

Women's History Movement, 8, 16

Women's History Sources, 209, 390n115

Women's History Sources Survey (WHSS), 209, 241–42, 261–63, 319. See also *Women's History Sources*

Women's History Week: Molly Murphy McGregor and origins of, 323, 330; Gerda Lerner and origins of, 312, 216

women's liberation movement: and critiques of patriarchal structures in academe, 187; and demand for women's